I

LOVE

NEW YORK

GUIDE

I
LOVE
NEW YORK
GUIDE

NEW EDITION

Marilyn J. Appleberg

Illustrations by **Albert Pfeiffer**

COLLIER BOOKS
Macmillan Publishing Company
New York

Maxwell Macmillan Canada • Toronto
Maxwell Macmillan International • New York • Oxford • Singapore • Sydney

Collier Books
Macmillan Publishing Company
866 Third Avenue, New York, NY 10022

Maxwell Macmillan Canada, Inc.
1200 Eglinton Avenue East, Suite 200
Don Mills, Ontario M3C 3N1

Macmillan Publishing Company is part of the Maxwell Communication Group of Companies.

Library of Congress Cataloging-in-Publication Data
Appleberg, Marilyn J.
   I love New York guide / Marilyn J. Appleberg; illustrations by
Albert Pfeiffer.—5th ed.
      p.   cm.
   Includes index.
   ISBN 0-02-097304-7
   1. New York (N.Y.)—Description—1981–   —Guide-books.   I. Title.
F128.18.A78   1992
917.47'10443—dc20   91-31441

Macmillan books are available at special discounts for bulk purchases for sales promotions, premiums, fund-raising, or educational use. For details, contact:

Special Sales Director
Macmillan Publishing Company
866 Third Avenue
New York, NY 10022

10 9 8 7 6 5 4 3 2 1

ACKNOWLEDGMENTS

The comprehensive nature of this book makes it imperative to have a great deal of help in researching, writing, and editing—I was blessed to have the best in all areas. Thank you to Assistant Commissioner Jack Linn and Len Shebar, City of New York Parks & Recreation; Lula Ward, New York Convention & Visitors Bureau; Kathleen Roche, Hagstrom American Map Corporation; Joan Johnson, New York City Transit Authority; Beth and Richard Flusser, Jeremiah Shea, Ruth Sager, Marilyn G. Haft, Letty Simon, Jennifer and Daniel Moyer, Sam Borkow, Carl Freed, Roger Feuerman, Jane Kalmus, Miriam Berman, Merise Nelson, Bill Collier, David Small, John Rothschild, and Barrie and Michael Pribyl. Special gratitude goes to Theresa A. Czajkowska, Carlo DeVito, Sharon L. Gonzalez, Jane Herman, and Margaret May. And thanks to my illustrator and friend, Albert Pfeiffer, still in a category of his own.

ACKNOWLEDGMENTS

CONTENTS

HOW TO USE THIS BOOK

General categories are listed in the table of contents; for more specific information on what is included in the book, use the index.

Unless otherwise noted, all shops are OPEN Monday to Saturday, from approximately 9am to 6pm, and CLOSED Sunday. Small shops, if in busy shopping areas, usually conform to the policies of their larger neighbors; the hours of the department stores are listed, as the only major change occurs during the Christmas shopping season, when they are all open every evening starting the day after Thanksgiving Day. Others conform to the eccentricities of their area of town. If unsure, call ahead.

To save space, abbreviations have been used for the days of the week and for the months. The area code is given for Brooklyn and Queens only; if none appears, the number is in the 212 area.

Where a shop or restaurant accepts credit cards, the following key is used. If no symbols appear, only cash or personal checks are accepted:

AE   American Express
CB   Carte Blanche
DC   Diners' Club
MC   MasterCard
V   Visa

INTRODUCTION

New York! It's the ultimate urban experience—reviled by those who hate it and revered by those who love it (a distinct majority).

More than anything else, New York is a city of superlatives, a place where the best, the brightest, the biggest is the norm. That's what comes of having world-class theater, music, museums, and galleries. Add to this an even longer agenda of world-renowned shops and restaurants, and you know why it's a magnet for tourists and why its natives are so fiercely proud.

But remember that New York has always been defined by its diversity, so after you have done the expected—the Met, the Modern, Mad Ave, Lincoln Center, the Empire State Building, and on- and off-Broadway theater—go exploring. See a tiger in the Bronx, visit a Tibetan temple on Staten Island, sail the East River on a 70-foot yawl, have a drink above the clouds at Windows on the World, eat a meal in Chinatown, cross the "border" into Little Italy for a pastry and coffee, then walk across the Brooklyn Bridge and gaze back at the picture-postcard-perfect view of what this native New Yorker knows to be the greatest city in the world.

If I could, I would take every visitor to the city by the hand and show him or her my New York—this book is the next best thing; as for natives, it was written for me and, by extension, for them. It is intended to make your relationship with New York, whether you are a visitor or a native, more than it could otherwise be. To know New York is to love New York, and this book is dedicated to that end.

Author's Note: Budget crises come and budget crises go; New York is rarely down and never out. Even in the worst of times there is more energy, more excitement, more enthusiasm—more of almost anything—here than anywhere else in the world. Visitors continue to flock here, and those of us who are lucky enough to call New York home know that all of the above is *still* true.

—New York, 1992

I

LOVE

NEW YORK

GUIDE

BASIC
INFORMATION

HELPFUL HINTS

New York City is comprised of five boroughs—Manhattan, Staten Island, Brooklyn, Queens, and the Bronx—that are linked by a series of bridges, tunnels, and ferries. Visitors will most likely spend the bulk of their time in Manhattan, an island that is a mere 13.4 miles long and, at its widest, 2.3 miles. With its grid-pattern layout, getting around is easy. Avenues run north and south, with Fifth Avenue the divider between the East and West sides of the island (the lower the house address, be it East or West, the closer it is to Fifth Avenue). Broadway, a former wagon trail, is the grand exception to the rule—it cuts diagonally through Manhattan as it moves downtown from the West Side to the East. As it intersects other avenues on its way downtown, Broadway creates Columbus Circle (at 59 Street), Times Square (at 42 Street), Herald Square (at 34 Street), Madison Square (at 23 Street), and Union Square (at 14 Street). Streets in Manhattan run east or west and ascend in numerical order as one travels north.

Downtown areas of the city, roughly 14 Street on the west and 1 Street on the east, were settled before the grid system and follow no particular pattern. These are among the city's oldest districts and include the Financial District, the Seaport, Greenwich Village, and Chinatown. A good map, a knowledgeable guide, or a fearless reliance on serendipity is recommended.

See Manhattan Address Locator, page 4.
NOTE: Sixth Avenue and Avenue of the Americas are used interchangeably.

WEATHER

New York has four distinct seasons, and a visit during any one of them will have its own character. Spring and fall offer moderate temperatures; the summer average is 75° F (23° C) with fairly high humidity, and the winter temperatures often hover near 32° F (0° C). But remember that indoor temperatures are often the opposite of outdoor—very cool in summer due to air-conditioning and warm in winter because of central heating. Therefore, layering of clothing is best; dress for comfort.

GETTING AROUND

New York's mass-transit system is extensive and efficient. Subways offer speed but can offend the eye and ear—and should be avoided late in the pm. Buses offer a view while you are getting to your destination at a slower pace. Taxis can be expensive during rush-hour traffic jams and elusive during rainstorms but a blessing when your feet hurt.

CAVEAT

First, about the city. Common sense must prevail regarding where you go and at what time you go there. Specifics: Secure your wallet or purse, do not flaunt cash or gold jewelry, and under no circumstances play three-card monte—a shell game with cards played on city streets by modern-day charlatans—it's for suckers. Second, about the book. New York is ever-moving, ever-changing, ever-growing—that's what makes it so special. It's also what makes the city so difficult to document. Though at press time all information contained herein is correct, changes will surely take place. Phone numbers are included and it is recommended always to call ahead.

NO SMOKING

In April 1988, New York City put into effect one of the toughest antismoking policies in the country. Places where it is illegal to puff include hotel lobbies, banks, sports stadiums, racetracks, public rest rooms, and taxis. Smoking has also been restricted in restaurants seating more than 50 people, in retail stores, and in schools.

TOURIST INFORMATION CENTERS

These are the main information sources for tourists about places, events, or travel.

Free daily events in the city parks, recorded information 360-1333.

New York Convention and Visitors Bureau
2 Columbus Circle at West 59 St & Broadway (10019). 397-8222. The bureau's helpful multilingual staff will answer questions and provide printed guides and maps in six languages, tickets for TV shows, discount coupons for theater tickets, and a current list of the city's hotel rates and weekend packages, major attractions, and seasonal events. *OPEN Mon-Fri 9am-6pm; Sat, Sun & Holidays 10am-6pm.*

New York State Department of Economic Development, Division of Tourism
1515 Broadway near West 44 St, 51st floor (10036). 827-6100. Information on tour packages in the city and statewide vacation and recreational activities. These folks are the creators of "I ♥ New York." *OPEN Mon-Fri 9am-5pm.*

Tourist Information Carts
In the Grand Central area, near Vanderbilt & East 42 Street, and on the concourse level of the terminal, carts stocked with visitor information and brochures from various attractions in the city. Tended by knowledgeable multilingual folks who are very helpful; sponsored by the Grand Central Partnership. Also to be found on 34 Street

between Park and Tenth avenues, as well as on the concourse level of Penn Station; sponsored by the 34th Street Partnership. *OPEN 7 days 9am–6pm.*

World Trade Center Information Kiosk
World Trade Center, Austin J. Tobin Plaza near Church Street. Staffed by volunteers who dispense transportation advice, maps, brochures, and listings of attractions and events in Lower Manhattan. *OPEN June–Sept, Mon–Sat 10am–6pm.*

PARKING

Street parking in Manhattan, if you can find a spot, is subject to a variety of restrictions, always posted. Metered street parking ranges from 20 minutes to one hour. Be sure to read the signs carefully: Your car may be ticketed or towed away if illegally parked; both can be expensive and the latter extremely troublesome. To find out whether alternate side of the street rules are in effect on any given day, call 566-4121.

There are hundreds of private parking facilities in Manhattan, with costs varying according to location and time of day and week. Be sure to always check the closing times or you may be left without your car till morning. The following is a list of short-term parking facilities with long hours and affordable prices.

Downtown

756 Parking Corp
756 Washington Street near West 12 St. Parking lot. *OPEN 24 hours.*

Midtown East

Real Pro Parking Corp
325 East 38 Street at First Ave. Garage. *OPEN 24 hours.*
River Edge Sutton Garden Garage
425 East 54 Street near First Ave. Garage. *OPEN 24 hours.*
50 Sutton Place Garage
East 54 Street & Sutton Place. Garage. *OPEN 7am–1am.*

Midtown West

Rapid 63 Street Corp.
408 West 57 Street near Tenth Ave. Garage. *OPEN Sun–Thurs 7am–1am; Fri & Sat 7am–1am.*
Allure
500 West 43 Street near Tenth Ave. Garage. *OPEN 24 hours.*

Upper East Side

Waterview
10 East End Avenue at East 80 St. Garage. *OPEN Mon–Fri 6am–1am; Sat 24 hours; Sun till 2am.*

222 East 69 Street Garage Corp.
East 69 Street & Second Avenue. Garage. *OPEN 7am–1am.*

Upper West Side

Hudson West Garage
101 West 90 Street near Columbus Ave. Garage. *OPEN Mon–Thurs & Sun 7am–1am; Fri & Sat 7am–2am.*
Alexander Parking Corp.
35–101 West End Avenue near West 61 St. Parking lot. *OPEN 24 hours.*

GAS STATIONS

Downtown

Amoco
Broadway & Houston Street. 473-5924. DC, Amoco card.
Citgo
Bowery & East 3 Street. 254-7790. No credit cards.
Gaseteria
East Houston & Lafayette Streets. 226-9530. No credit cards.
Gulf
FDR Drive & East 23 Street. 686-4546. AE, MC, V, Gulf card.
Mobil
Pike Street & East Broadway; 966-0571. And Sixth Avenue & Spring Street; 925-6126. AE, MC, V, Mobil card.

Uptown

Gaseteria
West End Avenue & West 59 Street; 245-9830. And Broadway & West 193 Street; 567-9345. No credit cards.
Merit
Seventh Avenue & West 145 Street. 283-9354. MC, V.
Mobil
Eleventh Avenue & West 57 Street. 582-9269. AE, MC, V, Mobil card.
Shell
Amsterdam Avenue & West 181 Street; 928-3100. And Amsterdam Avenue & West 167 Street; 923-9139. Shell card only.

GETTING TO JAVITS CONVENTION CENTER

Javits Convention Center
Eleventh Avenue between West 34 & West 39 Streets. (212) 216-2000. Fax (212) 216-2588. There is no nearby subway stop, but the M42 bus from Grand Central Station and the M34 bus from Penn Station both stop at the Center. There is no parking at the Center but plenty of parking in lots and garages in the immediate neighborhood.

MANHATTAN ADDRESS LOCATOR

To locate avenue addresses, take the address, drop the last figure, divide by 2, add or subtract the number indicated below. The answer is the nearest numbered cross street.

To find addresses on numbered cross streets, remember: Numbers increase east or west from Fifth Avenue, which runs north-south.

Ave A, B, C & D	Add 3
1st Ave & 2nd Ave	Add 3
3rd Ave	Add 10
4th Ave	Add 8
5th Ave	
Up to 200	Add 13
Up to 400	Add 16
Up to 600	Add 18
Up to 775	Add 20
From 775 to 1286	Drop last figure and subtract 18
Up to 1500	Add 45
Above 2000	Add 24
Ave of the Americas	Subt 12
7th Ave	Add 12
Above 110 St	Add 20
8th Ave	Add 10
9th Ave	Add 13
10th Ave	Add 14
Amsterdam Ave	Add 60
Audubon Ave	Add 165
Broadway (23 to 192 St)	Subt 30
Columbus Ave	Add 60
Convent Ave	Add 127
Central Park West	Divide house number by 10 and add 60
Edgecombe Ave	Add 134
Ft. Washington Ave	Add 158
Lenox Ave	Add 110
Lexington Ave	Add 22
Madison Ave	Add 26
Manhattan Ave	Add 100
Park Ave	Add 35
Pleasant Ave	Add 101
Riverside Drive	Divide house number by 10 and add 72 up to 165 St
St. Nicholas Ave	Add 110
Wadsworth Ave	Add 173
West End Ave	Add 60

BUS & SUBWAY INFORMATION

Information and directions to anywhere by subway or bus are available Monday to Sunday between 6am and 9pm from the Travel Information Bureau. *Call* (718) 330-1234. *There are also satellite centers at Penn Station, Grand Central Station, Port Authority at West 42 Street, and the lobby of 370 Jay Street, Brooklyn.*

Buses
Fare $1.25. For senior citizens and handicapped, 60¢ at all times. Exact change or subway tokens only, no bills, pennies, or 50-cent pieces. Bus stops are marked with signs that display the bus numbers, the approximate time schedules, and route maps. North-south (uptown-downtown) buses usually stop every two to three blocks; east-west (crosstown) stops are usually every block. There are yellow lines on the curb; glass-enclosed bus shelters are provided at many stops. Bus route maps are available at most subway stations.

Board at the front of the bus and deposit fare, exit in the rear. Smoking is not allowed. Animals (except Seeing Eye dogs or pets in carrying cases) are not permitted to travel on buses. Free transfers are available, see below.

Most buses run 24 hours a day, 7 days a week, albeit on reduced schedules in nonpeak hours and days.

Free Transfers
If you wish to transfer from an uptown or downtown bus to a crosstown bus, or vice versa, ask the bus driver for a transfer *upon boarding;* they are free.

Long-Distance & Commuter Buses
George Washington Bus Terminal: 564-1114
Port Authority Bus Terminal: 564-8484

Subways
Fare $1.25. Free return coupons for senior citizens and handicapped, good for three months.

Tokens must be purchased for entry. The token-booth operator can supply you with a free subway map and information. He can make change up to a $20 bill only. If you plan on using public transportation, buy a supply of tokens to save time (they are also sold at McDonald's fast-food emporiums). Buses also take subway tokens.

There is only one train class on the subway. Smoking is not allowed in the station or on the train. Animals (except Seeing Eye dogs or pets in carrying cases) are not permitted to travel on trains.

Subway trains run 24 hours a day, 7 days a week, although on reduced schedules in non-peak hours and days.

Staten Island Rapid Transit
Fare $1.25. Train information for Staten Island is available 24 hours a day, 7 days a week, call (718) 447-8601.

PATH (Hudson Tubes)
Fare $1 (four quarters or a dollar bill; pay at the turnstile). Trains to and from New Jersey. Information is available 24 hours a day, 7 days a week, call (800) 234-7284.

TAXIS

Taxicabs are readily available in New York City, except perhaps during peak rush hours and in the rain. Simply walk to the curb and extend your arm. Licensed taxis are always yellow (avoid gypsy caps, which are not); a lighted sign on its roof indicates it's available. Off-duty taxis will not stop. The first "drop of the flag" is $1.50 and 25¢ each additional ⅕ of a mile as well as 20¢ for each minute of waiting time. Pay only what's on the meter (there is an additional 50¢ night charge from 8pm to 6am) plus a 15-20 percent gratuity. According to regulations, drivers must take you anywhere in the five boroughs, Nassau or Westchester counties, or to Newark International Airport. Any problems or complaints should be made to the New York City Taxi and Limousine Commission, 221-8294.

RAILROAD INFORMATION

Long-Distance Rail Travel
All long-distance rail service leaves from Penn Station.
Amtrak: (800) 872-7245
Commuter Rail Service
Metro-North: Harlem, Hudson, New Haven, Port Jervis (Grand Central): 532-4900
Outside of New York, call (800) 638-7646
Long Island Rail Road (Penn Station): (718) 217-5477

GETTING TO & FROM THE AIRPORTS

For information on transportation to the three New York City airports, call the Port Authority of New York and New Jersey (800) 247-7433.

Bus/Subway
This is the most economical way, but it can be slow and, in summer, hot. During the rush hour, it's crowded. For bus and subway information, call (718) 330-1234.

To JFK from midtown and Queens take the E or F train to Kew Gardens/Union Turnpike, then the Green Lines Q10 bus to the airport; also, the A train from the West Side, Lower Manhattan, and Brooklyn to the Howard Beach-JFK Airport Station and there pick up the free airport shuttle bus (every 10 minutes from 5am to midnight, every 30 minutes at all other times).

From JFK, reverse the above directions or you can take the Q3 bus from the airport Main Terminal to the 179 Street Station, where it connects to the F or R lines to Manhattan and Brooklyn. Buses run every 15 minutes till midnight, then every 40 minutes till 5am.

The Triboro Coach Lines Q33 bus runs between LaGuardia's Main Terminal and the 74 Street/Roosevelt Avenue subway station, Jackson Heights, Queens, every 12 minutes during the day and evening, and every 40 minuts after midnight. At this station you can take the E, F, G, R, and #7 trains to Manhattan or Brooklyn. The

Triboro Coach Q47 bus departs from La-Guardia's Marine Terminal every 20 minutes between 5:20am and 12:45am for the 74 Street/Roosevelt Avenue station.

Express Bus
Carey Airport Express
Service to JFK and LaGuardia airports from six midtown Manhattan stops: Park Avenue between East 41 & East 42 Streets, opposite Grand Central Station; the Port Authority Bus Terminal, West 42 Street between Eighth & Ninth Avenues; the New York Hilton Hotel, West 53 Street off Sixth Ave; Sheraton City Squire, Seventh Avenue at West 51 St; the Marriott Marquis Hotel, Broadway between West 45 & West 46 Streets; Holiday Crowne Plaza, West 48 Street & Broadway. Fare (depending on where you board) is $9.50 or $11 to or from JFK; $7.50 or $9 to or from LaGuardia.

From Park Avenue, buses run nonstop to JFK every 30 minutes 5am-1am; from JFK, 6am-midnight. Nonstop to LaGuardia, every 20 minutes 6am-midnight; from LaGuardia, 6:45am-midnight. For complete schedule from all departure points, call (718) 632-0509.
Olympia Trails Airport Express
To and from Newark Airport from Penn Station, 34th Street & Eighth Avenue (3 blocks from the Javits Convention Center); Grand Central Station; Park Avenue & East 41 Street; and World Trade Center #1, West Street across from the World Financial Center. From all airport terminals to Penn Station and Grand Central Station, every 20 minutes 6:15am to midnight; to the World Trade Center, every 20-30 minutes 6am to 10pm. Fare $7. For further schedule information, call 964-6233.
New Jersey Transit
Airport Bus Center at Port Authority Bus Terminal, West 42 Street between Eighth and Ninth Avenues, ground floor. Airport Express bus service operates 24 hours a day, every 10-20 minutes, to and from Newark International Airport. The trip takes 30 minutes. Fare $7 one way; round trip $12.
Gray Line Air Shuttle
A door-to-door shared minibus service that is available between Manhattan hotels from 23 to 63 streets. Buses to JFK, LaGuardia, and Newark airports operate 7am-11pm. Fare to JFK, $14 per person; fare to LaGuardia, $11 per person; fare to Newark, $16 per person. For information, call 757-6840.

By Air
NOTE: Some carriers offer free helicopter service to first-class fliers; check with them.
New York Helicopter
(800) 645-3494. Wide-body Sikorsky copters. From East 34 Street at the East River to JFK in 10 minutes: Mon-Fri at 8:30, 9:50am, noon, 2:20, 2:50, 3:25, 4, 4:35, 5:10, 5:45, 6:20, 6:55, 7:30pm; Sat & Sun at noon, 2:20, 3:25, 4:35, 5:45, 6:55, 7:30pm. From JFK (TWA Interna-

tional) Mon-Fri at 8:45, 9:30, 10:15am, 12:15, 2:35, 3:05; 3:45, 4:15, 4:55, 5:25, 6:05, 6:35, 7:15pm; Sat & Sun at 12:15, 2:35, 4:55, 6:05, 7:15pm. The cost: $71.50 inclusive of tax.

TELEPHONE SERVICES

Emergency: Dial 911
Area Codes for the five boroughs of New York City
Manhattan and Bronx: 1-212
Brooklyn, Queens, and Staten Island: 1-718
Telephone Information
Manhattan and Bronx: 411
Brooklyn, Queens, and Staten Island from Manhattan and the Bronx: (1-718) 555-1212
Operator Assistance: 0
Out-of-Town: 1 + area code + 555-1212
International Calls
Many countries can now be dialed direct. Dial 0 (operator) for information concerning the code number of a particular country. Otherwise have the operator assist in placing the call. For information on international telephone service, call (1-800) 874-4000.
Direct   Access: 011 + country   code + city
code + number
Person-to-person, collect, or AT&T Credit Cards: 011
Foreign Credit Cards: 0
Pay Telephones
Local calls are 25¢ for the first three minutes. Information and 911 Emergency are FREE.
Recorded Telephone Services
(NOTE: There is a charge for each of these recorded services.)
Dow Jones Market Report: 976-4141
Inspiration, Norman Vincent Peale: 532-2266
Jazz-Line: (718) 465-7500
Lottery and Lotto Winners: 976-2020
OTB Results: 976-2121
Parking Regulations: 566-4121
Parks Department Information: 360-1333
Sky Report Hayden Planetarium: 769-5917
Sportsphone: 976-1313 or 976-2525
Time: 976-1616
Weather: 976-1212
Horoscopes by Phone
Aries: 976-5050
Taurus: 976-5151
Gemini: 976-5252
Cancer: 976-5353
Leo: 976-5454
Virgo: 976-5656
Libra: 976-5757
Scorpio: 976-5858
Sagittarius: 976-5959
Capricorn: 976-6060
Aquarius: 976-6161
Pisces: 976-6262
New York Public Library
    Telephone Reference Information Service
    They will answer any ready reference question you may have. It's an invaluable service.

Tip: Manhattan is usually busy, try the others first.
Manhattan: 340-0849. *Mon-Thurs 9am-6pm; Fri & Sat 10am-6pm.*
Brooklyn: (718) 780-7700. *Mon-Thurs 9am-8pm; Fri & Sat 10am-6pm; Sun 1-5pm (no Sunday in summer).*
Queens: (718) 990-0714. *Mon-Fri 10am-8:45pm; Sat 10am-5:15 pm; Sun noon-4:45pm (no Sunday in summer).*
Homework Hotline
(718) 780-7766. Teachers and librarians help children answer difficult homework questions. *Mon-Thurs 5-8pm during school year.* In Westchester: 682-9759.
Grammar Hotline
Dial (718) REWRITE—(718) 739-7483. *Mon-Wed 1-4pm during school year.*

BANKS

All commercial banks are *OPEN Mon-Fri 9am-3pm.* They are *CLOSED Sat & Sun and all legal holidays.* Some savings institutions are open Friday evening and Saturday morning, but they are the exceptions. If you intend to change a traveler's check, be sure you have proper identification with you. Most banks do not exchange foreign currency—Bank Leumi, with branches throughout the city, does. *See* TRAVEL & VACATION INFORMATION, Traveler's Checks, for addresses.

LEGAL HOLIDAYS

On these days, banks, post offices, schools, offices, and most businesses are CLOSED. But the good news is that many special events take place. *See* ANNUAL EVENTS, Calendar, for specific listings.
New Year's Day: January 1
Martin Luther King's Birthday: 3rd Monday in January
President's Day: 3rd Monday in Febuary
Memorial Day: last Monday in May
Independence Day: July 4
Labor Day: 1st Monday in September
Columbus Day: 2nd Monday in October
Election Day: 1st Tuesday in November
Veteran's Day: November 11
Thanksgiving Day: 4th Thursday in November
Christmas Day: December 25

NEW YORK PUBLICATIONS

For current happenings in New York at any given time, these are the best sources. They are available at any newsstand.

The Daily News
Daily, am and pm
New York Magazine
Weekly every Monday; great for current cultural goings-on
The New Yorker
Weekly every Monday; New York's most literate source
The New York Post
Monday to Saturday, am and pm
The New York Times
Daily; on Friday, the best for that weekend's events
The Village Voice
Weekly every Wednesday; great source for music and nightlife information—leans toward the cultural and political left

POSTAL SERVICES

Call the Postal Answer Line, 330-4000 (from a touch-tone phone only), for basic inquiries about postal services, delivery, and rate information.
Post Offices
General Post Office, 421 Eighth Avenue at West 33 St. 967-8585. Full service. *OPEN 7 days 7:30am-6pm*. Stamps available from self-service machines in the lobby *24 hours a day, 7 days a week*. See the list of Manhattan Post Office Stations for location of the post office nearest you.
Stamps
Available at all post offices. *OPEN Mon-Fri 8am-6pm* and at the General Post Office, 421 Eighth Avenue at West 33 St, *24 hours a day, 7 days a week* from self-service machines. Otherwise, stamps may be obtained from vending machines in most pharmacies, though at a premium. You may order stamps by phone and charge them to MasterCard or Visa; there is a $3 handling charge. Call (1-800) 782-6724 (STAMP 24). *Available 24 hours a day, 7 days a week.*
Express Letters
Guaranteed 24-hour delivery of any mail brought to one of the specially designated post offices before 5pm; to major cities only. For location of post office nearest you that features this service, call 967-8585.

Zip Codes
For zip code information, call 967-8585 during business hours. See also full-color fold-out map following Index.
Manhattan Post Office Stations

Zip Code	Station	Address
10001	James A. Farley	421 Eighth Avenue
10002	Knickerbocker	128 East Broadway
10003	Cooper	93 Fourth Avenue
10004	Bowling Green	25 Broadway
10005	Wall Street	73 Pine Street
10006	Trinity	25 Broadway
10007	Church Street	90 Church Street
10009	Peter Stuyvesant	432 East 14 Street
10010	Madison Square	149 East 23 Street
10011	Old Chelsea	217 West 18 Street
10012	Prince	103 Prince Street
10013	Canal Street	350 Canal Street
10014	Village	201 Varick Street
10016	Murray Hill	115 East 34 Street
10017	Grand Central	450 Lexington Avenue
10018	Midtown	221 West 38 Street
10019	Radio City	322 West 52 Street
10020	Rockefeller Center	610 Fifth Avenue
10021	Lenox Hill	217 East 70 Street
10022	Franklin D. Roosevelt	909 Third Avenue
10023	Ansonia	1980 Broadway
10024	Planetarium	127 West 83 Street
10025	Cathedral	215 West 104 Street
10026	Morningside	232 West 116 Street
10027	Manhattanville	365 West 125 Street
10028	Gracie	229 East 85 Street
10029	Hell Gate	153 East 110 Street
10030	College	217 West 140 Street
10031	Hamilton Grange	521 West 146 Street
10032	Audubon	515 West 165 Street
10033	Washington Bridge	555 West 180 Street
10034	Inwood	90 Vermilyea Avenue
10035	Triborough	167 East 124 Street
10036	Times Square	340 West 42 Street
10037	Lincolnton	2266 Fifth Avenue
10038	Peck Slip	1 Peck Slip
10039	Colonial Park	99 Macombs Place
10040	Fort George	4558 Broadway
10128	Yorkville	1691 Third Avenue

HOTELS

Plaza Hotel

When choosing where to stay, remember that Manhattan is only 13.4 miles long and 2.3 miles at its widest, so your choice of location will be more a matter of your interests and your desire for either tranquillity or frenzy. In any case, in New York, distance is measured by time, not space.

THINGS TO KNOW

- All prices are subject to change; that's why they're not quoted.
- The rate you will be quoted by the hotel does not include a sales tax of 8.25 percent, a city hotel tax of 5 percent, plus a $2 charge per room and a new 5 percent state tax on rooms costing more than $100 per night.
- Valuables should be deposited in the hotel safe when not in use.
- You keep your key when going out.
- Write the New York Convention and Visitors Bureau, Two Columbus Circle, New York, NY 10019, for their "New York City Tour Package Directory," which lists the weekend (as well as some weekday) bargains available at almost all the city's hotels. Or, call the hotel directly using the 800 toll-free number listed in each entry.

DELUXE

Yes, these are expensive—but they're also so much more.

Carlyle
35 East 76 Street (10021). (212) 744-1600; (800) 227-5737. Fax (212) 717-4682. The superb "small" hotel on upper Madison Avenue. Exclusive and European in manner, it's a permanent home to many who can afford the best. Impeccable service, tastefully decorated large rooms, and its location in the heart of auction and antique country is a boon to art lovers. Afternoon tea, a fine restaurant, and, in the Cafe Carlyle for much of the cabaret season, Bobby Short, a New York institution not to be missed. Also special, the cozy little Bemelmans Bar for cocktails and piano music. 24-hour room service; foreign exchange till midnight. Small pets permitted. Garage facilities. 503 rooms, 177 available to transients.

The Drake Hotel (Swissotel)
440 Park Avenue at East 56 St (10022). (212) 421-0900; (800) 372-5369. Fax (212) 371-4190. Casual elegance, beautifully located, perfectly Swiss-run. Newly remodeled pretty rooms have refrigerators, cable TV with first-run movies, telephone in bathroom; some have wraparound terraces. On premises, the excellent Lafayette restaurant (see RESTAURANTS, French) and the new Drake Bar for cocktails and piano music. Off-premises health club and pool privileges. Concierge; 24-hour room service. Complimentary morning limo to Wall Street. 583 rooms. Weekend package.

The Helmsley Palace
455 Madison Avenue at East 50 St (10022). (212) 888-7000; (800) 221-4982. Fax (212) 355-0820. Overlooking St. Patrick's Cathedral, a deluxe 55-story glass tower atop the historic 19th-century Villard Houses, now the hotel's exquisite public rooms retaining the original fireplaces, Tiffany glass, mosaic ceilings, and wood paneling. Plush spacious period-style rooms; superior concierge services and multilingual staff; 24-hour room service. Harry's New York Bar, private dining facilities, afternoon tea and cocktails in the opulent Gold Room (see RESTAURANTS, Afternoon Tea). 1,050 rooms and suites (including four triplexes above the 37th floor). P.S.: Go in spite of Leona. Weekend package.

The Helmsley Park Lane
36 Central Park South (10019). (212) 371-4000; (800) 221-4982. Fax (212) 319-9065. A beautiful, 46-story modern hotel, it is the one in which owner Harry Helmsley had chosen to reside. Good service, breathtaking views of Central Park (high up on the park side) from elegantly appointed rooms. All the amenities, plus underground garage. An earnest, multilingual staff. Good restaurant and bar; afternoon tea. Banquet ballroom. 640 rooms. Weekend package.

Inter-Continental New York
111 East 48 Street (10017). (212) 755-5900; (800) 327-0200. Fax (212) 755-5900. The Barclay (built in 1926) underwent a $30 million restoration; the result: this wonderful hotel, gracious and elegant, calm and comfortable. The staff is firmly committed to excellence. 24-hour con-

cierge and room service, laundry/valet as well as international communications, secretarial and translation services available. The re-created 1926 lobby with its brass birdcage and original skylight is a perfect setting for afternoon tea; the Barclay Restaurant is a popular spot for breakfast (choice of traditional American and Japanese) and business lunches. Recent updates include video message retrieval and check-out, three no-smoking floors, and, best of all, a modern health facility with circuit training, steam, sauna, and massage—open from 6am weekdays. Meeting and conference rooms. 692 rooms and suites (some with working fireplaces). Weekend package.

Lowell
28 East 63 Street (10021). (212) 838-1400; (800) 221-4444. Fax (212) 319-4230. This impressively located, old-world hotel, transformed by a sky's-the-limit renovation, is a luxurious and discreet little gem. The landmark building was completely and elegantly restored; many of the studio and one- and two-bedroom suites have wood-burning fireplaces and terraces, all have fully equipped kitchens. A well-stocked library; on the second floor, the Pembroke Room for breakfast, lunch, afternoon tea, and an English Sunday brunch. 24-hour concierge; room service; complimentary morning paper and shoeshine. 10 rooms plus 49 suites. Weekend package.

The Mark
25 East 77 Street (10021). (212) 744-4300; (800) 843-6275. Fax (212) 744-2749. The old Madison Avenue Hotel, prestigiously located, elegantly restored. Most of the accommodations are suites (the most desirable are high up) with plush furnishings, Frette linens and down pillows, high-tech kitchens, and marble baths; some have terraces. Extras include a VCR, fresh flowers, terry robes, twice-daily maid service, complimentary shoe shine and newspapers; 24-hour room service; valet service. Sumptuous restaurant; lobby bar. 120 rooms; 60 suites. Weekend package.

Mayfair Regent
610 Park Avenue at East 65 St (10021). (212) 288-0800; (800) 545-4000. Fax (212) 737-0538. One of the "baby grands," small and quietly elegant with a continental air. The luxury service and surroundings draw a sophisticated mainly European clientele. Spacious, sumptuously decorated high-ceilinged rooms; some suites have fireplaces. In the bathrooms, plush terry robes for guest use. Concierge; 24-hour room service; secretarial and limousine arrangements. Lovely inviting Lobby Lounge for breakfast, cocktails, and afternoon tea and next door the fine Le Cirque restaurant (see RESTAURANTS, Afternoon Tea: Mayfair Regent and Deluxe: Le Cirque). Banquet room. 96 rooms; 105 suites. Weekend package.

Peninsula New York
700 Fifth Avenue at 55 St (10019). (212) 247-2200; (800) 262-9467. Fax (212) 903-3949. Be-

hind the glorious classic Beaux Arts facade of what was once the Gotham Hotel (and briefly Maxim's) is a multimillion-dollar interpretation of the Art Nouveau style and spirit, now owned and operated by renowned Hong Kong–based Peninsula chain. Opulent decor, elegant style, and European service, all in addition to a perfect location. Rooms boast designer nouveau appointments as well as a mini bar and three telephones. On premises is the Adrienne restaurant, a bistro, and a lounge in the sumptuous lobby for tea and cocktails. A true exclusive is the Peninsula Spa, a glass-enclosed, trilevel health club/ spa with indoor rooftop swimming pool, steam room, sauna, and state-of-the-art exercise and spa facilities. 250 rooms, including 30 suites. Weekend package.

The Pierre
Fifth Avenue at 61 St (10021). (212) 838-8000; (800) 332-3442. Fax (212) 940-8109. Built in 1930 as an exclusive hotel and now newly renovated and under Four Seasons auspices, it's a consistent best. Glorious spacious rooms; upper levels have views of Central Park just across Fifth Avenue. Elegant and extremely worldly with an excellent, attentive, multilingual staff; concierge; valet service; twice-daily maid service; 24-hour room service. Cafe Pierre for fine dining; light menus and afternoon tea in the classic Rotunda daily from noon to 8pm. Valet parking; dogs allowed. 196 rooms and suites available for transient use.

The Plaza
Fifth Avenue at 59 St (10019). (212) 759-3000; (800) 228-3000. Fax (212) 759-3167. Ernest Hemingway is said to have advised F. Scott Fitzgerald to bequeath his liver to Princeton but his heart to the Plaza. This grande dame had lost some of her allure, but newest owner Donald— and ex-wife, Ivana—Trump is remedying that, and she's still a sentimental and elegant New York landmark, drawing the famous, the rich, and the royal since 1907. High-ceilinged rooms—the best are the ones with Central Park views. Improving restaurants, especially the Edwardian Room; the Palm Court for brunch and afternoon tea with violins in another-era feeling; the clubby Oak Bar for drinks with little elbow room (see RESTAURANTS, Afternoon Tea: The Plaza and Bars & Burgers: Oak Bar). 24-hour room service; on-premises money exchange, beauty salon, and theater desk. No-smoking floor available. NOTE: The Donald is planning to take the Plaza condominium—what would Eloise say! 800 rooms and suites. Weekend package.

Plaza Athenee
37 East 64 Street (10021). (212) 734-9100; (800) 447-8800. Fax (212) 772-0958. The dowager Alrae Hotel, with its enviable address, underwent a $40 million renovation under the auspices of Trusthouse Forte and was renamed for its glamorous Parisian sister. The 16-story luxury hotel's rooms are decorated with Louis XV reproductions and Directoire-style furnishings. European-trained staff; sophisticated interna-

tional clientele. Handsome lounge for drinks or afternoon tea; the wonderful Le Regence restaurant and bar (*see* RESTAURANTS, French); 24-hour room service. 119 rooms; 80 suites.

Ritz-Carlton
112 Central Park South (10019). (212) 757-1900; (800) 241-3333. Fax (212) 757-9620. Formerly the Navarro, this "small," luxurious hotel has a sedate English country-home feel. The rooms, with traditional 18th- and 19th-century reproduction furnishings, are small but charming, and 96 of them offer spectacular views of Central Park, just across the road. Twice-daily maid service; 24-hour room and valet service. The multilingual staff serves a large, discerning, European clientele. On premises, the Jockey Club restaurant and bar with its million-dollar art collection on its pine-paneled walls is a power broker's choice. Complimentary limousine to Wall Street in the am. 205 rooms and 23 suites. Weekend package.

St. Regis
2 East 55 Street (10022). 753-4500; (800) 325-3535. Fax 541-4736. Old-world landmark hotel at Fifth Avenue built in 1904 by John Jacob Astor for those who could appreciate and afford the "best of everything." Once home to Marlene Dietrich, William and "Babe" Paley, and Salvador Dali, the hotel recently reopened following a four-year, $100 million renovation. Now a Sheraton property, it has been returned to its original splendor, for which guests will pay handsomely. The high-ceilinged, exquisitely decorated guest rooms have been enlarged; there is butler service on every floor, 24-hour room service, and four floors for nonsmokers. The Astor Court in the lobby with piano music is oh-so-inviting and the fascinating King Cole Bar and Lounge with its Maxfield Parrish mural is once more serving cocktails to sophisticates. New amenities include a lower-level health club with gym, sauna, and massage rooms, and an executive business center. It continues to boast the most elegant lobby shops in town. Welcome back. 363 rooms, including 52 suites. Weekend package.

Stanhope
995 Fifth Avenue at 81 St (10028). (212) 288-5800; (800) 828-1123. Fax (212) 517-0088. Enviably situated opposite the Metropolitan Museum of Art and Central Park. Spacious and serene accommodations, lovingly refurbished with Louis XVI–style furnishings, to create a European ambience. A variety of personal services: 24-hour room service; concierge service; terry robes for guests' use; multilingual staff; babysitting, dog walking; free limo service 7:30 to 9:30am and 5:30 to 7:30pm. Charming seasonal sidewalk-terrace cafe for sophisticated people-watching and a quite good restaurant. If money is no object this is the perfect choice. 141 rooms, including 81 suites. Weekend package.

United Nations Plaza
One United Nations Plaza at East 44 Street & First Avenue (10017). (212) 355-3400; (800)

228-9000. Fax (212) 702-5051. Beginning on the 28th floor of two sleek skyscraper towers, a dazzling 13-story hotel; now a Park Hyatt property. Understated elegance adding up to pure luxury. Modern decor, absolutely breathtaking views of the city, international ambience (concierge and 29 languages available at front desk). Health club on the 39th floor for 24-hour indoor tennis, swimming pool on the 27th floor; underground garage; 24-hour room service; twice-daily maid service. Very good Ambassador Grill restaurant and lounge (*see* RESTAURANTS, Breakfast/Brunch). Complimentary limo service weekdays to Wall Street and the garment district, in the pm to the theater. 442 rooms (includes 115 apartments). Weekend package.

The Waldorf-Astoria & Waldorf Towers
301 Park Avenue at East 50 St (10022). (212) 355-3000; (800) 445-8667. Fax (212) 421-8103. Every inch the venerable institution, and now, after a $100 million refurbishing, the vast lobbies are once again Art Deco gems. Among its permanent residents (in the Towers, floors 28 to 42), the American representative to the UN and Frank Sinatra. Every president since Hoover has slept here (the nightly tab for the Presidential Suite is $2,000). Special consideration for special situations; 30 languages available; 24-hour room service; children in parents' room free. More boutiques, boîtes, and ballrooms than in some small cities. Despite its size and popularity, service still tends to be quite good. Flagship of the Hilton Hotels chain. 1,753 rooms. Weekend package.

Westbury
East 69 Street at Madison Ave (10021). (212) 535-2000; (800) 225-5843. Fax (212) 535-5058. Stylish yet serene, recently refurbished Trusthouse Forte hotel with well-appointed, spacious accommodations in excellent Upper East Side location convenient to the city's prestigious art galleries and auction houses. Old-world luxury feel; concierge service; 24-hour room service. The wonderful Polo restaurant (*see* RESTAURANTS, American). Recent updates include health club with sauna and whirlpool. Banquet facilities. 300 rooms and suites. Weekend package.

EXPENSIVE

Algonquin
59 West 44 Street (10036). (212) 840-6800; (800) 548-0345. Fax (212) 944-1419. A magnet for literary and theatrical folk since 1902; setting of the famed Round Table of wits and critics. Traditional and fascinating—and that's just the lobby. New owners are renovating the smallish rooms so they are now as inviting as the clubby oak-paneled lobby, where overstuffed sofas and easy chairs induce lolling over cocktails and conversation or afternoon tea. The Rose Room for late-night supper (*see* RESTAURANTS, Late Night/24 Hours), the Algonquin Oak Room for

sophisticated supperclub entertainment (see NIGHTLIFE, Cabaret), and the tiny Blue Bar, where you're always in good company. Hamlet, the house cat, completes the civilized picture. 165 rooms. Weekend package.

Barbizon
140 East 63 Street (10021). (212) 838-5700; (800) 223-1020. Fax (212) 753-0360. At Lexington Avenue, just three blocks from Bloomies. Formerly the all-women Barbizon, where the likes of Liza Minnelli and Candice Bergen once resided, the classic exterior was retained while the interior was thoroughly modernized. Concierge, multilingual staff, HBO, and health club with Olympic-size swimming pool. Now part of the Morgan's Hotel Group (Paramount, Royalton, Morgans), which plans to convert this property to a spa. Cafe Barbizon and Barbizon restaurant with fireplace. 350 rooms plus 12 tower suites, some with terraces. Weekend package.

Bedford
118 East 40 Street (10016). (212) 697-4800; (800) 221-6881. Comfortable, good location west of Lexington Avenue, popular with businesspeople and diplomats. Pleasant albeit modest rooms and suites have fully equipped kitchenettes, air-conditioning, color cable TV, direct-dial phones. Restaurant on premises. Family rates and monthly rates available. 138 rooms and suites. Weekend package.

Beekman Tower
3 Mitchell Place, East 49 Street & First Avenue (10017). (212) 355-7300; (800) 637-8483. Fax (212) 753-9366. Like a home away from home. Comfortable, attractively decorated all-suites hotel in United Nations area. Fully equipped kitchen facilities, air-conditioning, color TV. Top of the Tower penthouse lounge for cocktails and sweeping views. Multilingual staff; valet and limo service. 160 suites. Weekend package.

Beverly
125 East 50 Street (10022). (212) 753-2700; (800) 223-0945. Fax (212) 753-2700. Quiet, unpretentious, and rather plain surroundings but convenient East Side location, personalized service, and lower rates than its posher neighbor the Waldorf. Renovated rooms have air-conditioning, color cable TV; many have fully equipped kitchenettes and terraces. Room service, laundry/valet; multilingual concierge. On-premises lounge and restaurant; 24-hour pharmacy. Children under age 10 in parents' room free. Two meeting rooms. 300 rooms. Weekend package.

Days Inn-New York
440 West 57 Street (10019). (212) 581-8100; (800) 325-2525. Fax (212) 581-8719. Far west location, between unglamorous Ninth and Tenth avenues. Large rooms all have two doubles or a king-size bed, cable color TV, direct-dial phones, mini-bar/refrigerator. On-premises restaurant and cocktail bar; room service; multilingual staff. Free indoor garage. Children under age 17 stay in parents' room free. The outdoor rooftop swimming pool and cafe make this fine

for a summer stay. Ask about the bargain-priced (especially for families) "Bonanza Days Package." Group and convention rates also available. 600 rooms. Weekend rates.

Doral Court Hotel
130 East 39 Street (10016). (212) 685-1100; (800) 624-0607. Fax (212) 779-0287. Intimate and charming hotel carved out of the former Tuscany Towers is highly recommended. Spacious and plush accommodations in the quiet Murray Hill area just below midtown. Access to their nearby private fitness center a plus. On premises, the attractive and popular Courtyard Cafe. 199 rooms. Weekend package.

Doral Inn
541 Lexington Avenue at East 49 St (10022). (212) 755-1200; (800) 223-5823. Fax (212) 319-8344. Large renewed hotel, well located, efficient, modern, and bustling. In addition to the basic amenities, there is a health club with squash courts, sauna, game room. Bar, restaurant, 24-hour coffee shop. Fourteen languages spoken. 617 rooms and 35 suites. Weekend package.

Doral Park Avenue
70 Park Avenue at East 38 St (10016). (212) 687-7050; (800) 847-4135. Fax (212) 949-5924. Traditional elegance, meticulous service; beautiful rooms, some with serving pantries, all with refrigerators. Situated in quiet Murray Hill just below the frenzy of midtown. Charming sidewalk cafe in season, nice restaurant and bar. Free guest use of nearby health club facilities. Meeting facilities. Airport pickup on request. 200 rooms. Weekend package.

Doral Tuscany
120 East 39 Street (10016). (212) 686-1600; (800) 847-4078. Fax (212) 779-7822. Solicitous staff, a quiet tree-lined Murray Hill block just off Park Avenue, and one of the most inviting restaurants in the area (see RESTAURANTS, Continental: Time & Again) make this an extremely civilized place to stay. Large, traditionally decorated rooms have cable TV, mini-bars, and exercycles. Nightly shoeshine and turn-down service. Multilingual staff. The well-priced accommodations draw primarily a business clientele. 136 rooms and suites. Weekend package.

Dorset
30 West 54 Street (10019). (212) 247-7300; (800) 227-2348. Fax (212) 581-0153. This Museum of Modern Art neighbor, located between Fifth and Sixth avenues, is a quiet, discreet, and comfortable choice with many permanent residents. All rooms are air-conditioned and have cable TV; children under age 14 in parents' room free. Attentive staff. Restaurant and bar, beauty salon and gift shop. 200 rooms available for transients. Weekend package.

Dumont Plaza
150 East 34 Street (10016). (212) 481-7600; (800) 637-8483. Fax (212) 889-8856. A brand-new, 37-story hotel on Murray Hill's main thoroughfare, between Lexington and Third ave-

nues. The all-suites accommodations, part of the respected Manhattan East Suite Hotels chain, include studios and one- and two-bedroom units, all with fully equipped kitchens. Children under age 12 stay in parents' room free. Guests have free use of the on-premises health club with sauna. 250 suites. Weekend package.

Eastgate Tower
222 East 39 Street (10016). (212) 687-8000; (800) 637-8483. Fax (212) 490-2634. Between Second and Third avenues, a motor hotel with full apartment/hotel facilities located on charming plaza in Murray Hill area. All suites have fully equipped kitchens. On-premises garage; restaurant, outdoor cafe in summer. Good services for travelers. 192 apartments. Weekend package.

Hotel Elysee
60 East 54 Street (10022). (212) 753-1066; (800) 535-9733. Fax (212) 980-9278. Between Madison and Park avenues, this very well located, small, nonchaotic "artsy" hotel is a friendly choice. Comfortable, individually decorated rooms, gracious service. Children under age 12 in parents' room free. On premises the famed Monkey Bar and Lounge for meals, drinks, and late-night entertainment. 120 rooms.

Embassy Suites
1568 Broadway at West 47 St (10036). (212) 719-1600; (800) 362-2779. Fax (212) 921-5212. Right on the Great White Way, built atop the landmark Palace Theater, the first New York property and now the flagship of this national all-suites chain geared to the business traveler. Accommodations in this 43-story modern hotel consist of two-room suites—a living room/work area and a full-size bedroom. All have a wet bar, microwave, coffee maker, refrigerator, two TVs, two telephones with three incoming lines, computer/fax jacks, and an automated message system. Multilingual staff; a complimentary full American breakfast. 461 suites. Weekend package.

Essex House
160 Central Park South (10019). (212) 247-0300; (800) 645-5687. Fax (212) 315-1839. This large, traditional New York hotel now under the banner of Nikko Hotels International, a subsidiary of Japan Airlines, has undergone a multimillion dollar renovation. Accommodations are elegant and spacious, and with Central Park at its frontyard, the rooms overlooking it are choice (request when booking). Multilingual staff; 24-hour room service. Updates include a fully equipped business center. Lovely Art Deco lobby, but convention facilities make it hectic. Two restaurants; cocktail lounge. 590 rooms and suites. Weekend package.

Grand Hyatt New York
Park Avenue & East 42 Street at Grand Central Terminal (10017). (212) 883-1234; (800) 233-1234. Fax (212) 697-3772. The 30-story shell of the former Commodore Hotel sheathed in mirrored glass; the interior, a modern cosmopolitan hotel adjacent to Grand Central Station. Favored by businesspeople for its location and 44 meet-

ing rooms. The Regency Club for special attention on 31st and 32nd floors. A glamorous Hyatt-signature—a four-story atrium lobby; Trumpets and Crystal Fountain restaurants; Sun Garden cocktail lounge cantilevered over bustling 42 Street. Health club facilities available including tennis, squash, racquetball, sauna. 24-hour room service. 1,407 rooms. Weekend package.

Helmsley Middletowne
148 East 48 Street (10017). (212) 755-3000; (800) 221-4982. Fax (212) 832-0261. Apartment block refurbished in 1976 with an eye toward the executive or diplomat drawn to the location between Lexington and Third. Full kitchens in all rooms, some suites with fireplaces and terraces; cable TV. Pleasant and efficient multilingual staff albeit no room service. Residential feeling; reasonable rates for the area. 192 rooms including 45 suites. Weekend rates.

Helmsley Windsor
100 West 58 Street (10019). (212) 265-2100; (800) 221-4982. Fax (212) 315-0371. Remodeled, well-located (at Sixth Avenue), and gracious member of the Helmsley hotel family. Attractive, spacious accommodations; all feature two double or one king-size bed. Excellent service albeit no room service. Restaurant and lounge on premises. 274 rooms, including 53 suites. Weekend rates.

Holiday Inn Crowne Plaza
1605 Broadway at West 49 St (10019). (212) 947-4000; (800) 465-4329. Fax (212) 333-7393. Towering 46 stories above the Great White Way, this upscale Holiday Inn is part of the revitalization of the Broadway–Times Square area, although it might look more at home in Las Vegas. The full-service, highly self-contained environment includes a state-of-the-art fitness center with a 50-foot glass-domed indoor swimming pool, Manhattan's largest; extra special pampering in the Crowne Plaza Club, with concierge service, complimentary continental breakfast, and private lounge; a business center with fax, computer, and secretarial services. No-smoking rooms are available. Weekend package.

The Kimberly
145 East 50 Street (10022). (212) 755-0400; (800) 683-0400. Fax (212) 486-6915. Hotel residence with comfortable, fully furnished suites. Amenities include modern marble baths, remote-control cable TV, fully equipped designer kitchens with china and dishwasher; 24-hour concierge, valet, and executive services. Conference and meeting rooms. Guest privileges at a nearby New York Health & Racquet Club with swimming pool. Nightly, weekly, and monthly rates. 158 suites.

Hotel Lexington
511 Lexington Avenue at East 48 St (10017). (212) 755-4400; (800) 448-4471. Fax (212) 751-4091. Large, well-located older hotel recently tastefully updated. Comfortable albeit smallish rooms have cable TV, in-room movies, direct-dial phones, refrigerators. Two restaurants on premises. 800 rooms.

Loews New York
529 Lexington Avenue at East 51 St (10022). (212) 752-7000; (800) 223-0888. Fax (212) 758-6311. Modern, slick, well-contained East Side favorite with lively lobby lounge restaurant, shopping arcade, and garage. Concierge floor with lounge; a no-smoking floor; complimentary health club with Nautilus, Stair Master, sauna, and Jacuzzi. Children under age 18 in parents' room free. Executive Business Center. Meeting and banquet facilities. 729 rooms. Weekend package.

Lombardy
111 East 56 Street (10022). (212) 753-8600; (800) 223-5254. Fax (212) 754-5683. For complete privacy, a residential co-op hotel with room decors to appeal to a myriad of tastes. Top location just off Park Avenue. Spacious accommodations with serving pantries and refrigerators. Its on-premises restaurant is the fine Laurent (see RESTAURANTS, French). 176 units.

Hotel Macklowe/Macklowe Conference Center
145 West 44 Street (10036). (212) 768-4400; (800) 622-5569. Fax (212) 768-0847. In the heart of the Times Square renewal area, a major player in attracting business travelers. In the lower 8 floors of the 52-story building, the state-of-the-art conference center with 100,000 square feet of meeting space, computer, fax, and secretarial services; guest rooms have dual line phones plus Macktel, in-room computer access to airlines, theaters, and sports events in four languages. Pampering includes down pillows, all-cotton sheets, nightly turn-down, oversized tubs, and full valet services. A fitness center with personal trainers for one-on-one work. Multilingual staff; 24-hour concierge and room service. Adjacent to the hotel, the fully restored historic landmark Hudson Theater, now a full-service auditorium for corporate, fashion, and special event presentations. 638 rooms and suites. Weekend package.

Murray Hill East
149 East 39 Street (10016). (212) 661-2100; (800) 221-3037. Fax (212) 818-0724. All-suites hotel between Third and Lexington (formerly the Lyden), with daily and monthly rates. Pleasantly furnished studios, with or without dining areas, and one- and two-bedroom suites are great for family visits or corporate use. Maid service. 125 units. Weekend rates.

New York Helmsley
212 East 42 Street (10017). (212) 490-8900; (800) 221-4982. Fax (212) 986-4792. Forty-story modern Helmsley hotel in the UN area combines elegant European comfort (down pillows, linen towels) with New York–style efficiency. Top-level executive features include fast check in and out, translation and typing facilities, seven meeting rooms, underground parking, bathroom phones, and 24-hour room and concierge service. Mindy's Restaurant and Harry's New York Bar. 800 rooms. Weekend package.

New York Hilton & Towers
1335 Avenue of the Americas at West 53 St (10019). (212) 586-7000; (800) 445-8667. Fax (212) 315-1374. Army-sized 46-story hotel that grows better with age. Big with conventions; good business and foreign traveler services (30 languages spoken!). The Executive Towers, the top six floors, for special pampering including private registration, complimentary continental breakfast and afternoon tea in a private lounge. Recent additions include a business center with computer work station, fax machines, typewriter rental, and secretarial services; The Spa, with state-of-the-art fitness equipment, sauna, herbal wraps, massage, and more—starting weekdays at 6:30am. Several no-smoking floors. Cafe New York, open 6am–midnight, offers a huge Japanese buffet breakfast as well as American fare. Children in parents' or grandparents' room free. 2,131 rooms. Weekend package.

New York Marriott East Side
525 Lexington Avenue at East 49 St (10017). (212) 755-4000; (800) 228-9290. Fax (212) 980-6175. The newly upscaled historic hotel (formerly the Halloran House) boasts a prime midtown location and Marriott reliability. Rooms have cable TV, in-room safe, two telephones; no-smoking rooms available. Children under age 18 in parents' room free. Activities/tour desk; three restaurants and lounges. Concierge level occupying the top six floors complete with business center and private lounge for complimentary continental breakfast and afternoon hors d'oeuvres. Meeting and banquet facilities, including two on the 16th floor with outdoor terraces. 665 rooms. Weekend package.

New York Marriott Financial Center
85 West Street (10006). (212) 385-4900; (800) 228-9290. Fax (212) 385-9174. A classic Marriott right in the Financial District; adjacent to the World Trade Center, across the street from the World Financial Center, a short walk to Wall Street. Rooms have two phones, remote control TV with HBO, mini-bar; most boast sweeping Hudson River views. Indoor swimming pool and health club; restaurant and lounge; concierge and business center. 504 rooms, including 7 suites. Weekend package.

New York Marriott Marquis
1535 Broadway at West 45 St (10036). (212) 704-8745; (800) 228-9290. Fax (212) 704-8930. Right on the Great White Way, this modern, 50-story convention hotel is a major part of the rehabilitation of Times Square. The largest of the Marriotts, it contains the world's tallest (37 stories) atrium on the 8th-floor lobby level, reached by glass elevators (with the fastest closing doors). Also featured: a three-story revolving restaurant and lounge on the 46th floor, a 24-hour restaurant among several others, health club facilities, and a 1,600-seat legitimate theater (it will never make up for the loss of the Morosco and Helen Hayes, which were demolished for this project); meeting rooms and ballrooms galore. 1,876 rooms. Weekend package.

New York Penta
401 Seventh Avenue at West 33 St (10001).
(212) 736-5000; (800) 223-8585. Fax (212) 502-
8712. Built as the New York Statler in 1919, this
huge, refurbished landmark hotel near Macy's
and Madison Square Garden caters to the convention trade; it's the closest large-sized hotel to
the Javits Center. Multilingual staff; valet parking. 1,755 rooms. Weekend package.

New York Vista
3 World Trade Center (10048). (212) 938-9100;
(800) 258-2505. Fax (212) 321-2237. This 22-
story Hilton International hotel was the first major
one to be built in Lower Manhattan since 1836.
Sandwiched between its twin towering neighbors, it offers views of the Statue of Liberty to
upper-floor guests, direct access to the World
Trade Center concourse of shops, a shuttle bus
to midtown on weekends—not to mention a jogging track, indoor swimming pool, and fitness
center. Its proximity to Wall Street, the World Financial Headquarters, the Seaport, and other
downtown business and cultural attractions
makes it an interesting choice. Extra pampering
for execs on the 19th, 20th, and 21st floors. Multilingual staff. Lobby cafe for breakfast or tea; the
American Harvest restaurant and the Greenhouse, which features a wonderful seafood buffet Friday nights. 825 rooms; 4 duplex suites.
Weekend package.

Novotel/New York
226 West 52 Street (10019). (212) 315-0100;
(800) 221-3185. Fax (212) 765-5369. This 26-
story member of a French-based hotel, right in
the theater district, is built atop a preexisting
four-story commercial building. The sound-
proofed rooms all have individually controlled
air-conditioning; cable TV with in-room first-run
films. Laundry and valet service; hospitality
suites. Restaurant, brasserie, and wine bar on
premises. Children under age 16 stay in parents'
room free. 470 rooms and suites. Weekend
package.

Omni Berkshire Place
21 East 52 Street (10022). (212) 753-5800;
(800) 843-6664. Fax (212) 355-7646. Desirable
small hotel between Fifth and Madison avenues.
Personalized service; spacious, tastefully decorated rooms. Popular Rendez-Vous Bistro restaurant and the sunlit Atrium Bar; inviting lobby
for afternoon tea with harp music. NOTE: When
the business folk vacate, weekend values
abound for families and romantics. 400 rooms.
Weekend package.

Omni Park Central
870 Seventh Avenue at West 56 St (10019).
(212) 484-3300; (800) 843-6664. Fax (212) 484-
3374. Formerly the New York Sheraton, this is an
extremely large, no-nonsense hotel catering to a
convention crowd. In-room first-run movies, a
bar, several restaurants, nightly entertainment.
Two children under age 12 in parents' room free.
1,500 rooms. Weekend package.

Parc Fifty-One Hotel
152 West 51 Street (10019). (212) 765-1900;

(800) 338-1338. Fax (212) 581-7618. What was
once the old Taft Hotel and then briefly the Grand
Bay Hotel is now a luxury hotel well situated in
the emerging midtown west business corridor,
just above the theater district. Beautifully decorated rooms have two multiline phones, fax hook-
up, and TV in the bathroom. Personalized services include a concierge on every guest level;
24-hour room service; valet, business, and secretarial services. Valet parking; complimentary
limo service to Wall Street in the am. No-smoking
rooms available. On premises the Mezzanine
restaurant and the sophisticated Bellini by Cipriani (see RESTAURANTS, Italian). 172 rooms,
including 52 suites. Weekend package.

Parker Meridien
118 West 57 Street (10019). (212) 245-5000;
(800) 543-4300. Fax (212) 708-7477. Modern
40-story hotel is French-owned and -operated.
Fine location close to Fifth Avenue shopping,
Central Park, and Carnegie Hall; smallish rooms
are soundproof. There is a fitness club on the
premises that includes racquetball and squash
courts, a running track, and a glass-enclosed
rooftop swimming pool. Concierge service; multilingual staff; 24-hour room service. Maurice for
French dining (see RESTAURANTS, French),
and the lovely lobby lounge for breakfast and
drinks. Corporate rates available. 700 rooms,
600 available to transients. Weekend package.

Plaza Fifty
155 East 50 Street (10022). (212) 751-5710;
(800) 637-8483. Fax (212) 753-1468. Good economical (relatively speaking) East Side business
location between Lexington and Third avenues.
Air-conditioned all-suites hotel (part of the Manhattan East Suites chain), full kitchens, color TV,
some private terraces. Laundry facilities available; full hotel services. 118 rooms. Weekend
package.

Ramada Renaissance Times Square
Broadway to Seventh Avenue, West 47 to West
48 Streets. (212) 765-7676; (800) 228-9898. Fax
(212) 765-1962. On a trapezoidal block, the site
of the famed old Coca-Cola sign, not to mention
the famed old Latin Quarter, a 25-story structure
with two floors of upscale retail shops, a health
club, meeting rooms, and 21 floors of deluxe
accommodations with butler/valet service on
each floor and a fax machine in each room. The
Renaissance Club, on the third floor, for extra-
special personalized service, features the Club
Lounge, and the Club Restaurant & Bar. A new
Coca-Cola sign on the building's exterior is part
of a program to make sure the Great White Way
stays lit and lively after being "revitalized" as a
business as well as tourist destination. 305
rooms.

Regency Hotel
Park Avenue at East 61 St (10022). (212) 759-
4100; (800) 223-0607. Fax (212) 826-5674.
Tasteful modern Upper East Side Loew's hotel
with a refined European flair, a low-key location,
and a high-powered corporate reputation.
Rooms elegantly furnished with Louis XVI repro-

ductions; bathrooms have phones, TVs, and refrigerators. Its restaurant is a favorite power broker's breakfast spot (see RESTAURANTS, Breakfast/Brunch). Also, a congenial piano lounge; multilingual staff; 24-hour room service; lower-lobby fitness center. 500 rooms and suites.

Rihga Royal Hotel
151 West 54 Street (10036). (212) 307-5000; (800) 937-5454. Fax (212) 765-6530. At 54 stories, this handsome skyscraper hotel in Manhattan's rapidly growing midtown west business corridor (and the first American property of the Japan-based Royal Hotel group) weighs in as New York's tallest hotel—to date. The deluxe all-suites accommodations are classically decorated, spacious, and quiet, with VCRs, refrigerators, three separate phone lines, computer and fax hookups. There is the now-required full-service business and fitness centers, essentials for the busy executive traveler; complimentary shuttle to Wall Street. Concierge and valet services. Banquet and meeting facilities are on the top floors with stupendous views of the city. Attractive lobby lounge and bar; large restaurant. 500 one- and two-bedroom suites.

Roosevelt on Madison Avenue
Madison Avenue at East 45 St (10017). (212) 661-9600; (800) 223-1870. Fax (212) 687-5064. No glitz here, simply a redecorated older hotel located right in the middle of it all. Attractive, large, comfortable, quiet rooms. Two restaurants, a bar, coffee shop. Geared to an executive and international clientele. Extensive meeting facilities. Staff speaks several languages including Farsi, Japanese, Chinese, and Urdu. 1,070 rooms; 43 suites. Weekend package.

Royalton
44 West 44 Street (10036). (212) 869-4400; (800) 635-9013. Built in 1898 (it was designed by architect Stanford White as a private club), the Royalton recently underwent a $30 million reconstruction under the auspices of Ian Schrager of Studio 54 and Palladium fame, who went on to produce hotels. The results, in this case, a sophisticated but extremely offbeat, luxury hotel created by cutting-edge French designer Philippe Starck. Chic minimalism in the rooms, which all have queen- or king-sized beds, VCR (a 300-choice tape library available), stereo cassette, and two-line phones; 40 rooms have working fireplaces (wood comes via room service). The block-long multilevel stage-set lobby promotes itself as the gathering space of the 90s, with seating and dining rooms, a bar, a library, and recreation area complete with chess and checkers sets. The on-premises restaurant, "44," is a see and be seen spot for high profile diners (see also RESTAURANTS, American). 24-hour room service; multilingual staff. 205 rooms. Weekend rates.

St. Moritz on Central Park
50 Central Park South at Sixth Ave (10019). (212) 755-5800; (800) 221-4774. Fax (212) 751-2952. Very small rooms in a nostalgic setting, the best of which face north with views of Central Park, essentially the hotel's front lawn. Very European sidewalk Cafe de la Paix, and Rumpelmeyer's for those with a sweet tooth or for afternoon tea. 773 rooms and suites. Weekend package.

Shelburne Murray Hill
303 Lexington Avenue at East 37 St (10016). (212) 689-5200; (800) 637-8483. Fax (212) 779-7068. Full hotel services and long-term residency available in lovely, quiet Murray Hill location. All units in this member of an all-suites hotel chain have fully equipped kitchens; many one- and two-bedroom suites. Billy Budd restaurant on premises. 252 apartments. Weekend package.

Sheraton Centre Hotel & Towers
811 Seventh Avenue at West 52 St (10019). (212) 581-1000; (800) 325-3535. Fax (212) 262-4410. Formerly the Americana, this large, busy, and highly commercial hotel is in the midst of it all: Broadway, shopping, dining. Conveniences include valet parking and in-room first-run movies. Excels in convention and business group accommodations. The Towers, on the 46th floor for extra pampering, is less frenetic, for an added tariff. Four restaurants; lounge and disco. Pool privileges at the nearby Sheraton City Squire. 1,850 rooms; 73 suites. Weekend package.

Sheraton City Squire Hotel
790 Seventh Avenue at West 51 St (10019). (212) 581-3300; (800) 325-3535. Fax (212) 541-9219. Comfortable low-frills rooms, color TV, some have private terraces. Great location for theatergoers and the best feature: a glass-enclosed, year-round swimming pool. 24-hour room service; valet parking, enclosed garage. Children free if extra bed not required. 724 rooms and suites. Weekend package.

Sheraton Park Avenue
Park Avenue at East 37 St (10016). (212) 685-7676; (800) 325-3535. Fax (212) 889-3193. Formerly the Sheraton Russell, this serene, off-the-beaten-track Sheraton was originally a 1920s apartment hotel. Handsome welcoming oak-paneled lobby; quiet, comfortable rooms, some with fireplaces. In sum, a lovely, gracious small hotel with a good bar and restaurant. Concierge; multilingual staff; 24-hour room service. Free parking. 175 rooms. Weekend package.

Southgate Tower
371 Seventh Avenue at West 31 St (10001). (212) 563-1800; (800) 637-8483. Fax (212) 643-8028. Refurbished 30-story structure opposite Madison Square Garden, near Penn Plaza, convenient to the Javits Convention Center. All units of this chain hotel have fully equipped kitchens or serving pantries; some have terraces. Full hotel services; valet, maid, and room service; multilingual staff; two restaurants; fitness center. Nice lobby shops. Geared to a business clientele. Parking facilities. Meeting and banquet rooms. 525 rooms. Weekend package.

The Surrey Hotel
20 East 76 Street (10021). (212) 288-3700; (800) 637-8483. Fax (212) 628-1549. Exclusive Upper East Side location between Fifth and Madison avenues close to the Whitney Museum, Central Park, and European-style shops. Well-appointed apartment hotel features very large units, all with fully equipped kitchens. Room service; multilingual staff. On premises is the comfortable Les Pleiades restaurant; cocktail lounge and bar. 111 apartments.

The Tudor
304 East 42 Street (10017). (212) 986-8800; (800) 879-8836. Fax (212) 986-1758. This formerly sleepy old UN neighbor, now under the auspices of the London-based Sarova Hotels, has had a "gut" rehab bringing it into the 90s. Each of the newly enlarged rooms has electronic door lock, two-line speaker phone, fax outlet, in-room safe, and mini-bar. 24-hour room service; restaurant, coffee lounge, and bar. Fitness and business center facilities. 303 rooms, including 14 suites.

Warwick
65 West 54 Street (10019). (212) 247-2700; (800) 223-4099. Fax (212) 957-8915. Built in 1927, by William Randolph Hearst, this good midtown choice has recently been undergoing renovation. Quite large, comfortable rooms, some have serving pantries or refrigerators; all have two-line phones. Helpful multilingual staff. Good restaurant and cozy bar; on-premises beauty salon and barber shop. Popular with TV people and clothing buyers because of its location. (It's difficult to believe the Beatles once stayed here.) 500 rooms. Weekend package.

MODERATE

Chatwal Inn on 45 Street
132 West 45 Street (10036). (212) 921-7600; (800) 826-4667. Fax (212) 719-0171. Between Broadway and Sixth Avenue, in the theater district, one of the Chatwal chain's affordably priced hotels. Rooms are pleasant with cable TV, direct-dial phones, air-conditioning. Complimentary continental breakfast. 24-hour room service. 80 rooms; 5 suites.

Chelsea Hotel
222 West 23 Street (10011). (212) 243-3700. A lively landmark; home to the famous and infamous of every era since 1833. Suggested for the adventuresome and offbeat—dare I say bohemian? The rooms—large, high-ceilinged, soundproof with kitchens—are as checkered as its past—some excellent, some condemnable. Former tenants include Mark Twain, Sarah Bernhardt, Eugene O'Neill, Thomas Wolfe, Brendan Behan, Arthur Miller, Dylan Thomas (he died here), and Sid Vicious. Still a magnet for struggling artistic types. 400 rooms.

Comfort Inn Murray Hill
42 West 35 Street (10001). (212) 947-0200;

Chelsea Hotel

(800) 228-5150. Charming and highly affordable European-style choice located in a renovated 1920s building, just off Fifth Avenue, close to Macy's and the Empire State Building. Convenient to the Javits Center; popular with fashion buyers. Complimentary continental breakfast in the lobby, daily newspapers. No-smoking rooms available. 118 rooms.

Hotel Edison
228 West 47 Street (10036). (212) 840-5000; (800) 637-7070. Fax (212) 719-9541. At the low end of moderate, a longtime tourist mecca smack in the middle of the theater district, between Broadway and Eighth Avenue. Busy but comfortable; the rooms, though aging, are spacious, air-conditioned, and have direct-dial phones and cable TV. On premises a coffee shop, dubbed "the Polish Tea Room" by regulars, many of whom are in show business; also, a restaurant and cocktail lounge. Garage facilities. 1,000 rooms.

Hotel Esplanade
305 West End Avenue at West 74 St (10023). (212) 874-5000; (800) 367-1763. Fax (212) 496-0367. A superior close-to-budget choice on a tranquil Upper West Side residential street. Spacious accommodations good for families (two children under age 17 in parents' room free) range from large studios to two- and three-room suites, all with air-conditioning and cable color TV; some have Hudson River views. Full kitchenettes are available. Restaurant and cocktail lounge on premises. Very convenient to Lincoln Center. 140 rooms. Weekend package.

Gorham Hotel
136 West 55 Street (10019). (212) 245-1800; (800) 735-0710. Fax (212) 245-1800. Small, quiet, easy hotel built in 1938. Many of the rooms have been newly renovated; they have wet bars, microwaves, two-line phones, and whirlpool bath. Personal service, on-premises restaurant. Underground garage. Good value (on the low end of moderate) for prime location (between Sixth and Seventh avenues). 165 rooms.

Gramercy Park Hotel
2 Lexington Avenue at East 21 St (10010). (212) 475-4320; (800) 221-4083. Fax (212) 505-0535. Away from midtown bustle, this old-world hotel in a stylish and historic location draws a European clientele. Air-conditioning, color TV, access to New York's only private park. Newer rooms face the park, some have kitchenettes. Traditional restaurant, cocktail lounge, and piano bar. 500 rooms. Weekend rates.

Howard Johnson
851 Eighth Avenue at West 51 St (10019). (212) 581-4100; (800) 223-0888. Fax (212) 974-7502. Well known, reliable, and comfortable, at the edge of the theater district (a mixed blessing). In-room first-run movies; cocktail lounges, restaurant. Children under age 18 in parents' room free. Valet and baby-sitting services. Free parking (but in-out charge). 300 rooms. Weekend package.

Journey's End
3 East 40 Street (10016). (212) 447-1500; (800) 668-4200. Fax (212) 827-0464. Wonderfully positioned a few steps from Fifth Avenue, near the Public Library, Lord & Taylor, and other smart shops, this brand-new Canadian chain hotel caters to the individual business and pleasure traveler. Rooms have individually controlled heat and air-conditioning, remote cable TV; complimentary coffee and newspapers in the am in the lobby mezzanine. Children under age 12 in parents' room free. 189 rooms. Weekend package.

Kitano
66 Park Avenue at East 38 St (10016). (212) 685-0022; (800) 223-5823. Fax (212) 532-5615. This Japanese-owned and -operated hotel presents an interesting mix of efficiency and serenity. Rooms have color TV and refrigerator; a few authentic tatami suites with traditional tubs are available. Japanese restaurant and ceremonial tearoom (no room service). Peaceful Murray Hill location. Slated to undergo a major expansion. 90 rooms. Weekend package.

Madison Towers Hotel
22 East 38 Street (10016). (212) 685-3700; (800) 225-4340. Fax (212) 477-0747. Renovated oldie (formerly the Lancaster Hotel) in good, residential Murray Hill location. Small, nicely decorated rooms, color TV, individually controlled heat and air-conditioning. Draws fashion buyers, business travelers, and tour groups. Health club on premises. The Whaler Bar, with wood-burning fireplace in winter, for food, drink, entertainment; coffee shop. Banquet facilities; meeting rooms. 251 rooms and suites. Weekend package.

Mayflower Hotel
15 Central Park West at 61 St (10023). (212) 265-0060; (800) 223-4164. Fax (212) 265-5098. In the vicinity of Lincoln Center, facing Central Park. Newly renovated, the large albeit lackluster rooms all have private baths and serving pantries; color cable TV available; room service. Conservatory restaurant is a good choice for Sunday brunch with music. Free shuttle bus to Javits Center. 577 rooms. Weekend package.

Milford Plaza
270 West 45 Street (10036). (212) 869-3600; (800) 221-2690. Fax (212) 944-8357. (On Eighth Ave.) The theater district location makes this bustling Best Western hotel convenient for frequent Broadway theatergoers, but it's a noisy choice, especially on the lower floors where they house the tour groups. Small rooms, contemporary decor, three-story marble atrium lobby, show-biz motif. Good value package, check for availability. Mama Leone's restaurant on premises (see RESTAURANTS, Italian). 1,310 rooms. Corporate rates available. Weekend package.

Morgans
237 Madison Avenue at East 37 St (10016). (212) 686-0300; (800) 334-3408. Fax (212) 779-8352. In Murray Hill, the 50-year-old Executive Hotel refurbished and brought into the modern age—by the creators of Studio 54 and the Palladium no less. The sleek, ultramodern, subtle-hued design of the smallish rooms is up-to-the-minute (by famed French designer Andreé Putman), with all-built-in furnishings; Brooks Brothers shirting fabric on the duvets; stocked refrigerators, TV with HBO, cassette players, and VCR. 24-hour room and valet service. Service-oriented to the entertainment and fashion crowd. Note the address—there's no identifying name on the exterior. 154 rooms. Weekend package.

Paramount Hotel
235 West 46 Street (10036). (212) 764-5500; (800) 225-7474. Fax 354-5237. This oldie tourist-class theater district hotel has been no less than metamorphosed into an exciting affordable destination—hotel as theater—for the young, the hip. French designer Philippe Starck has created a dramatic multilevel lobby as town square. The tiny rooms, with a playful tongue-in-cheek quality, are highly functional with cable TV, VCR, call waiting. 24-hour room service; multilingual staff. Nightly turn-down service, fresh flowers daily. Other amenities of this boutique hotel: a Dean & DeLuca gourmet shop, a 24-hour brasserie, a 24-hour state-of-the-art fitness room (designed, my dears, by Madonna's personal trainer), a children's playroom, a business center. 610 rooms.

The President Hotel
234 West 48 Street (10036). (212) 246-8800; (800) 826-4667. Fax (212) 974-3922. In the theater district, between Eighth Avenue and Broadway, this oldie—now completely updated—is another very affordable link in the Chatwal hotel chain. Newly renovated rooms, some have terraces, all have cable TV and direct-dial phones. Complimentary continental breakfast in the skylit Atrium Court. Concierge service; multilingual staff. 400 rooms.

Radisson Empire Hotel New York
44 West 63 Street (10023). (212) 265-7400; (800) 333-3333. Fax (212) 765-6125. For music and dance lovers, the location just across Co-

lumbus Avenue from Lincoln Center is a boon. Now under new management (Radisson), this amiable hotel has been nicely upgraded and provides excellent value. All rooms have 20-inch color TV with VCR, CD/cassette stereo system, two-line direct-dial phones, bathroom phone, hair dryer, heated towel racks, and extra-large tubs. Four-story health club gratis for guests. Concierge; 24-hour room service; multilingual staff; valet parking. Meeting and banquet facilities. 375 rooms.

Ramada Hotel
790 Eighth Avenue at West 48 St (10019). (212) 581-7000; (800) 228-2828. Fax (212) 974-0291. In theater district, standard Ramada hotel, good for families: all rooms have two double beds or a king, children under age 18 in parents' room free. Pluses: in-room first-run movies, open-air rooftop swimming pool, free parking (but in-out charge). Drawback: the neighborhood. 366 rooms. Weekend package.

Roger Smith Winthrop
501 Lexington Avenue at East 47 St (10017). (212) 755-1400; (800) 445-0277. Fax (212) 319-9130. Lovely serene welcoming older hotel undergoing loving renovation; perfectly situated for business or pleasure. The large, nicely decorated rooms all have refrigerators and coffee makers; some suites have fireplaces, all have servicing pantries. No room service, but there is a complimentary continental breakfast. Restaurant and lounge located off the lobby. No charge for children in parents' room. Small pets welcome. 180 rooms and suites. Weekend package.

Salisbury
123 West 57 Street (10019). (212) 246-1300; (800) 223-0680. Fax (212) 977-7752. Across from Carnegie Hall, this quiet, traditionally decorated hotel is a good bet for families. Most of the spacious rooms have serving pantries with refrigerators, all have direct-dial phones, air-conditioning, and color TV. Children under age 12 in parents' room free. Room and valet service; restaurant but no bar (evidence of ownership by the adjacent Calvary Baptist Church). Banquet and meeting facilities. 322 rooms and suites. Weekend rates.

San Carlos Hotel
150 East 50 Street (10022). (212) 755-1800; (800) 722-2012. Fax (212) 688-9778. Comfortable hotel between Lexington and Third avenues; a good business location; amiable staff. Most rooms have fully equipped serving pantries; all have air-conditioning, color TV, direct-dial phones. Restaurant on premises. Parking facilities. Monthly rates available. 200 rooms.

Hotel Shoreham
33 West 55 Street (10019). (212) 247-6700; (800) 553-3347. Fax (212) 765-9741. Comfortable, practical rooms (mostly suites) with serving pantries, air-conditioning, cable TV—at reasonable rates. Excellent location, just off Fifth Avenue, for fine dining and shopping. On-premises restaurant is the famed La Caravelle (see RESTAURANTS, Deluxe). Courteous man-

agement; European clientele. 76 rooms and suites available for transients.

Travel Inn and Motor Hotel
515 West 42 Street (10036). (212) 695-7171; (800) 223-1900. Fax (212) 967-5025. Courteous, efficient choice close to Theater Row on the far west side. Popular with families and tour groups. Enormous rooms have been newly redecorated; all the amenities plus an Olympic-sized outdoor pool, saunas, solarium, rooftop sun deck. Great for summer stays. From Memorial Day to Labor Day up to five children in parents' room free. Pets allowed. Free self park. 250 rooms. Weekend package.

Wales
1295 Madison Avenue at East 92 St (10028). (212) 876-6000; (800) 223-0888. Fax (212) 860-7000. This longtime (1901) small homey hotel in the quiet Carnegie Hill residential neighborhood has undergone a major face-lift, restoring much of its original architectural features. The results are charming and inevitably has moved it from budget to low-end moderate. Spacious airy rooms; some boast Central Park–filled views. All are now air-conditioned, have TV and phone, some have refrigerators. Complimentary continental breakfast served in the new second-floor lounge. To come: a roof garden for guest use. Off the intimate European-styled lobby is Busby's restaurant and Sarabeth's Kitchen (see RESTAURANTS, Breakfast/Brunch). 93 rooms and suites.

Hotel Wellington
871 Seventh Avenue at West 55 St (10019). (212) 247-3900; (800) 652-1212. Fax (212) 979-8373. Nice tourist hotel near Carnegie Hall, which may be why it attracts musicians, as well as European and American tour groups. Friendly ambience. All rooms, though small, are air-conditioned and have color TV, some have kitchenettes. On-premises cafe and restaurant/lounge; lobby shops. Low end of moderate. 700 rooms.

Wentworth Hotel
59 West 46 Street (10036). (212) 719-2300; (800) 223-1900 (only weekdays 9am to 5pm). Fax (212) 768-3477. Old hotel, a bit tatty, but in the process of upgrading. Comfortable and clean; good location for theatergoing; popular with fashion buyers and frugal tourists from Europe and Latin America. Close to budget rates. Multilingual staff. 254 rooms and suites.

Westpark Hotel
308 West 58 Street at Columbus Circle (10019). (212) 246-6440; (800) 228-1122. Fax (212) 246-3131. Attractive, modest, almost-budget choice well situated on the West Side. Completely renovated rooms are charming; higher-up, higher-priced ones have Central Park views. Multilingual staff. No room service. 90 rooms.

Wyndham
42 West 58 Street (10019). (212) 753-3500. A word-of-mouth find near Fifth Avenue and Central Park. Privately owned and discreetly run, this well-appointed hotel—so well located and well

priced—caters to an American and British theatrical and literary clientele. Each room is individually decorated, quiet, and impeccably maintained. Great value, albeit no room service or direct-dial phones. Elevators still manned by operator, a locked lobby at all times. 200 rooms.

BUDGET

The rates of the hotels listed in this category range in price from $35 per person for a single to $75 to $80 for a double. In most cases the least expensive have shared bath.
See also Hostels & Y's and Bed & Breakfast.

Aberdeen Hotel
17 West 32 Street (10001). (212) 736-1600; (800) 826-4667. Fax (212) 695-1813. Between Broadway and Fifth Avenue, part of the Chatwal chain of pleasant, affordably priced hotels. The smallish rooms all have cable TV and airconditioning. Complimentary continental breakfast. Restaurant and lounge on premises. Group rates available. 200 rooms.

Allerton House
130 East 57 Street (10022). (212) 753-8841. Homey and secure for women only; many are older, permanent residents. Well located for East Side shopping, convenient to all transportation. Some rooms have private bath, none have airconditioning. But there is a TV room, a wraparound sun terrace, and a laundromat. The popular longtime Irish Pavilion restaurant on premises, as well as a fitness club (independently operated). NOTE: No credit cards accepted. 500 rooms.

Carlton Arms
160 East 25 Street (10010). (212) 679-0680. Off Third Avenue; an offbeat choice and, according to *Elle* magazine, "the hippest deal in town." The tiny, bare-essential rooms have been individually decorated by an international array of up-and-coming artists. If avant-garde art and funky bargains are your thing, and you're young, at least in spirit, this is the place for you. International and student discounts. No air-conditioning; not all rooms have private bath. 42 rooms.

Chatwal Inn on Park Avenue
429 Park Avenue South at East 30 St (10016). (212) 532-4860; (800) 826-4667. Fax (212) 545-9727. Formerly a residential property, now a small comfortable homey hotel below midtown; part of the Chatwal chain of affordable Manhattan hotels. Pleasant rooms have color TV, direct-dial phones, and individually controlled airconditioning. Complimentary continental breakfast. Valet parking. 53 rooms.

Excelsior
45 West 81 Street (10024). (212) 362-9200. Terrific budget choice on pretty tree-lined Upper West Side residential street, directly across the street from the American Museum of Natural History, and just a half block from Central Park. Sedate surroundings, clean and tidy rooms, air-

conditioning, private bath, color TV, suites are kitchenette-equipped; south-facing rooms on upper floors have park views. Room service from coffee shop. Secure and well operated; popular with frugal Europeans and space-cramped West Siders who house out-of-town visitors here. 300 rooms.

Herald Square Hotel
19 West 31 Street (10001). (212) 279-4017; (800) 727-1888. Fax (212) 643-9208. A ninestory 1893 landmark Beaux Arts building, the orignial home of *Life* magazine, has been recently transformed into a welcoming budgetpriced hotel. Nondescript location, albeit close to Macy's and the Empire State Building. Comfortably decorated rooms vary in size and price, and some have shared bath (these are rockbottom cheap), but all have cable TV, direct-dial phones, and individually controlled airconditioning. 130 rooms.

Iroquois Hotel
49 West 44 Street (10036). (212) 840-3080. Comfortable, pleasant family-style hotel in the process of being upgraded. All rooms have private bath, color cable TV, air-conditioning; some have kitchenettes. Children under age 12 in parents' room free. Theater district location just two doors from the famed Algonquin Hotel and across the street from the newly chic Royalton. On premises: Jan Wallman's restaurant and cabaret. 86 rooms, including 60 suites.

Mansfield Fifth Avenue Hotel
12 West 44 Street (10036). (212) 944-6050; (800) 255-5167. Fax (212) 764-4477. Just off Fifth Avenue, a simple standard tourist hotel located in a 1907 Stanford White building. Not all of the smallish rooms have private bath or airconditioning. Cable TV but few other amenities. Popular with European, Japanese, and South American tourists; multilingual staff. Restaurant and bar on premises. 200 rooms.

Martha Washington Hotel
30 East 30 Street (10016). (212) 689-1900. For women only (*see also* Allerton House); comfortable and secure but quality of rooms varies greatly. Not all have private bath. Airconditioning and TV may be rented. Rooftop sun deck. 451 rooms.

Olcott Hotel
27 West 72 Street (10023). (212) 877-4200. Fax (212) 580-0511. Just off Central Park West, near trendy Columbus Avenue, is this longtime residential hotel with some rooms for transients. Proximity to Lincoln Center draws ballet and opera clientele. Comfortable plain accommodations, studios and suites, all with private bath, cooking pantry, direct-dial phones, cable TV, airconditioning. Maid service. Very good value. Reserve well in advance. Weekly rates available. No pets allowed; no credit cards accepted. Approximately 130 units of 250 available for transients.

Pickwick Arms
230 East 51 Street (10022). (212) 355-0300; (800) 742-5945. Fax (212) 755-5029. Between Second and Third avenues, a pleasant, newly

refurbished oldie popular with foreign tourists. Some rooms have shared bath (they are the real bargains), all are air-conditioned, have direct-dial phones and cable TV. There is also a delightful rooftop garden; a lounge and restaurant on premises; courteous multilingual staff; room service. A plus is the East Side Turtle Bay neighborhood (where a frequently sighted Katharine Hepburn resides). 400 rooms.

The Portland Square Hotel
132 West 47 Street (10036). (212) 382-0600; (800) 388-8988. Fax (212) 382-0684. Built in 1904 as the Rio Hotel, this theater district hotel and its immediate area between Sixth and Seventh avenues have undergone a renaissance. Rooms are quite small but neat and each has color TV, direct-dial phones, individually regulated air-conditioning; singles have sinks but no bath (incredibly low-priced). Service is limited but management is caring. 100 rooms.

Remington
129 West 46 Street (10036). (212) 221-2600. Fax (212) 764-7481. A small theater district budget hotel, recently renovated. Pleasant rooms have cable color TV, direct-dial phones, double windows for quiet. Not all rooms have private bath. Latin American and European clientele. Good low-frills value. 80 rooms.

Roger Williams Hotel
28 East 31 Street (10016). (212) 684-7500. A terrific budget find in quiet Murray Hill, this longtime budget choice is in the process of renovating. The newly redone lobby is inviting, and the atmosphere is friendly and personal. All rooms have full bath, kitchenettes, cable TV, direct-dial phones, some even have terraces. Children under age 14 in parents' room free. Group rates upon request. 211 rooms.

Stanford Hotel
43 West 32 Street (10001). (212) 563-1480; (800) 365-1114. Fax (212) 629-0043. Between Broadway and Fifth Avenue, a completely renovated Korean-owned hotel attracts a Latin American and Japanese clientele. Close neighbor to Macy's and A&S Plaza shopping. Rooms have air-conditioning, cable TV, and refrigerator. Two restaurants and a piano bar. 135 rooms.

Washington Square Hotel
103 Waverly Place (10011). (212) 777-9515; (800) 222-0418. Fax (212) 979-8373. Originally built in 1902, the building has been upgraded into a pleasant budget choice, the only hotel in Greenwich Village. Rooms are small but all have private bath, air-conditioning, cable TV, and direct-dial phones. Located just across from Washington Square Park, during the day a lively urban oasis but a bit dicey after dark. 200 rooms.

HOSTELS & Y'S

American Youth Hostels/NY International Youth Hostel
891 Amsterdam Avenue at West 103 St (10025). (212) 932-2300. Clean, comfortable, and very secure accommodations located in a newly renovated landmark building with a large private garden and handsome common rooms. Cafeteria, restaurant, and self-service kitchen. And they are not for students only—anyone, including families, may take advantage of the rock-bottom prices. Also on premises conference facilities available for nonprofit groups. 480 beds, including 90 large two- to eight-person dormitory rooms. No curfew, guests may arrive at any hour.

International House of New York
500 Riverside Drive at West 122 St (10027). (212) 316-8400. Available during summer and mid-winter vacation periods to anyone in academic life. Accommodations are all singles with shared baths. Daily, weekly, monthly rates. Cafeteria, pub, dancing, gym, sun terrace, study facilities. Write or call in advance. 500 rooms.

International Student Center
38 West 88 Street (10024). (212) 787-7706. Between Central Park West and Columbus Avenue; sponsored by the Association for World Travel Exchange. Year-round dormitory-style accommodations for men and women students, age 18 to 30. (International only, no Americans or Canadians, passports are required.) Rock-bottom prices, limit of five nights. Cooking facilities available. No advance booking; open daily 8am to 11pm.

McBurney YMCA
215 West 23 Street (10011). (212) 741-9210. For men over 18 only. Coed gymnasium, swimming pool, track, and sauna. 279 rooms.

92 Street Y
1395 Lexington Avenue (10028). (212) 427-6000, ext. 126. Available to college-age students, men and women, ages 18 to 26. In an attractive residential area. Single and double dormlike rooms; weekly and monthly rates. Shared kitchen and bath facilities on each floor. During school year, a three-month minimum, other times three weeks. Proof of job or study program required, as is a personal interview. Access to adjoining gymnasium and pool, exercise rooms, and equipment, as well as reduced-rate tickets to the myriad cultural attractions for which this Y is known. 350 rooms.

Sloan House YMCA
356 West 34 Street (10001). (212) 760-5856. Fax (212) 967-7308. Large coed international young adult residence facilities. Singles, doubles, some with private bath. Weekly rates for students. On-premises cafeteria, gift shop, checkroom, safe-deposit boxes, laundry facilities. 1,400 rooms.

Vanderbilt YMCA
224 East 47 Street (10017). (212) 755-2410. Fax (212) 752-0210. Great location. Coed residence facilities with single, double, and quad rooms (upper and lower bunks); some with semi-private baths. Health club, swimming pool, sauna; excellent cafeteria. Self-service laundry facilities. Several languages spoken. 430 rooms.

West Side YMCA
5 West 63 Street (10023). (212) 787-4400. Fax (212) 580-0441. Men over 18; two floors reserved for women students only. Coed gymnasium, two swimming pools, track, racquetball/squash courts, sauna; cafeteria. French- and Spanish-speaking staff. 561 rooms.

HOTELS NEAR THE AIRPORT

By virtue of their location, these tend to be frenetic.

JFK International Airport

Hilton JFK Airport
JFK International Airport, 138-10 135 Avenue near 138 St, Jamaica, Queens (11436). (718) 322-8700; (800) 445-8667. Fax (718) 529-0749. Friendly, modern, and efficient. Provides transportation to and from terminals. Restaurant and lounge on premises. 330 rooms.

Holiday Inn JFK Airport
144-02 135 Avenue, Jamaica, Queens (11436). (718) 659-0200; (800) 465-4329. Adjacent to the airport. Spacious rooms with king-sized beds with work tables; in-room movies, no-smoking rooms; indoor/outdoor pool, sauna and whirlpool, and fitness center. 24-hour courtesy airport transport. Restaurant and lounge with entertainment. 360 rooms.

JFK Plaza Hotel
135-30 140 Street, Jamaica, Queens (11436). (718) 659-6000; (800) 445-7177. Fax (718) 659-4755. Hotel not far from airport with contemporary decor and facilities. Concierge level for extra pampering. Shuttle service to and from the airport terminals. Restaurant open 6am to 1am. Small indoor swimming pool, sauna, weight room open from 4 to 10pm, weekends from 10am to 10pm. Free indoor parking. 370 rooms.

Kennedy Inn at JFK
151-20 Baisley Boulevard, Jamaica, Queens (11434). (718) 276-6666; (800) 826-4667. Fax (718) 276-7777. Close to Kennedy International. All rooms have cable TV, individual climate control, direct-dial phones. Restaurant, lounge, and coffee shop on premises. 200 rooms and suites.

Travelodge International JFK
JFK International Airport, Van Wyck Expressway, Jamaica, Queens (11430). (718) 995-9000; (800) 255-3050. Fax (718) 995-9075. Modern hotel right at the airport geared to the executive trade complete with meeting/banquet facilities. Free airport limo to LaGuardia and JFK. Free parking; multilingual staff; secretarial services available. No-smoking rooms; children under age 18 in parents' room free. Restaurant and lounge on premises. 485 rooms.

LaGuardia Airport

Days Inn La Guardia
100-15 Ditmars Boulevard, East Elmhurst, Queens (11369). (718) 898-1225. Fax (718) 898-

8337. Modern hotel with all the conveniences. Outdoor swimming pool in season. Restaurant/lounge open 6:30am to 10pm. A courtesy van picks up guests from their flights. 224 rooms.

King's Inn at LaGuardia Airport
87-02 23 Avenue, East Elmhurst, Queens (11369). (718) 672-7900. Comfortable. Free transportation to and from your flight. Restaurant, coffee shop, and nightclub on premises. 75 rooms.

La Guardia Marriott
102-05 Ditmars Boulevard, East Elmhurst, Queens. (718) 565-8900; (800) 287-8900. Fax (718) 899-0764. All the comforts of Marriott. Opposite the airport. Two restaurants; fitness equipment, hydropathy pool, sauna; indoor swimming pool. 444 rooms.

Ramada at LaGuardia Airport
90-10 Grand Central Parkway, East Elmhurst, Queens (11370). (718) 446-4800; (800) 228-2828. Clean, modern, newly renovated, and quiet facilities, convenient to the airport. Shuttle service to airport. Restaurant and lounge; outdoor pool in summer. Corporate rates; weekend rates. 288 rooms.

BED & BREAKFAST

Want to save money, stay in comfortable accommodations, and perhaps meet your "average" New Yorker. In lieu of a hotel, try a Bed & Breakfast in the Big Apple. Accommodations and rates vary—be very specific regarding your needs: no smoking; no cats, dogs; quiet; no loft ladders, steps, etc.

In all cases a deposit is required to confirm a reservation. NOTE: *Call the following at reasonable hours.*

. . . Aaah! Bed & Breakfast #1, Ltd.
P.O. Box 200, New York, NY (10108). (212) 246-4000. Fax (212) 265-4346. A bed-and-breakfast reservations agency offering accommodations not only in New York but London and Paris as well. Hosted and unhosted apartments are available, a continental breakfast is included. The range per day is $60 for a single, $80 for doubles; for unhosted apartments the range is $80 to $250. All reservations require a deposit; all require a minimum stay of two nights. Payment by corporate and personal checks and by American Express.

Bed & Breakfast (& Books)
c/o Judy Goldberg, 35 West 92 Street, apt 2C, New York, NY (10025). (212) 865-8740. Representing about 20 hosted and unhosted apartments concentrated on the Upper West Side but also on the East Side and in Greenwich Village. The range for a hosted single is $57.50 to $80; doubles run from $67.50 to $150. Unhosted studio for $100 to $175 for a luxurious one-bedroom. Monthly availability as well. One night's deposit in advance. Payment by cash or traveler's check only.

City Lights Bed & Breakfast Ltd

P.O. Box 20355, Cherokee Station, New York, NY (10028). (212) 737-7049 or -8251. Over 400 listings in Manhattan and Park Slope and Brooklyn Heights (Brooklyn). Rates range from $60 to $75 for singles, $70 to $90 for doubles. Unhosted accommodations also available with rates dependent upon length of stay and number of people. A deposit of 25 percent of the total bill is required.

New World Bed and Breakfast

150 Fifth Avenue, New York, NY (10011). (212) 675-5600; (800) 443-3800. Over 100 listings in Manhattan only from 96 Street to the Battery. A deposit of 25 percent of the full cost is requested for unhosted apartments.

Urban Ventures

P.O. Box 426, Planetarium Station, New York, NY (10024). (212) 594-5650. The pioneer bed-and-breakfast people in New York. Over 700 listings in Manhattan, some in Brooklyn and Queens. Several levels of accommodations, including some with private bath. Unhosted apartments—studios, one- and two-bedroom apartments—are also available. Deposit of $40 per person required in advance. No credit cards

SIGHTSEEING

Brooklyn Bridge

For more sightseeing opportunities, see also AN-NUAL EVENTS *and* HISTORIC & NEW NEW YORK.

VIEWPOINTS

A view from the top is one of the best ways to acquaint yourself with New York City. See also From the Air.

Brooklyn Bridge
City Hall Park in Manhattan to Cadman Plaza West in Brooklyn Heights. There was no bridge in the world that had an elevated promenade when John Roebling planned the one for his bridge in 1869. This boardwalk for the exclusive use of pedestrians (and now, of course, bicycles) was to afford uninterrupted views in every direction. When the bridge was opened in 1883, 150,300 pedestrians paid one penny each to walk the one-mile-plus across the Great East River Bridge, as it was then called. It's free now, and the view is considerably different from what it was 100 years ago, but it's no less magnificent. Don't miss this walk, even if you only go to the first tower. If you do walk across to Brooklyn, head over to the Brooklyn Heights Esplanade for another famous view. (*See also* HISTORIC & NEW NEW YORK, Bridges.)
Brooklyn Heights Esplanade (Promenade)
From Remsen to Orange Streets, Brooklyn. The

esplanade, or as natives call it, the promenade, provides the most celebrated skyline view of the city, from across the East River. (*See also* RES-TAURANTS, Rooms with a View: River Cafe.)
Empire State Building
350 Fifth Avenue at 34 St. 736-3100. At 102 stories (1,250 feet), it's now the third-tallest building in the world, but it's still the most elegant. There are two observation decks—one outdoors on the 86th floor and one, glass-enclosed, on the 102nd. It's a 360-degree view with 80 miles of visibility on a clear day. Day or night it's quite an eyeful. *OPEN 7 days 9:30am-midnight.* Last ticket sold 11:25pm. (*See also* HISTORIC & NEW NEW YORK, Modern Architecture.) Admission charge; discount for children under 12. Group rates by reservations.
Metropolitan Museum of Art Rooftop Sculpture Garden
Fifth Avenue at 82 St. 535-7710. Atop the 10,000-square-foot Lila Acheson Wallace wing, New York's newest viewpoint: an outdoor rooftop sculpture garden with Central Park and the skyline as breathtaking backdrop. Perfect at twilight. *OPEN May-Oct weather permitting.* It's not easy to locate the elevator to reach this spot, but persevere, it's worth it. (*See also* MUSEUMS & GALLERIES, General Art Museums.)
Pier 17, South Street Seaport
Fulton Street at the East River. This shopping and dining pier juts 500 yards into the river pro-

viding superb views of the Brooklyn Bridge and the harbor. Best time and place: at sunset from a deck chair on the upper-level outdoor promenade. (*See also* SIGHTSEEING, On Your Own: South Street Seaport Marketplace *and* MUSEUMS & GALLERIES, Historic Museums: South Street Seaport Museum.)

Rainbow Room
30 Rockefeller Plaza. (*See* NIGHTLIFE, Dining & Dancing.)

Riverside Church
West 120 Street & Riverside Drive. 222-5900. The enclosed observation platform, 392 feet up, affords a lovely view of the Manhattan skyline. *OPEN (weather permitting) Mon-Sat 11am-3pm; Sun noon-4pm.* Nominal admission charge; children under age 6 not admitted. (*See also* HISTORIC & NEW NEW YORK, Churches & Synagogues.)

Statue of Liberty National Monument
Liberty Island. Ferry information: 269-5755; Statue information: 363-3200. A restored and resplendent Lady Liberty captured the nation's attention on her 100th birthday, and retains it still. The 20-minute boat ride provides lovely vistas and the view from her crown is unforgettable— expect a wait to ascend. The Statue is free (a plan by the federal government to charge admission has, for now, wisely been tabled); round-trip boat fare, half price for children under age 12. *Boats leave for the island daily on the hour from 9am to 4pm; last boat returns 5:15pm (call for slightly different hours in winter).* Buy tickets at Castle Clinton in Battery Park. NOTE: You can also visit Ellis Island by buying a combination boat fare. (*See also* HISTORIC & NEW NEW YORK, Statues & Monuments.)

Top of the Sixes
666 Fifth Avenue. (*See* RESTAURANTS, Rooms with a View.)

Windows on the World
World Trade Center, North Tower (#1). (*See* RESTAURANTS, Rooms with a View.)

The Winter Garden
World Financial Center, West Street just south of Vesey Street, at the North Pedestrian Bridge. From one of the most breathtaking public spaces to be found in any city, amid a stand of bamboo trees, a view of the Hudson River at sunset is a perfect way to end a day in Lower Manhattan. Also, the site of free musician and arts programs, call 945-0505 for details. (*See also* On Your Own, World Financial Center.)

World Trade Center, Observation Deck
South Tower (#2). 466-7397. This is the world's second-tallest building, measuring in at 1,377 feet, and when you get to the top you'll find it's quite high enough. There's an enclosed observation deck on the 107th floor, but the outdoor observation deck above the 110th (a quarter of a mile high!) is the world's highest open-air viewing platform. Day or night, the view is literally breathtaking. *OPEN (outdoors, wind and weather permitting) 7 days 9:30am-9:30pm.* NOTE: Shorter hours Christmas and New Year's

Eve and Day. Admission charge; half price for children age 6-12 and senior citizens; children under age 6 free. Call two weeks in advance for groups of 10 or more.

NEW YORK TOURS

By Coach

A great variety of escorted coach tours are offered in comfortable air-conditioned buses. Commentaries are given en route.

Brooklyn Day Tour
Gray Line Terminal, 8th Avenue & West 54 Street. 397-2600. A 6-hour bus tour of the famed borough leaves from the terminal and includes stops at the Brooklyn Museum, Brooklyn Heights, and the Botanic Gardens. AE, MC. V. *June-Oct, Thurs & Sat at 9:30am.*

Gray Line of New York
Main office, 900 Eighth Avenue at West 54 St. 397-2600. A choice of 24 different tours uptown (including Harlem), downtown, and out-of-town. From 2 hours to all day, from $14.75 to $45, rates lower for children under age 12. A new feature is an all-day tour of Brooklyn (see above). Foreign language tours available. AE, MC, V. *Tours available every day throughout the year except Christmas Day.*

Harlem Spirituals
Departs from 1697 Broadway at West 53 St (use 53 Street entrance). For information and reservations, call 302-2594. Fascinating bus tours that focus on the past and present of the 5¼ square miles of New York known as Harlem. *Harlem on Sunday, 9am-1pm:* Black Harlem, from 110 to

Statue of Liberty

162 streets, with visits to a historic house and a walk through the lovely Sugar Hill area; includes visit to a gospel-singing church service. *Harlem Weekday Tour, Thurs 9am-1:30pm:* Visits Aunt Len's Doll and Toy Museum; Hamilton Grange, former home of America's first treasury secretary, Alexander Hamilton; the Schomburg Center for black cultural research, walk through Sugar Hill, and finish with a soul-food lunch. *Gospel on a Weekday, Wed 9am-1pm:* In addition to a walk through Sugar Hill, attend a midweek church service and hear a gospel choir. *Soul Foods & Jazz, Thurs, Fri & Sat, 7pm-midnight:* Nighttime view of Harlem, includes a soul-food feast and a visit to a jazz cabaret. Call for reservations. Prices range from $27 to $65 (for the pm tour). AE only. Group rates available. NOTE: Proper dress required to attend church service. (*See also* Harlem Your Way!)

New York Big Apple Tours
203 East 94 Street, suite 1D (10128). 410-4190. Primarily for foreign tourists. Tours conducted in French and German every Tuesday, Thursday, and Saturday; Italian and Spanish, Wednesday, Friday, and Sunday. The standard tours are a 3-hour Lower Manhattan Tour and a 4-hour Upper and Lower Manhattan Tour. They also feature a Sunday Gospel Tour of Harlem. They can tailor a tour for groups. Call or write for further details. Tours leave from West 46 Street and Seventh Avenue (upper level Sbarro restaurant) at 9am Tuesday to Sunday. Reserve one day in advance. Cash and traveler's checks only.

Short Line-American Sightseeing International
166 West 46 Street (10036). 354-5122. Modern glass-top coaches make the views even more dramatic. Twenty tours daily from 2 to 8 hours in length with commentary available in Japanese, French, German, Spanish, and Italian. Also, day trips to Atlantic City's casinos. AE, MC, V.

Specialized Tours

Art Horizons International
14 East 63 Street (10021). 888-2299. They organize New York art tours for museums across the country. The focus is on what's current in the SoHo and uptown galleries and the city's museums. For travel groups only. Call or write for details.

Art Tours of Manhattan
(609) 683-0881. Grads with art degrees guide you through the cultural side of New York. Galleries, museums, music, and theater—often behind the scenes. Custom-designed for groups or individuals according to your interests; from half a day to a week.

Backstage on Broadway Tours
228 West 47 Street (10036). 575-8065. Go behind the scenes of a Broadway show—onstage and backstage for a 60- to 90-minute tour escorted by a professional actor, director, stage manager, or lighting director. For groups or individuals. Reserve.

Eye on Art Tours
10 West 66 Street, suite 21F (10023). 877-5117. Conducted by art consultant Stacey Winston and her associates, programs offer a look at what's current in painting, sculpture, and photography, with visits to galleries, artist studios, museums, auction houses, and even a dealer's or collector's home. Every two weeks on Monday and Wednesday in spring and fall. There are also customized half- or full-day excursions for a maximum of three persons.

Gallery Passport, Ltd.
211 East 70 Street (10021). 288-3578. Begun in 1960, these people offered the first art tours in America. Their unique tours of museums, galleries, and historic mansions are for groups of 10 or more. Expert guides give a preparatory lecture. Deluxe motor coach transport and luncheon are included. There are fall and spring tours. Multilingual guides available. Also, a fall to spring series of Art Talks in Manhattan; write or call for brochure.

Harlem Your Way! Tours Unlimited
129 West 130 Street. 690-1687. Harlem-based group shows you the soul of the black American community: the food, the gospel music, the cultural institutions, the brownstones, the nightlife. Customized walk, bike, or limo tours all conducted by knowledgeable Harlemites. Walks: *Mon-Sat at 12:30pm.* Gospel Tour: *Sun at 10:30am.* Champagne Safaris to the Apollo: *Wed at 6pm;* to jazz spots: *Fri & Sat at 9pm.* Bus tours for groups as well. All tours leave from midtown. Reserve.

Inside New York
203 East 72 Street (10021). 861-0709. An "insider" view of New York as fashion, art, and interior design capital—from Seventh Avenue to SoHo to the Lower East Side. Fashion shows, luncheons, beauty make-overs, shopping at wholesale prices. All tours escorted by fashion professionals. Half-day and full-day tours; multilingual tours available. Twenty-person minimum.

Passkey Associates
230 East 44 Street, suite 9K (10017). 697-4070. Custom-designed, multilingual programs, events, and activities for conventions, corporate meetings, or travel groups.

Planner's New Your Tours
772-5605. Unusual tours from a planner's point of view of rarely visited areas of lower Manhattan, central Manhattan, Brooklyn, Harlem, Bronx, and Queens in a glass-roofed bus. Guides are Hunter College graduate students in urban planning. The emphasis of the 3-hour tour is on history and architecture. For groups by advance registration.

Rothschild Fine Arts
205 West End Avenue (10023). 873-9142. For those very serious about art. Knowledgeable experts escort you to galleries, artists' studios, and museums in chauffeured limo. Tour custom-tailored to your special art interests. Very expensive.

Singer's Tours
130 St. Edward Street, Brooklyn (11201). (718) 875-9084. With enthusiastic native son Louis Singer take highly personal mini-bus tours of Brooklyn areas rich in brownstone architecture: Park Slope, Bedford Village, Stuyvesant Heights, Fort Greene, Cobble Hill, Boerum Hill, and Brooklyn Heights. Lou also leads a gastronomic tour of Manhattan, called "Noshing in New York." Tours leave from 325 East 41 Street in Manhattan. Call him between 7 and 11pm or write for details and reservations. Group rates.

Tours de Force
71 West 23 Street, suite 1825 (10010). 924-0320. The creative life of New York: art, theater, fashion. Visit galleries and artists' studios, meet the performers after the show, shop in Bloomies before the doors open to the public. Multilingual programs. Groups only, minimum of 25 people.

ViewPoint International
1414 Avenue of the Americas (10019). 355-1055. Well-regarded organizer of corporate and VIP tours. Originators of the "Big Apple Caper," a custom-designed city tour covering the city's visible and "hidden" sites. Multilingual guides. Call or write for information.

Your Way Visitor Services
P.O. Box 1232, New York, NY (10022). (516) 883-4560. Custom-designed tourist arrangements based on your needs. "New York Your Way" escorted or self-directed preplanned itineraries. Multilingual guides.

WALKING TOURS

Adventure on a Shoestring, Inc.
300 West 53 Street (10019). 265-2663. The motto of this 29-year-old organization: "Exploring the world within our reach, within our means." Off-the-beaten-path views of New York life and people, as popular with natives as with visitors. There is an annual membership fee and a low per-event fee. There are periodic walking tours of unique areas open to nonmembers. Write or call for details.

Chinatown Walking Tour
Center for Community Studies, 70 Mulberry Street, one block south of Canal Street, 2nd floor. 619-4785. **The Chinatown History Museum** provides walking tours of the largest Chinatown in the Western Hemisphere. The one-hour walk is preceded by a 20-minute slide presentation. Tours: *Mon-Fri between 10am & 4pm.* Advance reservations are required for weekend tours. Special rates for groups and schools by previous arrangement.

Citywalks
410 West 20 Street (10011). 989-2456. Walking tours of Greenwich Village, lower Broadway, the Lower East Side, Fifth Avenue, and Chelsea by extremely knowledgeable citywalker John Wilson. Tours: *year-round, nearly every Sat & Sun at 1pm.* Call or write for current schedule; personalized tours as well.

Classical America
P.O. Box 821, Times Square Station, New York, NY (10108). 753-4376. A national club, one of whose founders, Henry Hope Reed, is known as "the dean of informed walks." They sponsor tours focusing on architecture, sculpture, and garden design in the classical style—that is, Beaux Arts, American Renaissance, neoclassicism. For true New York architecture aficionados there are Stanford White and Charles McKim birthday tours. Lectures during the winter. Tours: *spring & fall, Sat & Sun afternoons.* Call or write for details.

Fulton Fish Market
South Street Seaport Museum. 669-9416. This is for early birds who want to see the catch. A 1¾-hour walking tour of the Fulton Fish Market, which was begun in 1823 and is still going strong. The proceeds of the tour go directly to the restoration, now under way at the Seaport, of the *Lettie G. Howard*, a Gloucester fishing schooner. *Apr-Oct, 1st & 3rd Thurs of each month at 6am.* Reserve two weeks in advance with full payment ($10 for nonmembers); call for details.

Grand Central Terminal Tour
A guided walk through New York's newly restored grand Beaux Arts beauty, sponsored by the Municipal Art Society, instrumental in the battle to preserve the station as a landmark. *Year-round every Wed, 12:30-1:30pm.* Meet at the Main Terminal, in front of the Chemical Bank Commuter Express. For further information, call 935-3960. No reservations necessary and it's FREE. (*See also* HISTORIC & NEW NEW YORK, Historic Buildings & Areas: Grand Central Terminal.)

Grand Tour
A Grand Central District tour, sponsored by the Grand Central Partnership and led by "urban detective" and historian Justin Ferate. A walking tour of the station and its environs, including the Art Deco interiors of the Chanin and Chrysler buildings, the Lincoln Building, the Helmsley Building, and more. The free 90-minute tour *every Fri at 12:30pm* leaves from the front of the Philip Morris Building on 42 Street at Park Avenue. For information, call 986-9217. For group tours, call Paula Horowitz in advance at 818-1777.

Hope Cooke's NY Walking Tours
(718) 852-3316. Take a thinking person's tour of New York with the American-born historian and writer (and former queen of Sikkim) Hope Cooke. They focus on the social, political, and cultural history of the city, on how the architecture reveals the dynamics of what built a neighborhood, and how the people lived. Architecture is the key to bringing past to present. Call for information on public and customized private tours.

Lower East Side
The Lower East Side Tenement Museum, 97 Orchard Street. 431-0233. The echo of the immigrant experience resonates on the streets of the Lower East Side. "Peddler's Pack Walk," the museum's living history tour of the Lower East Side

neighborhood led by a costumed actor, highlights the area's rich immigrant history. *Every Sun at noon.* "The Street Where We Lived," a 2-hour historical walk with Columbia professor James Shenton, explores the backgrounds and local experiences of six groups of the area's early residents: Eastern European Jews, the Chinese, free Africans, Germans, the Irish, and Italians. *Every Sun at 1pm.* Reservations required for each program. Admission charge, lower for seniors and students. (*See also* MUSEUMS & GALLERIES, Historic Museums.)

Manhattan History
242-5762. Teacher and Manhattan historian Joyce Gold offers highly informed public and private tours of lower Manhattan: the Financial District, the Lower East Side, TriBeCa, Greenwich Village, the East Village, Chelsea, Ladies Mile, and Gramercy Park. *Spring, summer, and fall; usually Sun at noon.* Rain or shine; no reservations necessary, except for her very special Ellis Island Tour. Call or write for schedule. 141 West 17 Street (10011).

Municipal Art Society
457 Madison Avenue at East 51 St. (10022). 935-3960. The premier preservationist civic group leads knowledgeably guided walks examining the city's architecture in the context of its social history and current goings-on in New York City-scaping. Great way to discover New York's neighborhoods. Shine only; reservations necessary; call or write for schedule. Tours: *Jan-Nov (usually on Sun at 2pm).* Cost lower for members. They also sponsor a free Grand Central Terminal tour every week, see above.

Museum of the City of New York
Fifth Avenue & 103 Street (10029). 534-1672. For over 30 years the museum has sponsored leisurely paced knowledgeable explorations of New York neighborhoods, highlighting the social, historical, and architectural. *Apr-Oct, bimonthly Sun.* Rain or shine. Advance registration required. Call or write for schedule. Admission lower for members.

92 Street Y
1395 Lexington Avenue at East 92 St (10128). 415-5600. Fun and fascinating thematic journeys to areas of historic, social, and architectural importance. *Early spring to fall, Sun mornings.* Rain or shine. Reservations required. Call or write for schedule.

River-to-River Downtown Walking Tours
321-2823. Ruth Alcher-Green's excursions through lower Manhattan are highly personal, chatty, informal yet informed glimpses of the area between the rivers below 14 Street. Two-hour walks by appointment only for one, two, or a group. Call or write for details: 375 South End Avenue (10280).

Sidewalks of New York
517-0201. These atypical 2-hour tours of Greenwich Village, midtown, and the Upper West Side delve into history, scandal, and trivia and include such offbeat themes as "Hollywood on the Hudson," "Ghosts After Sunset," "Famous Murder Sites," and "Death Scenes of the Famous." There is also the more straightforward "Ye Olde Tavern Tour" and a "Greenwich Village Brunch Tour." Tours: *nearly every Sat & Sun, day and evening.* No reservations required; call for schedule or mail a stamped, self-addressed envelope to Sidewalks of New York, P.O. Box 1660, Cathedral Station, New York, NY 10025. Private and group tours are available Monday to Friday by appointment.

South Street Seaport Museum
Daily guided tours of the museum complex: from the Pilothouse, a tour of the district itself and a visit to the *Peking;* a tour of the *Wavetree* restoration; also, from the museum gallery, a tour of the back streets; a walk along Water Street for a look at the history of the area. All tours are free with museum admission. For information, call 669-9400. (*See also* MUSEUMS & GALLERIES, Historic Museums: South Street Seaport Museum.)

Urban Park Rangers
The Rangers give tours that focus on every facet of that urban miracle, Central Park. Depending on the specialty of your particular guide, it may be a bird walk, a lake tour, tree identification, or a historical and geological tour. For details on *tours available year-round,* call 427-4040.

Self-guided

Flushing Freedom Mile
Queens Historical Society, 43-35 37th Avenue, Flushing, Queens (11354). (718) 939-0647. The society offers a brochure for a self-guided walking tour of the Flushing Freedom Mile, including visits to three historic houses. Send a stamped, self-addressed envelope to the society. Admission charge to the houses.

Friends of Cast-Iron Architecture
A lovely printed self-guided tour and map is available for $3 postpaid, to acquaint people with the splendid 19th-century iron-front architecture of New York, predominantly in SoHo and TriBeCa. For information, call 369-6004, or send your check to Friends of Cast-Iron Architecture, 235 East 87 Street, room 6C, New York, NY 10128.

Heritage Trail
Lower Manhattan from Civic Center to the South Street Seaport. A 3-mile do-it-yourself walking tour. Buildings, open spaces, and monuments representing key elements in the economic, social, and political evolution of New York have signposts presenting a brief history of each. A map of the trail is available at the Convention and Visitor's Bureau, 2 Columbus Circle at West 59 Street, or the New York Vista Hotel, 3 World Trade Center.

FROM THE AIR

Island Helicopter Corp.
The Heliport, East 34 Street at the East River. 683-4575 (recorded); 925-8807. The world's largest

sightseeing copter service. An expensive but unforgettable bird's-eye view of the city from a sightseeing helicopter. Fasten your seat belt and choose from flights lasting 7, 14, 22, or 35 minutes and covering sites from the United Nations and Statue of Liberty to midtown skyscrapers. Costs vary per flight—ranging from $41 to $94, with the most expensive being the Photographer's Delight, covering Central Park, Harlem, Yonkers, the Hudson River, and George Washington Bridge, plus lower Manhattan, the Statue, and midtown. Minimum two people. Cost is per person including children. No reservations necessary. For groups, call (718) 895-1626. Remember to bring your camera. Free parking. *Available Apr-Dec, 7 days 9am-9pm; Jan-Mar 9am-6pm. CLOSED Christmas & New Year's Day.*

ON YOUR OWN

For those of you who prefer to make your own way. Make sure you also check the HISTORIC & NEW YORK and ANNUAL EVENTS chapters for more to do on your own in New York.

Atriums
Foliage-bedecked, glass-topped, or enclosed oases in midtown where one can sit, sometimes sip or sup, and reflect—often made easy by the presence of reflecting pools and waterfalls. They are open free to the public and they are secure places to cool off in summer and get warm in winter; there's even free entertainment on occasion. Listed below are some of these very special urban spaces. NOTE: * indicates the best of them.

AT&T Building
Madison Avenue between East 55 & East 56 Sts. *OPEN Mon-Fri 8am-10pm; Sat & Sun 10am-6pm.*

Chemcourt
277 Park Avenue at East 47 St. The city's largest indoor green space—a three-story, block-long greenhouse. The greenery surrounding terraced pools is changed with the seasons. No food allowed. *OPEN 7 days, 24 hours a day.*

*Citicorp Center Market
Lexington Avenue between East 53 & East 54 Sts. 559-2330. Lively seven-story-high skylit atrium-agora; 27 shops and restaurants. Free classical concerts midday and in the evening, call for current roster. *OPEN Mon-Fri 7am-midnight; Sat 8am-midnight; Sun 10pm-midnight.*

*Ford Foundation
320 East 43 Street. This verdant habitat was one of the first of the city's public atriums—130-feet tall, surrounded by glass-enclosed offices. No food allowed. *OPEN Mon-Fri 8am-5pm.*

Galleria
East 57 Street between Park & Lexington Aves. Cafe Galleria for snacks and drinks. *OPEN Mon-Sat 8am-10pm; Sun 8am-6pm.*

*IBM Garden Plaza
Madison Avenue at East 57 St. A four-story gardenlike setting complete with a forest of 45-foot bamboo trees. The IBM Gallery of Science & Art is here (*see* MUSEUMS & GALLERIES, Science Museums), also, a New York Botanical Garden outlet shop. Monday to Friday a kiosk for snacks and beverages. Atrium: *OPEN 7 days 8am-10pm. Museum: OPEN Tues-Sat 11am-6pm.*

Olympic Tower
Fifth Avenue at East 51 St. A three-story waterfall and a cafe for food and drink, Monday to Friday from 8am to 9pm and Saturday from 9am to 8pm. Atrium *OPEN 7 days 8am-midnight.*

Park Atrium
East 46 to East 47 Street between Park & Lexington Aves. A 23-story plant-bedecked atrium; shops and restaurants. *OPEN Mon-Fri 8am-6pm.*

*Park Avenue Plaza
East 52 to East 53 Street between Park & Madison Aves. A shopping arcade, a dramatic waterfall, public seating, flowers, special events, and the Cafe Marguery for snacks, Monday to Friday from 8am to 7:30pm. Atrium *OPEN 7 days 8am-10pm.*

Trump Tower
Fifth Avenue & East 56 Street. Posh vertical shopping plaza with a five-story waterfall. Best spot: landscaped outdoor terraces with tables and chairs on the fourth and fifth levels; cafe on the fifth level as well. Atrium *OPEN Mon-Sat 10am-6pm.*

Whitney Museum Sculpture Court
Philip Morris Building, East 42 Street at Park Ave. 878-2550 or -2453. Seats and tables amid large-scale sculpture from the Whitney collection. *OPEN Mon-Sat 7:30am-9:30pm; Sun 11am-7pm.*

Carnegie Hall
154 West 57 Street. 247-7800. Take a 45-minute tour of the famed 100-year-old concert hall covering history and behind-the-scenes anecdotes. *Every Mon, Tues & Thurs at 11:30am, 2 & 3pm.* Also available "Tour & Tea," a package that includes the afternoon tour and tea service at the neighboring Russian Tea Room. Tickets may be bought at the Tour Window. Admission lower for seniors, children, and students. (*See also* HISTORIC & NEW NEW YORK, Historic Buildings & Areas, Manhattan: Carnegie Hall.)

Central Park: The Dairy
In the Park at East 64 St. 397-3156. An 1870 Gothic Revival building designed as a milk dispensary for working-class mothers and their babies. Newly restored, it serves as the park's **Visitor's Center** with a permanent exhibit on the park, a time-travel video every half hour, free literature and maps, also a gift shop with cards and books for sale. Weekend programs for families; starting point for lectures and tours on all aspects of Central Park given by the Urban Park Rangers (*see* Walking Tours). *OPEN Feb 1-Oct*

31, Tues-Thurs & Sat & Sun 11am-5pm, Fri 1-5pm; Nov 1-Jan 31, Tues-Sun 11am-4pm. CLOSED Mon.

Ellis Island
Battery Park & South Ferry. 269-5755. The 30-minute boat ride to Ellis Island is a trip worth taking. It's a poignant reminder of New York's role as adopted home of 12 million people from other lands. The "Island of Tears," as it was called by those who for one reason or another did not make it through, was designated an immigration station in 1892. The present building dates from 1900 and has just undergone a $156 million restoration, serving now as a museum celebrating American immigration. Start in the Baggage Room for an orientation, then ascend a staircase to the impressive two-story Registry Room, where 80 percent of those who arrived were deemed fit to remain (another 18 percent remained following appeal). A film chronicles the history of immigration but most evocative are the taped recordings of immigrant remembrances placed throughout the exhibition and the glass cases containing clothing and other items cherished by families descended from immigrants. **The American Immigrant Wall of Honor** records the names of 200,000 immigrants whose families honored them by contributing to the Island restoration. Boats operate to the Island daily 9:30am-3pm every half hour. Last boat returns at 5:15pm. Boats stop at the Statue of Liberty before going on to Ellis; you can book passage for visits to both. Fare lower for senior and children. (See also HISTORIC & NEW NEW YORK, Historic Buildings & Areas, Manhattan: Ellis Island.)

Federal Reserve Bank
33 Liberty Street near William St (10045). 720-6130. The largest of the Federal Reserve System's banks, located in a block-long 14-story stone structure. The tour provides an overview of the bank's operations and insight into its role in the economy. Visitors see the gold vault (where the world's largest known accumulation of that precious metal is stored), currency processing, the security area, and a brief film about the cash processing. For reservations, call or write c/o Public Information at least one week in advance. One-hour tours Mon-Fri 10:30 & 11:30am, 1:30 & 2:30pm. FREE.

Guinness World Records Exhibit Hall
Empire State Building, Fifth Avenue at 34 Street, concourse level. 947-2335. Memorabilia, minutiae, and videotapes of the amazing facts and feats chronicled in the Guinness Book of World Records. OPEN 7 days 9am-8pm; in summer and during the Christmas season Sat & Sun till 10pm. Allow 45 minutes. Combined, of course, with a trip up to see the view from the 86th- or 102nd-floor observation decks. Admission charge; lower for children under age 11 and senior citizens.

Intrepid Sea-Air-Space Museum
Pier 86, West 46 Street & 12th Avenue. 245-0072. Christened in 1943, this well-traveled 900-foot aircraft carrier—formerly the U.S.S. Intrepid—is

now a National Historic Landmark and a fascinating museum. In addition to more than 70 historic aircraft on board, there are crew area exhibits, an audiovisual presentation, and the Hall of Honor, dedicated to America's Congressional Medal of Honor recipients. The Intrepid had an illustrious 31-year career in World War II and Southeast Asia; it was also the rescue ship for the Mercury and Gemini space missions. Gift shop and cafeteria. Handicapped access. OPEN Wed-Sun 10am-5pm (last ticket sold 4pm). CLOSED Mon, Tues & all federal holidays. Admission charge; lower for senior citizens and children age 7-13; children under age 6 free. Military and members free. Group rates available, call 245-2533.

Manhattan Neighborhood Trolley
677-7269 (recorded). Hop on and off this new sightseeing trolley making hourly narrated tours around lower Manhattan. Start at the South Street Seaport (South & Fulton streets), then on to Peter Minuet Plaza, Battery Park, the World Financial Center (Vesey Street), World Trade Center (Church & Vesey streets), City Hall (Spruce Street & Park Row), Chinatown (Chatham Square, east side of Bowery), Little Italy (Grand & Bowery), and the final stop, Delancey & Orchard streets (south side) on the Lower East Side. One-time fare of $4 ($3 for seniors and children under age 12) allows you unlimited on and off at designated stops. Apr-Oct, weekends & holidays 10am-6pm.

Metropolitan Opera Backstage
Lincoln Center, Broadway & West 64 Street. 769-7020. Opera singers love this six-tiered, 3,800-seat auditorium—and so does the Opera Guild. They will take you for a fascinating 90-minute tour of the ofttimes bustling scenic and costume shops, auditorium, stage area, and rehearsal facilities. They don't promise Pavarotti, but who knows. . . . Admission charge; lower for students and Opera Guild members. Oct-June, Mon-Fri at 3:45pm; Sat at 10:30am. Reservations are encouraged as far in advance as possible. (See also HISTORIC & NEW NEW YORK, Modern Architecture: Lincoln Center for the Performing Arts.)

NBC Studio Tour
RCA Building, 30 Rockefeller Plaza at 50 St. 664-7174. Fifty-five-minute guided tours of the network's TV and radio stations located for more than 50 years in the RCA Building. Visit the sets of "The Today Show," "The Donahue Show," "Saturday Night Live," and the local news. Tours year-round Mon-Sat 9:30am-4:30pm. CLOSED Labor Day, Thanksgiving, Christmas & New Year's Day. Admission charge. Tickets sold on first-come, first-served basis. Reserve for groups of 10 or more. Children under age 6 not admitted.

New York Stock Exchange
20 Broad Street near Wall St. 656-3000. In front of what is now 60 Wall Street, 24 brokers met in 1792 under a buttonwood tree and agreed to a strict conduct of business, creating the New York Stock Exchange. The building that houses it

dates from 1903. There is a self-guided tour of the exhibit hall and gallery overlooking the trading floor, a continuous tape gives a brief explanation of the hectic goings-on. Advance reservations are necessary for groups of 10 or more. NOTE: Tickets are distributed on a first-come, first-served basis at the Visitor's Center starting at 9am. *OPEN to the public Mon-Fri 9:15am-4pm.* FREE.

New York Transit Museum
Schermerhorn Street & Boerum Place (northwest corner), Brooklyn. (718) 330-3060. In the Borough Hall section of Brooklyn, memorabilia covering a century of transit development. Situated in a 1936 subway station, the museum features 18 fully restored classic subway cars dating back to 1903, including the wooden cars with rattan seating, as well as trolley models, fare-collection devices, antique turnstyles, and a working signal tower. The authentic museum station is also used for film and photo shoots. *OPEN Tues-Fri 10am-4pm; Sat 11am-4pm. CLOSED Sun & Mon & legal holidays.* Admission charge; half price for children under age 17; lower for seniors. Group tours must be arranged in advance. Take the IND, A, F, or C trains to Jay Street; the IRT, 2, 3, 4, or 5 to Boro Hall; or the BMT, M or R to Court Street.

Radio City Music Hall
Avenue of the Americas at West 50 Street. 757-3100. The "Showplace of the Nation" threatened with the wrecker's ball a decade ago, thrives with spectaculars for the whole family: live shows on the block-long Great Stage with colorful costumes, scenery, and the incomparable 36—collectively known as the Rockettes. Their Christ-

New York Stock Exchange

mas show is a not-to-be-missed seasonal treat. There are fascinating hour-long backstage tours, departing from the lobby *year-round, Mon-Sat 10:15am-4:45pm; Sun 11:15am-4:45pm.* For information, call 632-4041 Monday to Friday from 9am to 4:30pm, ask for the Tour Desk. Admission charge lower for children under age 6. Group discounts available.

Schapiro's Winery
126 Rivington Street at Essex St. 674-4404. It's not the Napa Valley, but it's the only working winery in Manhattan. Founded in 1899, its motto (no joke) is "The wine you can cut with a knife." Tour the wine cellars, see the presses, taste the wine. *Twenty-minute tours Sun every hour 11am-4pm (from noon in summer). CLOSED Jewish holidays.* Reservations for groups only. $1 admission. Of course, as long as you're on the Lower East Side, you might as well go shopping for bargains.

South Street Seaport Marketplace
At Fulton & South Streets. New York's hottest new attraction is one of the oldest areas of the city. The 19th-century seaport area has been renewed; the remaining historic buildings are squeaky clean, and the tall ships have been joined by chic boutiques and a mind-boggling array of food stalls, restaurants, and cafes. There's plenty to do and see year-round, but many New Yorkers miss the prechic gritty, more authentic old seaport. Sociological note: Thursday and Friday evenings in summer over 6,000 young professionals descend on the seaport to imbibe and "network." Marketplace: *OPEN Mon-Sat 10am-10pm; Sun noon-6pm.* For information, call SEA-PORT. (*See also* HISTORIC & NEW NEW YORK, Historic Buildings & Areas, Manhattan: Schermerhorn Row *and* MUSEUMS & GALLERIES, Historic Museums: South Street Seaport Museum.) Accessible via subway to Fulton Street or World Trade Center.

United Nations Headquarters
First Avenue between East 42 & East 48 Streets. 963-7713. Visitor's entrance at East 46 Street. The monolithic Secretariat Building, the General Assembly Building, and the Dag Hammarskjold Library make up the distinguished complex. Free tickets for meetings of the General Assembly and Councils when in session; call for information. *OPEN 7 days 9:15am-4:45pm.* Hour-long guided tours start from the first floor of the General Assembly Building every half hour. Admission charge for tours; lower for seniors, children, and full-time students. (No children under age 5 admitted.) For foreign language tours, call 963-7539 on the day you wish to visit. To reserve in advance for groups of 15 or more, call 963-4440, Monday to Friday. Don't miss the well-stocked International Gift Shop on the lower level and try to have lunch in the Delegate's Dining Room, buffet or à la carte, Monday to Friday from 11:30am to 2:30pm; reservations required a day in advance, call 963-7625. (*See also* HISTORIC & NEW NEW YORK, Modern Architecture.)

The World Financial Center
Battery Park City on the Hudson River (across the West Side Highway from the World Trade Center). 945-0505. A lovely addition to lower Manhattan. Forty upscale boutiques, cafes, fine restaurants, and sweeping Hudson River–filled vistas. Plus, in the striking 120-foot-high Winter Garden, the Center's "Main Street," an ongoing free Arts & Events Program, with performing and visual art, including top theater, dance, and musical stars (seating on a first-come basis). Center *OPEN Mon-Fri 10am-7pm; Sat & Sun noon-5pm.* Restaurant hours vary. Accessible via the M9, M10, M22 bus lines to Battery Park City, via the IRT no. 1 local or the BMT, R or N trains to Cortlandt/World Trade Center. (*See also* HISTORIC & NEW NEW YORK, Modern Architecture: Battery Park City.)

BOAT TRIPS

Andrew Fletcher **and** *DeWitt Clinton*
South Street Seaport, Pier 16. 406-3434. Board one of these triple-decked re-created 19th-century sidewheel excursion boats and relax for 90 minutes while seeing the sights of New York Harbor, including a closeup view of the Statue of Liberty, and listening to a historical narrative. It's a relative bargain excursion and a pure delight, especially on the upper deck on a sunny day with a piña colada in hand. Food as well as drink available. *Sails Apr-Dec Mon-Fri 12:30, 2:30, 4:30pm; Sat & Sun hourly 11am-5pm (hours may vary with season, call for confirmation).* There are also non-narrated Twilight Cruises, Thursday evening jazz and Saturday evening rock cruises with live music, d.j., dancing, and a cash bar. Buy tickets at the Pilot House; groups of 20 or more should call 669-9405 in advance to reserve. Available for charter and private parties.

Circle Line Sightseeing Cruise
Circle Line Plaza, West 42 Street & the Hudson River. 563-3200. The best way to cover 35 miles of sightseeing and view areas you would never otherwise visit without becoming footsore. A relaxing—and, in summer, refreshing—3 hours. Narration often amusing as well as informative. Junk food available; soft drinks and beer, too. Children under age 12 half price. AE, MC, V. *Mid-Mar-mid-Nov, 7 days. Sailings every 45 minutes 9:45am-5:50pm.*

Ellis Island Ferry
See On Your Own: Ellis Island.

Harbor Lights Cruise
Circle Line Plaza, Pier 83, West 42 Street & the Hudson River. 563-3200. Two-hour twilight cruise with the world's most dazzling views as backdrop. Order drinks and snacks (extra). *Sat & Sun at 7pm.* No reservations necessary except for groups. AE, DC, MC, V. (No refunds.)

Petrel
From Battery Park. 825-1976. Sail New York Harbor on the spectacular 70-foot yawl that JFK

sailed when he was president. *Mid-Apr-mid-Oct, during the week there is a variety of lunchtime (1¾ hours), happy hour (1½ hours), sunset (1¼ hours), and moonlight outings. Weekends there are two harbor sails during the day as well.* Reservations and payment must be made well in advance (it's very popular with city-wise NYers); be forewarned they go rain or shine even if you don't, so be prepared to get wet or lose your money (or you can pay an extra 25 percent for rain insurance), because there are no refunds or date changes unless the captain wills it. Bar on board, you may bring food. Wear soft-soled shoes. Maximum number of people on board, 36. Available for private charter.

Pioneer
South Street Seaport, Pier 16, Fulton & South Streets. 669-9417. Sail New York Harbor for 2 to 3 hours on a 102-foot twin-masted schooner built in 1885. The *Pioneer* is the only active sailing vessel of the South Street Seaport's fleet of historic ships. Course—and, therefore, time—depends on wind and tides. You may bring food and drink, do dress appropriately, and remember to leave your radios at home. Maximum 40 passengers. *Sails May-mid-Sept, 7 days (unless privately chartered) noon, 3 & 6pm.* Charters Monday to Saturday 9pm to midnight only, call 233-5010. Call ahead for reservations and payment. Rates lower for children and members of the Seaport Museum.

Spirit of New York
Pier 9, at the foot of Wall Street. 279-1890. This 192-foot ship is a newcomer to the fleet of cruising-while-dining boats. The added attraction to the food with a view is a revue called "Salute to Broadway," performed by your waiters and waitresses. There is also a weekend "floating nightclub" cruise. *Sails Mar-Dec. Buffet lunch Mon-Fri noon-2:30pm; buffet dinner & dancing 7 nights 7-10pm; Saturday & Sunday buffet brunch noon-2:30pm; Moonlight Cruise Fri & Sat 11:30pm-2am.* Call in advance to reserve and pay with major credit card. Group rates for 20 or more, call 742-2789.

Staten Island Ferry
In Manhattan: South Ferry at the foot of Whitehall Street at Battery Park. In Staten Island: at the foot of Bay Street, St. George. (718) 727-2508. This 25-minute boat ride crosses Upper New York Bay and offers wonderful panoramic views for only a penny a minute (each way now that the fare has been increased to 50¢). It remains New York's premier sightseeing bargain and it's awfully romantic at dawn or sunset in summer. Snack bar on board. Passengers & autos 24 hours, 7 days. *Weekends every 15 minutes, weekdays every 20 minutes. In the wee hours every hour*, at which time the waiting room on Staten Island is anything but romantic.

Statue of Liberty Ferry
See Viewpoints: Statue of Liberty National Monument.

Venetian Gondola
Loeb Boathouse, Central Park at 74 Street. 517-

3623. (Enter at Fifth Avenue & 72 Street.) On a lovely summer evening why not glide the waters of Central Park Lake in an authentic Venetian gondola—the 37½ foot *Daughter of Venice*—expertly navigated by a traditionally trained and attired gondolier. It's expensive but it's pure magic. Half hour rides for up to six people. *Available May-Sept, 7 nights 5-10pm.* Reserve in advance or combine with dinner at the Boathouse Cafe (*see* RESTAURANTS, Rooms with a View).

World Yacht Cruises
Pier 62, West 23 Street at the Hudson River. 929-7090. Take a cruise around the tip of Manhattan and back again on New York's first luxury restaurant yachts. The *Empress, Riveranda, Princess,* and *Duchess* are plush, carpeted, and climate-controlled, with large observation windows (make sure you are next to one). The dining experience is unique, the food is passable (it's not why you're here). *Sailings year-round. Buffet lunch Mon-Sat noon-2pm; dinner & dancing 7 nights 7-10pm; Sunday buffet brunch 12:30-2:30pm.* You may board one hour before sailing for cocktails (not included in the prix fixe). You must call in advance to reserve and make payment with a major credit card.

DAY TRIPS FROM NEW YORK CITY

Escorted

Long Island Rail Road Tours
Penn Station, 34 Street & Eighth Avenue. *From June-mid-Nov.* The LIRR offers escorted combination rail, bus, and boat tours of Long Island. Spring Flower Tour: Planting Field Arboretum, Oyster Bay, the Vanderbilt Museum and Mansion. Great South Bay Boat Cruise: all-day train, bus, boat tour. Bridgeport Ferry Tour: 150-mile land/water cruise. Famous Homes and Garden Tour: Sagamore Hill and Old Westbury Gardens. Lands End: the Hamptons and Montauk. Island Hopping: Greenport, Shelter Island, and Sag Harbor. Also special tours, July and August, Monday, Tuesday, and Wednesday (to the Hamptons). Most of these tours include meals. For details, call (718) 990-7498; for train schedules, call (718) 454-5477.

On Your Own

(*See also* PARKS & GARDENS, Beaches.)
Atlantic City, N.J.
Though it's out of New York State, it deserves a mention because it's the only place on the East Coast (so far) that has legalized gambling. Besides casinos, name entertainers (such as Sinatra and Minnelli), and restaurants, there's the famed saltwater taffy. Gray Line (397-2600) has round-trip one-day excursion trips.

Boscobel Restoration
Garrison-on-Hudson, N.Y. (914) 265-3638. Lo-

cated on 36 acres of formal gardens and lawns overlooking the Hudson, a grand Federal-style mansion built in 1806 by States Morris Dyckman, a Loyalist. Elegant 19th-century furnishings include some Duncan Phyfe. A calendar of special events is available. The annual Christmas candlelight tour is memorable. *OPEN Apr-Oct, Mon, Wed-Sun 9:30am-4:15pm; Nov, Dec & Mar, Mon, Wed-Sun 9:30am-3:15pm. CLOSED Tues, Thanksgiving & Christmas Day & all of Jan & Feb.* Admission includes 45-minute tour; lower for seniors and children age 6-14 ; children under age 6 free.

Brotherhood Winery
Washingtonville, N.Y. (914) 496-9101. Founded by monks, it's America's oldest winery. Tour the caves, taste the wine, and learn about winemaking. Needless to say, harvest time is an extra special treat. *OPEN Jan-Apr & Nov, Dec, Sat & Sun only, 11am-5pm; May-Oct, 7 days 11am-5pm.*

FDR Home
Hyde Park, N.Y. (914) 229-9115. Franklin D. Roosevelt was born and reared in this large, rather plain country house built in 1826 (remodeled 1915). The museum contains a wealth of memorabilia from the Roosevelt presidency (tape-cassette tours available). In the Rose Garden, a simple slab of white Vermont marble marks the resting place of FDR and his wife, Eleanor. *OPEN Apr-Oct, 7 days 9am-5pm; Nov-Mar, Thurs-Mon 9am-5pm. CLOSED Thanksgiving, Christmas & New Year's Day.* Admission charge; children under age 16 and senior citizens free. Groups of 10 or more must reserve in advance.

Lyndhurst
Tarrytown, N.Y. (914) 631-0046. A Gothic Revival castle designed in 1838 by Alexander Jackson Davis for Gen. William Paulding, an early NYC mayor. Enlarged in 1864, it was purchased by railroad tycoon Jay Gould in 1870. Opulent interiors, period furnishings, a carriage house, and the remains of one of the world's largest greenhouses. *OPEN Mar-Oct, Tues-Sun 10am-5pm; Nov-Dec, Sat & Sun only, 10am-3:30pm; 10am-4:15pm (Mar & Apr). CLOSED Jan & Feb.* Admission charge includes house tour (last tour 45 minutes before closing); children under age 6 free.

Old Bethpage Village
Round Swamp Road, Old Bethpage, Long Island. (516) 420-5280 (for directions). This outdoor living historical museum is a restoration of a pre–Civil War rural Long Island village. Active village of craftsmen and a working historical 1850s farm. Site of the big Long Island Fair in October. Cafeteria and picnic facilities available. Nearby: Bethpage State Park. *OPEN June-Labor Day, Sat-Thurs 10am-5pm; CLOSED Fri. OPEN Sept-May, Sun-Thurs 10am-4pm; CLOSED Fri & Sat & some winter holidays.* Admission charge; lower for children. For group reservations, call (516) 420-5288.

Old Westbury Gardens
Old Westbury, Long Island. (516) 333-0048.

Several hundred acres of formal English gardens on the grounds of a beautifully furnished, Georgian-style manor house built in 1909, once the property of millionaire John S. Phipps. *OPEN only late Apr-Oct, Wed-Sun 10am-5pm; in June & July till twilight.* Admission charge; lower for children age 6-12; children under age 6 free.

Planting Fields Arboretum

Oyster Bay, Long Island. (516) 922-9200. A 409-acre country estate laid out into European-style gardens (the azalea walk is magnificent). It's a tranquil oasis, and on the grounds, Coe Hall, a 65-room Tudor-style mansion, contains an eclectic collection of artifacts from all over the world. Gardens and greenhouse *OPEN year-round, 7 days 10am-4:30pm. CLOSED Christmas Day.* Admission charge (free on weekdays from September to May). Mansion: *OPEN Apr-end of Sept only, Tues-Thurs 1-3:30pm.* Admission charge.

Sag Harbor, Long Island

(516) 725-0540 or -0011. A charming 19th-century waterside whaling center with historic houses and buildings. A 1793 Customs House, old cemetery, and Whaling Museum. Of course, chic boutiques and dining.

Sleepy Hollow Restorations

(914) 631-8200. In the lower Hudson Valley as immortalized in Washington Irving's *Legend of Sleepy Hollow.* All three of the following are *OPEN Apr-Nov, Mon, Wed-Sun 10am-5pm. CLOSED Tues, Dec-March & Thanksgiving, Christmas & New Year's Day.* Separate admission to each; lower for children age 6-14 and senior citizens; children under age 6 free. Picnicking permitted at all three sites.

Philipsburg Manor

North Tarrytown, N.Y. Restored early-1700s Dutch-American water-powered gristmill, barn, and stone manor house. Spinning and weaving demonstrations, costumed guides.

Sunnyside

Tarrytown, N.Y. Located on 20 acres is the 19th-century estate of Washington Irving. Personal memorabilia and furnishings, including over 3,000 books!

Van Cortlandt Manor

Croton-on-Hudson, N.Y. The Revolutionary War estate of one of America's Founding Fa-

thers. Such notables as Ben Franklin and Lafayette dined here. Original furnishings and paintings.

Vanderbilt Mansion

Hyde Park, N.Y. (914) 229-9115. Sumptuous 1898 Italian Renaissance residence of Frederick Vanderbilt, the commodore's son, designed by McKim, Mead & White. Opulent furnishings and paintings from the 16th to 18th centuries. *OPEN Apr-Oct, 7 days 10am-5:30pm; Nov-Mar, Thurs-Mon 9am-5pm. CLOSED Thanksgiving, Christmas & New Year's Day.* Admission charge; children under age 16 and senior citizens free. Groups of 10 or more must reserve. Combine with a visit to FDR's home.

Vanderbilt Museum and Planetarium

Little Neck Road, Centerport, Long Island. Planetarium: (516) 757-7500 (recorded information and sky show times). Museum & directions: (516) 262-7888. William K. Vanderbilt's "Eagle's Nest." The 24-room Spanish Baroque mansion situated on 43 acres overlooking the harbor now functions as a museum with wonderful art and antique treasures, and over 4,000 sea specimens. Planetarium: *OPEN Sept-June, Fri, Sat & Sun; July-Aug, Tues-Sun.* Call for show times and theme; special programs for children. Admission charge; lower for children and senior citizens. Museum: *OPEN May-Oct, Tues-Sat 10am-4pm, Sun & holidays 10am-5pm; Nov-Apr, Tues-Sun noon-4pm. CLOSED Mon except Mon holidays.* Admission charge; lower for senior citizens.

West Point, N.Y.

U.S. Military Academy. (914) 938-2638. The famed military academy and National Historic Site magnificently perched above the Hudson River. The colorful cadet dress parades, a must-see, take place from early September to November and from April to May (call for information on these). Start at the Visitor's Center. Fort Putnam *OPEN late May-mid-Nov, check for days & hours.* Museum *OPEN year-round, 7 days 10:30am-4:15pm. CLOSED Thanksgiving, Christmas & New Year's Day.* The **Chapel and Visitor's Center** *OPEN 7 days 8:30am-4pm.* NOTE: Access to Trophy Point by foot or shuttle bus only, no cars.

ANNUAL EVENTS

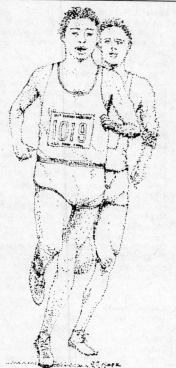

New York Marathon Runner

CALENDAR

The following is a list of annual events in the city that cover every area of interest. They are the great and small happenings that give the Big Apple its flavor, and many of them are FREE.

January

Legal Holidays
New Year's Day, January 1; Martin Luther King, Jr., Birthday, 3rd Monday.

Poetry Project
St. Mark's Church, Second Avenue & East 10 Street. January 1 from 7pm to 3am. The Annual New Year's Benefit for the resident Poetry Project at this treasure of a landmark church. Over 100 poets, dancers, and musicians perform. Admission charge; tickets may be reserved. For information, call 674-0910.

National Boat Show
Javits Convention Center, 11th Avenue at West 35 Street. 216-2000. Mid-January for approximately ten days. All the latest pleasure craft and equipment, the perfect cure for cabin fever. Admission charge.

Chinese New Year—"Kung Ha Fa Choy"
Early January to mid-February (based on the lunar calendar). A ten-day celebration ushered in by a barrage of fireworks and a colorful paper-dragon dance through the narrow always colorful streets of Chinatown. Many area restaurants have extravagant banquets for the occasion. For particulars, call 397-8222. Street celebrations are FREE.

Ice Capades
Madison Square Garden, 4 Penn Plaza. 465-6741. Late January for approximately two weeks. Artistry on ice, always a colorful and entertaining extravaganza to delight adults and children. Tickets can be purchased in advance.

Winter Antiques Show
7th Regiment Armory, Park Avenue & East 67 Street. Late January to early February for approximately 8 days. Prestigious annual antique show, with quality dealers from all over the country. Sponsored by the East Side Settlement House. For information, call 665-5250. Admission charge.

February

Note: In honor of Lincoln's and Washington's birthdays, the large department stores traditionally run fantastic sales. Check the daily newspapers for particulars.

Legal Holidays
Lincoln's Birthday, February 12 (a New York State holiday); Presidents' Day, 3rd Monday.

Black History Month
The entire month of February is devoted to a celebration of black American history and culture. There are events in all the boroughs; check the newspapers or call 397-8222 for specifics.

Chinese Lantern-Day Parade
On the 15th day of the Lunar New Year, sometime in mid-February (depending on the moon). Chinatown's schoolchildren parade to City Hall to present handmade paper lanterns to the mayor. Singing, dancing, and Kung Fu demonstrations. For exact date, call 397-8222. FREE.

Westminster Kennel Club Dog Show
Madison Square Garden, 4 Penn Plaza. 465-6741. Early February for two days it's a dog's life. The show of shows for canine lovers. Nearly 3,000 competing dogs from every state of the union. Call for exact date. Admission charge.

Empire State Building Run-Up
Start: the lobby. Finish: the 86th-floor observation deck. Mid-February. An invitational run up this unique course. The prize, a model of the building sans steps. Sponsored by the New York Road Runners Club. For information, call 860-4455.

Central Park Winter Carnival
Central Park, Great Lawn at 81 Street. One Saturday in mid-February from 10am to 4pm. Sports

activities and fun for the whole family. For information, call 360-8126. FREE.

March

The Spring Armory Antiques Show
7th Regiment Armory, Park Avenue & East 67 Street. Early March, preview plus 4 days. Renowned international antiques show for the benefit of WNET, New York's public television station. For information, call 777-5218. Admission charge.

St. Patrick's Day Parade
Fifth Avenue from 44 to 86 Street. March 17 starting at 11:30am. The first parade in this city in honor of St. Patrick took place in 1762, and what a grand tradition it is. A spirited wearin' of the green (including the green-for-the-occasion line down the avenue), with marching bands and smiling politicians. "Kiss Me I'm Irish" buttons abound. For details, call 397-8222. Good FREE viewing all along the route.

Vernal Equinox
World Trade Center Plaza. On March 20 at the *moment* spring arrives is the right time to—at least make an attempt—balance an egg on end. The event traces back to ancient China folk—or yoke—tradition, reputed to bring you good luck for the year. The eggs are free. For details, call the person who initiated this annual event 17 years ago, performance artist Donna Henes, at (718) 857-5619.

Model Yachting
Central Park, Conservatory Water near Fifth Avenue & 76 Street. Mid-March to mid-November, every Saturday (rain date Sunday). Races of beautifully crafted radio-controlled boats. Sponsored by the Model Yacht Club.

Ringling Bros. and Barnum & Bailey Circus
Madison Square Garden, 4 Penn Plaza. 465-6741. The world-famous three-ring circus comes to town every year, usually at the end of March, and stays until the end of April. It's a sure sign of spring. Tickets to the shows may be purchased in advance. Also, find out the date of the Animal Walk to the Garden; it's usually late in the pm, but it's quite a show in itself.

—March or April

Depending on when Easter falls.

Ukrainian Easter Egg Exhibit
Ukrainian Museum, 203 Second Avenue near East 13 St. 228-0110. Mid-March to mid-April, from Wednesday to Sunday, from 1 to 5 pm. A display of over 200 colorful Ukrainian Easter eggs—*pysanky*—decorated using the wax-resistant method. The designs are representative of various regions and most have symbolic meanings, such as prosperity or health. Decorating the eggs is a tradition that stems from pagan times. There are workshops, too, from mid-March to Easter. Call for exact dates. Admission charge.

Easter Lilies Display
Channel Gardens, Rockefeller Center, Fifth Avenue, 49 to 50 Street. An annual Easter treat, always dazzling for the eye and the spirit. FREE.

Macy's Spring Flower Show
Macy's Herald Square, 151 West 34 Street. From Palm Sunday to Easter Sunday. In the windows, on the main and 6th floors, and in The Cellar, this huge emporium literally blooms. Lectures by floral designers and interior decorators. For recorded information, call 560-4060. FREE.

Easter Egg Roll
Central Park, East Meadow, Fifth Avenue & 96 Street. Sponsored by the Department of Parks and Recreation. On the Saturday of Easter weekend from 9am to 2pm. For children age 4-11. A traditional Easter event but, wisely, wooden eggs are used. Refreshments, prizes, and entertainment. For information, call 360-8126. FREE.

Easter Sunrise Service
The 86th-floor observatory of the Empire State Building is the site of a very special high-rise sunrise (6am) service, led by Reverend Frank Rafter, who began the tradition in 1973. Space is limited, reservations are necessary; call (718) 849-3580. FREE

Easter Parade
Fifth Avenue from 44 to 57 Street. Easter Sunday, from 11am to 2:30pm. This traditional New York event is more a display of Easter-inspired finery—especially millinery—than a parade. The major focus is in front of St. Patrick's Cathedral at 51 Street.

April

It's time for the New York Mets and New York Yankees baseball teams to begin to play ball and for Coney Island Amusement Park to start its season. For exact dates, call 397-8222.

Street Entertainers
A sure sign of spring's arrival is the profusion of street performers that appear along with the daffodils. The street theater tends to be where the crowds are, always weather permitting. Here are a few of the main "stages":

Battery Park & Wall Street
Monday to Friday, noon.

Central Park
The Mall near 72 Street. Monday to Sunday.

Fifth Avenue
From Rockefeller Center (50 Street) to Central Park (59 Street). Monday to Sunday, noon and 5pm.

Greenwich Village
Washington Square Park. Monday to Sunday.

The New York Public Library
Fifth Avenue at 42 Street. Monday to Friday, noon.

Theater District
Intermission: matinee and evening performances.

Greater New York International Auto Show
Javits Convention Center, 11th Avenue at West 35 Street. 216-2000. Early April for approximately 9 days. The latest-model cars. Admission charge; lower for children under age 12.

Broadway Show League
Heckscher Diamond in Central Park at East 62 Street. From mid-April to July (weather permitting), every Thursday at noon and 2pm. A 20-team softball league comprised of theater people. At times the cast and crew of one Broadway show plays another. Among those who have pitched in recent years are Jack Lemmon, Lily Tomlin, and Glenda Jackson. FREE.

Stuyvesant Park Festival
Second Avenue, East 15 to East 17 Street. 684-4543. The third Sunday in April. The very first of the spring season's outdoor fairs—and none too soon. A lovely historic park setting for buying antiques, collectibles, *chotchkes*, rare books, and crafts; new merchandise, too. FREE.

New York Antiquarian Book Fair
7th Regiment Armory, Park Avenue & East 67 Street. One weekend in April. First editions, manuscripts, autographs, atlases, drawings, prints, maps. Prices range from $25 to $25,000. For information, call 757-9395. Admission charge.

Spring Flower Display
The Channel Gardens, Rockefeller Plaza near Fifth Avenue. From mid-April to mid-May. A small, superb garden in the middle of Manhattan right where and when you need it. FREE.

Cherry Blossom Festival
Brooklyn Botanic Garden, 100 Washington Avenue, Brooklyn. (718) 622-4433. Late April (depending on the weather). Go to Brooklyn for one of Mother Nature's most spectacular limited engagements. Call for exact date. Voluntary donation.

Five Boro Bike Tour
End of April/beginning of May, one Sunday at 7:30am. Starts and ends at Battery Park, Manhattan. An annual rite of spring—what the marathon is to runners, this is to pedalers. Through the five boroughs, over asphalt hills and dales, covering 36 miles. Over 20,000 participants make this the world's largest bicycle event. Sponsored by Citibank and American Youth Hostels. For information, call 932-2300.

May

Check the April listings for ongoing events.

Legal Holiday
Memorial Day, last Monday.

Parades
  Armed Forces Day Parade
  Bronx Day Parade
  Salute to Israel Parade
  Norwegian Constitution Day Parade
For exact dates and routes, call 397-8222.

Block Fairs
From May to October uptown, downtown, and all around the town, street fairs and block parties have become traditional weekend summer fare. Music, games, food, rummage, antiques, and collectibles—often for the benefit of neighborhood and block beautification projects. Some of the best are included in this calendar. For a current list of each weekend's fairs and festivals, check the *New York Times* Weekend section on Friday, also check notices on billboards and lampposts. FREE.

Greenmarkets
In all the boroughs. From May to December. The Council on the Environment introduced the idea and it's a gem. Farm-fresh produce and baked goods sold in inner-city neighborhood parks by farmers, dairymen, butchers, and bakers from New York, New Jersey, and Pennsylvania. Union Square Park is the biggest and busiest every Wednesday, Friday, and Saturday from 8am to late afternoon, year-round. For information, call 566-0990.

Citicorp Center
The Market, East 53 Street & Lexington Avenue. Entertainment events and concerts, including jazz, Shakespeare, musical sing-alongs, and more. In either the atrium or the outdoor plaza. Calendar available there or call 559-2330 for recorded information. *OPEN 7 days.* FREE.

Historic House Tours
May is the month that several historic neighborhoods offer tours of private houses. Park Slope Civic Council sponsors an annual tour of ten historic Brooklyn houses the third Sunday in May; call (718) 788-9150 (daytime only). The Brooklyn Heights Association features a self-guided afternoon tour, usually the second Saturday in May, of five historic homes and private gardens that often includes the sanctuary of the landmark Plymouth Church of the Pilgrims; call (718) 858-9193 for specifics. The Village Community School sponsors a tour of six Manhattan residences to benefit its school fund; call 691-5146 for details. Also check the *New York Times* Weekend section for offerings of other area tours. (*See also* SIGHTSEEING, Walking Tours.)

Brooklyn Heights Promenade Art Show
Along the East River, Remsen to Clark Street. (718) 783-3077. The first weekend in May (Mother's Day weekend) from 11am to 6pm. Over 100 artists, photographers, and artisans display their work with the New York skyline as backdrop. A beautifully situated, quality show. (Also, first weekend in October.) FREE.

Welcome Back to Brooklyn Festival
From Grand Army Plaza, at the north end of Prospect Park, down Eastern Parkway to the Brooklyn Museum. The second Sunday in May, noon to 5pm. An annual event promising you can go home again, at least if you were once (and always will be) a Brooklynite. Exhibits on local history, street games, street food, Junior's famous cheesecake and Nathan's famous hot dogs; continuous entertainment. Considering that one in seven Americans has his or her roots in Brooklyn (including this author), it's a crowded festival. For information, call (718) 855-7882. FREE.

Ninth Avenue International Food Festival

Ninth Avenue from West 37 to West 59 Street. The third weekend in May from 11am to 7pm. In midtown's international food market, a mile-long annual gustatory celebration of New York's ethnic diversity. Savor kebobs and sausages, souvlaki and gazpacho, tempura and falafel, moussaka and ravioli. There's merchandise, crafts, and entertainment but the emphasis is on eating, so go hungry! For information, call 581-7217. FREE.

Sephardic Fair

Spanish and Portuguese (Shearith Israel) Synagogue, Central Park West at West 70 Street. 873-0300. One Sunday in mid-May from 10am to 5pm. Tour the landmark home of America's oldest Jewish congregation and see prayer shawls being loomed, jewelry being crafted, potters vending wine cups, and scribes penning marriage contracts. Also, sample Sephardic delicacies. Call for exact date.

Ye Olde Village Fair

Between Seventh Avenue South & Hudson Street, two blocks south of Sheridan Square. One Saturday in mid-May from noon to 8pm, come to Bedford, Barrow, and Commerce—archetypal narrow Greenwich Village streets—for their crowded fun—and food-filled annual community bash. There are antiques, juried crafts, an outdoor cafe, a street of games for kids, a big band, and dancing in the evening under the stars. It's about as old-fashioned and homey as New York can get, and in the growing glut of fairs, this is the best. FREE.

You Gotta Have Park!

Central Park. The third weekend in May. A variety of park-related festivities—races, concerts, games—to reinforce the tradition of Central Park as urban oasis. The fun-filled day is a fund-raiser for the Central Park Conservancy, a wonderful nonprofit group that assists in park maintenance and renovation. For information, call 315-0385. $1 donation requested.

Ukrainian Festival

East 7 Street between Second Avenue & the Bowery. Usually the third weekend in May. Pierogi, polkas, and pysanky. Old-country music and dance in the heart of New York's East Village Ukrainian community. For exact date, call 674-1615. FREE.

Storytelling Hour

Central Park, Hans Christian Andersen Statue near Conservatory Water (East 74 Street). An appropriate and charming site for storytelling from late May to September every Saturday at 11am for one hour. Of interest to children age 3-7. For information, call 397-3156. FREE.

Advil Mini Marathon

Start: Central Park's west drive about 66 Street. Finish: Tavern-on-the-Green. End of May or early June. The world's biggest race for women only—over 6,000 participants—a 6.2 mile (10-kilometer) course. For information, call the New York Road Runners Club, 860-4455.

—Memorial Day Weekend

Last weekend in May. The unofficial start of summer. All New York City beaches open (see PARKS & GARDENS, Beaches).

Washington Square Outdoor Art Exhibit

Fifth Avenue, Washington Square Park, and environs. Memorial Day weekend and early June for three weekends from noon to sundown. For over 60 years the streets of Greenwich Village in the Washington Square area have become an arts and crafts gallery with 600 exhibitors of varying levels of talent. For exact dates, call 982-6255. (*See also* September, Labor Day Weekend.) FREE.

June

Check the April and May listings for ongoing summer events.

Parades

Puerto Rican Day Parade
For exact date, call 397-8222.

The Met in the Parks

Central Park, Great Lawn, Manhattan
Snug Harbor, Staten Island
Cunningham Park, Queens
Marine Park, Brooklyn
Prospect Park, Brooklyn
Van Cortlandt Park, Bronx

Picnic and Puccini (or Verdi or Mozart . . .), an annual New York summer joy. Outdoor evening performances starting at 8pm in the city's parks by the Metropolitan Opera Company. The acoustics are better elsewhere, but the ambience is unbeatable. For information, call 362-6000. FREE.

Museum Mile Festival

Fifth Avenue from 82 to 104 Street. Second Tuesday in June. A grand open house when, for one evening, ten of New York's prized cultural institutions located along one mile of upper Fifth Avenue are open free of charge from 6 to 9pm. Musicians, clowns, and jugglers entertain strollers along the avenue, which is closed to traffic. FREE.

Music in St. Mark's Park

St. Mark's Park, Second Avenue & East 10 Street. From June to July, every Thursday at noon. In front of the oldest site of continuous worship in the city, a series of musical interludes: jazz, classical, and pop. Intermission snacks courtesy of the famed Second Avenue Deli. Sponsored by the Third Street Music School and the 10th & Stuyvesant Streets Block Association. For information, call 777-3240. FREE.

Lower East Side Jewish Festival

East Broadway from Rutgers to Montgomery Street. One Sunday in late May. The Old World still lives on the Lower East Side, albeit these days there is Spanish and Chinese mixed in with the Yiddish. Books, baked goods, kosher food, continuous entertainment. Go, you'll enjoy. For information, call the Educational Alliance, 475-6200. FREE.

Basically Bach
Avery Fisher Hall, Broadway & West 65 Street.
874-2424. In early June for 6 days. Tickets can
be purchased in advance.

Belmont Stakes
Belmont Park Racetrack, Hempstead Turnpike
and Plainfield Avenue, Elmont, Long Island. In
early June, New York's thoroughbred of horse
races and a jewel in the Triple Crown. For exact
date, call (718) 641-4700. Admission charge.

Goldman Memorial Band
Damrosch Park, West 62 Street & Amsterdam
Avenue. From June to mid-August, Sunday, at
7:30pm. Since 1917, popular traditional band
concerts. Enduring and endearing. For information, call 875-5400. FREE.

Central Park SummerStage
Mid-park at 72 Street. Sponsored by the Central
Park Conservancy and the New York City Department of Parks & Recreation. From June to
August, weekday evening and weekend afternoon events. Blues, opera, Latin, pop, African,
rock, country, dance, opera, and literary
readings—something for everyone all summer
long. For exact location and information, call
360-2777. FREE.

Feast of St. Anthony of Padua
Sullivan Street between West Houston & Spring
Streets. Early June for two weeks. An Italian
street *festa,* with music, games of chance, rides
for the kids, but mostly glorious aromatic food for
sale. A spring must. For exact date, call 777-
2755. FREE.

JVC Jazz Festival New York
The end of June: Hot and cool jazz in the concert
halls and clubs of New York City and environs.
Check the newspapers for who and where. Tickets available at Ticketron outlets. For details, call
787-2020 Monday to Friday, from 10am to 6pm.

Shakespeare in the Park
Delacorte Theater, Central Park. Enter from either East or West 81 Street. From late June to
early September. Productions of Shakespeare in
a lovely outdoor theater that Joe (Papp) built.
Tickets distributed at 6:30pm to very early comers for that evening's performance. For information, call 861-PAPP. FREE (although you may be
asked for a contribution; better yet, to be sure of
a seat, become a sponsor).

Celebrate Brooklyn Performing Arts Festival
Prospect Park Band Shell, Prospect Park West &
9th Street, Park Slope, Brooklyn. From mid-June
to late September, a summer season-long potpourri of musical events—pop, jazz, rock, classical, Klezmer, African, Latin, calypso, and Caribbean music; dance; Shakespeare, and more.
For information, call (718) 768-0699.

Midsummer Night Swing
Lincoln Center Plaza, Broadway and West 65
Street. From late June to late July, Wednesday to
Saturday at 8:15pm. A new summer tradition.
Top big bands provide the Dixieland, jazz, R&B,
calypso, and Latin rhythms for swinging with
your partner, either on the checkerboard dance
floor for a fee or for free on the periphery. Every

Wednesday free dance lessons 6:30 to 7:30pm.
For details, call 875-5397.

July

*Check the April, May, and June listings for on-
going summer events.*

Legal Holiday
Independence Day, July 4.

**—Independence Day (July 4) Weekend
Celebrations**

Macy's Fireworks Display
On barges in the East River. The best view:
FDR Drive (closed to traffic) from East 14 to
East 41 Street. Access via East 23, East 34,
and East 48 streets. America's biggest fireworks display and a cherished New York July
4th tradition. The spectacular pyrotechnics
begin at 9:15pm. For information, call 560-
4060. FREE.

Harbor Festival
OP Sail '76 started it; now there's always a
nautical event as part of the July 4 celebration.
For exact time and place, call 397-8222.
FREE.

Great Fourth of July Festival
Water Street from Battery Park to John Street.
On July 4, from 11am to 7pm. In the oldest
part of New York: arts, crafts, ethnic food, live
entertainment, patriotic ceremonies, and a parade from Bowling Green to City Hall. For information, call 397-8222. FREE.

**South Street Seaport Independence
Weekend**
The Seaport area is awash in celebrations of
independence with live concerts and special
events including a rousing fireworks display
over the East River on July 3.

American Crafts Festival
Lincoln Center Plaza, West 64 Street & Columbus Avenue. First two weekends in July, from
noon to 9pm. In a beautiful outdoor setting, 400
skilled artisans display their crafts: leather, jewelry, blown and stained glass, quilts, baskets,
furniture, toys, and so much more. All for sale.
There's also a children's festival within the larger
crafts festival. Puppets, magic, mime, clowns,
singing, playing, maskmaking, and a sheepshearing demonstration followed by spinning
and weaving of the wool. For information, call
677-4627. FREE.

New York Philharmonic Park Concerts
Central Park, Great Lawn, Manhattan
Snug Harbor, Staten Island
Cunningham Park, Queens
Prospect Park, Brooklyn
Van Cortlandt Park, Bronx
One of New York's special summer treats. The
New York Philharmonic Orchestra under the
stars; the first concert of the season usually a
spirited event accompanied by a fabulous fire-
works display. There's a different program each
week in July. Good picnic time and place. For
information, call 875-5709 or 875-5400. FREE.

Summerpier
South Street Seaport Museum, Pier 16 at Fulton St. Early July to mid-August, Friday and Saturday at 8pm. Jazz on the waterfront with lower Manhattan as the backdrop. Open seating begins one hour before the performance. Bring a blanket. For information, call 669-9400. FREE.

Summergarden
Museum of Modern Art Sculpture Garden, 14 West 54 Street. 708-9840. Early July to mid-August, every Friday at 6pm. Music amid the sculpture and fountains as background in a very special serene New York space. FREE.

Washington Square Music Festival
Washington Square Park, at the foot of Fifth Avenue. From mid-July to mid-August, Tuesdays at 8pm. One of the oldest open-air concert series in New York. Chamber music in Greenwich Village—outdoors and FREE. For information, call 431-1088.

Brooklyn Philharmonic
Six evenings of beautiful music at various outdoor Brooklyn locations. For dates and places, call (718) 622-1000. FREE.

Mostly Mozart Festival
Lincoln Center, Avery Fisher Hall, Broadway & West 65 Street. 874-2424. Mid-July to August for 6 weeks. Mozart lives! Beginning with a free outdoor afternoon concert, then mainly evening concerts in a relaxed atmosphere at bargain prices.

Fiesta de Santiago Apostel
West 14 Street between Seventh & Eighth Avenues. In late July. A week-long celebration in the downtown West Side neighborhood known as Little Spain. Entertainment including Flamenco dancers; Iberian food. A bilingual outdoor mass at Our Lady of Guadalupe Church. FREE.

Festa Italiana
Our Lady of Pompeii at Carmine & Bleecker Streets. Last two weeks in July. A colorful street *festa* in the old Greenwich Village Italian community. Food, games of chance, live music. For information, call 989-6805.

August

Check the April, May, June, and July listings for ongoing summer events.

Harlem Week
At various sites in the community. Early August for one week, Harlem struts its stuff in the largest black and Hispanic festival in the world. Indoor and outdoor activities for every age in salute to the black community's past, present, and future. Culminates with Harlem Day. Sponsored by the Uptown Chamber of Commerce. For information, call 427-3315. FREE.

Lincoln Center Out-of-Doors
Lincoln Center Plaza, Broadway & West 65 Street. The entire month of August to Labor Day, daily, from 11am to 8pm. The annual four-week alfresco smorgasbord of music, dance, and theater at Lincoln Center. For information, call 875-5400. FREE.

Tap-O-Mania
Macy's Herald Square, Broadway & West 34 Street. Second Sunday in August. Be part of Broadway's longest tapping chorus line and try to displace the previous year's group from the *Guinness Book of World Records*. Register at 8am. FREE.

Greenwich Village Jazz Festival
End of August for 11 days (more precisely two Fridays before Labor Day). The kick-off is a free concert in Washington Square Park, then a club-hopping marathon to see some greats. Films and lectures, too. Reservations advised. Tip: Buy a festival pass in advance for discounts and freebies. For information, call 242-1785.

Governor's Cup Race
Battery Park City Esplanade. Late August. A 16-mile sailing race in New York Bay to the Verrazano Narrows Bridge and back to Pier A. Best viewing—Manhattan: the Esplanade, Battery Park; Brooklyn: Shore Road (Belt Parkway), 69 Street Pier to Bay 8 Street; Staten Island: Von Briesen Park in Fort Wadsworth, Edgewater Street in Rosewater.

American Crafts Festival
Lincoln Center, West 64 Street & Broadway. Last two weeks in August through Labor Day weekend. One-of-a-kind wares from over 400 talented craftspeople. Performers and demonstrations of sheepshearing and basket weaving. For information, call 677-4627.

U.S. Open
National Tennis Center, Flushing Meadows Park. (718) 592-8000. Annually, end of August/beginning of September. The greats of tennis meet on the courts in Queens. It's nirvana for tennis buffs. Buy tickets well in advance.

September

Broadway, the New York City and Metropolitan Opera companies, and the New York Philharmonic launch their new seasons. In general, the pace of the city quickens and New York's cultural life begins anew.

Legal Holiday
Labor Day, 1st Monday.

Parades
　Labor Day Parade, 1st Monday
　Steuben Day (German) Parade
For information, call 397-8222.

—Labor Day Weekend

The unofficial end of summer. Check the newspapers for special events marking this last weekend hurrah of summer. See August for events that continue through this holiday weekend.

Washington Square Outdoor Art Exhibit
Fifth Avenue, from 14 to Houston Street, University & LaGuardia Place & the vicinity of Washington Square Park. Labor Day weekend and the two following weekends, from noon to dusk. The streets of Greenwich Village in the Washington Square area become an alfresco

art gallery. The art is of varying levels. For information, call 982-6255. FREE.

West Indian American Day Carnival & Parade

Labor Day weekend. A colorful, spirited Caribbean carnival modeled after the harvest carnival of Trinidad and Tobago, a tradition in New York since the 1940s (originally in Harlem). The festivities begin with a salsa, reggae, and calypso musical extravaganza Friday evening at the Brooklyn Museum (admission charge) and culminates on Monday, from noon to 6pm, with a gigantic Mardi Gras–style parade of floats, dancers in elaborate costumes, stiltwalkers, and West Indian food and music from Eastern Parkway and Utica Avenue to the Brooklyn Museum. For information, call 397-8222. FREE.

TAMA Fair

Third Avenue, East 14 to East 34 Street. The first Sunday after Labor Day, from 11am to dusk. Food, crafts, antiques, general merchandise, junk, art, rides, and games take the place of cars on one mile of the avenue. For information, call 689-4543. FREE.

New York Is Book Country

Fifth Avenue, 48 to 57 Street. The third Sunday in September, from 11am to 5pm. For book lovers. The avenue contains the country's largest concentration of bookstores and on this day the street is filled with kiosks representing major publishers. Previews of new books, authors, and live entertainment; bookbinding demonstrations. Bring the kids. FREE.

Feast of San Gennaro

Mulberry Street from Canal to Prince Street, Little Italy. Mid- to late September for 11 days, from noon to midnight. Eating and gaming are the major activities at the oldest, grandest, largest, and most crowded *festa* of them all. In honor of the patron saint of Naples, it begins with the Triumphant March from *Aida* and draws over 3 million intrepid New Yorkers and visitors. For exact dates, call 226-9546. FREE.

Flatbush Frolic

Cortelyou Road between Coney Island Avenue & East 17 Street, Brooklyn. One Sunday in mid-September, from noon to 6pm. A community celebration with an old-fashioned, small-town flavor. Ethnic food, entertainment, arts and crafts. For exact date, call 397-8222. FREE.

Schooner Regatta

Battery Park, Fireboat House, Pier A. Third Saturday in September at 10am. An annual New York Harbor schooner race sponsored by the South Street Seaport Museum to commemorate a 19th-century sailing tradition when fishing schooners raced back to port with their catch; first in received the best prices. Rain or shine. For information about the event and passage on the Seaport Line spectator boat, call 669-9400.

Atlantic Antic

Atlantic Avenue between Fourth Avenue & the East River, Brooklyn Heights. One Sunday late September, from 10am to 6pm. A 12-block-long community festival to celebrate downtown Brooklyn. Food, entertainment, lots to do and see, including a parade at 11:30am. For exact date, call 397-8222. FREE.

Third Avenue Festival

Third Avenue between East 68 & East 90 Streets. One Sunday late September, from 11am to dusk. Arts and crafts, antiques, exotic food, entertainment. Fun for all. FREE.

New York Film Festival

Alice Tully Hall, Broadway & West 65 Street. 362-1911. Beginning the third week in September and lasting two weeks. A fine film festival; since 1963 a fall tradition for cinephiles. Afternoon and evening screenings. Tickets can be bought in advance.

Fifth Avenue Mile

82 to 62 Street on Fifth Avenue. One Saturday late September. The world's fastest runners on New York's chicest avenue. Thousands of spectators line the course for this brief but exhilarating, elite event. For information, call 860-4455.

October

The New York Rangers (hockey) and New York Knicks (basketball) begin their seasons at Madison Square Garden. For information, call 564-4400.

Legal Holiday

Columbus Day, 2nd Monday.

Parades

Columbus Day Parade
Hispanic Day Parade
Pulaski Day Parade

Early to mid-October. For exact dates and routes, call 397-8222.

Brooklyn Heights Promenade Art Show

Along the East River, Remsen to Clark Street. First weekend in October. (See May for details.)

Harvest Festival

Jacques Marchais Center of Tibetan Art, 338 Lighthouse Avenue, Staten Island. Mid-October for one weekend, from noon to 6 pm. A Tibetan festival in and around this lovely replica of a Tibetan monastery. For information, call (718) 987-3478.

Old Home Day

Richmondtown Restoration, 441 Clarke Avenue near Arthur Kill Rd, Staten Island. Third Sunday in October, from 10am to 5pm. All the period houses are open for this fall festival. Crafts demonstrations in each building, homemade foods and gifts, square dancing. Admission charge. For information, call (718) 351-1611.

Fall Antiques Show at the Pier

Pier 92, West 52 Street & the Hudson River. End of October, preview plus four days. Over 100 dealers from 21 states. The foremost American antiques show in the country, a bonanza for Americana collectors. Benefits the Museum of American Folk Art. Parking available; restaurant and bar. For information, call 777-5218 or 581-2676. Admission charge; children under age 16 free.

New York City Marathon
Starting point: the Staten Island side of the Verrazano Narrows Bridge at 10:30am. Finish line: Tavern-on-the-Green, West Drive in Central Park, Manhattan, at 12:53pm—and until the last runner finishes! Last Sunday in October (or first Sunday in November). See how they run: 25,000-plus men, women, and teens cover a 26-plus-mile course through all five boroughs. It's the largest spectator sporting event in the world with an estimated 2.5 million viewers lining the route. Come and cheer them on, exhausting enough for those not in shape. For exact date, call 860-4455.

Houdini Pilgrimage
Machpelah Cemetery, 82-30 Cypress Hills Street, Glendale, Queens. On the afternoon of October 31, 1926, at 1:26pm, master magician Harry Houdini died. Led by the Society of American Magicians, there is an annual visit every Halloween to his grave for a dignified wand-breaking ceremony at the exact moment that he died. (If Halloween falls on Saturday, the Jewish sabbath, the ceremony takes place on Sunday.) FREE.

Annual Village Halloween Parade
Assembles: West & West Houston Streets. Moves east on Houston Street, north on Sixth Avenue to 14th, east to Union Square. October 31 at 6pm. Join in or just watch the massive, wacky spectacle from the sidelines. For ghouls and goblins of all ages and persuasions. The annual procession features generally bizarre costumes and exuberant live music. What started with a handful of people now draws 50,000 participants. Finale approximately 10pm. FREE.

November

Legal Holidays
Veteran's Day, November 11; Thanksgiving Day, 4th Thursday.

Radio City Music Hall
Avenue of the Americas at West 50 Street. 247-7777. Mid-November to early January. The famed Music Hall's Christmas Spectacular—a huge entertainment extravaganza featuring the world-famous Rockettes. Highlight: the traditional living Nativity Pageant with live donkeys, camels, and sheep. Buy your tickets in advance.

Triple Pier Show
Piers 88, 90, 92 on the Hudson River, West 48 to West 55 Street. The weekend before Thanksgiving and Thanksgiving weekend. The annual collectibles and antiques extravaganza at the cavernous Passenger Ship Terminals gives new meaning to the phrase shop till you drop. Featuring Art Deco furniture, 19th-century decorative arts, American quilts, memorabilia, silver, prints, jewelry, dolls, and much more. Wide price and quality range. Admission charge. For information, call (201) 768-2773.

Christmas Star Show
Hayden Planetarium, Central Park West & West 81 Street. Late November to early January. A fascinating special 45-minute holiday season planetarium show conjures up the sky over Bethlehem at the time of Christ's birth. "The Star of Christmas" program has been presented here for more than 50 years. For information, call 769-5920. Admission charge.

Lord & Taylor's Christmas Windows
424 Fifth Avenue at 39 St. From the Tuesday before Thanksgiving to January 1. Lavish, animated scenes on a New York Christmas–holiday theme fill this store's Fifth Avenue windows (instead of merchandise!) to the delight of all. The queue moves quickly but best viewing is after 9pm when the shoppers have gone. For information, call 391-3344. FREE.

Macy's Thanksgiving Day Parade
South from Central Park West & West 77 Street to Columbus Circle, down Broadway to the reviewing stand at Macy's Herald Square (West 34 Street). Thanksgiving Day (4th Thursday in November) from 9am to noon. See the grandest, most spectacular parade of them all. The biggest stars are the gigantic balloons (inflation the night before on 77 Street between Central Park West and Columbus Avenue from 7pm to the wee hours is a gas), although big-name TV, movie, and rock entertainers are there, too. The finale: Santa's official arrival in town. Dress warmly and be in postion by 8am. Call Macy's Special Events hotline, 560-4060. FREE.

Origami Holiday Tree
American Museum of Natural History, West 79 Street & Central Park West. From Thanksgiving to the 12th day of Christmas, in the main-floor rotunda, the museum displays a 25-foot artificial tree decorated with 4,000 origami decorations. Workshops are given in this art of Japanese paper-folding in conjunction with the exhibition. For information, call 873-1300.

Macy's Santa Land & Marionette Show
Macy's Herald Square, West 34 Street & Broadway. From the day after Thanksgiving to December 24, Santa is in residence here to greet and be photographed with youngsters. There is a delightful 20-minute marionette show every hour from 10:30am to 4:30pm. For information, call 695-4400.

Big Apple Circus
Damrosch Park, Lincoln Center. Late November to early January. A new New York holiday season treat tips its hat to the classical American circus. Simplicity, charm, and magic in one ring under a heated little big top. Frequent performances. Tickets can be purchased in advance. For information, call 362-2229.

December

There are fairs, festivals, musical programs, and Messiahs galore throughout the city during the holiday season. Check the newspapers for specifics. See also November for ongoing festivities.

Legal Holiday
Christmas Day, December 25.

Tree-Lighting Ceremony
Rockefeller Center, Fifth Avenue between 50 & 51 Streets. This New York tradition began in 1933 and has become New York's yuletide centerpiece. On the first Monday in December at 5:30pm, 20,000 lights strung on five miles of wire on the mammoth Rockefeller Center Christmas tree are lit, accompanied by music, caroling, and figure skating. It's a magical sight and it's FREE. For exact date, call 397-8222.

Madison Avenue Xmas for Children's Day
Madison Avenue between East 62 & East 72 Streets. The first Sunday in December, from noon to 5pm. The avenue is closed to traffic for an afternoon of holiday shopping, with participating stores donating 20 percent of every sale to charities for children. Gaily decorated heated tents with strolling musicians, hot cider and cookies for sale. For information, call 988-4001. Admission is FREE.

Christmas in Richmondtown
Richmondtown Restoration, 441 Clarke Avenue near Arthur Kill Rd, Staten Island. The first or second Sunday in December, from 10am to 4pm. The restoration buildings are all open and specially decorated in period fashion for Christmas as it was celebrated in the 18th and 19th centuries. Costumed guides, parlor games, popcorn stringing, and homemade foods and gift items for sale. For exact dates, call (718) 351-1611. FREE.

The Christmas Revels
Symphony Space, Broadway at West 95 Street. 864-5400. Early December. Celebration of the winter solstice. A variety of fascinating groups. Five performances. Reserve in advance. Admission charge.

Carousel and Holiday Display
Lever House Lobby, 390 Park Avenue at East 53 St. Early December to January 2. An animated carousel and colorful display to delight youngsters. For information, call 688-6000. FREE.

WBAI Holiday Crafts Fair
Ferris Booth Hall, Columbia University, West 115 Street & Broadway. For three weekends preceding Christmas, America's oldest and largest winter crafts event. More than 300 artisans from 35 states partake in the annual holiday crafts fair for the benefit of (very) independent radio station WBAI. Excellent for Christmas gift shopping. Homemade food and drink; entertainment, too. For exact dates, call 279-0707. Admission charge; half price for children under age 10.

Metropolitan Museum Christmas Tree
Metropolitan Museum of Art, Fifth Avenue & 82 Street. 879-5500. Early December to early January. In the solemn Medieval Sculpture Hall, a 30-foot Baroque tree decorated with 18th-century cherubs and angels and an elaborate Neapolitan nativity scene.

Nutcracker Ballet
Lincoln Center, New York State Theater, Broadway & West 65 Street. 870-5570. Early December to early January. Tchaikovsky's Christmas gift to us all, it's the most popular ballet in the world, and a New York holiday season tradition.

The magical ballet performed by the famed New York City Ballet, ably assisted by children from the School of American Ballet. Extremely popular, be sure to purchase tickets early.

City Spirit Holiday Bazaar
Urban Center Galleries, 457 Madison Avenue at East 51 St. 935-3592. In mid-December, a 3-day shopping spree with wares from the gift shops of museums from all parts of the city. It's a convenient and interesting selection for the pressed holiday shopper.

Fifth Avenue Holiday Festival
Fifth Avenue, 34 to 57 Street. The Sunday before Christmas, from 11am to 3pm. The avenue, decked in holiday finery (even the Public Library lions, Patience and Fortitude, are adorned with holiday wreaths), is closed to traffic, becoming a Christmas shopping and entertainment mall. There are also participatory activities for kids. For information, call the Fifth Avenue Association, 736-7900. FREE.

"'Twas the Night Before Christmas"
Church of the Intercession, West 155 Street & Broadway. 283-6200. On the Sunday before Christmas at 4pm, a procession of carolers visits the Trinity Cemetery grave of Clement Clarke Moore to read his beloved poem, "A Visit from St. Nicholas," and lay a wreath.

Chanukah Celebrations
Grand Army Plaza, Fifth Avenue & 59 Street. A giant 32-foot menorah is the site of a candle-lighting ceremony each night at sundown of the eight-day Festival of Lights. Also at the 92 Street YM-YWHA, 1395 Lexington Avenue, 427-6000, the first night of Chanukah: candle-lighting ceremony; children's storytelling; puppet and magic shows; holiday play, music, and refreshments. FREE.

Messiah Sing-In
Lincoln Center, Avery Fisher Hall. 874-2424. A week before Christmas, for one evening at 7:30pm. Twenty-one guest conductors lead the chorus—you, me, and 3,000 others—in a run-through and then a performance of Handel's Messiah. Loud, enthusiastic, joyful, thrilling! Bring the score or purchase one in the lobby. No experience necessary. Admission charge.

Kwanzaa
December 26 to January 1. A 7-day citywide holiday tribute to the cultural roots of African-Americans. Check the newspapers for specific events, many of which are FREE.

—New Year's Eve

First Night
Within the area around Grand Central Station. December 31, noon through midnight. Sponsored by the Grand Central Partnership, New York's First Night—a New Year's celebration of the arts—is a wonderful new tradition, begun in 1991. A family-oriented alternative to high-priced, high-octane celebrations. Choose from over 40 events, such as storytelling, ice skating, music, circus arts, dancing, and more, in places like the Pan Am Build-

ing and the Grand Ballroom of the Roosevelt Hotel. When was the last time you waltzed in Grand Central Station? Purchase a First Night button for admission to all events, children age 5 and under free. Call 818-1777 for details.

New Year's Eve Concert for Peace
St. John the Divine, 1047 Amsterdam Avenue at West 112 St. Founded by the late conductor and composer Leonard Bernstein, the program like the cathedral itself usually soars. The 2-hour performance begins at 7:30pm but get there early if you want a seat. Doors open at 6pm. For information, call 662-2133. FREE.

Times Square
Times Square, up Broadway to West 49 Street. It's the Main Event. Every December 31 since 1907, a six-foot illuminated wrought-iron ball has moved down a flagpole atop the Times Tower (now 1 Times Square Building). It takes the last 59 seconds of the old year to make its descent, and at midnight the new year is illuminated at the pole's base. Over a quarter of a million people begin to gather at 10pm to see it happen in Times Square; the less hardy watch on television. For information, call 397-8222. (The Tower, and this tradition, may be lost in the Times Square Redevelopment Project.) FREE.

Midnight Run
Start and finish: Tavern-on-the-Green, Central Park at West 67 Street. At midnight more than 3,000 men and women, many in evening dress, others in costume, have a chilly run around Central Park. Prizes for the fastest runners and best costumed; champagne and T-shirts for all who run. Registration fee. For information, call the New York Road Runners Club, 860-4455.

Fireworks
Fireworks greet the New Year in Central Park at midnight. Best viewing: Bethesda Fountain, 72 Street; Central Park West and West 96 Street; Tavern-on-the-Green, West 67 Street and Central Park West; and Fifth Avenue at 90 Street. Also, Prospect Park, Grand Army Plaza, Brooklyn, fireworks accompanied by music, hot cider, and cookies. Festivities there begin at 11:30pm. Fireworks also light the sky above the South Street Seaport at 11:30pm. For information, call 397-3111. FREE.

The Empire State Building
Fifth Avenue & 34 Street. It's a grand place to be at midnight—way above the madding crowd. Last ticket sold 11:25pm. Admission charge.

HISTORIC & NEW
NEW YORK

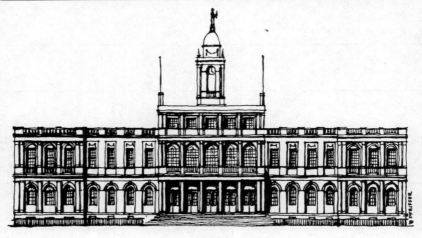

City Hall

NEW YORK CITY: THE FIVE BOROUGHS

The Bronx
The only one of the five boroughs connected to the American mainland—all of the others are islands or part of Long Island. In 1874, the western portion of the Bronx became part of the city, and in 1895, the eastern part followed suit. Named for founder Jonas Bronck, but famed for its Yankees, its zoo, and its cheer.

Brooklyn
One out of seven Americans is said to have roots here. Established as a town in 1658 and as a city in 1834, by 1860 Brooklyn was America's third-largest city. It was consolidated into Greater New York City in 1898. Breukelen—as it was called by the Dutch—covers 70 square miles at the southwest end of Long Island. Probably the best-known borough after Manhattan, its colorful image no doubt stems from having spawned Mario Lanza, Mae West, the original Brooklyn Dodgers, Woody Allen, and Nathan's hot dogs.

Manhattan
The smallest of the five boroughs, the island is a mere 13.4 miles long and 2.3 miles at its widest point. Despite its size, Manhattan is the city's, and to a great extent the world's, nerve center in finance, art, fashion, and theater.

Queens
Queens is the largest borough, comprising almost one-third of the city's land mass, 114.7 square miles. Named for Catherine de Braganza, wife of Charles II, it is the gateway to New York City for anyone arriving by plane at either Kennedy International Airport or La-Guardia Airport.

Staten Island
The third-largest borough in area, it is the least densely populated, although that has been changing since the construction of the Verrazano Narrows Bridge, which joins the Island to Brooklyn. Still just a famed ferry ride from Manhattan, Staten Island is historically rich (*see* Historic Buildings & Areas, Staten Island) and is blessed with large areas of untouched natural beauty (*see* PARKS & GARDENS).

HISTORIC BUILDINGS & AREAS

This list covers New York's most historic buildings, monuments, and houses as well as notable structures and districts. Historic sites open to the public under city or federal government auspices are subject to changes in budget allocations, which can affect days and times of access. Always call before visiting one unless you are in the vicinity. Unless otherwise noted, national sites are closed on federal holidays.

If no hours are indicated there is no public access. For convenience, the listings in this section are by borough.

The Metropolitan Historic Structures Association is a coalition of small history museums, including historic houses, religious sites, military sites, and historical societies throughout the city's five boroughs. For information about these sites write or call the association at One World Trade Center, suite 2611, New York, NY 10048; 432-5450.

Manhattan

Abigail Adams Smith Museum
421 East 61 Street near First Ave. 838-6878. An elegant Federal-style stone carriage house built in 1799. It was converted into a hotel in 1826 and into a residence in 1833. It is one of the few 18th-century historic structures remaining on Manhattan Island. Rooms contain Federal/Empire furniture; surrounding the house is a charming Colonial-style garden. Restored by the Colonial Dames of America. Special programs reflect 19th-century history and life-styles. Membership available. *OPEN Mon-Fri noon-4pm; June & July, Tues 5:30-8pm as well; Sept-May, Sun 1-5pm as well. CLOSED Sat, Sun (Apr-July), Aug & legal holidays.* Groups Monday to Friday, from 10am to noon, by appointment only. Admission charge includes conducted tour; lower for senior citizens and students; children under age 12 free when accompanied by an adult.

Ansonia Hotel
2109 Broadway between West 73 & West 74 Sts. (Graves & Duboy.) An exuberant architectural masterpiece finished in 1904. Constructed to be fireproof, this apartment hotel turned out to be virtually soundproof, drawing such music world notables as Enrico Caruso, Ezio Pinza, Igor Stravinsky, Lily Pons, and Arturo Toscanini.

Arsenal
Central Park, Fifth Avenue at 64 Street. (Martin E. Thompson, 1848.) Predating the park itself, the Arsenal was built to house the state's cache of artillery and ammunition. Troops were quartered here during the Civil War. Home of the city's Department of Parks and Recreation.

Audubon Terrace Historic District
Broadway between West 155 & West 156 Streets. Originally part of the estate belonging to noted ornithologist J. J. Audubon, now a cultural and historic section comprised of several small museums: the American Numismatic Society, the Hispanic Society of America, the Museum of the American Indian, and the American Academy & Institute of Arts & Letters (*see* MUSEUMS & GALLERIES, Museums, General Art *and* Historic).

Beekman Place
East 49 to East 51 Street, east of First Avenue. A retreat from Manhattan's bustle so near yet so

Abigail Adams Smith Museum

Ansonia Hotel

far. This quiet enclave on a bluff overlooking the river is one of New York's nearly hidden special places.

Bouwerie Lane Theater
330 Bowery at Bond St. (Henry Englebert, 1874.) Originally the Bond Street Savings Bank. French Second Empire in cast iron, no less.

Bowery
Third Avenue from Cooper Square (East 7 Street) to Canal Street. From Dutch farm (*bouwerie*) to entertainment center to derelicts' skid row—remnants of all these incarnations survive amid the commercial kitchen-equipment stores and the cash-and-carry discount lighting-fixture and lamp emporiums.

Broadway
Synonymous with legitimate theater in New York, though that district is just a small part of what is the city's longest street. It runs north from the Battery, at the tip of Manhattan, up into Yonkers. (*See also* Historic Buildings & Areas, Manhattan: Times Square.)

Carnegie Hall
154 West 57 Street at Seventh Ave. 247-7459. (William B. Tuthill.) Built under the direction of steel magnate Andrew Carnegie, the hall made its debut May 5, 1891, with a concert conducted by Tchaikovsky. Not only has it survived the competition of Lincoln Center, it thrives. In 1987, it reopened triumphantly following a long renovation and restoration and it joyfully celebrated its centennial in 1991. Bravo! Catch a performance, and don't miss the wonderful new museum; a 45-minute tour is given *every Mon, Tues & Thurs at 11:30am, 2 & 3pm (buy tickets in main lobby 11am-3pm.)*

Cast-Iron District
Broadway and West Broadway from Canal to Duane Streets. Many of New York's commercial buildings in the 1850s and 1860s were constructed in cast iron—elaborate yet inexpensive and the forerunner of today's skyscraper, with a supporting core and curtain walls. This area, combined with SoHo to the north, constitutes the

largest concentration of 19th-century cast-iron architecture in the world. **Friends of Cast-Iron Architecture** will send you a self-guided tour of this area. Call longtime cast-iron architecture champion Margot Gayle, 369-6004.

Castle Clinton National Monument
Battery Park. 344-7220. (John McComb, Jr., 1807-11.) Originally West Battery, an island defense post. Given to the city in 1823, it became successively Castle Garden, the concert hall where impresario P. T. Barnum presented "Swedish nightingale" Jenny Lind in 1850, the Emigrant Landing Depot (1855-90), and then, until 1941, the city's aquarium. Restored, it's now a National Historic Monument, and since 1987 ticket office for boats to the Statue of Liberty and Ellis Island. *OPEN 7 days 8:30am-5pm. CLOSED Christmas Day.* FREE.

Centre Market Place
Between Broome & Grand Streets. Gun sellers clustered here because of the proximity to the old police headquarters. Several survive. Note the "John Jovino Co." sign at No. 5.

Chamber of Commerce of the State of New York
65 Liberty Street at Liberty Pl. (James B. Baker.) An ornate Beaux Arts landmark building dating from 1901.

Charlton-King-Vandam Historic District
9-43 and 20-42 Charlton Street; 1-49 and 16-54 King Street; 9-29 Vandam Street; 43-51 MacDougal Street. The city's largest concentration of Federal-style houses, on a site that belonged first to Aaron Burr and later to John Jacob Astor.

Chelsea Historic District
West 20 to West 22 Street, Ninth to Tenth Avenue. Comprised mainly of land from the estate of Clement Clark Moore (author of "A Visit from St. Nicholas"), this area, developed in the 1830s and containing lovely Greek Revival and Italianate residences, has been making a fashionable comeback as bodegas give way to boutiques. Reactions are mixed.

Chelsea Hotel
222 West 23 Street between Seventh & Eighth Aves. 243-3700. (Hubert, Pirsson & Co.) A literary landmark built in 1884 as a cooperative

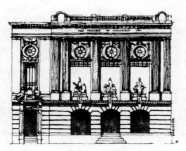

Chamber of Commerce

apartment house. It became a hotel in 1905. Among its former residents: Thomas Wolfe, Dylan Thomas, Mark Twain, and O. Henry. Haven still for struggling artists. (*See also* HOTELS, Moderate.)

Chinatown
Historically centered within the boundaries of Canal, Worth & Mulberry Streets, the Bowery & Chatham Square, but currently expanding on all sides. New York's colorful and bustling Chinese enclave is a feast for the senses, with streets of restaurants serving every type of Chinese food imaginable, from Cantonese to Fookinese. For tours, *see* SIGHTSEEING, Walking Tours. For individual restaurant selections, *see* RESTAURANTS, Chinese.

City Hall
City Hall Park, Broadway & Park Row. 566-8681. (Mangin and McComb, 1802-11.) Federal-period architecture enriched by French Renaissance detailing. New York City's seat of government since 1811. The governor's rooms containing original 19th-century furnishings are *OPEN Mon-Fri 10am-4pm.* Tours are given during those hours. Groups of 10 or more by appointment; call two weeks in advance. FREE.

William Clark House
51 Market Street between Monroe & Madison Sts. A superb, four-story Federal house built in 1824.

Colonnade Row (La Grange Terrace)
428-434 Lafayette Street between East 4 St & Astor Pl. (Attributed to Alexander Jackson Davis, 1833.) Across from Joseph Papp's Public Theater, some of the city's best examples of Greek Revival town houses. Only four of the original nine survive and they're more than just a little bit shabby. At one time home to New York's elite: · the Astors, the Delanos, the Vanderbilts.

Dakota Apartments
1 West 72 Street at Central Park West. (Henry J. Hardenbergh, 1884.) New York's first luxury apartment house, built for Singer Sewing Machine heir Edward Clark, amid run-down farms and shanties. It was thought to be as remote as "Dakotas in Indian territory," but it became, and remains, a prestigious address. Present-day tenants include Lauren Bacall. John Lennon lived and died here; Yoko and son, Sean, are still in residence.

Diamond & Jewelry Way
West 47 Street between Fifth & Sixth Avenues.

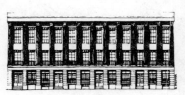

Colonnade Row

Dakota Apartments

Contrary to popular mythology, this is the only street in America that comes close to being paved with gold and diamonds. Shop after shop offer a dazzling assortment of jewelry, but almost as fascinating is the constant action among dealers, mainly Hasidic Jews, buying and selling 80 percent of all the diamonds in the country. Weekdays the area bustles with activity.

Dyckman House
4881 Broadway at West 204 St. 304-9422. Built in 1725 (addition in 1783), this is the only 18th-century Dutch farmhouse remaining in Manhattan. Restored and furnished with Dutch and English Colonial antiques and household items. Now it serves as a museum of Dutch New York. Lovely informal garden. *OPEN Tues-Sun 11am-4pm. Group tours by appointment. FREE.*

East Village
East 14 to East Houston Street, east of University Place to the river. For a short time in the 1820-30s, this was an aristocratic area; later in the century a large German community thrived here; at the turn of the century it became an extension of the immigrant-packed Lower East Side, dominated by Eastern Europeans (Jews and Gentiles), with enclaves of Italians and Irish. In the 1960s, hippies and flower children put the area on the cultural and sociological map, under its present name. Remnants of all of these eras exist today along with a predominant Puerto Rican population east of Avenue A, which has renamed their turf **Loisaida**. It's an area marked by individuality, creativity, and strong community-based activism. (*See also* St. Mark's Historic District, St. Marks Place, Renwick Triangle, the Stuyvesant-Fish House; *and* Churches & Synagogues: St. Mark's-in-the-Bowery; *and* Graveyards: New York City Marble Cemetery *and* New York Marble Cemetery.)

Ellis Island
New York Harbor, southwest of Manhattan's tip. (Boring & Tilton, 1898; restored 1991.) Entry point to America for more than 17 million European immigrants beginning in 1892 (the original building burned down) until 1954. The magnificent red-brick and limestone Beaux Arts build-

ing underwent an extraordinarily ambitious restoration. The enormous Registry Hall, the Baggage Room, and the Ticket Office have been restored, and visitors are able to retrace the steps of those early Americans-to-be. The major exhibits are in galleries around the Registry Room. Artifacts, tapes of immigrant reminiscences; wall drawings and graffiti, too. In all, a poignant reminder of the roots of many who call themselves Americans today; don't miss. On the island's eastern seawall, the **American Immigrant Wall of Honor,** copper plaques inscribed with the names of more than 200,000 immigrants whose descendants contributed at least $100 to the museum in their honor. *Boats depart for the island 7 days 9:30am-3pm every half hour; last boat returns at 5:15pm.* Fare lower for seniors and children; under age 3 free. For boat information, call 269-5755.

English Terrace Row
20-38 West 10 Street between Fifth & Sixth Aves. (James Renwick, Jr., 1856-58.) Modeled after England's row houses, abandoning the high Dutch stoop. Standouts on a lovely Greenwich Village street.

Federal Hall National Memorial
26 Wall Street at Nassau St. 264-8711. (Town & Davis, 1934-42.) This Greek Revival building occupies the site of New York's original city hall (1699), which later (1788) served as the new country's first capitol, where George Washington took the presidential oath in 1789. The present building served as a customs house and later as the subtreasury. Now a National Historic Site housing mementos of colonial and early federal New York, including Washington's inaugural suit. Classical concerts performed year-round on Wednesdays at 12:30pm. *OPEN Mon-Fri 9am-5pm. CLOSED federal holidays except George Washington's birthday & July 4. FREE.*

Fire Watchtower
Marcus Garvey Park, Madison Avenue & East 100 Street. A cast-iron octagonal structure built in 1856. The last remaining fire tower in the city.

Flatiron Building
175 Fifth Avenue at East 23 St. (D. H. Burnham

Fire Watchtower

& Co., 1892.) Originally known as the Fuller Building, its obvious nickname stuck. At 286 feet, it was one of New York's first steel skeleton skyscrapers. Designed in an Italian Renaissance manner and covered by a limestone skin, the shiplike structure, which appears to sail up the avenue, was the most popular picture postcard subject at the turn of the century. The phrase "23 Skiddoo" originated at the prow of the building, where policemen were assigned to chase away men who stopped to gaze at the upturned skirts of ladies at this, the windiest corner in the city. The prow has recently been restored and now houses an Italian sportswear shop, C.P. Shades.

Gainsborough Studios
154 West 57 Street. (Charles W. Buckham, 1908.) Built as an artist studio-cooperative, the front park-facing apartments are all duplexes, each with a two-story living room overlooked by a sleeping balcony. Recently restored ornate exterior.

General Post Office
West 31 to West 33 Street, Eighth to Ninth Avenue. 330-3601. (McKim, Mead & White, 1913.) A Corinthian-columned facade that bears the well-known, overblown, and too often untrue inscription "Neither snow, nor rain, nor heat, nor gloom of night stays these couriers from the swift completion of their appointed rounds." Tours available. Write Manager of Communications, New York Post Office, J. A. F. Building, room 3023, New York, NY 10199-9641, give dates and number of people. No children under age 12.

Governor's House
Governor's Island, Andes & Barry Roads. A true Georgian-style building, built circa 1708, that housed the British colonial governors. (*See also* Governor's Island.)

Governor's Island
New York Harbor, south of Manhattan's tip. In 1652, it was set aside as the Dutch governor's estate (see above), but it is best known as a military fortification from the 1790s. In 1966 the U.S. Coast Guard took command of it. Now a National Historic Landmark, it is *OPEN to the public only two days a year, one in mid-May & one in mid-Sept, noon-4pm.* For information, call 668-7255.

Gracie Mansion (mayors' residence)
In Carl Schurz Park, East 88 Street & East End Avenue. A Federal-style country villa built in 1799 by wealthy merchant Archibald Gracie. The 18th- and 19th-century furnishings have provided a graceful residence for New York's mayors since 1942. Tours of the public rooms, the garden, and the private quarters (except the mayor's bedroom) are offered to the public *Apr-Oct 10am-2pm by appointment only.* There is also a tour specifically designed for children on Thursdays. Admission charge; free for school-age children and senior citizens. No school groups below third grade. Write well in advance: Tour Program, Gracie Mansion, East 88 Street & East End Avenue, New York, NY 10128, or call 570-4751.

Gracie Mansion

Grand Central Terminal
East 42 Street & Vanderbilt Avenue. (Warren & Wetmore, Reed & Stem, 1913.) This massive Beaux Arts structure, completed in 1913, was the "gateway to the continent," in the heyday of rail travel. Now undergoing restoration, its majestic cathedral-like main concourse, with a 116-foot-high vaulted ceiling decorated with a mural of the night sky, is traversed by half a million people a day, albeit now all of them commuters not long-distance travelers. There are long-range plans afoot to make the station a destination in itself, with fancy restaurants and upscale shops; stay tuned. Fascinating free guided tours are given every Wednesday at 12:30pm by the Municipal Art Society. (*See* SIGHTSEEING, Walking Tours.)

General Grant National Memorial
Riverside Drive & West 122 Street. 666-1640. (John H. Duncan, 1897.) Where Ulysses S. Grant and his wife are entombed. Photographic exhibits of his life as general and president plus a collection of Civil War artifacts. Mosaic benches ringing the monument, done by neighborhood youths, are controversial to those who do not recognize urban folk art. *OPEN Wed-Sun 9am-5pm.* FREE.

Greenwich Village
Approximately west of University Place to the river, from East 14 to Spring Street. The largest designated historic district in New York City. Historically rich, traditional home of artists and writers. The area and its residents range from the offbeat to the upbeat. Its winding streets offer a wealth of architectural treasures, charming bistros, coffeehouses, and trendy and ethnic boutiques. Best way to experience it: meander. (*See also* Charlton-King-Vandam Historic District, English Terrace Row, Grove Court, Isaacs-Hendricks House, Jefferson Market Library, MacDougal Alley, MacDougal Street, Milligan Place/Patchin Place, Narrowest House, St. Luke's Place, Washington Mews, Washington Square North.)

Grove Court
South side of Grove Street between Bedford & Hudson Streets. (View through gates between nos. 10 & 12 Grove Street.) Built in 1854 as laborer's quarters, this charming secluded mews in Greenwich Village was then known as Mixed Ale Alley.

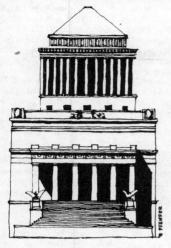

General Grant National Memorial (Grant's Tomb)

Hamilton Grange National Memorial
287 Convent Avenue near West 141 St. 283-5154. Founding Father and the first secretary of the treasury Alexander Hamilton's Harlem Heights "country" retreat, designed by John McComb, Jr. Built in 1801, it's one of the few Federal-period mansions remaining in Manhattan. Now a National Historic Site administered by the National Park Service. *OPEN Wed-Sun 9am-5pm.* FREE.

Harlem
North of West 110 Street to West 155 Street, west of Fifth Avenue to Broadway. A small 18th-century farm community that grew to be the largest black community in America. Vestiges of a proud past—elegant row houses, fine commercial structures, historic churches—exist within a blighted present. Interesting and enlightening. Take a tour and see for yourself. (*See* SIGHTSEEING, New York Tours, By Coach: Harlem Spirituals, *and* Specialized Tours: Harlem Your Way! *See also* RESTAURANTS, Soul/ Southern: Sylvia's.)

Harlem Courthouse
170 East 121 Street at Sylvan Pl. (Thom & Wilson, 1893.) A richly decorated brick-and-stone courthouse; now a landmark but mainly dormant.

Haughwout Building
488 Broadway at Broome St. (J. P. Gaynor, 1857.) This Palladio-inspired cast-iron building houses what was the first practical safety elevator in the world, by Otis.

Isaacs-Hendricks House
77 Bedford Street at Commerce St. Built in 1799, it's the oldest surviving house in Greenwich Village, but only the side and rear retain the original clapboard structure. Adjacent is the Narrowest House.

Harlem Courthouse

Jefferson Market Library
425 Avenue of the Americas at West 10 St. 243-4334. (Vaux & Withers, 1877; renovated interiors: Giorgio Cavaglieri, 1967.) Originally a courthouse built on the site of an old market, this extraordinary building is a Victorian Gothic celebration. Saved by determined Greenwich Villagers to become a branch of the New York Public Library. Call for current hours. Don't miss a look at the adjacent community garden.

Ladies' Mile Historic District
Roughly from Sixth Avenue to Broadway, West 15 to West 24 Street, from Union Square to Madison Square. The heart of the Gilded Age, an area once graced by well-known department stores and carriage trade specialty shops, as well as early "skyscrapers."

Little Italy
Houston south to Canal Street, and Lafayette Street east to the Bowery. New York's old Italian community settled between 1880 and 1924 is shrinking as Chinatown expands. But visitors still

Haughwout Building

Jefferson Market Library

clog the narrow streets in search of hearty Neapolitan fare, cappuccino and pastry at one of the many outdoor cafes, the colorful street *festa*, music, and atmosphere. Mulberry is the main street. The Feast of San Gennaro is the biggest (*see* ANNUAL EVENTS, September).

Little Red Lighthouse (Jeffrey's Hook Light)
Fort Washington Park. In Washington Heights, under the George Washington Bridge, the 40-foot-tall namesake of the beloved children's story, "The Little Red Lighthouse and the Great Gray Bridge." Built in 1926, recently designated an official landmark.

Lower East Side
Below Houston Street east of the Bowery to the East River. Historically the area that absorbed the masses of Jewish immigrants who flooded these shores in the 1880s and 1890s, becoming the world's largest Jewish community. The pushcarts are gone, but it's still a bargain hunter's paradise (principally, Orchard Street) and home to New York's newest immigrants—the Puerto Ricans. For a deeper look at this area take one of the fascinating tours presented by the Lower East Side Tenement Museum (*See also* SIGHTSEEING, Walking Tours *and* MUSEUMS & GALLERIES, Museums, Historic Museums.)

MacDougal Alley
MacDougal Street between West 8 Street & Washington Square North. A charming cul-de-sac adjacent to Greenwich Village's busiest thoroughfare, 8th Street.

MacDougal Street
Between West 3 & Bleecker Streets. Everchanging, busy Greenwich Village street reflects shifts in fashion, food, and music. Falls between colorful and bizarre. People-watch at the best of the old authentic coffeehouses—Cafe Reggio.

Merchants' Exchange (Citibank)
55 Wall Street between William & Hanover Sts.

(Isaiah Rogers, 1836-42; remodeled, McKim, Mead & White, 1907.) First a merchants' exchange, then the Customs House (1863-99), this massive double-colonnaded (second set of columns added 1907) building has housed a bank since 1907.

Milligan Place/Patchin Place
Sixth Avenue (west side) between West 10 & West 11 Streets; West 10 Street (north side) between Greenwich & Sixth Avenues. Two peaceful cul-de-sacs built originally as boardinghouses for the Basque employees of a nearby hotel. Writers Theodore Dreiser and e. e. cummings have been Patchin Place residents.

Mooney House
18 Bowery at Pell St. In Chinatown, Manhattan's oldest surviving row house. It was built between the British evacuation (1783) and Washington's inauguration (1789) by merchant Edward Mooney, who had been a breeder of racehorses. Restored in 1971.

Morris-Jumel Mansion
Roger Morris Park, Edgecombe Avenue at West 160 Street. 923-8008. The Georgian Colonial mansion, built in the Palladian-style in 1765 (remodeled 1810) as the Roger Morris family's "summer villa," is the oldest private dwelling extant on Manhattan. It served briefly as Gen. George Washington's headquarters in 1776. Bought in 1810 by wealthy French merchant Stephen Jumel, it was occupied by his widow (who, in 1833, married Aaron Burr) until 1865. Contains nine rooms of magnificent Georgian, Federal, and French Empire-style furnishings, silver, and china, a restored Colonial kitchen, and a lovely herb and rose garden. Third-floor museum area has changing exhibits. *OPEN Tues-Sun 10am-4pm. CLOSED Thanksgiving, Christmas & New Year's Day.* Admission charge; lower for students and groups of 10 or more. Special programs are offered, including jazz and classical concerts.

Mount Morris Fire Watchtower
Marcus Garvey Park, Madison Avenue & East 122 Street. A graceful cast-iron octagonal structure built in 1856. The last remaining fire tower in the city.

Municipal Building
Centre Street at Chambers Street. (McKim, Mead & White, 1914.) Straddling a city street, this is an imposing, almost imperial civic skyscraper. Each year thousands of couples get married in a civil chapel on the second floor of this building. (The ceremony takes 66 seconds and costs $25.) Atop the exterior, Adolph A. Weinman's Civic Fame.

Narrowest House
75½ Bedford Street between Morton & Commerce Sts. Built in 1873. Only 9½ feet wide, spanning what was once a carriageway, it was home to poet Edna St. Vincent Millay in 1923. Adjacent to the oldest house in Greenwich Village, the Isaacs-Hendricks House, no. 77.

New York Public Library, Main Branch
Fifth Avenue at 42 Street. 930-0800. (Carrere &

Hastings, 1911.) A magnificent Beaux Arts building, it houses one of the world's most extensive libraries, the result of a merger in 1895 of three large private libraries—the Astor, the Tilden, and the Lenox. The 5.5 million books are mainly for reference, and it's completely FREE. Free one-hour tours from main lobby Monday to Saturday at 11am and 2pm. (*See also* MUSEUMS & GALLERIES, Libraries.)

New York Yacht Club
37 West 44 Street between Fifth & Sixth Aves. (Warren & Wetmore, 1899.) Built on land donated by member J. P. Morgan, this Beaux Arts structure, with three bay windows fashioned after the stern of 18th-century sailing ships, was home to the America's Cup until 1983. (The cup now resides in San Diego.)

Old Merchant's House
29 East 4 Street between Lafayette St & the Bowery. 777-1089. (Attributed to Minard Lafever.) A true treasure. A completely intact, four-story Greek Revival house built in 1832, a remnant of a time when the area was fashionably residential. The property of wealthy merchant and hardware importer Seabury Tredwell from 1835. It retains most of its original fittings and furniture, as well as clothing belonging to Tredwell's daughter Gertrude, who lived here until she died in 1933 at age 93. Very special times to visit are during the Christmas season for a 19th-century holiday party, including the traditional open house on New Year's Day. *OPEN Sun 1-4pm. Call for additional hours following current restoration.* Group tours weekdays by appointment. Admission charge; special rates for senior citizens and students. Membership available.

Old New York City Courthouse
52 Chambers Street between Broadway & Centre St backing City Hall. (John Kellum, 1872.) A stately Italianate edifice better known as the "Tweed Courthouse" as a result of nine years of construction costing $8-$12 million, most of

which lined the pockets of politician "Boss" William Tweed and his ring of cronies. Now houses the Municipal Archives.

Patchin Place
See Milligan Place/Patchin Place.

Pearl Street
In Dutch colonial times, this street, now in the Financial District, was the original shoreline of the East River, and was so named because of the mother-of-pearl oyster shells scattered along the beach.

Players Club
16 Gramercy Park South between Irving Pl & Park Ave South. 475-6116. Built in 1845, it was remodeled by Stanford White in 1888 when famed actor Edwin Booth bought it to serve as an actors' club. Staid Gramercy Park residents were aghast. *OPEN for groups only by appointment only.*

The Plaza Hotel
Fifth Avenue & 59 Street. (Henry J. Hardenbergh, 1907.) This 18-story French Renaissance building by the same architect as the Dakota is more than an architectural landmark. Its exuberant style, its fortuitous location on a spacious plaza across from Central Park, and its legendary past make it a sentimental favorite. Ernest Hemingway is reported to have recommended to Scott Fitzgerald that he leave his liver to Princeton but his heart to the Plaza; quite understandable. New owner Donald Trump plans to convert most of the hotel to pricey condos—New Yorkers resent the idea and what would Eloise say? (*See also* HOTELS, Deluxe.)

Police Headquarters (former)
240 Centre Street between Grand & Broome Sts. (Hoppin & Koen, 1909.) A Beaux Arts beauty of a bygone era. The police moved in 1973; in the

Old Merchant's House

Players Club

booming 1980s it became luxury co-op residences.

Public Baths, City of New York
East 23 Street near FDR Drive. (Arnold W. Brunner and William Martin Aiken, 1906.) A public bath worthy of ancient Rome. Recently restored, it's the Asser Levy municipal swimming pool now.

Public Theater
425 Lafayette Street between East 4 St & Astor Pl. (Alexander Saeltzer, 1849; additions, Griffith Thomas, 1859, and Thomas Sent, 1881.) Originally New York's first free library—the Astor—it is now home to the creative legacy of Joseph Papp. Seven theaters are housed within; it's downtown's Lincoln Center for off-Broadway (where *Hair* and *Chorus Line* were born); film, jazz, and more. (*See also* ENTERTAINMENT, Off-Broadway.)

Puck Building
295 Lafayette Street between Houston & Mulberry Sts. (Albert Wagner, 1885.) Since 1983, it is a condo complex devoted to arts and design tenants, but this brick Romanesque Revival building once housed the world's largest concentration of lithographers and printers. From 1887 to 1916 it was home to the satirical weekly *Puck*. The two gold-leafed Pucks remain to remind.

Renwick Triangle
Nos. 112-128 East Tenth Street & 23-35 Stuyvesant Street. Attributed to James Renwick, Jr., the architect of St. Patrick's Cathedral and Grace Church. Built in 1861, they stand much as they were when completed and form a handsome, historic enclave in the bustling East Village. New York University's post-modern dormitory, bitterly contested by area residents, is an ungainly unworthy addition at the triangle's Third Avenue base.

Riverside–West 105th Street Historic District
Riverside Drive between West 105 & West 106 Streets. A 1899-1902 enclave of French Beaux Arts town houses overlooking the Hudson River.

Sara Delano Roosevelt Memorial House
47 East 65 Street. In 1910, Mrs. Roosevelt commissioned an architect to build twin town houses—one (no. 49) for her son, Franklin, and his future wife, Eleanor, and one for herself next door. FDR lived there until he became governor of New York in 1928; his mother lived at no. 47 until her death in 1941.

Theodore Roosevelt Birthplace
28 East 20 Street between Broadway & Park Ave South. 260-1616. Where Roosevelt, the 26th president, was born in 1858. The original 1848 building was demolished in 1916; this replica was built in 1923. Fascinating collection of "Teddy" memorabilia in five Victorian-period rooms containing some of the original house's furnishings. Lovely concerts every Saturday at 2pm (except July and August). Now a National Historic Site administered by the National Park Service. *OPEN Wed-Sun 9am-5pm.* Small admission charge; children under age 12 and senior citizens free.

St. Luke's Place
Between Seventh Avenue South & Hudson Street. (1852-53.) In Greenwich Village, a handsome block of brick and brownstone row houses. No. 6 was home of New York's colorful mayor Jimmy Walker.

St. Mark's Historic District
East 10 & Stuyvesant Streets between Second & Third Avenues. This historic East Village oasis contains three of the earliest Federal buildings standing in Manhattan: St. Mark's-in-the-Bowery (1799), the Stuyvesant-Fish House (1804), and 44 Stuyvesant Street (1795), all traceable back to Dutch governor Peter Stuyvesant, on whose farmland the district rests. Stuyvesant Street, the only true east-west street in Manhattan, was the driveway to the governor's mansion. (*See also* Renwick Triangle *and* Stuyvesant-Fish House; *and* Churches & Synagogues: St. Mark's-in-the-Bowery.)

St. Marks Place
East 8 Street from Third Avenue to Tompkins Square Park. In the 1960s, these 1830s Greek Revival row houses went psychedelic, forming the main street of the hippie phenomenon. Now

Public Baths

Theodore Roosevelt Birthplace

a punk haven, it remains the East Village's gritty main thoroughfare.

Schermerhorn Row
2-18 Fulton, 91-92 South, 159-171 John, and 189-195 Front Streets. Dating from the early 19th century, these Georgian-Federal and Greek Revival buildings were originally warehouses and countinghouses in the bustling seaport. Now a part of the South Street Seaport Museum project to evoke the area's rich history. The 12 buildings have been sanitized and now house mainly commercial tenants. Facing cobbled Fulton Street, they are the rich architectural legacy of a time long gone. (*See also* MUSEUMS & GALLERIES, Museums, Historic Museums: South Street Seaport Museum.)

7th Regiment Armory
Park Avenue between East 66 & East 67 Streets. (Charles W. Clinton, 1880.) A Victorian incarnation of a medieval fortress. Outstanding: a great drill hall—187 by 290 feet—and the Veterans' Room and library decorated under the direction of Louis Comfort Tiffany. Site of the prestigious Winter Antiques Show every January (*see* ANNUAL EVENTS).

Shubert Alley
West 44 to West 45 Street between Seventh & Eighth Avenues. A short private alley where many an actor cooled his heels awaiting the verdict of J. J. and Lee Shubert, theatrical impresarios. Now houses a theatrical memorabilia gift shop.

Singer Building (Paul Building)
561 Broadway between Spring & Prince Sts. In 1907, Ernest Flagg designed this as office and loft space for the Singer Sewing Machine Co. Highly innovative use of cast iron, terra-cotta paneling, and plate glass.

Sniffen Court Historic District
150-158 East 36 Street between Third & Lexington Aves. A charming 19th-century Murray Hill mews of ten Romanesque Revival brick carriage houses.

SoHo
An acronym meaning south of Houston Street, the term covers New York's once-grimy-now-chic art-colony neighborhood. Bounded by West Broadway, Canal, Lafayette, and Houston streets. Rich in galleries, trendy boutiques, restaurants, and most enduring of all, a splendid treasure trove of 19th-century cast-iron architecture. Rapidly rising rents have started an eastward migration of galleries.

"Strivers Row"
West 138 to West 139 Street between Adam Clayton Powell & Frederick Douglass Boulevards. In 1891, builder David H. King commissioned several leading architects of the day—James Brown Lord, Bruce Price and Clarence S. Luce, and McKim, Mead & White. The results, the King Model Houses, a harmonious grouping of row houses and apartments. Originally built to house well-to-do white residents, in the 20s and 30s they became home to successful blacks and acquired the nickname "Strivers Row."

Stuyvesant-Fish House
21 Stuyvesant Street at East 9 St between Second & Third Aves. A restored Federal house built in 1804 by Dutch governor Peter Stuyvesant's great-grandson as a wedding gift to his daughter Elizabeth. A city, state, and national landmark. Now used as commercial offices.

Surrogate's Court Hall of Records
31 Chambers Street at Centre St. (John R. Thomas, Horgan & Slattery, 1899-1907.) An impressive civic monument; its central hall is one of the finest Beaux Arts rooms this side of the Paris Opera House.

Sutton Place
East of First Avenue from East 49 to East 59 Street. A prestigious area of elegant town houses and cooperative apartment houses, overlooking the East River. Synonymous with status and affluence and, in the case of former resident Greta Garbo, mystery.

Times Square
West 42 to West 47 Street at the intersection of Broadway and Seventh Avenue. Named for the Times Tower—which is no longer there—the area is synonymous with theater, bright lights, honky-tonk, and tourists. For better or worse (the worst: between Broadway and Eighth Avenue), it's a hub of this city and its most democratic space—akin to a public square. Presently scheduled for a huge redevelopment that will forever change the character of this world-renowned area, it is stirring debate: Is no life really the only alternative to low life?

Triangle Fire Plaque
Washington Place & Greene Street. On the building that housed the Triangle Shirtwaist Co., where a tragic fire on March 25, 1911, claimed the lives of 146 young women. The tragedy led to improved safety conditions in factories.

Stuyvesant-Fish House

Surrogate's Court

U.S. Custom House

TriBeCa
Below Canal Street, west of Broadway. Translation: the Triangle Below Canal. It's the city's newest fashionably metamorphosized neighborhood. In reality it's the once-thriving Washington Market commercial district that's become residential and trendy. Dining in this area has also been raised to an art.

Tudor City
(H. Douglas Ives, 1926-30.) A towering residential enclave—a city within a city. Recently declared a landmark.

Turtle Bay Gardens
226-246 East 49 Street & 227-247 East 48 Street between Second & Third Avenues. In 1920, the four-story Italianate houses on two Turtle Bay–area blocks came to share a common garden on a cooperative basis. All living rooms face the gardens, kitchens are on the street side. Counted among its present-day residents is a frequently sighted Katharine Hepburn.

Union Club
101 East 69 Street at Park Ave. (Delano & Aldrich, 1932.) The oldest private club in New York.

U.S. Custom House
Bowling Green. (Cass Gilbert, 1907.) In the luxurious Beaux Arts style: four massive limestone sculptures representing the four continents are an integral part of the facade. Inside, a huge oval rotunda with 1937 WPA murals by Reginald Marsh. Vacant since 1971, when Customs moved to the World Trade Center. Possible future use: the new home of the American Indian Museum.

Villard Houses
451-455 Madison Avenue between East 50 & East 51 Sts (McKim, Mead & White, 1884). 24 East 51 Street (Babb, Cook & Willard, 1866). 29½ East 50 Street (McKim, Mead & White, 1909). Italian Renaissance buildings modeled after Rome's Palazzo della Cancelleria, built by newspaper owner Henry Villard. They have variously seen service as home to the New York Catholic Archdiocese and to Random House Publishing Co. Now the entrance and public rooms of the appropriately named Helmsley Palace Hotel (*see* HOTELS, Deluxe). Also, houses

the Urban Center (*see* MUSEUMS & GALLERIES, Museums, General Art Museums).

Wall Street
In 1653, the northern frontier of the city was here—a Dutch wall of thick wooden planks for protection against attack. The wall was completely dismantled by the English in 1699, but the name remained. It's now the world-renowned center of high finance. (*See also* SIGHTSEEING, On Your Own: New York Stock Exchange.)

Washington Mews
University Place to Fifth Avenue between East 8 Street & Washington Square North. A 19th-century Greenwich Village mews lined with converted stables on the north side, many of which now belong to New York University.

Washington Square North
1-13 and 21-26 Square North between Fifth Ave and University Pl. (Town & Davis, ca. 1831.) Made famous by Henry James's novel *Washington Square*. "The Row," when built, housed New York's socially prominent. No. 8 was once the mayor's official residence. Now most of the buildings belong to New York University. (It is rumored that one resident has bequeathed his house to Harvard.)

Woolworth Building
233 Broadway between Park Pl & Barclay St. (Cass Gilbert, 1913.) One of New York's most dramatic commercial buildings, this neo-Gothic tower rises 792 feet in the air and is the jewel of the downtown skyline. Fittingly dubbed a "cathedral of commerce," it was the world's tallest building until 1930. Don't miss the lobby: In the ceiling's carved figures you'll see representations of the architect holding a model of the building and of F. W. Woolworth himself, counting his 5s & 10s. (He paid $13 million in cash to

Villard Houses

Washington Square North

have it built.) Given landmark status in 1983, its crown now lights the downtown night sky.

Yorkville
East 75 to East 88 Street, Lexington to York Avenue. A *klein Deutschland*—little Germany—within Manhattan's chic Upper East Side. The boundaries are loose, but the main street is still East 86.

Brooklyn

Albemarle Terrace
East of 21 Street between Church Avenue & Albemarle Road, Brooklyn. Landmark Georgian Revival row houses in a charming cul-de-sac.

Brooklyn Heights
Roughly between Cadman Plaza West & the East River (the esplanade) and Atlantic Avenue and Poplar Street, Brooklyn. Called Ihpetonga—"high, sandy bank"—by the Canarsie Indians. Fifty blocks of rich 19th-century architecture and charm overlooking the East River. The breathtaking vista of lower Manhattan's skyline from the esplanade is a must see. (*See also* Grace Court Alley, Middagh Street, Montague Terrace, and Willow Place.)

Grace Court Alley
East of Hicks Street near Joralemon Street, Brooklyn Heights. A charming mews, formerly a stable alley for the Remsen Street mansions.

Grand Army Plaza
At the intersection of Flatbush Avenue, Prospect Park West, Eastern Parkway & Vanderbilt Avenue, Brooklyn. (Frederick Law Olmsted and Calvert Vaux, 1870.) The plaza is designed in the spirit of L'Etoile in Paris. The Soldiers' and Sailors' Memorial Arch (1892) honors the Union effort in the Civil War.

Jennie Jerome House
197 Amity Street, Brooklyn. Birthplace of Jennie Jerome (January 9, 1854), wife of Lord Randolph Churchill, mother of Winston.

Lefferts Homestead
In Prospect Park, Flatbush Avenue at Empire Boulevard, Brooklyn. (718) 965-6505. An English "Dutch Colonial" farmhouse, built in 1783. Transferred to the park in 1918, it's now a historic museum with period furnishings. Special programs for children and adults. Presently undergoing restoration; call for update.

Grand Army Plaza

Litchfield Villa
In Prospect Park, Prospect Park West between 4 & 5 Streets, Brooklyn. (Alexander Jackson Davis, 1857.) A romantic Italianate villa built for wealthy lawyer Edwin C. Litchfield. It now serves as the Department of Parks and Recreation's Brooklyn headquarters.

Middagh Street
Between Willow & Hicks Streets, Brooklyn Heights. One of the Heights's earliest streets, circa 1817. Many of the remaining houses are of wood. No. 24 (1824) on the southeast corner of Willow, is a wooden Federal house in exquisite condition.

Montague Terrace
1-13 Montague Terrace between Remsen & Montague Sts, Brooklyn Heights. An English-style terrace row beautifully preserved. Author Thomas Wolfe lived at no. 5.

Park Slope Historic District
Grand Army Plaza to Bartel-Pritchard Square along Prospect Park West. Brooklyn's former "Gold Coast," a residential area containing 1,900 structures of architectural interest dating from the 1860s to World War II.

Sheepshead Bay
Emmons Avenue from Knapp Street to Shore Boulevard, Brooklyn. A small active fishing port with boats coming and going and fine fish res-

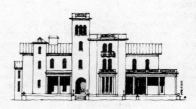

Litchfield Villa

taurants. Nice for an early-evening weekend outing. But the charm may be fleeting; scheduled for commercial redevelopment. Stay tuned.

Van Nuyse House (Coe House)
1128 East 34 Street between Flatbush Ave & Ave J, Brooklyn. Parts of this landmark Dutch house date back to 1744. Completed by Johannes Van Nuyse in 1806.

Van Nuyse-Magaw House
1041 East 22 Street between Aves I & J, Brooklyn. A Dutch Colonial house built circa 1800. Moved to its present site in 1916.

Willow Place
43-49 Willow Place, Brooklyn Heights. Built in 1846, this is Brooklyn's last surviving colonnade row. An imitation of the "classy" row on Lafayette Place in Manhattan.

Wyckoff-Bennett House
1669 East 22 Street at Kings Highway, Brooklyn. Built circa 1766, this is considered the finest example of Dutch Colonial architecture in Brooklyn. Two glass windowpanes are etched with the name and rank of two Hessian soldiers quartered there during the Revolution. A Bennett descendant still lives there.

Bronx

Bartow-Pell Mansion
Shore Road, Pelham Bay Park, Bronx. 885-1461. A Greek Revival country house built circa 1836. Filled with period furnishings. Beautiful sunken gardens, a breathtaking view of Long Island Sound. *OPEN Wed, Sat & Sun noon-4pm; Tues, Thurs & Fri by appointment only. CLOSED Mon and the month of Aug.* Small admission charge; children under age 12 free when accompanied by an adult.

City Island
A narrow, 230-acre island with a salty New England flavor, complete with weathered bungalows, Victorian houses, boatyards, and marinas right here in the city, specifically, the Bronx. Good for seafood dining and sea breezes. Attached to the mainland by a single narrow bridge, difficult to reach without a car—in summer, even harder with one.

Lorillard Snuff Mill
New York Botanical Garden, Bronx Park. Built on the Bronx River in 1840 by the Lorillard tobacco family as a mill to grind snuff, this fieldstone building now serves as a public restaurant in summer.

Poe Cottage
Grand Concourse at East Kingsbridge Road, Bronx. 881-8900. Built in 1816, it was the home of Edgar Allan Poe and his consumptive wife, Virginia, from 1846 to 1849, and the place where he wrote "Annabelle Lee" and "The Bells." Administered by the Bronx Historical Society. *OPEN Wed-Fri 9am-5pm; Sat 10am-4pm; Sun 1-5pm.* Small admission charge; children under age 12 free when accompanied by an adult. Groups by appointment only.

Valentine-Varian House (Bronx County Historical Society Museum)
3266 Bainbridge Avenue between Van Cortlandt Ave & East 208 St, Bronx. 881-8900. A two-story fieldstone farmhouse, dating from 1775, that now serves as a museum of local history. *OPEN Sat 10am-4pm; Sun 1-5pm.* Small admission charge; children under age 12 free when accompanied by an adult. Groups by appointment.

Van Cortlandt Mansion
In Van Cortlandt Park, Broadway north of West 242 Street, Riverdale, Bronx. 543-3344. A Georgian-style fieldstone manor house built in 1748. Washington's headquarters at various times during the American Revolution (yes, he slept here, too). The interior is a treasure house of colonial artifacts and furnishings. *OPEN Tues-Sat 11am-3pm; Sun 1-5pm.* Small admission charge; lower for senior citizens; children free when accompanied by an adult. Groups by appointment.

Queens

Bowne House
37-01 Bowne Street between 37 & 38 Aves, Flushing, Queens. (718) 359-0528. Quaker John Bowne's home, the oldest building in Queens, built in 1661, used as a clandestine meeting place for the then-forbidden Society of Friends. Contains colonial furnishings. Guided tours (last one 4:10pm). *OPEN Tues, Sat & Sun 2:30-4:30pm.* Admission charge. (*See also* Kingsland Homestead, which is nearby.)

Hunter's Point Historic District
45 Avenue between 21 & 23 Streets, Long Island City, Queens. A complete block of well-preserved row houses dating from the 1870s.

King Manor
King Park, Jamaica Avenue between 150 & 153 Streets, Jamaica, Queens. (718) 291-0282. Home of Rufus King, Federalist statesman, member of the Continental Congress, senator, and unsuccessful candidate for president. Its oldest section dates back to 1750. Period rooms. Now a new history museum with innovative exhibits and public programs for visitors of all ages. Call for update.

Kingsland Homestead
Weeping Beech Park, 143-35 37 Avenue & Parson's Blvd, Flushing, Queens. (718) 939-0647. Location of the **Queens Historical Society**, this farmhouse, built in 1774 by a wealthy Quaker farmer, is an interesting mix of Dutch and English architectural traditions. Moved from its original location on 155 Street, it's now a museum containing period rooms plus changing exhibits. *OPEN Tues, Sat & Sun 2:30-4:30pm.* Contribution suggested. (*See also* Bowne House, which is nearby.)

Cornelius Van Wyck House
37-04 Douglaston Parkway at Alston Pl, Douglaston, Queens. A 1735 Dutch farmhouse built by Revolutionary War patriot Cornelius Van Wyck. A landmark, but unfortunately renovated.

Lent Homestead
78-03 19 Road at 78 St, Astoria, Queens. A well-preserved, simple, Dutch Colonial farmhouse built in 1729. It still retains its original stonework.

Weeping Beech Tree
37 Avenue between Parsons Boulevard & Bowne Street, Flushing, Queens. A shoot from a rare Belgian tree was purchased by Samuel Parsons, a Flushing nurseryman, in 1847. It became the first tree ever designated a New York City landmark. It is over 60 feet high, with an 85-foot spread and a trunk circumference of 14 feet. (See also Kingsland Homestead.)

Staten Island

Alice Austen House (Clear Comfort)
2 Hylan Boulevard, Rosebank, Staten Island. (718) 816-4506. Built circa 1691 by a Dutch merchant, it was bought in 1844 by wealthy John Austen, whose granddaughter Alice was a pioneer in the field of photography. Her legacy: 3,000 glass-plate negatives of pictures taken between 1880 and 1930. Prints from those plates are on view, so are Victorian furnishings, and the view of the harbor and Manhattan is spectacular. Special events year-round. Call for schedule or join and receive the newsletter. OPEN Thurs-Sun noon-5pm. Suggested donation. Membership available.

Conference House (Billopp House)
7455 Hylan Boulevard, Tottenville, Staten Island. (718) 984-2086. This 1680 manor house built by a British naval captain, Christopher Billopp, was the site of the only Revolutionary War conference. Rebels Ben Franklin, John Adams, and Edward Rutledge turned down British offers of clemency in return for a cease-fire. OPEN Mar 16-Dec 14, Wed-Sun 1-4 pm. CLOSED Dec 15-Mar 15. Admission charge lower for children and senior citizens; children under age 6 free when accompanied by an adult.

Gardiner-Tyler Residence
27 Tyler Street between Clove Rd & Broadway intersection, West Brighton, Staten Island. A grand mansion built in 1835. Home of Julia Gardiner Tyler, widow of President John Tyler, from 1868 to 1874.

Weeping Beech Tree

Housman House
308 St. John Avenue at Watchogue Rd, Westerleigh, Staten Island. The original small, one-room stone section of this farmhouse was built in 1730. In 1760, the clapboard section was added.

Kreuzer-Pelton House
1262 Richmond Terrace near Pelton Pl, Livingston, Staten Island. Three distinct architectural periods are visible in the construction: the 1722 stone cottage, a shingled addition from 1770, and the two-story back section dating from 1836.

Neville House
806 Richmond Terrace between Clinton Ave & Tysen St, Livingston, Staten Island. One of the few remaining pre-Revolutionary War homes in New York. John Neville, a retired sea captain, had visited the Caribbean; his 1770 house reflects what he saw. Later a tavern, the Old Stone Jug.

Poillon House
4515 Hylan Boulevard between Hales Ave & Woods of Arden Rd, Annadale, Staten Island. Built in 1720, although there are remnants of a 1696 structure in the basement. Noted landscape architect Frederick Law Olmsted lived here and made extensive changes in the structure in 1848.

Richmondtown Restoration
Arthur Kill & Richmond Roads, Richmondtown, Staten Island. (718) 351-9414. Originally known as Cocclestown when founded in 1685 by Dutch, French Walloon, and English settlers, Richmondtown is now the site of approximately 26 buildings of major historical interest covering the years of 1690-1890 (not all are open to the public), including the **Voorlezer's House** (1695), the oldest known elementary school building in the U.S. The **Stephens General Store & House**, a reconstructed 19th-century store, stocks all the needs of its day. In July and August, costumed interpreters and craftspeople, such as a tinsmith, basketmaker, and a shoemaker, re-create the atmosphere of a small working period village; Labor Day weekend it's the site of a County Fair; at the end of December, it's Candlelight Tours and holiday revels; from January to April, there are Tavern Concerts in a period tavern lit by candle and heated by a wood-burning stove. From the Staten Island Ferry, take the no. 74 bus. OPEN Apr-June & Sept-Dec, Wed-Fri & Sun 1-5pm; July & Aug, Wed-Fri 10am-5pm, Sat & Sun 1-5 pm; Jan-Mar call for hours. Admission charge. Group tours are available.

Snug Harbor Cultural Center
Richmond Terrace from Tysen Street to Kissel Avenue, Livingston, Staten Island. (718) 448-2500. Sailor's Snug Harbor originally consisted of five magnificent Greek Revival buildings built in the 1830s-40s as a home for "aged, decrepit and worn-out sailors" by wealthy captain Robert Richard Randall. In all, there are 28 buildings on 80 acres of park, and they now serve as a performing and visual arts facility with a maritime historic heritage. Art, theater, recitals, outdoor sculpture, and concerts are presented in a land-

mark setting. Components include the Staten Island Botanical Garden and the Staten Island Children's Museum (*see* PARKS & GARDENS, Botanical Gardens *and* KIDS' NEW YORK, Museums for Children). *OPEN 7 days 9am-5pm.* Admission to the grounds is FREE. In summer, paid tours Sunday, at 2pm, from the main gate. In summer, the **Snug Harbor Trolley** runs from the Ferry Terminal every half hour on the hour from Wednesday to Sunday, noon to 6pm.

STATUES & MONUMENTS

Abingdon Square Memorial
Abingdon Square, Eighth Avenue & West 12 Street. (Philip Martiny, 1921.) Memorial to World War I dead features the "doughboy" planting an American flag.

Alice in Wonderland
Central Park, 76 Street near Fifth Avenue. (Jose de Creeft, 1959.) A bronze statue created for children to enjoy and experience by climbing and crawling—and so they do. The artist admits to pressure from his daughter to take the commission.

Alma Mater
Low Library, Columbia University. (Daniel Chester French, 1903.) This eight-foot-tall seated bronze lady has presided over graduations and, in the 1960s, riots.

Hans Christian Andersen
Central Park, Conservatory Water. (Georg John Lober, 1956.) This bronze statue, a gift from Danish and American schoolchildren, provides the natural place for the reading of Andersen's fairy tales (*see* KIDS' NEW YORK, Children's Entertainment: Storytelling). The two-foot-tall "Ugly Duckling" was stolen in 1974 but was soon recovered and returned to its creator's side.

Angel of the Waters (Bethesda Fountain)
Central Park, Bethesda Terrace near 72 Street. (Emma Stebbins, 1868.) The park's centerpiece, the newly refurbished bronze lady of the fountain usually watches over some interesting city rites. The cherubs represent Temperance, Purity, Health, and Peace.

Armillary Sphere
Flushing Meadows–Corona Park, Queens. (Paul Manship, 1964.) Bronze group on granite base, commissioned for 1964 World's Fair.

Atlas
International Building, Rockefeller Center, Fifth Avenue near West 51 Street. (Lee Lawrie, 1937.) The 15-foot-tall bronze figure resides on a 9-foot granite pedestal. It was picketed at its installation because of Atlas's reputed resemblance to Fascist dictator Mussolini.

Balto
Central Park, near Fifth Avenue & 66 Street. (Frederick George Richard Roth, 1925.) Schoolchildren's money helped erect this bronze statue of the sled dog that led the team of huskies that carried serum through a blizzard to Nome,

*Angel of the Waters
(Bethesda Fountain)*

Alaska, during a 1925 diphtheria epidemic. Note the shine where children have "petted" his snout and sat on his back.

Henry Ward Beecher
Fulton Street between Court & Joralemon Streets, Brooklyn. (John Quincy Adams Ward, 1891.) A fine bronze work of an abolitionist by an abolitionist.

James Gordon Bennett Memorial
Herald Square. (Antonin Jean Carles, 1940.) The bronze figure and clock (Bell Ringers Monument) once graced the top of Bennett's *New York Herald* building before it was razed.

Simon Bolivar
Central Park South at Avenue of the Americas. (Sally James Farnham, 1921.) The South American liberator on horseback in bronze on a polished-granite pedestal.

Edwin Booth as Hamlet
Gramercy Park. (Edmond T. Quinn, 1918.) Booth, America's leading Shakespearean actor of his time, lived at 16 Gramercy Park South from 1888 until his death in 1906.

William Cullen Bryant
Bryant Park. (Herbert Adams, 1911.) Bronze statue of the famed poet and journalist in a classical marble setting.

Central Park Mall at 72 Street
   Robert Burns
   Bronze. (Sir John Steell, 1880.)
   Fitz-Greene Halleck
   Bronze. (James Wilson Alexander MacDonald, 1877.)
   Victor Herbert
   Bronze. (Edmond T. Quinn, 1927.)
   Samuel F. B. Morse
   Bronze. (Byron M. Pickett, 1871.)
   Sir Walter Scott
   Bronze. (Sir John Steell, 1871.)
   William Shakespeare
   Bronze. (John Quincy Adams Ward, 1870.) The sculptor was paid $20,000 for this work.

Civic Virtue
Richard S. Newcomb Square, Queens. (Frederick William MacMonnies, 1922.) This male (as opposed to the usual female) embodiment of virtue was banished from City Hall Park in 1941 by women protesters.

Cleopatra's Needle
In Central Park behind the Metropolitan Museum of Art. Dating from 1600 B.C., this obelisk was a gift from Egypt in 1880. Pollution is taking its toll where time had not.

George M. Cohan
Broadway & West 46 Street. (Georg John Lober, 1959.) The famed song-and-dance man in bronze, permanently giving his "regards to Broadway."

Columbus Monument
Columbus Circle. (Gaetano Russo, 1892.) White marble statue atop a 26-foot granite column honoring Columbus (one of four in the city), erected on the 400th anniversary of America's discovery.

Peter Cooper
Cooper Square, Bowery at East 7 Street. (Augustus Saint-Gaudens, 1897.) Philanthropist Cooper in bronze sits proudly within a templelike structure by architect Stanford White, in front of Cooper Union, the free institution he founded to teach practical arts and sciences.

Delacorte Musical Clock
Central Park Zoo. (Andrea Spadini, 1965.) Almost as popular as the zoo's live residents, these bronze denizens do a dance every hour to the tune of one of 32 nursery tunes.

Abraham de Peyster
Bowling Green. (George Edwin Bissell, 1896.) Bronze statue of prosperous colonial merchant de Peyster stands where an ill-fated one of George III once stood.

Father Duffy Memorial
Duffy Square, Broadway between West 46 & West 47 Streets. (Charles Keck, 1937.) A bronze statue with a polished granite base and cross whose subject is straight out of Damon Runyon. Duffy, whose parish was honky-tonk Times Square of the 20s, was chaplain to the Fighting 69th in World War I.

Eagles and Prey
Central Park, northwest of the Mall. (Kristin Fratin, 1850.) One of the earliest pieces to grace the park.

The Falconer
Central Park, 72 Street Transverse. (George B. Simonds, 1871.) The graceful ten-foot bronze statue is back after a 30-year absence.

Firemen's Memorial
Riverside Drive at West 100 Street. (Attilio Piccirilli, 1912.) Representations of Duty and Courage in tribute to the men, and a bronze plaque in tribute to the horses, of the Fire Department.

Benjamin Franklin
Park Row at Nassau & Spruce Streets. (Ernst Plassmann, 1872.) In Franklin's left hand is a copy of his paper the *Pennsylvania Gazette*.

Mohandas Gandhi
Union Square, West 14 Street & Broadway. (Kantilal B. Patel, 1986.) Indian nationalist and nonviolent rebel against British rule, depicted as the devout Hindu ascetic he was.

Giuseppe Garibaldi
Washington Square Park. (Giovanni Turini, 1888.) A tribute from Italian Americans to Garibaldi's victorious efforts to unite Italy.

Good Defeats Evil
United Nations. (Zurab Tsereteli, 1990.) The dragon St. George is spearing is made of slices of what were once Soviet SS-20 and American Pershing ballistic missiles, chopped up in accordance with the 1988 treaty eliminating intermediate-range missiles. A gift from the Soviet government.

Horace Greeley
City Hall Park. (John Quincy Adams Ward, 1916.) Bronze statue of famed editor and unsuccessful presidential candidate. Seated in an armchair, Greeley holds a copy of the *New York Tribune*—not surprising, since he owned it.

Nathan Hale
City Hall Park. (Frederick MacMonnies, 1890.) An imaginary portrait in bronze of a very real hero, who was executed by the British as a spy in 1776.

Alexander Hamilton
Central Park, East Drive at 83 Street. (Carl Conrads, 1880.) This granite statue of the famed Federalist was presented to the city by Hamilton's son John C. Hamilton.

Alexander Lyman Holley
Washington Square Park. (John Quincy Adams Ward, 1889.) Bronze bust of inventor and engineer Holley is reputed to be one of the prolific sculptor's best public works.

Hudson Memorial Column
Henry Hudson Parkway & West 227 Street, Bronx. (Karl Bitter, 1909-39.) Commissioned to commemorate the 300th anniversary of Hudson's discovery of the river that bears his name.

Indian Hunter
Central Park northwest of the Mall. (John Quincy Adams Ward, 1866.) This bronze group, initially cast in plaster, was done from sketches made during a visit to the West. It was the first by an American to be placed in the park.

Washington Irving
Terrace Garden, Prospect Park, Brooklyn. (James Wilson Alexander MacDonald, 1871.) A bronze bust of "the father of American literature."

Joan of Arc
Riverside Drive at West 93 Street. (Anna Vaughn Hyatt Huntington, 1915.) Bronze statue on granite pedestal contains fragments of stone from the tower where Joan was imprisoned in Rouen and from Rheims Cathedral.

John F. Kennedy Memorial
Grand Army Plaza, Brooklyn. (Neil Estern, 1965.) This bronze bust is New York's only official memorial to the late president.

Lafayette
Union Square. (Frederic-Auguste Bartholdi, 1876.) Inscription: "As soon as I heard of American independence my heart was enlisted."

Lafayette and Washington
Morningside Park. (Frederic-Auguste Bartholdi, 1890.) The allies in independence by the famed French sculptor.

Abraham Lincoln
Terrace Garden, Prospect Park, Brooklyn. (Henry Kirke Brown, 1869.) Abe's right hand points to a manuscript now missing.

Lions
New York Public Library, Fifth Avenue & 41 Street. (Edward Clark Potter, 1911.) The closest thing New York has to a mascot—a matched pair no less. Dubbed Patience and Fortitude by Mayor Fiorello LaGuardia, they are dear to the hearts of all New Yorkers and are especially resplendent at Christmas, when they are bedecked with large beribboned wreaths.

Maine Monument
Columbus Circle at West 59 Street. (Attilio Piccirilli, 1913.) A dramatic Beaux Arts bronze-and-marble memorial to those who perished on the battleship Maine in 1898. Recently refurbished.

Manhattan & Brooklyn
Brooklyn Museum, Eastern Parkway, Brooklyn. (Daniel Chester French, 1916.) Symbolic representations of the two boroughs. Their original site, the Brooklyn end of the Manhattan Bridge.

Thomas Moore
Terrace Garden, Prospect Park, Brooklyn. (John G. Draddy, 1879.) Erin's beloved poet in bronze.

Mother Goose
Central Park near East Drive at 72 Street. (Frederick G. R. Roth, 1938.) This eight-foot granite embodiment of Mother and her goose stands on the site of the old Central Park Casino.

New York Vietnam Veterans Memorial
Vietnam Veterans Plaza, 55 Water Street. (Pete Wormser, William Fellows.) New York's Vietnam Veterans Memorial, unveiled May 6, 1985, ten years after the war ended, is a translucent glass-block wall, 14 feet high and 70 feet long, inscribed with excerpts of letters to and from those who served—only some of whom came home. On the granite shelves are left candles, notes, and flowers. It is a poignant tribute.

107th Infantry
Fifth Avenue at 67 Street. (Karl M. Illava, 1927.) The sculptor, an alumnus of the 107th in World War I, is depicted in this bronze work.

Peace
United Nations Gardens. (Antun Augustincic, 1954.) This heroic bronze statue was presented to the United Nations by the government of Yugoslavia.

Prison Ship Martyrs' Monument
Fort Greene Park, Brooklyn. (McKim, Mead & White, 1908.) The world's tallest Doric column: 148 feet 8 inches. A memorial to American patriots who died on British prison ships anchored in the bay during the Revolution.

Prometheus
Lower Plaza, Rockefeller Center. (Paul Manship, 1934.) The fire-giver in bronze with gold-leaf covering set in a flashing fountain-pool oversees ice skaters in winter, alfresco diners in summer.

Pulitzer Fountain
Grand Army Plaza, Fifth Avenue between West 58 & West 59 Streets. (Carrere & Hastings; Sculptor: Karl Bitter, 1916.) The fountain became a legendary part of the Roaring 20s when F. Scott and Zelda Fitzgerald went wading in it. Originally built of limestone, it had so badly deteriorated that it was crumbling; virtually rebuilt in more durable granite. The goddess Pomona was given a new patina.

Rocket Thrower
Flushing Meadows–Corona Park, Flushing, Queens. (Donald DeLue, 1964.) This bronze work was commissioned for the 1964 World's Fair as a permanent fixture for the park.

Roosevelt Memorial
American Museum of Natural History, Central Park West at 79 Street. (James Earle Fraser, 1940.) This bronze group, 16 feet tall, is one of the largest and best equestrian statues in the world.

Sculpture Garden
Brooklyn Museum, Eastern Parkway at Washington Avenue, Brooklyn. (718) 638-5000. An outdoor garden display of architectural ornamentation and sculpture salvaged from demolition sites in the city.

Seventh Regiment Memorial
Central Park, West Drive near West 67 Street. (John Quincy Adams Ward, 1873.) In memory of the 58 members of this New York State regiment who died in the Civil War.

William H. Seward
Madison Square Park. (Randolph Rogers, 1876.) Truth or fiction? Secretary of State Seward's head on President Lincoln's body, done previously by the sculptor in Philadelphia.

Sherman Monument
Grand Army Plaza, Fifth Avenue at 59 Street. (Augustus Saint-Gaudens, 1903.) A graceful bronze equestrian group in tribute to the Civil War general. Recently given a dazzling coat of gold said to replicate the original; part of the renewal of the entire plaza.

Soldiers' and Sailors' Memorial
Riverside Drive at West 89 Street. A 96-foot-high white marble monument was built in 1902 to commemorate the Civil War dead.

Statue of Liberty National Monument
Liberty Island, New York Harbor. Probably the most famous statue in the world, "Liberty Enlightening the World," sculpted by Frederic-Auguste Bartholdi, is better known as the Statue of Liberty. The proud lady stands 152 feet high atop a 150-foot pedestal executed by Richard Morris Hunt, paid for by American citizens. Gustav Eiffel designed the interior iron skeleton frame. A gift from France to the U.S. in 1886, she has since become a symbolic representation of freedom. In 1986, she underwent a long-overdue restoration and emerged, with great fanfare on July 4, more beautiful and awe-inspiring than ever. (See also SIGHTSEEING, Viewpoints.)

Still Hunt
Central Park, East Drive at 76 Street. (Edward

Kemeys, 1883.) Crouched bronze panther on natural rock—very realistic.

Straus Memorial
Broadway at West 106 Street. (Henry Augustus Lukeman, 1915.) In memory: Ida Straus chose to stay with her husband, Isador, and both perished on the maiden voyage of the *Titanic*. The philanthropists had lived close by the site chosen.

Peter Stuyvesant
Stuyvesant Square. (Gertrude Vanderbilt Whitney, 1941.) A life-size bronze statue of New York's last Dutch governor, peg-legged Peter Stuyvesant, on land that formed his farm. He's buried in nearby St. Mark's-in-the-Bowery. (*See* Churches & Synagogues.)

Swords into Plowshares
United Nations, North Gardens, East River Terrace. (Evgeniy Vuchetich, 1958.) This dramatc nine-foot-tall bronze statue was a gift from the U.S.S.R.

Tempest
Central Park near Delacorte Theater, Central Park West & West 81 Street. (Milton Hebald, 1966.) Depicting Shakespeare's Prospero, it's dedicated to Joseph Papp, the theatrical genius who among other joys presented free Shakespeare in the Park. When unveiled, this statue violated an 1876 law prohibiting commemorative statues until five years after the subject or dedicatee's death. No one complained. Papp died in 1991.

Albert Bertil Thorvalsden, Self-Portrait
Central Park off East 96 Street. (Donated by Denmark, 1894.) The great neoclassical sculptor. Made from the marble original, it was donated by the Danes in recognition of Thorvalsden's influence on early American sculpture.

Untermeyer Fountain (Dancing Girls)
Central Park, Conservatory Gardens, Fifth Avenue & 104 Street. (Walter Schott, 1947.) Beautifully sculpted spirited maidens; from Untermeyer's Yonkers estate.

Giuseppi Verdi
Verdi Square, Broadway & West 73 Street. (Pasquale Civiletti, 1906.) Carrara marble statue of the great 19th-century Italian composer.

Giovanni da Verrazano
Battery Park. (Ettore Ximenes, 1909.) Erected by proud Italian Americans honoring this man who is thought to have sighted New York Harbor before Henry Hudson did.

George Washington
Union Square Park. (Henry Kirke Brown, with John Quincy Adams Ward, 1856.) A beautiful bronze equestrian statue.

George Washington
Steps of Federal Hall, Wall & Broad Streets. (John Quincy Adams Ward, 1833.) On the site of Washington's inauguration. The statue's pedestal is said to contain a stone from the spot where he stood on that day.

Washington Arch
Foot of Fifth Avenue, Washington Square Park. (McKim, Mead & White, 1892.) First erected in

Washington Arch

wood in 1889 for the centennial celebration of Washington's inauguration. Pianist Paderewski gave a benefit concert to raise money for a permanent one. Now in sad state of disrepair.

Daniel Webster
Central Park, West Drive near 72 Street. (Thomas Ball, 1876.) Bronze statue of the famed American statesman and orator, with his memorable words "Liberty and union, now and forever, one and inseparable."

CHURCHES & SYNAGOGUES

There are more than 2,250 churches and 600 synagogues in New York City. The following are the most historic or architecturally interesting in all five boroughs.

Anshe Chesed (Old Congregation) (Jewish)
172-176 Norfolk Street between Stanton & East Houston Streets. (Alexander Saeltzer, 1849.) The city's oldest and, at one time, largest synagogue. Today, sadly, it is a mess. The congregation has long since moved uptown.

Bialystoker Synagogue

Bialystoker Synagogue
7 Willet Street between Grand & Broome Sts. A freestanding Federal-style building (1826), originally a rural Methodist church. Since 1908, a place of worship for Lower East Side Jews.

Brighton Heights Reformed Church
320 St. Mark's Place at Fort Place, Staten Island. A lovely white-wood-framed church built in 1866.

Brotherhood Synagogue (originally Friends' Meeting House)
28 Gramercy Park South between Irving Pl & Third Ave. Built in 1859 and remodeled as a synagogue in 1975. Now a landmark.

Cathedral of St. John the Divine (Episcopal)
Amsterdam Avenue at West 112 Street. 316-7540. Begun on St. John's Day, December 27, 1892, the work continued until 1941 and has now resumed—in the medieval manner, each stone is being hand-cut. This massive (the length of two football fields—601 feet—and 14 stories high) eclectic building will be the world's largest Gothic cathedral when completed. Special events throughout the year but two highlights are the blessing of the animals in honor of St. Francis (October) and the New Year's Eve Peace Concert. Don't miss the Rose Window (40 feet in diameter, it is comprised of 10,000 pieces of glass), the English and Italian 17th-century tapestries, and the lovely Biblical Garden (*see* PARKS & GARDENS, Gardens). Tours available. *OPEN Mon-Sat 11am-5pm; Sun (after service) 12:45-5pm.*

Central Synagogue (Reform Jewish)
652 Lexington Avenue at East 55 St. (Henry Fernbach.) A Moorish Revival edifice. Since 1872, the city's oldest synagogue in continuous use. Its Eternal Light, kindled in 1872, replaced by electricity in 1946, still burns.

Christ Church (Episcopal)
Henry Hudson Parkway at West 252 Street, Riverdale, Bronx. (Richard Upjohn, 1866.) A small, picturesque parish church.

Church of the Ascension (Episcopal)
36-38 Fifth Avenue at 10 St. (Richard Upjohn,

1841; interior remodeled: McKim, Mead & White, 1889.) New York's first Gothic Revival church. Beautiful altar mural and stained glass by John La Farge.

Church of the Holy Apostles (Episcopal)
300 Ninth Avenue at West 28 St. (Minard Lafever, 1848; transepts: Richard Upjohn & Son, 1858.) A handsome spire crowns this gem of a church. Stained-glass windows by William Jay Bolton.

Church of the Intercession (Episcopal)
Broadway at West 155 Street. 283-6200. (Cram, Goodhue & Ferguson, 1914.) The church was founded in 1846 as an independent congregation of the Episcopal church. The large English Gothic-style country church is beautifully situated in rural Trinity Cemetery (*see* Graveyards). The land was once the bird-watching farm of famed ornithologist James J. Audubon. The main altar was designed by Louis Comfort Tiffany and is inlaid with stones from Christianity's most revered sources.

Church of St. Andrew (Episcopal)
4 Arthur Kill Road at Old Mill Rd, Richmondtown, Staten Island. (William H. Mersereau, 1872.) As if transplanted, a picturesque random-fieldstone English parish church with graveyard in a lovely setting.

Church of St. Ignatius Loyola (Roman Catholic)
980 Park Avenue at East 84 St. (Ditmas & Schickel, 1898.) The lower church was dedicated initially to St. Laurence O'Toole; the main altar was later dedicated to St. Ignatius Loyola, founder of the Jesuits. A reflection of the parish's changing character.

Church of St. Mary the Virgin (Episcopal)
145 West 46 Street between Sixth Ave & Broadway. This theater district church is very high Episcopal—incense and all.

Church of St. Vincent Ferrer (Roman Catholic)
869 Lexington Avenue at East 66 St. (Bertram Grosvenor Goodhue, 1923.) Goodhue himself regarded this as one of his best. It has a magnificent rose window.

Central Synagogue

Church of St. Ignatius Loyola

Civic Center Synagogue (Shaare Zedek)
49 White Street between Church St & Broadway. (William N. Breger Assocs., 1967.) An incongruous marble swirl tucked between two tenements.

Congregation B'nai Jeshurun (Jewish)
257 West 88 Street between Broadway & West End Ave. (Henry B. Herts & Walter Schneider, 1918.) An exotic Byzantine edifice.

Congregation Chasam Sofer (Jewish)
8-10 Clinton Street between Stanton & East Houston Sts. Dating from 1853, it's the city's second-oldest surviving synagogue.

Congregation K'hal Adath Jeshurun (Jewish)
14 Eldridge Street between Forsyth & Canal Sts. (Herter Brothers, 1887.) Ornate Lower East Side synagogue now being restored after years of disuse.

Congregation Shearith Israel (Jewish)
99 Central Park West at West 70 St. (Brunner & Tryon, 1897.) Founded by North America's oldest Jewish congregation. The Sephardic (of Spanish and Portuguese origins) synagogue contains religious articles from three centuries. Site of an annual Sephardic Fair. (*See* ANNUAL EVENTS, May; *see also* Graveyards: First Shearith Israel Graveyard.)

Fifth Avenue Synagogue
5 East 62 Street between Fifth & Madison Aves. (Percival Goodman, 1959.) Modern limestone temple with stained-glass windows that can be appreciated only after dark when the interior lights come on.

First Moravian Church
154 Lexington Avenue at East 30 St. Small, lovely brick church, built circa 1845.

First Presbyterian Church
48 Fifth Avenue between West 11 & West 12 Sts. (Joseph C. Wells, 1846.) Gothic Revival church with a lovely cast-iron and wood fence.

First Reformed Church of College Point
14 Avenue at 119 Street, Queens. A beautiful wooden country church built in 1872.

First Warsaw Congregation (Jewish)
58-60 Rivington Street between Eldridge & Allen Sts. Built in 1903, originally Congregation Adath Jeshurun of Jassy. Lovely—but, sadly, it has been vandalized.

Flatbush Dutch Reformed Church
890 Flatbush Avenue at Church Ave, Brooklyn. Built 1793-98, the third church on the site, it's an elegant Federal-style building. The steeple has its original bell (imported from Holland), which tolled the death of President Washington and continues to do so on the demise of a chief executive.

Flatlands Dutch Reformed Church
3931 Kings Highway between Flatbush Ave & East 40 St, Brooklyn. A beautifully situated New England–like white-painted clapboard church built in 1848 for a cost of $5,506.29.

Friends' Meeting House
137-16 Northern Boulevard between Main & Union Sts, Flushing, Queens. (718) 358-9636. It is the oldest house of worship in the United

Flatbush Dutch Reformed Church

States. Used continuously since 1694, except for 1776-83 when the British used it successively as prison, storehouse, and hospital. In the rear, separate doors for men and women. The Quakers of Flushing were pioneers in demands for religious freedom. *OPEN first Sun of every month 11am.*

Friends' Meeting House & Seminary
221 East 15 Street & Rutherford Pl. (Charles T. Bunting, 1860.) Quaker conservative.

Grace Church & Rectory (Episcopal)
800 Broadway at East 10 St. (James Renwick, Jr., 1846.) This is Renwick's magnificent example of Gothic Revival architecture predating his later masterpiece, St. Patrick's Cathedral. Its serene English garden was landscaped by Vaux & Company. Its staid congregation was scandalized in 1863 when the sanctuary was used for the marriage of P. T. Barnum's little trouper Tom Thumb.

Grace Episcopal Church
155-03 Jamaica Avenue between 155 St & Parsons Blvd, Jamaica, Queens. The congregation was founded in 1702. This, the third church on this site, is a rugged Gothic Revival edifice. Statesman and four-time New York senator Ru-

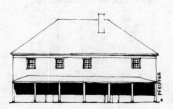

Friends' Meeting House

Grace Church

fus King is buried in a charming churchyard, which dates from 1734.

John Street United Methodist Church
44 John Street between Nassau & William Sts. This church dates from 1841, but the first Methodist church was on this site in 1766, making it America's oldest Methodist congregation.

Judson Memorial Baptist Church
55 Washington Square South between Thompson & Sullivan Sts. (McKim, Mead & White, 1892.) This neo-Italian-Renaissance-style church and campanile are very much a part of the Greenwich Village skyline.

John Street United Methodist Church

Judson Memorial Baptist Church

The Little Church Around the Corner (Church of the Transfiguration) (Episcopal)
1 East 29 Street between Fifth & Madison Aves. Built 1849-61. In 1870, a local pastor refused funeral services for an actor and suggested the "little church around the corner." Its name and its popularity with theater people are now tradition. The stained-glass windows are dedicated to past actors. Beautifully landscaped.

Marble Collegiate Church (Reformed)
272 Fifth Avenue at 29 St. (S. A. Warner, 1854.) Limestone Gothic Revival. Noted primarily for one of its former pastors, Dr. Norman Vincent Peale, and one of its former parishioners, Richard Nixon.

Mariners' Temple (Baptist)
12 Oliver Street at Henry St. (Minard Lafever, 1842.) Originally it was a Baptist seamen's church; historically, it is noted as a haven for immigrants of all nations. This church, reflecting the area's changing character, now conducts services in both Spanish and Chinese.

Mosque of New York
Islamic Cultural Center of New York, 1711 Third Avenue at East 96 St. 722-5234. (Main Building: Skidmore, Owings, Merrill; Minaret: Swanke, Hayden, Connell, Ltd, 1991.) A new focal point for Muslims in New York, this granite-and-glass building, topped with a copper dome and a thin gold crescent, is the first building in New York to be built as a mosque. The cornerstone of the 130-foot minaret was laid by the Emir of Kuwait in 1988. Eventually the complex will also house a school.

New Lots Reformed Church
620 New Lots Avenue at Schenck Ave, Brooklyn. Built in 1824 of wood, it stands virtually unaltered. Records show that the Dutch farmers of New Lots built it for $35 in out-of-pocket expenses.

New Utrecht Reformed Church
18 Avenue between 83 & 84 Sts, Brooklyn. The

Marble Collegiate Church

fieldstone for this Georgian Gothic edifice came from the original 1699 church on this spot, demolished to build this one in 1828. The windows are of Victorian milk glass.

Old St. Patrick's Cathedral (Roman Catholic)
260-264 Mulberry Street between Prince & East Houston Sts. (Joseph Mangin, 1815.) New York's original Roman Catholic cathedral, replaced by uptown St. Patrick's (1879) after a disastrous fire. It was restored in 1868 but demoted to a parish church. (*See also* Graveyards.)

Our Lady of Lebanon Roman Catholic Church
Remsen & Henry Streets, Brooklyn Heights. (Richard Upjohn, 1846.) Originally Congregational Church of the Pilgrims: a fragment of Plymouth Rock projects from one of its walls. The west and south doors are salvage from the ill-fated liner *Normandie.*

Plymouth Church of the Pilgrims
Orange Street between Henry & Hicks Streets, Brooklyn Heights. (718) 624-4743. Abolitionist Henry Ward Beecher's church from 1847 to 1887. Pew 89 is where Abraham Lincoln once worshiped. A piece of Plymouth Rock is preserved in its arcade. Tours Sunday at 12:30pm, following services.

Reformed Dutch Church of Newtown
85-15 Broadway at Corona Ave, Elmhurst, Queens. Dating from 1831, it is one of the oldest wooden churches in the city.

Riverdale Presbyterian Church
4765 Henry Hudson Parkway West at West 249

St, Bronx. (James Renwick, Jr., 1863.) A charming Gothic Revival building. Very much the English parish church.

Riverside Church (Interdenominational)
490 Riverside Drive at West 122 St. 222-5900. (Allen & Collens and Henry C. Pelton, 1930.) The church, endowed by John D. Rockefeller, Jr., occupies a prominent site along the Hudson. The tower of this steel-framed structure, 392 feet high, serves as an office building and houses the world's largest carillon and bell. (*See also* SIGHTSEEING, Viewpoints.) A one-hour guided tour of the church is offered most Sundays at 12:30pm beginning in Christ Chapel. Visitor's Center in the South Lobby: *OPEN Mon-Fri 11am-3pm; Sun 1-4pm.* Sunday service: 10:45am. Church *CLOSED Mon.*

Roman Catholic Church of the Transfiguration
25 Mott Street at Pell St. This unpretentious little Georgian-style house of worship was built in 1801 by English Lutherans.

St. Ann & the Holy Trinity
157 Montague Street at Clinton St, Brooklyn. (Minard Lafever, 1847) Neo-Gothic brownstone church currently undergoing restoration. Recently unveiled restorations of its stained-glass windows, America's first.

St. Ann's Church (Episcopal)
Clinton Street at Livingston Street, Brooklyn Heights. (James Renwick, Jr., 1869.) Renwick gave Brooklyn its only example of "Venetian" Gothic architecture with the facade's varying colors and textures of stone.

St. Ann's Church (Episcopal)
295 St. Ann's Avenue between East 139 & East 141 Sts, Bronx. Gouverneur Morris, Jr., built this fieldstone church on his estate for family worship. Consecrated in 1841, it's the earliest church building surviving in the Bronx. The cemetery and crypts contain many members of the Morris family. (Gouverneur Morris, Sr., drafted the final version of the Constitution.)

St. Augustine's Chapel (Episcopal)
290 Henry Street between Montgomery & Jackson Sts. An 1828 Georgian fieldstone building, originally All Saints' Free Church.

St. Bartholomew's Church (Episcopal)
Park Avenue between East 50 & East 51 Streets. (Bertram Grosvenor Goodhue, 1919.) This congregation followed New York's inexorable move uptown with locations at Great Jones Street, then 44 Street, and finally this Byzantine splendor with terraced gardens in the midst of Park Avenue's skyscrapers. The Romanesque porch, from the former building, is by McKim, Mead & White, 1902. The battle to prevent the landmark community house and garden from becoming a skyscraper has been won by preservationists.

St. Benedict's Church (Roman Catholic)
342 West 53 Street between Eighth & Ninth Aves. This congregation for black Catholics was founded in 1883. It was moved in the 1890s to this Italianate building.

St. Bartholomew's Church

St. Clement's Church (Episcopal)
423 West 46 Street between Ninth & Tenth Aves. Picturesque parish church built circa 1870. Perhaps reflecting its theater district location, dance and dramatic presentations are often offered here.

St. George's Episcopal Church
Rutherford Place at East 16 Street off Stuyvesant Square. (Blesch & Eidlitz, 1856.) Romanesque brownstone known as "Morgan's Church" after tough church elder, financier J. P. Morgan.

St. George's Ukrainian Catholic Church
East 7 Street & Hall Place. New (1977) religious centerpiece of old Ukrainian neighborhood and focal point of the annual Ukrainian folk festival (*see* ANNUAL EVENTS, May.)

St. James Church (Roman Catholic)
32 James Street between St. James Pl & Madison St. (Attributed to Minard Lafever, 1837.) Greek Revival in Connecticut brownstone, a cheap and easy-to-carve material that unfortunately weathers poorly. The community is raising money for structural repairs.

St. Jean Baptiste Church (Roman Catholic)
Lexington Avenue at East 76 Street. (Nicholas Serracino, 1913.) A single patron, the story goes, named Thomas Fortune Ryan, endowed this building when the little church on the site offered him standing-room-only one Sunday. The original congregation was French Canadian.

St. John the Baptist Church (Roman Catholic)
211 West 30 Street between Seventh & Eighth Aves. (Napoleon Le Brun, 1872.) A single-spired brownstone church with lovely white marble interior.

St. John's Episcopal Church
1331 Bay Street at New Lane, Rosebank, Staten Island. (Arthur D. Gilman, 1871.) A lovely rose-colored Victorian Gothic church.

St. Joseph's Roman Catholic Church
365 Avenue of the Americas at Washington Pl. (John Doran, 1834.) An imposing Greek Revival "temple" in Greenwich Village.

St. Luke-in-the-Fields Church (Episcopal)
485 Hudson Street between Barrow & Christopher Sts. (James N. Wells, 1822.) This area was rural to parishioners living at Manhattan's tip, hence the name of what was then a charming country parish church. A tragic fire devastated it in 1981. A successful restoration was completed in 1986.

St. Mark's Church-in-the-Bowery (Episcopal)
East 10 Street & Second Avenue. 674-6377. Built on the 1601 site of Dutch governor Peter Stuyvesant's family chapel, which makes it the oldest site of continuous worship in New York. Originally a stark Georgian structure (1799), it served as the first parish in Manhattan independent of Trinity Church. The Greek Revival steeple was completed in 1836; the Italianate portico was added in 1854. Beautifully restored following a devastating fire in 1978, it's a historical, architectural, and cultural treasure where Isadora Duncan danced and Edna St. Vincent Millay and

St. James Church

St. Luke-in-the-Fields Church

Robert Frost read their works. **Danspace** and the **Poetry Project** continue the tradition. A National Historic Landmark and centerpiece of the St. Mark's Historic District.

St. Patrick's Cathedral (Roman Catholic)
Fifth Avenue & East 50 Street. 753-2261. (James Renwick, Jr., 1858-79.) A Renwick masterpiece. The cathedral, a mix of English and French Gothic, took 21 years to complete. The seat of New York's Catholic Archdiocese. *OPEN 7 days 7am-9pm. Mass Mon-Fri at 7, 7:30, 8, 8:30am & noon, 12:30 & 1pm; Sat at 8 & 8:30am, noon, 12:30 & 5:30pm; Sun 7, 8, 9, 10:15am, noon, 1, 4 & 5:30pm.*

St. Patrick's Roman Catholic Church
53 St. Patrick's Place between Center St & Clarke Ave, Richmondtown, Staten Island. A white-painted brick church built in 1862.

St. Paul's Chapel (Episcopal)
Columbia University, Amsterdam Avenue between West 116 & West 117 Streets. (Howells & Stokes, 1907.) Considered one of the best of Columbia's buildings. The 24 windows in the dome are decorated with the coats of arms of old New York families associated with city and university history.

St. Paul's Chapel (Episcopal)
Broadway & Fulton Street. 602-0874. (Archibald Thomas McBean, 1764-66; tower, steeple, porch: James Crommelin Lawrence, 1794.) This Georgian-style church is New York's oldest surviving public building. Distinguished worshipers included George Washington, Gov. George Clinton, Lafayette, and General Cornwallis. Surrounded by its peaceful old cemetery (*see also* Graveyards). *OPEN Mon-Sat 8am-4pm; Sun 7am-3pm.* Musical program every Monday and Thursday afternoon at noon.

St. Peter's Church (Episcopal)
344 West 20 Street between Eighth & Ninth Aves.

St. Patrick's Cathedral

(James W. Smith, 1836-38.) Based on designs by Clement Clarke Moore, this Chelsea church is one of the earliest examples of an English Gothic parish church that was to become so popular in years to follow.

St. Peter's Church (Episcopal)
2500 Westchester Avenue near St. Peter's Ave, Bronx. Picturesque 1855 Gothic Revival church.

St. Peter's Church (Lutheran)
East 54 Street & Lexington Avenue. 935-2200. (Hugh Stubbins & Assocs., 1977.) The old church building came down to make way for the

St. Mark's Church-in-the-Bowery

St. Paul's Chapel

St. Peter's Church
(Chelsea)

St. Thomas's Church

Citicorp complex, and a new, ultra-modern church complete with a chapel by Louise Nevelson, on the same site, nests within the skyscraper's shadow. Still renowned for its Sunday jazz vespers. Also, jazz every Wednesday at 12:30pm for a small suggested donation. Call for other events.

St. Peter's Church (Roman Catholic)
22 Barclay Street at Church St. (John R. Haggerty and Thomas Thomas, 1838.) An impressive granite Greek Revival edifice. Its first incarnation on this site in 1786 was only the second Roman Catholic church to be built in the city.

St. Stephen's Church (Roman Catholic)
149 East 28 Street. (James Renwick, Jr., 1854.) Romanesque Revival in brownstone. Interior mural by Constantino Brumidi.

St. Teresa's Roman Catholic Church
16-18 Rutgers Street at Henry St. Built in 1841, originally the First Presbyterian Church of New York. It conducts services in English, Spanish, and Chinese.

St. Thomas's Church (Episcopal)
1 West 53 Street at Fifth Ave. (Cram, Goodhue & Ferguson, 1914.) Richly detailed French Gothic church; many feel it's New York's most beautiful. Popular with the city's fashionable rich for weddings; its "Bride's Door" ornamentation contains both a lover's knot and a dollar sign—the stonemason's commentary went unnoticed for three years.

Sea and Land Church
61 Henry Street at Market St. A Georgian-Federal church with Gothic windows, built in 1817. It's now the First Chinese Presbyterian Church.

Serbian Orthodox Cathedral of St. Sava
15 West 25 Street between Fifth & Sixth Aves. (Richard Upjohn, 1855.) Originally Trinity Chapel, part of Trinity Parish, this brownstone church is now a Croation sanctuary.

Temple Emanu-El (Reform Jewish)
1 East 65 Street at Fifth Ave. 744-1400. (Robert D. Kohn, Charles Butler, and Clarence Stein, 1929.) New York's "fashionable" synagogue, founded by wealthy German Jews. Built in the Byzantine-Romanesque style, it is the largest synagogue in America, with a seating capacity of 2,500. OPEN 7 days 10am-5:15pm. Services: Fri 5:15 pm & Sat 10:30am.

Trinity Church (Episcopal)
Broadway & Wall Street. 602-0872. (Richard Upjohn, 1846.) This church was founded by royal charter of England's King William III. The first two churches on the site were destroyed. The 280-foot spire of the present Gothic Revival edifice made it New York's tallest until the turn of the century; its old cemetery is a quiet green oasis in summertime. Tours daily at 2pm. Concerts year-round on Tuesday at 1pm. Museum OPEN Mon-Fri 9-11:45am, 1-3:45pm; Sat 10am-3:45pm; Sun 1-3:45pm. Church OPEN Mon-Fri 7am-6pm; Sat 8am-4pm; Sun 7am-4pm. (See also Graveyards.)

Village Community Church
143 West 13 Street between Sixth & Seventh Aves. (Samuel Thompson, 1846.) An excellent Greek Revival structure that now stands empty. A synagogue and church used to share these quarters, but unfortunately the ecumenical spirit did not last. Now part of a residential co-op complex.

Woodrow United Methodist Church
1109 Woodrow Road near Rossville Ave, Woodrow, Staten Island. Built in 1842, it is pure Greek Revival, except for the added tower and belfry.

GRAVEYARDS

In the 18th and early 19th centuries, New Yorkers buried their dead in churchyards or in nearby

Woodrow United Methodist Church

Green-Wood Cemetery

cemeteries. Of some 90 burial grounds, only a bare few remain, especially within the confines of "the City." After 1830, one needed a special permit for burial south of Canal Street, and after 1852 burial within Manhattan was completely prohibited. Trinity Cemetery is still active, but interment is aboveground in crypts. (According to the sales brochure, those with a view are extremely expensive.)

First Shearith Israel Graveyard
55 St. James Place between Oliver & James Sts. 1683-1828. Dating from their arrival in 1654, the Congregation Beth Shearith is the oldest Jewish congregation in America. This is the earliest surviving burial ground of these Spanish and Portuguese Jews. (*See also* Second *and* Third Cemetery of the Spanish & Portuguese Synagogue.) Consecrated in 1656; the oldest gravestone is dated 1683. The English translation on one of the tombstones reads:

> Here lies buried
> The unmarried man Walter J. Judah
> Old in wisdom, tender in years

Green-Wood Cemetery
Main Gate: Fifth Avenue & 25 Street, Brooklyn. (1-718) 768-7300. (Gates: Richard Upjohn, 1861-65.) Breaking with the traditional forms of interment—churchyards, family plots, or compact enclosures—this cemetery's 478 acres were opened in 1838. Beautifully landscaped and encompassing Brooklyn's highest point, 216 feet above sea level, the natural setting and view are unsurpassed. Magnificent Gothic Revival mausoleums and monuments decorate many of the 500,000 graves, including those of Currier and Ives, Peter Cooper, Samuel Morse, Horace Greeley, DeWitt Clinton, "Boss" Tweed, the infamous Lola Montez (Eliza Gilbert). It still operates as a full-service, nonsectarian, nonprofit cemetery, where in 1990 maestro Leonard Bernstein was laid to rest. *OPEN 7 days 8am-4pm.* For information regarding 3-hour Sunday walking tours of the cemetery in the spring and fall, call Marge Ward, (718) 439-8828.

Lawrence Family Graveyard
20 Road & 35 Street, Steinway, Queens. The private burial ground of a distinguished Queens family. The earliest grave is dated 1703, the rest span 2½ centuries of family history. The Lawrences were related to George Washington.

Lawrence Memorial Park
216 Street & 42 Avenue, Bayside, Queens. A second Lawrence family graveyard begun in 1832 contains the remains of a New York City mayor and Stock Exchange president, as well as an Indian named Moccasin, given the first name Lawrence and buried with the family.

New York City Marble Cemetery
52-74 East 2 Street between First & Second Aves. In this marble cemetery, opened in 1832, there are markers and headstones that can be seen through a handsome iron fence (not open to the public). Members of the Kips, Roosevelt, and Fish families are buried here.

New York Marble Cemetery
Entrance on Second Avenue between East 2 & East 3 Streets (west side). Opened in 1830, giving 156 prominent New Yorkers an opportunity for burial in what was then a fashionable area. Among them the Scribners, the Hoyts, the Varicks, and the Beekmans. Tablets on the brick wall served as the only markers. Only slightly visible through a fence on the avenue.

Old St. Patrick's Cemetery
Mulberry Street between Prince & East Houston Streets. On a quiet street in Little Italy, a nine-foot brick wall hides most of the churchyard from view; the earliest graves date from 1804. The crypt beneath the church holds the remains of two early bishops of the Catholic church, as well as those of early Irish settlers in this country. The remains of Pierre Toussaint (1766-1863) were recently exhumed, a step toward possible canonization of the former slave who secretly supported the family of his deceased former owner.

Old West Farms Soldier Cemetery
East 180 Street at Bryant Avenue, Bronx. Veterans of the War of 1812, the Civil War, the Spanish-American War, and World War I are buried here.

St. Mark's-in-the Bowery East & West Yards
East 10 Street & Second Avenue. Although the

graveyard was covered over by cobblestones, it is still a peaceful, historically rich spot. Some memorial tablets and markers are visible on this former site of Peter Stuyvesant's country chapel. Stuyvesant himself is buried in a crypt beneath the church. The East Yard is now a children's play area.

St. Paul's Churchyard
Broadway & Fulton Street. 602-0874. Though not as old as Trinity's graveyard, St. Paul's yard offers a pleasant, albeit somber, spot to reflect upon the past within the shadow of the present—the World Trade Center towers above. *OPEN 7 days 8am-3:30pm.*

Second Cemetery of the Spanish & Portuguese Synagogue Shearith Israel
72-76 West 11 Street between Fifth Ave & Ave of the Americas. 1805-29. Burials began here in 1805, but the large cemetery was reduced by the laying out of West 11 Street in 1830. The displaced graves were moved to West 21 Street.

Sleight Family Graveyard
Arthur Kill Road at Rossville Avenue, Rossville, Staten Island. 1750-1850. Also known as the Rossville or Blazing Star Burial Ground. Many of the island's early settlers are buried here, in what was originally a family plot.

Third Cemetery of the Spanish & Portuguese Synagogue
West 21 Street between Avenue of the Americas & Seventh Avenue. The northernmost burial ground of the Congregation Shearith Israel; consecrated in 1829.

Trinity Cemetery
Riverside Drive to Amsterdam Avenue, West 153 to West 155 Street. 368-1600. Once part of the farm belonging to naturalist J. J. Audubon, who is buried here, it became, in 1842, the rural burial place of Wall Street's Trinity Church and is still active, offering aboveground (crypt) resting places. Clement Clarke Moore, author of "A Visit from St. Nicholas," is also buried here. His grave is visited every Christmas by carolers (*see* ANNUAL EVENTS, December: "'Twas the Night Before Christmas"). *OPEN 7 days 8am-4:30pm.*

Trinity Church Graveyard
Broadway & Wall Street. 602-0872. In this historic graveyard, Manhattan's earliest, the oldest stone is dated 1681, predating the church itself. Two tombstones of note: those of Alexander Hamilton and inventor Robert Fulton. Also of note is the Martyr's Monument honoring the men who died imprisoned at the old Sugarhouse during the American Revolution and who are interred here. At the north end a faded stone reads:

Hark from tombs a doleful sound
Mine ears attend the cry
Ye living men come view the ground
Where you must shortly lie

OPEN Mon-Fri 7am-5pm (till 4pm in winter); Sat 8am-3pm; Sun 7am-3pm.

Vanderbilt Mausoleum
Moravian Cemetery, Todt Hill Road, New Dorp, Staten Island. (Richard Morris Hunt, 1866; landscaped by Frederick Law Olmsted.) Burial site of Cornelius Vanderbilt and family.

Van Pelt-Rezeau Cemetery
Tysen Court, Richmondtown, Staten Island. (ca. 1780). A homestead burial plot containing five generations of the Van Pelt-Rezeau families.

Woodlawn Cemetery
Entrance Jerome Avenue north of Bainbridge Avenue, Bronx. 920-0500. Elaborate tombs, in some cases replicas of European chapels and monuments, fill this 400-acre Gilded Age cemetery founded in 1863. Among the distinguished buried here: Mayor Fiorello LaGuardia, Bat Masterson, the Woolworths, Jay Gould, Joseph Pulitzer, Damon Runyon. It's also a bird sanctuary. Map available at office. Guided tours in spring and fall. *OPEN 7 days 9am-4:30pm.*

MODERN ARCHITECTURE

Almost everything's up-to-date in New York City—here are some of the best and/or most interesting examples.

AT&T Building
550 Madison Avenue at East 56 St. (Philip Johnson, John Burgee, Architects, 1984.) This monumental corporate statement is, per square foot, the most expensive office building ever constructed—and at press time AT&T is leasing it to Sony and moving elsewhere! Its 36 stories, climbing 660 feet (equivalent to 60 stories), of pinky beige stoney creek granite is topped by a much ballyhooed Classical pediment. Enormous archways, worthy of ancient imperial Rome, lead to a six-story-high public arcade. Don't miss the fabulous Infoquest Center in the arcade. (*See also* MUSEUMS & GALLERIES, Museums: Science Museums.) Plaza *OPEN Mon-Fri 8am-10pm; Sat & Sun 10am-6pm.*

Battery Park City
Not since Rockefeller Center has such an ambitious project been undertaken in New York. A city within a city built on a 92-acre stretch of landfill along the Hudson River at the tip of Manhattan (reversing the historic uptown movement of commercial and luxury-residential activity). When completed, it will contain 25,000 apartments and 30,000 office workers amid glorious open spaces, parks, promenades, and outdoor artwork. The results so far are impressive. The stone, ceramic, glass, and bronze buildings in shapes evocative of the 30s are a spectacular addition to the skyline. The four-tower **World Financial Center** (Cesar Pelli, 1988) provides 6 million square feet of office space, 220,000 square feet of shops and restaurants. Its centerpiece, the **Wintergarden**, a towering glass pavilion cum urban greenhouse, contains 16 palm trees (New York's first) under its 120-foot vaulted roof and overlooks a 3-acre river plaza and yacht marina. It connects to the World Trade Center by an enclosed pedestrian bridge.

Burlington House
1345 Avenue of the Americas at West 54 St. A

A T & T Building

50-story tower. The spacious plaza features two unique spherical fountains.

CBS Building
51 West 52 Street. (Eero Saarinen & Assocs., 1965.) A freestanding concrete-framed tower, called "Black Rock" by most.

Chanin Building
122 East 42 Street at Lexington Ave. (Sloan & Robertson, 1929.) Like the nearby Chrysler Building, an Art Deco winner. Wonderful bas-relief facade.

Chase Manhattan Bank & Plaza
1 Chase Manhattan Plaza between Nassau & William Streets. (Skidmore, Owings & Merrill, 1960.) One of lower Manhattan's first aluminum-and-glass high rises on one of the first "name it after yourself" plazas that tells you absolutely nothing about where it is actually located.

Chrysler Building
405 Lexington Avenue at East 42 St. (William Van Alen, 1930.) One of the first skyscrapers with stainless steel on its outside, including the gargoyles modeled after car-hood ornaments. For a few months—before the Empire State Building's completion—it was the world's tallest building at 1,048 feet to the top of its Art Deco spire. The elevators and lobby are Art Deco jewels. Don't miss taking a good look at them. *OPEN Mon-Fri 8am-6pm.*

Citicorp Center
Lexington Avenue between East 53 & East 54 Streets. 559-2319. (Hugh Stubbins & Assocs., 1977.) Although its unique silhouette stems from a summit solar heat collector that never came to pass, its addition to the city's skyline was a welcome respite from the flattop boxes of the 50s and 60s. Its satiny silver veneer is another eyecatcher. An interesting array of shops and restaurants, and a sunlit atrium public space for relaxing and enjoying free entertainment events comprise the Citicorp Market, a modern agora on its first three levels. Atrium *OPEN Mon-Fri 7am-midnight; Sat 8am-midnight; Sun 10am-midnight.*

Cityspire
150 West 56 Street. (Murphy/John, 1987.) Wind whistling through the louvers of this mixed-use residential and commercial tower's dome, 800 feet high, has caused it to be dubbed the "Whistling Skyscraper." Complaints brought a court order for it to be silenced; it already broke the law by exceeding its authorized height by 11 feet.

Daily News Building
220 East 42 Street between Second & Third Aves. (Howells & Hood, 1930.) Art Deco ornamentation graces the street floor's interior and exterior. In the lobby, a huge revolving globe.

88 Pine Street
Between Water & Front Streets. (I. M. Pei & Assocs., 1974.) Elegant aluminum-and-glass structure.

Empire State Building
350 Fifth Avenue at 34 St. (Shreve, Lamb & Harmon, 1931.) Although at 1,250 feet it's no longer the world's tallest, it remains the enduring symbol of this city and state. Its romantic image is now enhanced by the colored lights on its majestic peak changing for seasonal and ceremonial occasions. Examples: red and green at Christmas; red, white, and blue for July 4; blue and white when the Yankees win big (blue and orange for the Mets); and, of course, red on Valentine's Day. (*See also* SIGHTSEEING, Viewpoints.)

Equitable Building
120 Broadway at Cedar St. (Ernest R. Graham, 1915.) An unrelenting mass whose sheer volume was responsible for the city's first zoning law in 1916.

Ford Foundation Building
320 East 42 Street between First & Second Aves. (Kevin Roche, John Dinkeloo & Assocs., 1967.) Brick and glass with tree-filled, 130-foot-high enclosed central garden, the first real atrium in the city. Unique. *OPEN Mon-Fri 8am-5pm.*

Galleria
117 East 57 Street between Park & Lexington Aves. (David Kenneth Specter, Philip Birnbaum, 1975.) Mixed-use extravaganza. A skylit public gallery through to 58 Street with offices, luxury apartments, and a private health club atop. Millionaire Stewart Mott is its most famous nonresident. Atrium: *OPEN Mon-Sat 8am-10pm; Sun 8am-6pm.*

General Motors Building
767 Fifth Avenue between East 58 & East 59 Sts. (Edward Durell Stone, Emery Roth & Sons, 1968.) Down came the beautiful old Savoy Plaza Hotel in 1966 and up came this 50-story white Georgian marble tower. Unfair trade-in.

Grace Building
41 West 42 Street at Ave of the Americas. (Skidmore, Owings & Merrill, 1974.) A swooping glass structure.

Guggenheim Museum
Fifth Avenue between East 88 & East 89 Streets. (Frank Lloyd Wright, 1959.) The master was Wright. Go for the building as much as for the art. (*See also* MUSEUMS & GALLERIES, Museums, General Art Museums.) NOTE: The design of an addition to the building for much-needed gallery space is generating controversy.

IBM
590 Madison Avenue at East 57 St. (Edward Larrabee Barnes, 1982.) A sleek, 43-story, green-granite and glass tower, its entry is set back under 40 cantilevered floors. The huge bamboo-tree-filled glass shed is a tranquil public plaza for sitting or sipping; it also houses a New York Botanical Garden outlet shop. Adjacent to the atrium is the IBM Gallery of Science & Art (*see* MUSEUMS & GALLERIES, Art-&-Science Museums). Atrium *OPEN 7 days 8am-10pm.*

Jacob K. Javits Convention Center
Eleventh to Twelfth Avenue, West 34 to West 39 Street. 216-2000. (I. M. Pei & Partners, 1986.) Enormous and impressive. On a 22-acre site, an enclosed space of 1.8 million square feet; at the heart of the building is a 150-foot-high, 60,000-square-foot lobby. The dark green crystalline-glass walls contain 16,100 glass panes—100-square-feet of skylights. It's abuzz with trade show and convention activity year-round.

Kips Bay Branch, New York Public Library
446 Third Avenue at East 31 St. (Giorgio Cavaglieri, 1971.) A public building with style and books.

Kips Bay Plaza
East 30 to East 33 Street, First to Second Avenue. (I. M. Pei & Assocs. & S. J. Kessler, 1960 & 1965.) New York's first exposed-concrete apartment buildings.

Lescaze House
211 East 48 Street between Second & Third Aves. (William Lescaze, 1934.) Office and house of architect Lescaze combined in this pioneer example of modern town house architecture.

Lever House
390 Park Avenue between East 53 & East 54 Sts. (Skidmore, Owings & Merrill, 1952.) One of the first metal-and-glass-walled structures. Very avant-garde at its time. Recently and deservedly

designated a landmark to the dismay of its owners, who would have preferred to raze it in favor of a taller (read: more profitable) building.

Lincoln Center for the Performing Arts
West 62 to West 66 Street, Columbus to Amsterdam Avenue. 875-5400. Architecturally, the whole is greater than the sum of its parts; most impressive at night. Note especially the Met's murals by Chagall. Culturally, unsurpassed for variety and integrity, try to see at least one performance. Gift shops, one-hour paid guided tours from the concourse of the Metropolitan Opera House, New York State Theater, and Avery Fisher Hall. Tours: *7 days 10am-5pm.* Discount rates and "Meet the Artist" programs for groups of 20 or more.

The "Lipstick Building"
885 Third Avenue between East 53 & East 54 Sts. (John Burgee Architects with Philip Johnson, 1986.) It's an obvious nickname for this 34-story red-brown and pink elliptical office tower that seems to thumb its nose at its context.

Madison Square Garden
West 31 to West 33 Street, Seventh to Eighth Avenue. (Charles Luckman Assocs., 1968.) An entertainment-and-office complex composed of the 20,000-seat Garden, the 1,000-seat new Paramount, as well as a 500-seat cinema, a bowling center, and an office building on the site of the former—and sorely missed—old Penn Station.

Marine Midland Building
140 Broadway at Cedar St. (Skidmore, Owings & Merrill, 1967.) A sleek, elegant skyscraper rising 52 orderly stories above an attractive plaza.

McGraw-Hill Building (former)
330 West 42 Street between Eighth & Ninth Avenues. (Raymond Hood, Godley & Fouilhoux, 1931.) International-style masterpiece in sea-green terra-cotta with Art Deco details at street level.

Paul Mellon House
125 East 70 Street between Park & Lexington Aves. One of Manhattan's most recent (1965) millionaire's town houses, on one of the city's most beautiful residential blocks.

Mobil Building
150 East 42 Street between Lexington & Third Aves. (Harrison & Abramovitz.) This 1955 stainless-steel skyscraper was the first in the world to be fully air-conditioned.

NYC Department of Cultural Affairs
2 Columbus Circle between Broadway & Eighth Aves. (Edward Durell Stone, 1965.) A Huntington Hartford conceit that has always looked vacant. Now put to good use: home of the NYC Convention & Visitors Bureau and upstairs the City Gallery. (*See* MUSEUMS & GALLERIES, Museums, General Art Museums.)

919 Third Avenue
Entrances on East 55 & East 56 Streets. What's most interesting about this brown-glass office structure is the little red-brick 1890 building that seems to stand as its sentry box on the corner of East 55 Street and Third Avenue—P. J. Clarke's Tavern, famed watering hole and holdout against

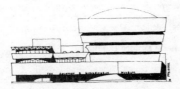

Guggenheim Museum

Tishman Realty. (*See* RESTAURANTS, Bars & Burgers.)

Olympic Tower
645 Fifth Avenue at 51 St. (Skidmore, Owings & Merrill, 1976.) A multipurpose building. Shops, offices, apartments—with a ground-level landscaped public arcade that, happily, is no longer a secret. Arcade *OPEN 7 days 8am-midnight.*

100 William Street
At John Street. (Davis, Brody & Assocs., 1973.) Elegant natural slate building.

135 East 57 Street
(Kohn Pedersen Fox, 1988.) A classically inspired edifice whose curve creates a plaza worthy of Delphi.

127 John Street
At Water Street. (Emery Roth & Sons, 1969; lobby & plaza: Corchia deHarak Assocs.) Whimsical urban design tips its hat to the pedestrian. Canvas-and-pipe structures to sit and climb on; a 45-by-50-foot digital timepiece involves you on the Water Street side.

One & Two United Nations Plaza
First Avenue at East 44 Street. (Kevin Roche, John Dinkeloo & Assocs., One: 1976, Two: 1984.) Elegant aluminum-and-glass combo of offices and the sleek UN Plaza Hotel (*see* HOTELS, Deluxe). Much style.

Pan Am Building
200 Park Avenue at East 46 St. (Emery Roth & Sons, Pietro Belluschi, and Walther Gropius, 1963.) Perched in the midst of the Grand Central complex, it was controversial for its size and site (New Yorkers lost a cherished vista) but now it's very much a part of the city skyline. Helicopters no longer land on its roof.

Philip Morris
Park Avenue between East 41 & East 42 Streets. (Ulrich Franzen & Assocs., 1983.) This 26-story gray granite corporate facility is the first to use its building bonus (public amenity in exchange for extra bulk) as a cultural facility. Its appealing pedestrian space is a 42-foot-high enclosed sculpture court—a branch of the Whitney Museum of Modern Art (*see* MUSEUMS & GALLERIES, General Art Museums). Also notable: the offices are elegantly appointed with such energy-wise features as ceiling fans and windows that actually open!

Police Headquarters
Between Park Row, Pearl, Henry & New Streets. (Gruzen & Partners, M. Paul Friedberg & Assocs., 1973.) Brick-and-concrete plazas and terraces—modern civic design at its best. There's an 1890 paddy wagon on display in the lobby.

Radio City Music Hall
Avenue of the Americas at West 50 Street. 246-4600. Part of the Rockefeller Center complex, this 1932 theater, dubbed the nation's showplace, can seat 6,000. Its interior is magnificence on a grand scale, from the world's largest chandeliers in a 50-foot-high foyer to the 32-foot-high organ pipes. Fine Art Deco details. There is a tour available (*see* SIGHTSEEING, On Your Own).

River House
435 East 52 Street at Sutton Pl. (Bottomly, Wagner & White, 1931.) Then and now, classic residential building for the very rich. The original private yacht mooring was displaced by the FDR Drive.

Rockefeller Center
West 48 to West 51 Street, Fifth to Sixth Avenue. A building complex of harmony and grace, erected mainly between 1931 and 1940. Functionalism and elegance combined: underground passages/shopping arcades, soaring towers each an individual yet very much a part of the whole, an outdoor plaza of gardens, skaters, cafes, and something its architects seemed very much to have in mind—people. (*See also* Radio City Music Hall.)

Roosevelt Island
East River, from about East 50 to East 86 Street. Known earlier as Welfare Island, where the city's poor and chronically ill were housed, it is now the site of a new community. Getting there on the aerial tramway (from Second Avenue and East 60 Street) is more than half the fun—cost: one subway token.

Seagram Building
375 Park Avenue between East 52 & East 53 Sts. (Ludwig Mies van der Rohe and Philip Johnson, Kahn & Jacobs, 1958.) A bronze-and-glass tribute to modernity by the master.

17 State Street
(Emery Roth & Sons, 1988.) A sleek, wedge-shaped reflective-glass tower that follows the arc of State Street. High-tech glass-enclosed lobby 25 feet up.

77 Water Street
Between Old Slip, Gouverneur Lane & Front Street. (Emery Roth & Sons, 1970.) In the Seaport area, a sleek building whose arcade of pools and bridges invites and involves the pedestrian at street level.

666 Fifth Avenue
Between West 52 & West 53 Streets. (Carson & Lundin, 1967.) Embossed aluminum-coated skyscraper. Isamu Noguchi waterfall in the arcade. Top of the Sixes on the 39th floor offers city-filled views (*see* RESTAURANTS, Rooms with a View).

747 Third Avenue
At East 47 Street. (Emery Roth & Co., 1972.) What's interesting here is not so much the building as the Streetscape. Designer Pamela Waters (1971) brings humor and functionalism together in her treatment of sidewalk seats, trash bins, and telephone booths.

Stuyvesant Town
East 14 to East 20 Street, First Avenue to FDR Drive. (Irwin Clavan and Gilmore Clarke, 1947.) A huge densely populated apartment complex built by Metropolitan Life Insurance Company for returning WWII servicemen. Every September it's the site of the best and biggest "garage" sale.

Time-Life Building
1271 Avenue of the Americas at West 50 St.
(Harrison & Abramovitz, 1960.) This one began
the Sixth Avenue—that is, Avenue of the
Americas—building boom. More of the same includes the Exxon (at 1251), McGraw-Hill (at
1221), and Celanese (at 1211) buildings. Part of
the Rockefeller Center complex in a geographic
sense only.

Trump Tower
725 Fifth Avenue at 56 St. (Swanke, Hayden,
Connell & Partners, 1983.) A 68-story, bronze-
glass mixed-use megastructure famed for the
cost of its condos (90 percent above $1 million—
albeit all with views in three directions) and the
pricey pride of shops housed in its ritzy, glitzy,
80,000-square-foot skylight-capped atrium of
peach marble (chosen for its complexion-
flattering qualities) and brass. Manhattan's first
vertical shopping mall features a dazzling but
overdone environment complete with a five-story
waterfall. Cafes lower level and top level, where
there is also a nearly secret outdoor spot to
brown bag it. Atrium OPEN Mon-Sat 10am-6pm.

Tudor City
East 40 to East 43 Street, First to Second Avenue. (Fred F. French Co., 1925-28; H. Douglas
Ives.) Twelve buildings containing 3,000 apartments form the crux of a private "city" surrounding two parks on a perch above First Avenue.

Union Carbide Building
270 Park Avenue between East 47 & East 48 Sts.
(Skidmore, Owings & Merrill, 1960.) A gray-
glass-and-black-steel tower.

United Nations Headquarters
First Avenue between East 42 & East 48 Streets.
Visitors' entrance at East 46 Street. 963-7713.
(International Committee of Architects, Wallace
K. Harrison, chairman, 1947-53.) These buildings became the UN's permanent headquarters
in 1952. The monolithic **Secretariat Building,**
the **General Assembly Building,** and the **Dag
Hammarskjold Library** (1963) make up the
complex. Flags of the 138 member nations fly in
alphabetical order when the General Assembly
is in session. OPEN 7 days, 9:15am-4:45pm.
Hour-long paid tours start from the first floor of
the General Assembly Building every half hour.
(No children under age 5.) To reserve for groups
of 15 or more, call 963-4440. For foreign language tours, call 963-7625. A small number of
free tickets are available for General Assembly
and Security Council sessions. There is also a
well-stocked international gift shop, and you may
have lunch in the **Delegate's Dining Room,**
Monday to Friday from 12:30 to 2:30pm, call to
reserve a day ahead, 963-7625.

Washington Square Village, Nos. 1 & 2
West 3 to Bleecker Street, West Broadway to
Mercer Street. (S. J. Kessler, 1956-58.) Very
large and colorful but very un-Greenwich Village.
Happily, zoning restrictions followed to prevent a
repetition.

Waterside Plaza
FDR Drive between East 25 & East 30 Streets.

(Davis Brody & Assocs., 1974.) One of the first
efforts to utilize the Manhattan waterfront for living. Handsome buildings (1,600 apartments)
surrounded by shopping and pedestrian plazas
and an adjacent marina. A bit isolated.

World Financial Center
See Battery Park City.

World Trade Center
West, Washington, Barclay, West Broadway, Vesey, Church & Liberty Streets. (Minoru Yamasaki
& Assocs. and Emery Roth & Sons, 1962-77.) It
seems that all downtown roads lead to these
twin 110-story monoliths that now dominate the
lower Manhattan skyline. New city folklore: Philippe Petit's hair-raising tightrope walk between
the towers, and George Willig's daring climb up
the side. For an unsurpassed view of the Apple
and more, go to the observation deck (see
SIGHTSEEING, Viewpoints) or to the spectacular restaurant on the 107th floor (see RESTAU-
RANTS, Rooms with a View: Windows on the
World).

World Wide Plaza
Eighth to Ninth Avenue between West 48 & West
49 Streets. (Skidmore, Owings & Merrill, 1990)
The former site of the old Madision Square Garden, razed in 1968, creating Manhattan's largest
parking lot. Now hosts a mammoth office (48-
story) and residential (38-story with low-rise
wings) condominium complex. A pioneering
project on still-tawdry Eighth Avenue, akin to
taming the the wild west—midtown west in this
case.

Zeckendorf Towers
Irving Place between East 14 and East 15
Streets. (Davis, Brody & Assocs., 1987.) Four
separate apartment towers set on a massive
commercial base and each topped by an illuminated pyramid, blocks the Con Ed Clocktower
from everyone else's view.

OUTDOOR SCULPTURE

Locations of some changing exhibits:
Hammarskjold Plaza
866 Second Avenue at East 47 Street.
Robert Moses Plaza
Fordham University at Lincoln Center, Colum-
bus Avenue at West 62 Street.
Waterside Plaza
East River Drive at 23 Street.
Wave Hill
Entrance Independence Avenue and West
249 Street, Bronx.
Alamo
Cooper Square at Astor Place. (Bernard J.
Rosenthal, 1967.) This was one of the first
"sculpture in environment" pieces to stand in a
public place. The cube, as it is commonly re-
ferred to, revolves on its axis when pushed. Graffiti is a constant problem; it has now been
adopted by nearby Cooper Union, which looks
after its maintenance.

Bust of Sylvette
100 Bleecker Street. (Pablo Picasso, adapted by sculptor Carl Nesjar, 1968.) In Greenwich Village. Concrete with black basalt pebbles. It is 36 feet high, 20 feet long, 12½ inches thick, and weighs 60 tons. It is New York's only public Picasso.

Cube
140 Broadway. (Isamu Noguchi, 1973.) Brilliant red steel covered in sheet aluminum, 28 feet tall. Because the form is an enclosed mass, a building permit had to be issued to allow its construction.

Cubed Curve
Time-Life Building, 1271 Avenue of the Americas. (William Crovello, 1971.) Hollow-steel sculpture, 12 feet high and 8 feet wide, painted blue.

Delacorte Fountain
Roosevelt Island. An artificial geyser reaching a maximum height of 250 feet.

5 in One
Police Plaza at the Municipal Building. (Bernard Rosenthal, 1974.) The interlocking disks represent the city's five boroughs. Symbolically, they are made of a weathering steel.

Group of Four Trees
Chase Manhattan Plaza. (Jean Dubuffet, 1972.) A steel framework covered in fiberglass and plastic resin, painted with polyurethane. The prefabricated sections were made in France and assembled here. It was Dubuffet's first outdoor sculpture in the U.S.

Helix
Plaza, 77 Water Street. (Rudolph de Harak, 1969.) A stainless-steel-and-marble contemporary version of an ornamental spiral.

Martin Luther King, Jr., Memorial
Martin Luther King High School, Amsterdam Avenue at West 66 Street. (William Tarr, 1974.) In weathering steel, a personal yet powerful tribute to the slain black leader.

Le Quichet (The Ticket Window)
Library and Museum of the Performing Arts, Lincoln Center. (Alexander Calder, 1972.) Blackened steel stabile created for a public space.

Night Presence IV
Park Avenue at East 92 Street. (Louise Nevelson, 1972.) In steel, 22 feet high, weighing 4½ tons; from a 1944 model. A gift to the city from the artist.

Peace Form One
Ralph Bunche Park, First Avenue at East 43 Street. (Daniel La Rue Johnson, 1980.) A 50-foot, stainless-steel obelisk dedicated to late Nobel Peace Prize laureate and former UN undersecretary Ralph J. Bunche.

Queen Elizabeth I Memorial
Orient Overseas Building Plaza, 88 Pine Street. (Yu Yu Yang, 1974.) Two unjoined stainless-steel units, and a pedestal of Italian marble as a plaque, serve as a commemorative to the late great ocean liner, not the monarch.

Reclining Figure
Lincoln Center, Reflecting Pool. (Henry Moore, 1965.) A bronze sculpture in two sections in the reflecting pool. It's the largest piece ever created by Moore; very dramatic.

Rejected Skin
77 Water Street. (William Tarr, 1971.) Rejected aluminum from the building's construction, compacted, make up this put-on sculpture. The touch of red is from a junked ambulance.

Seuil Configuration
Fifth Avenue at East 79 Street. (Jean Arp, 1972.) Up for interpretation by park visitors, its stainless-steel construction reflects its surroundings.

Shadows and Flags
Louise Nevelson Plaza, junction of William & Liberty Streets. (Louise Nevelson, 1979.) On round columns, seven black-painted steel vertical sculptures.

Single Form
Secretariat Building, United Nations. (Barbara Hepworth, 1964.) A powerful bronze piece, 21 feet high and weighing 5 tons. In memory of the late Dag Hammarskjold.

Sun Triangle
McGraw-Hill Building, 1221 Avenue of the Americas. (Athelstan Spilhaus, 1973.) Various parts of this mirror-polished stainless-steel modern sundial point to the noon sun on the winter and summer solstice and on the spring and fall equinox.

Taxi
Chemical Bank, 277 Park Avenue at East 48 St. (J. Seward Johnson, Jr., 1983.) A most realistic "dashing Dan," in mid-flight.

(212) 127-1972 Telephone Booth
127 John Street. (Albert Wilson, 1972.) This steel cutout is a totally original and functional piece of public sculpture.

Unisphere
Flushing Meadows–Corona Park, Flushing, Queens. (Peter Muller-Munk, Inc., 1964.) The symbol of the 1964 World's Fair in stainless steel.

OUTDOOR ARTWORK

Many buildings, especially in lower Manhattan, have become "canvas" for talented city artists. Standouts are Richard Haas's trompe l'oeil murals, which never fail to amuse or delight.

Arcade
Con Edison Substation, Peck Slip & South Street. Bridging the gap. Probably Haas's best mural to date.

Barney's
West 17 Street at Seventh Avenue. Only the first-floor windows are fake.

Central Park Health Bar
Sheep Meadow at 69 Street. Imaginary latticework light as the food sold.

Mulberry Street
Between Hester & Grand Streets. Two storefronts that are not.

114 Prince Street
In SoHo, two real windows are among the 53 painted ones. Note, too, the cat.

SCHOOLS

City University Graduate Center
33 West 42 Street between Fifth & Sixth Aves. Former concert hall, Aeolian Hall, 1912, put to good, practical use by CUNY. Remodeled in 1970 by Carl J. Petrilli & Assocs. An elegant pedestrian arcade cuts through to West 43 Street.

Columbia University
West 114 to West 120 Street between Broadway & Amsterdam Avenue. (Original design and buildings: McKim, Mead & White, 1897.) The university's growth beyond what the original architectural plan called for led to much deviation, but ultimately a happy coexistence between old and new. Best of the old, Low Memorial Library (1897); best of the new, Sherman Fairchild Center for the Life Sciences (1977).

Cooper Union Foundation Building
Cooper Square at East 7 Street between Lafayette Street & the Bowery. (Frederick A. Peterson, 1859; interior reconstructed: John Hejduk, 1975.) Endowed by inventor-philanthropist Peter Cooper, it's one of the earliest free institutions of education in America. Its emphasis was on trades and useful arts to afford students a livelihood. The **Great Hall** is where Abraham Lincoln delivered his historic "right makes might" speech February 27, 1860. Still a thriving institution, still tuition-free.

Fashion Institute of Technology
West 26 to West 28 Street, Seventh to Eighth Avenue. This city campus, having taken 20 years to complete, reflects the architectural styles of several seasons.

Hunter College
Park Avenue between East 68 & East 69 Streets. (Shreve, Lamb & Harmon, Harrison & Fouilhoux, Associated Architects, 1940.) Still too new-looking for the grand-dowager appearance of that area of Park Avenue. Especially intrusive is the pedestrian bridge across Lexington Avenue.

Cooper Union Foundation Building

New School for Social Research
66 West 12 Street between Fifth Ave & Ave of the Americas. (Joseph Urban, 1930.) Formed by Europe's refugee intelligentsia in the 1930s, it is no longer an exile in academic or architectural terms. The school has become an integral part of Greenwich Village and New York City life.

New York University
Most of the area on all sides of Washington Square Park belong to the university, forming a hodgepodge of architectural styles. The restored buildings are more successful than many of their thoroughly modern neighbors; Bobst Library, one of the worst additions, casts an unfortunate shadow on Washington Square Park. Although the park itself is public property, it serves as unofficial campus; site of NYU's outdoor graduation ceremonies in May.

Yeshiva University
Amsterdam Avenue from West 183 to West 187 Street. (Main Building: Charles B. Meyers Assocs., 1928). A grab bag of architectural tricks and treats, with the Main Building remaining the visual highpoint.

BRIDGES

New York has 65 bridges connecting its boroughs and islands to each other and to the world beyond the city and state limits. Listed are a few of the major ones.

Brooklyn Bridge
City Hall Park, Manhattan, to Cadman Plaza, Brooklyn. (John A. Washington Roebling, 1867-83.) This beautiful and graceful 1,595-foot suspension bridge, the world's longest when completed, is a 109-year-old monument to the builder's ingenuity and imagination. Fittingly,

Low Memorial Library, Columbia University

the city threw it a heck of a birthday party when it turned 100. (*See also* SIGHTSEEING, Viewpoints.)

Manhattan Bridge
Between Canal Street & the Bowery in Manhattan to Flatbush Avenue Extension in Brooklyn. (O. F. Nichols, 1909.) Entered through a regal Beaux Arts colonnade by Carrere and Hastings, the bridge spans 1,470 feet.

Queensborough Bridge
From East 59 & East 60 Streets in Manhattan to Queens Plaza. (Gustav Lindenthal, engineer; Palmer & Hornbostel, architects, 1909.) An ornate cantilevered bridge spanning 1,182 feet.

Triborough Bridge
(O. H. Ammann, engineer; Aymar Embury II, architect, 1936.) More accurately a series of interconnecting bridges from Queens to Wards Island and from Manhattan and the Bronx to Randalls Island, crossing the East and Harlem rivers and the Bronx Kill.

Verrazano Narrows Bridge
Fort Hamilton & 92 Street, Brooklyn, to Lily Pond Road, Fort Wadsworth, Staten Island. (O. H. Ammann, 1964.) The world's second-longest suspension bridge, 4,260 feet, links Brooklyn to Staten Island. Named for Giovanni de Verrazano, the first European to sight New York Harbor, 1524. Before it was built, the borough was accessible only via the Staten Island Ferry.

George Washington Bridge
Hudson River at West 178 Street to Fort Lee, N.J. (O. H. Ammann & Cass Gilbert, 1931.) New York's only bridge link to New Jersey—one pure 3,500-foot line spanning the Hudson.

Williamsburg Bridge
From Delancey & Clinton Streets in Manhattan to Washington Plaza in Brooklyn. (Leffert L. Buck, 1903.) This 1,600-foot span replaced the Brooklyn Bridge as the world's longest and had a telling effect on the Brooklyn side, as the bridge allowed Lower East Side immigrants easy access to a new promised land—Brooklyn. But time and tides have not been kind to this structure; at press time, the deteriorating bridge is undergoing extensive repair.

HAUNTED NEW YORK

Listed below are sites in New York City where lively spriits are reported to dwell.

Morris-Jumel Mansion

428 West 44 Street
This former residence of actress June Havoc was the scene of several seances conducted to find the source of mysterious tapping sounds. At least two spirits were allegedly "contacted."

Morris-Jumel Mansion
Edgecombe Avenue & West 160 Street. Washington's headquarters during the Battle of Harlem Heights in 1776 and later home of French merchant Stephen Jumel and wife. Schoolchildren and their teachers have seen a woman's form and, on another occasion, the ghost of a soldier. (*See also* Historic Buildings & Areas, Manhattan.)

Old Merchant's House
29 East 4 Street near the Bowery. This house, once owned by wealthy merchant Seabury Tredwell, is reputed to be haunted by a lovely young woman in 19th-century dress. She is assumed to be Tredwell's daughter, Gertrude, who became a spinster recluse following a romance thwarted by her father. A white aura has been reported above the third-floor fireplace. (*See also* Historic Buildings & Areas, Manhattan.)

St. Mark's-in-the-Bowery
East 10 Street at Second Avenue. The shimmering image of a woman and a tapping sound attributed to Peter Stuyvesant's peg leg have given people pause. (*See also* Churches & Synagogues.)

12 Gay Street
A well-dressed ghost in evening clothes appeared here one night, presumably looking for old friend Jimmy Walker, the colorful mayor of New York who once owned the house.

MUSEUMS & GALLERIES

Metropolitan Museum of Art

ANNUAL ART EVENTS

Brooklyn Heights Promenade Art Show
See ANNUAL EVENTS, Calendar, May *and* October.

Washington Square Outdoor Art Show
See ANNUAL EVENTS, Calendar, May: Memorial Day Weekend *and* September: Labor Day Weekend.

Museum Mile Festival
Upper Fifth Avenue between 82 & 104 Streets. The first Tuesday in June, from 6 to 9pm. A celebration of the unmatched cultural riches of this part of the city. The avenue is closed to traffic; there's music, mime, and dance performances, and best of all, the ten museums along the Mile (El Museo del Barrio, Museum of the City of New York, International Center of Photography, Jewish Museum, Cooper-Hewitt Museum, National Academy of Design, Solomon R. Guggenheim Museum, YIVO Institute for Jewish Research, Goethe House New York, Metropolitan Museum of Art) are open to the public free of charge. For information, call 397-8222.

41 Union Square/Open Studios
41 Union Square West. One weekend in mid-October, from 11am to 5pm, this building, which houses over 80 artists in an area of the city with a rich artistic heritage, hosts an Open House. Professional artists of every discipline open their working studios. Browse, buy, or simply chat with the artists. For information, call 807-6257.

ART TOURS

Tours that offer an opportunity to visit galleries, museums, artists' studios and lofts in unusual parts of the city are available year-round; for a selection of some of these, *see* SIGHTSEEING, New York Tours, Specialized.

MUSEUMS

Each of the larger museums has a shop where you can purchase adaptations, reproductions, books, posters, and postcards.

Suggested contribution means just that. Don't be embarrassed to give less if you cannot afford what is posted.

General Art Museums

See also HISTORIC & NEW NEW YORK *for landmark buildings and mansions that now house collections of art and period furnishings.*

American Academy & Institute of Arts & Letters
Broadway & West 155 Street. Entrance Audubon Terrace. 368-5900. Three exhibits a year of American sculpture, painting, and architecture. Call for schedule.

American Craft Museum
40 West 53 Street. 956-6047. America's only museum devoted solely to crafts. A unique permanent collection recording American craft activity from 1900 to the present, emphasis on work created since World War II. Plus changing exhibitions in metal, wood, glass, and fiber. *OPEN Tues 10am-8pm; Wed-Sun 10am-5pm. CLOSED Mon.* Admission charge; lower for students and senior citizens; free for children under age 12.

Americas Society
680 Park Avenue at East 68 St. 249-8950. Exhibits from South and Central America, the Caribbean, and Canada, ranging from pre-Columbian to contemporary painting, sculpture, photography, and decorative arts. *OPEN Tues-Sun noon-6pm.* Suggested contribution.

Asia Society Gallery
725 Park Avenue at East 70 St. 288-6400. Fascinating aspects of traditional Asian art are highlighted in several exhibitions each year. On permanent view are objects from the Mr. and Mrs. John D. Rockefeller III collection. A fascinating

selection of film, dance, and musical programs. Membership available. *OPEN Tues-Sat 11am-6pm; Sun noon-5pm.* Admission charge; lower for students and senior citizens. Group tours by reservations, call 288-6400, ext. 237.

Bronx Museum of the Arts
1040 Grand Concourse near East 165 St, Bronx. 681-6000. The permanent collection consists of 20th-century works on paper by artists from Africa, Latin America, and Southern Asia, as well as American descendants of these areas. Approximately 12 exhibits annually with a focus on contemporary works; cultural and social history of the Bronx as well as international artists. Membership available. *OPEN Mon-Thurs & Sat 10am-4:30pm; Sun 11-4:30pm. CLOSED Fri.* Suggested contribution.

Brooklyn Museum
200 Eastern Parkway at Washington Ave, Brooklyn. (718) 638-5000. An outstanding museum begun in 1823 covering a wide range of interests: Egyptian, Classical, Middle Eastern, Oriental, American, and European art; Oceanic and New World cultures; prints and drawings; period rooms from 1675; a sculpture garden with 19th-century architectural ornaments and so much more. Free gallery talks Wednesday, Thursday, and Friday at 2pm begin in the Grand Lobby. An active community department presents a wide range of special events and activities, check the monthly newsletter. Painting and sculpture classes. Membership available. Wonderful gift shop; cafe. Museum *OPEN Wed-Sun 10-5pm.* Suggested contribution. Free for children under age 12 when accompanied by an adult.

Center for African Art
54 East 68 Street. 861-1200. In a town house setting, a new museum devoted exclusively to the broad geographic, cultural, and temporal range of African art. Two to three exhibitions a year. Films and lectures. *OPEN Tues-Fri 10am-5pm; Sat 11am-5pm; Sun noon-5pm.* Suggested contribution. Membership available.

China House Gallery
China Institute of America, 125 East 65 Street. 744-8181. Twice a year, exhibits featuring traditional and contemporary Chinese arts and crafts, all media. Exhibitions April to May and late Oc-tober to January. *OPEN Mon-Sat 10am-5pm.* Suggested contribution.

City Gallery
2 Columbus Circle at West 59 St, 2nd floor. 974-1150. Operated by the City of New York Department of Cultural Affairs, dedicated to exhibiting art that is an expression of the city's diverse communities and its cultural vitality. Curated by nonprofit arts organizations throughout New York City's five boroughs. *OPEN Mon-Fri 10am-5:30pm.* FREE.

The Cloisters
Fort Tryon Park. 923-3700. One of New York's artistic and spiritual treasures, beautifully situated high on a hill above the Hudson River. Medieval art and architecture comprise this branch of the Metropolitan Museum of Art. Opened in 1938, the medieval-style structure incorporates parts of five cloisters from medieval monasteries, a Romanesque chapel, and a 12th-century Spanish apse. A unique environment in which to see the famed Unicorn Tapestries, frescoes, illuminated manuscripts, and the Chalice of Antioch. The gardens in the cloistered courtyards hold more than 250 species of plant grown in the Middle Ages. Recorded medieval music enhances the mood. Live concerts and lectures are offered in spring and fall. Free tours Tuesday to Friday at 3pm; Sunday at noon; gallery talks Saturday, noon and 2pm. Group tours by appointment. Book shop. NOTE: The Madison Avenue M4 bus is a scenic route to the door of the Cloisters. *OPEN Mar-Oct, Tues-Sun 9:30am-5:15pm; Nov-Feb, Tues-Sun 9:30am-4:45pm.* Suggested contribution.

Cooper-Hewitt Museum (The Smithsonian Institution's National Museum of Design)
2 East 91 Street, at Fifth Ave. 860-6868. The beautifully restored, landmark, 64-room Andrew Carnegie mansion houses the most important collection of design and decorative arts in the world. Major categories include ceramics, textiles, drawings, prints, glass, furniture, metalwork, book papers, woodwork, wall coverings, embroidery, and lace. The drawings and prints collection is America's largest. The museum spans 3,000 years of design history with a collection of over 300,000 objects. The library con-

Brooklyn Museum

tains over 40,000 books. Workshops, seminars, classes, lectures, performances. Research facilities by appointment. *OPEN Tues 10am-9pm; Wed-Sat 10am-5pm; Sun noon-5pm.* Admission charge; half price for senior citizens and students over age 12; children under age 12 free. Tuesday from 5 to 9pm FREE for everyone.

Frick Collection
1 East 70 Street. 288-0700. Don't miss this little jewel of a museum. Henry Clay Frick's residence (built 1913-14) houses masterpieces of 14th- to 19th-century European paintings, exquisite 18th-century French and Italian Renaissance furniture, Oriental porcelain, and Limoges enamel. Chamber music concerts and lecture programs. *OPEN Tues-Sat 10am-6pm; Sun 1-6pm.* Admission charge; lower for students and senior citizens; children age 10-16 must be accompanied by an adult; children under age 10 not admitted.

Goethe House New York
1014 Fifth Avenue at 82 St. 439-8700. On Museum Mile, housed in a newly renovated 1907 Beaux Arts town house. New York arm of Munich, Germany, Institute to promote German culture. Exhibitions of German artists, film programs, lectures, library. Gallery *OPEN Tues & Thurs noon-7pm; Wed, Fri & Sat noon-5pm.* FREE.

Guggenheim Museum
1071 Fifth Avenue at 88 Street. 423-3500. The Frank Lloyd Wright building provides a unique setting for modern art, Impressionist to present-day, and the world's largest Vasily Kandinsky collection. There are 8 to 12 shows a year. There are also films, lectures, and performances. The recent renovation has resulted in increased exhibition space, an outdoor sculpture terrace, and an enlarged bookstore and cafe. An annex now affords space for more contemporary art exhibitions. Membership available. Museum *OPEN Mon-Wed & Fri-Sun 10am-8pm. CLOSED Thurs.* Admission charge; lower for students and senior citizens; children under age 12 free. Tuesday from 5 to 8pm pay-as-you-wish. **Guggenheim Soho**, 575 Broadway at Prince St., an additional exhibition site, call for hours.

Hispanic Society of America
Audubon Terrace, Broadway at West 155 St. 926-2234. The culture of Spanish and Portuguese peoples as seen through paintings, sculpture, and the decorative arts from prehistoric times to the present. Important reference library. *OPEN Tues-Sat 10am-4:30pm; Sun 1-4pm. CLOSED Aug.* FREE.

International Center of Photography (ICP)
1130 Fifth Avenue at 94 St. 860-1777. Located in a lovely landmark building; devoted exclusively to the field of photography as an art form and medium of communication. Works by important 20th-century photographers including Robert Capa, W. Eugene Smith, Henri Cartier-Bresson, Yousuf Karsh, Man Ray, Lee Miller, Gordon Parks, Roman Vishniac, and Ernst Haas comprise the permanent collection. There are also changing exhibitions, lectures, conservation programs, archives, resource library, work-shops, seminars, courses. Excellent museum shop. Membership available. *OPEN Tues noon-8pm; Wed-Fri noon-5pm; Sat & Sun 11am-6pm.* Admission charge; lower for students and senior citizens. Tuesday from 5 to 8 pm FREE for everyone. *See also* ICP Midtown.

ICP Midtown
1133 Avenue of the Americas at West 43 St. 768-4680. A four-level, 16,000-square-foot branch of the original but smaller uptown ICP. Selections from the extensive permanent collection plus changing exhibits; also an education program, a screening room, and a bookstore. *OPEN Tues & Wed 11am-6pm; Thurs 11am-8pm; Fri-Sun 11am-6pm.* FREE.

Isamu Noguchi Garden Museum
32-37 Vernon Boulevard at 33 Rd, Long Island City, Queens. (718) 204-7088. A large tranquil open-air garden and 12 gallery spaces on two floors contain over 250 pieces of sculpture by the octogenarian American-born sculptor, as well as models, drawings, and stage sets for dances by Martha Graham. Originally a photo-engraving plant, the building was converted by Noguchi for use as a studio as well as museum. *OPEN Apr-Nov, Wed & Sat noon-5pm.* Suggested contribution. Shuttle bus from the Asia Society, Park Avenue and East 70 Street, on Saturdays from 11:30am to 3:30pm every hour on the hour; $5 fare round trip; for information, call 721-1932.

Jacques Marchais Center of Tibetan Art
338 Lighthouse Avenue off Richmond Rd, Lighthouse Hill, Staten Island. (718) 987-3500. A major collection of Tibetan art housed in a replica of a Buddhist temple surrounded by lovely gardens, perfect for contemplation. Bronzes, paintings, ritual objects; library. Every Sunday at 2pm there is a special program. NOTE: The authenticity of the experience is enhanced by a quarter-mile walk up Lighthouse Hill if you take the S74 bus from the ferry. *OPEN only mid-Apr-mid-Nov Wed-Sun 1-5pm.* Admission charge; lower for senior citizens and children under age 12.

Jamaica Arts Center
161-04 Jamaica Avenue at 161 St, Jamaica, Queens. (718) 658-7400. Performing and visual arts programs and exhibits. Print, photography, and arts and crafts. Workshops, lectures, performances. Gallery *OPEN Tues-Sat 10am-5pm.* FREE.

Japan Society Gallery
333 East 47 Street. 752-0824. The only museum in America devoted exclusively to Japanese art; in a serene and spare space. Three loan exhibitions a year of Japanese art (ancient as well as contemporary); also No robes and masks, swords and packaging. *OPEN during exhibitions Tues-Sun 11am-5pm.* Suggested contribution.

The Jewish Museum
1109 Fifth Avenue at 92 St. 399-3344. One of the largest and most beautiful collections of Judaica in America includes ceremonial objects, paintings, prints, drawings, sculpture, photos, and antiquities, all housed in a French Renaissance

mansion, which is undergoing renovation in conjunction with the addition for a new annex building, to be completed in 1993. Exhibitions are temporarily housed at The New-York Historical Society, 170 Central Park West at West 77 St. *OPEN Tues & Wed 11am-5pm; Thurs 11am-8pm; Fri 11am-3pm. CLOSED Mon, Sat & major Jewish holidays.* Admission charge; lower for children age 6-16, students, and senior citizens. Tuesday from 5 to 8pm FREE for everyone.

Metropolitan Museum of Art
Fifth Avenue at 82 Street. 535-7710 (recorded). Quite simply one of the world's great museums. Five thousand years of art magnificently displayed. Comprehensive collections of Greek and Roman art; the most extensive display of Egyptian treasures and the largest collection of Islamic art in the world, plus major collections of Far Eastern, European, and American art. Don't miss the Temple of Dendur in its impressive setting, the new Lila Acheson Wallace Wing for 20th-century art, the Sackler Wing, and the spectacular American Wing, which houses the finest, most comprehensive collection of American art and artifacts; the eye-catching 70-foot-high glass-roofed garden court housing large-scale decorative arts and the living room of a Frank Lloyd Wright house (1912-14). Also special: the serene Astor Court and the sunlit atrium housing the Lehman Collection, the rooftop sculpture garden (May to October, weather permitting), especially at twilight, and several of the best of all possible gift shops. Cafeteria/restaurant and bar for lunch, brunch, dinner, or cocktails on the balcony with music by a Juilliard quartet (Friday and Saturday pm only). Membership available. Concerts, lectures, films, call 570-3949 for current roster. Facilities for sight and hearing impaired and wheelchairs available, call 535-7710. Hourly rate parking garage. *OPEN Sun & Tues-Thurs 9:30am-5:15pm; Fri & Sat 9:30am-8:45pm. CLOSED Mon.* Suggested contribution. FREE to children under age 12 when accompanied by an adult. Advance reservations required for group tours, call 570-3916.

El Museo del Barrio
1230 Fifth Avenue at 104 Street. 831-7272. The art, culture, and heritage of Puerto Rico and Latin America through artifacts, photographs, and paintings. *OPEN Wed-Sun 11am-5pm.* Suggested contribution, lower for seniors and students.

Museum of American Folk Art
2 Lincoln Square, Columbus Avenue between West 65 & West 66 Streets. 595-9533. American folk art, textiles, paintings, sculpture from colonial times to the present in changing exhibitions based on a theme. Lovely shop. *OPEN Tues-Sun 11:30am-7:30pm.* FREE. Don't pass up a chance to visit their wonderful gift and book shop at 62 West 50 Street, *OPEN Mon-Sat 10:30am-5:30pm.*

Museum of Modern Art
11 West 53 Street. 708-9400. Opened in 1929, this museum developed into the greatest repository of modern art in the world, covering the movement from the 1880s to the present. The handsome new MOMA has more than double the space; escalators in a glass-enclosed atrium now carry the public to six floors of galleries. On display are over 100,000 works of art: paintings and sculpture, architecture and design, drawings, prints and illustrated books, photography, film and video. As the first museum to recognize film as an art form, it has documented the development of motion pictures for nearly 50 years; two film theaters, six screenings daily (for film listings, call 708-9490). The Philip Johnson Gallery is devoted to a permanent exhibition of architectural drawings and models. The **Sculpture Garden** remains one of New York's most treasured spaces; two new restaurants—the Garden Cafe and the Member's Dining Room—overlook it. Don't miss the **Museum Store** and its Annex at 37 West 53 Street for gifts, art books, and design objects, many of which are represented in the museum's collections. Gallery talks: Monday to Friday at 12:30pm; Thursday also at 5:30 and 7pm. Membership available. *OPEN Fri-Tues 11am-6pm; Thurs 11am-9pm. CLOSED Wed.* Admission charge; lower for students with I.D., children under age 16 when accompanied by an adult. On Thursday from 5 to 9pm it's pay-what-you-wish.

National Academy of Design
1083 Fifth Avenue at 89 St. 369-4880. Founded in 1825 as a drawing society and school; exhibits are devoted to America's art heritage. Extensive holdings of 19th- and 20th-century paintings, prints, drawings, photography, and sculpture as well as an annual juried show of contemporary work. Library and resource center for serious research, all in a Beaux Arts mansion. *OPEN Tues noon-8pm; Wed-Sun noon-5pm.* Admission charge; lower for senior citizens and students. Tuesday from 5 to 8pm FREE for everyone.

New Museum of Contemporary Art
583 Broadway near Houston St. 219-1222. Founded in 1977, this experimental center for art and ideas is now located in the landmark Astor Building. It's the city's only museum concerned exclusively with contemporary art, showing emerging artists or lesser-known works of established artists. Library, archives, auditorium. *OPEN Wed, Thurs & Sun noon-6pm; Fri & Sat noon-8pm.* Suggested contribution; lower for students, senior citizens, and artists; children under age 12 free.

Nicholas Roerich Museum
319 West 107 Street. 864-7752. In a former town house, artist Nicholas Roerich's expedition to the Himalayas, Tibet, and India, 1923-28, is the subject of his paintings. Every month a new exhibition of a contemporary artist. Lectures and free recitals. Membership available. *OPEN Tues-Sun 2-5pm.* FREE.

Queens Museum
New York City Building, Flushing Meadows–Corona Park, Flushing, Queens. (718) 592-5555.

A center for visual arts on the site of two famed World Fairs. On permanent view is **Panorama**, a detailed (9,000-square-foot) scale model of New York City's five boroughs that includes nearly every building—it's fascinating. Changing fine arts and sculpture exhibitions from the classical to the avant-garde. Gallery talks, workshops, lectures, and performances. Groups must reserve, call (718) 592-9700. Membership available. Free parking. *OPEN Tues-Fri 10am-5pm; Sat & Sun noon-5pm.* Suggested contribution; lower for children; senior citizens and children under age 5 free.

Society of Illustrators
128 East 63 Street. 838-2560. Founded in 1901 to "promote and stimulate interest in the art of illustration, past, present, and future." Interesting and informative shows in a comfortable environment. Every three weeks there is a new exhibition of illustrations. *OPEN Mon & Wed-Fri 10am-5pm; Tues 10am-8pm. CLOSED Sat, Sun & Aug.* FREE.

Studio Museum in Harlem
144 West 125 Street. 864-4500. A distingushed museum devoted solely to the study, documentation, collection, promotion, and exhibition of the arts and artifacts of black America. Exhibitions of the works of established and emerging black artists from America, the Caribbean, and Africa. Tour groups by appointment. Membership available. *OPEN Wed-Fri 10am-5pm; Sat & Sun 1-6pm.* Admission charge; lower for children, students, and senior citizens. Free for seniors on Wednesday.

Ukrainian Museum
203 Second Avenue near East 13 St. 228-0110. Rich and colorful displays of Ukrainian folk art from the 19th and 20th centuries. Programs, workshops, and lectures available. *OPEN Wed-Sun 1-5 pm.* Admission charge; lower for children and senior citizens; children under age 6 free.

Urban Center
Municipal Art Society, 457 Madison Avenue at East 51 St. 935-3960. Housed in the north wing of the historic Villard Houses (1884). Exhibitions reflect issues related to urban development: past, present, and future. Home of the Municipal Art Society's programs and a public forum for the livable city. Galleries: downstairs and 2nd floor. *OPEN Mon-Wed, Fri & Sat 11am-5pm. CLOSED Thurs & Sun.* (*See also* SIGHTSEEING, Walking Tours: Municipal Art Society.)

Whitney Museum of American Art
945 Madison Avenue at East 75 St. 570-3676. Founded in 1930 by Gertrude Vanderbilt Whitney to emphasize the work of living American artists. In a fine Marcel Breuer building since 1966. Works by 20th-century American artists comprise the bulk of the permanent collection. Special exhibitions are of major events in photography, folk or contemporary art, film and video. Free gallery talks every Tuesday at 1:30, 3:30, and 6:15pm; Wednesday, Thursday, and Friday at 1:30 and 3:30pm; Saturday and Sunday at 2 and 3:30pm. Sculpture garden and Sarabeth's Restaurant, outdoors in summer. For details on foreign language tours, call 570-3652. *OPEN Tues 1-8 pm; Wed-Sat 11am-5pm; Sun noon-6pm.* Admission charge; half price for senior citizens; free for college students with I.D. and children under age 12 when accompanied by an adult. Tuesday from 6 to 8 pm FREE for everyone.

Whitney Museum of American Art Downtown
33 Maiden Lane at Nassau St. 943-5655. At Federal Reserve Plaza, a 3,200-square-foot satellite gallery tucked beneath a 26-story building. Five exhibitions a year of painting and sculpture. Gallery talks on Monday, Wednesday, and Friday at 12:30pm. *OPEN Mon-Fri 11am-6pm.* FREE.

Whitney Museum of American Art at Equitable Center
787 Seventh Avenue at West 51 St. 554-1113. Two galleries. One contains works from the Whitney permanent collection, the other is for changing exhibits. Gallery talks Tuesday to Friday at 12:30 and 2:30pm; Saturday at 1pm. *OPEN Tues, Wed & Fri 11am-6pm; Thurs 11am-7:30pm; Sat noon-5pm.* FREE.

Whitney Museum of American Art at Philip Morris
120 Park Avenue at East 42 St. 878-2550. A wonderful respite from midtown's maddening crowds. A 42-foot-high Sculpture Court for outstanding examples of 20th-century sculpture, many of which are too big for the uptown Whitney. On permanent view are works by Oldenberg, Nevelson, Lichtenstein, Calder, and Bourgeois. In the adjacent gallery six shows a year covering all aspects of American art; lectures and performances. Gallery talks on Monday, Wednesday, and Friday at 1pm. Espresso bar. Gallery *OPEN Mon-Wed, Fri & Sat 11am-6pm; Thurs 11am-7:30pm.* Sculpture Court *OPEN Mon-Sat 7:30am-9:30pm; Sun 11am-7pm.* FREE.

Art-&-Science Museums

Brooklyn Children's Museum
See KIDS' NEW YORK, Museums for Children.

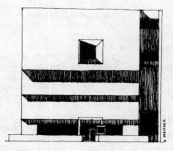

Whitney Museum of American Art

Children's Museum of Manhattan
See KIDS' NEW YORK, Museums for Children.

IBM Gallery of Science & Art
590 Madison Avenue at East 57 St. 745-6100.
This large (13,000 square feet) exhibition space brings high-quality science and art exhibits to New York that otherwise might not be seen here. Exhibitions throughout the year reflect recent developments in the sciences and change periodically. Guided tours are conducted during the day. Relax in the wonderful garden plaza atrium afterward. For group visits, call 745-5214 (Tuesday to Friday from 10am-5pm). *OPEN Tues-Sat 11am-6pm.* FREE.

Staten Island Children's Museum
See KIDS' NEW YORK, Museums for Children.

Staten Island Institute of Art & Science
75 Stuyvesant Place near Wall St, St. George, Staten Island. (718) 727-1135. A museum of art, science, and history founded in 1881. Records the natural history of Staten Island with its collection ranging from anthropology to zoology. Paintings, prints, sculpture, textiles. Also under its auspices: the Davis Wildlife Refuge and High Rock Park Conservation Center (see PARKS & GARDENS, Nature Trails & Wildlife Preserves). Archives and library for researchers by appointment only. Programs for schoolchildren. Membership available. *OPEN Mon-Sat 9am-5pm; Sun 1-5pm.* Suggested contribution.

Science Museums

American Museum of Natural History
Central Park West at West 79 Street. 769-5100. A wonderful wonder-filled place. The evolution of life on earth: huge dinosaur skeletons, lifelike animals shown in their natural habitat, and various world cultures depicted through their artifacts, clothing, sculpture, and crafts. Special: Naturemax, New York's largest movie screen—40 feet high, 60 feet wide—for spectacular views of earth and the creatures that inhabit it. Admission; half price for children; members 40 percent off. Call for schedule, 769-5200. Also a spectacular collection of some of the world's largest and best-known gems. Good gift shop. The **Whale's Lair**, Friday and Saturday from 3 to 8pm, Sunday and holidays from noon to 5pm, for drinks and snacks under the blue whale. Museum *OPEN Sun-Tues & Thurs 10am-5:45pm; Wed, Fri & Sat 10am-9pm. CLOSED Thanksgiving & Christmas Day.* Suggested contribution.

Hayden Planetarium
Central Park West at West 81 Street. 769-5920. In the 75-foot, domed Sky Theater, over 100 computer-controlled special effects projectors show you the night sky from anywhere on earth, take you past black holes and exploding stars. Special shows also for preschoolers feature the Sesame Street Muppets, other shows for kids age 6-9 (call 769-5900). Sky shows *Oct-June, Mon-Fri 1:30 & 3:30pm; Sat 11am, 1, 2, 3, 4, 5pm; Sun 1, 2, 3, 4, 5pm. From July to Sept there are extra shows.* Also, two floors of exhibits re-

American Museum of Natural History

lating to the history of astronomy and navigation, a 360-degree slide presentation, the Hall of the Sun with participatory exhibits, and a reference library. There are courses for adults and children. A shop for space-related gifts (769-5910). Admission charge (includes entry into the American Museum of Natural History); lower for children under age 12, students, senior citizens, and members. Special: cosmic laser-light shows with rock music Friday and Saturday at 7:30, 8:30, and 10:30pm. For details, call the Laser Hotline, 769-5921. Admission charge, tickets available through Ticketron. For group reservations, call 769-5900.

Infoquest Center
AT&T Building Arcade, Madison Avenue at East 56 St, 4th floor. 605-5555. Take the glass elevator to this permanent exhibition dedicated to the technology of the Information Age. Forty interactive exhibits on three levels afford insights into the wonders and joys of fiber optics, holograms, computer software, and microelectronics. Program Gordon, the talking robot; direct a music video; see your voice and picture transmitted on a fiberoptic videophone; and tour New York in a video-taxi (updated weekly). Also, in the auditorium, a 10-minute laserdisc presentation on a 300-square-foot screen. *OPEN Tues 10am-9pm; Wed-Sun 10am-6pm.* FREE.

Museum of Holography
11 Mercer Street near Canal St, a half block west of Broadway. 925-0526. Founded in 1976, housed in a landmark cast-iron building in SoHo, it's the only museum of its kind in the world. Holograms are three-dimensional images made with lasers. The museum shows how they are made, how they work, and the work of individual artists, plus historic prototypes. Membership available; gift shop. *OPEN Mon, Tues, Thurs-Sun 11am-6pm; Wed 11am-8pm.* Admission charge; lower for children under age 12 and senior citizens.

New York Hall of Science
Flushing Meadows–Corona Park, 47-01 111 Street & 48 Avenue, Flushing, Queens. (718) 699-0005. The only hands-on museum in the New York Metropolitan area devoted exclusively to science and technology; done with imagina-

tion and ingenuity. Lectures and workshops. Group visits on Tuesday only from 10am to 2pm. *OPEN Wed-Sun 10am-5pm.* Suggested contribution; lower for children age 3-18 and senior citizens.

Historic Museums

American Museum of the Moving Image
35 Avenue at 36 St, Astoria, Queens. (718) 784-4520. Adjacent to the Kaufman-Astoria (originally Paramount) Studio 1920 building this is the first museum in the United States devoted to the art, technology, history, and impact of moving image media. It contains a state-of-the-art 190-seat theater as well as a 60-seat experimental video and film screening room, and 25,000 square feet of space for permanent and changing interactive exhibits. There are over 700 film and video programs each year. Membership available. Museum shop and cafe. Call and get on their mailing list. P.S. It's only three subway stops from Bloomies. *OPEN Tues-Fri noon-4pm; Sat & Sun noon-6pm.* Admission charge; half price for students and senior citizens.

American Numismatic Society
Audubon Terrace, Broadway at West 155 Street. 234-3130. Two exhibit halls show a portion of the world's largest collection devoted solely to numismatics. Strongest aspect is ancient coins. Appointments can be made for special interests; excellent library houses one of the world's most comprehensive collections of numismatic literature. *OPEN Tues-Sat 9am-4:30pm; Sun 1-4pm (library closed).* FREE.

Aunt Len's Doll and Toy Museum
6 Hamilton Terrace between St. Nicholas & Convent Aves. 926-4172; 281-4143. In a Harlem brownstone, a feast for eye and heart. Over 5,000 dolls, accessories, miniatures, and toys. *OPEN by appointment only.* Admission charge.

Bible House
American Bible Society, 1865 Broadway near West 61 St. 581-7400. Exhibits of rare and historic Bibles; leaves of the original Gutenberg Bible, Helen Keller's braille Bible, a Kai Feng Fu Torah scroll. Nearly 50,000 scripture items in nearly 2,000 languages and dialects. *OPEN Mon-Fri 9am-4:30pm.* FREE.

Black Fashion Museum
155 West 126 Street. 666-1320. This museum, located in a Harlem brownstone, is devoted to notable contributions by blacks—many of whom were slaves—to the evolution of American fashion—for example, a line-for-line copy of Mary Todd Lincoln's inaugural dress, which was made by a former slave. Exhibits change every six months. *OPEN 7 days noon-8pm by appointment only.* Suggested contribution; lower for senior citizens and children.

Brooklyn Historical Society
128 Pierrepont Street near Clinton St, Brooklyn. (718) 624-0890. (Formerly the Long Island Historical Society.) One of the largest collections of documentation pertaining to the history of Brooklyn and the lives of Brooklynites imaginatively displayed. Changing exhibits and lectures on such diverse but universally recognizable subjects as the Brooklyn Bridge and the Brooklyn Dodgers. Membership available. *OPEN Wed-Sun noon-5pm.* FREE. Nominal charge for use of the library.

Carnegie Hall Museum
Carnegie Hall, 154 West 57 Street. 903-9620. A wonderful new aspect of the hall, which opened 100 years to the day from when the hall debuted. A permanent exhibition of memorabilia (1891-present) and changing exhibits pertaining to aspects of Carnegie Hall history. Visit it in conjunction with a performance, the tour, or on its own. *OPEN during the performance season Tues-Sun 11am-4pm.* FREE.

Chinatown History Museum
70 Mulberry Street, 2nd floor. 619-4785. Chinatown as a symbol of the cultural richness and complexity of Chinese American history. "Remembering New York's Chinatown," an interactive permanent exhibition on the history and culture of the area through the eyes and voices of Chinatown residents; Chinatown Walking Tours (*see* SIGHTSEEING, Walking Tours); library, archives, and bookstore. Gallery *OPEN Sun-Wed noon-5pm.*

Energy Museum
145 East 14 Street. 460-6244. Push-button exhibits depict the stages of electrical development from an 1878 arc lamp to the present. Groups by appointment only. *OPEN Tues-Sat 10am-4pm.* FREE.

Fashion Institute Gallery
Fashion Institute of Technology, Shirley Goodman Resource Center & Design Laboratory, southwest corner Seventh Avenue & West 27 Street. 760-7760. Located in the garment district off "Fashion Avenue," the textile collection contains more than 3 million indexed swatches, ½ million costumes and accessories from the 18th century to the present. Frequent fascinating fashion-theme exhibitions (past shows have highlighted the fashion duds for Snoopy and the fabulous creation of Fortuny). Library of related books and periodicals. *OPEN Tues-Fri noon-8pm; Sat 10am-5pm.*

Forbes Magazine Galleries
Forbes Building, 62 Fifth Avenue at 12 St, main floor. 620-2389. This eclectic mini-museum in Greenwich Village displaying the Forbes family collectibles is pure delight. Toys, including 12,000 toy soldiers and hundreds of toy boats made between 1870 and 1950, trophy memorabilia, Fabergé treasures (including ten of the imperial eggs made for the last two Russian czars), and a gallery devoted to American historical manuscripts, presidential papers, including letters from Abraham Lincoln; his stove pipe hat is here, too. A large gallery for changing art exhibitions. *OPEN Tues-Sat 10am-4pm. (Thurs is reserved for group tours and advance reservations.)* Children under age 16 must be

accompanied by an adult, no more than four children per adult. FREE.

Fraunces Tavern Museum

54 Pearl Street at Broad St. 425-1778. The site of the original tavern of Samuel Fraunces, where George Washington bade farewell to his officers in 1783; reconstructed in 1927. A present-day archaeological dig in its basement has unearthed remnants of New York's Dutch past. The museum, founded in 1907 and housed in five 18th- and 19th-century buildings, interprets the history and culture of 18th-century America through its permanent collection of Revolutionary War artifacts and memorabilia; decorative arts, prints, and paintings are displayed. Throughout the year there are fascinating lunchtime lectures, performances, walking tours, concerts, celebrations, and family entertainment. For group tours, call 425-1778. Operated by the Sons of the Revolution. Also on premises, a restaurant with traditional fare (*see* RESTAURANTS, American). *OPEN Mon-Fri 10am-4pm; Oct-May, Sun as well, noon-5pm.* Admission charge, lower for students, senior citizens, children under age 12 accompanied by an adult.

Lower East Side Tenement Museum

97 Orchard Street. 431-0233. The preservation of a typical threadbare tenement in honor of the urban pioneers who inhabited it and others like it at the turn-of-the-century. The Lower East Side was the place most immigrants to this country came when they passed through Ellis Island; most of them lived in a tenement such as this. Exhibition gallery, forums on immigrant history, and fascinating tours (*see* SIGHTSEEING, Walking Tours). Membership available. Gallery *OPEN Tues-Fri 11am-4pm; Sun 10am-3pm. CLOSED Sat & Mon.* FREE.

Museum of Television & Radio

23 West 52 Street. 621-6800. Founded in 1975 by William S. Paley as the Museum of Broadcasting to be a vital public repository of radio and television broadcasting. The institution collects, preserves, presents, interprets, and exhibits an American cultural treasure chest of video and audio tape 1920s to present. Newly esconsed in a Philip Johnson–designed building, the museum now has the proper facilities to accommodate the throngs drawn throughout the year to special-focus exhibitions, programming series, seminars, and workshops. There are now 96 television consoles to be used by the public (on a first-come-first-served basis) to monitor any of the programs in the collection (which is now cataloged by computer); a 200-seat theater, a 96-seat theater, two 45-seat screening rooms, and a listening room for radio programming. There are also galleries for related art, photos and artifacts, and a museum shop. Great fun and extremely popular, so get there early. Membership available. *OPEN Tues, Wed, Fri, Sat & Sun noon-6pm; Thurs noon-8pm.* Suggested contribution; lower for children under age 13, seniors, and students.

Museum of the City of New York

1220 Fifth Avenue at 103 St. 534-1672. Founded in 1923. The life and history of New York City dating back to the Indians and the Dutch seen through costumes, furniture, silver, paintings, decorative arts, ship models, a toy gallery, and period rooms. A full schedule of special exhibitions. Gallery talks, concerts, and a series of wonderful urban walks (*see* SIGHTSEEING, Walking Tours). Special children's programs (*see* KIDS' NEW YORK, Museums for Children). Guided and self-guided tours Tuesday to Friday with advance reservations. For group arrangements, call 534-1672, ext. 206. Gift shop. *OPEN Tues-Sat 10am-5pm; Sun & legal holidays 1-5pm. CLOSED Mon, Thanksgiving, Christmas & New Year's Day.* Suggested contribution.

National Museum of the American Indian

Audubon Terrace, Broadway at West 155 Street. 283-2420. The world's largest and best collection of ethnology and archaeology relating to the Indians of North, South, and Central America and the West Indies. (NOTE: New York came close to losing this cultural treasure, but soon it will have a much-needed additional space at the U.S. Customs House.) Now part of The Smithsonian Institution. *OPEN Tues-Sat 10am-5pm; Sun 1-5pm.* Admission charge; lower for students and senior citizens. Group tours by appointment.

Fraunces Tavern Museum

Museum of the City of New York

New York City Fire Museum
278 Spring Street. 691-1303. Outstanding collection of New York fire-fighting memorabilia and related historical records. *OPEN Tues-Sat 10am-4pm.* Groups by appointment only. Suggested donation.

New-York Historical Society
170 Central Park West at West 77 St. 873-3400. Founded in 1804, it's the oldest museum in New York State, the second oldest historical society in America. Devoted to American history, and New York in particular. Paintings, prints, and folk art, all elegantly displayed. A major research library of 600,000 volumes and an impressive collection of 18th-century New York newspapers; over a million maps, prints, photos, lithos, architectural drawings. Changing exhibitions drawn from the collections. Membership available. Museum shop. Museum *OPEN Tues-Sun 10am-5pm.* Library *OPEN Tues-Sat 10am-5pm; in summer OPEN Mon-Fri 10am-5pm.* Admission charge; lower for children and senior citizens. Tuesday admission is by donation. Nonmembers must pay for use of library.

Police Museum
235 East 20 Street, 2nd floor. 477-9753. World's largest collection of police memorabilia depicting the history of New York City's finest plus related historical items. *OPEN Mon-Fri 9am-3pm.* FREE.

South Street Seaport Museum
Visitor's Center, 207 Water Street. 669-9400; 669-9424 (recorded). A nautical museum within and without walls in an 11-block area that reflects New York's historic and vital past as a busy 19th-century seaport. Restored ships and buildings, shops selling models and charts, a printing museum and shop, excursion vessels, and a multiscreen 50-minute film, *South Street Venture* (211 Front Street). Concerts and special events especially during spring and summer. Piers, shops, and exhibits *OPEN year-round 7 days 10am-5pm.* Entry to the district is FREE; there is an admission charge to the museum's ships, walking tours, special programs, films, and exhibitions. Discount for children under age 12 and senior citizens; children under age 4 free. Tickets available at the Visitor's Center, the Pier 16 Pilothouse, and the *Titanic* Memorial Tower at Fulton and Water streets. Membership available. (*See also* SIGHTSEEING, On Your Own: South Street Seaport Marketplace.)

Yeshiva University Museum
2520 Amsterdam Avenue near West 185 St. 960-5390. Exhibitions that reflect Jewish historical and cultural experience. Paintings, photographs, ceremonial objects, architectural models of synagogues dating from ancient to modern times. Good museum shop. Membership available. *OPEN Tues-Thurs 10:30am-5pm; Sun noon-6pm. CLOSED Mon, Fri, Sat & all Jewish holidays.* Admission charge; lower for children and senior citizens; children under age 3 free.

LIBRARIES

In New York City's five boroughs, there are 82 branch and research libraries. The Main Branch of the New York Public Library is the world's largest research library.

Pierpont Morgan Library
33 East 36 Street. 685-0610. An Italian Renaissance palazzo (designed by McKim, Mead & White, 1906) that was built for an American prince of finance, J. Pierpont Morgan (1837-1913). His son opened it to the public as a museum and research library in 1924. The exterior stonework was done without cement; the opulent interior is rich, not only in furnishings and paintings but in medieval and Renaissance illuminated manuscripts, old master drawings and prints, rare books, and autographed manuscripts. Recently enhanced by a major renovation and the acquisition of the adjacent palatial 19th-century 45-room brownstone, once the residence of J. P. Morgan, Jr., resulting in a graceful 45–54-foot-tall glass-enclosed garden court connecting the two buildings, a Permanent Collections Gallery, and a large education center. In addition to the newly redesigned period rooms there is a continuing series of changing exhibits, as well as evening concerts and lectures throughout the year. Book shop. Membership available. *OPEN Tues-Sat 10:30am-5pm; Sun 1-5pm. CLOSED Mon, Sun in July, all of Aug.* Suggested contribution.

New York Public Library (Main Branch)
Fifth Avenue & 42 Street. 930-0800. A national historic landmark that covers two city blocks. A.k.a. the Central Research Library, it opened to the public May 24, 1911. It is quite simply one of the greatest research institutions in the world, containing 6 million books, 12 million manuscripts, 2.8 million pictures. Don't miss: the newly restored splendid **Gottesman Exhibition Hall** with its ornate carved oak paneling (*OPEN Tues-Sat 10am-6pm*); the **DeWitt Wallace Periodicals Room**, an elegant public room with 13 new murals by trompe l'oeil master Richard Haas; and most of all, for silence and solace, the **Main Reading Room**—it's 297 feet long, 78 feet deep, and contains the original chairs, tables, and bronze reading lamps (*OPEN Tues-Wed 11am-7:30pm; Thurs-Sat 10am-6pm*). One-hour free tours of the library leave daily at 11am and 2pm from Astor Hall just inside the main entrance on Fifth Avenue. For individual and group tours and exhibit information, call 930-0501. *CLOSED Sun.* (NOTE: Budget constraints may result in Monday closings for the duration.)

Schomburg Center
515 Lenox Avenue at West 135 St. 491-2200. A component of the Public Library's Research Library. This internationally renowned cultural facility, located in the heart of Harlem, began with the donated holdings of Arthur Schomburg, an Afro-Puerto Rican. Now the world's largest collection of documentation of black history and

New York Public Library

culture, it includes 20,000 reels of microfilm of news clippings, over 1,000 rare books, 30,000 photographs, 15,000 hours of taped oral history, 10,000 records, 3,000 videotapes and films. A permanent display of African and Afro-American art and artifacts. On West 135 Street, an outdoor sculpture garden; on West 136 Street, an outdoor amphitheater. The original building at 103 West 135 Street is to undergo restoration. *OPEN Tues-Wed noon-8pm; Fri & Sat 10am-6pm. CLOSED Mon, Thurs & Sun.* FREE.

YIVO Institute for Jewish Research
Fifth Avenue at 86 Street. 535-6700. Established in 1925 in Vilna, Lithuania, this academic research center for Eastern European Jewry and Jewish culture contains more than 22 million archival documents, 100,000 photographs, 300,000 books. *OPEN Mon, Tues, Thurs & Fri 9:30am-5:30pm. CLOSED Wed, Sat & Sun.* FREE.

GALLERIES

IMPORTANT NOTE: *The "art scene" slows during June, July, and August. Gallery hours and weeks may be shorter, and in many cases "Never in August" is the rule. In general, call for summer hours.*

Uptown Galleries

These are located primarily on and off Madison Avenue, from East 86 Street south to East 57 Street.

Dider Aaron
32 East 67 Street. 988-5248. Seventeenth- and 19th-century European paintings and drawings, decorative arts and furniture as well as Oriental arts. *OPEN Mon-Fri 10am-6pm.*

Aberbach Fine Art
980 Madison Avenue at East 77 St, 3rd floor. 988-1100. Contemporary American, European, and Latin art. *OPEN Tues-Fri 10am-5pm; Sat 11am-5pm.*

A.C.A. Galleries
41 East 57 Street, 7th floor. 644-8300. Early 20th-century and contemporary American works of art. *OPEN Tues-Sat 10am-5:30pm.*

Acquavella Galleries, Inc.
18 East 79 Street. 734-6300. Impressionist, Post-Impressionist: Monet, Matisse, Picasso, Miró, Pissarro. Downstairs for post–World War II and contemporary paintings: Guston, Gottlieb, Lichtenstein, Pollack. *OPEN Mon-Sat 10am-5pm.*

Rachel Adler Gallery
41 East 57 Street. 308-0511. Early 20th-century works. Italian Futurism (1909–World War II), Russian avant-garde, and European art of the 1920s; E. L. Lissitzky, Liubov Popova, F. W. Seiwert, Erika Giovanna Klein. *OPEN Tues-Sat 10am-5:30pm.*

Alexander Gallery
980 Madison Avenue near East 76 St, 3rd floor. 472-1636. Specializes in Hudson River landscapes. *OPEN year-round Tues-Fri 9:30am-5:30pm; Sat 9:30am-5pm.*

Jack Arnold Fine Arts
5 East 67 Street. 249-7218. Private dealer in prints, graphics, and paintings by such artists as George Blouin, Daniel Gelis, Gabriel Godard, Claude Hemeret, Li Zhong-Liang, Luis Mazorra, Malcolm Morley, Helen Rundell, and others. *By appointment only.*

Arras Gallery East
Trump Tower, 725 Fifth Avenue at 56 St, level A. 751-0080. And 24 West 57 Street, room 301. Contemporary painting, tapestry, sculpture, graphics and photography, Goudji objects and jewels, artists kaleidoscopes. *OPEN Tues-Sat 10am-5:30pm.*

Babcock Galleries
724 Fifth Avenue near 57 St, 11th floor. 535-9355. Established in 1852. American works of art of the 19th and 20th centuries. Contemporary paintings, drawings, and sculpture. *OPEN Tues-Sat 10am-5:30pm.*

William Beadleston Fine Art
60 East 91 Street. 348-7234. Impressionist, Post-Impressionist, and 20th-century paintings and sculpture. *By appointment only.*

Claude Bernard Gallery
33 East 74 Street. 988-2050. Works by 19th- and 20th-century South American, American, and European artists such as Fernando Botero, Balthus, Jim Dine, Jean Dubuffet, Ferdinand Leger, Miró, Picasso, Francisco Toledo, and many more. *OPEN Tues-Sat 9:30am-5:30pm.*

Berry-Hill Galleries, Inc.
11 East 70 Street. 371-6777. American painting and sculpture from the 19th and 20th centuries and 19th-century China Trade paintings. *OPEN Mon-Fri 9:30am-5:30pm; Sat 10am-5pm.*

Blum Helman Gallery
20 West 57 Street, 2nd & 8th floors. 245-2888. Twentieth-century and recent American painting and sculpture. *OPEN Tues-Sat 10am-6pm.*

Grace Borgenicht
724 Fifth Avenue near 56 St, 8th floor. 247-2111. Twentieth-century American art. *OPEN Tues-Fri 10am-5:30pm; Sat 11am-5:30pm.*

Brewster Gallery
41 West 57 Street, 6th floor. 980-1975. Twentieth-century European and Latin American masters; exclusive representative for Branko Bahunek, Leonora Carrington. Largest dealers in Miró and Chagall. Publisher of Francisco Zuñiga. *OPEN Mon-Sat 10:30am-5:30pm.*

Bruton Gallery
40 East 61 Street. 980-1640. French and European sculpture of the 19th and 20th centuries by Joseph Bernard, Antoine Bourdekke, Stephen Buxin, Jean Carton, Paul Cornet, Aristide Maillol, Auguste Rodin, and others. *By appointment only.*

Carus Gallery
872 Madison Avenue at East 71 St, 2nd floor. 879-4660. German Expressionists. Constructivists. Russian and European avant-garde (1910-30) watercolors, drawings, and prints. Beckmann, Kandinsky, Kirchner, Kupka. *OPEN Tues-Sat 11am-5pm; Aug by appointment only. CLOSED July.*

Chapellier Galleries
815 Park Avenue at East 75 St, apt. 5A. 988-8430. Works by American painters 1850 to the present. *By appointment only.*

Cordier & Ekstrom
417 East 75 Street, 1st floor. 988-8857. Contemporary art, painting, and sculpture. *OPEN Tues-Sat 10am-5pm.*

Eugenia Cucalon Gallery
145 East 72 Street, 2nd floor. 472-8741. Conceptual art: Dada, Man Ray, Oppenheimer, as well as contemporary Latin American artists. *By appointment only.*

Davis & Langdale Company
231 East 60 Street. 838-0333. Eighteenth-, 19th-, and 20th-century American and English paintings, watercolors, and drawings; as well as contemporary American artists: Lennart Anderson, Aaron Shikler, Albert York, Harry Roseman. *OPEN Tues-Sat 10am-5pm.*

Davlyn Gallery
975 Madison Avenue near East 76 St. 879-2075. Nineteenth- and 20th-century European paintings and sculpture. *OPEN year-round Tues-Sat 10:30am-5:30pm.*

Marisa del Re Gallery
41 East 57 Street, 4th floor. 688-1843. Nineteenth- and 20th-century European and American art. Karen Apel, Arman, Richard Pousette-Dart, Kenzo Okado, Arnaldo Pomodoro, Conrad Marca-Reli. *OPEN Tues-Fri 5:30pm, Sat 11am-5pm.*

Tibor de Nagy Gallery
41 West 57 Street, 7th floor. 421-3780. Contemporary art, both abstract and representational. *OPEN Tues-Sat 10am-5:30pm.*

Sid Deutsch Gallery
20 West 57 Street, 8th floor. 765-4722. Early 20th-century American art. *OPEN Tues-Sat 10am-5:30pm.*

Terry Dintenfass
50 West 57 Street, 10th floor. 581-2268. Twentieth-century painting and sculpture. *OPEN Tues-Sat 10am-5:30pm.*

Theodore B. Donson Ltd.
24 West 57 Street, 3rd floor. 245-7007. Fine old master and modern prints, 1450-1950. Author of an excellent book on prints. Collection includes Albrecht Dürer, Goya, William Hogarth, Rembrandt, Toulouse-Lautrec, Matisse. *OPEN year-round Tues-Sat 10am-5:30pm.*

Paul Drey Gallery
11 East 57 Street, 4th floor. 753-2551. Old master paintings, drawings, sculpture, and works of art. *OPEN Mon-Fri 10am-5:30pm.*

The Elkon Gallery
18 East 81 Street, 2nd floor. 535-3940. Twentieth-century masters, paintings, drawings, sculpture, and contemporary art. Balthus, Botero, Dubuffet, Ernst, Leger, Magritte, Matisse, Miró, Picasso. *OPEN Tues-Sat 9:30am-5:30pm.*

Andre Emmerich Gallery
41 East 57 Street, 5th & 6th floors. 752-0124. Contemporary American and European art; classical antiquities. Painters include Al Held, Hans Hofmann, Morris Louis, David Hockney, Helen Frankenthaler. Sculptors include Anthony Caro, Beverly Pepper, Anne Truitt. *OPEN Tues-Sat 10am-5:30pm; July & Aug by appointment only.*

Richard L. Feigen & Company
49 East 68 Street. 628-0700. Fifteenth- to 20th-century masters, paintings, drawings, sculpture. *OPEN Mon-Fri 10am-6pm.*

David Findlay Galleries
984 Madison Avenue near East 77 St. 249-2909. Nineteenth- and 20th-century European paintings. Sculpture and graphics as well. *OPEN Mon-Sat 10am-5pm.*

Wally Findlay
17 East 57 Street. 421-5390. French Impressionist, Post-Impressionist, contemporary art of the French school. Mass appeal. *OPEN year-round Mon-Sat 9:30am-5:30pm.*

Fischbach Gallery
24 West 57 Street, 8th floor. 759-2345. Twentieth-century American paintings, drawings. *OPEN Tues-Sat 10am-5:30pm; July-Aug, Mon-Fri 10am-5pm.*

Forum Gallery
1018 Madison Avenue near East 78 St, 5th floor.
772-7666. Contemporary American figurative
paintings and sculpture. *OPEN Tues-Sat 10am-5:30pm.*

Frumkin/Adams Gallery
50 West 57 Street, 2nd floor. 757-6655. Contemporary American paintings, Realism, West Coast
artists, ceramics, sculpture. Nineteenth- and
20th-century European drawings. *OPEN Tues-Fri 10am-6pm, Sat 11am-5:30pm.*

Galerie Felix Vercel Inc.
17 East 64 Street. 744-3131. School of Paris and
commercial contemporary art with some old
masters. *OPEN Tues-Sat 10am-6pm.*

Galerie Lelong
20 West 57 Street. 315-0470. Contemporary
American and European sculpture, drawings,
and paintings. *OPEN Tues-Sat 10am-5:30pm.*

Galerie St. Etienne
24 West 57 Street, 8th floor. 245-6734. Private
dealer. Nineteenth- and 20th-century Austrian
and German Expressionism; 19th- and 20th-century Naive art; Grandma Moses. *OPEN Tues-Sat 11am-5pm.*

Gimpel Weitzenhoffer Gallery
724 Fifth Avenue, 11th floor. 315-2033.
Twentieth-century American and European
paintings and sculpture. *OPEN Tues-Fri 10am-6pm, Sat 10am-5pm.*

James Goodman Gallery
41 East 57 Street, 8th floor. 593-3737. Twentieth-century American and European paintings,
drawings, watercolors, sculpture. Botero,
Calder, de Kooning, Dubuffet, Giacometti,
Leger, Lichtenstein, Matisse, Miró, Henry Moore,
Rauschenberg. *OPEN Tues-Sat 10am-6pm; Mon
by appointment.*

Graham Modern
1014 Madison Avenue near East 78 St, 3rd floor.
535-5767. Contemporary American art. *OPEN
Tues-Sat 10am-5pm.*

Grand Central Art Galleries
24 West 57 Street, 2nd floor. 867-3344. Late
19th-century American masters; early 20th-century representational American art. *OPEN
Mon-Fri 10am-6pm; Sat 10am-5pm.*

Daniel B. Grossman Gallery
1100 Madison Avenue near East 82 St. 861-9285. Impressionist, Post-Impressionist, and
neoclassical European and American paintings.
OPEN Mon-Sat 9:30am-6pm.

Stephen Hahn Inc.
9 East 79 Street. 570-0020. Private dealer.
Nineteenth- and 20th-century European works of
art. *By appointment only.*

Nohra Haime Gallery
41 East 57 Street, 6th floor. 772-7760. Contemporary Latin American, American, and European
art. *OPEN Mon-Sat 10am-6pm.*

Hammer Galleries
33 West 57 Street. 644-4400. Nineteenth- and
20th-century European and American paintings.
Hammer Graphics on 3rd floor; Leroy Neiman.
OPEN Mon-Fri 9:30am-5:30pm; Sat 10am-5pm.

Lillian Heidenberg Gallery
50 West 57 Street, 8th floor. 586-3808.
Twentieth-century modern masters and contemporary painting, sculpture, and graphics. *OPEN
Tues-Fri 10am-5:30pm; Sat 11am-5:30pm.*

Hirschl & Adler Folk
851 Madison Avenue at East 70 St. 988-3655.
Nineteenth-century American folk art. Paintings,
coverlets and quilts, furniture, weather vanes,
and glass. *OPEN Tues-Fri 9:30am-5:30pm; Sat
10am-4:45pm.*

Hirschl & Adler Galleries
21 East 70 Street. 535-8810. Top-quality 18th-,
19th-, and 20th-century American painting,
sculpture, and drawings. European Impressionist and modern painting and drawing. Mary Cassatt, Frederick Church, John Singleton Copley,
Childe Hassam, Homer, Hopper, Matisse,
O'Keeffe, Picasso, Renoir. *OPEN Tues-Fri
9:30am-5:15pm; Sat 9:30am-4:45pm.*

Hirschl & Adler Modern
851 Madison Avenue at East 70 St. 744-6700.
Twentieth-century American and European art.
OPEN Tues-Fri 9:30am-5:30pm; Sat 9:30am-5pm.

Leonard Hutton Galleries
33 East 74 Street, 2nd floor. 249-9700. Specializes in German Expressionists and Russian
avant-garde works of art. *OPEN Tues-Fri 10am-5:30pm; Sat 11am-5pm. Aug by appointment
only.*

Sidney Janis Gallery
110 West 57 Street, 6th floor. 586-0110. Four
generations of modern art from Cubism to Pop to
Minimalism painting to post-graffiti. *OPEN Mon-Sat 10am-5:30pm.*

Jaro Art Galleries
955 Madison Avenue near East 75 St. 734-5475.
Specializes in Yugoslavian Naives and American Primitive art; fine art glass. *OPEN Mon-Sat
10am-6pm.*

Jordan-Volpe Gallery
958 Madison Avenue near East 75 St. 570-9500.
American painting, 1840-1940. Late 19th-century, early 20th-century paintings. *OPEN
Tues-Sat 10am-5:30pm.*

Julie: Artisans' Gallery
687 Madison Avenue near East 62 St. 688-2345.
Fanciful, wearable arts and crafts. All one of a
kind. First gallery to show clothing as an art form
created by contemporary craftpeople. *OPEN 7
days 11am-6pm.*

Alexander Kahn Fine Arts
40 East 76 Street. 737-4230. Works by American
and European artists of the late 19th and 20th
centuries. *OPEN 7 days 10am-5pm.*

Kennedy Galleries
40 West 57 Street, 5th floor. 541-9600. American
paintings, sculpture, and graphics of the 18th,
19th, and 20th centuries plus European fine
prints. *OPEN Tues-Sat 9:30am-5:30pm.*

Coe Kerr Gallery
49 East 82 Street. 628-1340. Nineteenth- and
20th-century American paintings and sculpture.
All three Wyeths, Mary Cassatt, Childe Hassam,

Winslow Homer, Maurice Prendergast. *OPEN Mon-Fri 9am-5pm; Sat 10am-5pm.*

Knoedler & Company
19 East 70 Street. 794-0550. Contemporary European and American paintings and sculpture. *OPEN Tues-Fri 9:30am-5:30pm, Sat 10am-5:30pm.*

Kraushaar Galleries
724 Fifth Avenue near 57th St, 7th floor. 307-5730. Paintings, drawings, and sculpture by 20th-century American artists. Peggy Bacon, William Glackens, Leon Goldin, Elsie Manville, Ben Frank Moss, John Sloan. *OPEN Tues-Fri 9:30am-5:30pm; Sat 10am-5pm.*

La Boetie, Inc.
9 East 82 Street, 3rd floor. 535-4865. Early 20th-century European avant-garde paintings, drawings, watercolors, sculpture, and collages, including Expressionists, Surrealists, Constructivists, Art of the Bauhaus, and Dada. Grosz, Klee, Klimt, Leger, Matisse, Schiele. *OPEN Tues-Sat 10am-5:30pm.*

Lefebre Gallery
411 West End Avenue. 744-3384. Private dealer. Mainly European contemporary paintings and sculpture. *By appointment only.*

Littlejohn-Smith
245 East 72 Street. 420-6090. Works by contemporary emerging artists. *By appointment only.*

Marlborough Gallery
40 West 57 Street, 2nd floor. 541-4900. Twentieth-century and contemporary paintings, sculpture, photographs, graphics. Frank Auerbach, Francis Bacon, Fernando Botero, Red Grooms, Barbara Hepworth, Alex Katz, Antonio Lopez-Garcia, Henry Moore, Larry Rivers, Rufino Tamayo. *OPEN Mon-Sat 10am-5:30pm.*

James Maroney
129A East 74 Street. 879-2252. Private dealer. Nineteenth- and early 20th-century American paintings and watercolors. *By appointment only.*

Barbara Mathes Gallery
851 Madison Avenue near East 70 St, 2nd floor. 249-3600. Late 19th- and 20th-century American and European art: Avery, Cornell, de Kooning, Dine, Francis, Lichtenstein, Motherwell, Rothko, Stella, Hockney, Balthus, Gottlieb. *OPEN Tues-Fri 9:30am-5:30pm; Sat 10am-5:30pm.*

Pierre Matisse Gallery
41 East 57 Street, 4th floor. 355-6269. Contemporary paintings and sculpture, including Miró. *OPEN Tues-Sat 10am-5pm. CLOSED July & Aug.*

David McKee Gallery
41 East 57 Street. 688-5951. Contemporary paintings, drawings, sculpture, and prints. *OPEN Tues-Sat 10am-5:30pm.*

Midtown Galleries
11 East 57 Street, 3rd floor. 758-1900. Twentieth-century and contemporary American art, 1930-present. *OPEN Tues-Sat 10am-5:30pm.*

Eduard Nakhamkin Fine Arts
138 Greene Street. 473-2007. Contemporary Russian art-in-exile. Prints, graphics, oils, sculpture. *OPEN Mon-Sat 10am-6pm; Sun noon-5pm.*

Newhouse Galleries
19 East 66 Street. 879-2700. Dutch 17th-, Italian 15th-, and American 18th- and 19th-century paintings. Large and very good operation. Strong in old masters and American 19th century. *OPEN year-round Mon-Fri 9:30am-5pm.*

Pace Gallery of New York
32 East 57 Street, 2nd floor. 421-3292. Twentieth-century painting, drawings, sculpture. Dine, Nevelson, Schnabel, Calder, Samaris, Dubuffet. On the 10th floor, master prints and drawings. *OPEN Tues-Fri 9:30am-5:30pm; Sat 10am-6pm.*

William Pall Fine Arts
1175 Park Avenue near East 93 St. 860-3400. Nineteenth- and 20th-century European and American art. *By appointment only.*

Pannonia Gallery
21 East 82 Street. 628-1168. Nineteenth-century European flower, genre, and orientalist sculpture and painting. *OPEN Mon-Fri 10:30am-5pm.*

Peris Galleries
1016 Madison Avenue near East 78 St. 472-3200. Paintings and sculpture by 20th-century masters: Calder, Picasso, Braque, Chagall, Dufy. *OPEN Tues-Sat 10am-5pm. Aug by appointment only.*

Raydon Gallery
1091 Madison Avenue at East 82 St. 288-3555. Works from Renaissance to the present; 19th- and 20th-century art. *OPEN Mon-Sat 10am-6pm.*

Reinhold-Brown Gallery
26 East 78 Street. 734-7999. Twentieth-century graphic design, specializing in early avant-garde movements. *OPEN Tues-Sat 10:30am-5pm.*

Rosenberg & Stiebel, Inc.
32 East 57 Street, 5th floor. 753-4368. Fine paintings, drawings, works of art, and 18th-century French furniture and decorative arts. *OPEN Tues-Sat 10am-5pm, Mon by appointment only.*

Rothschild Fine Arts
205 West End Avenue. 873-9142. Private dealer. European and American paintings, drawings, sculpture. Impressionist, Post-Impressionist, modern, and contemporary art. *By appointment only.*

Serge Sabarsky
58 East 79 Street, 3rd floor. 628-6281. Twentieth-century German and Austrian Expressionists: Beckmann, Grosz, Feininger, Dix, Schiele, Klimt, Klee. *By appointment only.*

Sacks Fine Art
30 East 68 Street. 249-2121. Early 20th-century American paintings. Also vintage American illustrators. *By appointment only.*

Saidenberg Gallery
1018 Madison Avenue near East 79 St, 3rd floor. 288-3387. Twentieth-century European and American paintings, sculpture, and graphic art. Specialists in Picasso, Klee, Leger. *OPEN Tues-Fri 10am-5pm; Sat 1-5pm.*

Salander-O'Reilly Galleries
2 East 79 Street. 879-6606. Nineteenth- to 20th-century American modernist paintings: Ashcan School, Precisionist, New York School. Also contemporary painters and 19th-century European painters, antique European and American period frames. *OPEN Mon-Sat 10am-5:30pm.*

Spencer A. Samuels Gallery
39 East 72 Street, 5th floor. 288-9333. Master paintings from the 14th to 19th century, drawings and sculpture. *By appointment only.*

Schaeffer Galleries
983 Park Avenue near East 83 St, 2nd floor. 535-6410 or -6411. Old masters paintings and drawings of the 17th, 18th, and 19th centuries. *OPEN year-round Mon-Fri 10am-5pm.*

Schmidt Bingham Gallery
41 West 57 Street. 888-1122. Contemporary American Realism. *OPEN Mon-Sat 10am-6pm.*

Robert Schoelkopf Gallery
50 West 57 Street, suite 12A. 765-3540. Early 20th-century modernism. Contemporary realist painting, sculpture, and drawings. *OPEN Tues-Sat 10am-5pm.*

Schweitzer Gallery
1015 Madison Avenue near East 78 St, 3rd floor. 535-5430. European and American paintings from the old masters to the 20th century. *By appointment only.*

Shepherd Gallery
21 East 84 Street. 861-4050. Nineteenth-century (pre-Impressionist) European paintings, drawings, and sculpture. *OPEN Tues-Sat 10am-6pm. CLOSED mid-Aug-Labor Day.*

H. Shickman Gallery
980 Madison Avenue near East 76 St. 249-3800. Fine old masters paintings and drawings, 19th-century French paintings. *By appointment only.*

Smith Gallery
1045 Madison Avenue at East 79 St. 744-6171. Nineteenth- and 20th-century American marine paintings and Western art. *OPEN Mon-Sat 11am-6pm.*

Holly Solomon
724 Fifth Avenue at 56 St. 757-7777. Contemporary art with an emphasis on narrative and decorative patterns in all media. *OPEN Mon-Sat 10am-6pm.*

Solomon & Company Fine Art
959 Madison Avenue near East 75 St. 737-8200. Twentieth-century American and European painting and sculpture. Avery, Calder, de Kooning, Dubuffet, Hofman, Pollack, Stella. *OPEN Mon-Sat 11am-5:30pm.*

Soufer
1015 Madison Avenue near East 79 St. 628-3225. Post-Impressionist and European paintings of the 1920s-40s, including German Expressionist and Naive. *OPEN Tues-Sat 11am-5:30pm.*

Spanierman Gallery
50 East 78 Street. 879-7085. Nineteenth- and 20th-century American paintings, sculpture, and works on paper. *OPEN Tues-Sat 9:30am-5:30pm.*

Sportsman's Edge, Ltd.
136 East 74 Street. 249-5010. Contemporary sporting and wildlife art; original oils, watercolors, sculpture, and prints. *OPEN Mon-Sat 10am-6pm.*

Allan Stone Gallery
48 East 86 Street, 2nd floor. 988-6870. Twentieth-century masters and contemporary art with an emphasis on Abstract Expressionism. *OPEN Tues-Fri 10am-6pm; Sat 10am-5pm. CLOSED July & Aug.*

Tatistcheff & Company
50 West 57 Street, 8th floor. 664-0907. Contemporary American painting and works on paper. *OPEN Tues-Sat 10am-6pm.*

E. V. Thaw & Company, Inc.
726 Park Avenue at East 70 St. 535-6333. Private dealer; master paintings and drawings of all periods. *By appointment only.*

Jack Tilton Gallery
24 West 57 Street, 3rd floor. 247-7480. Contemporary sculpture, painting, drawing. *OPEN Tues-Sat 10am-5:30pm.*

Bertha Urdang Gallery
23 East 74 Street. 288-7004. Abstract works by Israeli, European, and American artists; photography. *OPEN Tues-Sat 10am-5:30pm.*

Vanderwoude/Tananbaum
24 East 81 Street. 879-8200. American modernist and post–World War II art; works by emerging artists; contemporary painting and sculpture. *OPEN Tues-Sat 10am-5:30pm.*

Viridian Gallery
52 West 57 Street, 2nd floor. 245-2882. Contemporary art, painting, sculpture, graphics. *OPEN Tues-Sat 11am-6:30pm.*

Washburn Gallery
41 East 57 Street, 8th floor. 753-0546. American abstract art 1930s and 1940s; folk art; contemporary paintings, sculpture, drawings. *OPEN Tues-Sat 10am-6pm.*

Phyllis Weil & Company
1065 Park Avenue. 369-0255. Contemporary figurative and abstract sculpture, paintings, and photography. *By appointment only.*

Weintraub Gallery
988 Madison Avenue near East 77 St. 879-1195. Modern paintings and sculpture. *OPEN Tues-Sat 10am-5pm.*

Wildenstein & Co
19 East 64 Street. 879-0500. The world's foremost selection of old and modern paintings, drawings, and objects of art. *OPEN year-round Mon-Fri 10am-5pm.*

Zabriskie Gallery
724 Fifth Avenue at 56 St, 12th floor. 307-7430. Early 20th-century American painting, sculpture, drawing. Contemporary large-scale sculpture; photography. Some European. *OPEN Mon-Sat 10am-5:30pm.*

SoHo Galleries

A.I.R. Gallery
63 Crosby Street. 966-0799. Women artists' co-

operative; art-related special events. *OPEN Tues-Sat 11am-6pm.*

Scott Alan Gallery
270 Lafayette Street, suite 204. 226-5145. Contemporary international painting, sculpture, and drawings. Mexican and Spanish artists emphasized. *OPEN Tues-Sat 11am-6pm.*

Brooke Alexander
59 Wooster, 2nd floor. 925-4338. Contemporary American and European paintings, drawings, and sculpture. *OPEN Tues-Sat 10am-6pm.*

Pamela Auchincloss Gallery
558 Broadway, 2nd floor. 966-7753. Contemporary American and European paintings, sculpture, and drawings. *OPEN Tues-Sat 10am-6pm & by appointment.*

Jayne H. Baum Gallery
588 Broadway. 219-9854. Contemporary art in all media. *OPEN Mon-Sat 10am-6pm.*

Mary Boone
417 West Broadway. 431-1818. Contemporary paintings, constructions, and drawings. *OPEN Tues-Sat 10am-6pm; July & Aug by appointment only.*

Leo Castelli Gallery
420 West Broadway, 2nd floor; 431-5160. And 578 Broadway, 3rd floor; 431-6279. Top gallery for contemporary paintings, drawings, and sculpture: Artschwager, Johns, Kelly, Lichtenstein, Oldenburg, Rauschenberg, Rosenquist, Stella, among others. *OPEN Tues-Sat 10am-6pm.*

Paula Cooper Gallery
155 Wooster Street. 674-0766. Contemporary paintings, sculpture, drawings, prints, and photography. Jennifer Barlett, Lynda Benglis, Peter Campus, Robert Gober, Michael Hurson, Robert Mangold, Joel Shapiro, Jackie Winsor. *OPEN Tues-Sat 10am-6pm.*

Charles Cowles
420 West Broadway. 925-3500. Contemporary paintings, photography, and sculpture. *OPEN Tues-Sat 10am-6pm.*

Bess Cutler Gallery
164 Mercer Street. 219-1577. Sculpture and contemporary paintings by emerging artists. *OPEN Tues-Sat 10am-6pm.*

Maxwell Davidson Gallery
415 West Broadway. 925-5300. Modern and contemporary paintings, drawings, and sculpture. *OPEN Tues-Sat 10am-6pm.*

DiLaurenti Gallery
383 West Broadway. 925-5100. Modern and contemporary masters and emerging artists: paintings, sculpture, and works on paper. *By appointment only.*

Dyansen Gallery of SoHo
122 Spring Street. 226-3384. Sculpture, paintings, and prints. *OPEN 7 days 11am-7pm.*

Rose Esman Gallery
70 Greene Street. 219-3044. Contemporary painting and sculpture and Russian avant-garde and Bauhaus works on paper; photographs. *OPEN Tues-Sat 10am-6pm.*

Facchetti
476 Broadway. 966-5991. Contemporary American and European art. *OPEN Tues-Sat 10am-6pm.*

Ronald Feldman Fine Arts
31 Mercer Street. 226-3232. Nineteenth- and 20th-century American and European art. *OPEN Tues-Sat 10am-6pm, Mon by appointment. July & Aug by appointment only.*

14 Sculptors Gallery
164 Mercer Street. 966-5790. Artist-run gallery exhibits advanced contemporary sculpture in all media. *OPEN Tues-Sun 11am-6pm. CLOSED mid-July-Aug.*

Pat Hearn
39 Wooster Street. 941-7055. Contemporary art. *OPEN Tues-Sat 10am-6pm.*

Heller Gallery
71 Greene Street. 966-5948. Contemporary glass sculpture. *OPEN Tues-Sat 11am-6pm; Sun noon-5pm.*

Carolyn Hill Gallery
109 Spring Street. 226-4611. Sculpture and paintings by contemporary international artists. *OPEN Wed-Sun noon-6pm.*

Nancy Hoffman
429 West Broadway. 966-6676. Good contemporary art, including works by Carolyn Brady, Don Eddy, Juan Gonzalez, Joseph Raffael, Rafael Ferrer, Howard Buchwald, John Okulick, and Alan Siegel. *OPEN Tues-Sat 10am-6pm.*

Jack Gallery
138 Prince Street. 226-1989. Contemporary paintings and sculpture. *OPEN year-round Mon-Fri 10am-6pm; Sat 11am-6pm; Sun noon-6pm.*

Phyllis Kind Gallery
136 Greene Street. 925-1200. Contemporary American, Soviet, and European art. Twentieth-century American and European art brut. *OPEN Tues-Sat 10am-6pm; Aug by appointment only.*

Koury Wingate
578 Broadway. 966-5777. Contemporary paintings, sculpture, and photography. *OPEN Tues-Sat 10am-6pm.*

Chuck Levitan Gallery
42 Grand Street. 966-2782. Contemporary American paintings and sculpture: Will Barnet, Romare Bearden, Marisol. *OPEN Tues-Sat 1-6pm. CLOSED July & Aug.*

Luhring Augustine Gallery
130 Prince Street. 219-9600. Sculpture, drawings, prints, and paintings by modern and contemporary American and European artists. *OPEN Tues-Sat 10am-6pm.*

Gracie Mansion Gallery
532 Broadway, 4th floor. 941-5580. Pioneer East Village gallery now in SoHo. Contemporary art. Buster Cleveland, Claudia DeMonte, Rodney Alan Greenblat, Al Hansen, Stephen Lack, Gary Panter, Hope Sandrow. *OPEN Tues-Sat 10am-6pm.*

Louis K. Meisel
141 Prince Street. 677-1340. Photorealist art by Audrey Flack, Charles Bell, Hilo Chen, Ron Kleemann. Abstract trompe l'oeil paintings by

James Havard and Jack Lembeck. Pop art by Mel Ramos. Also Theodoros Stamas, Abstract Expressionist. *OPEN Tues-Sat 10am-6pm.*

Alexander F. Milliken, Inc.
98 Prince Street. 966-7800. Contemporary painting and sculpture; drawings and prints. Wendell Castle, Mary Ann Currier, Steve Hawley, Kazuma Oshita, Lee Schuette, Lois Polansky, Richard Saba, Hendrick Brandtsoen, Randall Deihl. A very good eye for less familiar artists as well. *OPEN Tues-Sat 10am-6pm.*

Edward Nahamkin Limited
402 West Broadway. 219-8990. Original and limited edition 20th-century and contemporary Russian art. Limited edition lithographs from the State Museum in Leningrad. *OPEN Mon-Sat 10am-6pm; Sun noon-5pm.*

O.K. Harris Works of Art
383 West Broadway. 431-3600. Largest art gallery in the world. Presents four to five one-man shows every three weeks. Specializes in contemporary painting, sculpture, photography. Very good place to "discover" new artists. *OPEN Tues-Sat 10am-6pm. CLOSED mid-July-Labor Day.*

Marilyn Pearl Gallery
420 West Broadway. 966-5506. Contemporary American masters and emerging artists. Exhibits change monthly. *OPEN Tues-Sat 10am-6pm. CLOSED Aug.*

Pindar Gallery
127 Greene Street. 533-4881. Cooperative gallery representing contemporary American painters and sculptors. *OPEN Tues-Sat 11:30am-6pm; Sun 1-5pm.*

Pleiades Gallery
164 Mercer Street. 226-9093. Figurative, abstract, and experimental art. *OPEN Tues-Sun 11am-6pm.*

P.P.O.W.
532 Broadway, 3rd floor. 941-8642. Contemporary international artists. *OPEN Tues-Sat 10am-6pm.*

Prince Street Gallery
121 Wooster Street. 226-9402. Contemporary expressionist and representational paintings, sculpture, drawings. *OPEN Tues-Sun noon-6pm.*

Putumayo Folk Art Gallery
147 Spring Street. 431-7250. American and European Naive painting, masks, puppets, antique textiles, ceramics, and santos. *OPEN Tues-Sat 11am-6pm.*

Stephen Rosenberg Gallery
115 Wooster Street. 431-4838. Sculpture, drawings, and paintings by contemporary European and American artists. *OPEN Tues-Sat 11am-6pm or by appointment.*

Jeffrey Ruesch Fine Arts
134 Spring Street. 925-1137. Art Nouveau and Art Deco works on paper; contemporary prints. *OPEN Mon-Sat 11am-6pm.*

Tony Shafrazi Gallery
163 Mercer Street. 925-8732. Emerging and established contemporary artists in all media. *OPEN Tues-Sat 10am-6pm.*

Nathan Silberberg Fine Arts
382 West Broadway. 966-0611. Contemporary international artists. *OPEN 7 days 11am-6pm.*

Sonnabend Gallery
420 West Broadway, 3rd floor. 966-6160. Contemporary American and European paintings and sculpture: some contemporary photographs. *OPEN Tues-Sat 10am-6pm.*

Sperone Westwater
142 Greene Street, 2nd floor. 431-3685. European and American contemporary art. *OPEN Tues-Sat 10am-6pm.*

Staempfli Gallery
415 West Broadway. 941-7100. Contemporary American, European, and Asian art. *OPEN Tues-Sat 10am-6pm.*

Edward Thorp
103 Prince Street, 2nd floor. 431-6880. Contemporary American painting and sculpture. *OPEN Tues-Sat 10am-6pm.*

Barbara Toll Fine Arts
146 Greene Street. 431-1788. Contemporary sculpture, drawings, prints, and paintings by European and American artists. *OPEN Tues-Sat 10am-6pm.*

Vasarely Center
484 Bloome Street. 219-2275. Exhibits and sells sculpture, paintings, original serigraphs, and posters by Victor Vasarely. *OPEN Wed-Sun 11am-6pm.*

Vorpal SoHo
411 West Broadway. 334-3939. Contemporary paintings, sculpture, and prints. Largest collection of prints by M. C. Escher in the world. *OPEN year-round Mon-Fri 10am-6pm; Sat 10am-7pm; Sun 11am-7pm.*

Ward-Nasse Gallery
178 Prince Street. 925-6951. A cooperative art gallery; all media. *OPEN Tues-Sat 11am-6pm; Sun 1-4pm.*

John Weber Gallery
142 Greene Street, 3rd floor. 966-6115. European and contemporary artists, emphasis on minimalist and conceptual art. *OPEN Tues-Sat 10am-6pm.*

Wolff
560 Broadway. 431-7833. Contemporary painting and sculpture. *OPEN Tues-Sat noon-6pm.*

Eastern Art

Jacques Carcanagues
114 Spring Street. 925-8110. Ethnographic items from Afghanistan, Central America, Guatemala, India, Thailand, Indonesia, Japan, Korea, the Philippines, and more. *OPEN year-round Tues-Sat 11:30am-7pm.*

Frank Caro Gallery
41 East 57 Street, 2nd floor. 753-2166. Ancient art of China, India, and Southeast Asia. *OPEN Tues-Sat 10am-5:30pm.*

Ralph M. Chait Galleries, Inc.
12 East 56 Street. 758-0937. Top-quality Chinese works of art, porcelain, pottery from the Neolithic

period to 1800, and Chinese export silver. *OPEN Mon-Sat 10am-5:30pm.*

De Havenon, Inc.
160 East 65 Street, 29th floor. 249-9572. Primitive African and Oceanic art. *By appointment only.*

E & J Frankel, Ltd
1040 Madison Avenue at East 79 St. 879-5733. Specializes in Oriental art from China: Shang Dynasty–1840s porcelains and jade; from Japan, all-periods screen paintings and furnishings. *OPEN Mon-Sat 10am-5:30pm.*

Navin Kumar
1001 Madison Avenue near East 77 St. 734-4075. Works of art from India, Tibet, Nepal. Also Islamic and Chinese art. *OPEN 7 days 10:30am-6pm.*

Pace Primitive Art
32 East 57 Street, 10th floor. 421-3688. Antique African art, masks, and artifacts. *OPEN Tues-Fri 9:30am-5:30pm; Sat 10am-6pm.*

F. Rolin & Company, Inc
61 East 77 Street, apt. 9A. 879-0077. Top New York source for primitive art. *By appointment only.*

Ronin Gallery
605 Madison Avenue near East 57 St, 2nd floor. 688-0188. Large selection of 17th- to 20th-century Japanese woodblock prints; netsuke. *OPEN Mon-Sat 10am-6pm.*

Merton Simpson Gallery
1063 Madison Avenue near East 80 St, 3rd floor. 988-6290. Mainly African, also Oceanic and American Indian art. *OPEN Tues-Sat 10:30am-5:30pm.*

Temple Art
1242 Madison Avenue near East 89 St. 860-7070. Rare works from Nepal, Tibet, and India. *OPEN Mon-Sat 9:30am-6pm.*

Ed Waldman Collection, Inc.
231 East 58 Street, suite 2A. 838-2140. Art from India, Thailand, Burma, China, Japan, Korea, Indonesia: 14th century to contemporary. *OPEN Mon-Fri 9:30am-6pm.*

Prints & Original Posters

A Clean, Well-Lighted Place
363 Bleecker Street near Charles St. 255-3656. Contemporary prints, including works by Susan Rothenberg, Sean Scully, Hockney, Motherwell. *OPEN Tues-Sat noon-7pm; Sun 1-5pm.*

Brooke Alexander Editions
476 Broome Street. 925-2070. Contemporary prints, multiples, and illustrated books. Richard Artschwager, Richard Bosman, Jasper Johns, Claes Oldenburg, Andy Warhol. *OPEN Tues-Sat 10am-6pm.*

Associated American Artists (A.A.A.)
20 West 57 Street, 6th floor. 399-5510. America's largest print dealer. Sixteenth to 20th century. Original etchings, lithographs, woodcuts, and serigraphs, from the 15th to 20th century. *OPEN Sept-May, Tues-Sat 10am-6pm; June-Aug, Mon-Fri 10am-5pm.*

Castelli Graphics
578 Broadway; 941-9855. And 4 East 77 Street, 2nd floor; 288-3202. Publisher of prints by Artschwager, Johns, Kelly, Lichtenstein, Stella, as well as limited-edition photographic photofolios and books. *OPEN Tues-Sat 10am-6pm. Appointments preferred.*

Circle Gallery
SoHo, 468 West Broadway at Houston St.; 677-5100. And *Trump Tower, 725 Fifth Avenue, 4th floor; 980-5455. Also **South Street Seaport, 205-7 Front Street, 732-5625; and ***780 Seventh Avenue at West 51 St, 765-6975. Specializing in moderately priced graphics with mass appeal and art-to-wear jewelry. At Seventh Avenue, the specialty is animation and cartoon art. *OPEN Mon-Thurs 10am-6pm, Fri 10am-7pm, Sat 11am-7pm, Sun 11am-6pm; *Mon-Sat 10am-6pm *(CLOSED Sun); **Mon-Sat 10am-9pm, Sun 11am-8pm; ***Mon-Sat 10am-9pm, Sun noon-6pm.*

Margo Feiden Galleries
699 Madison Avenue near East 66 St. 223-4230. The complete collection of Al Hirschfield drawings, watercolors, lithographs, and etchings. *OPEN 7 days 10am-6pm.*

Fitch-Febvrel Gallery
5 East 57 Street, 12th floor. 688-8522. Nineteenth- and 20th-century fine prints and drawings. *OPEN Tues-Sat 11am-5:30pm; Aug by appointment only.*

Isselbacher Gallery
41 East 78 Street. 472-1766. Late 19th- and 20th-century prints, woodcuts, etchings: Beckmann, Bonnard, Chagall, Klee, Matisse, Miró, Picasso, Toulouse-Lautrec, Vuillard. *OPEN Tues-Sat 10:30am-5:30pm.*

Japan Gallery
1210 Lexington Avenue near East 82 St. 288-2241. Specializes in Japanese woodblock prints from the 18th century to the present. *OPEN Tues-Sat 11am-6pm.*

Jane Kahan Gallery
922 Madison Avenue at East 73 St, 2nd floor. 744-1490. Large collection of Chagall prints; also Appel, Calder, Delaunay, Dubuffet, Francis, Lichtenstein, Matisse, Matta, Miró, Picasso, Pissarro, Stella. *OPEN Mon-Sat 10am-5:30pm.*

Multiple Impressions, Ltd.
128 Spring Street at Greene St. 925-1313. Contemporary American and European original graphics: Kozo, Andre Masson, Johnny Friedlaender, Harold Altman, Elizabeth Schippert, Mikio Watanabe. Several one-man shows a year. *OPEN 7 days noon-7pm.*

Multiples Inc.
24 West 57 Street, 4th floor. 977-7160. Publisher of prints by John Baldessari, Sol Lewitt, Oldenburg, and other contemporary American and European artists. Paintings, drawings, sculpture. *OPEN Mon-Sat 10am-6pm.*

Old Print Shop
150 Lexington Avenue at East 30 St. 683-3950. Original old prints of Audubon, Currier & Ives, 18th-century maps, marines, and some Ameri-

can paintings. *OPEN Mon-Sat 9am-5pm; in summer, Mon-Fri 9am-5pm.*

Pace Master Prints and Drawings
32 East 57 Street, 10th floor. 421-3688. Old master prints and drawings from the 15th century; 19th- and 20th-century master prints. Canaletto, Dürer, Goya, Kandinsky, Matisse, Miró, Picasso, Piranesi, Rembrandt, Tiepolo, Toulouse-Lautrec, Whistler. *OPEN Tues-Sat 9:30am-5:30pm.*

Pace Prints
32 East 57 Street, 3rd floor. 421-3237. Contemporary prints, multiples; tapestries. *OPEN Tues-Fri 9:30am-5:30pm, Sat 10am-6pm. In summer, Mon-Fri 9:30am-5:30pm.*

Reiss-Cohen, Inc.
628-2496. Major graphics of the 19th and 20th centuries: Braque, Bonnard, Chagall, Kandinsky, Toulouse-Lautrec, Leger, Miró, Matisse, Picasso, Renoir, Rouault. *By appointment only.*

William H. Schab Gallery
11 East 57 Street, 5th floor. 758-0327. Old master and modern prints, lithographs, woodcuts, engravings, etchings: Dürer, Rembrandt, Goya; old master drawings: Tiepolo, Tintoretto. *OPEN Tues-Sat 9:30am-5:30pm.*

Sindin Galleries
1035 Madison Avenue at East 79 St. 288-7902. Twentieth-century master graphics, drawings, etchings, and sculpture: Botero, Miró, Motherwell, Picasso, Stella, Zuñiga. *OPEN Tues-Sat 10am-5:30pm.*

David Tunick, Inc.
21 East 81 Street. 570-0090. Fine old masters, modern prints, and drawings: Rembrandt, Dürer, Tiepolo, Bruegel, Canaletto; 19th-century prints: Bonnard, Goya, Cezanne, Degas, Delacroix, Gericault, Manet, Toulouse-Lautrec, Pissarro; 20th century: Picasso, Matisse, Braque, Whistler, Bellows, Villon. *OPEN Mon-Fri 10am-5pm; appointment advisable.*

Weyhe Gallery
794 Lexington Avenue near East 61 St. 838-5478. American fine prints and drawings 1920s and 1930s. *OPEN Tues-Sat 9:30am-4:30pm.*

Photography

Castelli Graphics, Paula Cooper, Charles Cowles, Rose Esman, Marlborough, O.K. Harris, and Zabriskie also show photography.

Robert Freidus Gallery
70 Greene Street near Spring St. 925-0113. Contemporary American photography, sculpture, and painting. Publishes photographic portfolios. *By appointment only.*

International Center of Photography
See Museums: General Art Museums.

Robert Miller
41 East 57 Street, 2nd floor. 980-5454. Contemporary American art, plus 19th- and 20th-century photography. Berenice Abbott, Diane Arbus, Jean Michel Basquiat, Walker Evans, Man Ray, Robert Mapplethorpe, David McDermott and Peter McGough, Alice Neel, Bruce Weber. *OPEN Tues-Sat 10am-5:30pm; Aug by appointment.*

Neikrug Gallery
224 East 68 Street. 288-7741. Town house setting for contemporary and vintage photographs including daguerreotypes. Appraisals. *OPEN Wed-Fri 1-5pm; Sat 1-6pm or by appointment.*

Marcuse Pfeifer Gallery
568 Broadway near Prince St, suite 102. 226-2251. Exhibits solely photographic art, 19th-20th century and contemporary: Allan Chasanoff, Mark Berghash, Joan Myers, Lilo Raymond, Holly Wright. *OPEN Tues-Sat 10:30am-6pm.*

Witkin Gallery
415 West Broadway near Prince St, 4th floor. 925-5510. Photographs and photographic books, including out-of-print photo literature. Vintage and contemporary prints: Andre Kertesz, Evelyn Hofer, Joel Meyerowitz, George Tice, Jerry Uelsmann. *OPEN Tues-Fri 11am-6pm; Sat noon-6pm.*

Daniel Wolf
52 East 78 Street, apt. 11C. 772-7721. Nineteenth- and 20th-century photography: Cameron, Watkins, Baldus, Fenton, Thompson. *By appointment only.*

ALTERNATIVE EXHIBITION SPACES

Devoted to assisting new or neglected artists and art forms, they are mainly nonprofit, multiple-discipline centers long on vision and, usually, short on funds.

Alternative Museum
17 White Street near Church St. 966-4444. In TriBeCa, exhibitions in all media by American and other world cultures; emphasis on artists outside the mainstream. A major presenter of world music: from non-Western, classical, and folk, to experimental. Poetry, too. Artist-founded and -operated. *OPEN Tues-Sat 11am-6pm.*

The Drawing Center
35 Wooster Street. 219-2166. Nonprofit institution dedicated to the study and exhibition of works on paper. Shows of promising and well-known artists; historical and theme exhibitions. Lectures, films, symposiums, twice-yearly conservation workshops. *OPEN Tues & Thurs-Sat 11am-6pm; Wed 11am-8pm.*

Global Village
431 Broome Street near Crosby St. 431-7261. Begun in 1969, it is the center for documentary video in New York. Workshops, internships, production. Large tape library. Video and film screenings in the spring and fall. Call to get on their mailing list.

Henry Street Settlement
466 Grand Street at Pitt St. 598-0400. Longtime (since 1888) social service institution houses arts and performance spaces to serve the Lower East Side community. Theaters, galleries, and classrooms for the visual and performing arts. Exhibitions of emerging minority and women art-

ists. Gallery *OPEN 7 days noon-6pm. Performances at 7:30pm.*

Institute for Contemporary Art
P.S. 1, 46-01 21 Street, Long Island City, Queens. (718) 784-2084. Large exhibition center located in an 1888 former public school. Painting, sculpture, photography, music, fashion, video, and film. Group shows and special projects by contemporary artists at P.S. 1. *OPEN Tues-Sun noon-6pm.*

The Kitchen
512 West 19 Street. 255-5793. Since 1971, inno-vative experimental dance, music, video (very strong), and performance and visual arts center. Membership available. *OPEN Tues-Sat 1-6pm.* Admission charge.

P.S. 122
150 First Avenue at East 9 St. 228-4249. Flourishing East Village showcase for new and experimental dance, music, film, theater, poetry, and performance art. Artist-run space. Gallery *OPEN Tues-Sun 1-5pm.* Admission charge for events.

PARKS & GARDENS

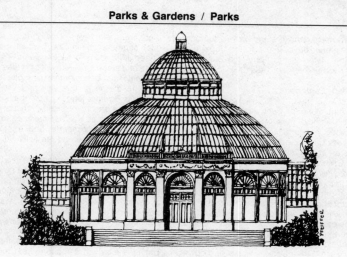

Enid Haupt Conservatory, NY Botanical Garden

Vast or vest-pocket, parks and gardens in a city like New York have an incalculable value. When canyons of steel and glass have to cease or go around small or large outposts of "country," a modern miracle is wrought. The effect of greenery and open space in New York on the mind and spirit cannot be overstated.

PARKS

CAVEAT: It is recommended that you confine your park visits to daylight hours unless a specific special event is scheduled.

General

New York City has 26,175 acres of parkland: 6,774 in the Bronx; 4,073 in Brooklyn; 2,614 in Manhattan; 6,999 in Queens; and 5,715 on Staten Island. For recorded information pertaining to events in the city's parks available on any given day in New York's five boroughs, call 360-1333.

For further information on the city's parks, call the individual borough office:
Brooklyn: (718) 965-8900
Bronx: 430-1800
Manhattan: 408-0100
Queens: (718) 520-5900
Staten Island: (718) 390-8000
Central Park Conservancy
830 Fifth Avenue, New York, NY 10021. 315-0385. A private nonprofit citizen's group dedicated to the physical restoration of Central Park as well as improved maintenance and security. Write for information.

Greensward Foundation
Box 610, Lenox Hill P.O., New York, NY 10021. An independent organization comprised of the Friends of Central, Carl Schurz, and Prospect Parks and dedicated to the care and restoration of historic trees and monuments within these parks. Walking tours, bicycle tours, and lectures are some of what's offered.
Urban Park Rangers
Trained in the history, design, geology, wildlife, and botany of the city's parks, they offer FREE walks and talks to encourage better use of them and to remind New Yorkers of the origins of the city's open spaces. For information on their fascinating and educational programs, call the appropriate number:
Brooklyn Parks: (718) 287-3400
Bronx (except Crotona) Parks: 548-7070
Crotona Park: 589-0096
Manhattan Parks: 397-3081
Queens Parks: (718) 699-4204
Staten Island Parks: (718) 816-5456

Manhattan

Battery Park
State Street & Battery Place. At the southern tip of Manhattan, 21 acres extending from Bowling Green to the junction of the Hudson and East rivers. Its name resulted from a row of guns along its old shoreline. Castle Clinton, then known as Southwest Battery, was erected offshore on a pile of rock for the occasion of the War of 1812 (nary a shot was ever fired). Landfill later joined it to the mainland, and Castle Clinton (*see* HISTORIC & NEW NEW YORK, Historic Buildings & Areas) now sits squarely in what has become Battery Park. Greenery, sea breezes, and great

vistas draw mainly bankers and brokers at noon on good weather days. It is also the departure point of the Staten Island Ferry, the Statue of Liberty Ferry, and the *Petrel* (see SIGHTSEEING, Boat Trips).

Battery Park Esplanade
Enter West & Liberty Streets. This 1.2-mile linear park that runs along the perimeter of the Battery Park landfill is one of the city's newest and best. Old-fashioned lampposts, shade trees, and benches facing unimpeded Hudson River views make this an inviting spirit-lifting spot.

Bowling Green
At the foot of Broadway. Opened in 1733, it was the city's first public park. The Common Council leased the park to three citizens who paid the annual sum of one peppercorn and in return improved it with trees and grass. Its simple iron fence was erected in 1771 to protect the statue of George III that stood there. It failed. The day the Declaration of Independence reached New York—July 9, 1776—the statue was pulled down and apart along with some royal ornamentation on the fence.

Bryant Park
Sixth Avenue, West 40 to West 42 Street, behind the New York Public Library. In 1823, these nine acres were set aside as a potter's field, but in 1853, New York's version of London's Crystal Palace was erected on the site; it burned down five years later. The land became a public park in 1882, and in 1847, it was named for William Cullen Bryant, poet and editor-journalist. Now midtown Manhattan's only public square is undergoing a major renovation in hopes of driving out the drug dealers who appropriated it in recent years. A pavilion-style restaurant is part of the proposed redesign. Book kiosks and a flower stall help draw desirables. There is also a half-price ticket booth for music and dance performances (see ENTERTAINMENT, Tickets: Music & Dance Half-Price Tickets Booth).

Carl Schurz Park
East 84 to East 90 Street, East End Avenue to East River. The site of Gracie Mansion (1799); now the official residence of New York City's mayor (see HISTORIC & NEW NEW YORK, Historic Buildings & Areas). The park, located in Yorkville, the city's German area, is named after Carl Schurz, prominent 19th-century German immigrant who was once a senator and secretary of the interior.

Central Park
59 to 110 Street, Fifth Avenue to Central Park West. America's premiere urban park, an 843-acre oasis, 2 1/2 miles long, 1/2 mile wide, smack in the middle of Manhattan. Farsighted journalist-poet William Cullen Bryant and others saw the need to preserve some country space near the inner city, and in 1858 Frederick Law Olmsted and Calvert Vaux submitted the best plan for how it should be done. The results, a skillful blend of man-made elements: lakes and ponds, hills and dales, secluded glens, wide meadows, a bird sanctuary, bridle paths, ram-

bles, and nature trails. Though large enough to offer serene pockets (the best of them is the Sheep Meadow), in recent years it's become more of a stage for New York's diverse interests, elements, and behavior than a respite from them. Over 16 million people visit and use the park annually. Rowing, jogging, horseback riding, bicycling, ice and roller skating, model-boat sailing, and tennis as well as Shakespeare, Philharmonic and pop concerts, and opera are just some of what is offered (see ANNUAL EVENTS, summer months).

Strawberry Fields, created by Yoko Ono as an International Peace Garden, is the new name of a tear-shaped area near West 72 Street and Central Park West in honor of John Lennon.

Tavern-on-the-Green, originally a sheepfold, now offers meals in elegant surroundings (see RESTAURANTS, Rooms with a View). The refreshment stand at the boathouse serves more traditional park snacks and the Boathouse Cafe provides a sylvan alfresco setting for lunch or dinner (see RESTAURANTS, Rooms with a View). Also try the Mineral Springs at the Sheep Meadow (69 Street) or the Ice Cream Cafe at Conservatory Water (76 Street).

The Park Drive is closed to motor traffic from Friday 7pm till Monday 6am; on legal holidays from 7pm the night before till 6am the morning after, *year-round*. In addition, from late April through October the prohibition extends from Monday to Friday 10am to 3pm and Monday to Thursday 7 to 10pm (exception: entry West 59 & Avenue of the Americas and exit East 72 & Fifth Avenue, closed only 7 to 10pm). NOTE: The first two digits of the number plate of each lamppost in the park indicates the nearest cross street, so you'll never be lost. But if you lose (or find) anything in the park, call the Dairy, 397-3183. (See also SIGHTSEEING, On Your Own: Central Park: The Dairy.)

City Hall Park
Broadway, Park Row & Chambers Street. Known, in colonial times, as the Fields or the Common, it now serves as City Hall's frontyard. Schoolchildren with picnics and office workers with sun visors populate the park in fine weather.

Fort Tryon Park
Riverside Drive to Broadway, West 192 to Dyckman Street. These 66 acres of wooded hills and dales overlooking the Hudson River were a Rockefeller family gift to the City of New York. It was formerly the site of C. K. G. Billings's estate. Fort Tryon, on the site of Fort Washington, the last holdout against the British invasion of Manhattan (it fell November 16, 1776), caps a hill 250 feet above the river. Its beautiful flower gardens and terracing make you feel miles away from the city. The Cloisters (see MUSEUMS & GALLERIES, General Art Museums), located in the park, has a garden with 230 varieties of herbs and plants known before 1520. Parking facilities and a cafeteria.

Gramercy Park
Lexington Avenue, East 20 to East 21 Street. The

land, originally swamp, was bought in 1831 by Samuel B. Ruggles, one of the city's first real estate developers. After it was drained, a private park was created for the exclusive use of those who would buy the surrounding lots. Sixty-six of the city's fashionable elite did just that and no less than golden keys were provided for them to use the park, which was surrounded by an eight-foot fence. Although no longer golden, keys are still needed and used by residents only. It's New York's only surviving private square.

Greenacre Park
East 51 Street between Second & Third Avenues. A 1971 addition to the city's roster of parks. Donated by Mrs. Jean Mauzi, daughter of John D. Rockefeller, Jr., this vest-pocket park provides an oasis of cool, calm visual beauty. Very popular with brown-baggers at lunchtime.

Highbridge Park
West 155 to Dyckman Street, from Edgecombe & Amsterdam Avenues to the Harlem River Drive. Steeply sloped and very rugged terrain at West 174 Street. High Bridge, built in 1842 (originally Aqueduct Bridge), is the oldest remaining bridge connecting Manhattan to the mainland. Originally it carried Croton River water to Manhattan. The Water Tower, built in 1872 to support a 47,000-gallon tank, now houses a carillon that plays from the tower's belfry. There is an imaginative Adventure Playground for children, a large outdoor public swimming pool dating from 1936, and spectacular views of the Harlem River valley.

Inwood Hill Park
Dyckman Street to the Harlem River, from Seaman to Payson Avenue. Algonquin Indians once dwelled in caves on this site; Henry Hudson possibly came ashore here (1609), and during the American Revolution it's where British and Hessian troops were quartered. It's located in a particularly rich historic district, with Dyckman House (1783) nearby (see HISTORIC & NEW NEW YORK, Historic Buildings & Areas, Manhattan). The 196-acre park, rugged, hilly, and densely wooded, contains the largest tulip trees and oldest geological formations in Manhattan and is a truly unspoiled urban wilderness. Added bonus: great views of the Hudson River.

Madison Square Park
East 23 to East 26 Street between Fifth & Madison Avenues. At various times in its history the area was a potter's field, the site of the city's first baseball games (1845), a luxurious residential area, and the site of the original Madison Square Garden (designed by Stanford White, who was shot dead on its roof garden by his lover's jealous husband). There are several splendid sculptures here including the famed one of William H. Seward (see HISTORIC & NEW NEW YORK, Statues & Monuments). The park is now primarily used by office workers from the nearby insurance companies and, unfortunately, drug dealers. Presently undergoing extensive renovation.

Marcus Garvey Memorial Park (formerly Mount Morris Park)
120 to 124 Street at Fifth Avenue. Squarely in the path of Fifth Avenue as it pushed northward in 1835 lay a 70-foot-high rocky eminence unsuitable to build on. Since no public place for "ornamentation and beauty" had yet been laid out in Harlem, the city acquired the property for just such a purpose in 1839. Its height and location made it a natural place to put a fire watchtower, and there it still stands (at 122 Street), the city's last remaining one, built in 1856 of cast iron (see HISTORIC & NEW NEW YORK, Historic Buildings & Areas, Manhattan: Mount Morris Fire Watchtower). The watchman would strike the bell if a fire was sighted, alerting other towers and the volunteer fire companies.

Morningside Park
West 110 to West 123 Street, from Morningside Drive to Manhattan & Morningside Avenues. Planned by Olmsted and Vaux, the architects of Central Park. Located in the Morningside Heights area, it follows the crest of the hills above Harlem. Nearby is the Cathedral of St. John the Divine (see HISTORIC & NEW NEW YORK, Churches & Synagogues). Designs for a multimillion dollar restoration have been completed.

Paley Park (Samuel Paley Plaza)
3 East 53 Street between Fifth & Madison Aves. As unlikely an oasis as one can find in the heart of midtown Manhattan. This vest-pocket park refreshes with just the sight and sound of its 20-foot recycling waterfall. There is a snack stand for hot dogs, coffee, and soft drinks and plenty of places to sit in the shade of 17 locust trees. OPEN May-Oct, Mon-Sat 8am-7pm; Nov-Apr, Mon-Sat 8am-6pm. CLOSED Sun & all of Jan & Feb.

Randalls Island
At the junction of the East & Harlem Rivers. Accessible via the Triborough Bridge. The stadium is the site of pop concerts in the summer and rugby games and track and field meets in spring. (See SPORTS, Sports Activities, Rugby.)

Riverside Park
West 72 to West 159 Street between Riverside Drive & the Hudson River. In the tradition of English landscaping, Frederick Law Olmsted in 1875 met the challenge of this sloping terrain to provide a playground with a view for Upper West Siders. It's the site of several important monuments including Soldiers' and Sailors' Memorial and Grant's Tomb (see HISTORIC & NEW NEW YORK, Statues & Monuments and Historic Buildings & Areas, Manhattan: General Grant National Memorial). A great spot for summer picnics, strolls, and jogging.

Stuyvesant Square
Second Avenue from East 15 to East 17 Street. This historic square, split by the avenue, was part of the farm of Peter Stuyvesant, Dutch governor of Nieuw Amsterdam, and was ceded to the city in 1836 by his great-great grandson. It comprised the core of fashionable New York in the late 19th century and has recently under-

gone a multimillion-dollar restoration. On its west side, St. George's Episcopal Church (1856) and the Friends Meeting House (1860). (*See* HISTORIC & NEW NEW YORK, Churches & Synagogues.) Scene of a spring fair.

Tompkins Square

East 7 to East 10 Street, Avenue A to Avenue B. Sixteen acres of what was originally laid out as a drill ground. It is the oldest park on the Lower East Side, dating from 1834 and named after Gov. Daniel P. Tompkins. In the 60s, the neighborhood became, for a brief but memorable time, haven and mecca for hippies and "flower children." Most recently, an uninviting scene of squalor—squatter shanties, garbage, and drugs. A microcosm of the area's present troubles, it was closed for renovation amid controversy regarding the fate of its homeless residents.

Union Square

East 14 to East 17 Street between Broadway & Park Avenue South. Once fashionable, the garden center of this square was fenced and locked à la Gramercy Park. It then became a commercial area with some of the city's finer shops in residence, Tiffany's among them, but soon became renowned as the scene of large, ofttimes unruly political gatherings—New York's Hyde Park of soapbox oratory. This former center of radicalism now sits amid a budget shopping enclave at the crossroads of a busy intersection on the verge of residential gentrification. Its western and northern edges are the site of a colorful Farmer's Market every Wednesday, Friday, and Saturday. Efforts to reclaim the 3.6-acre park from unsavory elements include a recent $3.6 million restoration.

Wards Island

Connected to Manhattan by a footbridge at East 102 Street & FDR Drive. Farm of the Ward family in the 1780s. A lovely, very rural park coexists on this island with Manhattan State Hospital.

Washington Square Park

At the foot of Fifth Avenue from MacDougal Street to University Place, West 4 Street to Waverly Place. A marshy area that was favored by duck hunters, then a potter's field, and next the site of hanging gallows. In 1828, it became a public park, precipitating the growth of a fashionable residential area. Now it is the emotional if not geographical heart of Greenwich Village. All the diverse elements within the area's boundaries can be found in the park.

The central fountain and recent redesign efforts give it a definite European flavor. Interesting children's play areas and always-in-use chess tables. The city's most diligent Frisbee throwers, skilled roller-dancers, dog walkers, guitar strummers, folk singers, and magicians share the turf with New York University students whose informal campus it has become (the scene of their graduation ceremonies in June). A very lively example of a city park.

Brooklyn

Dyker Beach Park

Shore Parkway, east of the Verrazano Narrows Bridge. A 216.7-acre park adjacent to the Fort Hamilton Military Reservation. Beautiful views of Gravesend Bay and the Verrazano Narrows Bridge. Fine expanses of lawn, sea breezes, and good fishing.

Fort Greene Park

Myrtle to DeKalb Avenue, St. Edward to Washington Park Avenue. The site of Fort Putnam during the Revolutionary War and Fort Greene during the War of 1812. In 1860, the team of Frederick Law Olmsted and Calvert Vaux transformed the 30-acre hill into elegant Washington Park, renamed in 1897. From the hill, the view of Brooklyn and the harbor is spectacular. In the center stands Prison Ship Martyrs' Monument, designed in 1908 by architect Stanford White (see HISTORIC & NEW NEW YORK, Statues & Monuments).

Marine Park

Rockaway Inlet between Gerritsen & Flatbush Avenues inland to Fillmore Avenue between Burnet & East 32 Streets. The park covers 798 acres.

Prospect Park

Flatbush, Ocean & Parkside Avenues, Prospect Park West, Prospect Park Southwest. Olmsted and Vaux's ode to Brooklyn (1866-74), covering 526 acres, has remained very much as they conceived it: broad meadows, gardens, terraces, and landscaped walks. Now in the midst of a 20-year, $200 million renovation to undo years of neglect of the park's formal structures. The main entrance to the park is Grand Army Plaza, planned in the spirit of L'Etoile in Paris, with its neo-Roman Soldiers' and Sailors' Arch, a Civil War memorial to the Union Army. Prominent among its attractions: a zoo (now undergoing redesign); the Palladian-style boathouse (1905); the Croquet Shelter, a fine classical structure designed by Stanford White; the Camperdown Elm, near the boathouse, designed by Mother Nature; and the Lefferts Homestead (1783) (*see* HISTORIC & NEW NEW YORK, Historic Buildings & Areas, Brooklyn). Activities in the park include riding, ice skating, row boating, and concerts. Nearby are the treasured Brooklyn Botanical Gardens (*see* Botanical Gardens), the Main Branch of the Brooklyn Public Library, and the well-respected Brooklyn Museum (*see* MUSEUMS & GALLERIES, General Art Museums).

Bronx

Many of what are now Bronx parks were once the private estates of prominent families.

Bronx Park

Bronx Park East & Brady Avenue. This park's 718 acres contain the New York Botanical Garden. Patterned after England's Kew Gardens, it occupies 240 acres in the park's northern extremity. Some wild and beautiful land is contained within its boundaries, including a virgin hemlock forest and the Bronx River Gorge. Another 252 acres are reserved for the animal inhabitants of the New York Zoological Park (the Bronx Zoo), opened 1899. Over 3,500 animals live in indoor and outdoor settings as close to their natural habitat as possible. Parking and cafeteria facilities. (*See* Zoos & Aquariums.)

Crotona Park
Fulton Avenue & East 175 Street. Formerly the estate of the Bathgate family known as Bathgate Woods, it was named after the ancient Greek city of Croton. Selected as a park site in 1883. The Play Center contains a bathhouse and pool dating back to the 1930s. The 142-acre park has its own Urban Park Ranger program. For information, call 589-0096.

Pelham Bay Park
East of Bruckner Boulevard & Middletown Road. The largest (2,764 acres) and one of the more versatile of New York City parks. Some relics of the past include Rice Memorial Stadium (1916) and the Bartow-Pell Mansion (*see* HISTORIC & NEW NEW YORK, Historic Buildings & Areas, Bronx). In addition, there are bridle paths; the Police Department's firing range; two golf courses (*see* SPORTS, Golf, Municipal Golf Courses); Orchard Beach, with bathhouse and cafeteria (*see* Beaches); as well as some natural wildlife-preserve areas.

Van Cortlandt Park
West 242 Street to city line between Broadway & Jerome Avenue. August Van Cortlandt, city clerk when the British occupied New York in 1776, is said to have hidden the municipal records in the family vault. It and the Van Cortlandt family mansion occupy a corner in the eastern end of the park (*see* HISTORIC & NEW NEW YORK, Historic Buildings & Areas, Bronx). Activities include cross-country skiing in winter and swimming and tennis in summer (*see* SPORTS).

Queens

Alley Pond Park
Grand Central Parkway, Northern Boulevard at 233 Street, Bayside. The "alley" was a row of 18th-century commercial buildings, including a gristmill and a general store. A nearby lake was then named Alley Pond. The buildings are long gone, but the parkland retains the name—135 acres of highlands, ponds, marsh, trees, and an amazing array of wildlife. On the northern boundary, the Alley Pond Environmental Center.

Astoria Park
Between 19 Street & the East River from Hoyt Avenue to Ditmars Boulevard, Astoria. Picnickers can get a great view of the Manhattan skyline. The Astoria Play Center and swimming pool; tennis, too.

Cunningham Park
193 to 210 Street, Long Island Expressway to Grand Central Parkway, Bayside. This large park offers a myriad of events and activities. In the summer months there are concerts by the New York Philharmonic plus opera and jazz. Volley-

ball courts, softball fields, tennis (indoor and outdoor), boccie courts, and picnic grounds.

Flushing Meadows–Corona Park
Union Turnpike from 111 Street & Grand Central Parkway to the Van Wyck Extension, Flushing. This 1,257-acre park has had a Cinderella history. Originally a swamp, then a garbage dump, the area was chosen as the site for the 1939 New York World's Fair. From 1946 to 1949, the United Nations General Assembly met here, and in 1964-65, it was again the site of a World's Fair. It has now become a complete recreation and entertainment park: tennis, golf, swimming, roller skating, boating, bicycling, ice skating (*see* SPORTS), the Queens Museum, the New York Hall of Science (*see* MUSEUMS & GALLERIES, General Art Museums *and* Science Museums), the Queens Botanical Garden, Queens Zoo & Children's Farm (*see* Botanical Gardens *and* Zoos & Aquariums), and an antique carousel. Also here, the Unisphere, symbol of the 1964 World's Fair.

Staten Island

Clove Lakes Park
1150 Clove Road near Victory Blvd, Sunnyside. A popular and picturesque park covering 195.25 acres. Among its unexpected delights: a brook, a waterfall, and a small lake with rowboats, providing picnickers with bucolic settings. For the more active there are facilities for ice skating, horseback riding, football, softball, jogging, bicycle riding, and fishing (*see* SPORTS). In summer, the New York Philharmonic and Metropolitan Opera concerts are held here (*see* ANNUAL EVENTS, June *and* July).

Latourette Park in the Greenbelt
Forest Hill & Richmond Hill Roads, Richmondtown. This 511-acre park features a beautiful golf course and clubhouse—once the farmland and mansion of the Latourette family—as well as wooded and uninterrupted wetland trails, the most notable of which is *Buck's Hollow*. Also, bridle paths (*see* SPORTS) and lovely picnic areas. (*See also* Nature Trails & Wildlife Preserves: Staten Island Greenbelt.)

Silver Lake Park
Hart Boulevard & Revere Street, Silver Lake. Children's play areas, a golf course, and a wide variety of recreational activities, including tennis, Ping-Pong, and rowing, on 209 acres (*see* SPORTS).

Von Briesen Park
Bay Street & Wadsworth Avenue, Fort Wadsworth. A meticulously groomed city park. Its elevated harbor-front location provides a stunning aerial view of lower Manhattan, both bays, and Brooklyn. A good picnic spot.

Willowbrook Park in the Greenbelt
Victory Boulevard & Richmond Avenue, Bull's Head. There are ample picnic facilities in this lovely 164-acre park popular with its lake with fishing for children, athletic fields, archery range, and horseshoe pitches (*see* SPORTS). Its exten-

sive wetland area was called Great Swamp when American patriots hid there during the Revolutionary War. (*See also* Nature Trails & Wildlife Preserves: Staten Island Greenbelt.)

BOTANICAL GARDENS

Biblical Garden
Cathedral of St. John the Divine, West 112 Street & Amsterdam Avenue. 316-7400. On the grounds of this grand Gothic cathedral, a 1/4-acre garden where only plants mentioned in the Bible are grown. Garden & Church: *OPEN 7 days 7am-5pm.* FREE. (*See also* HISTORIC & NEW NEW YORK, Churches & Synagogues.)

Brooklyn Botanical Garden
1000 Washington Avenue near Empire Blvd, Brooklyn. (718) 622-4433. Founded in 1910 on the site of a city dump; 50 acres of land heavily planted with the greatest variety of trees and bushes. The largest and one of the finest displays of Japanese flowering cherry trees in America as well as an unparalleled exhibition of bonsai trees. There are beautifully designed and serene Japanese Gardens (early April to late October; nominal admission); a wonderful display of magnolias in the spring; a medicinal herb garden; the Fragrance Garden, a unique garden for the blind; one of the country's largest public rose collections; a Shakespeare Garden with 80 plants cited in the Bard's works; and a local flora section featuring a 25-acre sampling of the ecology within a 100-mile radius of the city. The spectacular new Steinhardt Conservatory complex, for tropical plants and bonsai (admission charge). *OPEN Apr-Sept, Tues-Fri 8am-6pm, weekends & holidays 10am-6pm; Oct-Mar, Tues-Sat 8am-4:30pm. CLOSED Mon (unless Mon holiday).* FREE.

Channel Gardens
Rockefeller Center, enter Fifth Avenue between West 49 & West 50 Streets. A gently sloped and fountained space whose name is derived from its position between the French (La Maison Française) and English (British Empire Building) Pavilion buildings. Its beauty is usually a reflection of the season; especially dazzling are the Easter lilies in April and the Christmas display complementing the giant Rockefeller Center tree. The scene of concerts and musical performances in summer (*see* ANNUAL EVENTS, June). FREE.

Conservatory Garden
Central Park at Fifth Avenue & 105 Street. 397-3150. Established in 1937, four acres of English perennial gardens firmly, albeit almost secretly, ensconced in Central Park. These harmoniously designed gardens form an oasis within an oasis. Opening onto the main lawn is the handsome wrought-iron Vanderbilt Gate; it's a popular spot for wedding portraits. *OPEN 7 days 7:30am-4:30pm.* FREE.

Jefferson Market Garden
Greenwich Avenue at West 9 Street. Determined Greenwich Villagers planted this formal English garden on the site of the old Women's House of Detention. The fence is an unfortunate necessity but it is *OPEN to the public Sat & Sun 1-5pm.* FREE.

New York Botanical Garden
Bronx Park between Bedford Park Boulevard & Mosholu Parkway, Bronx. 220-8777 (recorded) for directions; 220-8700. This 250-acre garden, founded in 1891, was patterned after the Royal Botanical Gardens at Kew, England. Every season is spectacular here. The rose garden has 700 bushes of 400 different varieties; there is a magnolia dell, an azalea glen (spectacular in May), a pine grove, a rock garden (April to October; admission charge), and much more. The Museum Building houses an exhibit hall devoted to ecological and environmental studies, as well as a large botanical library, auditorium, and the Herbarium with dried plant specimens. The recently restored Enid Haupt Conservatory, a 90-foot central Palm Court rotunda with ten connecting greenhouses, is a glass paradise housing exotic desert plants, a medieval herb garden, a fun forest, and more. A restored 1840 Snuff Mill now serves as a cafe for modest-priced lunches and a terrace overlooking the Bronx River. Garden *OPEN year-round 7 days sunrise to sunset.* Conservatory *Tues-Sun 10am-4pm.* FREE admission to grounds, but there is a parking fee. Groups must reserve four weeks in advance, call 220-6775.

Peace Garden
Main public entrance, United Nations, First Avenue at East 46 Street. Adjacent to the UN headquarters, 12 acres of formal rose plantings overlooking the East River. Hybrid tea roses or prolific floribunda. Japanese cherry blossoms in May. *OPEN 7 days 9:30am-4:45pm.* FREE.

Queens Botanical Garden
43-50 Main Street, east end of Flushing Meadows–Corona Park, Flushing, Queens. (718) 886-3800. Thirty-nine acres of flora. Completely outdoors, so visits are very much a seasonal matter. In September, 10,000 chrysanthemums are in bloom; in April, 250,000 tulips put in an appearance. There is also a specialty garden to attract birds and a labeled vegetable garden. Free parking. *OPEN May-Sept, Tues-Sun 10am-7pm; Oct-Apr, Tues-Sun 10am-5pm. CLOSED Mon.* FREE.

St. John's in the Village
Waverly Place & West 11 Street. Enter garden through the church office, 224 Waverly Place. A lovely, peaceful garden. *OPEN after Sunday services & weekdays 9am-5pm.*

Shakespeare Garden
Central Park, south of Delacorte Theater near West 80 Street. There has been a Shakespeare Garden in the park since 1912. This one dates from 1936. Seeds and cuttings from the same mulberry and hawthorne trees Shakespeare himself once tended in his own Stratford-on-Avon garden formed the basis of the garden. Now tended by volunteers, Shakespearean blossoms

and Elizabethan herbs bloom once more. Pools, a bust of the Bard, and annual flowers provide a peaceful setting.

Staten Island Botanical Garden

Richmondtown Terrace from Tysen Street to Kissel Avenue, Livingston, Staten Island. (718) 273-8200. The Staten Island Botanical Garden lies within Snug Harbor Cultural Center's 80 acres. It includes an English perennial garden, formal annuals displays, a tropical and orchid greenhouse, and community fruit and vegetable garden. Tours by appointment. Classes, horticulture lectures, and workshops. *OPEN year-round 7 days 9am-4pm.*

BEACHES

Manhattan is the only one of the five boroughs that does not have a beach. Though much sunbathing goes on in Manhattan during summer, it is usually done on rooftops, affectionately known as a "tar beach"; on river piers, known as "splinter beach;" and in the parks, especially Central Park's Sheep Meadow. The other four boroughs are blessed with miles and miles of beaches, all easily accessible by bus, subway, or car. City beaches are officially open from Memorial Day weekend to Labor Day, sunrise to midnight, with swimming allowed 10am to 6:30pm, when lifeguards are on duty.

Brighton Beach

Brighton 15th Street to Ocean Parkway, Brooklyn. This is actually the "beginning" of the beach that due west becomes Coney Island. At this end you'll find locals: mothers with children, older retired folks, and Russians who have emigrated to this shore, now commonly referred to as "Little Odessa." The boardwalk has little but benches, so bring your lunch or buy it at a local deli on your way. As either warning or blessing: It has none of the honky-tonk atmosphere of Coney Island. The best entertainment here is the people; and it's only a short subway ride from Manhattan.

Coney Island Beach

From Ocean Parkway to West 37 Street, Brooklyn. (718) 946-1350. Originally called Rabbit Island after its only inhabitants, Coney Island, from the Dutch *Konijn Eiland*, began its resort days in the 1830s. At that time elegant hotels drew the elite. It evolved into a more popular entertainment area with the coming of the first roller coaster in 1884. A mere shadow of its former incarnations, against a backdrop of crumbling poverty, it still has a fine 2½-mile-long sandy beach and a boardwalk over 2 miles long with everything you would expect to find at a beach resort, from cotton candy to bumper cars. Hot summer days have drawn as many as a million people to Coney Island, which at times makes it a bit difficult to find a place in the sun without stepping on someone else's blanket. Still a must for Brooklyn color: Nathan's on Surf and Stillwell

avenues, a hot dog never tasted so good. There are many who feel the time is right for Coney's revival; let's hope so.

Great Kills Park

Hylan Boulevard & Hopkins Avenue, Great Kills, Staten Island. (718) 351-8700. The beach is part of Gateway National Recreation Area.

Manhattan Beach

Ocean Avenue between Oriental Boulevard & MacKenzie Street, Brooklyn. (718) 946-1373. This small beach, only three-tenths of a mile long, draws a young ethnically mixed crowd. There are changing rooms available and adjacent to the beach is a park with barbecue facilities as well as handball, tennis, and basketball.

Orchard Beach

Shore Road & City Island Road, Bronx. 885-2275. Popular beach on the East Shore of Pelham Bay Park fronts onto Long Island Sound. Cafeteria and changing rooms.

Riis Park

Beach 149 to Beach 169 Street, Queens. (718) 474-4600. Operated by the National Park Service as part of the Gateway National Recreation Area. There is a boardwalk for strolling and a mile-long sandy beach. Other facilities include handball, paddle tennis, shuffleboard. There are ample parking facilities as well as lockers and refreshments.

Rockaway Beach

Beach First Street to Beach 109 Street, Beach 126 to Beach 149 Street, Queens. (718) 318-4000. Nearly 10 miles of glorious sandy beach and 7½ miles of boardwalk fronting on the Atlantic form the core of this recreational area.

South & Midland Beach

Fort Wadsworth to Miller Field, New Dorp, Staten Island. On 638 acres. A 7,500-foot-long boardwalk, fishing, swimming, shuffleboard, and entertainment. Dressing rooms and parking facilities available.

Wolf's Pond Park

Holton to Cornelia Avenue on Raritan Bay, Prince's Bay, Staten Island. Not only saltwater swimming, but a wooded area and a lake offer fishing and rustic picnic settings.

Long Island Beaches

The Long Island Tourism Commission can provide any information needed on Long Island beaches, call (516) 794-4222.

Jones Beach State Park

Wantagh, Long Island. (516) 785-1600. On Long Island's south shore, 6½ miles of white sand beach fronting the Atlantic Ocean. One of the most beautiful and complete state parks. Parking facilities, cafeterias, boardwalk, dancing, theater, miniature golf, fishing, and bay, pool, or ocean swimming. Buses from Port Authority Bus Terminal and the Long Island Rail Road's trainbus service provide direct access. *OPEN Memorial Day-Labor Day.*

ZOOS & AQUARIUMS

(For Children's Zoos, see KIDS' NEW YORK.*)*
*All animals in the Central Park, Prospect Park,
and Queens zoos are given names. Although the
selection process is informal, there are some
traditions—for example, hippopotamus babies
in Central Park are always named for
Shakespearean characters.*

Bronx Zoo

Fordham Road & Bronx River Parkway, Bronx.
367-1010 (recorded); 220-5100. An extensive
265-acre zoological park (the world's largest urban zoo), it opened in 1899. Always considered
one of the world's best zoos, in recent years it's
become even better. Although the older buildings still house animals in indoor cages and exhibits, the real excitement and adventure comes
from seeing the animals roam in spacious simulated natural habitats, in some cases only a
moat away from visitors. The African Plains and
Lion Island are special treats. The Skyfari tramway (from April to October) affords an aerial
view. Not to be missed: the World of Birds, a
tropical rain forest home, complete with thunder-
storms each day at 2pm, for over 100 species;
and the World of Darkness, where nocturnal animals are awake in an artificially reversed night
for day. Wild Asia (from April to October), seen
from a 2-mile journey on the Bengali Express, a
slow-moving monorail, offers Asian elephants
and Siberian tigers living as if in the Asian heart-
land. The 2 1/2-acre Himalayan Highlands habitat, with 17 resident snow leopards, is a must-
see. There's also a Children's Zoo and camel
rides (from May to October) (*see* KIDS' NEW
YORK, Zoos & Animal Preserves). Zoo *OPEN
Feb-Oct, Mon-Sat 10am-5pm, Sun & holidays
10am-5:30pm; Nov-Jan, 7 days 10am-4:30pm.*
Admission charge from Friday to Monday; lower
for children under age 12. Tuesday, Wednesday, and Thursday FREE. Senior citizens free all
times. Friends of the Zoo (FOZ), 220-5141, offers free guided tours to the public on weekends
by appointment. All children under age 16 must
be accompanied by an adult. Leave radios and
pets home. Parking free; membership available.

Central Park Zoo

Central Park, East 64 Street & Fifth Avenue.
861-6030. Much of America's oldest zoo has
been demolished (several of the WPA-era
buildings have been restored) and a more
modern, more humane habitat has taken its
place. The new zoo is under the auspices of
the well-respected New York Zoological Society. There are polar bears in a glass-enclosed
pool, penguins in an arctic exhibit, prairie
dogs, and alligators, and the sea lions are in
their same old spot. *OPEN Apr-Oct, Mon-Fri
10am-5pm (May-Sept, Tues till 8 pm), Sat &
Sun & holidays 10am-5:30pm; Nov-Mar, 7 days
10am-4pm.* Last ticket sold half an hour before
closing time. Admission charge. Children under
age 16 must be accompanied by an adult.

New York Aquarium

Surf Avenue & West 8 Street, Coney Island,
Brooklyn. (718) 265-3474. Nearly 2500 sea creatures reside within view of the Atlantic Ocean at
Coney Island. Indoor and outdoor pools hold
seals, whales, dolphins, penguins, sea lions, pi-
ranhas, sharks, electric eels, and turtles. Feeding time is fun time here and from late April to
mid-October the bottlenose dolphins star in a
20-minute show, and there is a 10-minute sea
lion training session. *OPEN Sept-May, 7 days
10am-4:45pm; Memorial Day-Labor Day, Sat,
Sun & holidays 10am-5:45pm.* Admission
charge; senior citizens free after 2 pm weekdays
(except holidays). Group rates available, call
(718) 266-8540. Parking fee. Restaurant, snack
bar, outdoor picnic facilities, and gift shop.

Prospect Park Zoo

Empire Boulevard & Flatbush Avenue, Brooklyn.
Closed for renovation, will reopen in 1993.

Queens Zoo & Children's Farm

Flushing Meadows–Corona Park, 111 Street at
54 Avenue, Flushing, Queens. (718) 699-7239.
A large but not heavily populated zoo. There's a
natural habitat of North American wildlife and a
walk-thru aviary. The 47-acre farm provides the
most entertainment, especially for the kids.
OPEN year-round 7 days 10am-3:45pm. FREE.
(*See also* KIDS' NEW YORK, Zoos & Animal Preserves: Queens County Farm Museum.)

Staten Island Zoological Park

Barrett Park, 614 Broadway near Forrest Ave,
West Brighton, Staten Island. (718) 422-3100.
This small and highly unusual zoo has on exhibit
all 32 species of rattlesnake. It's the largest collection in the world and, what's more, all fangs
are still intact. In addition to the rattlers, there are
scorpions, Madagascan cockroaches, alligators, crocodiles, and snapping turtles, along with
the more usual zoo residents. Free parking.
OPEN year-round 7 days 10am-4:45pm. Admission charge; children under age 3, senior citizens, and handicapped free. Wednesday FREE
for everyone.

NATURE TRAILS & WILDLIFE PRESERVES

*In addition to those listed here, there are nature
trails in Kissena Park in Queens, Marine Park in
Brooklyn, and Van Cortlandt Park in the Bronx.*

William T. Davis Wildlife Refuge

Travis Avenue off Richmond Avenue, Travis,
Staten Island. Named for noted Staten Island
naturalist William Thompson Davis. These 260
acres of dry and wetland attract many rarely
seen birds, and its wide variety of habitats makes
it an ideal wildlife sanctuary. Trail guides are
available from the Staten Island Greenbelt, call
(718) 667-2165, *Mon-Fri 9am-5pm.* FREE.

Gateway National Recreation Area

Office: Floyd Bennett Field, Building 69, Brooklyn. (718) 338-3338. The first national park within

an urban setting. The area consists of 26,000 acres of land divided into four units: Staten Island (718-351-8700), includes the Great Kills Park beaches; Jamaica Bay, Queens (718-474-3799), includes the Jamaica Bay Wildlife Refuge; Breezy Point, Queens (718-474-4600), includes Jacob Riis Park and Beach; and Sandy Hook, N.J. (201-872-0115). There is a variety of free programs and happenings. Call for information. FREE.

High Rock Park at the Greenbelt
200 Nevada Avenue near Richmond Road & Rockland Avenue, Egbertville, Staten Island. (718) 667-2165. Ninety-two acres of natural hardwood forest, glacial ponds, and freshwater swamp to explore. Ongoing environmental education programs, workshops, and tours year-round. Great bird-watching area, best in April. *OPEN year-round 7 days 9am-5pm.* FREE.

Hunter Island Marine Zoology & Geology Sanctuary
Pelham Bay Park, north end of Orchard Beach, Bronx. A wooded rocky area of geological interest, plus dry, marshy, and underwater areas. Beautiful; popular with picnickers. FREE.

Inwood Hill Park
West 207 Street & Seaman Avenue. Three nature trails totaling one mile. Tree identification signs, trail-side displays, and Indian caves. FREE.

Jamaica Bay Wildlife Refuge
Cross Bay Boulevard between Howard Beach & Broad Channel, Jamaica, Queens. (718) 474-0613. The preserve's 2,868 acres of wetlands and uplands, carved out of Jamaica Bay's 16,000 acres, is reserved for nature walks and bird-watching. One trail, 1¾ miles long, runs around the West Pond. Over 300 species of land and waterfowl have been sighted, including ibis, egret, and eagles (best watching: May). Weekend exhibits, slide presentations, guide walks. Visitor's Center *OPEN Mon-Fri 8:30am-5pm; Sat 8am-5pm; Sun 8am-6pm. CLOSED Christmas & New Year's Day.* Permit necessary from Visitor's Center. FREE.

Thomas Pell Wildlife Refuge
Pelham Bay Park, Hutchinson River Parkway & Bartow Avenue, Bronx. Along the shoreline, a swampy and a wooded area. Popular spot for bird-watching. FREE.

Staten Island Greenbelt
(718) 667-2165. Located in central Staten Island, the Greenbelt is a contiguous expanse of approximately 2,500 acres. It is primarily a nature preserve with unique woodlands, wetlands, and open fields, providing a habitat for native wildlife and an inviting rest stop for many migratory birds. There are special programs throughout the year including bird-watching, hiking, cross-country skiing. The circular marked trail covering 28 miles is of much geological interest. Hardwood forest and glacial kettles, ponds formed by the last of the great glaciers.

Wave Hill Center for Environmental Studies
Main entrance West 249 Street & Independence Avenue, Riverdale, Bronx. 549-2055. The former 28-acre estate of conservation-minded financier George Perkins and at various times home to Theodore Roosevelt, Mark Twain, Arturo Toscanini, and the United Kingdom's ambassador to the UN. Perkins's descendants gave it to the city in 1960 to be used as a nonprofit center for the study of environmental sciences. It commands a magnificent view of the Hudson and the Palisades and there are nature trails, including a 1½-mile marked trail, greenhouses, and exquisite herb, wildflower, and aquatic gardens. A myriad of activities available including workshops, concerts, slide lectures, special events. Gardens *OPEN Sept-June, 7 days 10am-4:30pm; July & Aug, Mon, Tues & Thurs-Sat 10am-5:30pm, Wed 10am-dusk, Sun 10am-7pm. CLOSED Christmas & New Year's Day.* FREE except weekends. Memberships available. Lower for senior citizens; children under age 14 free.

BIRD-WATCHING

(*See also* Nature Trails & Wildlife Preserves.)

Rare Bird Alert
832-6523. A recorded service available 24 hours a day, 7 days a week, listing up-to-the-minute information on rare and interesting birds that have been sighted in the area.

American Museum of Natural History
Central Park West at 77 Street. 873-1300. Visits to Central Park, which is on one of the main bird migratory lines, for bird-watching during the times of heaviest movement. Call for information.

Brooklyn Botanical Garden
1000 Washington Avenue near Crown St, Brooklyn. (718) 622-4433 (Education Dept.). The garden is in the flyway of the Atlantic migration and a course is offered in both spring and fall for fledgling bird-watchers. For information, call *Mon-Fri 9am-4:30pm.*

High Rock in the Greenbelt
200 Nevada Avenue, Staten Island (10306). (718) 667-2165. This great bird-watching area has special programs, walks, and workshops year-round. Get on their mailing list; call or write. *OPEN year-round 7 days 9am-5pm.*

Linnaean Society of New York
15 West 77 Street, New York (10024). Active group founded in 1878, for amateurs and professionals. Open to all with interest in ornithology. There are meetings held at the American Museum of Natural History, local and long-distance field trips, a monthly newsletter. Write for more information.

New York Botanical Garden
Bronx Park, Bronx Park East & Brady Avenue. 220-8747. Spring and fall, a course given on different species of birds that can be seen in and around New York City. Guided field trips, mainly

for beginners. Call for information, *Mon-Thurs 9am-9pm, Fri 9am-5pm, Sat & Sun 9am-2pm.*

Queens County Bird Club
Queens Botanical Garden, 43-50 Main Street at Dalia St, Flushing, Queens. (718) 939-6224. An active club offering single or family membership. There are monthly meetings (third Wednesday, except July and August) and field trips all year (except July). New birders always welcome.

KIDS'
NEW YORK

Alice in Wonderland Statue, Central Park

SEEING NEW YORK

Here are some fun things to do with kids in the city. For more of New York's traditional attractions, see also: SIGHTSEEING, HISTORIC & NEW NEW YORK, *and* ANNUAL EVENTS *for parades, fairs, and festivals—many of which are* FREE.

Belvedere Castle
Central Park, West 79 Street, south of the Great Lawn. 772-0210. The restored castle is now the Central Park Learning Center as well as a station for the National Weather Service. In the Discovery Chamber learn about the park through activities and games. Gift shop with books and natural history items. *OPEN Tues-Thurs, Sat & Sun 9am-4pm, Fri 1-5pm; in spring and summer, Tues-Sun till 5pm.*

Carousel
Central Park, midway at 64 Street. 879-0244. Have a 3-minute whirl on a lovely elegantly carved antique merry-go-round. *OPEN year-round (weather permitting) Mon-Fri 10:30am-4:30pm; Sat & Sun 10:30am-5:45pm; Thanksgiving Day-mid-March weekends only.* Minimal charge.

Circle Line Cruise
Circle Line Plaza, West 42 Street & the Hudson River. 563-2000. A 3-hour, 35-mile circumnavigation of Manhattan Island with informative and ofttimes entertaining narration. Junk-food snack bar on board or bring a lunch. *Mid-Mar-mid-Nov, 7 days. Sailings every 45 minutes 9:45am-*

5:50pm. Call for schedule. Half price for children under age 12. AE, MC, V.

Empire State Building
350 Fifth Avenue at 34 St. 736-3100. The 86th-floor observation deck has an outside terrace for a broader view, the 102nd floor is enclosed. On clear days you can almost see forever. *OPEN 7 days 9:30am-midnight (last ticket sold 11:25pm).* Admission charge; lower for children age 5-11; children under age 5 free. Combine with a visit to the Guinness World Records Exhibit in the building's lobby (see below).

Federal Reserve Bank
33 Liberty Street near William St. 720-6130. For age 15 and up: a one-hour educational tour of the central banking operation, including a visit to the gold vault, where the world's largest known accumulation of that precious metal is stored. Call or write c/o Public Information for reservations at least a week in advance. *Tours: Mon-Fri 10:30 & 11:30am, 1:30 & 2:30pm.* FREE.

Guinness World Records Exhibit Hall
Empire State Building, 350 Fifth Avenue at 34 St, concourse level. 947-2335. Displays, models, film clips of record breakers: the world's smallest book, largest guitar, etc. Allow 45 minutes to see it all. *OPEN 7 days 9am-8pm (weekends in summer and during Christmas till 10pm).* Admission charge; lower for children age 5-11; children under age 5 free. Group rates available.

InfoQuest Center
AT&T Building, arcade, Madison Avenue at East 56 Street. 605-5555. An awesome new attrac-

tion. Take the glass elevator to the 4th floor for a permanent exhibition dedicated to the technology of the Information Age. Upon entry stop at the InfoGuide for a description of what you are about to visit. There are 40 interactive exhibits on three levels affording insight into the wonders and joys of fiber optics, computer software, and microelectronics. Sounds serious but it's great fun. Program a robot, direct a music video, scramble your face, see your voice and picture transmitted on the fiber-optic videophone, tour New York in a video-taxi and there's more. See a 10-minute laserdisc presentation on a 300-square-foot screen in the auditorium. Best for age 5 and older; children under age 12 must be accompanied by an adult. Groups must reserve in advance, call 605-5140. *OPEN Tues 10am-9pm; Wed-Sun 10am-6pm.* FREE.

Model Yachts
Central Park, Conservatory Water near 76 Street & Fifth Avenue. Sail your own model boat or watch most Saturdays, from 10am to 4pm, as the Central Park Model Yacht Club races magnificent radio-controlled sailboats. FREE.

Post Office
Tours of local post offices can be arranged by writing or calling the Manager of Communications, New York Post Office, J.A.F. Building, room 3023, New York, NY 10199-9641; 330-3604. Children age 5-12 visit only nonmechanized locations; children over age 12 are able to tour mechanized stations; in both cases an adult must accompany the child. FREE.

Roosevelt Island Tramway
Second Avenue at East 60 Street. 832-4555. A brief (4-minute) but exciting ride in an aerial car, 200 feet above Second Avenue and then the East River, to Roosevelt Island. Yes, getting there is all the fun—turn around and come right back. *Every 15 minutes on the quarter hour, 7 days 6am-2am.* Subway tokens required; children under age 6 ride free.

Rowing
Loeb Boathouse. Enter Central Park at East 72 Street. 517-2233. Rent an aluminum rowboat and spend a lovely day on Central Park Lake. Weather permitting *Apr-Sept, 7 days 10-5pm.* Limit four people to a boat and one must be age 16 or older. (Life preservers are supplied.) Hourly fee plus a refundable $20 deposit. Adjacent to the lovely outdoor Boathouse Cafe (*see* RESTAURANTS, Rooms with a View) and a lower-priced snack bar.

Staten Island Ferry
In Manhattan: at the foot of Whitehall Street at Battery Park; 806-6940. In Staten Island: at the foot of Bay Street, St. George; (718) 727-2508. It's no longer a nickel, but this 25-minute boat ride across Upper New York Bay is still New York's premier bargain. Wonderful views, a cooling breeze in summer, a snack bar on board, and it costs only a penny a minute (each way). *24 hours a day, 7 days a week. Weekends, every 30 minutes; weekdays, every 15 minutes during rush hours, other times*

every 20 to 30 minutes; in the wee hours, every hour.

Statue of Liberty
Circle Line Statue of Liberty Ferry, Battery Park. 269-5755; 363-3200 (about the Statue). The famed Lady has undergone a much-needed restoration in honor of her 100th birthday and a visit to this revered monument is more thrilling than ever. Allow 2 hours for the visit, but if you want to ascend the crown the wait may be anywhere from 2 to 4 hours. (Expect to wait most weekends, all holidays, and the whole summer.) *Boats leave 7 days 9:10am-4pm every 1/2 hour (there are more frequent sailings in fine weather).* Fare for the round-trip boat ride is half price for children under age 17. NOTE: For school groups there must be one chaperone for every 10 children. The Island itself is *OPEN 7 days 9:30am-5pm.* Admission to the island and the statue are FREE.

MUSEUMS FOR CHILDREN

Also included are general museums with special attractions for children.

American Museum of Natural History
Central Park West at West 79 Street. 769-5100 or -5315 (recorded). A vast complex of exhibit halls, most of which are of interest to children. It's such a wonder-filled place you will return again and again. Special: "The Discovery Room," open year-round except one month in summer, involves learning through use of discovered touchable items in a box. For children over age 5 accompanied by an adult; tickets given out on first-come basis at 11:45am at the first-floor information desk (accommodates 25 children). In "The Natural Science Center" children learn about plants, animals, and rocks found in New York City. In the Naturemax Theatre, movies are shown on a four-story-high screen daily from 10:30am (separate admission). Museum *OPEN Sun-Tues & Thurs 10am-5:45pm; Wed, Fri & Sat 10am-9pm. CLOSED only Thanksgiving & Christmas Day.* Suggested donation.

Aunt Len's Doll & Toy Museum
6 Hamilton Terrace between St. Nicholas & Convent Avenues. 926-4172; 281-4143. What began as a hobby for Lenon Holder Hoyte (now a youthful 85) became a museum. Four delightful rooms in a Harlem brownstone house, her very own collection of over 5,000 antique dolls, dollhouses and accessories, miniatures, and toys. She and the museum are a delight. *OPEN by appointment only.* Admission charge.

Brooklyn Children's Museum
145 Brooklyn Avenue at St. Mark's Ave, Crown Heights, Brooklyn. (718) 735-4400 or -4432 (recorded information). Established in 1899 as the world's first museum for children, it's an environment geared to learning through discovery. Children are involved in entertaining and interactive

activities, crafts handling, and the operating of museum displays. There are films, workshops, and more than 40,000 objects to involve and inform the child. A treat for all ages. Membership available. NOTE: The following are reduced hours due to budget cuts; they are hopefully temporary. *OPEN Wed-Fri 2pm-5pm; Sat & Sun noon-5pm. CLOSED Mon & Tues, except school holidays.* Suggested donation.

Brooklyn Museum
188 Eastern Parkway, Brooklyn. (718) 638-5000. "What's Up?": Through storytelling and art-making with simple materials, children (unaccompanied) age 8-12 learn at each class about a different one of the museum's collections. *Sat & Sun at 2pm.* "Arty Facts": Children age 4-7 accompanied by an adult meet in the Grand Lobby for monthly themes, parties, and participatory activities that make the museum's art and artifacts come to life. *Sat & Sun 11am-12:30pm.* No reservation necessary: Simply arrive 15 minutes before the start. All during the year there are events for parents and children that are FREE. The **Kids Mart**, a shop for unusual toys and other finds. Museum *OPEN Wed-Sun 10am-5pm. CLOSED Mon & Tues, Thanksgiving, Christmas & New Year's Day.* Suggested contribution.

Children's Museum of Manhattan
212 West 83 Street (off Amsterdam Avenue). 721-1234. In a wonderful old four-story building, a kid's-eye view with the focus on nature, culture, and perception. A colorful place for children to have fun and learn about the world around them through participatory events. Special Saturday workshops for age 4-12, among many other unique programs; call for specifics. Advance reservations are required for school groups. *OPEN Mon, Wed, Thurs & Fri 1-5pm; Sat & Sun 10am-5pm. CLOSED Tues.* Admission charge.

Chinese Museum
8 Mott Street near Chatham Sq. 964-1542. Chinese antiques, coins, musical instruments, temple artifacts, and an 18-foot-long Chinese dragon that lights up. Only worth a visit if you're dining in Chinatown. *OPEN 7 days 10am-6pm.* Admission charge (a bit steep for what you get).

Energy Museum
145 East 14 Street. 460-6244. Hands-on exhibits depicting the age of electricity—past, present, and future. Fun, educational, and nostalgic. Groups by appointment only. *OPEN Tues-Sat 10am-4pm.* FREE.

Forbes Magazine Galleries
62 Fifth Avenue at 12 St. 620-2389. A unique gallery of Forbes family collectibles including 12,000 toy soldiers and hundreds of toy boats, wonderfully displayed. It's very special, for age 5 and up. *OPEN Tues-Sat 10am-4pm. (Thurs is reserved for group tours and advance reservations.)* FREE.

Hayden Planetarium
Central Park West at 81 Street. 769-5920 for show times. A fascinating place to learn and have fun. Exhibits, many of them participatory

(touch one of the world's largest meteorites and step on scales to see what you weigh on different planets) demonstrate the workings of the universe in practical terms. Special: Sky Show, where the universe is projected on a huge dome, accompanied by narration: 7 days usually every hour on the hour, but call ahead. There are special shows for preschoolers by reservation, call 873-5714. Popular Laser Show with rock music for older children every Friday and Saturday at 7:30, 9, and 10:30pm (tickets go on sale in the lobby at 6pm). Also courses for children age 10 and older, such as "Stars, Black Holes and Galaxies." *OPEN 7 days noon-5pm. CLOSED Thanksgiving & Christmas Day.* Admission charge, lower for children and students. No children under age 2 admitted.

Intrepid Sea-Air-Space Museum
Pier 86, West 46 Street & the Hudson River. 245-2533. This 900-foot aircraft carrier—the former U.S.S. *Intrepid*—is now a fascinating museum. On board are vintage aircraft as well as luner landing modules, crew area exhibits, an audiovisual presentation, and lots of hands-on and changing exhibits to involve the kids. NOTE: Some of this may be intimidating for the very young or impressionable. Cafeteria on board. *OPEN Wed-Sun 10am-5pm* (last tickets sold 4pm). Admission charge; lower for children under age 13; free for age 5 and under. Membership available. Group rates available.

Metropolitan Museum of Art
Fifth Avenue at 82 Street. Education department, 570-3932. Family Programs include a lecture series for children age 6-12 and their parents, explore works of art through discussions and sketching, Friday from 7 to 8pm; "A First Look" introduces children age 6-12 and accompanying adults to the collections through discussions, sketching, and art projects on Saturday from 11am to 12:30pm and from 2:30 to 4pm, Sunday from 11am to 12:30pm. Also "Family Films" on Saturday from 12:30 to 1pm or from 2 to 2:30pm. There are also classes for junior high and high school students. Programs all FREE with museum admission. All materials are provided. No reservations are required. Museum *OPEN Sun & Tues-Thurs 9:30am-5:15pm; Fri & Sat 9:30am-8:45pm.* Suggested contribution; children under age 12 free when accompanied by an adult.

Museum of the City of New York
1220 Fifth Avenue at 103 St. 534-1672. An inviting relaxed museum depicting New York's past through rich and colorful exhibits. The museum sponsors frequent Family Programs. There are special events, puppet shows, entertaining programs for parents and children nearly every weekend throughout the year. Also, a lovely Toy and Doll Gallery to widen the eyes of any child. Tuesdays are reserved for school groups; call ext. 207 for reservations. *OPEN Wed-Sat 10am-5pm; Sun & legal holidays 1-5pm. CLOSED Mon, Thanksgiving, Christmas & New Year's Day.* Suggested contribution.

Museum of Holography
11 Mercer Street near Canal St. 925-0526. Holography? Why, it's simple: focused laser beams become 3-D images that float in space. The exhibits change periodically and a video explains the process. For the scientifically curious child or adult. There is an interesting gift shop. OPEN Sun-Tues & Thurs-Sat 11am-6pm; Wed 11am-8pm. Admission charge; lower for children under age 12 and senior citizens.

Museum of Television and Radio
23 West 52 Street. 621-6800. Radio and television broadcasting from the 1920s through the present are preserved here. Select tapes of historic moments or memorable entertainment programs to hear in the Radio Listening Room or view at an individual console. Workshops designed for the younger set, such as "Re-creating Radio," on Saturday mornings 10 to 11:30am, for children age 8-13, introduce children to the workings of classic radio programs through participation (the performance is recorded and an audiocassette is mailed to each child); Weekend Screenings for Children, every Saturday and Sunday, feature shows chosen for creativity and originality and appeal to a variety of ages. Always interesting and fun and therefore very popular, so get there early. Membership available. OPEN Tues, Wed, Fri, Sat & Sun noon-6pm; Thurs noon-8pm. CLOSED Mon & holidays. Suggested contribution; lower for children under age 13, senior citizens and students.

National Museum of the American Indian
Audubon Terrace, Broadway at West 155 Street. 283-2420. The world's largest collection of Indian artifacts (albeit only a fraction of it is on display), such as totem poles, drums, masks, and warbonnets. Occasional crafts demonstrations such as weaving and pottery making. OPEN Tues-Sat 10am-5pm; Sun 1-5pm. Admission charge; lower for children under age 12, students, and senior citizens.

New York Hall of Science
Flushing Meadows–Corona Park, 47-01 111 Street & 48 Avenue, Flushing, Queens. (718) 699-0005. Originally part of the 1964 New York World's Fair, it is now the only museum in the New York area devoted exclusively to science and technology. You are invited to explore, investigate, and experiment with the hundreds of mainly hands-on exhibits. Learning was never this much fun. OPEN Wed-Sun 10am-5pm. Admission charge. For group reservations, call 699-0301.

New-York Historical Society
170 Central Park West near West 77 St. 873-3400. The oldest museum in New York State, it is extremely welcoming to children. There are antique and vintage toys, dolls, carriages, mechanical banks, fire trucks, a replica of Noah's ark, and programs of special interest to children. OPEN Tues-Sun 10am-5pm. Admission charge; lower for children and senior citizens.

New York Transit Museum
Entrance: Schermerhorn Street & Boerum Place,

Brooklyn. (718) 330-3060. In the Borough Hall section of Brooklyn, no-longer-used station turned museum offers a unique opportunity to learn about the world's most complex mass transit system. Vintage subway cars and equipment from the early 1900s, including antique turnstiles, fare collection devices, and trolley models. There is a lunch area for school groups and a transit-related gift shop. OPEN Tues-Fri 10am-4pm; Sat 11am-4pm. Admission charge; half price for children under age 17. Take the IRT 2, 3, 4, or 5 or the IND A, F, or C to Jay Street station, or the BMT M or R trains to Court Street.

Police Museum
235 East 20 Street, 2nd floor. 477-9753. The museum contains one of the largest collections of antique and contemporary police paraphernalia, and though the tour of the facility is self-guided, there is someone on hand to answer questions. A tour of the police academy operations is sometimes available. Student group tours by reservation. OPEN Mon-Fri 9am-3pm. FREE.

Queens Museum
New York City Building, Flushing Meadows–Corona Park, Flushing, Queens. (718) 592-5555. Most fascinating is the **Panorama**, a 9,000-square-foot scale model of New York City's five boroughs that is constantly updated; light changes simulate day into night. Every Sunday afternoon there are family programs, with interesting and fun happenings; also on Sunday, there are Art Workshops, where kids age 5 and up can spend from 1 to 4pm creating a masterpiece. There are also frequently changing exhibits, some of which are of interest to children. OPEN Tues-Fri 10am-5pm, Sat & Sun noon-5pm. Admission charge; lower for children and senior citizens; children under age 5 free.

Richmondtown Restoration
441 Clarke Avenue near Arthur Kill Rd, Staten Island. (718) 351-1611. A charming re-creation of Richmondtown, founded originally as Cocclestown in 1685 by Dutch, French Walloon, and English settlers. In July and August, the best times to visit, there are costumed guides and craftspeople such as a tinsmith and basketmaker. There are 14 historic buildings open to the public, lovely grounds for strolling, ducks for feeding. There are special events during the year, call 351-9414 (see also ANNUAL EVENTS, October: Old Home Day and December: Christmas in Richmondtown). OPEN Apr-June & Sept-Dec, Wed-Fri & Sun 1-5pm; July & Aug, Wed-Fri 10am-5pm, Sat & Sun 1-5pm. Call for hours in Jan-Mar. Admission charge; half price for children age 3-18, students, and senior citizens. From the Staten Island Ferry take the S74 bus to the front door.

South Street Seaport Museum
207 Front Street. 669-9400. The seaport is a colorful and exciting place especially in fine weather when there are special events and alfresco entertainment galore. Don't miss the tall sailing ships at Pier 16, and if you want to be a sailor for the day, book passage on the Pioneer,

a 102-foot schooner built in 1885, the museum's only working vessel. At the **Children's Center**, 165 John Street, there's a 15-minute film; activities such as stitching a sail or plotting a course. Also have a look at the ongoing restoration of the *Lettie G. Howard*, an 1893 Gloucester fishing schooner (between Piers 15 and 16, John & South Streets). Museum *OPEN year-round 7 days 10am-5pm.* Purchase tickets at the **Visitor's Center**, 207 Water Street. Admission charge to museum and to board boats; lower for children age 6-12; children under age 6 free. Admission to the district is free.

Staten Island Children's Museum
Snug Harbor, 1000 Richmond Terrace, Staten Island. (718) 273-2060. Award-winning museum with changing thematic interactive exhibits put together with consulting artists and educators. Sample themes include "bugs and other insects," "news and the media." Hands-on exhibits, performances, workshops, and family activities. Terrific shop for "kids' stuff." Special events every weekend. *OPEN Wed-Fri 1-5pm, Sat, Sun & holidays 11am-5pm; July & Aug, Tues-Sun 11am-5pm.* Classes or group visits may reserve in advance. Admission charge; free for children under age 2.

ZOOS & ANIMAL PRESERVES

Bronx Zoo
Fordham Road & Bronx River Parkway, Bronx. 367-1010 (recorded information & directions). One of the world's largest and best zoological parks. Features 4,150 animals in natural habitat settings, including snow leopards in the Himalayan Highlands and a fascinating reversed day for night World of Darkness, where birds live in a simulated jungle setting. Upon entering the zoo, obtain a map and plan your itinerary. The Skyfari aerial tramway (OPEN from April to October) affords good views of most areas of the park; the Bengali Express, also seasonal, is a 2-mile-long monorail ride through the Wild Asia exhibit. Zoo *OPEN Apr-Oct, Mon-Fri 10am-5pm, Sat, Sun & holidays 10am-5:30pm; Nov-Mar, 7 days 10am-4:30pm.* Admission charge from Friday to Monday; lower for children under age 12; free for kids under age 2. Tuesday, Wednesday, and Thursday are on a donation basis. Friends of the Zoo (FOZ), 220-5141, offers free 90-minute guided walking tours on Saturday and Sunday by reservation. All children under age 16 must be accompanied by an adult. Please leave radios and pets home. Parking fee; membership available.

Bronx Zoo Children's Zoo
Fordham Road & Bronx River Parkway, Bronx. 367-1010 (recorded information). Within this large renowned zoological park there is a unique 3-acre Children's Zoo with participatory educational themes. Exhibits put children in the animals' places: burrowing like a prairie dog, perching on a nest like a bird, climbing a child-sized "spider's web"; they learn about animal defenses in a tree house and slide, about motion in a marsh area with alligators and wallabees, and, in a desert area, they learn about animal senses. In addition, there are domestic animals to pet and feed, a chick hatchery, and camel rides (not in winter). Animal Theater shows from 11am to 4pm (except during winter). Child-high signs (aimed at third graders with a 200-word vocabulary) with explanations and questions designed to make the child think. Fun and informative. *OPEN Apr-Oct, Mon-Fri 10am-5pm, Sat, Sun & holidays 10am-5:30pm; Nov-Mar, 7 days 10am-4:30pm.* Admission charge.

Central Park Children's Zoo
Central Park, enter Fifth Avenue & 64 Street. 360-8288. North of the main zoo is this haven for small children. Farm animals in a charming albeit at the moment poorly maintained setting (philanthrophy is coming to the rescue). Lobby exhibit of reptiles. *OPEN year-round 7 days 10am-5pm (last entry 4:30pm).* Tiny admission charge.

Central Park Zoo
Central Park, Fifth Avenue & 64 Street. 861-6030 (recorded information & directions). Much of America's oldest zoo has been demolished (several of the WPA-era buildings have been attractively restored) and a more modern, more humane habitat under the auspices of the well-respected New York Zoological Society has taken its place. The stars of the new zoo are definitely the polar bears, who may be viewed above and below water, and the penguins, in an enclosed polar exhibit with audio so you can hear their chatter. Of course the sea lions, in a new pool in their same old spot, are the all-time champs at getting the crowd's attention, especially at feeding time. There are educational programs (call 439-6538); an attractive cafeteria; Zoo Gift Shop for tees, books, and more. Membership available. *OPEN Apr-Oct, Mon-Fri 10am-5pm (May-Sept, Tues till 8pm), Sat, Sun & holidays 10am-5:30pm; Nov-Mar, 7 days 10am-4:30pm.* (Last ticket sold half an hour before closing.) Admission charge lower for children age 3-12 and seniors; free for children under age 3. Children under age 16 must be accompanied by an adult. Please leave your radios and pets home. School groups must call for advance reservations.

Jamaica Bay Wildlife Refuge
Cross Bay Boulevard between Howard Beach & Broad Channel, Queens. (718) 474-0613. A wonderful place for a close-to-nature walk. There are two trails, no bicycle paths, no picnics, no cross-country skiing, no jogging, but there are over 300 species of wildlife, including waterfowl, predatory birds, songbirds. Visitor's Center *OPEN year-round 7 days 8:30am-5pm; in summer, Mon-Sat 8am-5pm, Sun 8am-6pm. CLOSED Christmas & New Year's Day.* FREE, but a permit is necessary (obtain at the Visitor's Center).

Long Island Game Farm
Off the Long Island Expressway at Exit 70, Manorville, Long Island. (516) 878-6644. Nestled in a 300-acre pine forest. Children can touch and feed domestic animals, including deer and llamas, all in a lovely, friendly atmosphere. There is also an authentic 1865 "Iron Horse" train ride and an antique carousel, as well as a Sky Slide. In addition, at 11am, 1 & 3pm there is a Wild Bengal Tiger show. Picnic grounds and free parking. *OPEN mid-Apr-mid-Oct, 7 days 10am-6pm.* Admission charge; lower for children age 2-11 and senior citizens.

New York Aquarium
Surf Avenue & West 8 Street, Coney Island, Brooklyn. (718) 265-3474. Over 2,500 fantastic sea creatures in a colorful setting, with both indoor and outdoor exhibits including the new interactive **Discovery Cove**, with aquatic animals, video terminals, and walk-through underwater exhibits providing an overview of the coastal ecosystems. In the **Children's Cove**, kids touch live marine creatures and explore the wonders of a sand dune. From late April to mid-October there's a daily dolphin show in the Aquatheater. *OPEN Sept-May, 7 days 10am-4:45pm; Memorial Day-Labor Day, Sat, Sun & holidays 10am-5:45pm.* Admission charge; lower for children age 2-12; children under age 2 free.

Prospect Park Zoo
Empire Boulevard & Flatbush Avenue, Brooklyn. (718) 965-8900. Built in 1934, this zoo is undergoing a complete overhaul and will reopen in 1993 under the auspices of the New York Zoological Society. Call for an update.

Queens County Farm Museum
73-50 Little Neck Parkway, Floral Park, Queens. (718) 347-3276. One of New York City's last working farms. On 47 acres of city-owned farmland you will find a restored 18th-century farmhouse; sheep, geese, ducks, a donkey, and chickens; an orchard, greenhouses, and a cornfield. There are all sorts of special events during the year including fireside concerts, crafts courses, and an agricultural fair; call for schedule. Membership available. Museum open to school tours Monday to Friday only, although the public is admitted to the grounds. Museum: *OPEN to the public Sat & Sun only noon-5pm.* FREE.

Staten Island Zoo
Barrett Park, 614 Broadway near Forest Ave, West Brighton, Staten Island. (718) 442-3100 (directions). Besides housing the world's largest collection of rattlesnakes, there are reptiles of every kind, bats, birds, big cats, and an otter pool. There is also a South American Tropical Forest. A charming Children's Center features lectures, demonstrations, and saddle pony rides. For a complete schedule of programs, call 442-3174. To reserve for groups, call 442-3101. Membership available. *OPEN year-round 7 days 10am-4:45pm.* Admission charge; lower for children age 3-11 & senior citizens; children under age 3 and disabled always free. On Wednesdays from 2 to 4:45pm FREE for everyone. Free parking.

AMUSEMENT PARKS

Astroland Park
Coney Island, West 10 Street & Surf Avenue, Brooklyn. (718) 372-0275. A Kiddie Park with 14 rides and major attractions for adults including the now landmarked **Cyclone** roller coaster—the granddad of them all. Weather permitting *OPEN Palm Sun-mid-June, weekends only; mid-June-weekend after Labor Day, noon-midnight (later on weekends); until mid-Oct, weekends only. CLOSED mid-Oct-mid-Apr.* Admission to the midway FREE; cost per ride. Combine with a visit to the nearby New York Aquarium (see above).

Victory Park
Pier 84, West 44 Street & the Hudson River. 239-0796. Challenging and fun rides and amusements make this a fun place for children and adults. A 45-foot-high slide, a mini-roller coaster, bumper cars, and more at this riverside park. Of course, hot dogs, cotton candy, and games of chance, too. Admission charge, free for children under 36 inches tall. *OPEN Apr-Oct, Sun-Thurs 11am-11pm; Fri & Sat 11am-1am.*

PLAYGROUNDS

The Department of Parks and Recreation has 130 playgrounds throughout the five boroughs with supervised free play activities for children age 8-13 during the month of July. For location nearest you, call your borough recreation office: Brooklyn, (718) 965-8941; Bronx, 430-1826; Manhattan, 408-0210; Queens, (718) 520-5920; Staten Island, (718) 816-6421.

Adventure playgrounds reflect recent trends in innovative equipment and design for children's play areas. The following are in Central Park:

Adventure Playground
West 68 Street & Central Park West.

Adventure Playground
East 71 Street & Fifth Avenue.

New Adventure Playground
Central Park West between West 85 & West 86 Streets.

Sand Playground
East 85 Street & Fifth Avenue.

In addition to those in Central Park, the following are interesting play areas:

Abingdon Square Park & Playground
Hudson, Bank & Bleecker Streets, Greenwich Village.

Carl Schurz Playground
East End Avenue at East 84 Street.

P.S. 40 Playground
Second Avenue at East 19 Street.

May Matthews Playground
West 45 to West 46 Street, between Ninth & Tenth Avenues.
Playground
Central Park West at 100 Street.
Playground
Lenox Avenue at West 139 Street.
St. Catherine's Park
First Avenue between East 67 & East 68 Streets.
Stephen Wise Towers Play Area
West 90 to West 91 Street, Columbus to Amsterdam Avenue.
Washington Square Park
At the foot of Fifth Avenue, Greenwich Village.

LEARNING

Arts & Crafts

In addition to the following, many of the children's museums offer crafts classes for children.
92 Street YM-YWHA
1395 Lexington Avenue. 427-6000. For preschoolers 17 months to 5 years and for children age 6-12, adventures in arts and crafts, including ceramic sculpture and pottery.
Saturday Family Workshops
Belvedere Castle, Central Park, West 79 Street, south of the Great Lawn. 772-0210. Everything from meeting baby animals to planting herb gardens. FREE for children age 5-11 and their families. Year-round three Saturdays a month, from 1 to 2:30pm. Reservations are a must! Castle OPEN mid-March-Mid-Oct, Tues-Thurs, Sat & Sun 11am-5pm, Fri 1pm-5pm; balance of the year till 4pm.
YWCA
610 Lexington Avenue near East 53 St. 755-4500. A sampling of what's offered: ceramics workshop (ages 8-12), decoupage (13-16), stained glass (13-16), woodworking (13-16).

Dance

The Children's Center for Dance and Theater
Musical Theater Works, 440 Lafayette Street near Astor Pl, 3rd floor. 724-2977. Ballet, jazz, modern, tap, and rhythm and movement for age 7-17. Beginners welcome. Three sessions during the school year, call for schedule.
Neubert Ballet Institute
Carnegie Hall, 881 Seventh Avenue near West 57 St, studio 819. 246-3166; 685-7754. Age 4-20. A unique institution nurtures talent from childhood to culmination as adult performing artist. The 80 courses offer a full range; two divisions, one professional (the Neubert Ballet Company), the other educational. Training ground for the world-famous Children's Ballet Theater. Internationally known teachers and coaches; Christine Neubert, director.
YWCA
610 Lexington Avenue near East 53 Street. 755-

4500. Classes in modern, tap, and ballet. Designed to develop coordination. Individual and group performances display newly acquired skills. For boys and girls age 5-12. A program for teens as well.

Drama

ABC Productions, Inc.
P.O. Box 20136, Dag Hammarskjold Post Office, New York (10017). 832-6635. For young people age 10-18, adults 18-30, workshops in voice training, dance, movement, and acting techniques lead to performances for an audience. Call or write for information.
BACA/The Brooklyn Arts Council
200 Eastern Parkway, Brooklyn. (718) 783-4469. A series of theater and dance workshops for children age 8-18; call for further information. Performances are given in all five boroughs.
Lee Strasberg Theatre Institute
115 East 15 Street. 533-5500. "Young People's Program." an intense and diverse course of study for those serious about acting. Saturdays, fall, winter, and spring for age 7-17.
Preparatory Center for the Performing Arts at Brooklyn College
Brooklyn College, 114 Roosevelt Hall, Bedford Avenue & Avenue H, Brooklyn. (718) 780-4112. Professionally geared workshop classes in theater (age 7-18) and dance techniques (age 5-18). Private lessons in music—for children age 7-17. Also preschool program in music and movement including Susuki violin.
Weist-Barron School of Television
35 West 45 Street, 6th floor. 840-7025. New York's first school (founded 1956) specializing in acting for TV commercials and soap operas. A complete division for children age 4-7 and 8-12, and teens age 5-19.

Fencing

Fencers Club
154 West 71 Street. 977-4150 (day); 874-9800 (evening). A nonprofit organization founded in 1883. Membership is available to kids approximately 8 years old, depending on height. Olympic-level coaches on staff. Evenings only.
YWCA
610 Lexington Avenue near East 53 St. 755-4500, ext. 63. Balance and grace are enhanced by acquiring basic fencing skills. For children age 9-13.

French

French for Young People
French Institute/Alliance Française, 22 East 60 Street. 355-6100. Emphasis on conversational French; learn through audio and visual aids, games, poems, songs, creative activities—no English used. For age 8-10 and 11-13. Classes Saturday morning and afternoon. Not cheap.

Gardening

Brooklyn Botanical Garden
1000 Washington Avenue. (718) 622-4433. For over 75 years, the Children's Garden has introduced 7-18-year-olds to the joys of growing one's own plants and vegetables. Two sessions during the planting season.

New York Botanical Garden
200 Street & Kazimiroff (formerly Southern) Boulevard. 220-8982. In their Children's Garden, children age 5-16 raise vegetables, flowers, and herbs. There are also weekend workshops for ages 5-6, 7-9, and 10-12.

Gymnastics

Alzerrecas
210 East 23 Street, 4th floor. 683-1703. Long-time well-respected teachers of gymnastics classes for toddlers, preschoolers, and up to teens; parents, too. Children are grouped according to ability. Also Teen Aerobics, Jazz Dance, and Aerobikata (karate and aerobics combined). Available for birthday parties.

Asphalt Green
555 East 90 Street. 369-8890. A nonprofit sports, art, and education center. Classes in aerobics, gymnastics, karate, and yoga. Call for schedule.

Discovery Programs
749-8717. Locations on Upper East Side and Upper West Side. In existence for 19 years, offering gymnastics, dance, theater, art, karate, track and field for toddlers through teens. In addition to classes, they can create a fun birthday celebration at their 424 East 89 Street facility; call 348-5371.

Gymboree
505-2259. Call for information on this interesting weekly movement play program for parents and children 3 months to 4 years. Forty-five-minute sessions are designed to enhance active play and promote self-esteem. Well-supervised centers are filled with colorful tyke-sized equipment. There are locations on the Upper West Side, Upper East Side, Gramercy Park, and Greenwich Village.

Jodi's Gym
244 East 84 Street. 722-7633. Gymnastics specifically designed for young people age 18 months-12 years (parental supervision required for under 2 1/2). Small classes, special attention. Shop for children's dance and activewear. Available for birthday parties.

92 Street YM-YWHA
1395 Lexington Avenue. 427-6000. Wee Wizards: children age 2-3½ engage in climbing and running to develop confidence and coordination; instructor- and parent-supervised. Tumbling Tots: 12 months-4½, gymnastics to develop coordination and a sense of movement; instructor- and parent-supervised.

Sutton Gymnastics & Physical Fitness
440 Lafayette Street near East 8 St. 533-9390. Closely supervised, small gymnastics and phys-

ical fitness classes for age 6-teens. There's a baby gym for wee ones age 18-36 months; Rhythmic Gymnastics for age 7 and up; Kinder Camp, for five weeks in summer for age 3-5. Also, self-defense training. Fun birthday party space.

West Side YMCA
5 West 63 Street. 787-4400. Offers a gymnastics day camp for boys and girls age 7-14.

YWCA
610 Lexington Avenue near East 53 St. 755-4500. Excellent gymnastics program. Preschool gymnastics (ages 4-5), novice (5-6 and 7-12), and three-level beginner classes (5-6 and 7-12). Clinic, workshop, and competing/performing team. In summer, an intensive program for serious young gymnasts age 8-12. Classes limited to 30 students.

Ice Skating

For municipal skating rinks, both indoor and outdoor, see SPORTS, Ice Skating.

Ice Studio
1034 Lexington Avenue near East 73 St. 535-0304. Small friendly studio for instruction—private and group classes, primarily for kids age 6 and up, September to June, Monday to Friday, noon to 5pm. Kiddie Time, for age 5 and under, every Monday, Thursday, Friday, Saturday, and Sunday; call for exact times. *OPEN 7 days. CLOSED Sun & Mon in July & Aug.*

Rivergate Ice Rink
401 East 34 Street at First Ave. 689-0035. Pleasant new outdoor ice rink on the East Side. Skate rental. *OPEN Mon-Fri noon-10pm; Sat & Sun 10am-10pm.*

Rockefeller Center
601 Fifth Avenue at 50 St. 757-5731. Instruction for the not easily intimidated. A highly visible, beautifully situated outdoor rink. Private classes only for age 5 and up. *OPEN mid-Oct-mid-Apr.*

Sky Rink
450 West 33 Street, 16th floor. 695-6555. They're the tops. This sky-high Olympic-sized indoor rink is open year-round. Private instruction by appointment only. Call for exact dates.

Music

Dalcroze School of Music
161 East 73 Street. 879-0316. At this teacher's training college, rhythm classes for preschoolers (starting age 3), singing, sight-reading, and keyboard improvisation for children age 5 and older. Private and group instruction available; classes during school year and summer session, mid-July to August.

Growing Up with Opera
Metropolitan Opera Guild. 769-7022. For families with children age 5-12, the Guild offers (for a fee) to make opera accessible for children with this program, which consists of a specially produced-for-the-kids opera performance, a

cast party, a behind-the-scenes look at opera production, and an activity kit with at-home projects. Approximately three programs a year.

Hebrew Arts School
129 West 67 Street. 362-8060. Instruction in all orchestral instruments, plus guitar, recorder, and piano; classes in musical theory. Art and dance as well. For children age 6-17.

Little Orchestra Society
704-2100. A joyous listening and learning experience for more than four generations of New York youngsters. "Lollipops Concerts" teaches youngsters age 3-5 what to listen for in music and how to listen to it. Saturdays at 10:15 and 11:15am; Sundays at 1:15 and 2:30pm. At the Florence Gould Hall, French Institute/Alliance Française, 55 East 59 Street. "Happy Concerts for Young People," for age 6-12, take place on Saturdays at 11am and 1pm, Avery Fisher Hall, Lincoln Center. *Season runs from Oct-Apr.* Tickets may be purchased in advance.

92 Street YM-YWHA
1395 Lexington Avenue. 427-6000. This Y has a good music department with a wide range of programming for instrument or vocal instruction, both groups and private. There's a preinstrumental course for 3-year-olds.

Preparatory Center for the Performing Arts at Brooklyn College
114 Roosevelt Hall, Bedford Avenue & Avenue H. (718) 780-4112. Classes for age 3 and up in music and movement, Suzuki violin or cello, creative dance and the Arts Express, a balance of music and the visual arts. For age 7-18, private lessons in piano, all orchestral instruments, classical guitar, and voice.

Third Street Music School Settlement
233 East 11 Street. 777-3240. Founded in 1894. Instruction begins with arts for the very young (age 2½); nursery-school-age children take Suzuki violin or piano, or creative dance; for older children and adults there is a wide variety of programs including individual and group lessons in all instruments.

YWCA
610 Lexington Avenue near East 53 St. 755-4500. Flute and guitar lessons for children age 5-12, plus a teen program offering classes in basic music theory, songwriting, guitar, piano, and singing.

Painting & Drawing

Art Students' League
215 West 57 Street. 247-4510. Saturday classes in figure and still life for children age 10-16. Also, sculpture classes.

92 Street YM-YWHA
1395 Lexington Avenue. 427-6000. After-school Adventure in Art classes for age 6-8.

Riding

Claremont Riding Academy
175 West 89 Street. 724-5100. For children age 8-15. Monday to Saturday group and private

classes are offered in a small indoor ring and in Central Park.

Pelham Bit Stable
Pelham Bay Park, 9 Shore Road, Bronx. 885-0551. Riding instruction for age 8 and up in an outdoor ring; group or private. For younger children there are pony rides year-round; in summer there are wagon rides, too.

Van Cortlandt Stables
Broadway & West 254 Street, Bronx. 543-4433. Private or semiprivate (two children) lessons for age 8-12, group lessons thereafter. English or Western. Outdoor ring.

Running

New York Road Runners Club
9 East 89 Street. 860-4455. They sponsor a number of youth sports and fitness programs year-round, including City Sports for Kids, age 5-12; a track, field, and cross-country program; the New York Junior Road Runners series, including the "Pee-Wee" runs for age 2-6 and a one-mile run for age 6-18. In addition they sponsor a New York City Junior Marathon and a five-boro youth running network. Call for details.

Self-Defense

YWCA
610 Lexington Avenue near East 53 St. 755-4500. Provides full range of courses in judo and karate for children age 8-16. Separate program for older teens and adults.

Swimming

—Toddlers–5 Years

Aerobics West Fitness Club
131 West 86 Street. 787-3356. Infants, toddlers, and older children learn to swim by playing games. Parental supervision required. Four sessions throughout the year.

92 Street YM-YWHA
1395 Lexington Avenue. 427-6000. A swim program for toddlers 18 months to 5 years.

YWCA
610 Lexington Avenue near East 53 St. 755-4500. Classes in basic swimming skills for water babies age 18 months-4 years, sprites age 3-5, as well as various skill levels for age 5-12. There are also classes for babies under a year old to adjust to the water. Infants accepted with note from doctor.

—Various Age & Skill Levels

These two Y's also have swim programs for kids at various levels. Call for details.

McBurney YMCA
215 West 23 Street. 741-9221.

West Side Y
5 West 63 Street. 787-4400.

Tennis

Department of Parks and Recreation
For information, call (718) 699-4233. The City of

New York, under the auspices of the Parks Department, provides free tennis instruction for age 8-18 in the summer in parks throughout the city. They provide racquets and balls for use.

Midtown Tennis Club
341 Eighth Avenue at West 27 St. 989-8572. Junior development program. Private or group lessons for children age 5 and older.

Sutton East Tennis Club
488 East 60 Street. 751-3452. Has Manhattan's largest junior development program, starting at age 7. The season is from October to April.

CHILDREN'S CLOTHES

All of the major department stores in Manhattan have large departments for children's clothing. Unless otherwise stated, all shops are open Monday to Saturday.

Boutiques

Barneys
Seventh Avenue & West 17 Street. 929-9000. Pricey and precious European fashions for the young set, and a more affordable boutique for comfortably down-to-earth duds, newborn to age 6. MC,V, Barney's charge. *OPEN 7 days.*

Bebe Thompson
98 Thompson Street near Prince St. 925-1122. Lovely European and American clothing and shoes, newborn to 12 years. Especially nice are knits, including cashmere, in winter. AE, MC, V. *OPEN 7 days.*

Ben's Up 'N' Up
1335 Third Avenue near East 76 St. 744-2520. Beautiful imported and domestic children's wear newborn to size 10. Toys, too. AE, MC, V.

Cerutti
807 Madison Avenue near East 68 St. 737-7540. Popular shop for expensive European and American fashions, including one-of-a-kind made-to-order. Casual, school, and dress-up for infants, toddlers, girls to size 14, boys to size 16. Personal service; free gift wrap. AE, MC, V.

Children's Place
A&S Plaza, 901 Sixth Avenue at West 33 St, level C2. 268-7696. E. J. Gitano, Oshkosh B'Gosh, Bugel Boy, Mickey & Co, Lee, newborn to size 14. AE, MC, V. *OPEN 7 days.*

The Chocolate Soup
946 Madison Avenue near East 74 St. 861-2210. A fascinating small store for colorful clothes and accessories (infant to 12 years), many of which are handcrafted imports. Specialty: hand-knit sweaters. Also handpainted tees, fun shoes and accessories, handcrafted toys, and their best seller, the Danish schoolbag. Good value and *grrreat* sales. AE, MC, V. *OPEN 7 days.*

Citykids
130 Seventh Avenue near West 18 St. 620-0906. Lovely Chelsea shop for children's clothing newborn to size 12; shoes, too. They feature exclusive designs in natural fibers plus fun accessories. Toys, books, and audio and video tapes as well. AE, MC, V.

The Elder Craftsman
846 Lexington Avenue at East 64 St. 535-8030. This nonprofit showcase for the work of people over 60 years old is a worthwhile place to buy that special child a special present. All the clothing (infant to size 8), quilts, toys, and dolls are handmade with care and love, most are one of a kind. (*See also* Lighthouse Craft Shop.) MC, V.

GapKids
Lexington Avenue at East 75 Street; 988-4460. And 2370 Broadway near West 86 St; 873-2044. Also 215 Columbus Avenue near West 70 St, 874-3740; and elsewhere. "Real clothes" for boys and girls. Scaled-down durable versions of what's current for adults in denim, corduroy, and cotton, sizes 2-14. AE, MC, V. *OPEN 7 days.*

Glad Rags
1007 Madison Avenue near East 77 St. 988-1880. All the basic classics for children from underwear to outerwear, infant to size 20. AE, MC, V.

Greenstones et Cie
442 Columbus Avenue near West 81 St. 580-4322. Beautiful, in-depth selection of mainly European, mainly expensive, designer fashions—casual to elegant—for boys and girls 3 months to 16 years. AE, MC, V. *OPEN 7 days.*

The Hired Hand
1324 Lexington Avenue near East 88 St. 722- · 1355. Clothing infant to size 7, including Oshkosh, Mousefeathers, Echo Field, and some Absorba. Handmade toys, crafts; personalized gifts. AE, MC, V. *OPEN 7 days.*

Ibiza Kids
42 University Place near East 10 St. 505-9907. Children's clothing with an offbeat flair. Infants and ages 3-6. Molina, Widget Factory, Beth Schaeffer, Jean Bourget, Nini Bambini, Bubula, Kidstock. Also old-world, European-style toys, puzzles, and Victorian-style books. AE, MC, V. *OPEN 7 Days.*

K.I.D.S.
Saks Fifth Avenue, 611 Fifth Avenue at 50 St. 753-4000. Their own shop on 8, infants to preteen. Designer labels including Ralph Lauren and Calvin Klein. Toys, too. AE, DC, MC, V, Saks charge.

Kids Kids Kids
44 Greenwich Avenue near Sixth Ave. 366-0809. Newborn to size 8. Now in bigger and better quarters. Moderate to expensive clothing, shoes, accessories, toys, and more. Unique shop by phone service for busy parents. AE, MC, V. *OPEN 7 days.*

Kids 'R' Us
Herald Center, Broadway & West 34 Street, 2nd floor; 643-0714. And 8973 Bay Parkway, Brooklyn; (718) 373-0880. Famous-brand American clothing, including Bugle Boy, Health-Tex, and Oshkosh at discount prices. Girls, sizes new-

born to 14. Boys, to size 20. AE, MC, V. *OPEN 7 days*.

Kidz at Bendelz
Henri Bendel, 712 Fifth Avenue near 56 St, 2nd floor. 247-1100. Snappy, colorful, all-natural-fiber classic clothes for newborn to size 6. Also toys to encourage creativity. Stylish, of course. AE, MC, V, Bendel charge.

Laura Ashley
21 East 57 Street. 752-7300. Picture-perfect turnouts for little girls newborn to 6 months to 12 years. The same English-country look for young-at-heart mommies, too. AE, MC, V.

Lighthouse Craft Shop
111 East 59 Street. 355-2200. Another worthwhile nonprofit shop (*see* The Elder Craftsman) for handcrafted clothing, infant to size 4; dolls, bibs, and other little items. *Very* inexpensive. MC, V. *OPEN Mon-Fri 9am-5pm*

L'il Feet
1712 First Avenue near East 88 St. 410-2129. Children's fashion footwear boutique. Imported and domestic styles, infant to young adult. Certified podiatrist assures proper fit. AE, MC, V. *OPEN 7 days*.

Little Senli
30 Rockefeller Plaza, concourse level, 307-5352. Cheerful, fanciful clothing for newborn to size 14, as well as baby gifts and nursery accessories. Helpful staff. AE, DC, MC, V. *OPEN Mon-Fri 10am-6:30pm*.

Monkeys & Bears
506 Amsterdam Avenue near West 84 St. 873-2673. Classic comfortable clothing sizes newborn to 8. Also books, stuffed toys, and lovely accessories for baby's room. AE, MC, V. *OPEN 7 days*.

Morris Bros.
2322 Broadway near West 84 St. 724-9000. Carters, Oshkosh, Petit Bateau, and more at moderate prices. AE, MC, V. *OPEN 7 days*.

Mothercare
2305 Broadway near West 83 St. 877-1044. First New York branch of famed English chain, albeit everything here is made in America. Good source for layettes, clothes up to toddler size 4, stuffed animals, accessories. Maternity clothes, too. MC, V. *OPEN 7 days*.

Mouse 'N' Around
A&S Plaza, 901 Sixth Avenue at West 33 St, 7th floor. 947-3954. An ode to that famous mouse. Mickey everything, including clothing and accessories for infants, toddlers, kids to size 14, and adults, too. AE, MC, V. *OPEN 7 days*.

Peanut Butter & Jane
617 Hudson Street near Jane St. 620-7952. Their own and domestic designs plus French and Italian imports, newborn to size 8, all 100 percent cotton. Hand-decorated clothes and crafts, charming shop and owner. AE, MC, V. *OPEN 7 days*.

Petit Bateau Boutique
930 Madison Avenue near East 73 St. 288-1444. Owned by the French children's wear manufacturer Petit Bateau, this shop stocks a very up-to-date, very fine selection of underwear, play clothes, and party clothes, mostly in sizes 3 months to 8 years; some items to 14 years. Tartine et Chocolat, Matin Matine, Dan-Jean. AE, MC, V.

Pushbottom for Kids
255 East 62 Street; 888-3336. And A. Peter Pushbottom, 1157 Second Avenue near East 61 St; 879-2660. Wonderful cotton handloomed-knit crewneck and cardigan sweaters for boys and girls, newborn to 7 years. Second Avenue shop for other scaled-down versions of adult sportswear including coveralls, sweats, striped shirts, and tees. AE, MC, V.

Shoofly
506 Amsterdam Avenue near West 84 St. 580-4390. Children's shoes, infant to size 8, and enormous stock of accessories. AE, MC, V. *OPEN 7 days*.

Small Change
964 Lexington Avenue near East 70 St. 772-6455. Whimsical and imaginative clothes, much of it French and Italian imports; accessories, too. Infants and children to size 14. AE, MC, V.

Space Kiddets
46 East 21 Street. 420-9878. Charming, 100 percent natural-fiber kids clothes newborn to size 12. Also one-of-a-kind items like leather jumpers, 50s tuxedos for little boys, and circle skirts for girls. AE, MC, V.

Spring Flowers
1710 First Avenue near East 88 St. 876-0469. Well-priced dressy and casual European imports in infant to teen sizes. Also carries various school uniforms in sizes 4-14. AE, MC, V.

Trevi
141 Orchard Street near Delancey St. 529-9333. High-fashion European shoes for boys and girls, newborn to adult sizes. AE, MC, V. *OPEN 7 days*.

Wicker Garden's Children
1327 Madison Avenue near East 93 St. 410-7001. Spacious, beautifully appointed specialty shop for boys and girls clothing, ready-made or custom for play and party, infants up to size 10. Accessories for the girls including hats. Delicate crib and carriage linens. Complete layettes; gift items. Range: $10-$250. AE, MC, V.

—Camp Clothing

The Camp Shop
(800) 845-2267. These camp specialists are in New York each season from March through June, Friday from 1 to 8pm and Saturday from 9:30am to 4pm, at an East Side location—call for where. Customers are seated while salespeople bring out merchandise for approval. Clothing (including 250 camp uniforms), shoes, and gear are stocked. Free name-tagging before the seasonal rush.

Ideal Department Store
1814-16 Flatbush Avenue near Ave K, Flatbush, Brooklyn. (718) 252-5090. Features Boy Scout and Girl Scout supplies and school uniforms. Nationwide delivery. Sizes 4-44. AE, MC, V.

—Discount Clothes

A & G Children's Wear
261 Broome Street near Orchard St. 966-3775. Lower East Side source for name-brand merchandise from layettes to size 14 at up to 25 percent off list prices. Dorisa, Tickle Me, Carters, Bull Frog, Dijon, Muffling, Rothchild. *OPEN Sun-Thurs, Fri till 2pm. CLOSED Sat.*

Conways
1333-1345 Broadway near West 34 St; 560-9196. And nearby branches. Also 201 East 42 Street; 922-5030. This is a bargain hunter's dream but a nightmare for those who expect service and aisles you can walk through. There are buys to be had on layettes, clothing, and accessories for infants up to teens, including name brands. Caveat: seconds here means just that. AE, MC, V. *OPEN 7 days.*

Daffy's
111 Fifth Avenue at 18 St. 529-4477. A huge bargain emporium direct from New Jersey. On the children's floor everything your child could ever don—from underwear to leatherwear—most of it imported from Europe and sold at up to 40 percent off retail. Also accessories, toys, and stuffed animals. MC, V. *OPEN 7 days.*

M. Kreinen Sales
301 Grand Street near Allen St. 925-0239. Large selection of better children's clothes at 25 percent off retail. Sizes infant to 14. *OPEN Sun-Fri. CLOSED Sat.*

Nathan Borlam's
157 Havemeyer Street near South 2 St, Brooklyn. (718) 387-2983. Many mothers say it's well worth the trip to Williamsburg for up to 50 percent discount on children's clothes infant up to juniors. *OPEN Sun-Thurs & Fri morning. CLOSED Fri afternoon & Sat.*

Rice & Breskin
323 Grand Street near Orchard St. 925-5515. Vast inventory of famous-name infants' and children's wear at 20 percent discount. MC, V. *OPEN Sun-Fri. CLOSED Sat.*

—Resale Clothes

First & Second Cousin
147 Seventh Avenue South near West 10 St. 929-8048. Greenwich Village shop for good-condition used clothing on consignment. New clothes, too, infant to size 14. AE, MC, V. *OPEN 7 days.*

Once Upon a Time
171 East 92 Street. 831-7619. High-quality gently worn used clothing and accessories in a shop started by two grandmas. Also, great buys on new clothing from overstocks or sellouts from first-run kids stores. MC, V.

Second Act Children's Wear
1046 Madison Avenue near East 79 St, 2nd floor. 988-2440. Well-known longtime (25 years) shop with a large selection of inexpensive used clothing and shoes for both boys and girls, sizes infant to 14. Toys, books, and sporting goods, too. Bulletin board lists larger items.

Thrifty Threads for Kids
2082 East 13 Street near Ave U, Brooklyn. (718) 336-8037. Used clothing, toys, carriages, cribs, books. *OPEN Tues-Sat.*

CHILDREN'S SPECIALTY SHOPPING

Again, unless otherwise stated, all shops are OPEN Monday to Saturday. Call for hours; they tend to change with the season.

Bikes

Most of the larger toy stores also carry a good selection of bicycles.

Bicycle Renaissance
491 Amsterdam Avenue near West 83 St. 362-3388. Large selection of famous-name bikes in all sizes. Repairs, expert service. No rentals. AE, MC, V. *OPEN 7 days.*

Bicycles Plus
1400 Third Avenue near East 79 St; 794-2929. And 204 East 85 Street; 794-2201. High-quality children's bicycles. Large selection of clothing and accesories. AE, MC, V. *OPEN 7 days.*

Morris' Toy Land
1896 Third Avenue near East 105 St. 876-0740. Long-established shop offers an extensive line of bicycles including Ross and Schwin for children of every age. Low prices, all merchandise guaranteed. An extensive line of toys as well. AE, MC, V. *OPEN 7 days.*

Stuyvesant Bicycle
349 West 14 Street. 254-5200. Since 1939, the best-made American children's bikes at discount prices. Rentals, too. A full-service shop. AE, MC, V. *OPEN 7 days.*

Books

B. Dalton, 666 Fifth Avenue at East 52 Street, has a large children's book department. (See also SHOPPING, Specialty Shops & Services, Books.)

Barnes & Noble Jr.
Sales Annex, Fifth Avenue & 18 Street. 807-0099. A big store for little readers. Books and educational materials for preschoolers to 13-year-olds at discount prices. AE, MC, V. *OPEN 7 days.*

Books of Wonder
464 Hudson Street at Barrow St; 645-8006. And 132 Seventh Avenue at West 18 St; 989-3270. The largest collection of children's books in the city; new, used, out-of-print. Very special are the 19th- and early 20th-century picture books (mainly at the Seventh Avenue shop). Toys that are book-related. All knowledgeably purveyed. Gift wrap; will ship all over the world. At Hudson Street: Storytelling Sunday at 11:30am for age 3-7. Free newsletter. AE, MC. V. *OPEN 7 days.*

Corner Bookstore
1313 Madison Avenue at East 93 St. 831-3554.

Welcoming Carnegie Hill shop about one-third of which is devoted to children's books. Novel idea: children's account cards. MC, V. *OPEN 7 days.*

Cousin Arthur's
82 Montague Street near Hicks St, Brooklyn Heights. (718) 643-1232. A tiny but good children's bookstore right near the Promenade. In addition to the books there are classic audio- and videotapes, stuffed animals, and posters. Storytelling usually the first Sunday of the month at 1pm; also, Toddler Reading, the third Thursday of every month at 11am. AE, MC, V. *OPEN 7 days.*

Eeyore's Books for Children
25 East 83 Street; 988-3404. And 2212 Broadway near West 79 St; 362-0634. The city's first store to be completely devoted to children's books; baby books through young adult. Also cassettes, videos, educational games, locally handmade stuffed toys. Special events including story hours (during the school year) on Sunday at 12:30pm on the East Side and 11am on the West Side; author appearances. Put your name on their mailing list. AE, MC, V. *OPEN 7 days.*

Jeryl Metz Books
697 West End Avenue, apt 13A (10023). 864-3055. If you're looking for a beloved book from your childhood to share with your child, Ms. Metz will search for it; hardcover mainly. Allow six weeks minimum for the process. She also keeps a stock of approximately 600 books on hand, half of which are for children. She issues a catalog or you can browse. *By appointment only*

Storyland
1369 Third Avenue near East 78 St; 517-6951. And 379 Amsterdam Avenue near West 78 St; 769-2665. A tiny well-run bookstore filled with books for children through age 15. Casettes, videos, games, and puzzles. Every Sunday at 1:30pm there is a special event; on the West Side they take place Tuesdays at 7pm and Saturdays and Sundays at 12:30pm. AE, MC, V. *OPEN 7 days.*

Strand Book Store
828 Broadway at East 12 St. 473-1452. In the basement of this huge book emporium is a large stock of used children's books, organized in no particular order. In the Rare Book Room on the 5th floor there are children's book treasures, priced accordingly. AE, MC, V. *OPEN 7 days.*

—Comic Books

Funny Business
656 Amsterdam Avenue at West 92 St. 799-9477. For kids, for collectors, for collector kids. New, old, and the classics. Over 750,000 issues in stock! MC, V. *OPEN 7 days.*

Village Comics
163 Bleecker Street near Sullivan St. 777-2770. Excellent stock of in-print and collector's comics. New shipments every Thursday. Also related books, posters, and science fiction paperbacks. MC, V. *OPEN 7 days.*

West Side Comics
107 West 86 Street. 724-0432. Well stocked with new comics mainly; some back issues. AE, MC, V. *OPEN 7 days.*

Diapers

General Diaper Service
For all five boroughs, call (718) 417-1002. Home delivery of 100 percent cotton diapers with bacteria inhibitor. Gift certificates available. *OPEN Mon-Fri 9am-5pm.*

Dolls & Dollhouses

Dollhouse Antics
1343 Madison Avenue at East 94 St. 876-2288. A lovely gracious dollhouse shop geared to both children and collectors. Complete line of dollhouses, accessories, and furnishings. Broad price range. AE, MC, V.

Manhattan Doll House
176 Ninth Avenue near West 21 St. 989-5220. This Chelsea shop has a large selection of dolls, dollhouses and kits, miniatures, wallpaper, and lighting. Also lovely antique dolls for show and sale. Expert repairs of antique, cloth-body, even some rubber and plastic dolls. They'll even re-attach Teddy's torn limbs. AE, MC, V.

New York Doll Hospital
787 Lexington Avenue near East 61 St, upstairs. 838-7527. Repairs on all kinds of dolls (including battery-operated ones) with a reputation for care and concern since 1900. Also restores, buys, sells, rents, and appraises old and antique dolls. No credit cards.

Furniture

Albee
715 Amsterdam Avenue at West 95 St. 662-5740 or 662-8902. A quality discount store for over 50 years. Wide selection of well-priced infant and toddler furniture and accessories, including twin carriages. Complete layette department; toys, too. AE, MC, V.

Bellini
473 Columbus Avenue near West 82 St. 362-3700. Beautiful furniture that "grows with the child," which means they convert to other use as baby grows older. Accessories and gift items, as well. MC, V. *OPEN 7 days.*

Ben's Babyland
81 Avenue A near East 5 St. 674-1353. Anything you need for baby's room, carriages, strollers, car seats, all at discount. MC, V. *OPEN 7 days.*

Ben's for Kids
1380 Third Avenue near East 79 St. 794-2330. A large, very helpful, very friendly store for infant furniture and accessories, carriages, strollers, much you won't find elsewhere. Some clothing for newborns to age 4; toys, too. Free gift wrap, free local delivery, free assembly. Knowledgeable staff. AE, MC, V.

Children's Room
318 East 45 Street. 687-3868. Scandinavian fur-

niture for children: desks, bunk beds, modular systems—in basic functional designs. Brightly colored wall hangings, too. MC, V (there's a $300 minimum).

Hush-A-Bye
1459 First Avenue at East 76 St. 988-4500. Since 1943, respected retailers of imported and domestic nursery and juvenile furniture. Personalized accessories, made-to-order quilts, handpainting of furniture. Complete layettes, toys, books, videos. AE, MC, V. *OPEN 7 days.*

Lewis of London
215 East 51 Street; 688-3669. And 72-17 Austin Street, Queens; (718) 544-8003. Exclusive imported juvenile furniture, carriages, and accessories. Unique designs, large selection. Layette and infant clothing department, too. AE, MC, V.

Little Spaces
P.O. Box 247, Gracie Station (10028). 865-9281. They will customize your child's room and solve the space and storage problems of the urban child. Playhouses, sleeping lofts, built-in or free-standing. Call or write for details.

Schneider's
20 Avenue A at East 2 St. 228-3540. Nursery through teenage needs. Complete line of furniture, linens, bumpers, carriages, and toys all at very good prices. MC, V. *OPEN 7 days.*

—Furniture Rentals
The following rent children's furniture and accessories. Perfect for short stays at Grandma's house.

Keefe & Keefe
988-8800. Rents cribs with one day's notice—in Manhattan only.

Granny's
876-4310. Rents everything but the baby: from cribs to car seats.

Haircuts

Astor Place Hairstylists
2 Astor Place. 475-9854. The preteen or teen with a mind of his or her own will want a cut here. The Mohawk and the flattop were born here—they do *anything* the customer wants. Mom, don't be shocked. *OPEN 7 days.*

Michael's Children's Haircutting Salon
1263 Madison Avenue near East 90 St. 289-9612. Child haircutting specialists since 1910. European haircuts for boys and girls age 1-12. First haircut receives a certificate. Special seats, lollipop inducements. No appointment necessary.

Shooting Star
F.A.O. Schwartz, 767 Fifth Avenue at 58 St. 758-4344. Hair parlor on the second floor of the famed toy emporium for children's cuts and styling. Appointment necessary. AE only. *OPEN Tues-Sun.*

Short Cuts
104 West 83 Street. 877-2277. Cartoons and a play area for the kids; a diploma for first cuts to

cherish. There's a Parent/Child Special, too. Appointment preferred. AE, MC, V. *OPEN Tues-Sat*

Hobbies

Ace Hobbies
35 West 31 Street, 3rd floor. 268-4151. For the plastic model enthusiast. Hundreds of scale kits to choose from: aircraft, armor, autos, ships. Also paints, decals, books.

Kites

Big City Kite Company
1201 Lexington Avenue near East 82 St. 472-2623. Your spirits will soar upon entering this wonderful shop completely devoted to kites: every color, shape, material, and price. AE, MC, V ($15 minimum). *OPEN Mon-Sat; Sun in season.*

Magic, Jokes & Tricks

See also SHOPPING, Specialty Shops & Services, Magic.

Flosso-Hornmann Magic Company
45 West 34 Street, room 607. 279-6079. The oldest shop of its kind in America. Founded in 1865, it has a magic museum and they'll demonstrate tricks on request. MC, V. *CLOSES Sat at 4pm.*

Tannen Magic Company
6 West 32 Street, 4th floor. 239-8383. The world's largest magic store—need I say more? They run a magic camp every August. AE, MC, V. *CLOSES Sat at 4pm.*

School Supplies

*Inexpensive supplies can be found at **Woolworth** and **Lamston** stores.*

Toys

Dinosaur Hill
302 East 9 Street. 473-5850. Charming little East Village shop crammed with colorful handmade "wonderments"—quality toys and novelties, much of which is unusual, much of which demands involvement. Also natural-fiber clothing up to age 4. As you might expect, dinosaurs are well represented. Don't miss this one. AE, MC, V. *OPEN 7 days.*

The Enchanted Forest
85 Mercer Street near Spring St. 925-6677. An enchanting SoHo shop for young and old. Imported and handmade toys, stuffed animals, books of fairy tales and mythology. Extensive line of kaleidoscopes. Will ship anywhere. AE, MC, V. *OPEN 7 days.*

F.A.O. Schwarz
767 Fifth Avenue at 58 St. 644-9400. Now in new quarters, boasting child-sized boutiques. This large, world-famous toy emporium, established in 1862, still purveys much that is opulent for the affluent, including life-sized stuffed animals and

miniaturized powered autos. The standards, too, kites, dolls, games, and toys. All in a bustling, exciting setting. A must-visit. (If you can't visit, use their shop-by-phone service, just ask the operator for a Personal Shopper and your selections will be sent out the same day.) AE, CB, DC, MC, V. *OPEN 7 days.*

Forbidden Planet
821 Broadway at East 12 St; 473-1576. And 227 East 59 Street; 751-4386. A most complete stock of science fiction– and fantasy-related toys, games, and books. That covers everything from Masters of the Universe and Star Trek to Disney. For the uninitiated it's all pretty bizarre. AE, MC, V. *OPEN 7 days.*

The Last Wound Up
889 Broadway at West 19 St. 529-4197. Specializes in whimsical wind-up toys (if it winds, it winds up here), such as a walking camel, a chicken that lays eggs, a mooing cow, and a mouse that does flips. Also music boxes and some battery-operated toys. Extremely wide price range. AE, MC, V ($15 minimum). *OPEN 7 days.*

Laughing Giraffe
234 Court Street near Baltic St, Brooklyn. (718) 852-3635. A casualty of too-high Manhattan rents—now in Brooklyn, it's still an intelligent, well-thought-out shop for unique toys, books, games for newborns to teens. No "Do Not Touch" signs here. Baby-gift registry, too. Phone orders happily taken; UPS delivery. Price range $1-$300. MC, V. *OPEN Tues-Sat.*

Lilliput The Toy Store
8217 Fifth Avenue at 82 St, Brooklyn. (718) 833-3399. Unique selection of quality toys at affordable prices. Dolls, doll carriages and accessories, stuffed animals, preschool and educational toys. Handcrafted wooden table and chair sets, rocking horses, rocking chairs, and toy chests. AE, MC, V.

Macy's
West 34 Street & Broadway, 6th floor. 695-4400. One of the best toy stores in the city is located in its biggest department store. No wonder that it's Santa's official New York residence after he arrives in New York for the Thanksgiving Day parade. AE, MC, V, Macy's charge. *OPEN 7 days.*

Mary Arnold Toys
962 Lexington Avenue near East 70 St. 744-8510. Toys, stuffed animals, dolls and dollhouses, arts and crafts supplies, and books for all ages. A child can leave a "wish list" for special-occasion days. They also carry paper goods and helium balloons. AE, MC, V.

Penny Whistle
1283 Madison Avenue at East 91 St; 369-3868. And 448 Columbus Avenue near West 81 St; 873-9090. Also 132 Spring Street near Greene St, 925-2088. This was a pioneer concept in toy stores, where children were—and still are—encouraged to touch and play. Emphasis is on toys with high play value and unusual design. Prices start as low as 20¢ and go *way* up. Ex-

cellent informed service, including free gift wrap and delivery. AE, MC, V ($25 minimum). *OPEN 7 days.*

Star Magic
743 Broadway near East 8 St; 228-7770. And 275 Amsterdam Avenue at West 73 St; 769-2020. A wonderful array of all things space-y. Star charts, moon maps, toy space ships, books, postcards, and freeze-dried ice cream for would-be astronauts. AE, MC, V. *OPEN 7 days.*

Toy Park
112 East 86 Street; 427-6611. And 624 Columbus Avenue at West 90 St; 769-3880. Large, well-stocked store carrying more than 15,000 brand-name fun and educational toys for all ages, including a very large game department. They will gift wrap free, take phone orders, and deliver free (Upper West Side and Upper East Side) anything above $10. MC, V. *OPEN 7 days.*

West Side Kids
498 Amsterdam Avenue at West 84 St. 496-7282. Imaginative, artfully chosen playthings at fair prices. Play corner, birthday party registry. Personable and knowledgeable service. AE, MC, V. *OPEN 7 days.*

—Discount Toys

Hershey's Stationers
48 Clinton Street near Rivington St. 473-6391. For 50 years, a veritable Lower East Side institution. Toys and games, stuffed animals, sporting goods, and stationery, too—all at discount prices. *OPEN Sun-Thurs, Fri till 3pm. CLOSED Sat.*

Lionel Kiddie City Toys
35 West 34 Street; 629-3070 or -3089. And 24 Union Square East; 353-0215. A huge stock of famous name-brand toys; all at discount prices. On the first floor red-tag items are a steal (but do pay). AE, MC, V. *OPEN 7 days.*

Morris Toy Land
1896 Third Avenue at 105 St. 876-0470. Large, longtime discount toy store. Bikes, too. AE, V. *OPEN 7 days.*

Toys 'R' Us
Herald Center, Sixth Avenue & West 34 Street; 596-8697. And 2875 Flatbush Avenue near Kings Plaza, Brooklyn; (718) 258-2061. Also 8973 Bay Parkway, Brooklyn, (718) 372-4646. The nation's largest toy retailer in 45,000 square feet on three levels. Well-stocked supermarket for discount toys and games. AE, MC, V. *OPEN 7 days.*

Trains

Red Caboose
16 West 45 Street, 4th floor. 575-0155. Extensive collection of model trains and railroad equipment at 10 to 25 percent discount. All the latest models plus old tin-plate Lionel and American Flyer. Radio-controlled cars and boats, too. AE, MC, V.

CHILDREN'S ENTERTAINMENT

Most branches of the New York Public Library present special programs, many of which, especially on weekends, are of interest to children. Every branch has available a FREE calendar of these special activities; pick one up for current information. The New York Times *and* New York Daily News *on Friday and the* New York Post *on Saturday are good sources for happenings of special interest to kids. Also check* New York magazine *and the* Village Voice.

Big Apple Circus
220 West 42 Street. 391-0760. This one-ring circus performs in Damrosch Park at Lincoln Center in Manhattan during the Christmas season, November to early January. There's a general admission charge and worth every penny. For information on location schedule—they perform in the boroughs in spring—call the New York School for Circus Arts at the above number.

Bowlmor Lanes
110 University Place near East 12 St. 255-8188. In business since 1938, with 44 lanes on two floors and decor from the 50s. Kids 8 and up may bowl *Sat & Sun 10am-7pm.*

F.A.O. Schwarz
767 Fifth Avenue at 58 St. 644-9400. A variety of entertainment on weekdays, from clowns and puppet demonstrations to turtle races. Schedule varies, call for update. FREE.

Fourth Wall Theater
79 East 4 Street. 254-5060. Original musicals with a message for children. *Oct-May, Sat & Sun at 3:30pm.* For children age 5 to teen. Admission charge. Reserve. Also, *Tues at 7:30pm,* a political theater company for age 13 and up. Admission charge. Reserve.

Henry Street Settlement Louis Abrons Arts Center
466 Grand Street near Delancey St. 598-0400. Family theater for kids and their parents; performances *Oct-mid-June, Sat & Sun.* Admission charge. Reserve.

Little People's Theater Company
Courtyard Playhouse, 39 Grove Street, west of Sheridan Sq & Seventh Ave South. 765-9540. The company has been performing for over 20 years. Performances *Sat & Sun from the weekend after Labor Day to the end of June at 1:30pm & 3pm; daily during Christmas school holidays.* Admission charge. Reserve.

Marionette Theatre
Swedish Cottage, Central Park (enter from Central Park West & 81 Street). 988-9093. The cottage was built as a schoolhouse in Sweden in the 19th century; it was brought to America as part of the Swedish exhibition at the Centennial Fair in Philadelphia in 1876. When the fair closed, New York City purchased it for Central Park. Since 1947, the home to the Marionette Theatre Company. Performances for organized groups of 10 or more *Sept-June, Tues-Fri 10:30am &* noon. For the general public *Sat noon & 3pm.* Admission charge. Reservations are required. In addition, the Marionette Theatre travels to all the boroughs in July and August; contact your local borough office for time and place of performance. The cottage is available for birthday parties.

Mostly Magic
53 Carmine Street. 924-1472. Every Saturday, Magic Matinee at 2pm. Two magicians and lots of audience participation. For age 4-10. Reserve.

Off-Center Theater Company
768-3277. Updated versions of classical fairy tales with audience participation. Call for show times and location. Admission charge. Reserve.

On Stage Children Company
Hartley House Theater, 413 West 46 Street between Ninth & Tenth Ave. 666-1716. Four productions a year. *Mid-Sept-May, Sat 1:30 & 3pm, Sun 1 & 3:30pm.* For age 5 and up. Admission charge. Group rates available. Reserve.

Penny Bridge Players
Undercroft of the Assumption Church, 59 Cranberry Street, Brooklyn Heights. (718) 855-6346. Children's fairy tales performed on weekends—matinee hours. Admission charge. Reserve.

The Puppet Company
31 Union Square West, loft 2B. 741-1646. A wonderful loft setting for a new main production each year plus an ever-changing marionette revue. In addition, a lesson in puppet making. *Sun noon, 2 & 3:30pm.* For age 3-7. Admission charge. Reserve.

Storytelling
Hans Christian Andersen Statue, Central Park, near Conservatory Water (the Model Boat Pond) at 74 Street. The perfect setting for storytelling— *late May-late Sept, Sat 11am-noon.* For children age 4 and up. FREE.

Thirteenth Street Theater Company
50 West 13 Street between Fifth & Sixth Ave. 675-6677. One-hour performances of original musicals. *Year-round Sat & Sun 1 & 3pm.* Suitable for age 4-10. Admission charge. Reserve.

PARTIES

For party supplies and favors, see SHOPPING, Specialty Shops & Services, Party Paraphernalia.

Party Entertainment to Hire

New York's parks and plazas are used as impromptu stages during the summer by aspiring actors, mimes, magicians, fire-eaters, jugglers, and oompah and steel-drum bands. Any of them would be interested in entertaining indoors for a change.

Allie, Lady Rainbow Clown
966-5218. Two hours of participatory magic, face painting, games, balloon sculpture.

Eggroll the Clown
595-2347. An 18-year veteran. Traditional clowning and a colorful magic show. Balloons, too.

Jeremy's Place
See Special-Activity Parties & Places.

Jonathan the Storyteller
886-1811; (914) 265-9525. Jonathan, who has a master's degree in education, enchants with his tales, participatory stories, and creative organized games. An original tale especially personalized for the birthday child.

Ken Levy
(718) 857-6309. Levity and levitation. Clowning, participation, face painting, and balloons.

Magical David
799-1290. New York's only musical magician. Magic tricks and songs to tickle and delight.

Marcia the Magical Moose
567-0682. A puppet show with lifelike furry puppets, songs, and finger puppet party favors. Balloons, too. Participatory in nature. For age 1-7.

Michael Shall
724-5556. Will teach origami to a maximum of 20 kids age 6 and up for 1½ hours. He's a master at it. (He's responsible for the origami Christmas trees at the American Museum of Natural History and in the Japan Airlines windows.) Each child gets an instruction kit and a creation as a party favor. Gives private lessons, too.

Silly Billy
645-1299. A magic show and join-in storytelling with lots of participation. Balloon animals, too. According to WABC-TV, he's "king of the kiddie comedy circuit." For age 3-8.

Ups the Clown
989-7555. She's a lovable clown with magic, mime, balloons, and more up her sleeve.

Special-Activity Parties & Places

Birthdaybakers, Partymakers
195 East 76 Street. 288-7112. Experienced party specialist Linda Kaye really knows how to create a memorable event for your child's birthday. All the parties are participatory and everything is provided, from the theme—it could be a fairy tale come to life, baking the birthday cake, or a video "who dunnit" party—to the place. The magical toyland treasure hunt through F.A.O. Schwarz before it opens on Sunday is a dream come true for any child. Custom invitations, favors, balloons; she can also supply hayrides, fireworks, jukeboxes, a skywriter. . .you name it. Birthdays-to-go, a box of themed party paper goods: a convenient way to celebrate with schoolmates. There's also a party room on premises for 24 kids. Call for more ideas.

Children's Museum of Manhattan
212 West 83 Street. 721-1234. Children explore exhibits and create their own work of art. Music, entertainment, and refreshments in the Birthday Party Room. Call the party coordinator at 721-1223.

Discovery Center
424 East 89 Street. 348-5371. Gymnastics, Bal-

let, Rock 'n Roll, Dinosaurs, Science, Art & Magic are some of the Dance & Storytime parties from which to choose. They can handle all of the invites, favors, food, and decorations, too.

Gymboree
308-6353. At the Gymboree Center or your home. Music, games, sights, and sounds to delight 1- to 4-year-olds. Trained instructors help parents and children have fun together.

Jeremy's Place
322 East 81 Street. 628-1414. A party with Jeremy Sage is a rite of passage for many New York kids. They love the puppets, robots, wind tunnel, waterfall, electric trains, light show, and a magical performance by Jeremy himself. Accommodates 12 to 65 children, age 4 to 13. Book six to eight months in advance—he's that much in demand. Available to go as Jeremy's Place Party Bags, filled with inexpensive party favors from his huge inventory. OPEN 7 days.

Jodi's Place
244 East 84 Street. 772-7633. Party guests "work out" on bars, beams, mats, rings, and trapeze under supervision of trained instructors. Separate area for refreshments supplied by parent. Party favors available. For age 3-12.

McDonald's
1499 Third Avenue near East 85 St. 628-8100. A special private room for your McBirthday party where the McFood will be served to the guests by a McHostess, who will also lead the group in games. A birthday cake, party hats, and a present for the birthday child. Minimum of 10 kids. Call for reservations.

Mostly Magic
55 Carmine Street near Seventh Ave South. 924-1472. Magic club available on weekends for a private party. Price includes balloon party favors, cake, ice cream, unlimited soft drinks, and an hour-long performance by a professional magician. You can also have your party after the weekly Saturday magic show.

New York Hall of Science
Flushing Meadows–Corona Park, 47-01 111 Street & 48 Avenue, Flushing, Queens. (718) 699-0005. In this hands-on science and technology museum, the birthday party consists of a live laser or flight demonstration, a private tour of the exhibits, make-it-and-take-it activities, science theme party bags.

FOR PARENTS

General

Early Childhood Resource & Information Center
New York Public Library, 66 Leroy Street near Seventh Ave South (10014). 929-0815. A Family Room & Parent Involvement Program with workshops, parents' learning groups, and a family room. Stocked with books for adults who work with children from birth to age 5. And you don't

have to hush! To get on their mailing list, send a self-addressed stamped envelope. Library *OPEN Tues-Fri.*

Elisabeth Bing Center for Parents
164 West 79 Street. 362-5304. Pre- and postnatal exercise classes. Workshops for parents and babies. Lamaze instruction.

Homework Hotline
(718) 780-7766. A teacher or librarian will help elementary, junior high, and high school students (and their parents) find the solution to a difficult homework problem. *AVAILABLE during the school year Mon-Thurs 5-8pm.*

92 Street Y Parenting Center
1395 Lexington Avenue. 427-6000. Because parenting isn't easy, the center offers a variety of services, including workshops, classes, and lectures with other parents and professionals. *Year-round.*

Parents League of New York, Inc.
115 East 82 Street. 737-7385. A good source of information and services for the parent and child on such things as schools, summer camps, safety, and baby-sitters. Yearly fee and membership.

Volunteer Services for Children
867-2220. At eight community centers in Manhattan, volunteers tutor one child in reading, one evening a week during the school year.

Baby Care

Always personally interview a prospective baby nurse and thoroughly check out her references. A few agencies are listed below.

Avalon Registry
116 Central Park South. 245-0250.

Baby Sitters Guild
60 East 42 Street, suite 912. 682-0227. *OPEN 7 days 9am-9pm.*

Fox Agency
30 East 60 Street. 753-2686.

Park Avenue Home Employment Agency
16 East 79 Street. 737-7733.

Baby-sitters

Avalon Registry
116 Central Park South. 245-0250.

Baby Sitters Guild
60 East 42 Street, suite 912. 682-0227. Long-term source for experienced, referenced sitters. 24-hour notice preferred.

Barnard College Baby-sitting Service
Millbank Hall, 3009 Broadway at 119 St. 280-2035.

Gilbert Child Care Agency
111 West 57 Street. 757-7900. Referenced sitters, one-day notice preferred.

Lenox Hill Senior Citizens Service Center
343 East 70 Street. 744-5905

Sitters on Standby (SOS)
838-0134. A round-the-clock, last-minute service for Manhattan parents. Experienced sitters. For Brooklynites, call **Pinch Sitters Agency** (718) 622-0305.

Day Camps (Summer)

Many of the city parks run a free play group for children age 4-12 during July and August, Monday to Friday 9:30am-3:30pm. Activities and entertainment, including magicians and clowns. Call the appropriate borough office of the Department of Parks and Recreation for information.

—Information

Bureau for Day Camps & Recreation, New York City Department of Health
65 Worth Street, room 1003 (10013). 334-7735 or -3295. Write or call for information. Updated yearly. Indicate which borough's booklet you require.

Scouts

Girl Scouts Council of Greater New York
43 West 23 Street. 645-4000. Call for information about becoming a Girl Scout in one of New York's five boroughs.

Girl Scout Retail Shop
830 Third Avenue near East 50 St. 940-7380. Everything to do with Girl Scouting: uniforms, badges, camping equipment, and publications.

Boy Scouts
345 Hudson Street. 242-1100. Call for information about becoming a Boy Scout in one of New York's five boroughs.

SPORTS

The Yankees

GENERAL INFORMATION

For information regarding a park or activity, call the appropriate borough office of the Department of Parks and Recreation.
Brooklyn: (718) 965-8900
Bronx: 430-1800
Manhattan: 408-0100
Queens: (718) 520-5900
Staten Island: (718) 390-8000
For recorded information on what's happening in the city's parks, call 360-1333.

SPORTS STADIUMS

Byrne Meadowlands Sports Complex East (Rutherford, N.J.)
Box Office: (201) 935-3900
New York Giants (football): (201) 935-8222
New York Jets (football): (516) 538-7200
Fitzgerald Gymnasium (Queens College)
Kissena Boulevard & 65 Avenue, Flushing, Queens. (718) 520-7212.
John J. Downing Memorial Stadium
Randalls Island. 860-1828.
Madison Square Garden
West 33 Street & Seventh Avenue. 465-6741.
National Tennis Center
Flushing Meadows Park, Flushing, Queens. (718) 271-5100.

Shea Stadium
Roosevelt Avenue & 126 Street, Flushing, Queens. New York Mets (baseball): (718) 507-8499.
West Side Tennis Center
1 Tennis Place, Forest Hills, Queens. (718) 268-2300.
Yankee Stadium
West 161 Street & River Avenue, Bronx. 293-6000.

ANNUAL SPORTING EVENTS

See also the ANNUAL EVENTS chapter.
Madison Square Garden: 465-6741.
Millrose Track & Field Championships: January/February
Golden Gloves Boxing: January/February/March
Westminster Kennel Club Show: February
USA Indoor Track & Field Championships: February
National Invitational Basketball Tournament: March/April
World Figure-Skating Championships: April
National Tennis Center, Flushing Meadows Park. (718) 592-8000.
U.S. Open Tennis Championship: Late August/early September

SPORTS ACTIVITIES

Baseball

New York City has two professional baseball teams: **The New York Yankees** *play at* **Yankee Stadium***, Bronx, 293-6000, and the* **New York Mets** *at* **Shea Stadium***, Flushing, Queens,* (718) 507-8499.
The baseball season begins the first week in April and continues through mid-October. Call the stadiums for specific game or ticket information or check the local papers.

—Municipal Baseball Diamonds

There are hundreds of municipal baseball facilities in the city. A permit is required for use of a field. For details on use of ball fields in Central Park, call 408-0209.

—Baseball Information

The following league clubs will be able to give you information on current events and exhibition games of the major teams in the city.
American League of Professional Baseball Clubs
339-7600.
National League of Professional Baseball Clubs
339-7700.

Basketball

New York's professional basketball team is the **New York Knickerbockers***. Home court for the*

"Knicks" is **Madison Square Garden,** 465-6741. *The season starts in October and can run into June. The Garden is also the scene of a heavy college basketball schedule starting in January, including the Big East and ECAC championships. The many college courts also provide action.*

Although the Nets have moved to New Jersey they still have a New York following. You can see their games at the Byrne Meadowlands Arena, East Rutherford, N.J., (201) 935-3900.

—Municipal Basketball Courts

Call the Parks Department for the outdoor or indoor basketball court nearest you.

—Exhibition Basketball Games

Harlem Globetrotters
Madison Square Garden. 465-6741. A New York legend. Fun, frolic, and comedy on the court. Usually in February.

Harlem Wizards
757-6300. Exhibition team similar in style to the Harlem Globetrotters. Just as spunky, still unspoiled.

Bicycling

Central Park *is closed to vehicular traffic on weekends, which permits the cyclist an exhaust-free course for pedaling (albeit bicyclists are subject to all vehicular regulations, including a 15 m.p.h. speed limit). In addition, there are 91.1 miles of bikeways in New York City (every borough but Staten Island) including Broadway, West 59 to West 23 Street; Fifth Avenue, 23 Street to Waverly Place; Sixth Avenue, West 8 to West 59 Street; Brooklyn Bridge, Centre Street to Cadman Plaza East. Call the Department of Transportation for more information on existing bike lanes: 566-0751.* NOTE: *The Metropolitan Transportation Authority prohibits carrying bicycles on subways, buses, and the Metro-North commuter railroads.*

—Bicycle Tours

Country Cycling & Hiking Tours
140 West 83 Street (10024). 874-5151. For carless city-dweller bikers. Whisks riders and bikes into the country for weekend or four- to ten-day tours; international, too. Out-of-town tours as well. Send for a free brochure.

Transportation Alternatives
494 Broadway (10012). 941-4600. Bicycle and environmental advocacy group dedicated to expanding and maintaining bicycle-friendly routes in the metropolitan area. Education and outreach programs. Publishes "City Cyclist," listing local area rides; distributed free in bike shops. Very helpful.

—Bicycle Rental & Instruction

Bikes in Central Park
Central Park, Loeb Boathouse parking lot near Fifth Ave. & 76 St (enter 72 Street). 861-4137.

For biking in Central Park this is perfect. Three- and 10-speeds; also tandems, bicycles built for two. To rent you need to have either a major credit card, passport, or driver's license, and they require a $20 cash deposit. In lieu of photo I.D., a $50 deposit is required. Cash for payment only. *OPEN Apr-Oct, Mon-Fri 10am-6pm; Sat & Sun 9am-6pm.*

Bicycles Metro
1311 Lexington Avenue at East 88 St. 427-4450. A short ride to Central Park. Three-speed and 10-speed rentals; repairs, parts, and sales. *OPEN 7 days.*

Bicycles Plus
204 East 85 Street. 794-2201. Three- and 10-speed bike rentals. Sales and repairs, too. *OPEN 7 days.*

Pedal Pusher Bicycle Shop
1306 Second Avenue near East 69 St. 288-5592 (for rentals only). Largest fleet of rentals, 3- and 10-speed bikes at low prices. Expert private lessons by appointment. Sales and repairs; a full line of accessories for bike and biker. *CLOSED Tues.*

Billiards

Before it became upwardly mobile, known as pool.

Amsterdam Billiard Club
344 Amsterdam Avenue near West 76 St. 496-8180. Thirty-one Brunswick Gold Crown tables and a private room where co-owner comedian David Brenner can play with his buddies. Truly upscale decor and crowd. Convivial cafe and lounge area; working fireplace.(For those keeping track of Lost NY, this was once Beacon Lanes.) MC, V. *OPEN Sun-Thurs 11:30am-3am; Fri & Sat 11:30am-5am.*

The Billiard Club
220 West 19 Street. 206-7665. Thirty-three tables; lessons, too. Dark and high-ceilinged pseudo-Victoriana decor. Cafe beverages and snack food. *OPEN Mon-Thurs 10am-3am; Fri & Sat 10am-5am.*

Chelsea Billiards
54 West 21 Street. 989-0096. Low-key Chelsea spot with 44 tables for snooker and billiards; lessons, too. TV for major sporting events. AE, MC, V. *OPEN 7 days 24 hours.*

Corner Billiards
85 Fourth Avenue at East 11 St. 995-1314. East Village yuppie destination. Twenty-eight tables and a restaurant. AE only. *OPEN Mon-Thurs 11am-2am; Fri & Sat 11am-4am; Sun noon-2am.*

Jacks Billiards
614 Ninth Avenue near West 43 St. 315-5225. Pleasant oasis in the theater district with nine tables. No credit cards. *OPEN 7 days noon-2am.*

Julian's
138 East 14 Street. 475-9338. The oldest and last remaining authentic pool hall complete with sharks. Thirty tables, unlimited color. No credit cards. *OPEN 7 days noon-2am.*

Le Q
36 East 12 Street. 995-8512. Twenty-eight tables on two floors. Also video and pinball. MC, V. *OPEN 7 days 10am-4am.*

Pockets
7 West 18 Street. 727-2701. Attractive Chelsea parlor. Fourteen tables and a private room. Ping-Pong downstairs. *OPEN Mon-Thurs 11am-1am; Fri & Sat 11am-3am.*

Society Billiards
10 East 21 Street, downstairs. 529-8600. Twenty-five tables in a sedate upscale environment. No credit cards. *OPEN Sun-Thurs 11am-midnight; Fri & Sat 11am-4am.*

Boating

Central Park
Loeb Boathouse, Central Park, Fifth Avenue at East 76 St (enter 72 Street). 517-3623. Aluminum rowboats for rent. Must be over 16 years of age, with proof. Rather large deposit required. *OPEN May-Oct, 7 days 9am-6pm.*

Clove Lakes Park
Victory Boulevard & Clove Road, Staten Island. (718) 442-7451. Aluminum rowboat and peddleboat rental. Must be over 14 with proof of age or accompanied by an adult. Deposit required. *OPEN weather permitting Apr-mid-Oct, 7 days 10m-6pm.*

Pelham Bay Park
Hunter Island Lagoon, Bronx. 430-1890. The only regatta course in New York City for both canoeing and rowing; a canoe and kayak launch ramp. Competitions held by private rowing clubs during spring and summer.

Boccie

There are 100 boccie courts in the city. Just a few are listed.

—Brooklyn

Bushwick Park
Knickerbocker & Irving Avenues. 2 boccie courts.

Byrne Memorial Park
3 Street & 4 Avenue. 2 boccie courts.

McCarren Park
Driggs Avenue & Lorimer Street. 4 boccie courts.

Playground
Shore Parkway & 17 Avenue. 2 boccie courts.

—Manhattan

Culliver Park
East River & 125 Street. 8 boccie courts.

East River Park
At Broome Street. 3 boccie courts.

Highbridge Park
West 173 Street. 2 boccie courts.

Playground
Houston Street & First Avenue. 5 boccie courts.

Randalls Island
Sunken Meadow Park. 4 boccie courts.

Wards Island
Recreation Area. 4 boccie courts.

—Queens

Cunningham Park
196 Street & Union Turnpike, Flushing. 1 boccie court.

Flushing Meadows–Corona Park
2 boccie courts.

Highland Park
Lower Elton Street & Jamaica Avenue, Cypress Hills. 2 boccie courts.

Triborough Playground
66 East Hoyt Avenue, Long Island City. 2 boccie courts.

—Staten Island

DeMatti Playground
Tompkins Avenue & Chestnut Street. 1 boccie court.

Stapleton Houses Playground
Tompkins Street & Tompkins Avenue, Stapleton. 1 boccie court.

Bowling

Bowlmor Lanes
110 University Place near East 12 St. 255-8188. This lively old-time (1938) two-story bowling center—Manhattan only has two—has 44 lanes, pro shop, jukebox, bar, and grill. League bowling Monday to Thursday 5 to 11pm. *OPEN Sun-Thurs 10am-1am; Fri & Sat 10am-4am.*

Fiesta Lanes
2826 Westchester Avenue, Bronx. 824-2600. Call for league or open bowling times, mainly during the day. *OPEN 7 days 9am-midnight.*

Hollywood Lanes
99-23 Queens Boulevard, Rego Park, Queens. (718) 896-2121. An underground 30-lane facility. Open bowling only on Saturday, Sunday, and Monday from 10am to 1 am; on Tuesday to Friday from 10am to early evening. Bar and coffee shop. *OPEN Sun-Fri 10am-midnight; Sat 10am-3am.*

Leisure Time Bowling & Recreation
625 Eighth Avenue, at the Port Authority Bus Terminal, 2nd level (enter Ninth Ave). 268-6909. A cavernous modern recreation complex. Thirty bowling lanes with computerized scoring. Fully equipped pro shop. Also, billiard parlor, video lounge, sports bar, and cafe. *OPEN 7 days 10am-1am.*

Whitestone Lanes
30-05 Whitestone Parkway at Linden Pl, Flushing, Queens. (718) 353-6300. Open bowling, 48 lanes. Snack bar on premises. *OPEN 7 days, 24 hours.*

Boxing

*Major boxing events are held at **Madison Square Garden** (children under age 14 not admitted). For details, call 465-6741.*

Gleason's Gym
75 Front Street near Main St, Brooklyn. (718) 797-2872. Well known for 54 years (at their former location on West 30 Street) for rigorous training and workout facilities. Will supply everything for the boxer, including a sparring partner. Come in just to watch; it's all from another time. Lessons for pros and amateurs. Sociological note: Over 140 women take boxing lessons here. Nominal admission charge. *OPEN Mon-Fri 7am-8pm; Sat 9am-4pm.*

Cricket

Below is a listing of some municipal cricket pitches in the city.
Flushing Meadows–Corona Park
Northeast of amphitheater. 1 cricket pitch.
Marine Park
Avenue U & Stuart Street, Brooklyn. 4 cricket pitches.
Red Hook Recreation Area Stadium
Bay & Columbia Streets, Brooklyn. 1 cricket pitch.
Van Cortlandt Park
Broadway & West 250 Street, Bronx. 10 cricket pitches.
Walker Park
Delafield Place, Bard & Davis Avenues, Staten Island. 1 cricket pitch.

Croquet

To play croquet on a municipal green you must obtain a permit. Season runs from April to October. For information, call the permit office, 360-8133.
Central Park
North of Sheep Meadow, 67 Street near West Drive. Croquet players and lawn bowlers share two lawns and a clubhouse, the Sports Lawn Center. *Season May-Nov.*
New York Croquet Club
Jim Erwin. 860-5347. An athletic and social club that uses the Croquet Green in Central Park's Sheep Meadow near West 69 Street. Permit for use of the green is purchased by the club. Club dues cover equipment and permit costs.

Diving (Skin or Scuba)

Aqua-Lung School of New York
1089 Second Avenue. 582-2800. Taught by Fran Gaar, TV's "Sea Hunt" diving adviser; 12 professional assistants. P.A.D.I. W-M#1; N.A.U.I. #6609. All equipment provided. Semi-private classes year-round. Certifications. Pool at First Avenue and 88 Street. 24-hour answering service.
Central Skindivers Discount Center
160-09 Jamaica Avenue, Jamaica, Queens. (718) 739-5772; (516) 826-8888. Diving on Long Island in their own heated indoor pool. Class and private lessons. Equipment sales (at discount), rentals, and repairs.

Kings County Divers Corporation
2417 Avenue U, Brooklyn. (718) 648-4232. Basic and advanced scuba diving classes taught at indoor heated pools; 5 locations. Equipment rental, sales, and service.
Professional Diving Services Inc.
3662 Shore Parkway, Brooklyn. (718) 332-9574. Taught by diving expert Bill Reddan. Private, group, or semi-private lessons. Wreck trips, night dives, underwater photography, lobstering. Lessons in Brooklyn at the Shore Front YMHA; dive boat, the *Jeanne Too*, Marine Basin Marina.
Scuba Network
571-1800; (800) 287-2822. Lessons, dives, and travel. Locations in Manhattan, Brooklyn, and Queens. Professional equipment at discount prices.
Scuba World
167 West 72 Street, 2nd floor. 496-6983. Small and personalized classes for basic to advanced instruction. Equipment, rental, repair, sales. Travel, too.

Fencing

Blade Fencing
212 West 15 Street. 620-0114. Private and group instruction; recreational, competitive, and theatrical. Equipment, too.
Fencers Club, Inc.
174 West 71 Street. 977-4150; 874-9800 (evenings). This nonprofit organization, established in 1883, is America's oldest fencing club. For men and women all levels, all ages, group and individual. Olympic-level coaches. Professional fencing championship competitors. Call for appointment.
Santelli Salle D'Armes
40 West 27 Street. 683-2823. Expert instruction in foil, sabre, epee. Beginners, advanced, competitors; theatrical fencing, too. Equipment also for sale.
McBurney YMCA
215 West 23 Street. 741-9210. Expert fencing instruction for adults and teens. Free to members of the Y.

Fishing

*In order to freshwater fish in New York City, you must get a New York State freshwater fishing license, for age 16-70. You can obtain an application from tackle stores or the **Department of Environmental Conservation,** (718) 482-4999.*
    Saltwater fishing requires only a line and reel. Check the sports section of Friday's Daily News for what's "running" that particular week. Surf casting can be done year-round from any beach in the city without a license.

—Municipal Park Fishing

Central Park
72 Street Lake. Carp, catfish, bullheads.

Kissena Park Lake
Rose Avenue & 160 Street, Flushing, Queens.
Catfish.
Prospect Park Lake
Brooklyn. Designated areas. Catfish, carp.
Van Cortlandt Park
West 242 Street, east of Broadway. Catfish, bull-
heads.
Wolf's Pond
Wolf's Pond Park, Staten Island. Catfish, carp.

—Fishing Boats

*The following boats go out very early am daily;
call to see what pier they sail from.*
City Island: *North Star*, 822-0945.
Sheepshead Bay: *Betty W.II*, (718) 769-9815;
Dorothy B., (718) 646-4057; *Flamingo III*, (718)
891-3980; *Helen H.*, (718) 646-7030; *Zephyer
V*, (718) 743-6170.

—Fishing Equipment

Manhattan Custom Tackle
49 Market Street near Monroe St., 2nd floor. 964-
1590. Specializes in repairs of rods and reels.
Also, custom rods. MC, V.
Orvis
355 Madison Avenue at East 45 St. 697-3133.
The fisherman's friend. Fly rods, reels, and accessories. Free seminars at the start of the trout
season. AE, MC, V.
Urban Angler
118 East 25 Street, 3rd floor. 979-7600. New
York's most complete selection of fly-fishing
equipment for fresh- and saltwater. MC, V.

Flying

*In order to fly a plane in the New York City area,
you must have a single or multiengine license.*
Academics of Flight
43-49 45 Street, Sunnyside, Queens. (718) 937-
5716. FAA-approved ground school; will also arrange for flying lessons at MacArthur Airport, Is-
lip, Long Island.

Football

*New York has two professional football teams:
The **Jets** (421-6600) and the **Giants**, both of
which play across the border in Giants Stadium,
Meadowlands, East Rutherford, N.J. (201) 935-
3900.*
*The pro-football season extends from early
September through December.*

—Municipal Football Fields

*There are hundreds of municipal football/soccer
fields in New York City. Call your borough office
for fields in your area.*

Golf

*For no-frills golf there are 13 public golf courses
within five boroughs. Call the individual course*

*for tee-off waiting times. There is a small fee;
discount for juniors and senior citizens. Instruction is usually available. The golf season runs
from mid-March through November.*

—Municipal Golf Courses

Bronx
Mosholu Golf Course
Van Cortlandt Park, Jerome Avenue & 213
Street. 655-9164. 5,231 yards.
Pelham Golf Course
Pelham Bay Park, Shore Road & Split Rock
Road. 885-1258. 6,405 yards.
Split Rock Golf Course
Pelham Bay Park, Split Rock Road north of Bar-
tow Circle. 885-1258. 6,462 yards.
Van Cortlandt Golf Course
Van Cortlandt Park, Park South & Bailey Avenue.
543-4595. 5,702 yards. This is the oldest public
course in the country, opened in 1895.
Brooklyn
Dyker Beach Park
Seventh Avenue & 86 Street. (718) 836-9722.
6,317 yards.
Marine Park
Flatbush Avenue between Avenue U & Belt Park-
way. (718) 338-7113. 6,736 yards.
Queens
*In addition to the courses below there is a **Pitch
& Putt** in Flushing Meadows–Corona Park, (718)
271-8182.*
Clearview Park
23 Avenue & 202 Street, Bayside. (718) 229-
2570. 6,168 yards.
Douglaston Park
Commonwealth Boulevard & Marathon Parkway,
Douglaston. (718) 224-6566. 6,314 yards.
Forest Park
Park Lane South, Union Turnpike, Myrtle Avenue
& Interboro Parkway. (718) 296-0999. 5,492
yards.
Kissena Park
Rose Avenue, Oak Avenue & Fresh Meadow
Road at 164 Street, Flushing. (718) 939-4594.
4,367 yards.
Staten Island
LaTourette Golf Course & Driving Range
Forest Hill & London Roads near Rockland Av-
enue. (718) 351-1889. 6,540 yards. Reputed to
be the best of the public courses.
Silver Lake
Victory Boulevard, Park Road & Forest Avenue.
(718) 447-5686. 5,891 yards.
South Shore
Huguenot Avenue & Rally Street. (718) 984-
0101. 6,520 yards.

—Golfing Instruction

Al Lieber's World of Golf
147 East 47 Street. 751-7890. Astroturf putting
green and instant-replay TV camera. Complete
golf shop. Evenings and weekends by appointment.
Golf Master Studio & Pro Shop
7 West 44 Street, 4th Floor. 944-1120. Lessons

including computerized swing analysis. Major-brand equipment.

Richard Metz Golf Studio
425 Madison Avenue at East 49 St., 3rd floor. 759-6940. Individual and group instruction; instant replay video. Practice cage and sand traps for city-bound golfers. Glamour note: Metz has taught George Segal, Tom Brokaw, George C. Scott, and Jackie Mason for his role in *Caddyshack*.

Midtown Golf Club
7 West 45 Street, 2nd & 3rd floors. 869-3636. With the help of climate control and electronic technology, indoor golf that feels like outdoor. Practice your swing while "playing" Pebble Beach, Spy Glass, Pinehurst II.

—Miniature Golf

Gotham Golf
Central Park, Wollman Rink, East Drive & 63 Street, north of the Pond (shortest route—enter Sixth Avenue & 59 Street). 517-4800. An 18-hole course, which includes models of such New York landmarks as the Brooklyn Bridge and Empire State Building, takes the place of ice skaters on the rink in summer (sharing it with roller skating). Popular with businesspeople at lunchtime. Available on Monday evening for private events. Admission lower for children under age 12. *OPEN Apr-Sept, Mon 10am-5pm, Tues-Thurs & Sun 10am-9:30pm, Fri & Sat 10am-11pm.*

Hackers, Hitters & Hoops ·
123 West 18 Street. 929-7482. A potpourri of activities including an 18-hole miniature golf course and a driving range. Also, three Ping-Pong tables, one pool table, baseball and basketball cages. Snack bar. Popular with kids of all ages. Available for private parties. *OPEN Mon-Thurs 11am-11pm; Fri 11am-1am; Sat 10am-1am; Sun 10am-10pm.*

Putter's Paradise
48 West 21 Street. 727-7888. This tropical motif course in Chelsea is a popular date night destination. Admission lower for children under age 12. *OPEN Wed & Thurs 6pm-midnight; Fri 5:30pm-1am; Sat noon-1am; Sun noon-8pm. CLOSED Mon & Tues.*

Gymnastics

Alex & Walter Physical Fitness
30 West 56 Street, 3rd floor. 265-7270. The emphasis is on fitness through gymnastics for strength, coordination, and balance. For adults and children.

Alzerreca's Gym
210 East 23 Street. 683-1703. Well-equipped gym. Professionally taught, grouped by ability and strength. Toddlers, preschool, adults.

McBurney YMCA
215 West 23 Street. 741-9216. Coordination, flexibility, and strength taught in a coed class using Olympic regulation equipment. Year-round. Free for members.

Handball

Handball is usually played on a four-walled court. There are over 2,000 such municipal facilities throughout the boroughs. Call your local Parks Department office for one near you.

McBurney YMCA
215 West 23 Street. 741-9210. Members-only handball.

92 Street YM-YWHA
1395 Lexington Avenue. 427-6000. Five four-walled handball courts available on a first-come, first-served basis day and evening. Reservations accepted. Membership required.

Hockey

*New York has two professional hockey teams: the **New York Rangers** skate at **Madison Square Garden,** 465-6741; the **New York Islanders** at the **Nassau Coliseum,** Hempstead Turnpike, Uniondale, (516) 794-9300. The hockey season begins in October and ends in April.*

Catching the Rangers at practice can be fun, call (914) 967-2040 for information.

Horseracing

New York's best-attended spectator sport.

—Racetracks

Aqueduct
Rockaway Boulevard at 108 Street, Jamaica, Queens. (718) 641-4700. Nonstop bus service from 42 Street and Eighth Avenue during the racing season. For exact details on travel, call (718) 330-1234. Thoroughbreds race from October to May.

Belmont Park
Hempstead Turnpike & Plainfield Avenue, Elmont, Long Island. (718) 641-4700. Long Island Rail Road Special fare includes trip from Penn Station; Atlantic Avenue, Brooklyn; or Jamaica or Woodside, Queens; and discount admission to the park. On race days, trains leave from 10:30am to 1pm. For details, call (718) 217-5477. Thoroughbreds race from May to August and September to October. Special: **Breakfast at Belmont.** Trackside breakfast plus a minitrain tour of the paddock; watch the horses work out. A wonderful family outing especially in autumn when the park is ablaze in color. Available Saturday, Sunday, and holidays, or anytime for groups of 30 or more; call for more information.

Meadowlands
Meadowlands, East Rutherford, N.J. (eight miles from Manhattan). (201) 935-8500.
Trotters: January to August
Thoroughbreds: September to December
Post time from Tuesday to Saturday at 7:30pm; Sun 1:30pm. Totally enclosed track, bleacher seats outside. The Pegasus restaurant, with lounge overlooking the races.

Transportation: Port Authority Bus Terminal, Eighth Avenue and West 41 Street, 564-8484.
Yonkers Raceway
Yonkers, N.Y. (914) 968-4200.
Trotters: Year-round. Post time 8pm.
Transportation: Port Authority Bus Terminal, Eighth Avenue and West 41 Street. 564-8484.

—Off-Track Betting (OTB)

Located throughout the city, OTB are convenient places to bet without going to the track. Call Customer Service, 704-5620, for details on how to bet, or stop in at any branch and pick up a pamphlet. They will also provide information on the OTB parlor nearest your location. *OPEN Mon-Fri 9am-5pm; Sat 9am-2pm.*
Dial-a-Horse
Open an OTB telephone account to place bets on the phone. For information and application, call 704-5337.

Horseshoe Pitches

New York City has hundreds of horseshoe pitches throughout the boroughs. The best way to find the one closest to you is to call your borough's Department of Parks and Recreation office.

Juggling

The art of keeping several objects in motion at the same time. If you don't think this is a sport, just try it.
New York Jugglers
Carmine Street Gym, Clarkson Street & Seventh Avenue South. The time to be at the gym is Thursday from 7:30pm to 9:30pm, when an average of 20 to 45 jugglers, including World Champions, entertainers, and beginners, go to it. At any given time, 150 to 250 objects may be flying through the air! Drop in with a few things to juggle and someone will help you get started. For more information on the association, call (718) 398-3561.

Lawn Bowling

*The oldest sport played in New York City, dating back to 1626—at Bowling Green, of course. Seasonal permits are required to bowl on a municipal green. Inquire at the appropriate borough office of the Parks Department. For **Central Park**, call 360-8133.*
New York Lawn Bowling Club
997-5754. You must be a member in order to use the Bowling Greens in Central Park, north of the Sheep Meadow, 67 Street near West Drive. Lawn bowling and croquet share the greens and clubhouse.

Martial Arts

(Jiu-jitsu, judo, karate, tai chi chuan.) Martial arts is an Eastern mix of physical training and philosophy for self-defense and mental discipline.

McBurney YMCA
215 West 23 Street. 741-9210. Judo, karate, iaido for men and women.
Seido Karate
61 West 23 Street, 2nd floor. 924-0511. Self-defense, physical fitness, zen meditation. Classes early morning to evening seven days a week.
Tai Chi Chuan Center of New York
125 West 43 Street. 221-6110. All are welcome to come in and observe. Call for class times.

Paddleball

Paddleball can be played on one wall and requires very little expense to play, which is one reason for its popularity. There are over 400 paddleball courts in the city. Call your borough's Parks Department office for the one nearest you.
92 Street YM-YWHA
1395 Lexington Avenue. 427-6000. Five four-walled courts are available for paddleball and are also used to play handball. Call for details.

Racquetball

Easier than tennis or squash to learn; requires more skill than force.
BQE Racquetball Club
26-50 Brooklyn-Queens Expressway West, Woodside, Queens. (718) 726-4343. Seventeen racquetball courts, pro instruction, shop. Free nursery. Exercise room, complete aerobic conditioning program; Nautilus. Bar/lounge. Membership only.
Chelsea Racquet & Fitness Club
45 West 18 Street. 807-8899. Four racquetball courts, 2 for squash. Nautilus, whirlpool, sauna. Snack bar and lounge.
Club LaRaquette
Hotel Parker Meridien, 119 West 56 Street. 245-1144. Racquetball, handball, squash. Rooftop pool and slide. Membership only.
Courts of Appeal
300 West Service Road, Staten Island. (718) 698-4500. Eleven racquetball courts; 5 Hartru tennis courts. Daily round robins; league play.
Manhattan Plaza Racquet Club
450 West 43 Street. 594-0554. This private club offers 2 racquetball courts, lessons, a pro shop, and pool; 5 Elastoturf tennis courts. Open to the public by appointment in advance without membership.
St. George Health & Racquet
43 Clark Street, Brooklyn. (718) 625-0500. One of the largest multisport fitness centers in the city.

Riding

—Riding Instruction

Claremont Riding Academy
175 West 89 Street. 724-5100. Manhattan's only remaining riding academy (established in 1892)

for expert private and group instruction for adults and children in their large indoor ring. Central Park's 6 miles of bridle paths are 1½ blocks away for those qualified to ride the street-smart horses. *OPEN 7 days 6am-10pm.*

Happy Trails
1680 Pelham Parkway, Bronx. 822-8510. Outdoor instruction for beginners and those who need a brushup. Western only. Good riding facilities. Rentals. *OPEN year-round 8am-8pm.*

Jamaica Bay Riding Academy
7000 Shore Parkway, Brooklyn. (718) 531-8949. Western and English lessons, indoors and out. Rentals and trail rides (300 acres of riding land, including some on the beach). *OPEN year-round, 7 days 9:30am-4:30pm.*

Lynne's Riding School
88-03 70 Road, Forest Hills, Queens. (718) 261-7679. Specializes in English riding. Forest Park bridal paths. Indoors in winter. Lessons, rental, boarding. *OPEN 7 days 8am-4pm.*

Pelham Bit Stables
9 Shore Road, Bronx. 885-0551. Expert English and Western riding lessons, year-round. Trail rides along the waterfront. *OPEN year-round, 7 days 8am-dark.*

Van Cortlandt Park Riding Academy
Broadway & West 254 Street, Bronx. 543-4433. Specializes in English instruction. Private, semi-private, and group only. Rentals as well. Lounge with fireplace. *OPEN year-round 9am-dark.*

West Shore Stables
52 Hughes Avenue, Staten Island. (718) 494-9816. English riding lessons. Indoor and outdoor rings. No rental. *OPEN year-round, Tues-Sun 8am-9pm.*

Rugby

The Mad Hatter Pub
1485 Second Avenue near East 77 St. 628-4917. Unofficial "headquarters" for New York rugby players.

Randalls Island
Playing fields 100 yards to the right of ramp off the Triborough Bridge. Games every Saturday morning, spring to late fall.

Running & Jogging

Call the Department of Parks and Recreation office in your borough for the municipal running track nearest you.

McBurney YMCA
215 West 23 Street. 741-9216. This Y has many programs for the runner. Physical-fitness evaluation test. This branch has the best indoor running track in New York; 20 laps equal a mile. Runners' clinic and a 100-, 250-, and 500-mile jogging program for those who want to keep a record of their mileage.

New York Road Runners Club
9 East 89 Street. 860-4455. The largest runners club in the world; the sponsor of the New York City Marathon. Open to all, whether they want to run a marathon or not. Runners clinic, classes, and "roadways" maps available. Races almost every weekend year-round. Group runs in summer every Saturday at 10am and Monday and Wednesday at 6:30pm. Clubhouse *OPEN Mon-Fri 10am-8pm; Sat 10am-5pm; Sun 10am-3pm.*

Sailing

Bring Sailing Back
Battery Park. 825-1976. Sail on the *Petrel*, a 70-foot yawl, the fastest sailboat in New York Harbor. Classes are given on a group basis in the spring and fall. Call for details.

Manhattan Yacht Club
619-3656. This private membership club offers lessons, on their own fleet of boats, out of the South Street Seaport into New York Harbor. *June-Sept.*

New York Sailing School
560 Minneford Avenue, City Island, Bronx. 885-3103. Learn to sail, cruise, or race on Long Island Sound. *Apr-Oct.*

Offshore Sailing School, Ltd.
459 City Island Avenue, City Island, Bronx. 885-3200; (800) 221-4326. Instruction to beginner, intermediate, and advanced students of the sea. *Apr-Oct.*

Skating

—Ice Skating

Allowed on natural-ice park lakes and ponds in all boroughs when and if we have a "hard freeze"; call (800) 834-3832 for round-the-clock information on safe places to skate.

Municipal Rinks

The following rinks are operated by the Department of Parks and Recreation. OPEN Nov-Apr. They tend to be cheaper than the rest but more crowded, especially on weekends.

Brooklyn

Abe Stark Skating Rink (Indoor)
Boardwalk & West 19 Street, Coney Island, Brooklyn. (718) 946-6536. A 17,000-square-foot rink. General sessions *Fri 3:30-5:30pm; Sat 12:30-3:30pm; Sun noon-4pm.* Call for hockey schedule.

Kate Wollman Memorial Rink (Outdoor)
Prospect Park, East Drive near Lincoln Road & Parkside Avenue, Brooklyn. (718) 965-6561. Speed- and figure-skating sessions nightly. *OPEN Wed-Sun.*

Manhattan

Lasker Memorial Rink (Outdoor)
Central Park at 106 Street. 517-4800. Large (26,600 square feet) outdoor rink. A lot of racing skaters here. Separate rink for hockey. *OPEN Mon 10am-5pm; Tues-Thurs 10 am-9:30pm; Fri & Sat 10am-11pm; Sun noon-9:30pm.*

Wollman Ice Rink (Outdoor)
Central Park, East Drive & 63 Street, north of the pond. 517-4800. This 33,000-square-foot rink, which often draws 100,000 skaters a season, reopened in 1986 after a lengthy reconstruction. Manhattan's elegant skyline makes a romantic backdrop—especially evenings. Indoor and outdoor seating, snack bars, lockers, and lessons. *OPEN Mon 10am-5pm; Tues-Thurs 10am-9:30pm; Fri & Sat 10am-11pm; Sun noon-9:30pm.*

Queens

World's Fair Ice Rink (Indoor)
New York City Building, Long Island Expressway & Grand Central Parkway, Queens. (718) 271-1996. An 18,000-square-foot rink. Snack bar; lockers. Lessons available. *CLOSED Mon, Tues & Thurs.* Call for hours.

Staten Island

Staten Island War Memorial Rink (Outdoor)
Clove Lakes Park, Victory Boulevard & Clove Road, Staten Island. (718) 720-1010. A 28,000-square-foot rink.

Other Rinks

Ice Studio
1034 Lexington Avenue near East 74 St, 2nd floor. 535-0304. Primarily for kids. Private lessons year-round; groups September to June. *OPEN 7 days.* Call for hours.

Rivergate Ice Rink
401 East 34 Street. 689-0035. Manhattan's newest outdoor rink, comparable in size to Rockefeller Center's rink. Coat check, rest rooms, and a warming hut. Skate rental. *OPEN Mon-Fri noon-10pm; Sat & Sun 10am-10pm.*

The Rink at Rockefeller Center
1 Rockefeller Plaza, Fifth Avenue near 51 St. 757-5730. This very busy, highly visible outdoor rink is *the* classic place to skate in New York. Private lessons available for those who don't mind an audience; call 757-5731. Rental and free checking. Group rates. *OPEN Oct-Apr, 7 days 9am-11:30pm.*

Sky Rink
450 West 33 Street, 16th floor. 695-6556. City skating year-round on Olympic-sized rink in an office building between Ninth and Tenth avenues. A mixed crowd of hockey teams, figure skaters, skating parties. Weekend evenings there's a d.j. Excellent skate shop, group and private lessons (call 239-8385). Coffee shop. Hours vary with the seasons; call 695-6555 for schedule.

—Roller Skating

Roller skating is a year-round sport. Central Park affords 31 miles of paved walkways on which to skate.

Lezly Dance & Skate School
622-26 Broadway near Bleecker St. 777-3232. Roller-skating specialists—disco, jazz, figure, and free-style. Private or group lessons, outdoor and indoor. They sell skates as well. NOTE: They trained the skaters in *Starlight Express.*

Wollman Rink
Central Park, East Drive & 63 Street, north of the pond. 517-4800. During the warm months this wonderfully located ice skating rink is turned over to roller skaters. *OPEN May to Sept.*

Skiing

—Cross-Country Skiing

Flat-surface skiing requires untrampled snow and surprisingly more physical stamina than its more popular relative, downhill skiing. The following provide excellent opportunities for cross-country skiing right in the city. Skis, boats, and poles may be rented from ski shops in town.

Manhattan

Central Park
Great Lawn, 79 Street. Good for early comers only.

Bronx

Van Cortlandt Park
Jerome Avenue & Holly Lane. Vast terrain, untrampled and smooth.

Brooklyn

Marine Park
A 19-station fitness course.

Prospect Park
Flatbush Avenue & Empire Boulevard. The Long Meadow. Get there early for smooth surface.

Queens

Alley Pond Park
Grand Central Parkway & Winchester Boulevard, Douglaston.

Staten Island

Clove Lakes Park
A 2-mile course and 19-station fitness course.

High Rock Park
Rockland & Nevada Avenues. For experienced skiers.

Soccer

A season permit is required from the Department of Parks and Recreation if you wish to play soccer on any of the park fields. Call the appropriate borough office.

—Municipal Soccer Fields

Bronx

Van Cortlandt Park Parade Field
250 Street & Broadway. 7 fields.

Brooklyn

Red Hook Recreation Area Center
Bay & Columbia Streets. 2 soccer fields, one lighted.

Manhattan

Central Park: Great Lawn
West 81 Street. 1 soccer field.

Central Park: North Meadow
97 Street. 3 soccer fields.

Queens

Alley Pond Park
Springfield Boulevard & Union Turnpike, Queens Village. 1 soccer field.

Softball

Softball can be played on the baseball diamonds in the city. A permit is required. (See Baseball.) *Call your borough's Parks Department office for fields near you. There are 656 softball fields in the city. For a permit to use the ball fields in Central Park, call 408-0209.*

Squash

New York Health & Racquet Club
20 East 50 Street; 593-1500. And 39 Whitehall Street; 269-9800. Also other locations. Good facilities and extras like a sauna, steam room, and exercise room. Membership only.

New York Sports Club
404 Fifth Avenue near 37 St. 594-3120. Complete squash facilities and lessons for men and women. Nautilus center.

Park Avenue Athletic Complex
3 Park Avenue near East 34 St. 686-1085. Good facilities. 10 courts. Lessons for men and women; matching. Pro shop. Exercise equipment.

Park Place Squash Club
25 Park Place near Church St. 964-2677. Squash instructions and games on 5 courts. Men and women. Open to the public on an hourly basis.

West Side YMCA
5 West 63 Street. 787-4400. 2 squash courts, lessons available. Also, racquetball court and 3 handball courts.

Swimming

—Municipal Swimming Pools

Outdoor pools are open from the day after New York City public schools close through to Labor Day. Indoor pools are open year-round. At presstime, a city budget crunch is threatening to drain the pools—I'm taking the rosy view that all will be well—so call before going.

Bronx
Outdoor

Claremont Pool
170 Street & Clay Avenue. 822-4217. 75 by 60 feet.

Crotona Pool
173 Street & Fulton Avenue. 822-4440. 330 by 120 feet.

Haffen Pool
Ely & Burke Avenues. 822-4176. 75 by 60 feet.

Mullay Pool
East 165 Street at Jerome & River Avenues. 822-4343. 75 by 60 feet.

Van Cortlandt Pool
West 244 Street east of Broadway. 822-4222. 164 by 104 feet.

Indoor

St. Mary's Recreation Center
St. Ann's Avenue & East 145 Street. 822-4682. 75 by 40 feet.

Brooklyn
Outdoor

Betsy Head Pool
Betsy Head Park, Hopkinson & Dumont Avenues. (718) 965-6581. 330 by 165 feet.

Kosciuszko Pool
Marcy & DeKalb Avenues. (718) 965-6585. 75 by 60 feet.

Red Hook Pool
Bay & Henry Streets. (718) 965-6579. 330 by 160 feet.

Sunset Park Pool
Seventh Avenue & 43 Street. (718) 965-6578. 256 by 165 feet.

Indoor

Brownsville Playground Recreation Center
Linden Boulevard & Christopher Avenue. (718) 345-2706. 75 by 30 feet.

Metropolitan Avenue Pool
Metropolitan & Bedford Avenues. (718) 965-6576. 75 by 30 feet.

St. John's Recreation Center
1251 Prospect Place between Troy & Schenectady Avenues. (718) 965-6574. 75 by 42 feet.

Manhattan
Outdoor

Asser Levy Pool
Playground at Asser Levy Place. 447-2020. 115 by 47 feet.

Carmine Street Recreation Center
Clarkson Street & Seventh Avenue South. 397-3147. 100 by 50 feet.

Highbridge Park Pool
Amsterdam Avenue & West 173 Street. 397-3173. 228 by 165 feet.

Jackie Robinson Pool
Bradhurst Avenue & West 145 Street. 397-3146. 235 by 81 feet.

John Jay Park Pool
East 77 Street near York Ave. 397-3177. 145 by 50 feet.

Lasker Pool
Harlem Meer, south of West 110 Street in Central Park. 397-3106. 225 by 195 feet.

Marcus Garvey Park
Madison Avenue, East 121 & East 122 Streets. 397-3124. 75 by 60 feet.

Sheltering Arms Park
West 129 Street & Amsterdam Avenue. 397-3126. 75 by 60 feet.

Wagner Houses Pool
East 124 Street between First & Second Avenues. 397-3125. 75 by 60 feet.

West 59 Street Pool
West 59 Street between West End & Amsterdam Avenues. 397-3159. 100 by 75 feet.

Indoor

Asser Levy Pool
East 23 Street & Asser Levy Place. 447-2020. 60 by 30 feet.

Carmine Street Recreation Center
Clarkson Street & Seventh Avenue South. 397-3107. 70 by 20 feet.

East 54 Street Recreation Center
342 East 54 Street between First & Second Avenues. 397-3154. 54 by 50 feet. Diving permitted.
Hansborough Recreation Center
35 West 134 Street between Fifth & Lenox Avenues. 397-3134. 75 by 45 feet.
West 59 Street Recreation Center
West 59 Street between Amsterdam & West End Avenues. 397-3159. 60 by 34 feet.

Queens
Outdoor
Astoria Park Pool
19 Street & 23 Drive, Astoria. (718) 626-8620. 330 by 165 feet.
Liberty
172 Street south of Liberty Avenue, Jamaica. (718) 520-5354. 75 by 60 feet.

Staten Island
Outdoor
Faber Park Pool
Faber Street & Richmond Terrace, Port Richmond. (718) 816-5259. 140 by 75 feet.
Lyons Pool
Victory Boulevard east of Bay Street, Tompkinsville. (718) 816-9571. 165 by 100 feet.
Tottenville Pool
Hylan Boulevard & Joline Avenue, Tottenville. (718) 356-8242. 75 by 60 feet.
West Brighton Pool
Broadway & Henderson Avenue, West Brighton. (718) 816-5507. 75 by 60 feet.

Tennis

*New York is the scene of the **U.S. Open Championships** (late August/early September) at the National Tennis Center at Flushing Meadows Park, Flushing, Queens, (718) 592-8000.*

In order to play tennis on a municipal court during the season (March to November), you must get a season's permit (there are also single play tickets available) from the Arsenal, 830 Fifth Avenue at East 64 St, 360-8133, Monday to Friday, 9am to 4pm; April to June, Saturday, 9am to noon. You must register a week in advance and bring a passport or similar-type photo with you.

—Municipal Tennis Courts

Bronx
Bronx Park
Bronx Park East & Brady Avenue. 6 hard courts.
Crotona Park
East 173 Street & Crotona Avenue. Lockers, 5 hard and 20 clay courts.
Haffen Park
Hammersley, Ely & Gunther Avenues. 6 hard courts.
Mullaly Park
164 Street & Jerome Avenue. Lockers, 8 bubbled hard courts, 7 clay courts.
Pelham Bay Park: Rice Stadium
Bruckner Boulevard & Middletown Road. 10 hard courts.
St. James Park
Jerome Avenue & 193 Street. 8 clay courts.
Seton Park
West 232 to West 235 Streets, and Independence to Palisades Avenues. 6 hard courts.
Van Cortlandt Park Stadium
West 241 Street & Broadway. 4 hard courts.
Van Cortlandt Park-Woodlawn
233 Street & Jerome Avenue. 8 clay courts, lockers.
Williamsbridge Oval
East 208 Street & Bainbridge Avenue. 8 hard courts.

Brooklyn
Bensonhurst Park
Cropsey Avenue & Bay Parkway. 8 hard courts.
Fort Greene Park
Dekalb & South Portland Avenues. 6 hard courts.
Fort Hamilton Park
Shore Road & 95 Street. 10 hard courts.
Friends Field
Avenue L & East 4 Street. 2 hard courts.
Gravesend Playground
18 Avenue & 56 Street. 8 hard courts.
Kaiser Playground
Neptune Avenue & 25 Street. 12 hard courts.
Leif Ericson Park
Eighth Avenue & 66 Street. 9 hard courts.
Lincoln Terrace Park
Buffalo & Rochester Avenues. 8 hard courts.
Manhattan Beach
Oriental Boulevard. 6 hard courts.
Marine Park
Filmore Avenue & Stuart Street. 12 hard courts.
McCarren Park
Driggs Avenue & Lorimer Street. 7 hard courts.
McKinley Park
Seventh Avenue & 75 Street. 9 clay courts.
Playground
Bay 8 Street & Cropsey Avenue. 9 hard courts.
Playground
McDonald Avenue & Avenue S. 7 hard courts.
Playground
Shore Road & 95 Street. 4 hard courts.
Prospect Park Parade Ground
Coney Island & Caton Avenues. 10 bubble-topped courts.

Manhattan
Central Park
West 93 Street & West Drive. Locker facilities. 30 courts, 4 all-weather and 26 clay.
East River Park
Broome Street. 12 hard courts.
Inwood Hill Park
West 207 Street & Seaman Avenue. 9 hard courts.
Frederick Johnson Playground
West 151 Street near Seventh Avenue. 8 hard courts.
Randalls Island
4 bubble-topped hard courts, 7 clay courts.
Riverside Park
Riverside Park & West 96 Street. 10 hard courts.
Riverside Park & West 119 Street. 10 clay courts.

Queens

Alley Pond Park
Grand Central Parkway & Winchester Boulevard, Queens Village. Lockers, 6 hard courts.

Astoria Park
21 Street & Hoyt Avenue, Astoria. 14 hard courts.

Baisley Extension
150 Street & North Conduit Avenue. 4 hard courts.

Crocheron Park
215 Place & 33 Avenue, Bayside. 10 hard courts.

Cunningham Park
Union Turnpike & 193 Street, Hollis. Lockers, 20 hard courts.

Edgemere
Alameda Avenue near Beach 51 to Beach 54 Street, Rockaway. 8 clay courts.

Equity Park
89 Avenue & 90 Street. 3 hard courts.

Flushing Fields
149 Street & 25 Avenue, Flushing. 8 clay courts.

Forest Park
Park Lane South & 89 Street, Woodhaven. Lockers, 7 hard and 7 clay courts.

Highland Park Lower Playground (Brooklyn/Queens)
Jamaica Avenue & Elton Street, Cypress Hills. 13 hard and 13 clay courts.

Juniper Valley Park
62 Avenue & 80 Street, Middle Village. 8 hard courts.

Kissena Park
Rose & Oak Avenues, Flushing. 4 hard and 8 fast-dry courts.

Liberty Park
Liberty Avenue & 173 Street, Jamaica. 10 hard courts.

Rochdale Park
New York Boulevard & 134 Avenue. 6 hard courts.

St. Albans Park
Merrick Boulevard & 172 Street. 2 hard courts.

Staten Island

Silver Lake Park
Hart Boulevard & Revere Street. 4 clay courts.

Walker Park
Bard Avenue & Delafield Place. 6 hard courts.

—Other Tennis Courts

NOTE: *Tennis is the most expensive racquet sport.*
Unless otherwise indicated, the following are open to the public.

Alley Pond Tennis Club
7920 Winchester Boulevard, Grand Central Parkway, Queens Village. (718) 468-4420. 11 indoor hard courts under a bubble. *Seasonal: OPEN end Oct-early Apr, 24 hours (winter season).* Balance of the year the bubble comes down and there are 16 outdoor municipal courts requiring only a park permit. Lessons available year-round through the club.

Boulevard Gardens Tennis
51-26 Broadway, Woodside, Queens. (718) 545-7774. 6 clay courts. Lessons available. *OPEN 7 days 8am-11pm.*

Brooklyn Racquet Club
2781 Shell Road, Brooklyn. (718) 769-5167. 11 indoor Hartru and 3 outdoor courts. Lessons. *OPEN 7 days 7am-midnight.*

Crosstown Tennis at Fifth Avenue
14 West 31 Street. 947-5780. 4 Elastaturf courts. Daily or seasonal court rental. Junior development program. Private and group lessons. *OPEN 7 days 6am-midnight.*

East River Tennis Club
44-02 Vernon Boulevard, Long Island City, Queens. (718) 937-2381. This membership club is the largest tennis facility in the city and only 10 minutes from midtown. 22 Hartru and Omni courts. Clinics, tournaments, and frequent exhibitions. Also, a 70-foot heated outdoor pool, sauna, whirlpool, Nautilus. Restaurant and lounge on premises. Minibus service to Manhattan.

Midtown Tennis Club
341 Eighth Avenue at West 27 St. 989-8572. 8 Hartru courts, indoor and outdoor. Hourly and seasonal court rental. Individual and group lessons. Junior Tennis Academy. *OPEN 7 days 7am-midnight.*

Paerdegat Racquet Club
1500 Paerdegat Avenue North, Canarsie, Brooklyn. (718) 531-1111. 4 Elastaturf courts. Lessons. Daily junior program. *OPEN 7 days 8am-11pm.*

Stadium Tennis Center
11 East 162 Street near Jerome Ave, Bronx. 293-2386. 8 indoor Elastaturf courts. Seasonal: *OPEN end Oct-end Apr, 7 days 6am-midnight.*

Sutton East Tennis Club
488 East 60 Street. 751-3452. 8 clay courts, one bubble. Individual and group lessons. Has Manhattan's largest junior development program. Tennis parties. *OPEN 7 days 7am-midnight.*

Tennis Club Grand Central Terminal
15 Vanderbilt Avenue over Grand Central Station. 687-3841. The city's oldest and most uniquely located indoor facility. 2 Elastaturf courts. *OPEN 7 days 8am-10pm.*

Tennisport, Inc.
51-24 Second Street near Borden Ave, Long Island City, Queens. (718) 392-1880. There are 16 indoor courts and 14 outdoor courts of mixed surfaces. Lessons. Membership only. *OPEN Mon-Fri 8am-10pm; Sat & Sun 8am-8pm.*

Volleyball

The 1984 Olympics gave this sport new life. There are more than 330 volleyball courts in New York City. Call your borough's Parks Department office for the one nearest you.

Wrestling

Madison Square Garden *has championship, professional, and exhibition wrestling matches one weekend a month. For information, call 465-6741.*

McBurney YM-YWCA
215 West 23 Street. 741-9216. Classes for be-

ginners and better wrestlers. Free-style wrestling taught by national YMCA wrestling champ.

92 Street YM-YWHA
1395 Lexington Avenue. 427-6000. Free-style wrestling taught. Coed classes.

Yoga

Integral Yoga Institute
227 West 13 Street; 929-0585. And 200 West 72 Street; 721-4000. Beginner, intermediate, advanced; posture, meditation, breathing, relaxation. Single-class system, no advance registration required.

Sivananda Yoga Vedanta, Inc.
243 West 24 Street. 255-4560. Small instructional groups. From breathing exercises to the yoga postures. Meditation as well. Two-hour sessions.

Yoga Society of New York
94 Fulton Street, 4th floor. 233-3887. Relaxation, breathing exercises, and yoga taught as an alternate life-style along with meditation and philosophy.

Yoga Studio of New York
351 East 84 Street. 988-9474. Basic Hatha (physical) yoga. Firming, breathing, relaxation. Private and small classes for women only.

ENTERTAINMENT

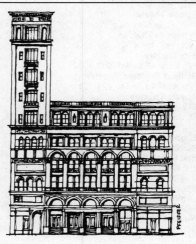

Carnegie Hall

TICKETS

Tickets can be bought in advance by mail or in person at the box office. Most theaters will take telephone orders and charge to a major credit card. Below are four discount ticket booths that sell half-price tickets for **Broadway** *and* **Off-Broadway** *shows as well as music and dance performances, same day only. Be prepared to line up and have alternate selections as shows may be sold out as the line progresses. (There are two transactions a minute at TKTS!) Cash or traveler's checks only.*

Times Square Theater Center (TKTS)
West 47 Street & Broadway. 354-5800 (recorded information about the booth only). Same-day evening performances: *Mon-Sat 3pm-8pm.* Matinee performances: *Wed & Sat 10am-2pm.* Sunday matinee and evening performances: *noon-8pm.*

Lower Manhattan Theater Center
#2 World Trade Center, mezzanine. 354-5800 (taped information). Same-day evening performances: *Mon-Fri 11am-5:30pm; Sat 11am-1pm.* Matinee and Sunday performances: sold one day prior to performance.

TKTS Brooklyn Information Booth
Boro Hall Park, Court & Montague Streets, Brooklyn. (718) 625-5015 (taped information). Same-day evening performances (off-Broadway sold till 1pm only): *Tues-Fri 11am-5:30pm; Sat 11am-3:30pm.* Matinee and Sunday performances: sold one day prior to performance date. Also sold here: full-price advance tickets to Brooklyn music, theater, and dance.

Music & Dance Half-Price Tickets Booth
Bryant Park, West 42 Street between Fifth & Sixth

Avenues. 382-2323 (taped information on ticket availability—after 12:30pm). Same-day evening performances for music and dance throughout the city. Monday tickets are sold on Sunday. *Tues, Thurs & Fri noon-2pm, 3-7pm; Wed & Sat 11am-2pm, 3-7pm; Sun noon-6pm.*

Ticketron
Tickets to Broadway shows: 246-0102.
Tickets for Broadway shows, special events, and concerts: 947-5850. AE, MC, V.

Ticketron Outlets

399-4444. To order tickets you must be calling from a touch-tone phone. Tickets for Broadway shows, special events, and concerts. Service charge per ticket. There are over 100 locations including:
   Grand Central Station, East 42 Street & Lexington Avenue
   Pennsylvania Station, West 33 Street & Seventh Avenue
   J&R Music World, 33 Park Row, opposite City Hall; 732-8600
   Tower Records, Broadway & West 4 Street and Broadway & West 66 Street

Ticketmaster
307-7171. Tickets for sporting events, concerts, and off-Broadway. AE, MC, V.

Ticket Central
406 West 42 Street. 279-4200. Tickets to all shows on Theater Row as well as other off-Broadway productions. *OPEN 7 days 1pm-8pm.*

BROADWAY

Theater in New York has traditionally referred to Broadway, the "Great White Way," but in recent years off-Broadway theater has come of age. Often thought of as more experimental, adventurous, and independent, many of Broadway's brightest lights in recent years were kindled off-Broadway. Even more avant-garde is the off-off-Broadway scene: unconventional in setting—church basements, coffeehouses, converted lofts—and in performance structure. The run is limited, often actors work for free, and admission is a donation.

For current theater and movie information, see the New Yorker; New York magazine; the New York Times, Friday's Weekend section and Sunday's Arts and Leisure section. For off- and off-off-Broadway, the Village Voice is best.

NOTE: *Stubs, $3.95, has the seating plans for all of New York's theaters, stadiums, and music halls.*

Ambassador Theater
215 West 49 Street. 239-6200.

Brooks Atkinson Theater
256 West 47 Street. 719-4098.

Ethel Barrymore Theater
243 West 47 Street. 239-6200.

Vivian Beaumont Theater
Lincoln Center, 150 West 65 Street. 239-6200.

Martin Beck Theater
302 West 45 Street. 246-6363.
Belasco Theater
111 West 44 Street. 239-6200.
Booth Theater
222 West 45 Street. 239-6200.
Broadhurst Theater
235 West 44 Street. 239-6200.
Broadway Theater
1681 Broadway near West 53 St. 239-6200.
Circle in the Square
235 West 50 Street. 239-6200.
Cort Theater
138 West 48 Street. 239-6200.
Edison Theater
240 West 47 Street. 302-2302.
Gershwin Theater
222 West 51 Street. 586-6510.
Golden Theater
252 West 45 Street. 239-6200.
Helen Hayes Theater
240 West 44 Street. 944-9450.
Imperial Theater
249 West 45 Street. 239-6200.
Walter Kerr Theater
219 West 48 Street. 582-4022.
Longacre Theater
220 West 48 Street. 239-6200.
Lunt-Fontanne Theater
205 West 46 Street. 575-9200.
Lyceum Theater
149 West 45 Street. 239-6200.
Majestic Theater
247 West 44 Street. 239-6200.
Marquis Theater
West 46 Street & Broadway. 382-0100.
Minskoff Theater
200 West 45 Street. 869-0550.
Music Box Theater
239 West 45 Street. 688-6022.
Nederlander Theater
208 West 41 Street. 921-8000
Eugene O'Neill Theater
230 West 49 Street. 246-0220.

Helen Hayes Theater
(formerly the Little Theater)

Palace Theater
1564 Broadway near West 47 St. 730-8200.
Plymouth Theater
236 West 45 Street. 239-6200.
Ritz Theater
225 West 48 Street. 582-4022.
Richard Rodgers Theater
226 West 46 Street. 221-1211.
Royale Theater
242 West 45 Street. 239-6200.
St. James Theater
246 West 44 Street. 239-6200.
Shubert Theater
225 West 44 Street. 239-6200.
Neil Simon Theater
250 West 52 Street. 757-8646.
Uris Theater
222 West 51 Street. 586-6510.
Virginia Theater
245 West 52 Street. 246-0102.
Winter Garden Theater
1634 Broadway near West 51 St. 239-6200.

OFF-BROADWAY

*Indicates Theater Row.
Abbey Theater
136 East 13 Street. 677-4120.
American Place Theater
111 West 46 Street. 840-3074.
Astor Place Theater
434 Lafayette Street. 254-4370.
Beacon Theater
2124 Broadway near West 74 St. 496-7070.
***Samuel Beckett Theater**
410 West 42 Street. 594-2826.
Susan Bloch Theater
307 West 26 Street. 633-9797.
Bouwerie Lane Theater
330 Bowery at Bond Street. 677-0060.
Cherry Lane Theater
38 Commerce Street near Bleecker St. 989-2020.
Circle in the Square Downtown
159 Bleecker Street near Thompson St. 254-6330.
Circle Repertory
99 Seventh Avenue South near West 4 St. 924-7100.
City Center, I & II
131 West 55 Street. 581-7907.
***Harold Clurman Theater**
412 West 42 Street. 594-2826.
CSC Repertory
136 East 13 Street. 677-4210.
Double Image Theater
15 Vandam Street. 924-1120.
Ensemble Studio Theater
549 West 52 Street. 247-4982.
Equity Library Theater
103 Street & Riverside Drive. 678-9505.
***Douglas Fairbanks Theater**
432 West 42 Street. 239-4321.

Folksbeine
123 East 55 Street. 755-2231.
47th Street Theater
304 West 47 Street. 265-0794.
Hartley House Theater
413 West 46 Street. 246-9872 or -9885.
*John Houseman Theater
450 West 42 Street. 967-9077.
Hudson Guild Theater
441 West 26 Street. 760-9810.
Intar Theater
420 West 42 Street. 695-6134.
Jewish Repertory Theater
344 East 14 Street. 505-2667.
La MaMa E.T.C.
74A East 4 Street. 475-7710.
Lambs Theater
130 West 44 Street. 997-1780.
Lucille Lortel Theater
121 Christopher Street near Hudson St. 924-8782
Majestic Theater
651 Fulton Street (two blocks from the Brooklyn Academy of Music), Brooklyn. (718) 636-4100.
Manhattan Theater Club
453 West 16 Street. 645-5590.
Minetta Lane Theater
18 Minetta Lane. 420-8000.
National Black Theater
2033 Fifth Avenue near 125 St. 426-5615.
Negro Ensemble Company
424 West 55 Street. 246-8545.
New Federal Theater
466 Grand Street. 598-0400.
Mitzie E. Newhouse Theater
Lincoln Center, 150 West 65 Street. 239-6200.
Ohio Theater
66 Wooster Street. 966-2509.
Perry Street Theater
31 Perry Street. 691-2509.
Players
115 MacDougal Street. 254-5076.
*Playwrights Horizons Main Stage
416 West 42 Street. 279-4200.
Promenade Theater
2162 Broadway at West 76 St. 580-1313.
Provincetown Playhouse
133 MacDougal Street. 477-5048.
Public Theater
425 Lafayette Street near Astor Pl. 598-7150.
Quiktix: For all Joseph Papp's Shakespeare Festival Public Theater attractions, half-price tickets on sale at 1pm for matinees, 6pm for evening performances; subject to availability. (*See also* HISTORIC & NEW NEW YORK, Historic Buildings & Areas, Manhattan.)
Quaigh Theater
110 West 43 Street. 382-0618.
Roundabout Theater Company
100 East 17 Street. 420-1883.
The 7th Regiment Armory
Park Avenue at East 66 St. 307-7171.
*South Street Theater
424 West 42 Street. 564-0660.

Public Theater

Sullivan Street Playhouse
181 Sullivan Street near Bleecker St. 674-3838.
For *The Fantasticks*, the world's longest-running musical—in its 32nd year.
Theater East
211 East 60 Street. 838-0177.
Theater Four
424 West 55 Street. 695-3401.
Theater off Park
224 Waverly Place. 627-2556.
The 13th Street Theater
50 West 13 Street. 627-2556.
Top of the Gate
160 Bleecker Street near Thompson St. 982-9292.
Variety Arts
Third Avenue & East 14 Street. 239-6200.
The Vineyard
108 East 15 Street. 353-3366.
Westbeth Theater Center
151 Bank Street. 924-7185.
Westside Arts Theater
407 West 43 Street. 246-6351.
WPA Theater
519 West 23 Street. 206-0523.

DANCE

Dance flourishes in New York year-round. Check the papers for current programs.
Brooklyn Academy of Music
30 Lafayette Avenue, Brooklyn. (718) 636-4100.
Next Wave Festival every fall featuring cutting edge dance groups from America and abroad. Traditional dance companies perform in the spring.
Brooklyn Center for the Performing Arts at Brooklyn College
Brooklyn College, Campus Road off Flatbush Avenue, Brooklyn. (718) 434-2222. Now in its 37th year, presenting dance, music, and popular entertainment. From October to May.
City Center
131 West 55 Street. 581-7907. Busy ballet theater. The following appear on a regular basis: the **Joffrey Ballet**, in December; **Paul Taylor Dance Company**, October; **Alvin Ailey American Dance Theater**, end of November.

Dance Theater Workshop (DTW)
Bessie Schoenberg Theater, 219 West 19 Street, upstairs. 691-6500. In Chelsea; the country's most active dance theater.
Danspace
St. Mark's Church, Second Avenue & East 10 Street. 529-2318. Where Isadora Duncan and Martha Graham once danced. Presents some of the most adventurous dance today in this historic sanctuary. Most weekends from September to June.
The Joyce Theater
175 Eighth Avenue at West 18 St. 242-0800. A fine dance venue. Home of the **Eliot Feld Ballet** and other modern companies.
The Kitchen
512 West 19 Street. 255-5793. Intriguing dance in what was the first and most forward-reaching performance center.
Metropolitan Opera House
Lincoln Center, Broadway & West 64 Street. 362-6000. The renowned **American Ballet Theatre**: new season every spring. Also Summer Dance features visiting national ballet companies including the Royal Ballet.
New York State Theater
Lincoln Center, Broadway & West 64 Street. 870-5570. The famed **New York City Ballet**: late April to late June; late November to late February.
P.S. 122
150 First Avenue at East 9 St. 477-5288. Fascinating experimental dance/performance space; year-round.

OPERA

After Dinner Opera Company
A movable feast of American opera only. For program and place, call 477-6212.
Amato Opera
319 Bowery near East 2 St. 228-8200. Since 1947. Season: September to June.
Light Opera of Manhattan
334 East 74 Street. 831-2000. Light opera year-round.
Metropolitan Opera Company
Metropolitan Opera House, Lincoln Center, Broadway & West 64 Street. 362-6000. New season: September to April. For fascinating backstage tour, call 582-3512.
New York City Opera
New York State Theater, Lincoln Center, Broadway & West 64 Street. 870-5570. A 20-week opera season July to November; musical theater for five weeks from late February to mid-April.

CONCERT HALLS

Alice Tully Hall
Broadway at West 65 Street. 362-1911.

Amato Opera Theater
319 Bowery near East 2 St. 228-8200.
Apollo Theater
253 West 125 Street. 749-5838.
Avery Fisher Hall
Lincoln Center, Broadway at West 65 Street. 874-2424.
Bargemusic Ltd.
Fulton Ferry Landing, Brooklyn. (718) 624-4061.
Beacon Theater
2124 Broadway near West 74 St. 496-7070.
Bloomingdale House of Music
323 West 108 Street. 663-6021.
Brooklyn Academy of Music (BAM)
30 Lafayette Avenue, Brooklyn. (718) 636-4100. Bus Express to Brooklyn from Manhattan and back. Call for details.
Carnegie Hall & Weill Recital Hall
154 West 57 Street. 247-7800.
Cooper Union Great Hall
Cooper Square at East 7 St. 254-6374.
Greenwich House Music School
46 Barrow Street near Seventh Ave South. 242-4770.
Juilliard School Theater
144 West 66 Street. 799-5000.
Kaufman Concert Hall
92 Street Y, 1395 Lexington Avenue. 996-1100.
The Kitchen
512 West 19 Street. 255-5793.
Lehman College Center for the Performing Arts
Bedford Park Boulevard West, Bronx. 960-8833.
Madison Square Garden
Seventh Avenue & West 33 Street. 563-8000.
Merkin Concert Hall
Abraham Goodman House, 129 West 67 Street. 362-8719.
Metropolitan Museum
Fifth Avenue & 82 Street. 879-5512 (box office); 570-3949 (auditorium information).
Metropolitan Opera House
Lincoln Center, Broadway & West 64 Street. 362-6000.
New School Auditorium
66 West 12 Street. 741-5689.
New York City Center
131 West 55 Street. 581-7907.
Queensborough Community College Theater
56 Avenue off Springfield Boulevard, Bayside, Queens. (718) 631-6321.
Radio City Entertainment Center
Avenue of the Americas at West 50 Street. 247-4777.
Symphony Space
2537 Broadway at West 95 St. 864-5400.
Third Street Music School Settlement
235 East 11 Street. 777-3240.
Town Hall
123 West 43 Street. 840-2824.
Wave Hill
249 Street & Independence Avenue, Riverdale, Bronx. 549-3200.

Weill Recital Hall at Carnegie Hall
154 West 57 Street. 247-7800.

MOVIE THEATERS: FIRST-RUN

In recent years, first-run movie theaters have proliferated throughout Manhattan, with multi-screen complexes sprouting in every neighborhood. Alas, while the theaters are more numerous, the screens have shrunk, the price has skyrocketed, and there are actually fewer films to choose from. Most of the complexes are owned by Cineplex Odeon or City Cinemas; for current listing check any of the daily newspapers, New York magazine, or the Village Voice.

MOVIE THEATERS: REVIVAL

Fewer and fewer. . .

American Museum of the Moving Image
35 Avenue at 36 Street, Astoria, Queens. (718) 784-0077.

Cinema Village
100 Third Avenue near East 12 St. 505-7320.

Film Forum
209 West Houston Street. 727-8110.

Museum of Modern Art
11 West 53 Street. 708-9490.

Public Theater
425 Lafayette Street near Astor Pl. 598-7150.

Theater 80 St. Marks
80 St. Marks Place near First Ave. 254-7400. A wonderfully quirky place features a new classic double-bill daily.

FREE ENTERTAINMENT

Call 360-1333 daily for a listing of free events in the parks on that day. In addition, check the ANNUAL EVENTS chapter for listings of many very special happenings, especially during the summer months, most of which are FREE.

CHURCH MUSIC

See Saturday's New York Times for current church musical programs.

TELEVISION SHOWS

For free tickets to TV programs go to the Convention & Visitor's Bureau, 2 Columbus Circle or in Times Square at 158 West 42 Street between Broadway and Seventh Avenue, 397-8222, or call or write the appropriate station:

WABC (Channel 7)
For tickets to "Live with Regis & Kathie Lee," send a postcard with name, address, phone number, and number of tickets (maximum 4; no one under age 18 admitted) to: Live Tickets, Ansonia Station, P.O. Box 777, New York, NY 10023-0777. NOTE: Eight-month wait. For Sally Jesse Raphael, write Sally Tickets, P.O. Box 1400, Radio City Station, New York, NY 10101.

WCBS (Channel 2)
CBS Ticket Bureau, 524 West 57 Street (10019). 975-2476.

WNBC (Channel 4)
NBC Guest Relations, 30 Rockefeller Plaza (10020). 664-3055 (recording) or 664-3056. "Saturday Night Live," "Late Night with David Letterman," "Donahue," "Cosby." Four hot shows, write many months in advance (postcards only; no one under age 16 admitted). NOTE: Standby tickets are a possibility for "Letterman," Tuesday to Friday, 8:15am, mezzanine level, 50 Street side.

WNET (Channel 13)
356 West 58 Street (10019). 560-2000.

RADIO STATIONS

Radio jargon: MOR = "middle of the road." AOR = "all over the road" or more traditionally "album-oriented radio."

AM-Radio

WABC-AM: 770. Talk
WADO-AM: 1280. Spanish, news/talk
WALK-AM: 1370. Adult contemporary (Long Island)
WCBS-AM: 880. All news
WEVD-AM: 1050. Talk/MOR
WFAS-AM: 1230. Contemporary/personalities & sports (Westchester)
WGBB-AM: 1240. News & sports (Long Island)
WGLI-AM: 1290. Oldies (Long Island)
WGRC-AM: 1300. Adult contemporary/news/ sports (Rockland)
WGSM-AM: 740. MOR (Long Island)
WHLI-AM: 1100. Big band (Long Island)
WINS-AM: 1010. All news
WZRC-AM: 1480. Heavy metal/rock
WKDM-AM: 1380. Spanish contemporary
WLIB-AM: 1190. Black news/information/ Caribbean music
WLNA-AM: 1420. MOR/news/talk (Westchester)
WMCA-AM: 570. Religious
WFAN-AM: 660. Imus/sports, Mets, Rangers, Knicks
WNEW-AM: 1130. Big band, NY Giants
WNYC-AM: 830. NYC public radio; information/ talk
WNYG-AM: 1440. Gospel (Long Island)

WOR-AM: 710. Talk
WPAT-AM: 930. "Beautiful music"
WQXR-AM: 1560. Classical
WSKQ-AM: 620. Spanish, MOR
WVIP-AM: 1310. News & information (Westchester)
WVOX-AM: 1460. Talk (Westchester)
WWDJ-AM: 970. Religious
WWRL-AM: 1600. Urban contemporary; NY Nets basketball

FM-Radio

WALK-FM: 97.5. Adult contemporary (Long Island)
WBAB-FM: 102.3. AOR (Long Island)
WBAI-FM: 99.5. Listener sponsored, noncommercial; talk/music
WBGO-FM: 88.3. Jazz (Newark)
WBLS-FM: 107.5. Urban contemporary
WCBS-FM: 101.1. Golden oldies 50s and 60s
WEVD-FM: 97.9. Foreign language/talk
WFME-FM: 94.7. Religious
WFUV-FM: 90.7. Black/jazz/ethnic (Fordham University)

WHTZ-FM: 100.3. Top 40, contemporary hit radio
WKCR-FM: 89.9. Jazz (Columbia University)
WKJY-FM: 98.3. Soft rock (Long Island)
WLTW-FM: 106.7. Light music
WNCN-FM: 104.3. Classical
WNEW-FM: 102.7. AOR
WNSR-FM: 105.1. Soft rock
WNYC-FM: 93.9. NYC public radio; classical/talk
WNYE-FM: 91.5. Educational/50s and 60s music
WNYU-FM: 89.1. Classical/jazz/alternative (New York University)
WPAT-FM: 93.1. "Beautiful music"
WQCD-FM: 101.9. Contemporary jazz/new age
WQHT-FM: 103.5. Contemporary hit radio/dance
WQXR-FM: 96.3. Classical
WRKS-FM: 98.7. Urban contemporary
WPLJ-FM: 95.5. Top 40/contemporary hit radio
WXRK-FM: 92.3. Personality/classic rock
WYNY-FM: 103.5 Crossover country
WSKQ-FM: 97.9. Spanish contemporary

NIGHTLIFE

Limelight

A NOTE ABOUT NIGHTLIFE

No aspect of life in New York changes as rapidly as this, and in no other area of the city's available pleasures is the term *hot* so short-lived. What's hot one month may just as easily be gone the next. Ask any of the young downtown set where the best in town is and they'll tell you it's the movable one—the outlaw party, advertised by word of mouth, that glows hot for the evening and then disappears as the sun rises, only to surface the next time somewhere else. Obviously they are undocumentable. With that in mind, this list covers what is classic and hot at presstime. Short of writing this section in pencil and supplying you with an eraser, this note will have to suffice.

NIGHTSPOTS INDEX

The following is an index of nightspots in this section. The categories appearing in alphabetical order are: Blues, Cabaret, Comedy, Country/Western, Dance Clubs, Dining & Dancing, Jazz, Nightclubs, Piano Bars, and Pop/Rock. The description of a particular nightspot can be found in the category that appears in parentheses. Full descriptions follow this index.

Abilene Cafe (Blues)
Algonquin Hotel (Piano Bars)
Algonquin Oak Room (Cabaret)
Amazonas (Nightclubs)
Angry Squire (Jazz)
Arthur's Tavern (Jazz)
Au Bar (Dance Clubs)
Back Fence (Pop/Rock)

Baja (Dance Clubs)
The Ballroom (Cabaret)
Bemelman's Bar (Piano Bars)
Birdland (Jazz)
The Bitter End (Pop/Rock)
Blue Note (Jazz)
Bottom Line (Pop/Rock)
Bradley's (Jazz)
Cafe Carlyle (Cabaret)
Cafe Feenjon (Nightclubs)
Cafe Pierre (Piano Bars)
Cafe Society (Nightclubs)
Catch a Rising Star (Comedy)
Cat Club (Dance Clubs)
Cave Canem (Dance Clubs)
CBGB and OMFUG (Pop/Rock)
Chez Josephine (Piano Bars)
Chicago City Limits (Comedy)
China Club (Dance Clubs)
Chippendale's (Nightclubs)
Club Broadway (Dance Clubs)
Club El Morocco (Dance Clubs)
Clubland (Dance Clubs)
The Comedy Cellar (Comedy)
Comic Strip (Comedy)
Condon's (Jazz)
Copacabana New York (Dance Clubs)
Dangerfield's (Comedy)
Dan Lynch's (Blues)
Don't Tell Mama (Cabaret)
The Duplex (Cabaret)
Eagle Tavern (Comedy)
Eighty Eights (Cabaret)
Emerald City (Dance Clubs)
Fat Tuesday's (Jazz)
Five Oaks (Piano Bars)
Greene Street Cafe (Jazz)
Hors D'Oeuvrerie (Dining & Dancing)

Improvisation (Comedy)
Jan Wallman's (Cabaret)
J's (Jazz)
Kenny's Castaways (Pop/Rock)
Knickerbocker Bar & Grill (Jazz)
The Knitting Factory (Pop/Rock)
Limelight (Dance Clubs)
Lone Star Road House (Country/Western)
Manny's Car Wash (Blues)
Maxim's de Paris (Dining & Dancing)
Michael's Pub (Jazz)
Monkey Bar (Piano Bars)
Mostly Magic (Nightclubs)
Nell's (Dance Clubs)
New York Roxy (Dance Clubs)
Palladium (Dance Clubs)
The Pyramid (Dance Clubs)
Rainbow and Stars (Cabaret)
Rainbow Room (Dining & Dancing)
Red Zone (Dance Clubs)
Reggae Lounge (Dance Clubs)
The Ritz (Pop/Rock)

Roma di Notte (Dining & Dancing)
Roseland (Dance Clubs)
S.O.B.'s (Sounds of Brazil) (Dance Clubs)
Stand-Up New York (Comedy)
Sweet Basil (Jazz)
Sweetwater's (Cabaret)
Texas (Country/Western)
Top of the Gate (Cabaret)
Top of the Tower (Piano Bars)
Tramps (Blues)
Upstairs at Greene Street (Cabaret)
The View Lounge (Jazz)
Village Corner (Jazz)
Village Gate (Jazz)
Village Vanguard (Jazz)
Visiones (Jazz)
West Bank Cafe (Cabaret)
West End Cafe (Jazz)
Wetlands (Dance Clubs)
World Yacht Cruises (Dining & Dancing)
Zinno (Jazz)

BLUES

The Manhattan Blues Alliance, 105 East 10 Street (10003), is a nonprofit organization dedicated to keeping blues music alive in New York. They sponsor a Blues Monday series; get on their mailing list.

Abilene Cafe
73 Eighth Avenue at West 13 St. 255-7373. In a stucco-and-wood ersatz Southwestern setting, traditional rhythm and blues. Draws a well-heeled crowd for dinner, more humble folks at the bar. Weekdays and Sunday, shows at 9:30 and 11:30pm; Friday and Saturday at 1am also. Menu of basic fare. No cover or minimum weekdays unless there's a hot act. Weekends cover and two-drink minimum. AE, MC, V.

Dan Lynch's
221 Second Avenue near East 14 St. 677-0911. In the East Village, an old-time no-frills neighborhood bar for low-priced drinks and some of the best blues in this city. During the week the music starts at 10pm and wails till 2am, Saturday till 3:30am. Sunday matinee music starts at 4pm and goes till 9pm. No food, but there is a well-used pool table. No cover during the week. No credit cards. *OPEN Mon-Fri 8am-2am; Sat 8am-3:30am; Sun noon-3am.*

Lone Star Roadhouse
See Country/Western.

Manny's Car Wash
1558 Third Avenue at East 87 St. 369-2583. Hard evidence of the proliferation of blues music in the city. A rowdy rough-and-ready audience of 25 to 45-year-olds flocks here for Chicago-style blues and one another. Shows Monday to Saturday from 9:15pm, on Sunday from 8:30pm. White Castle burgers (the real thing), microwaved in their boxes, available at the bar. No minimum, cover varies. AE only.

Tramps
45 West 21 Street. 727-7788. New sleeker Flatiron District location for this old reliable restaurant/bar that still features a wide range of musical talent in still casual friendly atmosphere. Top-flight rock and pop are featured but the soul of the club is R&B and New Orleans Zydeco. Shows Tuesday to Saturday at 8:30pm and 11:30pm. Inexpensive Cajun-Creole menu and a spacious floor for dancing. Cover varies; two-drink minimum at tables unless you dine; on selected evenings free admission with dinner reservations before 8pm. Pool table. AE, DC, MC, V. *OPEN on show nights till 4am.*

CABARET

Algonquin Oak Room
59 West 44 Street. 840-6800. Sophisticated New York setting and crowd. The attraction is usually a gifted song stylist, the likes of Julie Wilson, Michael Feinstein, Andrea Marcovicci. Shows Tuesday to Thursday at 9:15pm, Friday and Saturday at 9:15 and 11:15pm. Dinner rarely lives up to the talent or the surroundings. Reserve. Cover and minimum. Jacket and tie. AE, CB, DC, MC, V.

The Ballroom
253 West 28 Street near Eighth Ave. 244-3005. Longtime popular Chelsea cabaret regularly features such grand ladies as Peggy Lee, Karen Akkers, and Blossom Dearie. It also boasts the oldest tapas bar in America (*OPEN noon-1am*). Dine before the show in the dining room or at the bar on original and tasty tapas (*see* RESTAURANTS, Spanish: Tapas). Shows Tuesday to Thursday at 9pm; Friday and Saturday at 9 and 11pm; Sunday at 3 and 7pm. Cover charge and two-drink minimum for shows. Free parking for dinner guests. AE, DC, MC, V.

Cafe Carlyle
Carlyle Hotel, Madison Avenue & East 76 Street. 744-1600. The stylishly sophisticated bar/supper club is a must, especially when witty urbane entertainer Bobby Short is in residence (from September to December and April to June each year); he's as New York as a Gershwin tune. The rest of the year supremely talented jazz pianist George Shearing, among others, fills in. Intimate dining especially if seated on the comfy banquettes, basking in a romantic glow. Shows Tuesday to Saturday at 9:30 and 11:30pm. Jacket required. Stiff cover charge but you can sit at the bar for less than half the charge. AE, CB, DC, MC, V.

Don't Tell Mama
343 West 46 Street. 757-0788. Theater district cabaret and piano bar. Revues, comedy, and music in the long-running back-room cabaret; shows nightly at 8 and 10pm. Reservations necessary. Cover varies; two-drink minimum. The front room piano bar with its "open mike" is also popular, especially after theater nightly 9:30pm till 3 or 4am. There is a minimum at the tables. No food. No credit cards.

The Duplex
61 Christopher Street at Seventh Ave South. 255-5438. Longtime (40 years) lively Greenwich Village cabaret in new digs. Upstairs, shows Sunday to Thursday at 8 and 10pm, Friday and Saturday comedy at midnight as well. Casual, friendly crowd. Drinks only; cover and minimum. Downstairs, a packed piano bar nightly from 9pm to 4am for singing along. No cover here. No credit cards.

Eighty Eights
228 West 10 Street. 924-0088. Casual, inviting Greenwich Village cabaret/piano bar. Original musical revues and comedy are the usual features in the intimate upstairs Cabaret Room. Shows Monday through Thursday at 8 and 10pm, Friday and Saturday at 11pm and 1am; at the downstairs piano bar, the singing along can get raucous. Cover and two-drink minimum. No credit cards.

Jan Wallman's
49 West 44 Street. 764-8930. Intimate theater

district restaurant/cabaret of a long-known, well-thought-of Village cabaret owner. Shows Monday to Saturday at 9 and 11pm. Continental food. Cover and food or drink minimum. AE, CB, DC, MC, V.

Rainbow and Stars
30 Rockefeller Center, 65th floor. 632-5000. Around the bend from the Rainbow Room, this smartly situated Art Deco–detailed supper club overlooking Central Park presents most of the greats—including Rosemary Clooney, Tony Bennett, Mel Torme—against the city night. It's a sophisticated way to spend an evening. Shows Tuesday to Saturday at 9 and 11:15pm. Continental cuisine. Steep cover charge. AE only.

Sweetwater's
170 Amsterdam Avenue at West 68 St. 873-4100. Top entertainment in this Lincoln Center–area spot. Featured artists have included Arthur Prysock, Cissy Houston, Wilson Pickett, the Manhattans. Shows Thursday, Friday, and Saturday at 9 and 11pm. Sunday and Wednesday are Latin nights from 7pm to 3am. Jacket required. Cover and minimum varies. AE, DC, MC, V.

Top of the Gate
160 Bleeker Street near Thompson St. 982-9292. Theater cabaret with wide range of acts from comedy to political theater. Drinks only. Admission charge plus minimum (except for theater shows). Call for current attraction.

Upstairs at Greene Street
101 Greene Street near Prince St., upstairs. 925-2415. A popular SoHo showplace for music and comedy every Friday and Saturday starting at 8pm. Light menu, cocktails, or desserts. Cover charge. Dine to sophisticated piano music in the cavernous restaurant downstairs.

West Bank Cafe
407 West 42 Street. 695-6909. Go west to the **Downstairs Theatre Bar**, for plays, cabarets, musical revues, try-outs—a wide variety. Very friendly and casual. Cover and minimum. AE, MC, V.

COMEDY

Comedy is king in New York. At some of the following clubs each night is amateur night; you don't know what you'll get for the price of a drink, but you will have fun. At others, some of today's top stars got their start, and lightning keeps striking. Most are showcases for fledgling funny people to hone their skills while waiting for a stint with Letterman or Carson. At the more established clubs, top alumni occasionally drop by to try out new material. They are all popular, and reservations are recommended, especially on weekends.

Catch a Rising Star
1487 First Avenue near East 77 St. 794-1906. Extremely casual ambience in this Upper East Side showcase club known for its consistent good humor. Hosts of comics onstage, scouts in

the audience, and sometimes at the crowded bar a who's who of comedy (David Brenner and Robin Williams have been known to drop in). Continuous lineup Sunday to Thursday, 9pm till midnight; Friday at 8:30 and 11pm; Saturday at 8pm, 10:15pm, and 12:30am. Cover and two-drink minimum. AE only.

Chicago City Limits
Jan Hus Theater, 351 East 74 Street. 772-8707. For over 12 years, this improv troupe has been doing what they describe as "comedy without a net." Shows Wednesday and Thursday at 8:30pm, Friday and Saturday at 8 and 10:30pm. Soft drinks and snacks available. Tickets required. AE only.

The Comedy Cellar
117 MacDougal Street near Bleecker St. 254-3630. Tightly packed informal downstairs Village club for constant comedy. Shows Sunday to Thursday at 9pm; Friday at 9 and 11:30pm; Saturday at 8pm, 10pm, and midnight. Middle Eastern and American food. Cover and drinks minimum varies. No credit cards.

Comic Strip
1568 Second Avenue near East 81 St. 861-9386. Packed comedy showcase club, where Eddie Murphy began to make us laugh. Merriment Sunday to Thursday from 9pm to 1am; Friday and Saturday at 9 and 11pm. Monday night is open mike. Comfortable bar; Chinese food. Cover and two-drink minimum. AE, MC, V.

Dangerfield's
1118 First Avenue near East 61 St. 593-1650. Comedian Rodney "I don't get no respect" Dangerfield's popular club specializes, of course, in good comedy, often by some golden oldies. Newfound silver screen stardom keeps himself away more often than not. Shows Sunday to Thursday at 9pm; Friday at 9 and 11:30pm; Saturday at 8pm, 10:30pm, and 12:30am. New talent showcase on Sunday. American food. Cover and minimum. AE, CB, DC, MC, V. *OPEN 7 days 8pm-4am.*

Eagle Tavern
355 West 14 Street. 924-0275. Authentic working-class Irish bar for comedy every Thursday—open mike 6 to 8:30pm, show at 8:30pm. In addition, there's an "Irish Jam" Monday and Friday from 9pm to 1am and more music—jazz or folk—Saturday and Sunday, with shows at 8:30 and 10:30pm. Cover and one-drink minimum Thursday night only. MC, V.

Improvisation
358 West 44 Street. 765-8268. On the fringe of the theater district, the Improv is the oldest (1963) and most famed of the comedy showcase spots. Among those who honed their skills here: Joe Piscopo, Richard Pryor, Bette Midler. Very informal. Sunday to Thursday from 9pm to 2am; Friday at 9pm and midnight; Saturday at 8 and 10:30pm. Very crowded on weekends. Food available (burgers, soups, desserts). Cover and minimum. AE only.

Mostly Magic
See Nightclubs.

Stand-Up New York
236 West 78 Street. 595-0850. Good comedy
line-up in intimate bare bones Upper West Side
club. Three funny people nightly. Shows Sunday
to Thursday at 9pm; Friday at 8:30 and 11:30pm;
Saturday at 8pm, 10:15pm, 12:30am (reserve
for this night). Hot and cold heroes and pizza.
Cover and two-drink minimum. AE, MC, V.

COUNTRY/WESTERN

Lone Star Roadhouse
240 West 52 Street. 245-2950. It's uptown now,
but it's still the official Texas embassy in New
York; just look for the red Silver Eagle Tour Bus.
Raucous American-roots music—country, R&B,
and rockabilly, Monday to Saturday 9:30 and
11:30pm. Add one-, two-, or three-alarm chili
and Texas beers and you've got a hot spot. Almost always crowded. Two bars. Cover charge
and minimum at tables. AE, CB, DC, MC, V.
Texas
10 East 16 Street. 255-8880. Friendly bar/
restaurant features a little country in the city every Saturday night 9pm to midnight. AE, MC, V.

DANCE CLUBS

See also Pop/Rock.
Au Bar
41 East 58 Street. 308-9455. The first of the Nell's
clones; this one is from Howard Stein, the creator of that once-hot disco Xenon. It's small and
insulated with the look and feel of a Ralph Lauren ad. Nostalgic classics give way to contemporary music as the evening progresses. Supper and breakfast are served. Reserve. AE, CB,
DC, MC, V. OPEN 7 days 9pm-4am.
Baja
246 Columbus Avenue near West 72 St. 724-
8890. Casual dance club owned by a clutch of
investment bankers. Here, young (early 20s)
professionals can imbibe tropical drinks, dance,
or watch large-screen TV. A d.j. spins 60s to 90s
tunes. Private party venue. Cover varies. AE,
MC, V. OPEN Tues-Sat 9:30pm-4am.
Cat Club
76 East 13 Street. 505-0090. On Sundays, the
New York Swing Dance Society makes this
place jump with great swing dancing to live big
bands from 7pm to midnight. (For more information on the society, call 713-5148.) The rest of
the week it's a mixed bag: Monday night for funk;
Wednesday and Thursday, heavy metal and its
heavy fans; Friday, rock; and every Saturday
there's some avant-garde event. Shows at 11pm.
Cover varies. Drinks only. No credit cards.
Cave Canem
24 First Avenue near East 2 St. 529-9665. Architecturally fascinating East Village club/restaurant
in a renovated former bath house. Dining up-

stairs, dancing downstairs amid the "ruins."
Cover charge (weekends only). OPEN 7 nights
till 4am.
China Club
2130 Broadway at West 75 St, downstairs. 877-
1166. No glitz just great rock music for listening
and dancing. It is a music industry hangout and
impromptu after-hours jams have included the
likes of Julian Lennon, David Bowie, and Stevie
Wonder. Live music every night but Monday,
which is Disco Night for pretty people. Cover
charge. AE, MC, V. OPEN 7 nights 10pm-4am.
Club Broadway
2551 Broadway at West 96 St. 864-1660. Black
and Latino crowd, dancing and listening to pulsating Latin rhythms Thursday to Sunday from
9:30pm to 1am. No food. No credit cards.
Club El Morocco
307 East 54 Street. 750-1500. In its heyday, this
was the exclusive watering hole for the glittering
Hollywood/cafe society crowd. Still here are the
famed zebra banquettes, the white palms, and
the twinkling ceiling, but the music and the
young, affluent, hip crowd have a Latin flavor.
Thursday there are free mambo lessons and a
free buffet; Friday disco on the second floor, a
salsa d.j. on the first; Saturday and Sunday live
salsa bands draw major crowds. Admission varies. Jacket preferred; no denim or sneakers.
OPEN Thurs 6pm-midnight; Fri & Sat 10pm-4am;
Sun 4pm-midnight.
Clubland
254 West 54 Street. At the Ritz Wednesday to
Saturday at 10pm or immediately following the
show on concert nights. Loud music from Mo-
town to modern, dancing, elaborate video presentations, theatrics, lights, skits and bits, and
the Clubland Party Machinery. A new twist on
clubs (they hope) promising a new party every
week. Admission charge.
Copacabana New York
10 East 60 Street. 755-6010. At the famed Copa
Tuesdays, Fridays, and Saturdays are disco and
Latin nights featuring Latin bands downstairs
and disco music upstairs. Draws a dancing
crowd. Tuesday from 6 to 7pm free admission
and free buffet; cover varies thereafter and on
Friday and Saturday. No sneakers or denim; Saturday night jacket required. Balance of the week
private parties. OPEN Tues 6pm-3am; Fri 6pm-
4am; Sat 10pm-4am.
Emerald City
617 West 57 Street. 581-4432. Way way west,
between 11th and 12th avenues, one of the largest dance clubs in town. Disco—hot 97—every
Friday and Saturday 9:30pm to 4am. Admission
varies with the hour.
Limelight
660 Sixth Avenue at West 20 St. 807-7850.
Former church (1846) converted to accommodate dance floor, bar, and VIP lounge, leaving
stained-glass windows and other religious accoutrements intact. Middle of the new-wave
road, still popular with music and movie people
and those who like to go where they go. Best

after midnight. Sunday nights "Rock and Roll Church." Booze only. Admission charge. AE only. *OPEN 7 nights 10pm-4am.*

Nell's
246 West 14 Street. 675-1567. It's *intime* with all the trappings of a time past—overstuffed seating, subdued lighting, wood paneling, gilt mirrors, quiet places to drink, dine, and talk. Downstairs for the dance floor. No longer *the* club—as evidenced by the fact that it's not hard to get in to. AE, MC, V. Cash only at the door, admission ranges from $6-$12. *OPEN 7 nights 10pm-4am.*

New York Roxy
1018 West 18 Street. 645-5156. Between 10th and 11th avenues, but on Saturday nights it's the hottest spot in town if you can get into their Locomotion Party, with musclemen, drag queens, people in various stages of undress, and assorted other atypical New Yorkers on their 5,000-square-foot dance floor—it's a pulsating chaotic time. Tuesday (gay and lesbian night) and Wednesday there's roller skating from 8pm, lessons at 6:30pm; Thursday is a gay dance night; Friday is Disco Inferno with Jelly Bean Benitez in charge of the music. *OPEN Tues & Wed 6:30pm-4am; Thurs-Sat 10pm-4am.*

Palladium
126 East 14 Street. 473-7171. This mega multimedia club has cooled (limos no longer grace its seedy exterior), but it's still an eyeful. The main dance space is overlooked by an 800-seat balcony and mezzanine. There are suspended staircases, 50 video monitors, art by some of today's top downtown artists, and loads of theatrical dazzle. There are also quiet spaces, pillows and platforms and conversation nooks with soft music. Things usually heat up after midnight. The place holds 3,500 but now only for hot shows. Booze only. Cover. AE, MC, V. *OPEN Thurs-Sat 9pm-4am.*

The Pyramid
101 Avenue A near East 6 St. 420-1590. Downtown attitude still prevails in what passes for venerable in the East Village. Kitsch art shows, avant-garde theme parties, and an extremely unpredictable assortment of live performances including go-go boys and drag queens. Sunday is the hot night for this quintessential East Village club. Showtime 11:30pm. No food. No credit cards. *OPEN 7 days till 4am.*

Red Zone
440 West 54 Street. 582-2222. An enormous block-long club with a 10,000-square-foot dance floor. Forty speakers make sure the music is heard and felt; an under-25, well-dressed, up-and downtown crowd—gay and straight—dance the night away here, especially Monday and Saturday nights. Tuesday is gay and lesbian night, Wednesday is Latin night, Thursday it becomes **Daddy's House** for hot hip hop, Friday features reggae. Upstairs VIP room more mellow.

Reggae Lounge
285 West Broadway at Canal St. 226-4598. In TriBeCa, colorful grass-roots reggae music and dancing in a very basic, no-frills atmosphere.

Live bands on Sunday from 9pm. Drinks only. Admission charge. *OPEN Wed-Sat 10pm-4am; Sun 9pm-4am.* (Expect to go through a metal detector.)

Roseland
239 West 52 Street. 247-0200. It's no longer ten cents a dance, but it's still reminiscent of another time, and you can still see the best ballroom dancing—they're serious about it here. Newly refurbished and, at nearly 70, still lookin' good. Two bands (one American, one Latin) alternate Sunday 2:30 to 11pm. Thursday and Saturday from 2:30 to 11pm, the dancing is to taped music. Restaurant and bar. Jacket required. Admission charge. AE only.

S.O.B.'s
204 Varick Street at West Houston St. 243-4940. Like a night in Rio: regional Brazilian food 7 to 10:30pm; spirited live bands from Brazil, the Caribbean, and Africa; dancing on the small floor from 9pm till dawn. A joyful carnival atmosphere prevails year-round. Cover and minimum. AE, CB, DC, MC, V. Reserve. *OPEN Tues-Thurs 5pm-2am; Fri & Sat 5pm-4am.*

DINING & DANCING

Hors D'Oeuvrerie
Windows on the World, World Trade Center, Tower #1, 107th floor. 938-1111. This aerie is a fine spot to dance or just listen to a trio Monday to Saturday from 7pm to 1am; Sunday from 7:30pm to 12:30am. Extensive menu of hors d'oeuvres and wines and champagne by the glass. Small cover charge. No denim, jackets for men. *OPEN 7 days.*

Maxim's de Paris
680 Madison Avenue near East 61 St. 751-5111. Opulent Belle Epoque clone of the famed Maxim's in Paris. Elegant bar and two-tiered restaurant, with an intimate dance floor. Dancing to a live orchestra from 9pm to 1am. Draws a society crowd, Concorde commuters, and other well-heeled folks. A la carte French food and ambience is very pricey indeed. Jacket and tie. Reserve. AE, CB, DC, MC, V. *OPEN Tues-Sat 6pm-1am.*

Rainbow Room
30 Rockefeller Plaza, 65th floor. 632-5000. Welcome back to the supper club in the sky. Restored to its original 1934 splendor, the room—two stories high with 24 floor-to-ceiling windows providing stunning city views north, east, and south—has a revolving dance floor surrounded by three terraced levels of tables. The menu features classic and contemporary dishes. The dancing Tuesday to Saturday from 7:30pm to 1am, Sunday from 6 to 11pm is to a 12-piece orchestra. Reserve at least 6 weeks in advance for a Friday or Saturday, less time needed for weekdays, and be prepared to shell out $100 per person. Oh, but isn't it romantic? Jacket and tie required. Cover charge. AE only. *A prix-fixe*

pre-theater dinner is served Tues-Sat 5-6:15pm (no cover, no dancing). Dinner Tues-Sun 6:30-10:15pm. Supper Tues-Sat 10:30-11:30pm. (See also RESTAURANTS, Rooms with a View: Rainbow Promenade.)

Roma di Notte
137 East 55 Street. 832-1128. Marble dance floor amid Roman artifacts, private dining "caves." Strolling singers; Italian and continental cuisine and music. Dancing Monday to Thursday from 7:30pm to 1am; Friday and Saturday from 8pm to 1:30am. Minimum. AE, CB, DC. *OPEN Mon-Sat 5:30pm-2am.*

World Yacht Cruises
Pier 62, West 23 Street at the Hudson River. 929-7090. Splurge on this romantic evening cruising the harbor with a city lights backdrop. Prix-fixe dinner, dancing nightly from 7 to 10pm. Reservations and payment with a credit card required in advance. *(See also RESTAURANTS, Rooms with a View.)*

JAZZ

Throughout New York, jazz is back and more joints are jumpin' than ever—even Lincoln Center has gotten into the act by creating a jazz department, thereby recognizing jazz as the true American art form it is.

Angry Squire
216 Seventh Avenue near West 23 St. 242-9066. Longtime popular spot for jazz; convivial pub atmosphere. Happy hour Monday to Friday from 5 to 7pm features free hors d'oeuvres. Music Sunday to Thursday from 9:30pm, Friday and Saturday from 10pm. Jazz brunch with unlimited champagne Sunday from noon to 4pm. Music charge at the tables and two-drink minimum. AE, CB, DC.

Arthur's Tavern
77 Grove Street near Seventh Ave South. 675-6879. Smoky, dimly lit casual Village spot. Dixieland by the Grove Street Stompers on Monday from 9:30pm to 1am; Tuesday, Wednesday, Thursday Al Bundy on piano from 9:30pm to 3:30am; piano blues by Mabel Godwin on Friday and Saturday from 9:30pm to 3:30am; Sunday more Dixieland from 9:30pm to 1am. No food. No credit cards. *OPEN 7 days 8pm-4am.*

Birdland
2745 Broadway at West 105 St. 749-2228. Live jazz and Latin music. Basic dinner fare. Sundays a Jazz Brunch from noon to 4pm. Cover charge at bar and tables. AE, MC, V. *OPEN 7 nights 5pm-4am.*

Blue Note
131 West 3 Street near Sixth Ave. 475-8592. Large respected jazz club presents well-known artists—jazz, Latin, and blues. Shows Tuesday to Sunday at 9 and 11:30pm; Monday at 1am as well. Tuesday to Saturday there's an "After Hours" jam session following the last set till 4am. Kitchen open till 1am. Cover and minimum

(lower at the bar). Special: Jazz Brunch Saturday and Sunday from 2 to 6pm; sets at 3 and 5pm. Reserve. AE, MC, V. *OPEN Mon 7pm-2am; Tues-Sun 7pm-4am.*

Bradley's
70 University Place near East 11 St. 228-6440. For over 20 years this narrow, warm, casual, dark wood-paneled Village bar/restaurant has been featuring topflight jazz artists (the kind other musicians come to hear) nightly from 9:45pm. Minimum at the tables (if you can get one). Moderately priced pub menu. Crowded bar scene on weekends. Cover Friday and Saturday. AE, CB, DC, MC, V. *OPEN 7 days 11:30am-4am.*

Cajun
See RESTAURANTS, Soul/Southern.

Condon's
117 East 15 Street. 254-0960. Top-flight mainstream jazz and blues artists in a relaxed cozy setting. Sets Monday to Thursday at 9 and 11pm; Friday and Saturday also at 1am. Full bistro fare menu till midnight; Friday and Saturday until 1am. Outdoor garden. Minimum at bar; cover and minimum at tables.

Fat Tuesday's
190 Third Avenue near East 17 St, downstairs. 533-7902. Good food and drink in this top-notch mainstream jazz club, downstairs under Tuesday's restaurant. Easy listening especially Monday night, with the Les Paul Trio. Two sets Monday to Thursday and Sunday at 8 and 10pm; Friday and Saturday at midnight as well. Cover and minimum. AE, MC, V. *OPEN 7 days 7pm-3am.*

Greene Street Cafe
101 Greene Street near Prince St. 925-2415. Brick walls, wicker chairs, murals, and trees appoint this beautiful three-story-high former truck garage; lounge with tables, spacious dining area with small stage, and literally topping it all, a balcony. Good food and easy-listening jazz nightly from 7pm to 12:15am and at Sunday brunch (expensive à la carte menu) from noon to 4pm. Upstairs cabaret, too, Friday and Saturday. *(See* Cabaret: Upstairs at Greene Street.*)* AE, MC, V.

J's
2581 Broadway at West 97 St, 2nd floor. 666-3600. Charming, casual, comfortable upstairs West Side club for good lineup of talent. Features terrific jazz players nightly. Monday to Thursday from 8:30pm to 12:30am; Friday and Saturday from 9pm to 1am. Modestly priced eclectic menu. No cover; minimum at the bar and tables.

Knickerbocker Bar & Grill
33 University Place at East 9 St. 228-8490. Atmospheric Village restaurant/pub with jazz Wednesday to Saturday starting at 9:45pm till closing (Harry Connick used to play this room). American menu, great steaks. AE, CB, DC, MC, V. *OPEN 7 days noon-1 or 2am.*

Michael's Pub
211 East 55 Street. 758-2272. Good food and traditional jazz draw an uptown crowd. Shows

Tuesday to Saturday at 9:30 and 11:30pm. The worst kept secret in America: Woody Allen on clarinet with the New Orleans Funeral & Ragtime Band on Monday nights. Cover charge and two-drink minimum. Expensive. AE, DC, MC, V. *CLOSED Sun.*

Sweet Basil
88 Seventh Avenue South near Bleecker St. 242-1785. Popular Greenwich Village eatery and bar with good menu and mainstream jazz in comfortable, natural wood-and-brick surroundings. Three shows nightly at 10pm, 11:30pm, and 1am. Saturday and Sunday there's a jazz brunch (no cover) from noon to 6pm. Cover and minimum. AE, MC, V. *OPEN 7 days noon-3am.*

The View Lounge
Marriott Marquis, 1700 Broadway at West 44 St, 48th floor. 398-1900. A large, bilevel revolving (slowly) bar lounge with a view. A jazz trio for listening and dancing Tuesday to Friday from 9pm to 1am; Saturday from 10pm to 2am. AE, DC, MC, V.

Village Corner
142 Bleecker Street at LaGuardia Pl. 473-9762. Cozy casual Village spot for fine jazz piano nightly from 9pm to 1am. Sunday jazz brunch from 3 to 6pm. Generous drinks, American food. No credit cards. *OPEN Mon-Fri 4pm-4am; Sat & Sun noon-4am.*

Village Gate
160 Bleecker Street at Thompson St. 982-9292. The most-recorded jazz room in the world and there's always somethin' goin' on. Mondays at 9:30pm salsa meets jazz. On the Terrace there's jazz nightly from 10pm till closing (2 or 3am) as well as Saturday and Sunday jazz jams from 2 to 6pm. Bistro food. No music charge on the Terrace, just a two-drink minimum. AE, MC, V.

Village Vanguard
178 Seventh Avenue South near West 11 St. 255-4037. Since 1935, this renowned New York jazz institution has hung in. The quintessential noisy, smoky Greenwich Village basement club. It has featured all the greats and is still going strong. Three shows nightly at 9:30pm, 11:30pm, and 1am. No frills. No food. Cover charge and two-drink minimum. No credit cards. *OPEN 7 days 9pm-2am.*

Visiones
125 MacDougal Street at West 3 St. 673-5576. New small, intimate jazz venue in the Village. Spanish fare as well as American bistro menu. Shows Wednesday and Thursday at 9:30 and 11:30pm; Friday, Saturday, and Sunday at 1:15am as well. Sunday jazz brunch at 3pm. Tuesday nights, Latin bands take the stage. Happy hour 5 to 7pm. Cover and minimum. AE, MC, V.

West End Cafe
2911 Broadway near West 114 St. 662-8830. Back after an absence of a year—and all gussied up. No longer a purely student hang-out (gone are the 70 brands of beer), but there's good jazz Friday and Saturday nights starting at 9:30pm. Musical open mike nights are Wednes-

day and Sunday. Good eclectic menu; kitchen till 11:30pm. Cover sometimes. AE, V. *OPEN 7 days 11:30am-2am.*

Zinno
126 West 13 Street. 924-5182. Jazz nightly from 8pm to midnight in this Italian restaurant formerly the beloved Reno Sweeney's. Two dinner seatings in the music room: 7 and 9:45pm. Minimum at bar (you can dine there, too) as well as in the music room. AE, DC, MC, V. *CLOSED Sun.*

NIGHTCLUBS

Amazonas
492 Broome Street near West Broadway. 966-3371. Exotic tropical setting in SoHo for authentic Brazilian cuisine and music nightly from 8 to 11:30pm. It's a loud lively hot spot. Happy hour from 4 to 7pm. AE, CB, DC. *OPEN 7 days 4pm-2am.*

Cafe Feenjon
40 West 8 Street. 979-8686. Longtime popular Greenwich Village cafe (in new digs), Arabic and Israeli music (Friday and Saturday nights), and Middle Eastern food. Folk dancing early Sunday followed by disco dancing. Inexpensive, unpretentious good fun. Cover and minimum (except Tuesday and Sunday). No credit cards. *OPEN Tues-Sun 9pm-2am.*

Cafe Society
915 Broadway at East 21 St. 529-8282. In a stylish high-ceilinged, very pink setting, ballroom dancing to a big band Monday and Tuesday from 8pm; Wednesday is "oldies" night with a variety of bands from 9pm; Thursday the "La Cage aux Folles" show night; Friday and Saturday disco nights with club music. Cover charge. AE, MC, V. *CLOSED Sun.*

Chippendale's
1110 First Avenue at East 61 St. 935-6060. Unsophisticated—albeit popular—good fun. An all-male revue and teasing strip show "For Ladies Only." The titilated audience is split between the embarrassed and the bold. Shows Wednesday to Saturday at 8:15pm. From 10:30pm it's a disco with men allowed till 4am. No food. Cover charge. AE only. Bar *OPEN Wed-Sat 6pm-4am.*

Mostly Magic
55 Carmine Street near Seventh Ave South. 924-1472. Nightclub/theater. Interesting magic and illusions; some comedy thrown in for good measure, so call ahead for information. Shows Tuesday to Thursday at 9pm; Friday and Saturday 9 and 11pm. Cover and food or drink minimum. AE, DC, MC, V. *OPEN Tues-Sat 6pm-1am.*

PIANO BARS

Algonquin Hotel
59 West 44 Street. 840-6800. In the always so-

phisticated lobby Wednesday to Saturday from 5 to 8pm, Sunday till 10pm, sit in a cozy armchair, have a drink, and listen to Buck Buckholz at the piano. Cover; no minimum. AE, CB, DC, MC, V.

Bemelman's Bar
Carlyle Hotel, Madison Avenue at East 76 St. 744-1600. Piano music Tuesday to Saturday from 9:30pm to 12:45am. Easy listening in a sophisticated setting with the famed Bemelman's murals as backdrop; perfect for a cocktail or cognac. Cover; no minimum. AE, CB, DC, MC, V.

Cafe Pierre
2 East 61 Street. 838-8000. Dressy upscale international crowd, classy venue. Piano music nightly 8pm to 1am. Jacket and tie required. AE, CB, DC, MC, V.

Chez Josephine
414 West 42 Street. 594-1925. Homage to legendary entertainer Josephine Baker, it's a sophisticated spot to sip, not to mention sup, and listen to piano music before or after theater. AE, MC, V. (*See also* RESTAURANTS, French.)

Don't Tell Mama
See Cabaret.

Duplex
See Cabaret.

Eighty Eights
See Cabaret.

Five Oaks
49 Grove Street at Bleecker St. 243-8885. Forty-year-old casual Village cellar club features piano music nightly but best when veteran entertainer Marie Blake is at the piano Wednesday to Sunday from 10pm to 4am. Feel free to sing along. Open mike every night. Food till midnight (none on Monday night); Friday and Saturday till 1am. AE, MC, V. *OPEN 7 nights.*

Monkey Bar
Elysee Hotel, 60 East 54 Street. 753-1066. This atmospheric old hotel bar draws crowds for the sophisticated piano music Monday to Friday from 5:30 to 7:30pm. AE, CB, DC, MC, V.

Top of the Tower
Beekman Tower, Mitchell Place, East 49 Street & First Avenue. 355-7300. A seductive 26th-floor penthouse cocktail lounge filled with romantic duos gazing at one another and the twinkling city lights. Piano music Tuesday to Saturday from 9:30pm to 1am. No food. AE, CB, DC, MC, V. *OPEN 7 days 5pm-2:30am.*

POP/ROCK

See also Dance Clubs.

Back Fence
155 Bleecker Street at Thompson St. 475-9221. Sort of a throwback. Live folk, rock, country, or R&B music nightly from 8:30pm to 4am in low-key no-frills friendly Greenwich Village atmosphere. In addition, early shows Friday to Sunday from 5 to 8pm. No food. Cover Friday and Saturday only. No credit cards.

The Bitter End
149 Bleecker Street near LaGuardia Pl. 673-7030. Once upon a time Bob Dylan showcased here, now it offers middle-of-the-road rock, fusion jazz, folk, blues, and comedy (Friday and Saturday nights). Shows from 9pm to 2am. Admission and two-drink minimum at tables. No credit cards. *OPEN 7 days 8pm-4am.*

Bottom Line
15 West 4 Street at Mercer St. 228-6300. Once a top showcase club, it's still a good spot for rock, comedy, and whatever on-the-verge newcomer may be touring to plug a first album. Check for the current attraction. Fast food and drink available. Admission charge for table seats and standing room. Shows nightly at 8 and 11pm. Tickets sold in advance. No credit cards.

CBGB and OMFUG
315 Bowery at Bleecker St. 982-4052. The gritty, rough-edged birthplace of punk still showcases up-and-coming rock bands nightly from 9pm to 3am for young hardcore rockers and slam dancers. Music and crowd often way out. *Great* sound system. No food. Admission charge and two-drink minimum. No credit cards.

Kenny's Castaways
157 Bleecker Street near Thompson St. 473-9870. Good Greenwich Village spot for live rock music nightly. Wide range of styles; Wednesday nights belong to Gordon Edwards & Stuff II. Music nightly 8pm till 2:30am. Huge bar (no minimum). Cover (except Sunday to Tuesday); two-drink minimum at tables. No credit cards.

The Knitting Factory
47 East Houston near Mulberry St. 219-3035. Live performances in a small-capacity club. Adventurous music and performers, experimental jazz, progressive rock. Shows at 9pm and midnight. In the Knot Room spoken-word performances, video and acoustic solos and duos. No credit cards. Cover charge includes one drink. *OPEN 7 days 5:30pm-4am.*

The Ritz
254 West 54 Street. 541-8900. An East Village escapee, now firmly established in what was once the legendary Studio 54. Rock, new wave, R&B, by many nationally and internationally renowned bands. Check the *Voice* for who and when. No credit cards. On nonshow nights, and following performances, the Ritz becomes Clubland (*see* Dance Clubs).

Wetlands
161 Hudson Street. 966-4225. Tie-dye lives in this ode to the 60s. Live music—ranging from reggae and grass-roots rock to bluegrass—starts at 10pm. Eco message theme; networking for causes on Sunday. Vegetarian snacks, organic wine. AE, MC. V *OPEN Mon-Thurs 5pm-3am; Fri & Sat 9pm-4am; Sun 5pm-1am.*

RESTAURANTS

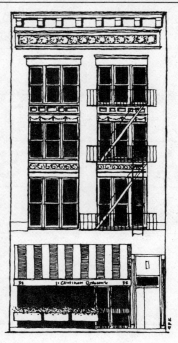

Il Cantinori

RESERVATIONS

Telephone ahead to make a reservation; this will determine that the particular restaurant is still in business and that a table will be available. If reservations are not accepted you can determine whether to expect a long wait prior to being seated.

TIPPING

The rule of thumb is approximately 15% of the total (exclusive of tax), easily calculated by doubling the amount of the 8¼% city sales tax. Generally, New York restaurants do not add a service charge.

NO SMOKING

All restaurants in New York City with seating for 50 or more diners are required to set aside at least half of those seats for nonsmokers. You might let your desire regarding smoking or nonsmoking be known when making your reserva-

tion. Restaurant owners or patrons who do not comply with the new law are subject to a fine. Call 285-9503 for information and complaints.

KEY

The price of dinner at these restaurants has been classified on the basis of a complete dinner (lunch is usually much less expensive) for two, excluding wine, tax, and tip, as follows:

$ $35 or less
$$ $35 to $60
$$$ $60 to $75
$$$$ $75 to $100
$$$$+   More than $100

The key used for meals served is:
B   Breakfast
L   Lunch
D   Dinner

The key used for credit cards is:
AE   American Express
CB   Carte Blanche
DC   Diners' Club
MC   MasterCard
V   Visa

RESTAURANTS: ALPHABETICAL INDEX

New York has nearly 30,000 restaurants! The following represent a good cross section of every type of food and price range. The category in which you will find a particular restaurant appears in parentheses after the name.

In addition to the traditional ethnic categories, I have included the following special listings for your convenience and pleasure: Afternoon Tea, Bars & Burgers, Breakfast/Brunch, Cafes, Deluxe, Fireplaces, Garden/Outdoor Dining, Inexpensive, Late Night & 24 Hours, Omelettes, Outdoor Dining, Pizza, Rooms with a View, Sidewalk Cafes, Stargazing, and Steak. A complete description of a particular restaurant can be found in the category that appears in parentheses. Categories are in alphabetical order starting with Afternoon Tea and going through Vietnamese.

Following the Alphabetical Index is a listing of restaurants by geographic area.

Abyssinia Restaurant (Ethiopian)
Acme Bar & Grill (Soul/Southern)
Adam's Rib (American)
Aggie's (Breakfast/Brunch)
Akasaka (Japanese)
Akbar (Indian)
Al Amir (Middle Eastern)
Alcala (Spanish)
Algonquin Hotel (Bars & Burgers)
Alison on Dominick Street (French)
Alo Alo (Italian)
Ambassador Grill (Breakfast/Brunch)
America (American)

American Festival Cafe (American *and*
  Breakfast/Brunch)
American Harvest Restaurant (American)
Amsterdam's Bar & Rotisserie (American)
An American Place (American)
Anatolia (Turkish)
Angelica Kitchen (Health & Vegetarian)
Angelo's (Italian)
Anglers & Writers (Afternoon Tea)
Anna's Harbor Restaurant (Rooms with a
  View)
Aperitivo (Italian)
Aquavit (Scandinavian)
Arcadia (American)
Arizona 206 & Cafe (American)
Around the Clock Cafe (Late Night & 24
  Hours)
Arqua' (Italian)
Arturo's Pizzeria (Pizza)
Assembly Steak House (Steak)
Asti (Italian)
Auntie Yuan (Chinese)
Aureole (American)
Au Troquet (French)
The Ballroom (Spanish: Tapas)
Bangkok Cuisine (Thai)
Bangkok House (Thai)
Barbetta (Italian)
Barney Greengrass (Jewish)
Barocco (Italian)
Barolo (Italian)
Bayamo (Latin American)
Beach House (Mexican)
Beatrice Inn (Italian)
Beijing Duck House (Chinese)
Bellini by Cipriani (Italian)
Benihana of Tokyo (Japanese)
Benny's Burritos (Mexican)
Bernstein-on-Essex Street (Delicatessen)
Berry's (Continental)
Bice (Italian)
Bienvenue (French)
Billy's (Bars & Burgers)
The Black Sheep (French)
The Blue Mill Tavern (Bars & Burgers)
The Blue Nile (Ethiopian)
The Boathouse Cafe (Rooms with a View)
Bombay Palace (Indian)
Bouley (French)
Box Tree (French)
Brasserie (Late Night & 24 Hours)
Brazilian Pavilion (Latin American)
Bridge Cafe (Continental)
Broome Street Bar (Bars & Burgers)
B. Smith (Soul/Southern)
Bukhara (Indian)
Cabana Carioca (Latin American)
Cafe de Bruxelles (Belgian)
Cafe de la Paix (Sidewalk Cafes)
Cafe des Artistes (Continental)
Cafe du Parc (French)
Cafe Europa (French)
Cafe La Fortuna (Cafes)
Cafe Loup (French)
Cafe Luxembourg (Late Night & 24 Hours)

Cafe Nicholson (Continental)
Cafe Orlin (Breakfast/Brunch)
Cafe Un Deux Trois (French)
Cafe Vivaldi (Cafes)
Caffe Biondo (Cafes)
Caffe Dante (Cafes)
Caffe Reggio (Cafes)
Caffe Roma (Cafes)
Cajun (Soul/Southern)
Canton (Chinese)
Capsouto Frères (French)
The Captain's Table (Fish & Seafood)
Caramba! & !! & !!! & !!!! (Mexican)
Caribe (Caribbean)
Carlyle Restaurant (Continental)
Carmine's (Italian)
Carnegie Delicatessen (Delicatessen)
Carolina (American)
Cedars of Lebanon (Middle Eastern)
Cellar in the Sky (Deluxe)
Cent'Anni (Italian)
Chalet Suisse (Swiss)
Chantal Cafe (French)
Chanterelle (French)
Chelsea Central (American)
Chelsea Place (Italian)
Cheyenne (Late Night & 24 Hours)
Chez Brigitte (Inexpensive)
Chez Josephine (French)
Chez Ma Tante (French)
Chez Michellat (French)
Chez Napoleon (French)
China Grill (Chinese)
Chin Chin (Chinese)
Choshi (Japanese)
Christ Cella (Steak)
Christine's (Polish)
Chumley's (Bars & Burgers)
Cinco de Mayo (Mexican)
City Lights Bar & Hors D'Oeuvrerie (Rooms
  with a View)
Claire (Fish & Seafood)
Cloister Cafe (Cafes)
Coach House (American)
Coco Pazzo (Italian)
Coffee Shop (Latin American)
Contrapunto (Italian)
Cornelia Street Cafe (Cafes)
Corner Bistro (Bars & Burgers)
Cottonwood Cafe (Breakfast/Brunch)
Courtyard Cafe & Bar (American)
Cucina di Pesce (Italian)
Cupping Room Cafe (Breakfast/Brunch)
Curtain Up! (American)
Danal (Afternoon Tea *and* Cafes)
Darbar (Indian)
Da Silvano (Italian)
David K's (Chinese)
Dawat (Indian)
Dock's Oyster Bar & Seafood Grill (Fish &
  Seafood)
Dolci on Park (Cafes)
Eclair Shop (Hungarian)
Elaine's (Stargazing)

El Coyote (Mexican)
Elephant & Castle (Omelettes)
El Faro (Spanish)
Elio's (Italian)
El Parador Cafe (Mexican)
El Rincon de Espana (Spanish)
El Teddy's (Mexican)
Empire Diner (Late Night & 24 Hours)
Ennio & Michael (Italian)
Erminia (Italian)
Eze (French)
Fanelli's Cafe (Bars & Burgers)
Felidia (Italian)
Ferrara's (Cafes)
Figaro Cafe (Sidewalk Cafes)
Fine & Shapiro (Delicatessen)
Fiorello's Roman Cafe (Sidewalk Cafes)
Florent (Late Night & 24 Hours)
Forlini's (Italian)
"44" (American)
Fountain Cafe (Sidewalk Cafes)
Four Seasons (Deluxe)
Francesca's (Italian)
Frank's (Steak)
Fraunces Tavern Restaurant (American)
Fulton Fish Market (Fish & Seafood)
Gage & Tollner (Fish & Seafood)
Gallagher's (Steak)
Gargiulo's (Italian)
Gascogne (French)
Gaylord (Indian)
Giambelli 50th Ristorante (Italian)
Gibbon (Japanese)
Ginger Man (American)
Giordano (Italian)
Good Enough to Eat (American)
Gotham Bar & Grill (American)
Grand Dairy Restaurant (Jewish)
Great American Health Bar (Health & Vegetarian)
Great Jones Cafe (Bars & Burgers)
Great Shanghai (Chinese)
Grotta Azzurra (Italian)
Grove Street Cafe (Continental)
Gulf Coast (Soul/Southern)
Hamburger Harry's (Bars & Burgers)
Hamilton House (Steak)
Hard Rock Cafe (Late Night & 24 Hours)
Harlequin (Spanish)
Harry Cipriani (Italian)
Harvey's Chelsea House (American)
Hatsuhana (Japanese)
Health Pub (Health & Vegetarian)
Hee Seung Fung (HSF) (Chinese: Dim Sum)
Helmsley Palace (Afternoon Tea)
Hong Fat (Chinese)
Hop Shing Restaurant (Chinese: Dim Sum)
Hors D'Oeuvrerie (Breakfast/Brunch)
Hudson River Club (Rooms with a View)
Hungarian Pastry Shop (Cafes)
Hwa Yuan Szechuan Inn (Chinese)
Il Cantinori (Italian)
Il Menestrello (Italian)
Il Monello (Italian)
Il Mulino (Italian)

Il Nido (Italian)
Il Ponte Vecchio (Italian)
Il Vagabondo (Italian)
India Pavilion (Indian)
Indochine (Vietnamese)
Jackson Hole Wyoming (Bars & Burgers)
Jane Street Seafood Cafe (Fish & Seafood)
Japonica (Japanese)
Jean Lafitte (French)
Jeremy's Ale House (Bars & Burgers)
Jerry's 103 (American)
Jezebel (Soul/Southern)
J. G. Melon (Bars & Burgers)
Jim McMullen (Bars & Burgers)
Joe Allen (Stargazing)
John Clancy's (Fish & Seafood)
John's Pizzeria (Pizza)
JoJo (French)
Junior's Restaurant (Inexpensive)
Kaplan's at the Delmonico (Delicatessen)
Karyatis (Greek)
Katz's Delicatessen (Delicatessen)
Kenny's Steak Pub (Steak)
Kiev International (Late Night & 24 Hours)
King Cole Bar (Bars & Burgers)
King Crab (Fish & Seafood)
Kleine Konditorei (German)
K-Paul's New York (Soul/Southern)
La Boheme (French)
La Bonne Soupe (Inexpensive)
La Caravelle (Deluxe)
La Colombe d'Or (French)
La Côte Basque (Deluxe)
Lafayette (French)
La Fondue (Swiss)
La Gauloise (French)
La Goulue (French)
La Grenouille (Deluxe)
La Kasbah (Middle Eastern)
La Mangeoire (French)
La Metairie (French)
Landmark Tavern (Bars & Burgers)
Lan Hong Kok Seafood House (Chinese: Dim Sum)
La Petite Ferme (French)
La Reserve (Deluxe)
Lattanzi (Italian)
Le Bernardin (French)
Le Bilboquet (French)
Le Boeuf a la Mode (French)
Le Chantilly (French)
Le Cirque (Deluxe)
Le Madri (Italian)
Le Pactole (French)
Le Perigord (French)
Le Regence (French)
Le Relais (French)
Les Halles (French)
Les Pyrenees (French)
Le Steak (Steak)
Le Veau d'Or (French)
Le Zinc (French)
Lion's Head (Bars & Burgers)
Lion's Rock (Continental)
Little Shanghai (Chinese)

Sido Abu Salim (Middle Eatern)
The Sign of the Dove (Continental)
SoHo Kitchen & Bar (Wine Bars)
Spark's Steak House (Steak)
Spring Street Natural Restaurant (Health & Vegetarian)
The Stage (Inexpensive)
Stage Deli (Delicatessen)
Sugar Reef (Caribbean)
Sukhathai West (Thai)
Summerhouse (Continental)
Sumptuary Restaurant (Continental)
Sushi Zen (Japanese)
Sweet's (Fish & Seafood)
Swiss Inn (Swiss)
Sylvia's (Soul/Southern)
Take-Sushi (Japanese)
Tang's Chariot (Chinese)
Taste of the Apple (Bars & Burgers)
Tavern-on-the-Green (Rooms with a View)
Telephone Bar & Grill (American)
Tennessee Mountain (American)
The Terrace (Rooms with a View)
Terrace Cafe (Sidewalk Cafes)
Time and Again (Continental)
Tommy Tang's (Thai)
Top of the Sixes (Rooms with a View)
Top of the Tower (Rooms with a View)
Tout Va Bien (French)
Trastevere & Trastevere 84 (Italian)
Trattoria dell'Arte (Italian)
TriBeCa Grill (Stargazing)
Triplets Roumanian Restaurant (Jewish)
Tripoli (Middle Eastern)
Tuesday's (Breakfast/Brunch)
20 Mott Street (Chinese: Dim Sum)
"21" Club (Stargazing)
Umberto's Clam House (Fish & Seafood)
Umeda (Japanese)
Vanessa (American)
Vasata (Czechoslovakian)
Veniero's (Cafes)
Veselka Coffee Shop (Breakfast/Brunch)
Victor's Cafe 52 (Latin American)
The View Restaurant (Rooms with a View)
Vivolo (Italian)
The Water Club (Rooms with a View)
Water's Edge Restaurant (Rooms with a View)
White Horse Tavern (Bars & Burgers)
Whole Wheat 'n' Wild Berries (Health & Vegetarian)
Windows on the World (Rooms with a View)
Woo Lae Oak of Seoul (Korean)
World Yacht Cruises (Rooms with a View)
Wylie's (Soul/Southern)
Yellowfingers di Nuovo (Italian)
Ye Waverly Inn (American)
Yonah Schimmel's (Jewish)
Zarela (Mexican)
Zinno (Italian)
Zula (Ethiopian)

RESTAURANTS: GEOGRAPHIC INDEX

Downtown (Financial District, Seaport Area, Lower East Side)

American Harvest Restaurant (American)
Bernstein-on-Essex Street (Delicatessen)
Bridge Cafe (Continental)
Cellar in the Sky (Deluxe)
Cinco de Mayo (Mexican)
City Lights Bar (Rooms with a View)
Fraunces Tavern Restaurant (American)
Fulton Fish Market (Fish & Seafood)
Grand Dairy Restaurant (Jewish)
Hamburger Harry's (Bars & Burgers)
Hors D'Oeuvrerie (Breakfast/Brunch)
Hudson River Club (Rooms with a View)
Jeremy's Ale House (Bars & Burgers)
Katz's Delicatessen (Delicatessen)
Ratner's Dairy Restaurant (Jewish)
Sammy's Roumanian (Jewish)
Sweets (Fish & Seafood)
Windows on the World (Rooms with a View)
Yonah Schimmel's (Jewish)

Chinatown

Canton (Chinese)
Chin Chin (Chinese)
Great Shanghai (Chinese)
Hee Seung Fung (HSF) (Chinese : Dim Sum)
Hong Fat (Chinese)
Hop Shing Restaurant (Chinese: Dim Sum)
Hwa Yuan Szechuan Inn (Chinese)
Lan Hong Kok Seafood House (Chinese: Dim Sum)
Little Shanghai (Chinese)
The Nice Restaurant (Chinese)
Nom Wah Tea Parlor (Chinese: Dim Sum)
Phoenix Garden (Chinese)
Pongsri Thai (Thai)
Saigon (Vietnamese)
Say Eng Look (Chinese)
20 Mott Street (Chinese: Dim Sum)

Little Italy

Angelo's (Italian)
Caffe Biondo (Cafes)
Caffe Roma (Cafes)
Ferrara's (Cafes)
Forlini's (Italian)
Grotta Azzurra (Italian)
Patrissey's (Italian)
Puglia's (Italian)
Triplet's Roumanian Restaurant (Jewish)
Umberto's Clam House (Fish & Seafood)

TriBeCa

Alison on Dominick Street (French)
Arqua' (Italian)
Barocco (Italian)

Beach House (Mexican)
Bouley (French)
Capsouto Frères (French)
Chanterelle (French)
El Teddy's (Mexican)
Le Zinc (French)
Montrachet (French)
Odeon (Late Night & 24 Hours)
Tommy Tang's (Thai)
TriBeCa Grill (Stargazing)

SoHo

Abyssinia Restaurant (Ethiopian)
Barolo (Italian)
Berry's (Continental)
Broome Street Bar (Bars & Burgers)
Cupping Room Cafe (Breakfast/Brunch)
Elephant & Castle (Omelettes)
Fanelli's Cafe (Bars & Burgers)
Manhattan Brewing Company (Bars & Burgers)
Mezzogiorno (Italian)
Moondance Diner (Inexpensive)
Omen (Japanese)
Raoul's (French)
SoHo Kitchen & Bar (Wine Bars)
Spring Street Natural Restaurant (Health & Vegetarian)
Tennessee Mountain (American)

Greenwich Village

Aggie's (Breakfast/Brunch)
Anglers & Writers (Afternoon Tea)
Arturo's Pizzeria (Pizza)
Asti (Italian)
Au Troquet (French)
Beatrice Inn (Italian)
Benny's Burritos (Mexican)
The Black Sheep (French)
The Blue Mill Tavern (Bars & Burgers)
Cafe de Bruxelles (Belgian)
Cafe Loup (French)
Cafe Vivaldi (Cafes)
Caffe Dante (Cafes)
Caffe Reggio (Cafes)
Caribe (Caribbean)
Cent'Anni (Italian)
Chez Brigitte (Inexpensive)
Chez Ma Tante (French)
Chez Michellat (French)
Chumley's (Bars & Burgers)
Coach House (American)
Cornelia Street Cafe (Cafes)
Corner Bistro (Bars & Burgers)
Cottonwood Cafe (Breakfast/Brunch)
Da Silvano (Italian)
Elephant & Castle (Omelettes)
El Faro (Spanish)
El Rincon de Espana (Spanish)
Ennio & Michael (Italian)
Figaro Cafe (Sidewalk Cafes)
Florent (Late Night & 24 Hours)

Gotham Bar & Grill (American)
Grove Street Cafe (Continental)
Gulf Coast (Soul/Southern)
Harlequin (Spanish)
Il Cantinori (Italian)
Il Mulino (Italian)
Il Ponte Vecchio (Italian)
Jane Street Seafood Cafe (Fish & Seafood)
Japonica (Japanese)
John Clancy's (Fish & Seafood)
John's Pizzeria (Pizza)
K-Paul's New York (Soul/Southern)
La Boheme (French)
La Gauloise (French)
La Metairie (French)
Lion's Head (Bars & Burgers)
Marylou's (Fish & Seafood)
Mary's (Italian)
One If by Land, Two If by Sea (Continental)
Paris Commune (Breakfast/Brunch)
Peacock (Cafes)
Pink Tea Cup (Breakfast/Brunch)
Provence (French)
Ray's Pizza (Pizza)
Riviera Cafe (Sidewalk Cafes)
Rumbuls (Cafes)
Sabor (Latin American)
Sazerac House (Soul/Southern)
Vanessa (American)
Vince & Eddie's (American)
White Horse Tavern (Bars & Burgers)
Whole Wheat 'n' Wild Berries (Health & Vegetarian)
Ye Waverly Inn (American)
Zinno (Italian)

East Village/NoHo

Acme Bar & Grill (Soul/Southern)
Angelica Kitchen (Health & Vegetarian)
Around the Clock Cafe (Late Night & 24 Hours)
Bayamo (Latin American)
Benny's Burritos (Mexican)
Cafe Orlin (Breakfast/Brunch)
Caramba!! (Mexican)
Christine's (Polish)
Cloister Cafe (Cafes)
Cucina di Pesce (Italian)
Danal (Afternoon Tea *and* Cafes)
De Robertis (Cafes)
El Coyote (Mexican)
Gaylord (Indian)
Great Jones Cafe (Bars & Burgers)
Indochine (Vietnamese)
Jerry's 103 (American)
Kiev International (Late Night & 24 Hours)
McSorley's Old Ale House (Bars & Burgers)
Mie (Japanese)
Mitali (Indian)
NoHo Star (American)
Pier Nine (Fish & Seafood)
PizzaPiazza (Breakfast/Brunch)
Rectangles (Middle Eastern)
Roettelle A.G. (German)

Rumbuls (Cafes)
Second Avenue Kosher Delicatessen
  (Delicatessen)
The Stage (Inexpensive)
Sugar Reef (Caribbean)
Telephone Bar & Grill (American)
Veniero's (Cafes)
Veselka Coffee Shop (Breakfast/Brunch)

East 14th-23rd Streets (Gramercy, Flatiron)

America (American)
Cafe du Parc (French)
Choshi (Japanese)
Coffee Shop (Latin American)
Health Pub (Health & Vegetarian)
Old Town Bar (Bars & Burgers)
Pete's Tavern (Bars & Burgers)
Positano (Italian)
Tuesday's (Breakfast/Brunch)
Umeda (Japanese)

West 14th-23rd Streets (Chelsea)

Cajun (Soul/Southern)
Chelsea Central (American)
Chelsea Place (Italian)
Claire (Fish & Seafood)
Empire Diner (Late Night & 24 Hours)
Eze (French)
Frank's (Steak)
Gascogne (French)
Harvey's Chelsea House (American)
Le Madri (Italian)
Lola (Caribbean)
Lox Around the Clock (Late Night & 24
  Hours)
Luma (Health & Vegetarian)
Man Ray (American)
Mesa Grill (American)
Moran's (Bars & Burgers)
Old Homestead Restaurant (Steak)
Periyali (Greek)
Quatorze (French)
World Yacht Cruises (Rooms with a View)

East 24th-42nd Streets

Akasaka (Japanese)
An American Place (American)
Bienvenue (French)
Cedars of Lebanon (Middle Eastern)
Christine's (Polish)
Courtyard Cafe & Bar (American)
Dock's Oyster Bar & Seafood Grill (Fish &
  Seafood)
Dolci on Park (Cafes)
El Parador Cafe (Mexican)
Francesca's (Italian)
Great American Health Bar (Health &
  Vegetarian)
Jackson Hole Wyoming (Bars & Burgers)
La Colombe d'Or (French)

Les Halles (French)
Mexico Lindo (Mexican)
Oyster Bar & Restaurant (Fish & Seafood)
Park Bistro (French)
Sido Abu Salim (Middle Eastern)
Sumptuary Restaurant (Continental)
Time and Again (Continental)
The Water Club (Rooms with a View)

West 24th-34th Streets

The Ballroom (Spanish: Tapas)
Cheyenne (Late Night & 24 Hours)

West 35th-49th Streets (Theater District)

Algonquin Hotel (Bars & Burgers)
Barbetta (Italian)
B. Smith's (Soul/Southern)
Cabana Carioca (Latin American)
Cafe Un Deux Trois (French)
Carolina (American)
Chez Josephine (French)
Curtain Up! (American)
"44" (American)
Giordano (Italian)
Hamburger Harry's (Bars & Burgers)
Jezebel (Soul/Southern)
Joe Allen (Stargazing)
Landmark Tavern (Bars & Burgers)
La Reserve (Deluxe)
Lattanzi (Italian)
Lou Siegel's (Jewish)
Mama Leone's (Italian)
Manganero's Grosseria Italiana
  (Inexpensive)
Moshe Peking (Jewish)
Orso (Italian)
Pongsri Thai (Thai)
Raga (Indian)
Rainbow Promenade (Rooms with a View)
Rose Room (Late Night & 24 Hours)
Sardi's (Stargazing)
Sea Grill (Fish & Seafood)
Sushi Zen (Japanese)
Swiss Inn (Swiss)
The View Restaurant (Rooms with a View)
Woo Lae Oak of Seoul (Korean)

East 43rd-59th Streets

Akbar (Indian)
Ambassador Grill (Breakfast/Brunch)
Beijing Duck House (Chinese)
Benihana of Tokyo (Japanese)
Bice (Italian)
Box Tree (French)
Brasserie (Late Night & 24 Hours)
Brazilian Pavilion (Latin American)
Bukhara (Indian)
Cafe Europa (French)
Cafe Nicholson (Continental)
The Captain's Table (Fish & Seafood)

Chalet Suisse (Swiss)
Christ Cella (Steak)
Cinco de Mayo (Mexican)
Dawat (Indian)
Felidia (Italian)
Four Seasons (Deluxe)
Giambelli 50th Ristorante (Italian)
Hatsuhana (Japanese)
Helmsley Palace (Afternoon Tea)
Il Menestrello (Italian)
Il Nido (Italian)
Indian Pavilion (Indian)
Kaplan's at the Delmonico (Delicatessen)
Kenny's Steak Pub (Steak)
La Côte Basque (Deluxe)
Lafayette (French)
La Grenouille (Deluxe)
La Mangeoire (French)
Le Chantilly (French)
Le Perigord (French)
Le Steak (Steak)
Louise Junior (Italian)
Lutece (Deluxe)
March (French)
Mr. Chow (Chinese)
Mitsukoshi (Japanese)
Nanni's (Italian)
Nippon (Japanese)
Nyborg Nelson (Inexpensive)
Palm Restaurant (Steak)
Paradis Barcelona (Spanish)
Pen & Pencil (Steak)
Pietro's (Steak)
P.J. Clarke's (Bars & Burgers)
Quilted Giraffe (American)
Rosa Mexicana (Mexican)
Seryna (Japanese)
Shun Lee Palace (Chinese)
Spark's Steak House (Steak)
Swiss Inn (Swiss)
Take-Sushi (Japanese)
Tang's Chariot (Chinese)
Taste of the Apple (Bars & Burgers)
Top of the Tower (Rooms with a View)
Wylie's (Soul/Southern)
Zarela (Mexican)

West 50th-57th Streets

American Festival Cafe (American *and*
  Breakfast/Brunch)
Aperitivo (Italian)
Aquavit (Scandinavian)
Assembly Steak House (Steak)
Bangkok Cuisine (Thai)
Bellini by Cipriani (Italian)
Benihana of Tokyo (Japanese)
Bombay Palace (Indian)
Caramba! (Mexican)
Carnegie Delicatessen (Delicatessen)
Chantal Cafe (French)
Chez Napoleon (French)
China Grill (Chinese)
Darbar (Indian)
Gallagher's (Steak)

Great American Health Bar (Health &
  Vegetarian)
Hard Rock Cafe (Late Night & 24 Hours)
Indian Pavilion (Indian)
King Crab (Fish & Seafood)
La Bonne Soup (Inexpensive)
La Caravelle (Deluxe)
La Fondue (Swiss)
Le Bernardin (French)
Les Pyrenees (French)
Maurice (French)
Palio (Italian)
Planet Hollywood (Stargazing)
Remi (Italian)
Rene Pujol (French)
Restaurant Raphael (French)
Russian Tea Room (Stargazing)
Sam's Restaurant (American)
Stage Deli (Delicatessen)
Top of the Sixes (Rooms with a View)
Tout Va Bien (French)
Trattoria dell'Arte (Italian)
"21" Club (Stargazing)
Victor's Cafe 52 (Latin American)

East 60th-79th Streets

Adam's Rib (American)
Al Amir (Middle Eastern)
Alo Alo (Italian)
Arcadia (American)
Arizona 206 & Cafe (American)
Auntie Yuan (Chinese)
Aureole (American)
Bangkok House (Thai)
The Boathouse Cafe (Rooms with a View)
Carlyle Restaurant (Continental)
Coco Pazzo (Italian)
Contrapunto (Italian)
David K's (Chinese)
Il Monello (Italian)
Il Vagabondo (Italian)
Jackson Hole Wyoming (Bars & Burgers)
J. G. Melon (Bars & Burgers)
Jim McMullen (Bars & Burgers)
John Clancy's (Fish & Seafood)
John's Pizzeria (Pizza)
JoJo (French)
La Goulue (French)
La Petite Ferme (French)
Le Biblioquet (French)
Le Cirque (Deluxe)
Le Regence (French)
Le Relais (French)
Le Veau d'Or (French)
Lion's Rock (Continental)
Madame Romaine de Lyon (Omelettes)
Mayfair Regent (Afternoon Tea)
Mezzaluna (Italian)
Mortimer's (Continental)
Nanni Il Valletto (Italian)
Pamir (Afghan)
Parma (Italian)
Petaluma (Italian)
The Polo (American)

The Post House (Steak)
Quatorze (French)
Ravelled Sleave (American)
Red Tulip (Hungarian)
Regency Hotel (Breakfast/Brunch)
Serendipity 3 (American)
The Sign of the Dove (Continental)
Vasata (Czechoslovakian)
Vivolo (Italian)
Yellowfingers di Nuovo (Italian)

West 58th-72nd Streets (Lincoln Center)

Cafe de la Paix (Sidewalk Cafes)
Cafe des Artistes (Continental)
Cafe La Fortuna (Cafes)
Cafe Luxembourg (Late Night & 24 Hours)
Eclair Shop (Hungarian)
Fine & Shapiro (Delicatessen)
Fiorello's Roman Cafe (Sidewalk Cafes)
Fountain Cafe (Sidewalk Cafes)
Ginger Man (American)
Jean Lafitte (French)
La Kasbah (Middle Eastern)
Manhattan Ocean Club (Fish & Seafood)
Nirvana (Rooms with a View)
Oak Bar (Bars & Burgers)
Petrossian (French)
The Plaza (Afternoon Tea)
The Saloon (Sidewalk Cafes)
San Domenico (Italian)
Santa Fe (Mexican)
Shun Lee West (Chinese)
Tavern-on-the-Green (Rooms with a View)
Vince & Eddie's (American)

East 80th-96th Streets

Anatolia (Turkish)
Caramba!!!! (Mexican)
Elaine's (Stargazing)
Elio's (Italian)
Erminia (Italian)
Gibbon (Japanese)
Jackson Hole Wyoming (Bars & Burgers)
Kleine Konditorei (German)
Le Boeuf a la Mode (French)
Parioli Romanissimo (Italian)
Pig Heaven (Chinese)
Pinocchio (Italian)
Sam's Cafe (American)
Sarabeth's Kitchen (Breakfast/Brunch)
Summerhouse (Continental)

Terrace Cafe (Sidewalk Cafes)
Trastevere & Trastevere 84 (Italian)

West 73rd-96th Streets

Alcala (Spanish)
Amsterdam's Bar & Rotisserie (American)
Barnery Greengrass (Jewish)
The Blue Nile (Ethiopian)
The Boathouse Cafe (Rooms with a View)
Caramba!!! (Mexican)
Carmine's (Italian)
Dock's Oyster Bar & Seafood Grill (Fish & Seafood)
Good Enough to Eat (American)
Jackson Hole Wyoming (Bars & Burgers)
J. G. Melon (Bars & Burgers)
Louie's Westside Cafe (American)
Memphis (Soul/Southern)
Museum Cafe (Bars & Burgers)
Popover Cafe (Breakfst/Brunch)
Sarabeth's Kitchen (Breakfast/Brunch)
Taste of the Apple (Bars & Burgers)

Above West 97th Street

Hungarian Pastry Shop (Cafes)
Sylvia's (Soul/Southern)
The Terrace (Rooms with a View)
Zula (Ethiopian)

Brooklyn

Gage & Tollner (Fish & Seafood)
Gargiulo's (Italian)
Hamilton House (Steak)
Junior's Restaurant (Inexpensive)
Nathan's Famous (Inexpensive)
New Prospect Cafe (Health & Vegetarian)
Peter Luger's (Steak)
River Cafe (Rooms with a View)
Tripoli (Middle Eastern)

Bronx

Anna's Harbor Restaurant (Rooms with a View)

Queens

Karyatis (Greek)
Roumeli Taverna (Greek))
Water's Edge Restaurant (Rooms with a View)

RESTAURANTS BY SPECIALTY

Afghan

Pamir
1437 Second Avenue near East 75 St. 734-3791. Dependable budget-priced hearty Afghan fare in a small exotic setting. Savory dishes include grilled meats and stews. Reserve. MC, V. *OPEN Tues-Sun 5pm-11pm. CLOSED Mon.* $

Afternoon Tea

Perhaps part of the recolonizing of America, afternoon tea is catching on and it's oh so civilized. In addition to the hotels described below, afternoon tea is also served at the **Algonquin,** *the* **Stanhope,** *the* **Carlyle,** *the* **Inter-Continental, Omni Berkshire Place,** *and the* **Pierre**—*all in extremely attractive settings.*

Anglers & Writers
420 Hudson Street at St. Luke's Pl. 675-0810. This charmingly sedate Greenwich Village cafe, attractively adorned with mismatched oak tables and chairs, vintage china, and fresh flowers, positively beckons you for afternoon tea. Fishing tackle baskets and other accoutrements of the sport, and the well-read books on the shelves, add to the country-inn mood. A wide choice of interesting teas, an enormous portion of scone, a plate of tasty open-face sandwiches, and a small finale sweet make up the prix-fixe repast. No credit cards. *Served 7 days 3pm-6pm.* $

Danal
90 East 10 Street. 982-6930. Whether seated on the sofa, at one of the country tables, or, in fine weather, in the rear garden, tea in this other time-other place cafe is a special treat. A selection of fine teas (coffee, too), delicate tea sandwiches, homebaked scones, and pastries make up the prix-fixe tea; by reservation only. *Tues-Sat 4pm-6pm.* $

Helmsley Palace
455 Madison Avenue at East 51 St. 888-7000. In the opulent 19th-century Gold Room a choice of Fortnum & Mason teas, tea sandwiches, scones with Devonshire cream and jam, miniature pastries, fruit tarts. The stiffest prix fixe but worth the view. Harpist as well. AE, MC, V. *Served 7 days 2pm-5pm.* $

Mayfair Regent
610 Park Avenue at East 65 St. 288-0800. In the intimate and elegant lobby lounge a wide choice of teas including herbal. Tea sandwiches, pastries, scones, cream, and jam. Also, espresso and cappuccino. Prix fixe. AE, MC, V. *Served 7 days 3pm-5:30pm.* $

The Plaza
Fifth Avenue & 59 Street. 759-3000. Tea in the old-world Palm Court is a New York tradition. High tea with crumpets, scones, open-face sandwiches, and pastries in the palm-bedecked enclave, serenaded by violins. A la carte (mini-

mum $6) or prix fixe. Reservations only for 8 or more. AE, MC, V. *Served Mon-Sat 3:45pm-6pm; Sun 4pm-6pm.* $

American

This list includes the traditional as well as new, nouvelle, and regional American cooking. See also Soul/Southern and Steak.

Adam's Rib
1338 First Avenue at East 72 St. 535-2112. Traditional restaurant specializes in superb prime ribs of beef on or off the bone. Burgers and omelettes at lunch. New attraction, the Cabaret Room, featuring entertainment Friday and Saturday nights (food or drink minimum, no cover). Reserve. AE, MC, V. *L Mon-Fri noon-3:30pm. D 7 days 5pm-11pm. Sun brunch noon-3:30pm.* $$

America
9-13 East 18 Street. 505-2110. A survivor of the restaurant-as-theater phenomenon of the 80s, and a noisy one at that. Huge is the key word here—the place, which seats 400; the plates; the portions. The copious menu with the widest price range in town features such basic all-American treats as macaroni and cheese, chili, sweet potato pancakes, Buffalo chicken wings, tasty individual pizza, and New Mexican black bean cakes. Don't take any of it too seriously and you'll have fun—albeit while going deaf. The elevated bar is still center stage in the pm. Reserve. AE, DC, MC, V. *OPEN Sun-Thurs 11:30am-11:30pm; Fri & Sat 12:30am.* $ and up

American Festival Cafe
Rockefeller Plaza, 20 West 50 Street, lower concourse. 246-6699. Well-located popular spot for a changing menu of seasonal American specials including Maine lobster gazpacho, fettuccine with crabmeat, and asparagus. In winter dine with a view of the ice skaters and outdoors in summer when the rink becomes an umbrella-shaded oasis. Reserve. AE, CB, DC, MC, V. *B Mon-Fri 7:30am-11am. L Mon-Fri 11am-4pm. D 7 days 4pm-11pm. Late supper 7 days 10pm-midnight. Weekend breakfast 9am-10:30am; brunch 10:30am-4pm. (See also* Breakfast/Brunch.) $$

American Harvest Restaurant
New York Vista Hotel, 3 World Trade Center. 432-9334; 938-9100. A serene choice for Wall Street business talk. Seasonal, truly American fare in a traditional Americana-appointed spacious setting. Menu changes monthly and may include soft-shelled crabs, medaillons of veal, Smithfield ham with ripe fruit garnishes, coal-broiled salmon. Prix-fixe lunch and dinner. Reasonably priced wine list. Reserve. AE, CB, DC, MC, V. *B Mon-Fri 7am-10am. L Mon-Fri noon-2:30pm. D Mon-Thurs 6pm-10pm. CLOSED Sat & Sun.* $$$

Amsterdam's Bar & Rotisserie
428 Amsterdam Avenue near West 80 St; 874-1377. And * 454 Broadway near Grand St; 925-6166. Stylish yet casual Upper West Side neighborhood meeting place that—more im-

portantly— serves good simple rotisserie cooking, salads, and lighter fare at unbeatable prices. Well-chosen selection of very affordable wines. As the crowds should tell you, no reservations. So successful, they have moved the formula downtown where they do take reservations. AE, DC, MC, V. *OPEN 7 days noon-midnight (bar till 1am). *OPEN Mon 11:30am-10pm; Tues-Thurs 11:30am-11pm; Fri 11:30am-1am; Sat 11:30am-midnight.* $

An American Place
2 Park Avenue at East 32 St. 684-2122. A handsome spacious setting in which to enjoy celebrated chef Larry Forgione's artfully presented American-grown foodstuff. Barbecued mallard, Key West shrimp with mustard sauce, chicken breast sauteed with apple-cider vinegar, savory duck sausage, three smoked-fish terrine, sweet potato ravioli. Expensive but tops of its genre. Excellent selection of American wines only. Jacket and tie; no denim. Prix fixe. Reserve! AE, DC, MC, V. *L Mon-Fri 11:45am-3pm. D Mon-Sat 5:30pm-10pm. CLOSED Sun.* $$$$ +

Arcadia
21 East 62 Street. 223-2900. Small and special and very fine indeed. Chef Anne Rosenzweig's home base, where she produces wonderfully creative American fare in an attractive, cozy (some say cramped), Paul Davis mural–enhanced setting. Seasonal menu; chimney-smoked lobster a house specialty. Well-chosen wine list. Reserve well in advance (request the main dining room). Jacket and tie. AE, MC, V. *L (two seatings) noon & 1:45pm. D Mon-Sat 6pm-midnight.* $$$$ +

Arizona 206 & Cafe
206 East 60 Street. 838-0440. Excellent inventive and tasty Southwestern-style cooking in a casual rustic setting. Savor the pan-roasted chicken, pistachio-coated rabbit, paella for two. A working fireplace adds to the charm. In the popular adjacent cafe, a scaled-down menu of dishes such as skirt steak tortilla or hacked chicken that come piping hot from the open grill. Reserve (not in the Cafe). AE, CB, DC, MC, V. *L Mon-Sat noon-3pm. D Mon-Sat 6pm-11pm; Sun 6pm-11:30pm.* $$$ (Cafe $)

Aureole
34 East 61 Street. 319-1660. Some of the city's best food is served in the elegant duplex dining room of this flower-bedecked town house. Charles Palmer, former chef of River Cafe (post-Forgione), prepares an exquisite array of dishes with the freshest seasonal ingredients. Menu changes daily. Prix-fixe dinner. Reserve! AE, MC, V. *L Mon-Fri 11:30am-2:30pm. D Mon-Thurs 5:30pm-10:30pm; Fri & Sat 5:30pm-11pm. CLOSED Sun.* $$$$ +

Carolina
355 West 46 Street. 245-0058. Smart Restaurant Row choice back after a detour, once again serving beautifully prepared Southern and Southwestern regional American dishes. Much of the meat is smoked over a wood-fired barbecue process called "hot smoke." Eclectic menu offers

crab cakes, rich and spicy beanless chili, beef brisket, red pepper shrimp. The Mudd Cake is a must! Quieter front and upstairs dining rooms but the mirrored skylit backroom is the preferred spot. American wines and champagnes. Reservations required. AE, MC, V. *L Mon-Sat 11:45am-3pm. D Mon 5:30pm-9pm; Tues-Sat 5:30pm-11:30pm. CLOSED Sun.* $$$$

Chelsea Central
227 Tenth Avenue near 23 St. 620-0230. A warm and welcoming Chelsea tavern cum bistro complete with ceiling fans, long mahogany bar, and tin ceiling for delicious American fare. Butternut squash ravioli, roast duck, grilled swordfish, roast leg of lamb, and, for dessert, flourless chocolate marquise. Reserve. AE, MC, V. *L Mon-Fri 11:30am-3pm. D Mon-Thurs 5:30pm-11pm; Fri & Sat 5:30pm-midnight; Sun 5:30pm-10pm. Sun brunch 11:30am-3pm.* $$

Coach House
110 Waverly Place near Sixth Ave. 777-0303. No longer lionized, this former coach house (c. 1843) still provides a handsome town house setting for Southern American dishes. Famed crab cakes, warm corn bread, black bean soup, rack of lamb; wonderful desserts. Gracious service; sedate clientele. Jacket required; no denim. Reserve. AE, CB, DC, MC, V. *OPEN Tues-Sat 5:30pm-10:30pm; Sun 4:30pm-10pm. CLOSED Mon & major holidays.* $$$

Courtyard Cafe & Bar
Doral Court Hotel, 130 East 39 Street. 779-0739. An inviting spot just below midtown for a tranquil lunch. A glass-enclosed patio overlooks a lovely latticed garden with a waterfall. Good salads and grilled dishes; keep it simple. Reserve. AE, DC, MC, V. *L Mon-Sat noon-2:30pm. D 7 nights 5pm-11pm. Sun brunch 11:30am-3pm.* $$

Curtain Up!
402 West 43 Street. 564-7272. Simple unpretentious spot with Broadway-theater theme; youthful show biz feel. Burgers, salads, chili, omelettes, steak, home-baked desserts. Sidewalk cafe in summer. AE, CB, DC, MC, V. *OPEN Sun-Thurs noon-11pm; Fri & Sat noon-midnight. Sun brunch noon-4:30pm.* $

"44"
Royalton Hotel, 44 West 44 Street. 944-8844. In the fascinating Philippe Starck–designed setting, a sophisticated stylish dining spot for New American fare, a nice well-priced wine list, great desserts, and more than a few famous faces. Reserve. AE, MC, V. *B Mon-Fri 7-11:45am. L Mon-Fri noon-2:30pm. D Sun-Thurs 6-11pm; Fri & Sat 6pm-midnight. Weekend brunch 8am-2:30pm.* $$

Fraunces Tavern Restaurant
54 Pearl Street near Broad St. 269-0144. Reconstructed on the site of Washington's farewell to his troops in 1783, the tavern is mainly of historic value. (There is a museum upstairs; *see* MUSEUMS & GALLERIES, Museums, Historic Museums.) The Colonial dining rooms, with wood-burning fireplaces, serve mainly forgettable yankee pot roast, steak, fish, baked chicken "à

la Washington." But it's a good Wall Street area breakfast choice, served 7:30am to 10:30am. Bar and lounge. Reserve. AE, CB, DC, MC, V. *OPEN Mon-Fri 7:30am-9:30pm. CLOSED Sat & Sun.* $$

Ginger Man
51 West 64 Street. 399-2358. For over 20 years this convivial Lincoln Center–vicinity pub/ restaurant with several dining rooms has drawn crowds, especially before and after perfor- mances. It has several things going for it— location, an ability to get you to the show on time, and perhaps a famous face or two. Stay with the simple fare and you'll do okay. It's an attractive weekday breakfast spot, 8am to 11:30am. En- closed sidewalk cafe. AE, CB, DC, MC, V. *OPEN Mon-Fri 8am-midnight; Sat & Sun 10am- midnight. Sun brunch 11am-4pm.* $$

Good Enough to Eat
483 Amsterdam Avenue near West 83 St. 496- 0163. Tiny Upper West Side restaurant serves simple, low-priced homey fare: soups, stews, meat loaf, pork chops with corn bread stuffing, roast chicken with sweet potatoes. Good breakfast/brunch with pancakes, French toast, waffles, homemade biscuits, requires queuing up on weekends. Reserve for dinner only. AE, MC, V ($30 minimum). *D Mon-Sat 6pm- 10:30pm; Sun 5:30pm-10pm. Breakfast/brunch Mon-Fri 8am-4pm; Sat & Sun 9am-4pm.* $

Gotham Bar & Grill
12 East 12 Street. 620-4020. Gorgeous multi- leveled postmodern brasserie with 17-foot-high ceilings, soft lighting, and cast-stone ledges that give the sense of an outdoor garden courtyard. The eclectic and pricey menu runs the gamut from an $11.50 (at this writing) hamburger and lunchtime omelette to stunningly presented so- phisticated offerings; glorious desserts. One of the best dining destinations in the Village. Re- serve! AE, CB, DC, MC, V. *L Mon-Fri noon- 2:30pm. D Mon-Thurs 6pm-11pm; Fri & Sat 6pm- 11:15am; Sun 5:30pm-9:30pm.* $$$

Harvey's Chelsea House
108 West 18 Street. 243-5644. Dating back to 1889, this beautiful atmospheric turn-of-the- century saloon with etched glass, mahogany paneling, and dark walls serves traditional Amer- ican and English pub fare. AE only. *OPEN Sun- Thurs noon-11:30pm; Fri & Sat noon-12:30am. Sun brunch noon-4pm.* $$

Jerry's 103
103 Second Avenue at East 6 St. 777-4120. Quite good reasonably priced newcomer to the East Village dining scene. Eclectic contempo- rary American menu—don't miss the sweet po- tato fries. Open front spills onto the avenue in good weather. Good people-watching spot es- pecially in the pm. Also a scene place in SoHo (Jerry's, 101 Prince Street, 966-9464.) Reserve for dinner. AE, MC, V. *L Mon-Fri 11:30am-3pm. D Sun -Thurs 6pm-midnight; Fri & Sat 6pm-1am. Weekend brunch 11:30am-3:30pm.* $$

Louie's Westside Cafe
441 Amsterdam Avenue at West 81 St. 877-

1900. Tiny (11 tables, 33 seats), friendly Upper West Side eatery for simple well-prepared Amer- ican food. The extremely low prices (especially their prix-fixe three-course lunch) for such qual- ity are hard to beat. It gets a bit tight at dinner- time; there are a few outside tables in summer. Reservations taken for dinner only. AE, DC, MC, V. *L Mon-Fri 11:30am-4pm. D 7 days 6pm- midnight. Weekend brunch 10am-4pm.* $

Man Ray
169 Eighth Avenue near West 19 St. 627-4220. Back in gear with a new owner and chef, this noisy bistro draws crowds for the good, reason- ably priced, hearty American food and the Chelsea scene. Reserve. AE only. *L 7 days 11:30am-3:30pm. D Mon-Thurs & Sun 5:30pm- 11pm; Fri & Sat 5:30pm-1am.* $$

Mesa Grill
102 Fifth Avenue near 15 St. 807-7400. Exit Sofi, enter this hot, boisterous, amusingly decorated spot for deliciously satisfying Southwestern cooking. Reserve! AE, MC, V. *L Mon-Sat noon- 2pm. D Mon-Thurs 5:30pm-10pm; Fri & Sat 5:30pm-10:30pm; Sun 5:30pm-9:30pm.* $$

NoHo Star
330 Lafayette at Bleecker St. 925-0070. Casual, reliable, albeit noisy NoHo neighborhood haunt offers wide selection of reasonably priced burg- ers, salads, sandwiches. Chinese specialties available beginning at 6pm, Monday to Satur- day. Weekday breakfast served from 8am to 11:30am. Service earnest but painfully slow. AE, MC, V. *OPEN Mon-Thurs 8am-midnight; Fri 8am- 12:30am; Sat 10:30am-12:30am; Sun 10:30am- 10:30pm. Weekend brunch 10:30am-4:30pm.* $

The Polo
Westbury Hotel, 840 Madison Avenue at East 69 St. 535-9141. In an attractive, calm, clubby at- mosphere, lovely elegant essentially American food: roasted squab, medaillons of veal with poached pears, rack of lamb in tarragon sauce with couscous for two. Reserve. AE, CB, DC, MC, V. *OPEN 7 days. L noon-2:30pm. D 6:30pm- 10:30pm.* $$$$

Quilted Giraffe
550 Madison Avenue at East 55 St. 593-1221. In the AT&T arcade. Stunning setting for highly ad- venturesome, artful, and always successful "Japanese-influenced nouvelle American" cui- sine by executive chef-owner Barry Wine. Sky- high prix fixe but true foodies know it's worth it. Impressive wine list. Jacket and tie. Reserva- tions required. AE, MC, V. *L Tues-Fri noon- 2:30pm. D Tues-Sat 5pm-10:30pm. CLOSED Sun & Mon.* $$$$ +

Ravelled Sleave
1387 Third Avenue near East 79 St. 628-8814. Popular and comfortable Upper East Side bar and restaurant with fireplace and piano music for traditional American dining. Rack of lamb, Long Island duckling, sole with lobster sauce. Reserve. AE, CB, DC, MC, V. *D Mon 5:30pm- 11pm; Tues-Sat 5:30pm-midnight; Sun 5pm- 10:30pm. Brunch Sat noon-3pm; Sun 11:30am- 3pm.* $

River Cafe
See Rooms with a View
Sam's Cafe & Sam's Restaurant
Cafe: 1406 Third Avenue at East 80 St; 988-5300. Restaurant: Equitable Center, 152 West 52 Street; 582-8700. The original cafe is an attractive uncluttered pretty-people place (opt for the quieter back dining room) for uncomplicated American fare: outstanding is Sam's salad, the grilled salmon steak, and the chargrilled burger with shoestrings. The West Side restaurant spawned by the cafe's success, a large beautiful bilevel open space with a busy bar, serves a more extensive menu of American foods: crab cakes, brick-oven pizzas, grilled duck breast with black beans, smoked turkey club sandwich, and much more. Both are co-owned by model/actress Mariel Hemingway. Reserve. AE, DC, MC, V. Cafe: *OPEN Mon-Sat 6pm-midnight; Sun 6pm-10pm.* Restaurant: *L Mon-Fri noon-3pm. D Mon-Sat 5:30pm-11:30pm. CLOSED Sun.* $$

Serendipity 3
225 East 60 Street. 838-3531. For over 35 years this combo restaurant/general store has been an inviting fun lunch or brunch spot or for late snacking, for burgers, salads, French toast, omelettes, and, of course, their frozen hot chocolate or banana split. Up front: clothing, gifts, and novelties. Popular at lunchtime with the ladies who shop and always with the young and young at heart. No alcohol. Reserve. AE, DC, MC, V. *OPEN Mon-Thurs 11:30am-midnight; Fri & Sat till 1am. Weekend brunch 11:30am-6pm.* $

Telephone Bar & Grill
149 Second Avenue near East 9 St. 529-5000. Authentic London phone booths form the facade of this new-fashioned pub that features nicely prepared, well-priced contemporary American and traditional English specialties including *New York Times* fish and chips, shepherd's pie, a great burger with choice of toppings, veal sausage, chicken and fish cakes with warm red cabbage, and outstanding flourless chocolate cake as well as trifle for dessert. Attractive busy bar, cacophonous in the pm. Sidewalk tables in good weather; cozy back room with fireplace in winter. AE only. *OPEN 7 days 11:30am-1am (bar weekdays till 2am, Fri & Sat till 4am). Weekend brunch 11:30am-4pm.* $

Tennessee Mountain
143 Spring Street at Wooster St. 431-3993. Popular smoky SoHo spot for excellent meaty beef and baby back ribs; wonderful onion loaf, corn bread, and vegetarian or meat chili. Apple walnut or pecan pie for desert. Reserve. AE, MC, V. *OPEN Mon-Thurs 11:30am-11pm; Fri & Sat 11:30am-midnight; Sun 11:30am-10pm.* $

Vanessa
289 Bleecker Street at Seventh Ave South. 243-4225. Stylish romantic Art Deco–inspired flower-bedecked setting for good American nouvelle. Shrimp and leek salad, calves' liver with pearl onions and bacon, sauteed salmon with sorrel sauce. Jacket and tie preferred. Reserve. AE,

DC, MC, V. *D 7 days 5:30pm-midnight. Sun brunch noon-4pm.* $$$

Vince & Eddie's
70 West 68 Street. 721-0068. Country-house homey surroundings and satisfying American fare from two veteran restaurateurs (Vincent Oregara and Ed Shoenfeld) make this close-by Lincoln Center spot a popular choice. Reserve especially for pre- or posttheater. AE, DC, MC, V. *L Mon-Sat 11:45am-3pm. D Mon-Sat 5pm-midnight; Sun 5pm-11pm. Sun Brunch 11:30am-4pm.* $$

Ye Waverly Inn
16 Bank Street at Waverly Pl. 929-4377. Authentic colonial-tavern feel in this original 148-year-old Greenwich Village town house (it's been a restaurant since 1920). Comfortable, simple ambience with food to match. Good pot pies, Southern fried chicken, and other traditional American dishes. Pleasant back garden, two working fireplaces in winter. Bargain-priced full dinner for early birds Monday to Thursday from 5:15pm to 6:30pm. AE, CB, DC, MC, V. *D Mon-Thurs 5:15pm-10pm; Fri & Sat 5:15pm-11pm; Sun 4:30pm-9pm. Sun brunch noon-3pm.* $

Bars & Burgers

This listing provides the best in atmospheric and classic New York bars plus the best burgers in town, which may or may not be located in a bar. See also NIGHTLIFE, Piano Bars, *for good spots to have a drink at musical accompaniment.*

Algonquin Hotel
59 West 44 Street. 840-6800. Home of the legendary literary Round Table, there is no more civilized place to have a cocktail when in the theater district—before or after the show. Choose either the clubby oak-paneled lobby with its inviting sofas and armchairs, or the tiny dimly lit atmospheric **Blue Bar**. AE, DC, MC, V. *OPEN 7 days 5pm-1am.* $

Billy's
948 First Avenue near East 52 St. 355-8920. Since 1870, an East Side neighborhood institution, cherished by locals. Stout on tap, blackboard menu, simple pub fare. AE, DC, MC, V. *OPEN 7 days noon-11pm.* $

The Blue Mill Tavern
50 Commerce Street near Barrow St. 243-7114. A never-out-of-fashion (opened in 1941) quintessential Greenwich Village watering hole on this quintessential Greenwich Village cul de sac. But here you get much more than booze—the welcome is warm, the crowd and service amiable, and the Portuguese specialties include calderada (a bouillabaisse) and frango a Mamarrosa (spicy chicken); the steaks are tasty and low priced. Reservations for parties of 6 or more only. AE, DC, MC, V. *OPEN Mon-Thurs 5pm-10pm; Fri & Sat 5pm-11pm. CLOSED Sun.* $

Broome Street Bar
363 West Broadway at Broome St. 925-2086. Comfortable busy bar/restaurant for the best burgers and biggest drinks in SoHo. Also good

homemade soup and desserts. Popular with locals especially during the week. No reservations. No credit cards. *OPEN Sun-Thurs noon-1:30am; Fri & Sat noon-2:30am. Bar weekdays till 2am; Fri & Sat till 3am. Weekend brunch 11am-4pm.* $

Chumley's
86 Bedford Street near Barrow St. 675-4449. Colorful old Greenwich Village speakeasy and literary landmark. No sign to indicate its presence (a remnant of Prohibition), but once you find it, comfort and inexpensive food and drink are yours. Fireplace ablaze in winter. AE, CB, DC, MC, V. *OPEN Sun-Thurs 5pm-midnight; Fri & Sat 5pm-1am.* $

Corner Bistro
331 West 4 Street at Jane St. 242-9502. This friendly West Village pub popular with neighborhood regulars is highly regarded for its burgers. Also good, the beef chili, not to mention the vintage jukebox. No credit cards. *OPEN 7 days noon-4am.* $

Dan Lynch's
See NIGHTLIFE, Blues.

Fanelli's Cafe
94 Prince Street at Mercer St. 226-9412. A popular 125-year-old neighborhood bar where the food and brew are basic and the atmosphere, predating SoHo chic, authentic. No credit cards. *OPEN Mon-Sat 10am-2am; Sun 11am-2am. Kitchen till 12:30am.* $

Great Jones Cafe
54 Great Jones Street near the Bowery. 674-9304. Downtown down-homey and crowded Bowery-area spot for flavorful burgers, chili, red- or bluefish filets, and the house drink—a jalapeno martini! To top it all off, a great jukebox. The noise is deafening but the young crowd doesn't seem to mind. No reservations. No credit cards. *D 7 nights 5pm-midnight; bar later. Weekend brunch noon-4pm.* $

Hamburger Harry's
145 West 45 Street; 840-2756. And * 157 Chambers Street near West Broadway; 267-4446. In the theater district, a terrific *haute* burger done to a turn on a mesquite grill with a selection of toppings (caviar and sour cream; bearnaise; chili, cheddar & guacamole). Wash it down with a beer, wine, or champagne. Counter or tables. In the back room, piano in the pm. Kids menu. No reservations. AE, MC, V. *OPEN Mon-Fri 11:30am-11pm; Sat noon-11:30pm. CLOSED Sun. *OPEN Sun-Thurs 11:30am-10pm; Fri & Sat 11:30am-11pm.* $

Jackson Hole Wyoming
*232 East 64 Street, 371-7187; ** 1633 Second Avenue at East 85 St, 737-8788; *** 521 Third Avenue near East 34 St, 679-3264; ****1270 Madison Avenue near East 90 St, 427-2820; and *****517 Columbus Avenue near West 85 St, 362-5177. Hamburger connoisseurs consider this the best in town (it's certainly one of the biggest). Twelve versions of burger; if you can resist those, there are omelettes, too. No reservations except for very large parties. *Garden dining in season. Beer & wine only. No

credit cards. *OPEN Mon-Sat 10:30am-1am; Sun noon-midnight.* **Sidewalk cafe. Full bar. AE, MC, V. *OPEN Mon-Thurs 10am-1am; Fri & Sat 10am-4am; Sun 10:30am-midnight.* ***Full bar. No credit cards. *OPEN 7 days 10:30am-1am.* ****Beer only. No credit cards. *OPEN Mon-Fri 7am-11pm; Sat & Sun 9am-11pm.* *****Full bar. AE only. *OPEN Mon-Thurs 11am-midnight; Fri 11am-4am; Sat 9am-4am; Sun 9am-2am.* $

Jeremy's Ale House
259 Front Street at Dover St. 964-3537. A few blocks north of the restored Seaport is a ramshackle 1806 landmark building housing this long narrow restaurant with a 60-foot bar popular with Wall Streeters at lunchtime and after work. Bare bones tavern decor, beer by the quart in Styrofoam "buckets," fried calamari, fish and chips, clam chowder, hero sandwiches, and chili. Atmospheric and convivial. No reservations. No credit cards. *OPEN Mon-Thurs 8am-9pm; Fri 8am-10pm; Sat & Sun 10am-7pm.* $

J. G. Melon
1291 Third Avenue at East 74 St; 650-1310. And * 340 Amsterdam Avenue at West 76 St; 874-8291. For years the best bar-burger on the Upper East Side; now on the West Side, too. Convivial pub settings. No reservations. *AE, CB, DC, MC, V ($20 minimum). *OPEN 7 days 11:30am-2:30am for food; bar till 4am. *OPEN 11:30am-1:30am; bar till 4am. Brunch Sat 11:30am-4:30pm; Sun 11am-4pm.* $

Jim McMullen
1341 Third Avenue near East 76 St. 861-4700. Handsome bar where pretty people find one another; crowded after work. In the dining room with Art Deco motif, okay steaks, chops, seafood; daily specials. No reservations, be prepared for a wait. AE, MC, V. *OPEN 7 days 11:30am-12:30am.* $$

King Cole Bar
St. Regis Hotel, Fifth Avenue & 55 Street. 753-4500. Once again Old King Cole—the central figure in the beloved Maxfield Parrish mural—gazes down on sophisticates sipping cocktails at the cherrywood bar. AE, DC, MC, V. *OPEN 7 days noon-4am.* $

Landmark Tavern
626 Eleventh Avenue at West 46 St. 757-8595. The tavern, which dates back to 1868, features traditional fare, including steak-and-kidney pie, fish and chips, and shepherd's pie. To warm you in winter the upstairs dining room has two fireplaces; the back room, a potbelly stove. Reserve. AE, MC, V. *L Mon-Fri noon-4:30pm. D Sun-Thurs 5pm-midnight; Fri & Sat noon-midnight. Sun brunch noon-4:15pm.* $$

Lion's Head
59 Christopher Street near Sheridan Sq. 929-0670. Longtime Village literary watering hole and gathering place. Burgers, shepherd's pie, steak. Wide selection of ales and beers on tap. AE, DC, MC, V. *L Mon-Fri noon-4pm. D Sun-Thurs 5:30pm-1am; Fri & Sat 5:30pm-2am. Weekend brunch noon-4pm.* $

Manhattan Brewing Company
40 Thompson Street near West Broadway. 219-9250. You can't get much closer to the brew than this. Former Con Ed substation converted to a brewery/bar/restaurant. Copper vats make for interesting ambience in the Tap Room. To eat—Texas barbecue done to a turn in a slow-smoke process. MC, V. *OPEN Tues-Thurs 5pm-1am; Fri & Sat noon-2am; Sun noon-10pm. CLOSED Mon.*
$

McSorley's Old Ale House
15 East 7 Street. 473-9148. This dusty memorabilia-bedecked landmark bar in the East Village, where Brendan Behan drank, has operated continuously—even through Prohibition—since 1854. Colorful, no-nonsense, formerly males-only ale house. (Women were reluctantly admitted August 10, 1970). Their own aged cream ale only, passable pub grub including corned beef and cabbage, Irish stew, sandwiches, and cheese plates. A collegiate clientele. Potbelly stove in winter. No reservations. No credit cards. *OPEN Mon-Sat 11am-1am; Sun 1pm-1am.*
$

Moran's
146 Tenth Avenue at West 19 St. 627-3030. No less than four fireplaces cozy up this old Chelsea neighborhood Irish bar. Their specialty is seafood, fresh clams and oysters, but steaks and chops, too. Great Irish coffee. Reserve. AE, DC, MC, V. *OPEN 7 days noon-midnight.*
$

Museum Cafe
366 Columbus Avenue near West 77 St. 799-0150. Bright popular glassed-in sidewalk cafe/bar/restaurant and survivor. Good burgers, omelettes, and Columbus Avenue viewing. Reserve. AE, DC, MC, V. *OPEN Mon-Fri 11:30am-1am; Sat 10:30am-2am; Sun 10:30am-1am. Weekend brunch 10:30am-5pm.*
$

Oak Bar
Plaza Hotel, 768 Fifth Avenue & 58 Street. 546-5330. Traditional wood-paneled bar in famed hotel is still one of the classiest spots in town for a drink. Also, light fare from a bar menu (or you can order from the Oak Room menu and be served in the bar). Jacket preferred. AE, CB, DC, MC, V. *OPEN 7 days 11am-2am. Food until midnight.*
$

Old Town Bar
45 East 18 Street. 473-8874. A lively tavern with a long old wooden bar, a 14-foot-high hammered-tin ceiling, tile floors, and a crowd that wouldn't be caught dead in any place termed trendy. Good brew, burgers, and fries. No credit cards. *OPEN 7 days 11:30am-12:30am.*
$

Pete's Tavern
129 East 18 Street at Irving Pl. 473-7676. Closeby Gramercy Park, a historic 1864 tavern where O. Henry, who lived across the street, penned "The Gift of the Magi." The original bar is quite popular, so is the sunny sidewalk cafe in summer. Mainly Italian food but you'll do well to have a burger. Reserve. AE, CB, DC, MC, V. *OPEN Sun-Thurs 11:30am-11:30pm; Fri & Sat 11:30am-12:30am. Weekend brunch 11am-4pm.*
$

P.J. Clarke's
915 Third Avenue at East 55 St. 759-1650. It's *the* classic old New York saloon. Quite literally rub shoulders with New Yorkers at the extremely popular front-room bar at noon and 5pm, or elbow your way to the atmospheric dark back-room dining room. Best bites: the burgers, home fries, chili, and spinach salad. Full menu till 3:30am. Reserve. AE, CB, DC. *OPEN 7 days noon-4am.*
$

Taste of the Apple
1000 Second Avenue near East 53 St. 751-1445. Maybe the best—as well as the best-priced—burger in midtown. Now also on the *West Side at 283 Columbus at West 73 Street; 873-8892. AE only. *OPEN Mon-Thurs 11am-midnight; Fri 11am-1am; Sat 10am-1am; Sun 10am-midnight. Weekend brunch 10am-4pm. *OPEN Sun-Thurs 8am-midnight; Fri & Sat 8am-1am.*

White Horse Tavern
560 Hudson Street at West 11 St. 243-9260. Friendly old Greenwich Village literary watering hole; Dylan Thomas and Norman Mailer are among the many who have imbibed here. To go with the booze, great burgers, fish and chips, and chili. In season, the largest outdoor cafe in Greenwich Village. No credit cards. *OPEN Sun-Thurs 11am-2am (cafe till 1am); Fri & Sat 11am-4am (cafe till 2am). Weekend brunch 11am-4pm.*
$

Belgian

Cafe de Bruxelles
118 Greenwich Avenue at West 13 St. 206-1830. In the West Village, the hearty cuisine of Belgium in a handsome European setting. Waterzooi de poulet, carbonnade flamanade, boudin blanc et frites; Belgian chocolate mousse; Belgian beers, and a good inexpensive wine selection. Lovely bar menu 5pm to 11:15pm. Reserve. AE, MC, V. *L Tues-Sun noon-3:30pm. D Mon-Sat 5pm-11:30pm; Sun 3:30pm-11:30pm.*
$$

Breakfast/Brunch

Aggie's
146 West Houston Street at MacDougal St. 673-8994. This updated but still basic luncheonette is just about the best place to have breakfast downtown—hearty and wholesome homey cooking. No credit cards. *OPEN Mon-Fri 7:30am-10pm; Sat & Sun 10am-11pm.*
$

Ambassador Grill
United Nations Plaza Hotel, First Avenue at East 44 St. 702-5014. Sophisticated dining in a beautiful black-and-white, prism-mirrored room. Sumptuous albeit pricey prix-fixe Sunday brunch buffet with lobster and unlimited champagne. Piano music. Reserve. AE, CB, DC, MC, V. *OPEN 7 days. Two sittings: 11:30am-1:30pm & 1:45pm-3pm.*
$$

American Festival Cafe
Rockefeller Center, 20 West 50 Street, lower concourse. 246-6699. A perfect spot in midtown for an early morning business breakfast, especially in summer when you can opt for outdoors in the gardenlike sunken plaza. For those of us not on an expense account, a tip: just around the bend is *Savories, where you can breakfast weekdays on essentially the same fare in more casual surroundings at lower prices; outdoors here, too. AE, DC, MC, V. *Breakfast served Mon-Fri 7:30am-10:30am; Sat & Sun 9am-10:30am. Weekend brunch 10:30am-3:30pm. *Breakfast Mon-Fri 7:30am-11am.* For lunch and dinner at American Festival Cafe, *see* American. $

Angry Squire
See NIGHTLIFE, Jazz.

Cafe Orlin
41 St. Marks Place near Second Ave. 777-1447. Brunch is a treat in this terrific East Village cafe. Egg dishes accompanied by great cappuccino and fresh-squeezed oj. In good weather the small European-style sidewalk cafe for the city's best bizarre-people watching. No reservations. No credit cards. *Weekend brunch 9:30am-4pm. OPEN Mon-Fri 9am-2am; Sat & Sun 9:30am-3am.* $

Cajun
See Soul/Southern.

Cottonwood Cafe
415 Bleecker Street near West 11 St. 924-6271. Downhome New York style. Noisy casual spot for a great Greenwich Village brunch. No reservations. No credit cards. *Weekend brunch Sat 10am-3pm; Sun 10am-4pm.* $

Cupping Room Cafe
359 West Broadway at Broome St. 925-2898. SoHo locals breakfast in this skylit brick and wood setting, you should, too. Go for the wonderful omelettes, homemade muffins, and the cafe au lait. A la carte brunch. AE, CB, DC, MC, V ($15 minimum). *Breakfast Mon-Fri 7:30am-11am; weekend brunch 8am-6pm. L Mon-Fri noon-5pm. D Sat & Sun 6pm-1am.* $

Hors D'Oeuvrerie
Windows on the World, #1 World Trade Center, 107th floor. 938-1111. There is no more spectacular breakfast/brunch venue in the city. The room, a quarter of a mile high, overlooks New York Harbor and Lady Liberty. Monday to Friday from 7am there is an à la carte breakfast menu including steak and eggs. On Sunday a choice of an international brunch—Mexico, China, or Scandinavia are featured—or one of several delicious egg dishes. In addition, on the weekend in the Restaurant dining room (where you'll find the most dazzling view) there is the copious Grand Buffet. Jacket required; no denim. Reserve for brunch. AE, CB, DC, MC, V. *Breakfast Mon-Fri 7am-10:30am (except holidays). Sun brunch noon-3pm. Windows brunch buffet Sat & Sun noon-3pm.* $

Paris Commune
411 Bleecker Street near West 11 St. 929-0509. The ground level of a Greenwich Village brown-

stone, with a warming fire in the hearth in winter, creates an inviting setting for a cozy weekend brunch. No reservations taken for brunch. AE, MC, V. *Weekend brunch 10am-3:30pm. D 7 days 6pm-11pm.* $

Pink Tea Cup
42 Grove Street near Bleecker St. 807-6755. Longtime unpretentious soul-food eatery in new still low-frills surroundings that still serves a satisfying breakfast (all day) of eggs, grits, homemade corn muffins. Followed by apple pie if you can handle it. Well-stocked jukebox. No credit cards. *OPEN Mon-Fri 8am-midnight; Sat & Sun 8am-1am.* $

PizzaPiazza
785 Broadway at East 10 St. 505-0977. Fine fun alternative to traditional brunch: a deep-dish brunch pizza! The Great Western with tomato, onion, eggs, jalapeno, and sausage, or the Florentine, a garlicky spinach and cheese pizza topped with two poached eggs (among other choices). Bloody Mary or mimosa, and coffee. All in a pink window-wrapped interior with a view of Renwick's marvelous Grace Church. Reserve for 6 or more only. AE, MC, V. *Weekend brunch 11:45am-3:30pm. OPEN Sun-Thurs 11:45am-11:30pm; Fri & Sat 11:45am-midnight.* $

Popover Cafe
551 Amsterdam Avenue near West 87 St. 595-8555. Country-cozy West Sider for copious helpings of well-prepared breakfast fixin's. Wonderful omelettes, cheese grits, and of course those gigantic popovers. Cappuccino, espresso, herbal teas. Also, sandwiches, hearty burgers, tasty salads. No reservations, expect a wait at peak times. AE, MC, V. *OPEN Mon-Fri 8:30am-11pm; Sat 9:30am-11pm; Sun 9:30am-10pm.* $

Regency Hotel
540 Park Avenue at East 61 St. 759-4100. The power breakfast was invented here where New York movers and shakers breakfast while their chauffeurs bide their time curbside. AE, DC, MC, V. *Breakfast 7 days 7am-11am.* $

Sarabeth's Kitchen
1295 Madison Avenue near East 92 St; 410-7335. And * 423 Amsterdam Avenue near West 80 St; 496-6280. Like a Vermont country kitchen. In addition to other tempting entrees, omelettes, homemade muffins, potato and cheese blintzes, pancakes with fresh fruit, and pumpkin waffles are served all day every day. Wonderful marmalades, Linzer tortes, and shortbreads. No smoking anywhere! Complete bar. AE, DC, MC, V. *Weekend brunch 9am-4pm. OPEN 7 days 9am-11pm. *Breakfast menu Tues-Fri 8:30am-4pm; weekend brunch 9am-4pm. D Mon-Thurs 6pm-10:30pm, Fri & Sat 6pm-11pm.* $

Tuesday's
190 Third Avenue near East 17 St. 533-7902. Former speakeasy with Tiffany lamps, wooden booths, marble-tiled floors. The popular weekend brunch, from 11:30am to 4pm, is a best only in the value-for-volume category, with mounds of just passable food and unlimited champagne for

one low price. Live jazz makes it a lively choice. Reserve. AE, MC, V. *OPEN 7 days 11:30am-1am.* $

Veselka Coffee Shop
144 Second Avenue at East 9 St. 228-9682. Where East Village natives (and that's quite a mix) eat breakfast (lunch and dinner, too). Those in the know head for the formerly private back room of this Polish luncheonette and order the blueberry or banana wheatcakes, challah French toast, blintzes, or pirogi. Breakfast specials are served Monday to Saturday from 7am to noon; Sunday from 7am to 5pm (they know their clientele sleeps late!) P.S.: The rest of the Eastern European home-cooking on the menu is delicious, satisfying, and inexpensive, too. No credit cards. *OPEN 7 days, 24 hours.* $

*The following also serve breakfast or brunch on Saturday and/or Sunday. An * indicates highly recommended:*

Abyssinia Restaurant (Ethiopian)
Acme Bar & Grill (Soul/Southern)
Adam's Rib (American)
Alo Alo (Italian)
Anglers & Writers (Afternoon Tea)
Around the Clock Cafe (Late Night & 24 Hours)
Bernstein-on-Essex Street (Delicatessen)
***Berry's** (Continental)
***The Black Sheep** (French)
Box Tree (French)
***Brasserie** (Late Night & 24 Hours)
Bridge Cafe (Continental)
Broome Street Bar (Bars & Burgers)
Cafe de Bruxelles (Belgian)
Cafe de la Paix (Sidewalk Cafes)
***Cafe des Artistes** (Continental)
Cafe Loup (French)
***Cafe Un Deux Trois** (French)
Caffe Reggio (Cafes)
***Cajun** (Soul/Southern)
Capsouto Frères (French)
Caramba! & !! & !!! & !!!! (Mexico)
Carlyle Restaurant (Continental)
Carnegie Delicatessen (Delicatessen)
Chez Ma Tante (French)
Claire (Fish & Seafood)
Cloister Cafe (Cafes)
Cornelia Street Cafe (Cafes)
Curtain Up! (American)
***Danal** (Afternoon Tea *and* Cafes)
David K's (Chinese)
Dock's Oyster Bar & Seafood Grill (Fish & Seafood)
Eclair Shop (Hungarian)
Elephant & Castle (Omelettes)
Fiorello's Roman Cafe (Sidewalk Cafes)
Florent (Late Night & 24 Hours)
Fraunces Tavern Restaurant (American)
Ginger Man (American)
Good Enough to Eat (American)
Gotham Bar & Grill (American)
Great Jones Cafe (Bars & Burgers)

Gulf Coast (Soul/Southern)
Hamilton House (Steak)
Harlequin (Spanish)
Harvey's Chelsea House (American)
Hee Seung Fung (HSF) (Chinese: Dim Sum)
Hop Shing Restaurant (Chinese: Dim Sum)
Hudson River Club (Rooms with a View)
Jerry's 103 (American)
J. G. Melon's (Bars & Burgers)
Kenny's Steak Pub (Steak)
La Boheme (French)
La Bonne Soupe (Inexpensive)
La Gauloise (French)
Landmark Tavern (Bars & Burgers)
Lan Hong Kok Seafood House (Chinese: Dim Sum)
***Le Regence** (French)
Lion's Head (Bars & Burgers)
***Lion's Rock** (Continental)
***Lola** (Caribbean)
Louie's Westside Cafe (American)
Marylou's (Fish & Seafood)
Maurice (French)
Memphis (Soul/Southern)
Moondance Diner (Inexpensive)
Mortimer's (Continental)
Museum Cafe (Bars & Burgers)
New Prospect Cafe (Health & Vegetarian)
The Nice Restaurant (Chinese)
NoHo Star (American)
Nom Wah Tea Parlor (Chinese: Dim Sum)
Odeon (Late Night & 24 Hours)
Omen (Japanese)
Petaluma (Italian)
Petrossian (French)
Pig Heaven (Chinese)
Rainbow Promenade (Rooms with a View)
Raoul's (French)
Ratner's Dairy Restaurant (Jewish)
Ravelled Sleave (American)
***River Cafe** (Rooms with a View)
Roettelle A. G. (German)
Rosa Mexicano (Mexican)
Russian Tea Room (Stargazing)
Sam's Cafe (American)
Sazerac House (Soul/Southern)
Second Avenue Kosher Delicatessen (Delicatessen)
Serendipity 3 (American)
Seryna (Japanese)
The Sign of the Dove (Continental)
SoHo Kitchen and Bar (Wine Bars)
Spring Street Natural Restaurant (Health & Vegetarian)
Stage Deli (Delicatessen)
Summerhouse (Continental)
Sumptuary Restaurant (Continental)
***Sylvia's** (Soul/Southern)
Telephone Bar & Grill (American)
Time and Again (Continental)
TriBeCa Grill (Stargazing)
20 Mott Street (Chinese: Dim Sum)
***Vanessa** (American)
The View Restaurant (Rooms with a View)
The Water Club (Rooms with a View)

Water's Edge Restaurant (Rooms with a View)
White Horse Tavern (Bars & Burgers)
Whole Wheat 'n' Wild Berries (Health & Vegetarian)
World Yacht Cruises (Rooms with a View)
Ye Waverly Inn (American)

Cafes

These are unique spots to have a coffee and pastry, most are old and full of atmosphere; all are perfect places to end an evening with a non-alcoholic nightcap (all serve decaf). See also Sidewalk Cafes.

Cafe La Fortuna
69 West 71 Street. 724-5846. Follow the enticing aroma to this understandably popular old-fashioned Lincoln Center–area cafe for coffees, pastries, teas, hot chocolate, and, in warm weather, a garden terrace for lingering. Opera memorabilia and music add to the atmosphere. No credit cards. *OPEN Mon-Thurs 1pm-1am; Fri 1pm-2am; Sat noon-2am; Sun noon-1am.* $

Cafe Vivaldi
32 Jones Street near Bleecker St. 929-9384. Cafe on a quiet Greenwich Village side street, serves tostini, coffees, teas, and desserts. Fireplace in winter, outside tables in fair weather. No credit cards. *OPEN 7 days 11am-1am.* $

Caffe Biondo
141 Mulberry Street near Hester St. 226-9285. Pretty Little Italy newcomer for snacks, desserts, coffees. Outdoor tables on still colorful Mulberry Street in summer. No credit cards. *OPEN 7 days 12:30pm-2am.* $

Caffe Dante
79-81 MacDougal Street near Bleecker St. 982-5275. Bracing espresso, frothy cappuccino, hot chocolate, iced drinks, teas, pastries, salads, and little sandwiches in one of the Village's more inviting Italian cafes. Sidewalk tables in summer. No credit cards. *OPEN Sun-Thurs 10am-2am; Fri & Sat 10am-3pm.*

Caffe Reggio
119 MacDougal Street near West 3 St. 475-9557. Wonderfully authentic and aromatic old-time Greenwich Village coffeehouse. Crowded, cramped, and cozy—it's the best for ambience with your espresso, cappuccino, and Italian pastries. Sidewalk tables in summer for the oft-times interesting street scene. No credit cards. *OPEN Sun-Thurs 9am-3am; Fri & Sat 10am-4am.* $

Caffe Roma
385 Broome Street at Mulberry St. 226-8413. Little Italy's best old pasticceria, tastefully redecorated. Cappuccino, cannoli, Sicilian cassata, and more. Busy, be prepared to wait on weekends. No credit cards. *OPEN 7 days 8am-midnight.* $

Cloister Cafe
238 East 9 Street. 777-9128. In the East Village; a mirage of a garden (late April to October) is the very special feature of this cafe. Stick to the salads—better yet, just linger over a wonderful bowl of cafe au lait and a pastry ($5 minimum in the garden). Day or evening it's a treat. In winter there's a potbelly stove inside. In or out you must suffer the service. Wine and beer. No reservations. No credit cards. *OPEN Sun-Thurs 11am-1am; Fri & Sat 11am-2am. Weekend brunch 11am-5pm.* $

Cornelia Street Cafe
29 Cornelia Street near Bleecker St. 989-9319. An oasis of calm in the Village for cappuccino and croissant; weekend brunch; cheese, fruit, and wine; or some of their lovely daily specials. Sidewalk tables in summer. Fireplace in winter. Poetry and prose spoken here every Sunday from 8pm. Full bar. AE, DC, MC. *OPEN 7 days 9am-1am. Kitchen till 12:30am. Weekend brunch 9:30am-4:30pm.* $

Danal
90 East 10 Street. 982-6930. The most inviting cafe in town, don't miss. During the week and Saturday for a continental breakfast, for a light lunch, or for their delightful reservation-only prix-fixe afternoon tea; on Sunday for their popular brunch. Soups, pâtés, tarts, brioche French toast (brunch only); cafe au lait served in a bowl, cappuccino, cafe filtre, and an exclusive selection of aromatic teas and enticing pastries. It's the perfect place for a private party. Up-front shop for a selection of imported gourmet and tabletop gifts. Charming secluded garden in summer. AE only. *OPEN Tues-Fri 9am-6:30pm; Sat noon-6:30pm; Sun 11:30am-3:30pm. CLOSED Mon.* $

De Robertis
176 First Avenue near East 11 St. 674-7137. In the East Village, wonderful, original 85-year-old pasticceria much as you would find in Rome. For espresso, cappuccino, and homemade Italian pastries. Weekends you'll wait. No credit cards. *OPEN Sun-Thurs 9am-11pm; Fri & Sat 9am-midnight.* $

Dolci on Park
12 Park Avenue near East 34 St. 686-4331. For light fare—pastas, salads, but best of all for cappuccino, pastries, and the city's best scones—a sedate enclave with a continental air. Outdoor tables in season. AE, MC, V. *OPEN Mon-Fri 7:30am-10:30pm; Sat 9:30am-10pm.* $

Ferrara's
195 Grand Street near Mulberry St. 226-6150. Famed very bright and lively Little Italy cafe is the granddaddy of them all and it spills out onto the colorful side street in summer. Espresso, cappuccino, delicious pastries, and gelati. Be prepared to wait in the pm. No credit cards. *OPEN 7 days 7:30am-midnight.* $

Hungarian Pastry Shop
1030 Amsterdam Avenue near West 111 St. 866-4230. Longtime Columbia University hangout. Cramped, cozy, and timeless, for wonderful linzer torte and cappuccino. No credit cards. *OPEN Mon-Fri 8am-11:15pm; Sat 9am-11:30pm; Sun 9am-10:30pm.*

Peacock
24 Greenwich Avenue near West 10 St. 242-9395. Antique tables, chairs, paintings, and opera music lend a Renaissance air to this longtime Village coffeehouse. You will have to be patient for good cappuccino and cannoli; light food, too. No credit cards. *OPEN Mon 1pm-midnight; Tues-Thurs 1pm-1am; Fri & Sat 1pm-2am; Sun 1pm-1am.* $

Rumbuls
20 Christopher Street near Gay St; 924-8900. And 559 Hudson Street near West 11 St; 929-8783. Also 128 East 7 Street, 473-8696. Coffee and sweets in a charming little 19th-century building (Christopher Street). Working fireplace in the back room. No credit cards. *OPEN 7 days 11am-midnight.* $

Veniero's
342 East 11 Street. 674-4415. Venerable Veniero's, here since 1894, continues to pack 'em in. Tables in the bakery for smokers, and the adjacent nonsmokers cafe for espresso, cappuccino, and a delectably rich pastry. Fresh fruit ices in summer, sidewalk tables, too. No credit cards. *OPEN Sun-Thurs 8am-midnight; Fri & Sat 8am-1am.* $

Caribbean

Caribe
117 Perry Street at Greenwich St. 255-9191. Good fun spot for spicy Jamaican cooking and exotic potent Island drinks, all to a reggae beat in a low-key jungle motif. Aromatic black bean soup, curried goat, Barbados codfish stew, spicy jerked chicken Caribe. No reservations taken; no credit cards. *OPEN Sun-Thurs 11:30am-11pm; Fri & Sat 11:30am-midnight.* $

Lola
30 West 22 Street. 675-6700. Inventive Caribbean cuisine in an elegant pastel environment in Chelsea. Extremely popular and noisy at peak times. Don't miss the Caribbean-fried chicken, the shrimp and chicken curry, the ribbon-thin cayenne-laced onion rings, or the Sunday brunch with rousing gospel music. Inviting bar area for tropical drinks accompanied by live music in the pm. Reserve! AE only. *L Mon-Fri noon-3pm. D Mon-Thurs 6pm-midnight; Fri & Sat 6pm-1am; Sun 6pm-10pm. Sun brunch, two sittings noon & 2:30pm.* $$

Sugar Reef
93 Second Avenue near East 5 St. 477-8427. Zesty Island cooking and potent multihued concoctions draw crowds to this tacky whacky East Village hot spot where six deep at the bar is not unusual. Recommended are the coconut shrimp, peppery jerk chicken, Baja kingfish, conch fritters, and barbecued shrimp wrapped in banana leaves. Warning: The din may be harmful to your hearing. Reservations Sunday to Thursday only for parties of more than 8 people. AE only. *OPEN Mon-Fri 5pm-11:30pm; Sat & Sun 3pm-12:30am. Bar later.* $

Chinese

Auntie Yuan
1191A First Avenue near East 64 St. 744-4040. Sophisticated Chinese cookery in a setting to match. Some fascinating dishes in addition to the standards, including an excellent Peking duck. Also good are the dumplings, shrimp with orange and ginger, and orange beef. A Cruvinet dispenses a choice of fine wines by the glass. AE, CB, DC, MC, V. Reserve. *OPEN 7 days noon-11:30pm.* $$$

Beijing Duck House
144 East 52 Street; 759-8260. And 22 Mott Street near Columbus Sq; 227-1810. For those who can't anticipate a craving for Peking duck 24 hours in advance. Always available (20-minute wait) whole duck, perfectly crisp, carved at the table. Also good is the duck soup. Don't let the uptown address fool you, it's informal Chinatown in spirit. Reserve. AE, DC, MC, V. *OPEN 7 days noon-9:30pm.* $$

Canton
45 Division Street near Market St. 226-4441. One of Chinatown's best. Those in the know come here for the authentic Cantonese food in clean spare surroundings. Seafood is the specialty; also good are the roast duck and the herbed chicken. Those in the know ask the gentlewoman owner for suggestions. Prices above Chinatown norm. No alcohol, but you may bring your own. Reserve. No credit cards. *OPEN Wed-Thurs noon-10pm; Fri & Sat noon-11pm; Sun noon-10pm. CLOSED Mon & Tues.* $$

China Grill
60 West 53 Street. 333-7788. This outpost of West Coast—Chinoise cooking (offshoot of Wolfgang Puck's L.A. Chinoise on Main)—in a dramatic block-long space with 20-foot-high ceilings, an extra-long bar, and an exposed kitchen—draws a trendy media and art crowd. Innovative choices: Chardonnay steamed mussels, tempura shashimi, Shanghai lobster, calamari salad, grilled squab; interesting desserts. Frenetic and loud in the pm. Reserve. AE, MC, V. *L Mon-Fri noon-2:30pm. D Mon-Thurs 5:30pm-11pm; Fri & Sat 5:30pm-midnight. CLOSED Sun.* $$$

Chin Chin
216 East 49 Street. 888-4555. Jimmy Chin's large, casual, but extremely stylish restaurant. Imaginatively prepared nouvelle Chinese offerings include shredded duck salad, vegetable duck pie with crepes, grilled baby quail, steamed or crispy whole bass, three-glass chicken, and veal medaillions with spicy pepper sauce. Good wine list. Reserve. AE, MC, V. *OPEN Mon-Fri 11:30am-11:30pm; Sat & Sun 5pm-11:30pm.* $$$

David K's
1115 Third Avenue near East 65 St. 371-9090. The latest from the famed restaurateur: health-conscious renditions of traditional Chinese fare using no MSG, little salt, less oil and fat. The menu is limited, the portions small but satisfying.

Specialty: Peking chicken served with whole wheat pancakes. Prix-fixe lunch and brunch. Good choice of wines. Reserve. AE, DC. *L Mon-Fri noon-3pm. D 7 days 5pm-11pm. Weekend brunch noon-3:30pm.* $$

Great Shanghai
27 Division Street at Market St. 966-7663. This busy Chinatown spot is a good bet for an extensive selection of quite good dishes. Seafood specialty standouts include the fried whole sea bass and fiery shrimp in garlic sauce. Also, Mongolian hot pots and well-priced Peking duck. Reserve for large parties only. AE only. *OPEN Sun-Thurs 11:30am-10pm; Fri & Sat 11:30am-11pm.* $

Hong Fat
63 Mott Street near Canal St. 962-9588. Tiny utilitarian Chinese restaurant; its specialty is noodles to the wee hours. No credit cards. *OPEN 7 days 11am-5am.* $

Hwa Yuan Szechuan Inn
40 East Broadway near Market St. 966-5534. This attractive cavernous, albeit cacophonous, restaurant in Chinatown is one of the area's best for spicy Szechuan dishes. Hot and sour soup, shredded chicken with pepper sauce, whole carp with hot sauce, and their cold noodles in sesame paste are the city's best. Crowded on weekends. Serves beer, bring your own wine. Reservations taken for 6 or more only. AE, DC, MC, V. *OPEN Sun-Thurs noon-10pm; Fri & Sat noon-11pm.* $

Little Shanghai
26 East Broadway near Division St. 925-4238. Small Chinatown find for wonderful, subtly spiced Shanghai-style cooking: dumplings, seafood specials, bean curd dishes. Low frills with prices to match. For dessert, exotic sherbets in season. Bring your own wine. No credit cards. *OPEN Mon-Thurs 10:30am-9:30pm; Fri, Sat & Sun 10:30am-10:30pm.* $

Mr. Chow
324 East 57 Street. 751-9030. Through the Lalique doors, a sleek old-money setting and crowd; noisy, busy ambience; wonderful but not very Chinese food. Reserve. AE, DC, MC, V. *OPEN 7 days 6pm-midnight.* $$$

Moshe Peking
See Jewish

The Nice Restaurant
35 East Broadway near Catherine St, upstairs. 406-9510. One of the newer Hong Kong-style Chinatown choices. The place and presentation are more festive and upscale than its neighbors; the food is quite good—especially the large scallops in hot pepper sauce, roast suckling pig, braised duck, barbecued pork ribs, and the salt-baked chicken. For dessert, choose the refreshing coconut tapioca soup with melon. Popular dim-sum lunch choice, served 8am to 4pm. Reserve, especially for large parties. Beer and wine. AE only. *OPEN 7 days 8am-11pm.* $$

Phoenix Garden ·
46 Bowery (in the arcade) below Canal St. 962-8934. *Authentic* Cantonese, not for chow mein aficionados. Extensive 16-page menu; shark fin soup, roast pigeon, fried milk with crab. No frills, no dessert, no reservations (except for parties of 7 or more). Yes, a wait. Bring your own wine, they have beer. Takeout, too. *OPEN 7 days 11:30am-10:30pm.* $

Pig Heaven
1540 Second Avenue at East 80 St. PIG-4333. David Keh's ode to the pig. Delicious and authentic food; silly decor. Though pork is the menu's mainstay, there's a great deal for nonpig fanciers. Don't miss the dumplings—fried, steamed, or boiled. Good family choice; Upper East Side prices. Shanghai-style brunch on weekends. Reserve. AE, DC. *OPEN Sun-Thurs noon-midnight; Fri & Sat noon-1am. Weekend brunch noon-3pm.* $$

Say Eng Look
5 East Broadway near Catherine St. 732-0796. This long-established Chinatown restaurant with its pagoda-inspired red walls still features well-prepared Shanghai specialties—fried fish roll in bean curd, Tai-chi chicken, orange-flavored beef, roasted whole carp. Reserve for more than 5 only. AE, DC, MC, V. *OPEN Sun-Thurs 11am-10pm; Fri & Sat 11am-11pm.* $

Shun Lee Palace
155 East 55 Street. 371-8844. Truly plush setting in which to enjoy excellent, impeccably served Hunan and Szechuan dishes. There's a low-calorie meal for dieters, but the temptations of the regular menu are too strong—hot and sour cabbage, lobster Szechuan, beggar's chicken, crispy whole sea bass, shrimp puffs, spicy Hunan duckling with smoke flavor. Very popular, it bustles; opt for the quieter back room. Reserve. AE, DC. *OPEN Sun-Thurs noon-11pm; Fri & Sat noon-11:30pm.* $$

Shun Lee West & Cafe
43 West 65 Street. 595-8895. This Shun Lee, in addition to well-prepared food and efficient service, boasts a dramatically designed setting. Good upbeat and consistent Lincoln Center choice. In the more casual **Shun Lee Cafe** (769-3888), dim sum from rolling carts. Reserve (especially for pretheater). AE, CB, DC, MC, V. *OPEN Mon-Sat noon-midnight; Sun noon-10pm. Cafe: 7 nights 5pm-midnight.* $$

Tang's Chariot
236 East 53 Street. 355-5096. Comfortable uptown relative of Chinatown's well-regarded Hwa Yuan Szechuan Inn. Here the interesting house specialty is beggar's chicken, which must be ordered a day in advance. Reserve. AE, DC, MC, V. *OPEN Mon-Fri 11am-11pm; Sat & Sun noon-11pm.* $$

—Dim Sum

Literally meaning "to take your heart's desire," it's the Chinese version of brunch. A tea lunch (tea is the beverage traditionally consumed with dim sum) consisting of dumplings, rolls, and buns filled with varieties of chicken, meat, fish, and vegetables; rice and noodle dishes; and sweet cakes. The food comes from the kitchen on rolling carts in a continuous stream, you beckon the server, and at the end of the meal the number of empty plates on your table are totaled to produce your bill. Listed are several Chinatown restaurants serving authentic dim sum. NOTE: This is one of the few times a seat near the kitchen is desirable. Also, pace yourself. Except for one, no credit cards for dim sum.

Hee Seung Fung (HSF)
46 Bowery near Canal St. 374-1319. Where almost every non-Chinese New Yorker had their first dim sum. Served 7 days 7:30am-5pm. $

Hop Shing Restaurant
9 Chatnam Square. 267-0220. Consistently good dim sum. Served 7 days 7am-3pm. $

Lan Hong Kok Seafood House
31 Division Street. 431-9063. One of the best for authentic dim sum. Served 7 days 7:30am-4pm.

Nom Wah Tea Parlor
13 Doyers Street near Pell St. 962-6047. The pioneer; for over 70 years, only dim sum. Aficionados disdain it, but it does have historic value. OPEN 7 days 11am-7pm.

20 Mott Street
20 Mott Street near Bowery. 964-0380. Three-story Chinatown eating emporium, winner hands down of the unofficial "where is the best dim sum" survey. AE, MC, V. Served 7 days 8am-4pm.

Continental

Berry's
180 Spring Street at Thompson St. 226-4394. A very good longtime SoHo dining choice is this charmingly cozy pub/restaurant. Imaginative, frequently changing menu. Excellent brunch choice. Front opens for alfresco dining in fine weather. Reserve. AE, MC, V. L Mon-Fri 11:30am-3:30pm. D Mon-Thurs 5:30pm-11:30pm; Fri & Sat 5:30pm-midnight; Sun 5:30pm-10:30pm. Brunch Sat 11:30am-3:30pm; Sun 11am-4pm. $$

Bridge Cafe
279 Water Street at Dover St. 227-3344. The kitchen of this early 19th-century waterfront-neighborhood saloon turns out some of the best and least expensive food in the South Street Seaport area; it's worth the short walk north. Best are the fish and seafood. Reserve. AE, DC, MC, V. L Mon-Fri 11:45am-5pm. D Sun & Mon 5pm-10pm; Tues-Sat 5pm-midnight. Sun brunch 11:45am-5pm. $

Cafe des Artistes
1 West 67 Street. 877-3500. The beautiful, nostalgic inviting ambience; the famed sweetly naughty murals by Howard Chandler Christy; and an imaginative menu of well-prepared hearty continental specialties understandably make this the preferred destination in the Lincoln Center area. If the object is romance, request one of the nooks surrounding the bar in the rear. Difficult as it may be, save room for dessert. Jacket required after 5pm. Reservations well ahead are a must, especially for pretheater dining. AE, CB, DC, MC, V. L Mon-Fri noon-3pm. D

Mon-Sat 5:30pm-12:30am; Sun 5pm-11pm. Brunch Sat noon-3pm; Sun 10am-4pm. $$$

Cafe Nicholson
323 East 58 Street. 355-6769. For a romantic evening this special spot can't be beat. But dining here requires some planning or good luck because it's open only when owner, John Nicholson, feels like it. The prix-fixe dinner includes a bottle of wine, and the hot chocolate souffle is one of the nicest desserts ever. Reserve well in advance. AE, DC, MC, V. As far as it can be pinned down, OPEN Wed-Sat, one seating 6pm-9pm. $$$$

Carlyle Restaurant
Madison Avenue at East 76 Street. 744-1600. The elegantly spacious dining room of this deluxe New York hotel serves very good continental dishes to an upscale clientele. Good spot for breakfast or prix-fixe Sunday brunch. Jacket and tie; no denim. Reserve. AE, CB, DC, MC, V. B Mon-Sat 7am-11am; Sun 8am-10:30am. L Mon-Sat noon-3pm. D 7 days 6pm-11pm. Sun brunch noon-3pm. $$$$

Grove Street Cafe
53 Grove Street near Bleecker St. 924-9501. Intimate charming Village bistro has no trouble filling its 12 candlelit tables. Dine on sweet red peppers stuffed with eggplant, roast duck with red cabbage, grilled seafood sausage, grilled filet mignon in green peppercorn sauce. For dessert, walnut ice cream. You may bring your own wine. Reserve well in advance. No credit cards. OPEN Mon-Sat 6pm-10:30pm. CLOSED Sun. $$

Lion's Rock
316 East 77 Street. 988-3610. Romantic little continental restaurant with amenities that make the food a runner-up. A wonderful large open-to-the-sky garden in summer (there resides the actual "lion's rock," a glacial remnant famed as a picnic spot for couples in love a century ago) and a blazing fireplace in each of the dining rooms on winter nights. Best meal: the interesting brunch. Reserve. AE, DC, MC, V. D Sun-Thurs 5pm-11pm; Fri & Sat 5pm-midnight. Weekend brunch 11:30am-3pm. $$

Mortimer's
1057 Lexington Avenue at East 75 St 861-2481. Fashionably clubby Upper East Side restaurant where the never-too-rich-never-too-thin-ladies-who-lunch lunch. Features fair continental fare: rack of lamb, chicken paillard, twin burgers, and, of course, a Women's Wear photographer. Don't expect to sit in the attractive main dining area if you are unknown to owner Glenn Bernbaum. Reserve for 5 or more only. AE, DC, MC, V. L Mon-Fri noon-3:30pm. D 7 days 6pm-midnight. Weekend brunch 12:15pm-4:30pm. $$

One If by Land, Two If by Sea
17 Barrow Street between West 4 St & Seventh Ave. South. 255-8649. In Greenwich Village, beautiful romantic dining in Aaron Burr's former carriage house. The continental entrees rarely fail to please, especially the beef Wellington. Fresh flowers, candlelight, and two working fire-

places in winter enhance the romantic glow. Piano music in the bar from 5:30pm makes this a swell place for an after-work cocktail or a wee-hours nightcap. Reserve. AE, CB, DC, MC, V. *OPEN Sun-Thurs 5:30pm-midnight; Fri & Sat 5:30pm-1am. Bar till 3am.* $$$

The Sign of the Dove
1110 Third Avenue at East 65 St. 861-8080. Extremely beautiful flower-bedecked restaurant with the look of a romantic indoor garden where, at last, the food measures up to the decor. Seasonal menu; well-chosen wine list. Attractive piano bar cafe. Jacket and tie preferred in the dining room. Reserve. AE, CB, DC, MC, V. *L Mon-Sat noon-2:30pm. D 7 days 6pm-11:30pm. Weekend brunch 11:30am-2:30pm. Bar till 1am.* $$$$

Summerhouse
50 East 86 Street. 249-6300. Sweet inviting Carnegie Hill restaurant popular with neighborhood locals. Simple fare; a wonderful apple tart for dessert. Complete bar. Reserve, for lunch 6 or more only. AE, MC, V. *OPEN 7 days 11:30am-11pm. Weekend brunch 11:30am-3:30pm.* $

Sumptuary Restaurant
400 Third Avenue near East 28 St. 889-6056. A very pretty setting either in the new street-level addition (open only Wednesday to Sunday) or the more cozy original upstairs with its open-to-the-sky dining terrace in summer and warming fireplaces in several of the romantic dining rooms in winter. Extremely pleasant dining on Italian and French Provençal dishes. Reserve. AE, MC, V. *L Mon-Fri noon-3pm. D Mon-Sat 4pm-10:30pm; Sun 4pm-9pm. Sun brunch noon-3pm.* $$

Time and Again
Doral Tuscany Hotel, 116 East 39 Street. 685-8887. Welcoming Murray Hill hotel dining room. Lovely creative food in a spacious, paneled dining room with crystal chandeliers. Attentive service and it's blessedly quiet; a great spot for a business breakfast. Comfortable bar. Jacket required. AE, DC, MC, V. *B Mon-Fri 7am-10:30pm; Sat & Sun 8am-noon. L Mon-Fri noon-2:30pm. D Mon-Thurs 6pm-10:30pm; Fri & Sat 6pm-11pm.* $$

Czechoslovakian

Vasata
339 East 75 Street. 988-7166. Comfortable family-run East Side restaurant has been serving hearty Czech national specialties for nearly 40 years. Famed for its roast duck (goose in winter), its bread dumplings, its dessert crepes (*palacinky*), and its old-fashioned European atmosphere. Jacket required. Reserve. AE, CB, DC, MC, V. *OPEN Tues-Sat 5pm-10:30pm; Sun 11am-9:30pm. CLOSED Mon.* $$

Delicatessen

Bernstein-on-Essex Street
135 Essex Street near Delancey St. 473-3900. Long-established informal Lower East Side

strictly kosher eatery (old-timers still call it Schmulka Bernstein). Unique feature: kosher Chinese food. Excellent deli sandwiches, especially the pastrami. Reserve. AE, CB, DC, MC, V. *OPEN Sun-Thurs 8am-1am; Fri 8am-2pm. CLOSED Sat.* $

Carnegie Delicatessen
854 Seventh Avenue near West 55 St. 757-2245. Considered the top New York deli by many. Good Jewish-style (not kosher) dishes (dairy and meat). The delicious pastrami and corned beef are made on premises. Generous-sized sandwiches. Friendly, extremely informal, generally chaotic. Beer only. No credit cards. *OPEN 7 days 6:30am-3:30am.* $

Fine & Shapiro
138 West 72 Street. 877-2874. Since 1920 (albeit now under new ownership), famed kosher delicatessen/restaurant serves very good, inexpensive sandwiches; wonderful chicken in the pot, matzoh ball soup, and stuffed cabbage. Reserve for more than 6 people. Take-out and phone orders, too. AE, MC, V. *OPEN 7 days 11am-10pm.* $

Kaplan's at the Delmonico
59 East 59 Street. 755-5959. Informal well-located spot for hearty Jewish-style food. Excellent delicatessen sandwiches. Take-out and catering. AE, CB, DC, MC, V. *OPEN 7 days 6am-10pm.* $

Katz's Delicatessen
205 East Houston Street at Ludlow St. 254-2246. A Lower East Side institution whose appeal is slipping. Still, they have terrific hot dogs, inexpensive pastrami and corned-beef sandwiches (not kosher), and on Sunday it's unbeatable for local New York color and informality, especially on the part of the waiters. Self-service, too. No credit cards. *OPEN Sun-Thurs 8am-10:45pm; Fri & Sat 7:45am-12:45am.* $

Second Avenue Kosher Delicatessen
156 Second Avenue at East 10 St. 677-0606. Bar none: the best kosher deli restaurant in the city. In a hectic setting, delicious hot meals vie with traditional deli delights. Great chopped liver, and, oh, those pastrami sandwiches. For lunch, a good bet is matzoh ball soup and half a sandwich; for dinner on cold winter nights, cholent (Jewish cassoulet) or chicken in the pot. Take-out and catering (beautiful platters and chopped liver in the shape of a heart). Beer and wine. No reservations, lineups are usual on weekends. Counter and tables. Take out; phone and fax orders. No credit cards. *OPEN Sun-Thurs 7am-midnight; Fri & Sat 7am-2am.* $

Stage Deli
834 Seventh Avenue near West 53 St. 245-7850. Show-biz hangout named for the stars who did and do eat here. Home-style cooking and delicious deli sandwiches, blintzes, stuffed cabbage. Bustling New York experience albeit not the same since Leo departed. Breakfast till 11am. No credit cards. *OPEN 7 days 6am-2am.* $

Deluxe

NOTE: These all require men to wear a jacket and, in most cases, tie.
Cellar in the Sky
1 World Trade Center, 107th floor. 938-1111. For a very special occasion. A romantic cloistered enclave within the famed Windows on the World that seats only 35 for an exquisite seven-course meal accompanied by five different complimentary wines and a classical guitarist. The prix-fixe menu changes every other Wednesday. Reserve! (A $20 deposit is required to reserve the table.) AE, CB, DC, MC, V. *OPEN Mon-Sat: one sitting only at 7:30pm. CLOSED Sun.* $$$$ +
Four Seasons
99 East 52 Street. 754-9494. Large, beautiful modern restaurant of considerable repute. The Grill Room has long been favored for power lunches by publishing, fashion, and financial movers and shakers. The more lavish and romantic dining room with illuminated marble pool for prix-fixe pretheater, 5pm to 6:30pm, as well as after-theater, 10pm to 11:15pm, dining. Menu changes with the seasons and in the Grill Room a spa menu for the health conscious. Reserve well in advance for dinner. AE, CB, DC, MC. Jacket required. Grill Room: *L Mon-Sat noon-2pm. D Mon-Fri 7:30pm-11:30pm. Pool Room: L Mon-Fri noon-2:30pm. D Mon-Sat 5pm-11:30pm. CLOSED Sun.* $$$$ +
La Caravelle
33 West 55 Street. 586-4252. For over 30 years, one of the city's most fashionable classic French restaurants, now revitalized. Pretty amiable setting; an expensive evening, although there is a prix-fixe pretheater dinner served from 5:30pm to 6:30pm. Reserve. AE, DC, MC, V. *L Mon-Fri noon-2:30pm. D Mon-Sat 5:30pm-10:30pm. CLOSED Sun & holidays.* $$$$ +
La Côte Basque
5 East 55 Street. 688-6525. A venerable New York dining institution, elegantly beautiful and inviting. Agreeable French menu with the classic dishes the most consistent, an impressive wine list, always perfect desserts. Expensive prix-fixe lunch and dinner. Reserve! AE, CB, DC, MC, V. *L Mon-Sat noon-2:30pm. D Mon-Sat 6pm-10:30pm. CLOSED Sun.* $$$$ +
La Grenouille
3 East 52 Street. 752-1495. At the very top. Lush flower-bedecked setting; impeccable service. Outstanding classic French cuisine, beautifully prepared and perfectly served. Prix-fixe lunch and dinner. Reserve! AE, DC. *L Tues-Sat noon-2:30pm. D Tues-Sat 6pm-10:30pm. CLOSED Sun & Mon.* $$$$ +
La Reserve
4 West 49 Street. 247-2993. One of the city's best. Imaginative French menu, airy romantic surroundings, and gracious service. Well-priced high-end pretheater dinner served from 5:30pm to 7pm. Reserve. AE, CB, DC, MC, V. *L Mon-Sat noon-3pm. D Mon-Thurs 5:30pm-10:30pm; Fri & Sat 5:30pm-11:30pm. CLOSED Sun.* $$$$

Le Cirque
58 East 65 Street. 794-9292. Now considered the city's premier dining destination. Stellar food, presentation, service, and clientele. The rich and powerful come for the divine classic French cuisine, the crème brulee, and one another. Only drawback: diners are packed like sardines. Reserve very well ahead! AE, CB, DC. *L Mon-Sat noon-3pm. D Mon-Sat 6pm-10:30pm. CLOSED Sun.* $$$
Lutece
249 East 50 Street. 752-2225. The word is best; the excellent traditional French food, the inviting town house setting, the polished service. Expensive prix-fixe lunch and dinner. Reserve very well ahead! AE, CB, DC, MC, V. *L Tues-Fri noon-1:45pm. D Mon-Sat 6pm-9:45pm. CLOSED Sun.* $$$$ +

Ethiopian

Abyssinia Restaurant
35 Grand Street at Thompson St. 226-5959. Unique dining experience awaits in this spartan SoHo storefront. Hearty spicy Ethiopian beef or chicken stew—*wot*—eaten in the traditional manner (sans silverware). The thin crepelike bread called *injera* is used to scoop the food. It's family-style dining and the helpful staff will aid the uninitiated. For dessert, refreshing melon or papaya. Try the native honey wine or bring your own. No reservations except for large groups. AE only. *OPEN Mon-Thurs 6pm-11pm; Fri 6pm-midnight; Sat & Sun 5pm-midnight. Weekend brunch noon-5pm.* $
The Blue Nile
103 West 77 Street. 580-3232. Sister restaurant to Abyssinia, it's the same unique and exotic eating experience in prettier surroundings. Be adventuresome—try it at least once. Seating is on traditional three-legged stools, those with bad backs be forewarned. No reservations. AE only. *OPEN Mon 5pm-10:30pm; Tues-Fri 5pm-11pm; Sat & Sun noon-11pm.* $
Zula
1260 Amsterdam Avenue near West 122 Street. 663-1670. Ethiopian dining in the Columbia University area. Popular with students who take easily to the native dishes eaten without silverware. AE, MC, V. *OPEN 7 days 11:30am-midnight.* $

Fireplaces

The following have working fireplaces:
Arizona 206 & Cafe (American)
Beatrice Inn (Italian)
The Black Sheep (French)
Box Tree (French)
Cafe Vivaldi (Cafes)
Chumley's (Bars & Burgers)
Cornelia Street Cafe (Cafes)
Fraunces Tavern Restaurant (American)
Gibbon (Japanese)
Ginger Man (American)
Jane Street Seafood Cafe (Fish & Seafood)

JoJo (French)
La Metairie (French)
Landmark Tavern (Bars & Burgers)
Les Pyrenees (French)
Lion's Rock (Continental)
Marylou's (Fish & Seafood)
Mary's (Italian)
Moran's (Bars & Burgers)
One If by Land, Two If by Sea (Continental)
Paris Commune (Breakfast/Brunch)
Ravelled Sleave (American)
Rene Pujol (French)
Restaurant Raphael (French)
Riviera Cafe (Sidewalk Cafes)
Rumbuls (Cafes)
Sazerac House (Soul/Southern)
Sumptuary Restaurant (Continental)
"21" Club (Stargazing)
Vivolo (Italian)
The Water Club (Rooms with a View)
Ye Waverly Inn (American)

Fish & Seafood

The Captain's Table
860 Second Avenue at East 46 St. 697-9538. This kitchy old-timer is still well regarded by many seafood lovers. Trays of the day's catch are brought to you for choosing, then broiled, poached, or grilled. Overpriced wine list. Cramped when crowded. Reserve. AE, MC, V. *L Mon-Fri noon-3pm. D Mon-Fri 5pm-11pm; Sat 5pm-midnight. CLOSED Sun.* $$

Claire
156 Seventh Avenue near West 19 St. 255-1955. High-ceilinged cool cousin of the Key West original. A good choice for mussels, squid salad, bay scallops, broiled fish Thai-style. For dessert, Mississippi Mud pie with whiskey sauce and, of course, the best Key lime pie. Busy with Chelsea locals and rightly so. A la carte weekend brunch. Reserve. AE, MC, V. *OPEN 7 days noon-12:30am. Bar till 2am. Weekend brunch noon-4:45pm.* $$

Dock's Oyster Bar & Seafood Grill
2427 Broadway near West 89 St; 724-5588. And * 633 Third Avenue at East 40 St; 986-8080. Fresh seafood in a casually stylish black-and-white-tiled decor. (From the folks at Murray's next door.) Best bets: the fried oysters, the fried clams, lobster, and the crunchy cole slaw. Save room for dessert. Reserve. AE, DC, MC, V. *L Mon-Sat 11:30am-3pm. D Sun-Thurs 5pm-11pm; Fri & Sat 5pm-midnight. Sun brunch 10:30am-3pm. *OPEN Mon-Thurs 11:30am-11pm; Fri 11:30am-midnight; Sat 5pm-11pm; Sun brunch 10:30am-3pm.* $$

Fulton Fish Market
11 Fulton Street near Front St, 2nd floor. 608-2920. You can't get much closer to the catch than the fish market's retail outlet. No-frills spot for the very best clams and oysters. Eat on the run or at the counter. No credit cards. *OPEN 7 days 11am-10pm.* $

Gage & Tollner
372 Fulton Street near Jay St, Brooklyn. (718) 875-5181. Credit Peter Ashkenasy for resusitating this landmark Brooklyn Heights seafood restaurant established in 1879. The handsome gas-lit mahogany dining room provides a charming old-fashioned atmosphere for well-prepared fish—steaks, too. Sunday brunch is served from noon to 4pm. Reserve. AE, MC, V. *OPEN Mon-Fri 11:30am-10:30pm; Sat 4pm-11pm; Sun 11:30am-9pm.* $$

Gloucester House
37 East 50 Street. 755-7394. Time-worn seafood house complete with New England decor. Fine broiled and fresh fish, homemade biscuits, good fries. (Don't veer from the aforementioned). Overpriced for such simple fare. Reserve. AE, DC, MC, V. *L Mon-Sat noon-3pm. D Mon-Sat 5:30pm-10pm. CLOSED Sun.* $$$

Jane Street Seafood Cafe
31 Eighth Avenue at Jane St. 242-0003. A Greenwich Village favorite for fresh seafood in a snug, authentically rustic New England tavernlike setting. Wonderful steamed mussels, deep-fried oysters, and soft-shelled clams. Over 36 daily specials; 86 wines to choose from. Fireplace in winter. No reservations often means a crowded wait. AE, MC, V. *OPEN Mon-Thurs 5:30pm-11pm; Fri & Sat 5:30pm-midnight; Sun 4pm-10pm.* $

John Clancy's
181 West 10 Street at Seventh Ave South; 242-7350. And * 206 East 63 Street; 752-6666. The specialty of this delightful, very special Village town house restaurant is grilled fish scented with the smoke of mesquite branches. Also recommended: poached Coho salmon, lobster Americaine, scallops en brochette, shrimps sauteed with jalapeño peppers. Copious servings, pace yourself so as to savor the Grand Marnier chocolate mousse cake or the city's best English trifle among other scrumptious dessert choices. Reserve! AE, CB, DC, MC, V. *OPEN Mon-Sat 6pm-11:30pm; Sun 5pm-10pm. *OPEN Mon-Sat 5:30pm-11:30pm; Sun 5:30pm-10pm.* $$$$

King Crab
871 Eighth Avenue at West 52 St. 765-4393. Handy (to the theater district), homey, and popular for good well-priced seafood. AE only. *OPEN Mon-Fri noon-midnight; Sat & Sun 5pm-midnight.* $$

Le Bernardin
See French.

Manhattan Ocean Club
57 West 58 Street. 371-7777. Considered one of New York's very best and most stylish for fresh albeit high-priced seafood. Good crab cakes, swordfish en brochette, blackened red fish. Quite good steaks and chops, too. Very fine wine list. Service genial but often very slow. Jacket required. Reserve. AE, CB, DC, MC, V. *OPEN Mon-Fri noon-midnight; Sat & Sun 5pm-midnight.* $$$$

Marylou's
21 West 9 Street. 533-0012. Attractive brown-

stone setting, two working fireplaces in season, and, best of all, excellent fresh fish served till the wee hours. Save room for New York's best rice pudding. Good brunch spot Sunday from noon to 3:30pm. Reserve. AE, CB, DC, MC, V. *OPEN Mon-Thurs 5:30pm-1am; Fri & Sat 5:30pm-4am; Sun 5:30pm-10:30pm.* $$

Oyster Bar & Restaurant
Grand Central Terminal, 42 Street & Vanderbilt Avenue, lower level. 490-6650. Unique comfortable but noisy (except for the quieter, less dramatic Tavern Room) landmark locale (since 1915) for very good oysters, six versions of clam chowder, and grilled fresh fish. Bouillabaisse daily. Wide variety, including the unusual. Fine desserts; impressive wine list. Oyster bar, dining room, tavern. Reserve! AE, CB, DC, MC, V. *OPEN Mon-Fri 11:30am-9:30pm. CLOSED Sat & Sun.*$$

Pier Nine
215 Second Avenue near East 14 St. 673-9263. Attractive East Village restaurant for the nicely prepared bargain-priced seafood, accompanied by hot garlic bread and salad. Well-priced ample early-bird special Monday to Saturday from 5pm to 6:30pm and Sunday from 4pm to 6pm. AE, MC, V. *OPEN Mon-Sat 5pm-11pm; Sun 4pm-10pm.*$

Sea Grill
Rockefeller Center, 19 West 49 Street. 246-9201. Elegant Rockefeller Center restaurant designed to draw the sophisticated New Yorker as well as the tourist. Good are the Sea Grill chowder, Maryland crab cakes with lobster and herb sauce, and grilled tuna steak. Excellent wine list. Reserve a window table for a view of the skaters in winter; outdoors in the Summer Garden in spring and summer. Complimentary parking at the Rockefeller Center Garage from Monday to Saturday after 5:30pm. Pretheater prix-fixe dinner served from 5pm to 6:30pm. Reserve. AE, CB, DC, MC, V. *L Mon-Fri noon-3pm. D Mon-Sat 5pm-10:45pm. CLOSED Sun.* $$$

Sweet's
2 Fulton Street near South St, upstairs. 344-9189. Though no longer worth making a special trip for, it's still the best place to eat fresh fish if you're in the Seaport area. The famed fish and seafood restaurant is housed in an 1842 building now gussied up to match the Seaport Marketplace—a bad idea. Note the early closing. AE, MC, V. *OPEN Mon-Fri 11:30am-8:30pm; Sat noon-8:30pm. CLOSED Sun.* $$

Umberto's Clam House
129 Mulberry Street near Hester St. 431-7545. Good seafood and sweet Italian pastries —till dawn—are the specialties. Best known as the place where Crazy Joey Gallo got "rubbed out." Outside tables in season. AE only. *OPEN 7 days 11am-6am.* $$

French

Alison on Dominick Street
38 Dominick Streeet near Varick St. 727-1188. Wonderful southwestern French food in an inviting stylish yet unpretentious setting in TriBeCa.

Try the ragout of mussels, braised lamb shank, sauteed sea bass in a tarragon flavored broth; chocolate hazelnut ice cream or crème brulee for dessert Reserve! AE, MC, V. *OPEN Mon-Thurs 5:30pm-10:30pm; Fri & Sat 5:30pm-11pm; Sun 5:30pm-9:30pm.* $$$$

Au Troquet
328 West 12 Street at Greenwich St. 924-3413. This romantic, *very* Parisian bistro in the far West Village is small and charming and fine. Choices are few but enticing. Reserve. AE, MC, V. *OPEN Mon-Sat 6pm-11pm. CLOSED Sun.* $$

Bienvenue
21 East 36 Street. 684-0215. Small longtime Murray Hill–area bistro long on authenticity but short on elbow room. Very busy at noon. Hearty, French country specialties include crepes, sausage en croute, beouf bourguignonne, coq au vin. Wine only. AE, MC, V. *L Mon-Fri 11:30am-2:30pm. D Mon-Sat 5:30pm-10pm. CLOSED Sun.* $

The Black Sheep
344 West 11 Street at Washington St. 242-1010. Far West Village restaurant for good-value country French food in a charming cozy French country inn setting complete with fireplace. Generous great value five-course prix-fixe dinner includes crudités, soup, pâté, entree, and dessert. Seasonal choices may include roast duck with grapes, venison with chestnuts, Provençal fish stew. Impressive wine list. Pleasant service. Good Sunday brunch choice. Fireplace in winter. Reserve. AE, MC, V—but there's a 10 percent discount for those paying cash. *OPEN Mon-Thurs 6pm-11pm; Fri & Sat 6pm-midnight; Sun noon-4pm & 6pm-10:30pm.* $$$

Bouley
165 Duane Street near Hudson St. 608-3852. Beautiful romantic flower-filled TriBeCa setting for chef David Bouley's (formerly of Montrachet) superb modern French cuisine— rotisserie duckling with nine spices, veal kidney and sweetbreads in cider vinegar sauce, braised roast pigeon with savory cabbage. For dessert, hot chocolate souffle. Game in season. Choose the multicourse prix-fixe tasting menu. Jacket and tie required. Reserve! AE, CB, DC, MC, V. *L Mon-Fri noon-2pm. D 7 nights 6pm-11pm.* $$$$ +

Box Tree
242 East 49 Street. 758-8320. Intimate romantic town house setting with lovely classic French food, attentive service, and a working fireplace in season. Steep prix-fixe lunch and dinner. Sunday brunch in the cafe from noon to 3:30pm. Jacket and tie required. Reserve! *L Mon-Fri noon-2pm. D 7 days 6pm-11pm.* $$$$

Cafe du Parc
106 East 19 Street. 777-7840. This attractive, quiet, well-priced traditional French bistro is one of this area's least trendy places to dine. It's busy at lunchtime, perfect in the pm for a leisurely intimate dinner. Prix-fixe pretheater dinner. Reserve. AE, CB, DC, MC, V. *L Mon-Fri noon-3pm. D Mon-Sat 5pm-10pm. CLOSED Sun.* $$

Cafe Europa
347 East 54 Street. 755-0160. Old-fashioned French bistro with an authentic charm. Reserve. AE, MC, V. *L Mon-Fri noon-2pm. D Mon-Sat 5pm-10pm.* $$

Cafe Loup
105 West 13 Street. 255-4746. Small reliable neighborhood French restaurant. Casual ambience, good bistro food: mushrooms à la Grecque, duck Montmorency, sauteed calves' liver. Reserve. AE, CB, DC, MC, V. *L Mon-Fri noon-3pm. D 7 days 6pm-11:30pm. Sun brunch noon-3:30pm.* $$

Cafe Un Deux Trois
123 West 44 Street. 354-4148. Large convivial Parisian brasserie-style eatery. Leftover Corinthian columns, Crayolas for doodling on the paper tablecloths, and a menu offering basic and better French fare at moderate prices. Proximity to the theater district a plus for nonhectic pretheater dining; just get there before 6:15pm. Also, a good value prix-fixe brunch. No reservations. AE, DC, MC, V. *OPEN Mon-Sat 11:30am-midnight; Sun 11:30am-11pm. Weekend brunch 11am-4pm.* $$

Capsouto Frères
451 Washington Street at Watts St. 966-4900. Remote casual French bistro in 1891 landmark TriBeCa warehouse building. Simple country French fare: sauteed calves' liver, blanquette de veau, coq au vin, ratatouille, mussels ravigote, breast of duck sauteed with ginger cassis, bouillabaisse. Handsome surroundings and crowd. Good brunch choice especially on the umbrella-shaded terrace in summer. Reserve. AE, CB, DC. *L Tues-Fri noon-3pm. D Sun-Thurs 6pm-11:30pm; Fri & Sat 6pm-12:30am. Bar till 4am. Weekend brunch noon-3pm.* $$$

Chantal Cafe
257 West 55 Street. 246-7076. Authentic informal theater district French bistro. Brick-walled, narrow front room, skylit rear dining area. Basic bistro staples, congenial service, great value for budget-priced four-course pretheater dinner served Monday to Friday from 5:30pm to 7pm. Reserve for dinner. AE, MC, V. *L Mon-Fri 11:30am-3pm. D Mon-Thurs 5:30pm-10:30pm; Fri & Sat 5:30pm-11:30pm.* $$

Chanterelle
2 Harrison Street at Hudson St. 966-6960. Now located in the historic Mercantile Exchange Building in TriBeCa, the ambitious nouvelle cuisine so adored in SoHo has critics carping, but its many admirers keep the faith—and justifiably so. Menu changes weekly. Prix-fixe lunch. Reserve. AE, MC, V. *L Tues-Sat noon-2:30pm. D Tues-Sat 6pm-10:30pm. CLOSED Sun & Mon.* $$$$ +

Chez Josephine
414 West 42 Street. 594-1925. A tribute to famed cabaret star Josephine Baker who made her mark on Paris in the 20s, from her adopted son, Jean-Claude. Lively theatrical air and crowd, good French bistro food. Boudin noir, lobster cassoulet, steak au poivre; enticing desserts. All à la carte. Jazz piano among other nightly entertainment. Festive choice for pretheater, where reservations are a must. AE, MC, V. *OPEN Mon-Sat 5pm-midnight. CLOSED Sun.* $$

Chez Ma Tante
189 West 10 Street. 620-0223. Tiny West Village French bistro with an authentic feel and consistently fine basic fare. Tightly packed in winter, in summer the storefront opens on to the sidewalk. Reserve. AE, MC, V. *OPEN Sun-Thurs 6pm-11:30pm; Fri & Sat 6pm-12:30am. Weekend brunch noon-3pm.* $$

Chez Michellat
90 Bedford Street at Grove St. 242-8309. A tiny charmer with a palpable Left Bank air (their answering machine gives their message in both English and French). Wonderful food, friendly professional service. Wine and beer. Reserve. AE, MC, V. *OPEN 7 nights 5:30pm-11pm.* $$

Chez Napoleon
365 West 50 Street. 265-6980. This old-time theater district staple serves always dependable, unpretentious bourgeois French fare in a warm and friendly setting. Boiled scallops, sweetbreads, coquille St. Jacques, cassoulet on Thursday; bouillabaisse Friday and Saturday. Reserve. AE, MC, V. *L Mon-Fri noon-2:30pm. D Mon-Thurs 5pm-10:30pm; Fri & Sat 5pm-11pm. CLOSED Sun.* $$

Eze
254 West 23 Street. 691-1140. Comfortable tranquil Chelsea town house for wonderfully flavorful Mediterranean cooking. Prix-fixe dinner menu changes every two weeks. Reserve. AE, MC, V. *OPEN Tues-Sat 6pm-10:15pm.* $$$$

Florent
See Late Night & 24 Hours.

Gascogne
158 Eighth Avenue near West 17 St. 675-6564. Delightful rustic French country farm house ambience in which to enjoy the hearty fare of the Gascony region of France. Cassoulet, game, confit. Backyard garden for dining in season. Reserve. AE only. *OPEN Mon-Sat 6pm-11pm.* $$

Jean Lafitte
68 West 58 Street. 751-2323. Pleasant Parisian Art Nouveau–inspired decor, tasty bourgeois bistro fare in the Carnegie Hall vicinity. Reliables like steak tartare, boiled short ribs, scallops poached in lobster sauce, calves' liver. Pleasant popular lunch spot. No denim. Reserve. AE, CB, DC, MC, V. *L Mon-Fri noon-3pm. D 7 days 5:30pm-midnight.* $$

JoJo
160 East 64 Street. 223-5656. In a congenial town house setting, renowned chef Jean-Georges Vongerichten (formerly of Lafayette) offers a limited but wonderful selection of delicately seasoned dishes prepared with low-fat, herb-infused oils. Upstairs, a Victorian-era rear parlor (with fireplace in winter) is the perfect place for your dessert and coffee. Reserve! AE, DC, MC, V. *L Mon-Sat noon-2:30pm. D Mon-Sat 6pm-10pm. CLOSED Sun.* $$$

La Boheme
24 Minetta Lane near Sixth Ave. 473-6447. Attractive little rustic Village bistro for wonderful thin-crusted individual pizzas topped with interesting choices and baked in wood-fired brick ovens. Also, saucisson chaud, roast duck, steak au poivre, and the like, all well accompanied. Reserve. AE only. *OPEN Tues-Fri 5pm-midnight; Sat & Sun 4pm-midnight. Sun brunch noon-4pm.* $$

La Colombe d'Or
134 East 26 Street. 689-0666. A small, charming, pretty Provençal restaurant in the Gramercy Park area has long been popular for imaginative regional offerings, beautifully prepared and served. Bouillabaisse, a house specialty, served daily. Reserve. AE, DC, MC, V. *L Mon-Fri noon-2:30pm. D Mon-Thurs 6pm-10:30pm; Fri & Sat 6:30pm-11pm. CLOSED Sun.* $$$

Lafayette
Drake Hotel, 65 East 56 Street. 832-1565. Elegant dining, refined French cuisine, gracious and tranquil setting, perfect service. *Very* expensive. Prix-fixe lunch and dinner; pretheater dinner served from 6pm to 6:30pm. Reserve. AE, CB, DC, MC, V. *L Tues-Sat noon-2pm. D Mon-Fri 6:30pm-10pm; Sat 6:30pm-10:30pm. CLOSED Sun.* $$$$+

La Gauloise
502 Sixth Avenue near West 13 St. 691-1363. This handsome Art Nouveau bistro in Greenwich Village features very good French bistro food and good ambience. Excellent pepper steak, pâté, sweetbreads, roast chicken, cassoulet on Sunday. For dessert, crème brulee. Good value pretheater prix-fixe dinner served from 5:30pm to 6:45pm. Jacket and tie required. Reservations required. AE, MC, V. *L Tues-Sun noon-3pm. D Tues-Sun 5:30pm-11:30pm. Weekend brunch Sat noon-3pm; Sun noon-4pm. CLOSED Mon.* $$$$

La Goulue
28 East 70 Street. 988-8169. Highly evocative Parisian Art Nouveau setting now more comfortable than chic. Traditional French brasserie food. The outdoor cafe in summer on a lovely side street is inviting. Reserve. AE, DC, MC, V. *L Mon-Sat noon-3pm. D Mon-Sat 6pm-10pm. CLOSED Sun & holidays.* $$$

La Mangeoire
1008 Second Avenue near East 53 St. 759-7086. Very pretty French country restaurant for simple French fare. Filet of sole, sauteed calves' liver, wonderful omelettes. Reserve. AE, MC, V. *L Mon-Fri noon-2:30pm. D Mon-Sat 6pm-11pm; Sun 5:30pm-10pm.* $$

La Metairie
189 West 10 Street near Bleecker St. 989-0343. Literally a handful of tables seating perhaps 16 in a rustic, country French setting. Delicious food including couscous, duck with calvados; tempting desserts. Menu changes daily. Reserve. AE, MC, V. *OPEN 7 days 6pm-11pm.* $$$

La Petite Ferme
973 Lexington Avenue near East 70 St. 249-

3272. Cuisine bourgeoise in a sweetly rustic French country setting, replete with a cage of cooing doves. Limited satisfying menu, tiny room and small garden—in sum a lovely dining experience. Recommended: the poached fish, moules vinaigrette, beef paillard. Wonderful desserts. Perfect for a romantic lunchtime assignation. Alas, all this simplicity does not come cheap. Reserve. AE, CB, DC, MC, V. *L Mon-Sat noon-2:30pm. D Mon-Sat 6pm-10:30pm. CLOSED Sun.* $$$

Le Bernardin
155 West 51 Street. 489-1515. Beautiful and spacious French restaurant in the Equitable Building serves what many seafood lovers consider the best fish in the city, and they are willing to pay handsomely for it. Innovative and influential cuisine. Prix-fixe dinner. Reserve well in advance! *L Mon-Sat noon-2:15pm. D Mon-Thurs 6pm-10:15pm; Fri & Sat 5:30pm-11pm. CLOSED Sun.* $$$$+

Le Bilboquet
25 East 63 Street. 751-3036. A small, informal, but very fashionable, very Parisian *cousine* to Le Relais for wonderful salads. Great for an alfresco lunch at the sidewalk cafe in season. In the pm, much joie de vivre—translates as noisy. Reservations for dinner only. AE only. *L 7 days noon-3pm. D 7 days 6pm-11pm.* $$

Le Boeuf a la Mode
539 East 81 Street. 650-9664. Unpretentious Yorkville neighborhood French restaurant. Friendly atmosphere, reliably good food. Duckling aux cerises, sweetbreads bearnaise, daily specials. Reserve. AE, DC, MC. *OPEN 7 days 5:30pm-11pm.* $$

Le Chantilly
106 East 57 Street. 751-2931. Longtime restaurant popular with the international set. Pretty, old-world plush, spacious, and serene. Quite good classic French cooking, gracious service. Popular pretheater prix-fixe dinner served from 5:30pm to 6:45pm. Reserve. AE, DC, MC, V. *L Mon-Sat noon-3pm. D Mon-Sat 5:30pm-11pm. CLOSED Sun.* $$$$

Le Perigord
405 East 52 Street. 755-6244. This longtime inviting and serene East Sider may not be innovative but it's always satisfying. Elegant classic French dining from a fine wide-ranging menu. Lunch and dinner prix fixe. Perfect service. Reserve! AE, CB, DC, MC, V. *L Mon-Fri noon-3pm. D Mon-Sat 5:30pm-10:30pm. CLOSED Sun.* $$$$

Le Regence
Hotel Plaza Athenee, 37 East 64 Street. 606-4647. Very fine French dining and beautifully served in a sumptuous, stately setting. Excellent expensive wine list. Choice spot for a business breakfast; very good Sunday brunch choice. Reserve, especially for dinner. AE, DC, MC, V. *OPEN 7 days: B 7am-10am; L noon-2:30pm; D 6pm-9pm. Sun brunch noon-3pm.* $$$

Le Relais
712 Madison Avenue near East 63 St. 751-5108.

Chic, beautifully appointed bistro-style restaurant. Features okay French food in a very European ambience; trendy young pretty people at the bar. Best when the cafe spills out onto Madison Avenue for chic-people watching. Reserve! AE. *L Mon-Sat noon-3pm; Sun 12:30pm-3:30pm. D Mon-Fri 6:30pm-11pm; Sat & Sun 7pm-11pm.* $$$

Les Halles
411 Park Avenue South near East 28 St. 679-4111. Very Parisian butcher shop and casual cacophonous bistro from the owners of Park Bistro. Diners packed tighter than sardines flock here for the authentic flavorful cassoulet, brandade de morue, tripes à la Portugaise, boudin noir with apples. Interesting, affordable wine list. Reserve! AE, MC, V. *OPEN 7 days noon-midnight.* $$$

Les Pyrenees
251 West 51 Street. 246-0044. One of the few surviving of the long-standing family-owned theater district French restaurants. Good country French cooking, excellent wine cellar; fireplace in winter. Pretheater prix-fixe dinner. Reserve. AE, CB, DC, MC, V. *L Mon-Sat noon-3pm. D Mon-Sat 5pm-midnight; Sun 4pm-10pm.* $$

Le Veau d'Or
129 East 60 Street. 838-8133. Consistently fine classic French fare in this well-established, popular, and amiable French restaurant. Tends to be extremely crowded with their loyal old guard. Reserve. AE only. *L Mon-Fri noon-3pm. D Mon-Sat 5:30pm-10:15pm. CLOSED Sun & holidays.* $$$

Le Zinc
139 Duane Street near West Broadway. 732-1226. When this former TriBeCa shoe factory turned Parisian brasserie, downtowners flocked to it like a mirage. But TriBeCa is no longer a dining desert and the French bistro fare here is not quite as good as before. The crowds have moved on, but it's still a lively spot where you can still have a pleasant meal if you stay simple and aren't bothered by the lackadaisical service. Reserve. AE only. *L Mon-Fri noon-3pm. D Mon-Thurs 6pm-midnight; Fri & Sat 6pm-12:30am. CLOSED Sun.* $$

March
405 East 58 Street. 838-9393. Elegant East Side town house for wonderful imaginative French fare from Wayne Nish, former longtime chef of La Colombe d'Or. Prix-fixe dinner. Reserve! AE, MC, V. *L Wed & Thurs noon-2pm. D Mon-Sat 6pm-10pm. CLOSED Sun.*

Maurice
Parker Meridien Hotel, 118 West 57 Street. 245-7788. The setting is still plush, but the reincarnated hotel restaurant is now an upscale brasserie, less pricey than its predecessor. Reserve. AE, CB, DC, MC, V. *L Mon-Fri noon-3pm. D 7 days 5:30pm-11pm.* $$$

Mondrian
7 East 59 Street. 935-3434. Handsome tranquil wood-paneled dining room for Thomas Colicchio's (Quilted Giraffe, Gotham, and Rakel) ex-cellent ambitious contemporary French cooking, especially the fish preparations. Expense account dining at its best. Reserve! AE, DC, MC, V. *L Mon-Fri noon-2:30pm. D Mon-Sat 5:30pm-10:30pm.* $$$$ +

Montrachet
239 West Broadway near White St. 219-2777. Lovely, highly recommended TriBeCa choice for fine imaginative French nouvelle in a spare high-ceilinged contemporary setting. Well-priced prix-fixe dinners; inventive fish choices, outstanding desserts. Good wine list. AE only. Reserve! *OPEN Mon-Thurs & Sat 6pm-11pm; Fri noon-3pm & 6pm-11pm. CLOSED Sun.* $$

Odeon
See Late Night & 24 Hours.

Park Bistro
414 Park Avenue South near East 28 St. 689-1360. Authentic French bistro highly tauted for chef Jean-Michael Diot's delectable Provençal fare, professionally served. So lively it hurts (the ears) at peak times. Reserve! AE, DC. *L Mon-Fri noon-3pm. D 7 days 6pm-11pm.* $$$

Petrossian
182 West 58 Street. 245-2214. Elegant Belle Epoque decor provides the proper setting for the city's first caviar cafe with a perfect provenance. In addition to the finest caviar, there is foie gras served with warm truffles, smoked salmon, and a small choice of quite good dinner specials. Champagne by the glass; fine vodkas. In all, an indulgent—and expensive—experience. Psst! There is an affordable pre- and posttheater prix fixe. Jacket required. Reserve. AE, MC, V. *L Mon-Sat noon-3:30pm. D Mon-Sat 5:30pm-midnight; Sun 5:30pm-10pm. Sun brunch 11:30am-3pm. Caviar Bar: 3:30pm-5:30pm.* $$$

Provence
38 MacDougal Street near Prince St. 475-7500. Rustic SoHo bistro wins high marks for its authentic Provençal food, moderate prices, and romantic little tented outdoor garden complete with flower-encircled stone fountain. Sea scallops with truffles; Bourride, a garlicky Mediterranean fish stew; steak and fries; morrels St. Tropez; braised rabbit; bouillabaisse. Well-priced Provençal wines. Service has improved. Reserve! AE only. *OPEN 7 days: L noon-3pm; D 6pm-11:30pm.* $$

Quatorze
240 West 14 Street. 206-7006. Long ago uptowners had discovered this off-the-beaten-track charmer (but they now have one of their own at 323 East 79 Street, 535-1414). The reasonably priced reliable bourgeoise French fare, the compatible wine list, and the casual authentic bistro setting will make you think you're in Paris. Noisy in the pm. AE only. Reservations required. *L Mon-Fri noon-2:30pm. D Mon-Sat 6pm-midnight; Sun 5pm-11pm.* $$

Raoul's
180 Prince Street near Sullivan St. 966-3518. Extremely hectic, crowded, and friendly longtime SoHo neighborhood bistro. Features good

traditional country French cooking and a wait. The skylit backroom is for nonsmokers. Reserve! AE, MC, V. *OPEN Sun-Thurs 6:30pm-11:30pm; Fri & Sat late-night supper till 2am. Bar till 2am.* $$$

Rene Pujol
321 West 51 Street. 246-3023. Cozy family-owned theater district French restaurant with a country-inn feel, serves good traditional bistro fare. Prix-fixe dinner. Very fine wine list. Wood-burning fireplace in season. Jacket required. Reserve. AE, DC, MC, V. *L Mon-Fri noon-3pm. D Mon-Sat 5pm-11:30pm. CLOSED Sun.* $$

Restaurant Raphael
33 West 54 Street. 582-8993. Small, sedate, romantic brownstone setting for very good French food. Carefully planned menu; dishes all beautifully prepared. Fireplace in winter, trellised garden in summer. Jacket required. Reserve. AE, CB, DC, MC, V. (Service charge added to bill.) *L Mon-Fri noon-2:30pm. D Mon-Fri 6pm-10pm; Sat 6pm-10:30pm. CLOSED Sun.* $$$$

Tout Va Bien
311 West 51 Street. 265-0190. A theater district reliable. Authentic French cafe, simple country food, small peaceful courtyard with umbrella-shaded tables. Steak au poivre, bouillabaisse, onion soup. Blessedly untrendy. Reserve. AE, MC, V. *L Mon-Sat noon-2:30pm. D Mon-Sat 5pm-11:30pm. CLOSED Sun.* $

Garden/Outdoor Dining

The following have outdoor dining facilities in the form of a garden or a sidewalk cafe. In season, usually May to October, weather permitting.

American Festival Cafe (American *and* Breakfast/Brunch)
Around the Clock Cafe (Late Night & 24 Hours)
Aureole (American)
Barbetta (Italian)
Barolo (Italian)
Boathouse Cafe (Rooms with a View)
Cafe La Fortuna (Cafes)
Cafe Orlin (Breakfast/Brunch)
Caffe Biondo (Cafes)
Caffe Dante (Cafes)
Caffe Reggio (Cafes)
Capsouto Frères (French)
Chez Ma Tante (French)
Cloister Cafe (Cafes)
Coffee Shop (Latin American)
Cornelia Street Cafe (Cafes)
Courtyard Cafe & Bar (American)
Curtain Up! (American)
Danal (Afternoon Tea *and* Cafes)
Da Silvano (Italian)
Dolci on Park (Italian)
Empire Diner (Late Night & 24 Hours)
Ennio & Michael (Italian)
Eze (French)
Ferrara's (Cafes)

Gascogne (French)
Giordano (Italian)
Il Cantinori (Italian)
Jackson Hole Wyoming (Bars & Burgers)
Jerry's 103 (American)
John's Pizzeria (Pizza)
La Goulue (French)
Le Bilboquet (French)
Le Madri (Italian)
Le Relais (French)
Le Zinc (French)
Lion's Rock (Continental)
Louie's Westside Cafe (American)
Lox Around the Clock (Late Night & 24 Hours)
Pete's Tavern (Bars & Burgers)
Provence (French)
Rectangles (Middle Eastern)
Restaurant Raphael (French)
River Cafe (Rooms with a View)
Roettelle A.G. (German)
Rumbuls (Cafes)
Sea Grill (Fish & Seafood)
Spring Street Natural Restaurant (Health & Vegetarian)
Sumptuary Restaurant (Continental)
Tavern-on-the-Green (Rooms with a View)
Telephone Bar & Grill (American)
Tout Va Bien (French)
Umberto's Clam House (Fish & Seafood)
Veniero's (Cafes)
The Water Club (Rooms with a View)
Water's Edge Restaurant (Rooms with a View)
White Horse Tavern (Bars & Burgers)
Yellowfingers di Nuovo (Italian)
Ye Waverly Inn (American)

German

Kleine Konditorei
234 East 86 Street. 737-7130. Since 1923, a friendly, informal Yorkville restaurant for simple, hearty fare. Spicy sauerbraten, potato dumplings, and red cabbage, wiener schnitzel, wursts; German beer. Homemade cakes and tortes tempt you in the entry bake shop. Reserve weekends. AE, DC. *OPEN Sun-Thurs 10am-midnight; Fri & Sat 10:30pm-1am.* $

Roettelle A.G.
126 East 7 Street. 674-4140. A charming cozy find in—but not of—the East Village for simple inexpensive satisfying dining. German, Swiss, Italian, and French cooking are represented nightly on the changing menu. Smoked mustard-infused pork chop with spaetzle and red cabbage, sauteed chicken breast with sun-dried tomatoes and hazelnuts, veal in mushroom cream sauce with wonderful Swiss-style rosti potato pancakes. Early-bird special is a real steal. The trellised garden is the special place to sit. Beer and wine. Take-out of light fare available. MC, V. *L Mon-Sat noon-2pm. D Mon-Sat 5:30pm-11pm. Sat Brunch noon-2:30pm. CLOSED Sun.* $

Greek

Karyatis
35-03 Broadway near 35 St, Astoria, Queens.
(718) 204-0666. As close to the Plaka as you
can get without leaving New York. Friendly very
fine choice in our own Little Athens. Well-priced.
Reserve. AE, MC, V. *OPEN 7 days 11:30am-
midnight.* $

Periyali
35 West 20 Street. 463-7890. Amiable upscale
version of a white-washed Greek taverna in
Chelsea serves very good grilled lamb and seafood dishes. Reserve. AE, MC, V. *L Mon-Fri
noon-3pm. D Mon-Thurs 6pm-11pm; Fri & Sat
6pm-11:30pm.* $$

Roumeli Taverna
33-04 Broadway, Astoria, Queens. (718) 278-
7533. Noisy festive authentic Greek dining in
New York's own Little Athens. Best are the grilled
fish dishes, washed down by a cold glass of
Domestica. Reserve. AE only. *OPEN 7 days
11:30am-1:30am.*

Health & Vegetarian

(*See also* Jewish *for several dairy restaurants.*)
Angelica Kitchen
300 East 12 Street. 228-2909. East Village
Mecca for macrobiotics. Fans of this "vegan"
establishment are legion. No animal products,
everything is organically grown. No alcohol, but
you may bring your own. Reservations taken for
6 or more only. No credit cards. *OPEN 7 days
11:30am-10:30pm.* $

Great American Health Bar
35 West 57 Street; 355-5177. And 154 East 40
Street; 682-5656. Also 10 East 44 Street, 661-
3430. Counter and table service. Specializes in
vegetarian soups, salads, sandwiches, and yo-
gurt. No alcohol. *OPEN Mon-Fri 7am-8:30pm;
Sat & Sun 8:30am-8pm.* $

Health Pub
371 Second Avenue at East 21 St. 529-9200.
Eggless, sugarless, nondairy, vegetarian restau-
rant. Surprise, even without all of the above the
food is not only good but imaginative. Great sal-
ads; Japanese buckwheat noodles; blue corn
enchiladas; tofu-sunflower burger on whole
wheat English muffin; black bean chili with
cilantro and tofu sour cream. Just go elsewhere
for dessert. No alcohol, no smoking anywhere,
no reservations. AE only. *OPEN 7 days 11am-
11pm.* $

Luma
200 Ninth Avenue near West 23 St. 633-8033. A
pricey Chelsea vegetarian whose fans are
mainly macrobiotic. Seafood vegetarian, free-
range chicken, all organic, naturally prepared.
Reserve. CB, DC, MC, V. *OPEN 7 days 5:45pm-
11pm.* $$

New Prospect Cafe
393 Flatbush Avenue at Eighth Ave, Brooklyn.
(718) 638-2148. A friendly find in Brooklyn.
Imaginative though healthy cooking, inexpen-

sively priced. Soups, specials, seafood. Beer
and wine. Reserve. AE only. *L Tues-Sat
11:30am-3:30pm. D Sun-Thurs 5pm-10pm; Fri &
Sat 5pm-11pm. Sun brunch 11:30am-4pm.* $

Spring Street Natural Restaurant
62 Spring Street at Lafayette St. 966-0290. Features fresh fish, fowl, and seafood cooked from
scratch. No chemicals or preservatives, no red
meat. Specials include vegetarian lasagna, sauteed chicken breast with shiitake mushrooms,
baked filet of bluefish, garlic chicken marinated
in raspberry vinegar. Wines by the glass. Sidewalk cafe in fine weather. No reservations. AE,
CB, DC, MC, V. *OPEN Sun-Thurs 11:30am-
midnight; Fri & Sat 11:30am-1am. Weekend
brunch 11:30am-4pm.* $

Whole Wheat 'n' Wild Berries
57 West 10 Street. 677-3410. Omelettes, daily
hot specials, fresh bread, salads, and great desserts. Reservations for 3 or more only. No credit
cards. *L Tues-Sat 11:30am-4:30pm. D 7 nights
5pm-11pm. Sun brunch 11:30am-4:30pm.* $

Hungarian

Eclair Shop
141 West 72 Street. 873-7700. Informal West
Side spot for Viennese/Hungarian dishes; steaks
and burgers, too. Best known for its pastries,
especially the sacher torte and Grand Marnier
cake, sold retail as well. Wine and beer. Reserve.
No credit cards. *OPEN 7 days 8am-9pm. Weekend brunch 8:30am-2pm.* $

Mocca Hungarian
1588 Second Avenue near East 82 St. 734-6470.
Old-world Yorkville outpost of hearty inexpensive Hungarian fare. No credit cards. *OPEN 7
days 4pm-11pm.* $

Red Tulip
439 East 75 Street. 734-4893; 650-0537. Old-
world Hungarian dining. Reasonably priced,
heaping portions accompanied by gypsy violins.
Reserve. AE only. *OPEN Wed-Sat 6pm-midnight;
Sun 5pm-midnight. CLOSED Mon & Tues.* $

Indian

*Sixth Street between Second and First avenues
has been dubbed "Little India" because of the
number of Indian restaurants it boasts. They are
all cheap and various levels of cheerful; a few of
the best are among those listed below.*
Akbar
475 Park Avenue near East 57 St; 838-1717. *
And 256 East 49 Street; 755-9100. Well priced
for the location; authentic well-seasoned food in
an attractive setting. A good buy is their prix-fixe
lunch. *L Mon-Sat 11:30am-2:45pm. D Sun-Thurs
5:30pm-10:45pm; Fri & Sat 5:30pm-11:30pm.*$$

Bombay Palace
30 West 52 Street. 541-7777. Handsomely dec-
orated midtown restaurant for the delicate, mildly
spiced cuisine of northern India. Expensive un-
less you opt for the incredibly low-priced all-you-
can-eat lunchtime buffet. Reserve. AE, DC, MC,

V. Free dinner parking. *OPEN 7 days: L noon-3pm; D 5:30pm-11pm.*　$

Bukhara
Helmsley Middletown Hotel, 148 East 48 Street. 838-1811. Comfortable, handsome choice in midtown for unusual and delicious Indian fare. Meats and fowl are first marinated in yogurt, herbs, and spices and then either charcoal grilled or seared in the tandoor ovens. Meals are meant—indeed encouraged—to be eaten with both hands (hot towels are brought to your table before you start as well as a bib to protect your clothing). Best are the chicken or duck bukhara, the mellow cream chicken, the veal chops; also the breads and grilled cubes of cottage cheese. Bargain prix-fixe lunch. Reserve. AE, CB, DC, MC, V. *OPEN 7 days: L noon-3pm; D 6pm-10:45pm.* Free dinner parking after 6pm.　$$

Darbar
44 West 56 Street. 432-7227. Consistent high praise for this quite beautiful and elegant duplex setting for the wonderful authentic Mogul cookery of northern India. Recommended: the soups, the lamb stew, all the tandoori dishes, and the rice pudding or fig ice cream for dessert. Bargain all-you-can-eat buffet lunch. Prix-fixe pre- and after-theater dinners. Reserve. AE, DC, MC, V. *L 7 days noon-3pm D Sun-Thurs 5:30pm-11pm; Fri & Sat 5:30pm-11:30pm.*　$$

Dawat
210 East 58 Street. 355-7555. Lovers of Indian food revere this spot. The extensive menu created by actress/food writer Madhur Jaffrey, the elegant setting, and extraordinary bargain-priced lunch make it a popular midtown choice, especially for lunch. Reserve. AE, MC, V. *L Mon-Sat 11:30am-3pm. D Sun-Thurs 5:30pm-11pm; Fri & Sat 5:30pm-11:30pm.* Free dinner parking.　$$

Gaylord
87 First Avenue near East 6 St. 529-7990. Good classic Indian cuisine in this most attractive newcomer to the East Village cluster of Indian eateries. Tandoori is the specialty. Live sitar music on weekends. Reserve. AE, MC, V. *OPEN 7 days noon-midnight.*　$

India Pavilion
240 West 56 Street; 489-0035. And * 35 West 13 Street; 243-8175. Small, informal, and pleasant. Serves good low-priced Indian curries and tandoori. Bring your own wine. Reserve. AE, MC, V. *L Mon-Fri noon-2:30pm. D Sun-Thurs 5pm-10:30pm; Fri & Sat 5pm-11pm.*　$

Mitali
334 East 6 Street; 533-2508. And 296 Bleecker Street at Seventh Ave South; 989-1367. One of the original 6th Street Indian eateries and still one of the best. Northern specialties include murgh tikka muslam, chicken tandoori, lamb dupiag—all at bargain prices. The West Village venue is more attractive. AE, MC, V. *OPEN 7 days noon-midnight.*　$

Nirvana
See Rooms with a View.

Raga
57 West 48 Street. 757-3450. One of the consistent bests. Excellent food in elegant spacious digs. Specifications as to how hot are followed. Live sitar music in the evening. Reserve. AE, DC, MC, V. *L Mon-Fri noon-3pm. D 7 days 5:30pm-11:15pm.*　$$

Inexpensive

Good meals at less than $10 per person. For more inexpensive dining see also Bars & Burgers, Delicatessen, and Pizza.

Cheyenne
See Late Night & 24 Hours.

Chez Brigitte
77 Greenwich Avenue near West 11 St. 929-6736. French-accented luncheonette, with only 11 seats at a counter, serves delicious inexpensive Provençal homemade specialties: leg of lamb, beef bourguignonne; omelettes and pies, too. No alcohol. No reservations. No credit cards. *OPEN Mon-Sat 11am-9pm. CLOSED Sun.*

Junior's Restaurant
386 Flatbush Avenue Extension at DeKalb Ave, Brooklyn. (718) 852-5257. Famous longtime Brooklyn restaurant for good sandwiches, snacks, and great cheesecake. Full bar. Reserve for parties of 8 or more only. AE, DC, MC, V. *OPEN Sun-Thurs 6:30am-1:30am; Fri & Sat 6:30am-3am.*

La Bonne Soupe
48 West 55 Street. 586-7650. Cozy casual bistro on two floors for soups (*l'oignon* daily, bouillabaisse Friday and Saturday in winter) with crusty French bread, fluffy omelettes, hamburgers, and wine by the carafe—it all adds up to a simple, low-priced (though just a credit card's throw away from Saks), French-accented dining experience. No reservations. AE only. *OPEN 7 days 11:30am-midnight. Sun brunch 11:30am-3pm.*

Manganaro's Grosseria Italiana
488 Ninth Avenue near West 37 St. 563-5331. Famous Italian grocery in business since 1893. It's fun, boisterous, and very, very Italian. Tables in rear and upstairs. The offerings are tasty homemade pasta dishes and a wide range of hero sandwiches (they invented the six-foot hero). Beer and wine, excellent cappuccino. AE only. *OPEN Mon-Sat 8am-7pm. CLOSED Sun.*

Moondance Diner
80 Sixth Avenue at Grand St. 226-1191. The old Tunnel Diner resurrected for modern times. Quality modest food at good prices: grilled sandwiches, potato skins and onion rings, spinach and swiss omelettes, fresh-fruit buttermilk pancakes. Some good New York specialties, too, like challah French toast and egg creams. Beer and wine, plus champagne by the glass. Outdoor tables in season. No reservations. No credit cards. *OPEN Sun-Thurs 8:30am-midnight; Fri & Sat 24 hours.*

Nathan's Famous
Surf & Stillwell Avenues, Brooklyn. (718) 946-2202. The neighborhood, Coney Island, just ain't

what it used to be, but the famed hot dogs, first served here by founder Nathan Handwerker in 1916, are. Still one of the best places for fresh oysters and clams, the fries are also must-haves. Dining room and counter service. No credit cards. *OPEN Sun-Thurs 8am-2am; Fri & Sat 8am-4am.*

Nyborg Nelson
Citicorp Market, 153 East 53 Street. 223-0700. A taste of Scandinavia. The smorgasbord plates, open-face sandwiches, and hot daily specials are extremely fresh and tasty treats. Draws crowds. Full bar. No reservations. AE, CB, DC, MC, V. *OPEN Mon-Fri 11:30am-8:30pm; Sat & Sun noon-6pm.*

The Stage
Second Avenue near St. Marks Pl. 473-8614. Friendly, clean, and extremely well-run Ukrainian luncheonette serves the best chicken soup in the East Village. Wonderful, too, are the potato pirogi, blintzes, kielbasa omelette, beef goulash, meat loaf, stuffed cabbage, and heaping portions of vegetables, including kasha and wonderful mashed potatoes topped with fried onions. Breakfast specials till noon. Counter only, seats 16. No credit cards. *OPEN Mon-Sat 7am-9:30pm. CLOSED Sun.*

Italian

Alo Alo
1030 Third Avenue at East 61 St. 838-4343. The fashionable Euros who used to flock to this glitzy grand Italian cafe now go elsewhere. Those who still come seem not to care that the kitchen has changed dramatically for the worse though the pastas can still satisfy and the bar scene is still lively in the pm. Live music. Jacket required. Reserve. AE, DC, MC, V. *OPEN 7 days noon-11:45pm. Sun brunch noon-3pm. Bar till 1am.* $$

Angelo's
146 Mulberry Street near Grand St. 966-1277. A hectic but good Southern Italian restaurant in Little Italy. Try the special antipasto di mare, a foot-long platter of squid, shrimp, scallops, and celery for two, or the angel hair pasta or cannelloni Amalfitani. Reserve for more than two, even then there's often a wait. AE, DC, MC, V. *OPEN Tues-Thurs noon-11:30pm; Fri noon-12:30am; Sat noon-1am; Sun noon-11:30pm. CLOSED Mon.* $$

Aperitivo
29 West 56 Street. 765-5155. An old standby with attractive decor, cozy atmosphere, and friendly service. Very good Northern Italian food; expense account crowd. Jacket and tie required. Reserve. AE, DC, V. *L Mon-Fri noon-3pm. D Mon-Fri 5:30pm-10:30pm; Sat 5:30pm-11pm. CLOSED Sun.* $$

Arqua'
281 Church Street near White St. 334-1888. TriBeCa restaurant rightly lauded for its excellent authentic *cucina nuova* offerings in a spacious inviting ambience. Pastas are heavenly, especially the gnocchi; a risotto daily; calves' liver

with onions and polenta, fish soup, grilled chicken. For dessert, ricotta cheesecake, tiramisu. Popular and noisy in the pm. Reserve. AE only. *L Mon-Fri noon-3pm. D Mon-Thurs 5:30pm-11pm; Fri & Sat 5:30pm-11:30pm. CLOSED Sun.* $$$

Asti
13 East 12 Street. 741-9105. Large musical-memorabilia-bedecked Italian restaurant where enthusiastic customers and waiters, hosts, and performers sing opera with your supper. Good old-fashioned fun for groups. Reserve. AE, CB, DC, MC, V. *OPEN Tues-Sun 5pm-12:30am. CLOSED Mon & July & Aug.* $$

Barbetta
321 West 46 Street. 246-9171. Longtime (1906) theater district Italian restaurant set in a sumptuously appointed town house, presents mainly Northern Italian Piedmontese specialties. Stay simple and the food may please, but everyone will tell you that in season the luxurious outdoor dining garden, Manhattan's prettiest, is a true oasis and Barbetta's best feature. Madness before the curtain rises and after it falls, indulgent service in between. Pretheater dinner from 5pm to 7pm. Reserve. AE, CB, DC, MC, V. *L Mon-Sat noon-2pm. D Mon-Sat 5:30pm-11:30pm. CLOSED Sun.* $$$

Barocco
301 Church Street near White St. 431-1445. This casual yet trendy warehouse-sized trattoria for Tuscan specialties is a TriBeCa scene stealer. The pastas here are wonderful and don't miss the breads—fettunta or bruschetta. They also have a retail outlet. Reserve. AE, DC, MC, V. *L Mon-Sat noon-3pm. D Mon-Sat 6pm-11:30pm; Sun 6:30pm-10:30pm.* $$$

Barolo
398 West Broadway near Spring St. 226-1102. The predominant feature of this starkly handsome heart of SoHo restaurant for okay Piedmontese Italian cooking is its glorious walled-in summer garden dominated by dramatically lit full-size cherry trees. Reserve. AE, MC, V. *OPEN Sun-Thurs noon-midnight; Fri & Sat noon-1am.* $$$

Beatrice Inn
285 West 12 Street near Eighth Ave. 929-6165; 243-9826. Convivial Greenwich Village basement restaurant serves good traditional Northern Italian dishes, notably the pastas. Casual cozy smaller dining room has a fireplace; lingering in the pm is encouraged. Reserve. AE, CB, DC, MC, V. *L Mon-Fri 11:45am-2:45pm. D Mon-Thurs 5pm-10pm; Fri & Sat 5pm-10:30pm. CLOSED Sun.* $$

Bellini by Cipriani
777 Seventh Avenue at West 51 St. 265-7770. Arrigo Cipriani's chic New York outpost draws a well-heeled, well-dressed international crowd. Stick to the traditional Venetian dishes, some of which—like carpaccio—were invented at Cipriani's famed Harry's Bar in Venice. Have at least one Bellini (at this writing $8 a pop)—peach nectar and sparkling Prosecco—and don't miss the

risottos. Perfect choice for pre- or posttheater dining; choice of three prix-fixe menus nightly. Take-out gourmet shop, too. Jacket required. Reserve! AE, MC, V. *L Mon-Sat 11:45am-3pm. D Mon-Sat 5:30pm-11:30pm; Sun 5:30pm-9pm.* **$$$$+**

Bice
7 East 54 Street. 688-1999. Extremely successful Italian bistro imported from Milan (the original Bice founded there in 1926), where the fashionable continue to flock to feast on heavenly but high-priced pasta, risotto, grilled dishes, and game in season. Reserve! AE only. *OPEN 7 days: L noon-3pm; D 6pm-11:30pm.* **$$$$+**

Carmine's
2450 Broadway near West 90 St. 362-2200. Good restaurants are hard to find in this neck of the island—so the crowds flocking to this newcomer Italian with a turn-of-the-century ambience are understandable. Huge portions of hearty, well-prepared food at nearly bargain prices. Reservations taken for parties of 6 or more. AE only. *OPEN Mon-Thurs 5pm-11pm; Fri & Sat 5pm-midnight; Sun 2pm-10pm.* **$**

Cent'Anni
50 Carmine Street near Bleecker St. 989-9494. Small, crowded, casual West Village storefront trattoria for very good simple Florentine cooking. Wonderful seafood salad, grilled veal chop, and pastas. Finish with the zabaglione. Reserve. AE only. *L Mon-Fri noon-2:30pm. D Mon-Sat 5:30pm-11pm; Sun 5pm-10:30pm.* **$$**

Chelsea Place
147 Eighth Avenue near West 17 St. 924-8413. You walk through an antique shop to get to this cramped popular noisy Chelsea restaurant complete with small dance floor and live music Monday to Saturday from 5pm to 4am. Well-prepared Italian dishes are served in the sedate downstairs dining room; good fish choices, too. Intimate upstairs bar for live jazz Wednesday to Saturday nights starting at 9:30pm. Reserve. AE, CB, DC, MC, V. *L Mon-Fri noon-2:30pm. D Mon-Sat 5:30pm-11:30pm; Sun 5:30pm-11pm.* **$$**

Coco Pazzo
23 East 74 Street. 794-0205. Lively unpretentious Italian East Sider for excellent robust regional Italian specialties. Large portions of satisfying delicious fare: the nightly array of hot and cold antipasto is wonderful, so too the semolina dumplings, the risotto, and the rigatoni with sausage and peas; for game lovers, the choices are fine. Weekends there are special prices on various dishes for two or more. Reserve. AE, MC, V. *L Mon-Fri noon-3pm. D Mon-Sat 5:30pm-11:30pm; Sun 5:30pm-10:30pm. B Sat & Sun 7am-10:30am; brunch noon-3:30pm.* **$$$**

Contrapunto
200 East 60 Street, upstairs (above Yellowfingers). 751-8616. Cheerful busy and at times cramped Bloomies neighbor is a good casual choice for an imaginative array of perfect pasta preparations, vino, and homemade gelati. No

reservations, be prepared to wait. AE, DC, MC, V. *OPEN Mon-Sat noon-midnight; Sun 4pm-10pm.* **$$**

Cucina di Pesce
87 East 4 Street. 260-6800. Hearty portions of bargain-priced Italian-accented fish specialties served with heaping portions of pasta draw a better-dressed-than-the-neighborhood crowd to this East Village basement dining room. A mound of free mussels at the always crowded bar. No reservations. No credit cards. *OPEN 7 days 5pm-midnight.* **$$**

Da Silvano
260 Sixth Avenue near Houston St. 982-0090. Attractive and reliable though tightly packed Village storefront restaurant serves quite good Tuscan specialties. Best for outdoor sidewalk dining in summer. Suffer the service, which can be slow. Reserve. AE only. *L Mon-Fri noon-3pm. D Mon-Thurs 6pm-11:30pm; Fri & Sat 6pm-midnight; Sun 5pm-11pm.* **$$**

Elio's
1621 Second Avenue near East 84 St. 772-2242. Extremely popular for its very good Northern Italian fare and its star-studded crowd. Handsome setting, lively, but noisy; expect a wait. Reserve. AE, MC, V. *D Mon-Sat 5:30pm-midnight; Sun 5pm-midnight.* **$$**

Ennio & Michael
539 La Guardia Place near Bleecker St. 677-8577. Popular, consistently good casual Greenwich Village choice for Italian fare all in an unpretentious way. Many neighborhood devotees. Outside patio in season. Reserve. AE, MC, V. *OPEN 7 days noon-11pm.* **$$**

Erminia
250 East 83 Street. 879-4284; 517-3410. Appealing, romantic, and cozy (40 seats) family-run (same owner as Trastevere and Lattanzi) restaurant for foods grilled over a Tuscan wood fire. Also tasty pastas and bruschetta, olive-oil-and-garlic-drenched toasted bread. Jacket and tie. Reservations required. AE only. *OPEN Mon-Sat 5pm-11pm. CLOSED Sun.* **$$$**

Felidia
243 East 58 Street. 758-1479. Handsome sparkling restaurant for wonderfully original Northern Italian creations. Tasty antipasti and homemade pastas with seasonal ingredients; rustic regional specialties; game in season. Exceptional Italian wine selection. Jacket required. Reservations required. AE, CB, DC, MC, V. *L Mon-Fri noon-3pm. D Mon-Sat 5pm-midnight. CLOSED Sun.* **$$$$+**

Forlini's
93 Baxter Street near Canal St. 349-6779. Popular casual spot on the Little Italy–Chinatown "border" for Northern Italian cooking. Be prepared to wait on weekends. Reserve for 6 or more. AE, CB, DC, MC, V. Reduced-rate parking. *OPEN Tues-Sat noon-1am; Sun & Mon noon-midnight.* **$$**

Francesca's
129 East 28 Street. 685-0256. Cozy old-time, a-few-steps-down Italian restaurant for basic home-style Italian cooking. Reserve. AE, MC, V.

L Mon-Fri noon-3pm. D Mon-Sat 6pm-11:30pm. CLOSED Sun. $$

Gargiulo's
2911 West 15 Street, Brooklyn. (718) 266-4891. In Coney Island, a huge boisterous family-run restaurant renowned for its home-style Neapolitan cooking, including mozzarella en carozza, baked clams, fettuccine Gargiulo, tortellini Michelangelo, and risotto with mushrooms. Worth a trip for the food and the local color. Free parking. Reserve. AE, DC, MC, V. *OPEN Sun, Mon, Wed & Thurs 11am-10:30pm; Fri & Sat 11am-11:30pm. CLOSED Tues.* $

Giambelli 50th Ristorante
46 East 50 Street. 688-2760. Longtime midtown Northern Italian restaurant whose food is improving now that ownership has passed to same owner as Il Nido and Il Monello. Elegant old-money ambience and clientele. Jacket required. Reserve. AE, CB, DC, MC, V. *OPEN Mon-Sat noon-midnight. CLOSED Sun.* $$$$ +

Giordano
409 West 39 Street. 947-9811 or -3883. Out-of-the-way Italian favorite of those who know it. Atrium garden beneath the stars. Pianist Tuesday to Saturday. Convenient to Madison Square Garden. Jacket required. Valet parking at dinnertime. Reserve. AE, CB, DC, MC, V. *OPEN Mon-Thurs noon-11pm; Fri & Sat noon-midnight; Sun 5pm-11pm.* $$

Grotta Azzurra
387 Broome Street at Mulberry St. 226-9283. Festive diners follow the aroma of garlic and head for this old (1908) well-known cellar restaurant in Little Italy for heaping servings of Southern Italian specialties—lobster fra diavolo, cacciatore, ravioli. No reservations, so expect a wait. No credit cards. *OPEN Tues-Sun noon-midnight. CLOSED Mon.* $$

Harry Cipriani
781 Fifth Avenue at East 59 St. 753-5566. Harry is back where he belongs on the East Side (*see also* Bellini by Cipriani). The atmosphere will make you homesick for Venice. The elegant well-heeled international set veritably floats through the revolving door and hardly misses a beat before a Bellini is in hand. Wonderful Northern Italian food, sophisticated setting and crowd. Reserve. AE, DC, MC, V. *OPEN 7 days: B 7am-10am; L noon-3pm; D Mon-Sat 6pm-10:45pm; Sun 6pm-9pm.* $$$$

Il Cantinori
32 East 10 Street. 673-6044. Top-rated Italian in the Village for lovely uncomplicated Tuscan specialties in two subtly charming rustic country dining rooms, the front one spills out onto the street in good weather. Wonderful unusual daily specials, cold antipasti, and grilled meats and vegetables. Reserve for dinner. *L Mon-Fri noon-3pm. D Mon-Thurs 6pm-11:15pm; Fri & Sat 6pm-midnight; Sun 6pm-11pm.* $$

Il Menestrello
14 East 52 Street. 421-7588. The food is good traditional Northern Italian, especially the pastas. A pleasant albeit pricey choice. Jacket required. AE, DC, MC, V. *OPEN Mon-Thurs noon-11pm; Fri & Sat noon-midnight. CLOSED Sun.* $$$

Il Monello
1460 Second Avenue near East 76 St. 535-9310. Well-thought-of longtime plush Upper East Side Northern Italian restaurant (same ownership as Il Nido) for expensive regional Italian fare. Excellent wine list. Reserve. AE, CB, DC, MC, V. *L Mon-Sat noon-3pm. D Mon-Sat 5pm-midnight. CLOSED Sun.* $$$

Il Mulino
86 West 3 Street near Thompson St. 673-3783. Word is out: This Village entry may be the very best for Italian food. A dark and some say cramped setting for fried zucchini to start with, then on to stuffed mushrooms, breaded clams, carpaccio, superb pastas. For dessert, the zabaglione, hot or cold. Extremely crowded in the pm, go for lunch if you can. Reserve! AE only. *L Mon-Fri noon-2:30pm. D Mon-Sat 5pm-11:30pm. CLOSED Sun.* $$$

Il Nido
251 East 53 Street. 753-8450. Excellent Tuscan regional dishes in an elegant, softly lit, rather formal setting. Excels in pastas and seafood dishes. Great wine list. Expense account prices. Jacket and tie. Reserve. AE, CB, DC, MC, V. *L Mon-Sat noon-2:30pm. D Mon-Sat 5:30pm-10:30pm. CLOSED Sun.* $$$

Il Ponte Vecchio
206 Thompson Street near Bleecker St. 228-7701. Low-priced tasty food draws the locals to this neighborhood Village Italian restaurant. Good mussels, clams, shrimps oreganata, and simply divine pastas. Reserve for dinner. AE only. *L Mon-Sat noon-3pm. D Mon-Sat 5pm-11pm; Sun 3pm-10pm.* $

Il Vagabondo
351 East 62 Street. 832-9221. Popular and boisterous longtime East Side neighborhood Italian restaurant. Low-priced traditional red-sauced and cheesy Southern Italian specialties, steaks, and chops. The unique feature: a well-used earth-floor boccie court. No reservations. AE, CB, DC, MC, V. *L Mon-Fri noon-3pm. D Mon-Sat 5:30pm-midnight; Sun 5:30pm-11pm.* $

Lattanzi
361 West 46 Street. 315-0980. On Restaurant Row in the theater district, a rustic, informal setting draws crowds for hearty classic Italian dining featuring traditional Roman Jewish specialties at lunchtime and in the evening starting at 8pm, the best time to go anyway. Reserve. AE only. *L Mon-Fri noon-2pm. D Mon-Thurs 5pm-11pm; Fri & Sat 5pm-midnight. CLOSED Sun.* $$

Le Madri
168 West 18 Street. 727-8022. Spacious high-celinged lively spot in Chelsea for consistently fine imaginative Tuscan-style cooking. Great pizzas from a central wood-burning oven. The seasonal outside dining patio is quieter. Reserve! AE only. *L Mon-Fri noon-3pm. D Mon-Sat 6-10:30pm; pizza and salad menu 10:30pm-12:30am.* $$$

Louise Junior
317 East 53 Street. 752-7832; 335-9172. Congenial longtime Upper East Side Italian restaurant. Meals start with a standout antipasto that includes shrimp and crabmeat, and end with a huge bowl of fresh fruit. Jacket appreciated; no denim. No reservations. AE, CB, DC. *L Mon-Fri noon-3pm. D Mon-Fri 5pm-10:30pm; Sat 5pm-11:00pm. CLOSED Sun.* $$

Mama Leone's
Milford Plaza Hotel, 261 West 44 Street at Broadway. 391-8270. The 82-year-old dining institution is back, after a brief hiatus, in new but smaller digs (they now seat "only" 650 instead of 1,250). Once again tourists can dine on copious portions of basic Italian fare served by good-natured waiters in painting-and-marble-sculpture-bedecked surroundings. It's festive good fun for families. Reserve. AE, CB, DC, MC, V. *L Mon-Sat 11:30am-2:30pm. D Mon-Sat 4:30pm-11:30pm; Sun 2:30pm-10pm.* $

Mary's
42 Bedford Street near Seventh Ave South. 741-3387. You won't find many yuppies at this atmospheric old Village restaurant with two fireplaces. Home-style Italian cooking; Abruzzi specialties. Very good pastas. Reserve weekends. AE, CB, DC, MC. *OPEN Sun & Mon 5pm-11pm; Tues-Thurs 5pm-midnight; Fri & Sat 5pm-1am.* $

Mezzaluna
1295 Third Avenue near East 74 St. 535-9600. Bustling trattoria still draws a crowd—even though it's not the "in" crowd. Elegant, celestial decor—cloud-painted ceiling, half moon (mezzaluna) theme; shoulder-to-shoulder seating; ear-blasting music. Limited boutique menu: beef carpaccio with a choice of fixings; pasta main courses that change daily; vegetable and herb pizzas from wood-burning ovens (at lunch and after 10:30pm only). Cheese, fruit, and sorbets for dessert. All-Italian wine list. All-Italian experience. No reservations, expect a long wait and you won't be disappointed. No credit cards. *L Mon-Fri noon-3pm; Sat & Sun noon-4pm. D 6pm-1am.* $$

Mezzogiorno
195 Spring Street at Sullivan St. 334-2112. From the owners of the miniscule Mezzaluna, another trendy, very Italian trattoria (this one with a bit more breathing room) for an excellent choice of carpaccios, thin-crusted brick-oven pizzas (served from noon to 4pm and 10pm to 1am), pastas, and salads; a great tiramisù for dessert. You can also dine at the long marble-topped bar. Reserve. No credit cards. *OPEN Mon-Fri noon-3pm & 6pm-1am; Sat & Sun noon-1am.* $$

Nanni Il Valletto
133 East 61 Street. 838-3939. Many upper-crust Italians consider this the tops for osso buco, spinach and ricotta ravioli, baked clams, and pasta, especially the carbonara. (For lower prices and pretentions see Nanni's.) AE, CB, DC, MC, V. *L Mon-Fri noon-3:30pm. D Mon-Sat 5:30pm-11:30pm. CLOSED Sun.* $$$

Nanni's
146 East 46 Street. 599-9684. Long-established convivial Italian restaurant with a cramped clubby feel. Classic Northern specials beautifully prepared daily; the town's best angel hair pasta. Reserve for lunch and dinner. AE, DC, MC, V. *OPEN Mon-Sat noon-11pm. CLOSED Sun.* $$$

Orso
322 West 46 Street. 489-7212. For theatergoers, on Restaurant Row, this wonderful, casual Northern Italian trattoria with its open kitchen garners raves for pre- or posttheater pastas, thin crust pizzas, and tasty grilled entrees. After theater attracts a Broadway show-biz crowd to its bar and vaulted whitewashed skylit back room. Reserve! MC, V. *OPEN Sun-Tues & Thurs-Fri noon-11:45pm; Wed & Sat 11:30am-11:30pm.* $$

Palio
Equitable Center, 151 West 51 Street. 245-4850. Have a drink in the bar with Sandro Chia's striking wraparound mural, then an elevator ride up to the spacious restaurant for elegant dining on inventive Italian fare. Risotto dumplings with truffles, fresh mussels in saffron broth, carpaccio, roast squab. Pre- and after-theater menus in the bar. Jacket and tie required, no denim or sneakers. Reserve! AE, DC, MC, V. *L Mon-Fri noon-2:30pm. D Mon-Sat 5:30pm-11pm. Bar: Mon-Fri 11:30am-midnight; Sat 4pm-midnight. CLOSED Sun.* $$$$

Paolucci's
149 Mulberry Street near Grand St. 226-9653; 925-2288. Dine in a homey two-story 1816 landmark Federal building in Little Italy. Reserve. AE, DC, MC, V. *OPEN Mon-Thurs 11:30am-10:30pm; Fri 11:30am-11pm; Sat 11am-1am; Sun 11am-9:30pm.* $$

Parioli Romanissimo
24 East 81 Street. 288-2391. This long-standing luxurious restaurant located in a turn-of-the-century brownstone serves some of the city's best Northern Italian dishes. Unequaled veal and pasta dishes. Infallible service. Reservations required. Jacket and tie. AE, DC. *OPEN Tues-Sat 6pm-11pm. CLOSED Sun & Mon.* $$$$+

Parma
1404 Third Avenue near East 79 St. 535-3520. Noisy informal East Side neighborhood standby serves good Northern Italian food to an East Side crowd of regulars. Highly recommended: the pastas. Reservations required. AE only. *OPEN 7 days 5pm-midnight.* $$

Patrissey's
98 Kenmare Street near Mulberry St. 226-8854. Substantial Little Italy fixture since the 1930s serves good Neapolitan specialties. No denim. Reserve. AE, CB, DC, MC, V. *OPEN 7 days noon-10:30pm.* $$

Petaluma
1354 First Avenue at East 73 St. 772-8800. They once came in droves to this convivial cafe for thin-crust pizza from wood-burning ovens and good pasta specials. There's the de rigueur open kitchen and the elevated front dining room

for the best "view." Alas the "in" crowd's gone elsewhere, but those who remain dine well. Reserve. AE, V. *L Mon-Fri 11:30am-3pm. D Mon-Sat 5:30pm-midnight; Sun 5pm-11pm. Weekend brunch 11:30am-3pm.* $

Pinocchio
168 East 81 Street. 650-1513; 879-0752. Tiny family-run storefront restaurant serves simple but well-prepared Northern Italian fare, including carpaccio, fegato Veneziano, paglia and fieno. Well-priced pretheater dinner served from 5pm to 6:30pm. Reserve. AE only. *OPEN Mon-Sat 5pm-11pm.* $$

Positano
250 Park Avenue South at East 20 St. 777-6211. This once so-hot trendy ode to the Amalfi Coast has cooled, but the sleek trilevel restaurant still attracts a crowd with its very good pastas and innovative daily specials. Best view: from the "summit" tables. As you would expect, the crowd is young, media-connected, and extremely noisy. Reserve! AE, CB, DC, MC, V. *L Mon-Fri noon-3pm. D Mon-Thurs 5:30pm-11:30pm; Fri & Sat 5:30pm-12:30am. CLOSED Sun.* $$

Puglia's
189 Hester Street at Mulberry St. 966-6006. Little Italy's most festive restaurant. Peasant-style home cooking, wine that's made in the basement, shared tables, camaraderie, and impromptu singing. The food will be better elsewhere but not the raucous fun. Colorful, unsophisticated Little Italy experience. No reservations. No credit cards. *OPEN Tues-Sun noon-midnight. CLOSED Mon.*

Remi
145 West 53 Street. 581-4242. The elegant new surroundings —a two-story dining room dominated by a spectacular mural of Venice—make dining on Venetian pastas, beef carpaccio, risottos, and wonderful vegetable antipastos, even more pleasureable. Without doubt the best Bellini's in town. Fine pre- or posttheater choice. Reserve! Also **Remi to Go** for breakfast and light meals in the glass-enclosed passageway adjacent to the restaurant. AE, MC, V. *L Mon-Fri 11:30am-2:30pm. D 7 days 5:30pm-11:30pm.* $$$

San Domenico
240 Central Park South. 265-5959. Beautifully presented traditional northern Italian cuisine in luxuriously elegant surroundings. Fettuccine with wild rabbit sauce, smoked breast of goose, pan-roasted sweetbreads with garlic, roast veal chop in a smoked-bacon-and-cream sauce. Prix-fixe lunch and dinner. Reserve. AE, CB, DC, MC, V. *OPEN 7 days: L 11:45am-2:30pm; D 5:45pm-11pm.* $$$$

Trastevere 83 & Trastevere 84
309 East 83 Street; 734-6343; And * 155 East 84 Street; 744-0210. Tiny romantic (albeit tightly packed) candlelit settings for the Lattanzi family's hearty Roman specialties. Pollo alla Romana, veal piccante, capellini primavera, and Napoleon for dessert. Wine only. *Kosher. Re-

serve. AE only. *D Mon-Sat 5pm-11pm; Sun 5pm-10pm. *OPEN Mon-Thurs 5:30pm-10:30pm; Sat one hour after sunset-1am; Sun 2pm-10pm. CLOSED Fri.* $$

Trattoria dell'Arte
900 Seventh Avenue near West 57 St. 245-9800. The amusing decor—oversized proboscises and other body parts—and the lively upbeat attitude of this casual Italian trattoria make it a best bite for pre- or post–Carnegie Hall. Antipasto platters for two, thin-crust pizzas, pastas in half portions, grilled meats and fish. Reserve. AE, MC, V. *OPEN 7 days noon-midnight.* $$

Vivolo
140 East 74 Street. 737-3533. Simple, old-fashioned Northern Italian fare in a handsome 100-year-old brownstone with two working fireplaces. Dark and romantic, especially upstairs for more intimacy. Good value early-bird dinner. Jacket required. Reserve. AE, CB, DC, MC, V. *L Mon-Fri noon-3pm. D Mon-Sat 5pm-11:15pm. CLOSED Sun.* $$

Yellowfingers di Nuovo
200 East 60 Street. 751-8615. Lively longtime standby with a new menu slant: Italian with California influences. Delicious herb-scented pizzas with interesting grilled vegetable toppings, roast chicken salad, grilled fish and meat. High quality, low tariff. Enclosed sidewalk cafe is best place to sit for a view of Bloomies' comings and goings. Good selection of wines by the glass. AE, MC, V. *OPEN 7 days noon-1am* $

Zinno
126 West 13 Street. 924-5182. Comfortable, convivial replacement for the old Reno Sweeney's. Simple Neapolitan dishes. Best are the linguine with vodka, fried zucchini, pork chop alla pizziola, calves' liver alla nonna. Fine jazz Monday to Saturday from 8pm. Reserve. AE, MC, V. *L Mon-Fri noon-2:30pm. D Mon-Thurs 5:30pm-11pm; Fri & Sat 5:30pm-11:30pm; Sun 5:30pm-10:30pm.* $$

Japanese

Akasaka
715 Second Avenue near East 38 St. 867-6410. Large, busy Japanese restaurant and sushi bar offers good traditional raw fish dishes and tempura. AE, DC, MC, V. *L Mon-Sat noon-2:30pm. D Mon-Sat 5pm-10pm. CLOSED Sun.* $

Benihana of Tokyo
47 West 56 Street; 581-0930. And 120 East 56 Street; 593-1627. The formula: chicken or steak, accompanied by stir-fired shrimp or vegetables, is prepared and cooked by adept chef-cum-showman at a table shared with others (unless there are eight people in your party). Fun when you have relatives visiting or an office birthday to celebrate. Warm saki and Japanese beer available. Full bar. Reserve. AE, CB, DC, MC, V. *L Mon-Fri noon-2:30pm. D Mon-Thurs 5:30pm-10:30pm; Fri & Sat 5:30pm-11:30pm; Sun 5pm-10:30pm.* $$

Choshi
77 Irving Place at East 19 St. 420-1419. Very good choice in the Gramercy Park neighborhood for tasty, extremely fresh sushi in a relaxed setting. AE, MC, V. *L noon-2:30pm. D 7 days 5:30pm-10:30pm.* $

Gibbon
24 East 80 Street. 861-4001. In a tranquil and spacious town house setting, convenient to the Met and Mad Ave galleries. French-influenced Japanese: mussels with garlic, cucumber stuffed with lobster, wonderful tataki (sliced filet mignon), negima (thin-sliced beef with onions and zucchini), prawns à la Kyoto, rack of lamb. Sushi and sashimi for purists. Extremely popular with the art crowd who know about the bargain-priced lunch. Working fireplace in the bar. Jacket required. Reserve. AE, DC, MC, V. *L Mon-Fri noon-2pm. D Mon-Sat 6pm-10pm. CLOSED Sun.* $$

Hatsuhana
17 East 48 Street; 355-3345. And 237 Park Avenue at East 46 St; 661-3400. Sushi connoisseurs know this is the very best (though pricey) and they wait in line for their conviction. Also very good, the teriyaki. Higher marks go to the original (48th Street) for comfort and consistency. Japanese beers. No reservations policy creates crowds. AE, DC, MC, V. *L Mon-Sat 11:45am-2:30pm. D 7 days 5pm-9:30pm.* $$

Japonica
90 University Place near East 11 St. 243-7752. Reliably excellent, cozy but noisy Greenwich Village choice for well-served and well-priced sushi. Also sashimi, tempura, and teriyaki. Line-ups are usual. No reservations taken. AE, DC. *OPEN Mon-Thurs noon-11pm; Fri & Sat noon-12:30am; Sun noon-10pm.* $

Mie
196 Second Avenue near East 12 St. 674-7060. One-flight-below-street-level East Village sushi bar and restaurant. Very popular because it serves some of the best sushi and sashimi; bar or table service. Also some original dishes including deep-fried oysters, hot pot of clams, oyako-don chicken, scallion omelette. Sapporo beer. AE, DC, MC, V. *OPEN Tues-Sun 5:30pm-12:30am.* $

Mitsukoshi
461 Park Avenue at East 57 St. 935-6444. An elegant choice for very fine traditional Japanese dining. Superb sushi, much of it flown in daily from Japan. Busy at lunchtime, more tranquil for dinner. Small sushi bar. Reserve. AE, DC, MC, V. *L Mon-Sat noon-2pm. D Mon-Sat 6pm-10pm.* $$$

Nippon
155 East 52 Street. 355-9020. This large, well-known Japanese restaurant has been a mainstay in New York. It still serves extremely fresh sushi and sashimi. The à la carte menu has some interesting authentic choices tailored for the Japanese client and the educated Westerner. Private tatami rooms perfect for wonderfully unique ceremonial dinners. Saki, Japanese beers. Re-

serve. AE, CB, DC, MC, V. *L Mon-Fri noon-2:30 pm. D Mon-Thurs 5:30pm-10pm; Fri & Sat 5:30pm-10:30pm. CLOSED Sun.* $$$

Omen
113 Thompson Street near Prince St. 925-8923. Top-rated rustic SoHo cafe for unusual Japanese country-style fare via the original in Kyoto. Omen, a hearty broth with noodles and vegetables, is the specialty. Reserve. AE, DC. *OPEN Tues-Sun 5:30pm-10:30pm. Weekend brunch 11:30am-4:30pm. CLOSED Mon.* $$

Seryna
11 East 53 Street. 980-9393. Beautiful serene spot in midtown for very good nonsushi Japanese dining. Especially popular, the sirloin or filet steak (ishiyaki) grilled on a hot stone at your table and served with two dipping sauces (accompanied by french fries!). Also good is the shabu-shabu. Reserve. AE, CB, DC, MC, V. *L Mon-Fri noon-2pm. D Mon-Fri 5pm-midnight; Sat 6pm-midnight. CLOSED Sun.* $$

Sushi Zen
57 West 46 Street. 302-0707. Sushi bar for beautiful to look at and taste sushi and sashimi. Limited menu for non-raw-fish lovers. A la carte or a four-course prix fixe. Reserve. AE, CB, DC. *L Mon-Fri noon-2:30pm. D Mon-Fri 5:30pm-10:30pm; Sat 3pm-9pm.* $$

Take-Sushi
71 Vanderbilt Avenue at Park Ave & East 45 St. 867-5120. Good midtown sushi choice. Counter, tables, plus two private tatami suites. Always busy at lunch. Downstairs is preferable. Reserve! AE, DC, MC, V. *L Mon-Fri noon-2:30pm. D Mon-Sat 5pm-10pm. CLOSED Sun & holidays.* $$

Umeda
102 East 22 Street. 505-1550. Imaginative Japanese dining in the Gramercy Park area. Attractive and inviting paneled dining room and New York's first sake bar. Reserve. AE, MC, V. *L Mon-Fri noon-2:30pm; D 7 days 6pm-midnight.* $$$

Jewish (Kosher & Nonkosher)

(See also Delicatessen.)

Barney Greengrass "The Sturgeon King"
541 Amsterdam Avenue near West 86 St. 724-4707. Over 53 years of serving wonderful borscht, lox, sturgeon, and white fish to Upper West Siders. Best bite: the house omelette of Nova, eggs, and onions. No reservations. No credit cards. *OPEN Tues-Fri 9am-4pm; Sat & Sun 9am-5pm. CLOSED Mon.* $

Grand Dairy Restaurant
341 Grand Street at Ludlow St. 673-1904. Informal old Lower East Side dairy restaurant for Jewish-style foods. Potato pirogen, fried herring, crisp apple blintzes, good rice pudding. No reservations. No credit cards. *OPEN Sun-Fri 6am-3:30pm. CLOSED Sat.* $

La Kasbah
See Middle Eastern

Lou Siegel's
209 West 38 Street. 921-4433. Large, informal

kosher restaurant featuring Jewish home-style cooking. Crowded lunchtime with garment manufacturers. No dairy. Reserve. AE, MC, V. *OPEN Sun-Thurs 11:30am-10pm; Fri noon-2:45pm. CLOSED Sat.* $

Moshe Peking
40 West 37 Street. 594-6500. Complete kosher-Chinese garment center restaurant features non-spicy Cantonese-style dishes including Peking duck for two. Kosher wine list. Take-out and catering. Reserve. AE, CB, DC, MC, V. *OPEN Sun-Thurs noon-11pm; Sat one hour after sunset-1am. CLOSED all day Fri & Sat until sunset.* $

Ratner's Dairy Restaurant
138 Delancey Street near Norfolk St. 677-5588. Famous Lower East Side Jewish dairy restaurant, now kosher, still offers an extensive range of well-prepared dishes—vegetable goulash, matzoh brie, stuffed cabbage, blintzes, mushroom cutlets, baked stuffed fish. The waiters are straight from central casting. Sundays here are hectic. AE, MC, V ($20 minimum). *OPEN Sun-Thurs 6am-11pm; Fri 6am till sundown; Sat from sundown till 2am.* $

Rectangles
See Middle Eastern

Sammy's Roumanian
157 Chrystie Street near Delancey St. 673-0330; 475-9131. Romanian tenderloin steak "with or without garlic," potatoes with gribenes, veal chops, stuffed cabbage, egg creams, and more. A schmaltzy New York institution; it's terribly entertaining and filling. Go with a hungry group, and give yourself up to it. Reserve. AE, CB, DC. *OPEN 7 days 4pm-midnight.* $$

Trastevere 84
See Italian.

Triplet's Roumanian Restaurant
Sixth Avenue at Grand Street. 925-9303. Owned by triplets (there's a story here, ask them about it), it's a younger better-run clone of Sammy's Roumanian. Those with high cholesterol stay home. Entertainment and dancing nightly from 6 pm. Reserve. AE, MC. *OPEN Sun-Fri 5pm-10pm; Sat dinner seatings 7, 8 & 9:30pm.* $$

Yonah Schimmel's
137 East Houston Street near Eldridge St; 477-2858. And 1275 Lexington Avenue near East 86 St; 722-4849. The place (here since 1895) and food are nostalgic remnants of the old Jewish East Side. Authentic knishes—the best are still potato and kasha, though good updates include cherry cheese. Other age-old treats: clabbered milk, borscht, and a glass of tea. There's an uptown branch on Lexington but downtown has the real taste of old New York. No credit cards. *OPEN 7 days 8am-6:30pm.* $

Korean

Woo Lae Oak of Seoul
77 West 46 Street. 869-9958. For more than 40 years, this large friendly attractive spot has been specializing in outstanding authentic, moderately priced Korean barbecue (beef, chicken,

pork, or organ meats) cooked by you at your table; served with soup, rice, and vegetables. One drawback: smoke gets in your eyes. Good for groups. Reserve for more than 5. AE, DC, MC, V. *OPEN 7 days 11:30am-10:30pm.* $

Late Night & 24 Hours

Around the Clock Cafe
8 Stuyvesant Street (Third Ave & East 9 St). 598-0402. Comfortable casual contemporary East Village cafe with a catch-as-catch-can eclectic menu. Very noisy; a few outside tables in good weather. No reservations. AE, MC, V. *OPEN 7 days, 24 hours.* $

Brasserie
100 East 53 Street. 751-4840. Huge, informal yet sophisticated French brasserie for good onion soup (you can't get it in Paris anymore at 3am, but you can here), burgers, quiches, salads. Also a civilized early business breakfast spot. Their croissants are still the city's flakiest. Counter and table service. Reserve for dinner only. Full bar service. AE, CB, DC, MC, V. *Ouvert a toute heure. NEVER CLOSES!* $

Cafe Luxembourg
200 West 70 Street. 873-7411. The Luxembourg, with its Art Deco-ish interior, evocative of 1930s Paris, continues to be one of the most popular see-and-be-seen late-night spots with plenty of celebrity gazing opportunities. But best of all you will also get a wonderful meal. Menu ranges from simple brasserie fare—steak and pommes frites—to imaginative seasonal creations. Also a good value prix-fixe pre-Lincoln Center dinner served from 5:30pm to 6:30pm. Bright, crowded, and noisy. Book well in advance and you'll wait anyway. AE, MC, V. *OPEN Mon-Thurs 5:30pm-12:30am; Fri & Sat 5:30pm-1:30am; Sun 11am-2:30pm & 6pm-11:30am.* $$$

Cheyenne
411 Ninth Avenue at West 33 St. 465-8750. A restored 1927 diner (formerly the Market), for eggs, omelettes (all day and night), burgers accompanied by a salad, hearty sandwiches, chili, wheatcakes, hot fudge sundaes, and other old-fashioned all-American basics. Domestic and imported beer in bottles and on tap. Take-out and delivery. No credit cards. *OPEN 7 days, 24 hours.* $

Empire Diner
210 Tenth Avenue at West 22 St. 243-2736. Attractive Art Deco-design diner in Chelsea, best for late-night snacking by homebound club crowd. Sunday brunch from 10am to 4pm. Outdoor seating in summer. Piano music early till late. No reservations. AE only. *OPEN 7 days, 24 hours.* $

Florent
69 Gansvoort Street near Washington St. 989-5779. Gritty meat-market-area diner turned trendy. This funky all-night bistro is a late-night mecca for its good food and the crowd, which is a stylish but egalitarian mixed bag of up- and downtowners. Well-priced items include won-

derful French onion soup, couscous, sweet-breads, mussels in white wine broth, duck mousse, boudin noir. Good wee hours breakfast spot. Counter and tables. Reserve for peak hours. No credit cards. *OPEN 7 days, 24 hours.* $$

Hard Rock Cafe
221 West 57 Street. 459-9320. Tennessee to New York via London; the famed Hard Rock provides down-homey cooking and rock and roll nostalgia—and for that 15,000 people a week line up outside to gain access. Burgers, chili, guacamole, gooey desserts, but most of all "the scene"; backed up by the loudest music this side of a rock concert. Just look for the 1960 Cadillac jutting from the facade, under which you will always find a gaggle of prepubescent girls, some boys. Adjacent gift shop where you purchase an expensive momento of the experience. No reservations. AE, MC, V. *OPEN 7 days 11:30am-3am.* $

Kiev International
117 Second Avenue at East 7 St. 674-4040. Queue up with the denizens of the East Village who know a good inexpensive meal when they can still find one. At this low-frills Ukrainian coffee shop get pirogi, New York's very best cheese blintzes, hearty entrees, homemade soups, challah French toast, apple pancakes, and more at any hour of the day or night. No reservations. No credit cards. *OPEN 7 days, 24 hours.* $

Lox Around the Clock
676 Sixth Avenue at West 21 St. 691-3535. Deliberate designer-dilapidated decor distinguishes this noisy 24-hour deli/coffee shop. You can get bagels and lox much cheaper elsewhere but maybe not at 3am in this desertlike area. Service is terrible even when empty. Sidewalk tables in season. No reservations. AE only. *OPEN Sun-Wed 7:30am-3am; Thurs-Sat 24 hours.* $

Odeon
145 West Broadway at Thomas St. 233-0507. This large remodeled 30s-style cafeteria remains an arty TriBeCa "in" spot. Reliable French bistro food; low-key, softly lit, low-frills ambience, and an interesting cast of characters especially late-night. Reserve! AE, CB, DC, MC, V. *L Mon-Fri noon-3pm. D Sun-Thurs 7pm-midnight; Fri & Sat 6pm-12:30am. Late supper Sun-Thurs till 2am; Fri & Sat till 3am. Sun brunch noon-3:30pm.* $$

Rose Room
Algonquin Hotel, 59 West 44 Street. 840-6800. This classic New York setting is mainly a nostalgic rather than culinary destination after the theater. The best thing on the menu is the apple pancakes with lingonberries and cream—it's dessert masquerading as an entree. Jacket required. Reserve. AE, CB, DC, MC, V. *Late supper Mon-Sat 9:30pm-12:30am.* $$

The following serve food at least UNTIL 11:30pm every night of the week. For other late-night spots see also Bars & Burgers.

Acme Bar & Grill (Soul/Southern)
Alcala (Spanish)
Alo Alo (Italian)
America (American)
American Festival Cafe (American)
Amsterdam's Bar & Rotisserie (American)
Angelo's (Italian)
Arcadia (American)
Arturo's Pizzeria (Pizza)
Asti (Italian)
Auntie Yuan (Chinese)
The Ballroom (Spanish: Tapas)
Bangkok Cuisine (Thai)
Barbetta (Italian)
Barocco (Italian)
Barolo (Italian)
Bayamo (Latin American)
Beach House (Mexican)
Bellini by Cipriani (Italian)
Benny's Burritos (Mexican)
Bernstein-on-Essex Street (Delicatessen)
Berry's (Continental)
Bice (Italian)
The Black Sheep (French)
Bridge Cafe (Continental)
Cafe de Bruxelles (Belgian)
Cafe des Artistes (Continental)
Cafe La Fortuna (Cafes)
Cafe Orlin (Breakfast/Brunch)
Cafe Un Deux Trois (French)
Cafe Vivaldi (Cafes)
Caffe Biondo (Cafes)
Caffe Dante (Cafes)
Caffe Reggio (Cafes)
Caffe Roma (Cafes)
Capsouto Frères (French)
Caramba! & !! & !!! & !!!! (Mexican)
Carnegie Delicatessen (Delicatessen)
Carolina (American)
Chelsea Place (Italian)
Chez Josephine (French)
Chez Ma Tante (French)
China Grill (Chinese)
Cinco de Mayo (Mexican)
City Lights Bar & Hors D'Oeuvrerie (Rooms with a View)
Claire (Fish & Seafood)
Cloister Cafe (Cafes)
Contrapunto (Italian)
Cornelia Street Cafe (Cafes)
Corner Bistro (Bars & Burgers)
Cottonwood Cafe (Breakfast/Brunch)
Cucina di Pesce (Italian)
Da Silvano (Italian)
De Robertis (Cafes)
Dock's Oyster Bar & Seafood Grill (Fish & Seafood)
Elaine's (Stargazing)
El Coyote (Mexican)
Elephant & Castle (Omelettes)
El Faro (Spanish)
Elio's (Italian)
El Rincon de Espana (Spanish)
Felidia (Italian)
Ferrara's (Cafes)

Figaro Cafe (Sidewalk Cafes)
Fiorello's Roman Cafe (Sidewalk Cafes)
Forlini's (Italian)
Fountain Cafe (Sidewalk Cafes)
Four Seasons (Deluxe)
Francesca's (Italian)
Gallagher's (Steak)
Gaylord (Indian)
Giambelli 50th Ristorante (Italian)
Ginger Man (American)
Giordano (Italian)
Grotta Azzurra (Italian)
Gulf Coast (Soul/Southern)
Harvey's Chelsea House (American)
Hong Fat (Chinese)
Il Monello (Italian)
Il Mulino (Italian)
Il Vagabondo (Italian)
Indochine (Vietnamese)
Jane Street Seafood Cafe (Fish & Seafood)
Jean Lafitte (French)
Jerry's 103 (American)
Jezebel (Soul/Southern)
Joe Allen (Stargazing)
John Clancy's (Fish & Seafood)
John's Pizzeria (Pizza)
Junior's Restaurant (Inexpensive)
Kenny's Steak Pub (Steak)
King Crab (Fish & Seafood)
Kleine Konditorei (German)
La Boheme (French)
La Bonne Soupe (Inexpensive)
La Fondue (Swiss)
La Gauloise (French)
Le Madri (Italian)
Les Pyrenees (French)
Le Zinc (French)
Lion's Rock (Continental)
Lola (Caribbean)
Louie's Westside Cafe (American)
Mamma Leone's (Italian)
Manhattan Brewing Company (Bars & Burgers)
Manhattan Ocean Club (Fish & Seafood)
Man Ray (American)
Marylou's (Fish & Seafood)
Memphis (Soul/Southern)
Mexico Lindo (Mexican)
Mezzaluna (Italian)
Mezzogiorno (Italian)
Mie (Japanese)
Mitali (Indian)
Moondance Diner (Inexpensive)
Mortimer's (Continental)
Mr. Chow (Chinese)
Nanni Il Valletto (Italian)
Nathan's Famous (Inexpensive)
Nirvana (Rooms with a View)
NoHo Star (American)
Odeon (Late Night & 24 Hours)
Old Homestead Restaurant (Steak)
One If by Land, Two If by Sea (Continental)
Orso (Italian)
Palm Restaurant (Steak)
Paradis Barcelona (Spanish)

Parma (Italian)
Peacock (Cafes)
Petaluma (Italian)
Petrossian (French)
Pig Heaven (Chinese)
Pink Tea Cup (Breakfast/Brunch)
PizzaPiazza (Breakfast/Brunch)
Planet Hollywood (Stargazing)
Pongsri Thai (Thai)
Positano (Italian)
Provence (French)
Puglia's (Italian)
Quatorze (French)
Rainbow Promenade (Rooms with a View)
Raoul's (French)
Ravelled Sleave (American)
Ray's Pizza (Pizza)
Red Tulip (Hungarian)
Remi (Italian)
Rene Pujol (French)
River Cafe (Rooms with a View)
Riviera Cafe (Sidewalk Cafes)
Rosa Mexicano (Mexican)
Roumeli Taverna (Greek)
Rumbuls (Cafes)
Russian Tea Room (Stargazing)
The Saloon (Sidewalk Cafes)
Sammy's Roumanian (Jewish)
Sam's Restaurant (American)
Santa Fe (Mexican)
Sardi's (Stargazing)
Sazerac House (Soul/Southern)
Second Avenue Kosher Delicatessen (Delicatessen)
Serendipity 3 (American)
Shun Lee West (Chinese)
The Sign of the Dove (Continental)
SoHo Kitchen and Bar (Wine Bars)
Spark's Steak House (Steak)
Spring Street Natural Restaurant (Health & Vegetarian)
Stage Deli (Delicatessen)
Sugar Reef (Caribbean)
Taste of the Apple (Bars & Burgers)
Tavern-on-the-Green (Rooms with a View)
Telephone Bar & Grill (American)
Tommy Tang's (Thai)
Top of the Sixes (Rooms with a View)
Top of the Tower (Rooms withh a View)
Tout Va Bien (French)
Trattoria dell'Arte (Italian)
Tuesday's (Breakfast/Brunch)
"21" Club (Stargazing)
Umberto's Clam House (Fish & Seafood)
Umeda (Japanese)
Vanessa (American)
Veniero's (Cafes)
Veselka Coffee Shop (Breakfast/Brunch)
Victor's Cafe 52 (Latin American)
World Yacht Cruises (Rooms with a View)
Wylie's (Soul/Southern)
Yellowfingers di Nuovo (Italian)
Zarela (Mexican)
Zinno (Italian)
Zula (Ethiopian)

Latin American

Amazonas
See NIGHTLIFE, Nightclubs.

Bayamo
704 Broadway near East 4 St. 475-5151. Huge funky upbeat Chino-Latino on lower Broadway. Stick to the Latino dishes or the light corn crust pizzas and you'll be nicely fed. There are also classic Cuban sandwiches and some interesting egg dishes. Frozen margaritas draw the boisterous collegiate bar crowd. Reserve. AE, CB, DC, MC, V. *OPEN 7 days 11:30am-2am. Bar till 4am.* $

Brazilian Pavilion
316 East 53 Street. 758-8129. More posh than its West Side "Little Brazil" counterparts. Popular for the unusual Brazilian cocktails, broiled lobster with garlic butter, and the feijoada every night. Reserve. AE, DC, MC, V. *OPEN Mon-Sat noon-11pm. CLOSED Sun.* $$

Cabana Carioca
123 West 45 Street. 561-8088. Close to the theater district, huge portions of simple hearty Brazilian food. The national dish, feijoada, served daily. All-you-can-eat bargain (cash only) lunch buffet from noon to 3pm. Predominately Brazilian national crowd. Convivial, and the food is the best. On two floors; stay downstairs. Reserve. AE, DC, MC, V. *OPEN Sun-Thurs noon-11pm; Fri & Sat noon-midnight.* $

Coffee Shop
29 Union Square West at East 16 St. 243-7969. An unlikely hot spot but just look at the velvet ropes. This coffee shop serves modest moderately priced Brazilian food to the beautiful people nightly till dawn. Sidewalk tables. Reserve! AE only. *OPEN Mon-Fri 7am-6am; Sat 9am-6am; Sun 10am-6am.* $

Sabor
20 Cornelia Street near West 4 St. 243-9579. This small (not for claustrophobics), lively Cuban storefront is the city's best for that island's food. Interesting menu: red snapper in green sauce, roast suckling pig, Cuban pot roast; fresh-fruit daiquiris. Reserve. AE, MC, V. *OPEN Sun-Thurs 5:30pm-11pm; Fri & Sat 5:30pm-midnight.* $$

S.O.B.'s
See NIGHTLIFE, Dance Clubs.

Victor's Cafe 52
236 West 52 Street. 586-7714. Victor was the pioneer purveyor of Cuban cuisine and atmosphere in his longtime cafe on Columbus. He's now firmly ensconced in the theater district. Hearty paella, ropa vieja, grilled pork chops, black bean soup, fried bananas, strong Cuban coffee. Entertainment nightly. AE, CB, DC, MC, V. *OPEN Sun-Thurs noon-1am; Fri & Sat noon-1am.* $$

Mexican

Beach House
399 Greenwich Street at Beach St. 226-7800. In TriBeCa, some of the city's best Mexican in a relaxed, inviting atmosphere. Beautiful Victorian bar, high ceilings, and banquettes from the late, lamented Belmore Cafeteria. Hearty, robust dishes: quite good guacamole, burritos, nachos, pollo mole poblano, and fine regional specialties. For dessert, the bunelos. Reserve for 8 or more. AE, CB, DC, MC, V. *OPEN Mon-Fri noon-10:30pm; Sat & Sun 4pm-10:30pm.* $

Benny's Burritos
113 Greenwich Street at Jane St; 633-9210. And *93 Avenue A at East 6 St; 254-2054. For cheap and cheerful Tex/Mex in either the East or West Villages, check out Benny's. Lava lights, Keen paintings, Formica, and a jukebox with period tunes make up the retro backdrop for humongous portions of satisfying traditional south of the border fare, including foot-long burritos. Popular, cramped, and rowdy. Takeout till midnight. No reservations. No credit cards. *OPEN Mon-Fri 11:30am-1am; Sat 11am-1am; Sun 11am-midnight. *Open 7 days 11am-midnight.* $

Caramba! & !! & !!! & !!!!
918 Eighth Avenue near West 54 St; 245-7910. And 684 Broadway at East 3 St; 420-9817. Also 2567 Broadway at West 96 St, 749-5055; and 1576 Third Avenue near East 88 St, 876-8838. Lively youthful mob scene for Tex-Mex food and slush margaritas (famed for the latter). Downtown is airier and lighter. Good huevos rancheros at weekend brunch. Bunelo is the gluttonous dessert. Be forewarned, the noise level is in direct proportion to margarita consumption. No reservations. AE, CB, DC, MC, V. *OPEN 7 days noon-midnight. Weekend brunch noon-4pm.* $

Cinco de Mayo
Citicorp Center, 153 East 53 Street; 755-5033. And * 114 Greenwich Street; 233-5055. Authentic still-good-but-not-great regional Mexican dishes. Good seafood, grilled meats; dangerous margaritas. Kahlua-based mousse for dessert. Reserve. AE, MC, V. *OPEN Mon-Sat noon-10pm. CLOSED Sun. *OPEN Mon-Fri 11:30am-10:30pm. Takeout Mon-Fri 8am-4pm. CLOSED Sat & Sun.* $$

El Coyote
774 Broadway near East 9 St. 677-4291. The best most inviting Mexican restaurant in the East Village (faint praise). Try the chalupa, chicken en mole, chile rellenos, shrimp con salsa verde, enchiladas suizas, and lobster. Always packed in the pm partly because no reservations are accepted. AE, MC, V. *OPEN Mon-Thurs 11:30am-11:30pm; Fri & Sat 11:30am-1am; Sun 11:30am-11:30pm.* $

El Parador Cafe
325 East 34 Street. 679-6812. Attractive and very popular old-timer. Serves consistently good interesting and inexpensive Mexican food and great margaritas. Has legions of loyal followers; be prepared to wait. No reservations. AE, DC, MC, V. *OPEN Mon-Sat noon-11pm; Sun 1pm-10pm.* $

El Teddy's
219 West Broadway near Franklin St. 941-7070. Funky downtown Mexican attracts a trendy

downtown crowd for made-to-measure margaritas and a mix of trendy and traditional Mexican dishes. The decor and name are a mix of two former tenents, Teddy's Steak House and El International Tapas Bar. Reserve! AE , DC, MC, V. *L Mon-Fri noon-3pm. D Sun-Thurs 6pm-11pm; Fri & Sat 6pm-midnight. Late supper menu Wed-Sat 11pm-2am.* $

Mexico Lindo
459 Second Avenue at East 26 St. 679-3665. Predating New York's Mexican restaurant revolution. Extremely good Mexican food in a pleasant, airy setting. Spanish wine, Mexican and domestic beers. AE, MC, V. *OPEN Mon-Thurs noon-11pm; Fri noon-midnight; Sat 3pm-midnight; Sun 3pm-11pm.* $

Rosa Mexicano
1063 First Avenue at East 58 St. 753-7407. Lively upscale Upper East Side Mexican restaurant held in high esteem by many. Mildly spiced regional dishes prevail; wonderful guacamole and their signature pomegranate margaritas. Reserve. AE, DC, MC, V. *L Mon-Sat noon-3:30pm; Sun buffet noon-3:30pm. D 7 nights 5pm-midnight.* $$

Santa Fe
72 West 69 Street. 724-0822. Nearby Lincoln Center makes this a well-located soothing town house ambience for satisfactory Tex-Mex, powerful margaritas. Reserve. AE, MC, V. *OPEN Sun-Thurs noon-midnight; Fri & Sat noon-12:30am.* $$

Zarela
953 Second Avenue near East 50 St. 644-6740. Zarela Martinez's own premises for her well-regarded, wonderfully authentic (real) Mexican home cooking in a festive environment (quieter upstairs). Good midtown lunch spot. Reservations. AE, CB, DC, MC, V. *L Mon-Fri noon-3pm. D Mon-Thurs 5pm-11pm; Fri & Sat 5pm-11:30pm; Sun 5pm-10pm.* $$

Middle Eastern

Al Amir
1431 Second Avenue at East 74 St. 737-1800. Bright spacious attractive setting for delicious lighter-than-usual Middle Eastern—with an emphasis on Lebanese fare. Reserve. AE, MC, V. *OPEN Mon-Sat 6pm-11pm; Sun noon-11pm.* $$

Cedars of Lebanon
39 East 30 Street. 725-9251. Long-established Lebanese restaurant for shish-kebab, falafel, and a belly dancer Friday and Saturday from 10pm to 3am. Jacket required; no denim. Reserve. AE, CB, DC, MC, V. *OPEN 7 days noon-11pm.* $

La Kasbah
70 West 71 Street. 769-1690. Bustling Glatt kosher Upper West Side spot for enormous portions of chicken, lamb, and vegetarian couscous, baba gannoush, falafel, tabbouleh, and Moroccan salad. Reserve. AE, MC, V. *OPEN Mon-Thurs 5pm-11pm; Sat (winter only after sunset) & Sun 6pm-1:30am. CLOSED Fri & Sat (except in winter).* $

Rectangles
159 Second Avenue at East 10 St. 677-8410. Popular spot for tasty Yemenite and Israeli food (kosher) in a casual cafe setting in the East Village. Outdoor tables on bustling Second Avenue in good weather. AE, MC. V. *OPEN Sun-Thurs 11am-midnight; Fri & Sat 11am-1am. Bar later.* $

Sido Abu Salim
81 Lexington Avenue at East 26 St. 686-2031. Gramercy Park–area eatery for low-priced reliably satisfying fare—especially the couscous—in a modest setting. AE, MC, V. *OPEN 7 days 11am-11pm.* $

Tripoli
156 Atlantic Avenue at Clinton St, Brooklyn. (718) 596-5800. An old-timer in this Middle Eastern neighborhood. Worth a trip to this interesting area for the very good authentic Middle Eastern fare. Reserve weekends. AE, DC. *OPEN 7 days 11am-11pm.* $

Omelettes

Elephant & Castle
68 Greenwich Avenue near West 11 St; 243-1400. And * 183 Prince Street at Sullivan St; 260-3600. Pleasant Village and SoHo restaurants feature 24 delicious variations of omelette. Great burgers, chowders and sandwiches, too; also delicious homemade desserts. Terrific brunch spots—as evidenced by the crowds. Beer and wine only. (*Full bar.) Expect to wait. No reservations. AE, CB, V. *OPEN Mon-Thurs 8:30am-midnight; Fri 8:30am-1am; Sat 10am-1am; Sun 11am-midnight. Breakfast Mon-Fri 8:30am-11:30am. Weekend brunch Sat 10am-5pm; Sun 11am-5pm. *OPEN Mon-Thurs 8am-midnight; Fri 8am-1am; Sat 10am-1am; Sun 10am-midnight. Breakfast Mon-Fri 8am-11:30am. Weekend brunch 10am-5pm.* $

Madame Romaine de Lyon
29 East 61 Street. 758-2422. In a new location (the tearoom setting is gone courtesy of the wrecker's ball) and there is now a French-continental menu at dinner, but for lunch, the 44-year-old tradition continues: exquisite fluffy omelettes from a choice of over 500, filled with caviar or foie gras, ham or spinach, pistacchios or chestnuts, or . . . Brioches, croissants, green salad, lovely desserts, and wine available. All à la carte, and it adds up. Reserve for 3 or more. AE, DC ($15 minimum). Omelettes: *Mon-Fri 11am-3pm; Sat & Sun 10:30am-3:30pm.* $$

Popover Cafe
See Breakfast/Brunch.

Sarabeth's Kitchen
See Breakfast/Brunch.

Pizza

Arturo's Pizzeria
106 West Houston Street at Thompson St. 677-3820. On the Greenwich Village/SoHo border. With the coal-ovens, this is most people's choice when they can't get into John's. There is live

music nightly starting at 6pm. Fun downmarket setting. Reservations taken Monday to Thursday only. AE, MC, V. *OPEN Mon-Thurs 4pm-1am; Fri & Sat 4pm-2am; Sun 3pm-midnight.* $

John's Pizzeria
278 Bleecker Street near Cornelia St; 243-1680. And * 408 East 64 Street; 935-2895. For purists, this longtime Greenwich Village pizzeria serves the city's best and only really authentic pizza, baked in stone-floor ovens—thin-crust, garlicky, topped with fresh ingredients. Pies only, no slices, devoured in the old-fashioned setting of booths, celebrity photos, and painted murals of Italy. (The Village annex alleviates the crowds but has less character.) Beer and wine. *Outdoor dining. No reservations and there's almost always a wait. No credit cards. *OPEN 7 days 11:30am-11:30pm.* *OPEN Sun-Thurs 11:30am-11:15pm; Fri & Sat 11:30am-12:15am.* $

Mezzaluna
See Italian.

Mezzogiorno
See Italian.

PizzaPiazza
See Breakfast/Brunch.

Ray's Pizza
465 Sixth Avenue at West 11 St. 243-2253. The Famous, the Original, the Best. When you hear people say that Ray's is the best slice, this is the Ray's they mean. The line moves quickly. *OPEN Sun-Thurs 11am-2am; Fri & Sat 11am-3am.* $

Polish

Christine's
344 Lexington Avenue near East 39 St; 953-1920. And, 438 Second Avenue at East 25 St; 684-1879. Also 208 First Avenue near East 12 St, 505-0376. Well-run Polish coffee shops for homemade soups, blintzes, borscht, pierogi, kielbasa, and other filling budget-priced—especially for midtown—fare. Reserve for dinner only for 4 or more. Beer and wine. AE only. *OPEN 7 days 11am-9pm.* $

Kiev International
See Late Night & 24 Hours.

The Stage
See Inexpensive.

Veselka Coffee Shop
See Breakfast/Brunch.

Rooms with a View

American Festival Cafe
See American.

Anna's Harbor Restaurant
565 City Island Avenue, City Island, Bronx. 885-1373. Very good Italian seafood specialties and bouillabaisse daily in New York's own salty little seaport. The glass-enclosed dining room affords views of the harbor. Reserve on weekends. AE, MC, V. *OPEN Sun-Fri 11am-11pm; Sat 11am-1am.* $$

The Boathouse Cafe
Loeb Boathouse, Central Park Lake at 74 Street (enter the park at 72 St). 517-3623. This seasonal cafe in an unmatched sylvan setting on the lake is pure delight when you can dine alfresco on the umbrella-shaded deck. The food—salads, pastas, and the like—is okay, the service slow but amiable—you won't mind sitting here. From 5pm nightly you can go for a ride on the lake in an authentic Venetian gondola, *The Daughter of Venice*, and have the cost added to your dinner bill —it's magical (*see* SIGHTSEEING, Boat Trips). Practical note: The Boathouse Cafe trolley picks up dinner patrons at 72 Street and Fifth Avenue. Reservations taken for groups of 6 or more. AE, DC, MC, V. *OPEN Tues-Fri noon-9:30pm; Fri, Sat & Sun noon-11pm. Cocktails 7 days 4pm-6pm.* $

City Lights Bar & Hors D'Oeuvrerie
Windows on the World, 1 World Trade Center. 938-1111. From 3pm each day, enjoy a cocktail and hors d'oeuvres (à la carte) and one of the world's most exciting views a quarter of a mile in the sky! Piano music from 4pm. Jacket required; no denim. Cover charge only after 7:30pm (4pm on Sunday). AE, CB, DC, MC, V. City Lights Bar: *OPEN Mon-Fri 3pm-1am; Sat noon-1am; Sun noon-9pm.* Hors D'Oeuvrerie: *OPEN Mon-Sat 3pm-1am; Sun 4pm-9pm.* $

Delegate's Dining Room
The United Nations, Visitor's Entrance, First Avenue & East 46 Street, Conference Building, 4th floor. (NOTE: You will need a pass, so a photo ID is required.) 963-7625. Whether or not you are visiting the UN, this is a fine place to lunch in the midtown east area. The food is good, the setting civilized, there is a view of the East River, and talk about a window on the world—representatives of the member nations dine here daily. Reserve. AE, DC, MC, V. *OPEN Mon-Fri 11:30am-2:30pm.* $

Hudson River Club
World Financial Center, 250 Vesey Street, second floor. 786-1500. One of the prettiest places to dine and imbibe in the Wall Street area. Posh but unpretentious dining rooms, overlooking the yacht marina and affording views of the Statue of Liberty and Ellis Island, in which to feast on food and wine originating in the Hudson Valley region. Lovely Sunday brunch from noon to 3pm. Jacket and tie. Reserve. AE, MC, V. *L Mon-Sat 11:30am-2:30pm. D Mon-Sat 5:30pm-9:30pm; Sun noon-6pm.* $$$$

Nirvana
30 Central Park South, 15th floor. 486-5700. Okay Indo-Bengali cuisine in an extremely romantic setting overlooking Central Park. Spectacular view; some interesting regional dishes. Live sitar music. Reserve. AE, CB, DC, MC, V. *OPEN year-round noon-1am.* $$

Rainbow Promenade
30 Rockefeller Plaza, 65th floor. 632-5000. On the 65th floor of 30 Rock, adjacent to the Rainbow Room (*see* NIGHTLIFE, Dining & Dancing: Rainbow Room), there's this "little meals" bar/

restaurant. With the city night as backdrop, a nightcap at the serpentine bar, with a Norman Bel Geddes model of a 1930s oceanliner suspended above it, or at one of the cozy terraced tables may very well be the most romantic part of the evening. No reservations required. Also in this venue a delightful prix-fixe brunch served from 11:30am to 3pm (reserve). AE only. *OPEN Mon-Thurs 3pm-1am; Fri 3pm-2am; Sat noon-2am; Sun 11:30am-11pm.* $

The Rainbow Room
See NIGHTLIFE, Dining & Dancing.

River Cafe
1 Water Street at the East River beside the Brooklyn Bridge, Brooklyn. (718) 522-5200. Located on a permanently moored barge adjacent to the Brooklyn Bridge. The spectacular view of Lower Manhattan's towers is picture-postcard perfect; the food is wonderfully original American fare. Fine weather offers light dining opportunities on the outdoor patio. If you can't afford the pricey prix-fixe dinner do go for a drink or brunch. Piano bar till 1am. It's oh so romantic. Jacket required. Reserve well in advance. AE, CB, DC. *L Mon-Fri noon-3pm. D 7 days 6pm-11pm. Weekend brunch Sat 11:30am-2:30pm; Sun noon-2:30pm.* $$$$

Sea Grill
See Fish & Seafood.

Tavern-on-the-Green
Central Park West at West 67 Street. 873-3200. The Central Park setting and the dazzling Crystal Room (accept no substitution) make this restaurant a must. It's hard to believe that this opulent building was once a sheepfold housing 200 sheep and a shepherd—from 1870 to 1934. The menu offers a wide variety of choice and price including a great value pretheater. In summer it's one of the city's most bucolic settings for dining and dancing to a live orchestra (May to October, Tuesday to Sunday from 9pm to 1am); anytime, it's a joyful place. Reserve (especially for the Crystal Room, none are taken for the Garden). AE, CB, DC, MC, V. *L Mon-Fri 11:30am-3:30pm. D Mon-Thurs 5:30pm-11pm; Fri & Sat 5pm-11:30pm; Sun 5:30pm-10pm. Pretheater menu Mon-Sat 5:30pm-6:15pm. Weekend brunch 10am-3:30pm.* $$

The Terrace
Butler Hall, 400 West 119 Street at Morningside Dr. 666-9490. Only 16 stories up, but it offers a glittering panoramic view of the city, the George Washington Bridge, and the Palisades. Good French food in a beautifully romantic skylight penthouse setting, outdoor terrace in summer. Harp music adds to the special-occasion feeling. Reserve. Jacket required. Free valet parking. AE, DC, MC, V. *L Tues-Fri noon-3:30pm. D Tues-Thurs 6pm-10pm; Fri & Sat 6pm-10:30pm. CLOSED Sun & Mon.* $$$

Top of the Sixes
666 Fifth Avenue at 53 St. 757-6662. A spacious clubby restaurant/lounge on the 39th floor for great city viewing. Great spot for after-work cocktails and the wonderful finger-food hors

d'oeuvres from 5pm to 7pm. Also some inexpensive albeit unmemorable lunch choices. No denim. Reserve for dining. AE, DC, MC, V. *OPEN Mon-Sat 11:30am-11pm (kitchen till 11:30pm). CLOSED Sun.* $$$

Top of the Tower
Beekman Tower, 3 Mitchell Place, East 49 St & First Ave, 26th floor. 355-7300. Glass-enclosed wraparound roof terrace, romantic cocktail-lounge ambience. Dazzling views in all directions of midtown and the river; perfect at sunset. Piano music Tuesday to Saturday from 9pm. AE, DC, MC, V. No cover or minimum. Cocktails and light snacks: *7 days 5pm-2am.* $

The View Restaurant
Marriott Marquis Hotel, 1535 Broadway at West 46 St. 704-8900. On the 47th floor of this remarkably ugly building a revolving restaurant and lounge smack in the middle of the Great White Way. Recommended for the fine continental cuisine, convenience for theatergoers, and the dazzling 360-degree midtown view. The prix-fixe pretheater dinner served nightly from 5pm to 7pm and the Sunday brunch buffet served from 10:30am to 2:30pm are the best times to find other New Yorkers there. On matinee days—Wednesday and Saturday—an all-you-can-eat lunch buffet. On the 48th floor, the revolving lounge with drink and light fare. Jacket required. Reserve. AE, CB, DC, MC, V. *L Wed & Sat 11am-2pm. D Sun-Thurs 5:30pm-11pm; Fri & Sat 5pm-midnight.* $$$

The Water Club
East River at East 30 Street (from FDR Drive enter service road at East 23 St). 683-3333. Sophisticated, albeit expensive, dining on the East River on a permanently moored glass-enclosed barge. Enhanced by fireplaces, skylights, and sweeping views of the river. Topside open-air deck for drinks and light fare in good weather. Jacket requested. Reserve. Valet parking. AE, CB, DC, MC, V. *L Mon-Fri noon-2pm. D Mon-Fri 5:30pm-11pm; Sat 5:45pm-11:15pm; Sun 5:45pm-10pm. Weekend brunch Sat noon-2:15pm; Sun 11:30am-2:45pm.* $$$

Water's Edge Restaurant
East River Yacht Club, East River & 44 Drive, Long Island City, Queens. (718) 482-0033. Lovely wood-paneled formal restaurant close by the 59 Street Bridge offers a wonderful East River/midtown Manhattan panorama and an eclectic menu with a seafood emphasis. Open-air deck; glass-enclosed dining room. Jacket required. Reserve. AE, DC. *L Mon-Fri noon-3pm. D Mon-Sat 6pm-11pm.* NOTE: In good weather months a ferry takes diners from the 23 Street Marina in Manhattan hourly from 6pm to 11pm, returning on the half hour. $$

Windows on the World
1 World Trade Center, 107th floor. 938-1111. Quite simply one of the world's most spectacular restaurants. The food, though secondary to the view, which is unsurpassed, is quite good, with a pleasing variety of entrees, prix fixe (a relative bargain) or à la carte. Also, the special Sunset

Supper, Monday though Saturday 5pm to 6:30pm, Sunday till 7:30pm, is a good bet. The wonderful service is a plus; the wine list is exceptional and unexpectedly affordable. Reserve very well in advance and then pray for a clear night. Jacket and tie required; no denim. AE, CB, DC, MC, V. *D Mon-Sat 5pm-10pm. Lunch buffet Sat noon-3pm; Sun noon-7:30pm.* For other dining options on the 107th floor, *see* City Lights Bar & Hors D'Oeuvrerie, *and* Deluxe: Cellar in the Sky. $$$

World Yacht Cruises
World Yacht Enterprises, Pier 62, West 23 Street at the Hudson River. 929-7090. For years Paris has had the Bateaux Mouches and New Yorkers have wondered why not here. Well, now we have our own version of the floating restaurant with a view (though the food is better in Paris). Even jaded New Yorkers enjoy the dazzle of the skyline, as the yacht (one of four) glides around the tip of Lower Manhattan. Dinner is served, lunch and brunch are buffet-style, and there's dancing in the pm. Pricey, but the experience if not the meal is worth it. You must reserve with a credit card (cancellations within 48 hours or you forfeit the cost). AE, DC, MC, V. You may board one hour before sailing for cocktails (not included in the prix fixe). Jacket required. Parking available. *Year-round, 7 days: L 12:30pm-2:30pm. D 7pm-10pm. Sun brunch 12:30pm-2:30pm.* $$

Scandinavian

Aquavit
13 West 54 Street. 307-7311. Handsome two-level town house (formerly belonging to Nelson Rockefeller) setting for wonderful Scandinavian dining. Downstairs the more formal dramatic atrium dining room for lovely simple fish dishes and deftly prepared meat choices. Upstairs a more casual less-expensive bar/cafe for light fare: Danish open sandwiches, Swedish meatballs, smorgasbord plates, a variety of aquavits. Jacket required downstairs only. Reserve downstairs. AE, MC, V. *L Mon-Fri noon-3pm. D Mon-Sat 5:30pm-10pm. CLOSED Sun.*
Downstairs prix-fixe lunch and dinner $$
Upstairs à la carte menu $

Sidewalk Cafes

Columbus Avenue and the South Street Seaport offer a variety of opportunities to sup outdoors. This selection represents the best in every neighborhood. For more alfresco dining opportunities, see also Cafes *and* Garden/Outdoor Dining.

Cafe de la Paix
St. Moritz Hotel, Central Park South at Sixth Avenue. 755-5800. Well-situated cafe—across from Central Park—for drinks or brunch. AE, CB, DC, MC, V. *L Mon-Fri noon-4pm. D 7 days 5:30pm-11pm. Sun brunch 11:30am-4pm.* $

Figaro Cafe
186 Bleecker Street at MacDougal St. 677-

1100. Reincarnation of long-established Village coffeehouse is a relaxed spot for good burgers, cheese and fruit board, a late-night cappuccino or espresso with pastry. Grab a seat at the outdoor sidewalk cafe in good weather at this busy Greenwich Village crossroad. On Wednesdays and weekends, live music. No reservations. No credit cards. *OPEN Mon-Thurs 11am-2am; Fri 11am-4am; Sat 9am-4am; Sun 9am-2am.* $

Fiorello's Roman Cafe
1900 Broadway near West 63 St. 595-5330. Bright, bustling cafe best for salads, pasta, and very good pizza in a pan (it gets too expensive for what you get if you go beyond these). Outdoor cafe in summer for Lincoln Center crowd-watching. Reserve. AE, MC, V. *OPEN Mon-Sat noon-midnight; Sun noon-11pm; Sun brunch 11am-3pm.* $

Fountain Cafe
Lincoln Center Plaza, Broadway & West 64 Street. 874-7000. As close to a Roman piazza as you can find in New York. A special spot for a light lunch, dinner, or just drinks, while the ballet and opera set head for the performances. AE, MC, V. *OPEN May-Sept, weather permitting, Sun-Thurs noon-9pm. Fri & Sat noon-9pm.* $

Riviera Cafe
225 West 4 Street at Seventh Ave South. 242-8732. Indoor/outdoor cafe best known as the best spot to see, and be seen, in Greenwich Village. In winter, two fireplaces make up for the sidewalk cafe's hibernation. *OPEN 7 days noon-3am or 4am.* $

The Saloon
1920 Broadway at West 64 St. 874-1500. Best when you can sit at the sidewalk terrace with all its seats facing front, and watch the West Side crowds go by. Satisfying—if you keep it simple—food. Reserve. AE, CB, DC, MC, V. *OPEN Sun-Thurs 11:30am-midnight (bar till 1am); Fri & Sat 11:30am-2am (bar till 3am).* $

Terrace Cafe
Stanhope Hotel, Fifth Avenue & 81 Street. 288-5800. Perhaps the most civilized sidewalk cafe in New York, for sophisticated-people watching and a view of the Metropolitan Museum of Art. A light menu and cocktails. AE, MC, V. In season, *OPEN 7 days noon-9:30pm.* $

Soul/Southern

Acme Bar & Grill
9 Great Jones Street (East 3 St west of Lafayette). 420-1934. Funky garagelike setting, "decorated" with hot sauce labels and bottles. The food is well priced, tasty (sometime tongue-searing), and home-style. Southern specialties include steamed oysters, fried shrimp, blackened trout, oyster po'boys, grilled pork chops, catfish sandwiches, sides of corn fritters, hush puppies, and black-eyed peas. No reservations. No credit cards. *OPEN Sun-Thurs 11:30am-midnight; Fri & Sat 11:30am-1am. Weekend brunch 11:30am-4pm.* $

B. Smith's
771 Eighth Avenue at West 47 St. 247-2222. Run by model Barbara Smith, it is a stylish multiracial theater district spot for hot food, cool jazz, and some very diverse pretty-people watching at the bar. P.S. Don't miss the sweet potato pie! Reserve. AE, DC, MC, V. *OPEN 7 days noon-midnight.* $$

Cajun
129 Eighth Avenue at West 16 St. 691-6174. Longtime Chelsea practitioner of Cajun cooking. Gumbo, jambalaya, shrimp Creole, and crab cakes in a convivial Chelsea bar/restaurant. Live Dixieland jazz Monday to Saturday from 8:30pm. The Sunday jazz brunch from noon to 4pm is great fun. Reserve for 6 or more. AE, DC, MC, V. *L Mon-Fri noon-3pm. D Mon-Thurs 6pm-11pm; Fri & Sat 6pm-1am; Sun 5:30pm-10:30pm.* $

Gulf Coast
489 West Street at the West Side Highway. 206-8790. Down-market, extremely funky, and noisy Louisiana-style restaurant in the far West Village. Features a changing menu of Cajun/Creole dishes: shrimp grilled over mesquite, crawfish etouffee, deep-fried catfish. The crowd is young, raucous, and oblivious. Sunday brunch from 12:30pm to 3:30pm. Live music Monday and Tuesday from 9:30pm. Reserve. AE only. *OPEN Mon-Thurs 5pm-11:30pm; Fri & Sat 5pm-1am; Sun 12:30pm-11:30pm.* $

Jezebel
630 Ninth Avenue at West 45 St. 582-1045. A mood-piece of a restaurant where fringed shawls, ceiling fans, and vintage linens form a unique nostalgic bordellolike backdrop for the satisfying Southern cooking. Yummy corn bread, spare ribs, honey chicken, shrimp Creole, curried goat, accompanied by grits, yams, sweet potato pie, and, for dessert, bread pudding. Prices higher than you'd expect for such homey fare, but it's a terrific theater district choice. It's madness for pretheater (be forewarned, service is akin to molasses) if you can get a reservation, more subdued after, but best around 9pm when the piano music helps set the mood. Jacket required. Reserve. AE only. *OPEN 7 days 5:30pm-11:45pm. Bar till 1am.* $$

K-Paul's New York
622 Broadway near Bleecker St. 460-9633. Northern outpost of famed New Orleans chef, Paul Prudhomme (he shuttles between both), considered one of the most authentic for deftly seasoned Cajun popcorn, roasted sweet andouille, and jambalaya. Portions are huge; the Cajun martinis lethal; and the desserts obscene after such a feast. Reserve. AE, MC, V. *OPEN Tues-Sat 5:30pm-11pm. CLOSED Sun & Mon.* $$$

Memphis
329 Columbus Avenue near West 75 St. 496-1840. Handsome bilevel cafe featuring Cajun/Creole cooking; star-studded stylish crowd (the owners are actors). Try the gumbo, Belle River crayfish plate, crunchy fried chicken, Cajun popcorn, jambalaya, and whiskey-soaked bread pudding. Noisy; joyful, socially active bar scene. Reserve. AE, CB, DC, MC, V. *OPEN Mon-Thurs 6pm-11pm; Fri & Sat 6pm-1:30am; Sun 6pm-10pm.* $$

Sazerac House
533 Hudson Street at Charles St. 989-0313. Relaxed old-fashioned tin-ceilinged Greenwich Village eatery with enclosed sidewalk cafe and fireplace. Serves American food with an emphasis on New Orleans–style specialties: jambalaya, Louisiana crab chops. Good burgers, too. Weekend brunch from 11am to 4:30pm. AE, DC, MC, V. *OPEN 7 days noon-midnight.* $

Sylvia's
328 Lenox Avenue near West 126 St. 996-0660. Sylvia Woods is known as the "Queen of Soul Food," and her restaurant has been a Harlem institution for more than 30 years. Don't hesitate to head uptown for some of her down-home Southern specialties, including her famed braised ribs, fried or smothered chicken with black-eyed peas, collard green, yams, sweet potato pie (a must!), fresh-baked corn bread. Bargained-priced Sunday brunch from 1pm to 3pm. Low-frills counter, pleasantly serviced tables. Two jukeboxes add to the 50s flavor. No reservations for parties of less than 8 people. No credit cards. *OPEN Mon-Sat 7:30am-10pm.* $

Wylie's
891 First Avenue at East 50 St. 751-0700. Terrific baby-back ribs, fried onion loaf in a raucous downhome East Side setting. No reservations. AE, DC, MC, V. *OPEN 7 days 11:30am-midnight.* $

Spanish

Alcala
349 Amsterdam Avenue near West 76 St. 769-9600. Upper West Siders are fans of this large contemporary Spanish restaurant serving terrific tapas, roast suckling pig, and Iberian standards such as paella. Good Spanish wine list. Reserve. AE, DC, MC, V. *OPEN Mon-Thurs 5:30pm-11pm (cold tapas till 11:30pm); Fri & Sat 5:30pm-midnight; Sun 2pm-10pm.* $$

El Faro
823 Greenwich Street at Horatio St. 929-8210. Extremely popular, longtime (over 30 years), small Spanish restaurant in the West Village redolent with garlic. No reservations, be prepared to wait. AE, CB, DC, MC, V. *OPEN Sun-Thurs 11am-midnight; Fri & Sat 11am-1am.* $$

El Rincon de Espana
226 Thompson Street near Bleecker St. 260-4950. Busy, congenial Greenwich Village standby. Authentic recommended dishes include the hearty paella, all seafood dishes, the arroz con pollo, and the octopus. From Wednesday to Saturday a strolling guitarist in the pm. Reserve. AE, CB, DC, MC, V. *OPEN Sun-Thurs 11am-11pm; Fri & Sat 11am-midnight.* $$

Harlequin
569 Hudson Street at West 11 St. 255-4950.

Tranquil, contemporary, very personally operated West Village restaurant for anything-but-run-of-the-mill Spanish fare. Regional dishes, imaginatively prepared, as well as the best paella this side of the Pyrenees. Good Spanish wine selection. Reserve. AE, DC, MC, V. *L Mon-Fri noon-3pm; Sat & Sun noon-4pm. D Mon-Sat 5:30pm-11pm; Sun 5:30pm-10:30pm. Sun brunch noon-4pm.*   **$$$$**

Paradis Barcelona
145 East 50 Street. 754-3333. The first American outpost of a Barcelona-based operation. Lavish spacious dining room, good Catalonia regional cuisine; tapas bar and a wide selection of Spanish wines. Pianist nightly. Jacket preferred. Reserve. AE, MC, V. *L Mon-Fri noon-3pm. D 7 days 5pm-11:30pm. Sun brunch noon-4pm.*   **$$$$**

—Tapas

Literally meaning lid, the term derives from the habit of Spaniards to put a slice of bread over an open bottle of wine to keep the flies out. Putting a piece of sausage on the bread was a logical next step. In any case, a new dining experience was born. Almost all of the Spanish restaurants listed above do some version of these.

The Ballroom
253 West 28 Street. 244-3005. Tapas, a Spanish tradition transplanted to this charming Chelsea setting by the late first chef Felipe Rojas-Lombardi. At the colorful bar or in the dining room eat your way through an exotic, mouthwatering selection of these morsels. The cooking is authentic; priced by the plate like dim sum—it can add up. Well-prepared entrees and specials as well. Tapas buffet prix-fixe lunch. This is also one of the best cabarets in the city (*see* NIGHTLIFE, Cabaret). Reserve. AE, CB, DC, MC, V. *OPEN Tues-Fri noon-1am; Sat 4:30pm-1am; Sun noon-9pm. CLOSED Mon.*   **$$$**

Stargazing

The following are some places where the "stars" are almost certain to be spotted—especially late pm or early am. But in New York you're just as likely to see someone famous next to you waiting for takeout at the Second Avenue Deli (where, to name only two, Mary Tyler Moore and Paul Newman—separately—have been seen getting chicken soup to go).

Elaine's
1703 Second Avenue near East 88 St. 534-8103. Overhyped "literary and theatrical watering hole." Small, crowded, informal, passable—mainly Italian—specialties. Your treatment depends on what best-selling author is ahead or even behind you in line. Woody Allen is a virtual fixture here but in this case you might question his taste. Other regulars include Sam Shepard and Norman Mailer. Reserve. AE only. *L Mon-Fri noon-3pm. D 7 days 5:30pm-2am.*   **$$**

Joe Allen
326 West 46 Street. 581-6464. Relaxed late-night bar and restaurant favored by theater crowd—both the actors and the audience. In the rear a skylight dining room. Basic fare: steaks, chili burgers, some daily specials. Bass Ale on tap. Reserve. MC, V. *OPEN Mon, Tues, Thurs, Fri & Sun noon-1am; Wed & Sat 11:30am-1am.*   **$**

Le Cirque
See Deluxe.

Planet Hollywood
140 West 57 Street. 333-7827. It's not easy to get in to dine at this museum of movie memorabilia unless you're a friend of one of the owners—Bruce, Arnold, Sly (Willis, Schwarzenegger, Stallone). Overhead flash snippets of film, and on the menu a hit parade of recent food fads—BBQ pizza, blackened shrimp, Buffalo wings. On display: E.T.'s bike, Dorothy's dress from *The Wizard of Oz*, Jack Lemmon's frock from *Some Like It Hot*, the knife from *Psycho*, and more. No reservations. AE, MC, V. *OPEN 7 days 11am-1am.* **$**

Russian Tea Room
150 West 57 Street. 265-0947. One of the best for some remarkably authentic Russian food and a colorful New York crowd—dancers, musicians, impresarios, you, and me. Stick with the blinis and caviar, the chicken Kiev, and don't miss the best borscht in the city. (Lighter, less caloric dishes are now also available.) Extremely celebratory possibly because there's a vodka menu and Christmas decorations year-round. Liza Minnelli and Rudolf Nureyev prefer downstairs and so should you. Don't let them steer you upstairs to Siberia (unless their cabaret series is on up there). Jacket required for dinner. NOTE: OPEN on holidays—even more festive times to go. A la carte supper menu from 9:30pm, brunch menu weekends 11am to 4pm. Reserve. AE, CB, DC, MC V. *OPEN Mon-Fri 11:30am-11:30pm; Sat & Sun 11am-11:30pm.*   **$$$**

Sardi's
234 West 44 Street. 221-8440. Long-revered traditional site for Broadway-opening parties to await reviews. Celebrity caricatures line the wall, and one or two stars grace the premises nightly. The food? Well, if it were located elsewhere no one would come. Reserve. AE, CB, DC, MC, V. *OPEN Mon-Sat 11:30am-12:30am. CLOSED Sun.*   **$$$**

TriBeCa Grill
375 Greenwich Street at Franklin St. 941-3900. This vibrant TriBeCa outpost qualifies as a stargazer for no other reason than its owners represent a stellar collection of Hollywood leading men including Robert DeNiro, Mikhail Baryshnikov, and Christopher Walken, among others. The spacious dining room, with its huge bar salvaged from Maxwell's Plum (if mahogany could only talk), is attractive, the contemporary American fare quite good, the service professional. Reserve. AE, DC, MC, V. *L Mon-Fri noon-2:30pm. D Mon-Thurs 6pm-10:45pm; Fri & Sat 6pm-11:15pm; Sun 6pm-9:45pm. Sun brunch 11:30pm-3pm.*   **$$$**

"21" Club
21 West 52 Street. 582-7200. Triple-parked limos mark the spot for this de facto club in a renewed but unchanged turn-of-the-century setting. Noisy celebrated downstairs bar is where the "power" people lunch and sup, upstairs is quieter, less interesting. The place and menu have undergone facelifts but there's still the famed oversized pricey "21" burger, the chicken hash, the steak tartare, and the lobster salad. Impressive wine list. Good pretheater special. Jacket and tie required. Reserve. AE, CB, DC, MC, "21" charge. *L Mon-Sat noon-3pm. D Mon-Sat 6pm-12:30am. CLOSED Sun.* $$$$

Steak

Assembly Steak House
16 West 51 Street. 581-3580. Popular and noisy at lunchtime. Known for good-quality steaks, done to your specification. Reserve. AE, CB, DC, MC, V. *OPEN Mon-Fri 11am-10pm. CLOSED Sat & Sun.* $$$$

Christ Cella
160 East 46 Street. 697-2479. Justly renowned for excellent steaks, chops, and lobsters. Conservative, almost Spartan environment and service. Jacket and tie required. Reserve. AE, CB, DC, MC, V. *OPEN Mon-Fri noon-10:30pm; Sat 5pm-10:45pm. CLOSED Sun.* $$$$

Frank's
431 West 14 Street. 243-1349 or -9641. This old Italian steak house has been around for 80 years—in the "colorful" (as in *Irma La Douce*) Gansevoort wholesale meat market district. The sawdust on the floor and the tin ceiling are authentic; the welcome is warm; the prime beef steaks and chops very fine; and the wonderful pasta appetizers large enough for two. Well-priced wine list. AE, CB, DC, MC, V. *L Mon-Fri 10am-3pm. D Mon-Thurs 5pm-10pm; Fri & Sat 5pm-11pm. CLOSED Sun.* $$

Gallagher's
228 West 52 Street. 245-5336. Popular old-time Broadway-area sports hangout complete with red-checkered tablecloths and sawdust on the floor, for humongous high-quality hickory-cooked steaks, good seafood as well; great rice pudding. Glass refrigerator to view the steaks aging. Jacket preferred. Reserve. AE, CB, DC, MC, V. *OPEN 7 days noon-midnight.* $$$$

Hamilton House
101 Street & Fourth Avenue off Belt Parkway, Fort Hamilton, Brooklyn. (718) 745-6359 or -0600. Old-fashioned elegance in Brooklyn for steaks, chops, and seafood with views overlooking the Verrazano Narrows Bridge. Parking facilities. No denim. Reserve. AE, MC. *OPEN Tues-Sat 4:30pm-11pm; Sun 3pm-10pm. Sun brunch noon-2:30pm. CLOSED Mon.* $$

Kenny's Steak Pub
565 Lexington Avenue near East 50 St. 355-0666. Comfortable, friendly, midtown steak house attracts a sports crowd. Very good steaks. For the hardy, steak and eggs (among other choices) breakfast from 7am to noon. Reserve. AE, CB, DC, MC, V. *OPEN 7 days 7am-midnight.* $$

Le Steak
1089 Second Avenue near East 57 St. 421-9072. Longtime cozy East Side bistro where decisions are kept to a minimum. French-style steak with a delicious mustard herb sauce, great pommes frites, and salad or onion soup; now also swordfish for noncarnivores. Good value. Reserve. AE, DC, MC, V. *OPEN Sun-Thurs 5:30pm-10:30pm; Fri & Sat 5:30pm-11pm* $$

Old Homestead Restaurant
56 Ninth Avenue at West 14 St. 242-9040. Open since 1868, it's New York's oldest steak house. In addition to the steaks—including Japanese Kobi steak at $100 a serving!—copious portions of shrimp, lobster, and prime rib. Reserve. AE, CB, DC, MC, V. *OPEN Mon-Fri noon-10:45pm; Sat 1pm-11:45pm; Sun 1pm-10:45pm.* $$

Palm Restaurant
837 Second Avenue near East 45 St. 687-2953. Sawdusted floors and caricature-covered walls create the nostalgic backdrop for this very noisy, upbeat steak and lobster house, considered the best by many. Excellent steaks and enormous lobsters, good cottage fries and crispy onion rings. Watch the bill add up, it's all à la carte, including the pedestrian vegetables. If too crowded, go across the street to **Palm, Too.** Reserve. AE, CB, DC, MC, V. *OPEN Mon-Fri noon-11:30pm; Sat 5pm-11:30pm. CLOSED Sun.* $$$$

Pen & Pencil
205 East 45 Street. 682-8660. Longtime reliable midtown steak house gets high marks from carnivores. Very popular at lunchtime. Reserve. AE, CB, DC, MC, V. *OPEN Mon-Fri 11:45am-10pm; Sat 4pm-11pm; Sun 4:30pm-10pm. Pretheater dinner 4:30pm-7pm.* $$$

Peter Luger
178 Broadway at Driggs Ave, Brooklyn. (718) 387-7400. Located for over 100 years in a now depressed edge of Brooklyn just across the Williamsburg Bridge, one of the legendary bests. Bare-essential decor and service, no-frills accompaniments to the huge delicious porterhouse steaks and double lamb chops. Reservations required and you will still have a wait. No credit cards. *OPEN Mon-Thurs 11:45am-9:45pm; Fri 11:30am-11pm; Sat 11:45am-11:45pm; Sun 1pm-10:45pm.* $$$

Pietro's
232 East 43 Street. 682-9760. Regulars still flock to this 50-year-old Italian steak house in relatively new quarters. Known for their quite good generous-sized steaks with delicious shoestring, Lyonnaise, or au gratin potatoes. Wide choice of veal and chicken dishes, Caesar salad, too. For dessert, don't miss the zabaglione. Reserve. AE, DC, MC, V. *OPEN Mon-Fri noon-10:30pm; Sat 5:30pm-10:30pm. CLOSED Sat & Sun in summer.* $$$$

The Post House
28 East 63 Street. 935-2888. Attractive albeit noisy place for steak, less macho than the rest. Good steak, chops, seafood, game in season. Fine desserts. Good wine list. Jacket requested. Reserve. AE, DC, MC, V. *OPEN Mon-Fri noon-midnight; Sat & Sun 5pm-11:30pm.* $$

Spark's Steak House
210 East 46 Street. 687-4855. Informal restaurant, well known for very fine steaks and lobsters and the excellent extensive wine list. Jacket required. Reserve. AE, CB, DC, MC, V. *L Mon-Fri noon-3pm. D Mon-Thurs 5pm-11pm; Fri & Sat 5pm-11:30pm. CLOSED Sun.* $$

Swiss

Chalet Suisse
6 East 48 Street. 355-0855. The city's oldest, most authentic, most charming and best Swiss restaurant. Try the bundnerfleisch, veal à la Suisse, rack of lamb, and wonderful rosti. Pricey unless you have the fondue; chocolate fondue for dessert. Jacket required. Reservations required. AE, DC, MC, V. *L Mon-Fri noon-2:30pm. D 5pm-9:30pm. CLOSED Sat & Sun.* $$$$

La Fondue
43 West 55 Street. 581-0820. A pleasant inexpensive° midtown spot, popular and casual, features Swiss fondue and light meals of fruit, cheese, bread, and wine, and of course, chocolate fondue. Heartier fare, too. Reservations for 4 or more. No credit cards. *OPEN Mon-Sat 11:45am-midnight; Sun 11:45am-11pm.* $

Swiss Inn
311 West 48 Street. 459-9280. In the theater district, comfort and good filling food at affordable prices. Cheese fondue for two, mixed grill, smoked pork chops. Reserve. AE, CB, DC, MC, V. *L Mon-Fri noon-2:30pm. D Mon-Sat 5pm-10pm. CLOSED Sun.* $

Thai

Bangkok Cuisine
885 Eighth Avenue near West 52 St. 581-6370. Authentic savory Thai cuisine. Interesting eating, courteous service, colorful setting. Good for pre- or posttheater dining. Reserve. AE, MC, V. *OPEN Mon-Sat 11:30am-11:30pm; Sun 5pm-11:30pm.* $

Bangkok House
1485 First Avenue near East 77 St. 249-5700. Top-rated for authentic Thai fare, much of which sizzles. Try the "jungle curry," the pork in green curry, or the barbecued chicken (gai yang). Thai beer. All in a pleasant setting. Reserve during the week only. AE, DC, MC, V. *OPEN 7 days 5pm-11pm.* $

Pongsri Thai
244 West 48 Street; 582-3392. And 106 Bayard Street near Mulberry St; 349-3132. Uptown in a spacious theater district locale or downtown in

the more spartan Chinatown location (formerly called Thailand), you will dine well on wonderful Thai seafood specialties. Full bar. Reserve. AE, CB, DC, MC, V. *OPEN 7 days 11:30am-11:30pm.* $

Sukhathai West
411 West 42 Street. 947-1930. Perfect for theater area dining. Savory and zesty Thai food in an attractive setting. Flavorful choices include tasty soups, charbroiled jumbo shrimp, steamed mussels, chicken satay, deep-fried shrimp in bean curd. Full bar. Reserve on weekends. AE, MC, V. *OPEN Sun-Thurs 5pm-11pm; Fri & Sat 5pm-midnight.* $

Tommy Tang's
323 Greenwich Street near Reade St. 334-9190. Via L.A., trendy spot for pricey California-accented Thai. Zesty choices include "naked shrimp," ginger beef with black beans, blackened whole chili fish, and, to cool the palate, homemade sorbets. Reserve. AE, MC, V. *L Mon-Fri 11:30am-3pm. D Mon-Thurs 6pm-11:30pm; Fri & Sat 6pm-midnight.* $$$

Turkish

Anatolia
1422 Third Avenue near East 80 St. 517-6262. A vibrantly painted, extremely lively Turkish delight on the Upper East Side. Tasty light specialties include mussels stuffed with currants, pan-fried eggplant with a garlic and yogurt sauce, skewers of char-grilled swordfish, stuffed Cornish hen, or quail wrapped in vine leaves. Reserve. AE, MC, V. *L Mon-Fri noon-2:30pm. D Mon-Thurs 5:30pm-11pm; Fri & Sat 5:30pm-11:30pm; Sun 5pm-10:30pm.* $$

Vietnamese

Indochine
430 Lafayette Street near Astor Pl. 505-5111. On the bones of the old Lady Astor (the bar not the dowager) Vietnamese/Cambodian cuisine in a clamorous Hollywoody-glamorous setting. Still a celebrity hot spot. As for the food, as long as you order only appetizers and share you can dine well. Vietnamese ravioli, stuffed boneless chicken wings, frogs' legs in coconut milk, scampi beignet. (Watch it, the tab can add up quickly.) Sit up front if you want it quieter. Reserve! AE, CB, DC, MC, V. *OPEN 7 days 6pm-midnight.* $$

Saigon Restaurant
60 Mulberry Street near Bayard St. 227-8825. Family-run Chinatown Vietnamese restaurant considered by most to be the best. No decor to speak of but wonderful appetizers, great big bowls of thin noodles; seafood cooked in beer; Saigon spiced beef. Full bar. AE, MC, V. *OPEN 7 days 11:30am-10:30pm.*

Wine Bars

SoHo Kitchen & Bar
103 Greene Street near Prince St. 925-1866. At-

tractive cavernous high-ceilinged SoHo wine bar with a 60-foot-long bar. The city's largest Cruvi-net dispenses over 120 choice wines by the glass including champagnes; nibbles include pizzas, pasta, salads, and burgers—available at the bar or tables. Also draft beer and ales. No reservations except for large parties. AE, CB, DC, MC, V. *OPEN Mon-Thurs 11:30am-11:45pm; Fri & Sat 11:30am-2am; Sun noon-10pm. Sun brunch all day.* $

SHOPPING

Macy's

SHOPPING INFORMATION

New York is an international center of art, food, fashion, antiques, and furnishings. This is only a selection of some of the best, most unique, and least expensive shops in each category. Good general shopping areas are West 34 Street, SoHo, Greenwich Village, 57 Street, upper Madison Avenue, Columbus Avenue, and the Lower East Side. Unless otherwise noted, all these shops are OPEN Monday to Saturday, approximately 9am to 6pm and CLOSED Sunday. NOTE: If no credit cards are mentioned in the description, none are taken.

Uptown, late-night shopping is usually Monday and Thursday. Downtown shops, such as those in Greenwich Village, the East Village, and SoHo, have a different rhythm, reflecting the slower pace in those areas: later openings but later closings; sometimes open Sunday, other times not; many Monday closings; often only a five-day schedule. In summer, many shops are closed on Saturday, often for all of August. It's therefore best to call ahead if you are coming any distance to a particular shop.

Price tags do not reflect the 8¼ percent city sales tax, which will be added by the salesperson or cashier upon purchase. NOTE: Street vendors selling anything from $2 umbrellas to $80 designer handbags have become a common sight, especially near the larger stores in popular shopping areas, much to the chagrin of the store managers. Bargains can be had; after all, the overhead is low. But check the merchandise carefully; what you think you are buying may not be what you get—forgeries abound—also re-

member these are migratory merchants and there are no returns or exchanges.

CONSUMER PROTECTION

The **New York City Department of Consumer Affairs**, 80 Lafayette Street, New York, NY 10013 (577-0111), mediates and arbitrates disputes, and can fine a merchant when warranted. If you have any problems with a merchant, call *Mon-Fri 9am-5pm*. The **Better Business Bureau**, 257 Park Avenue South, New York, NY 10010, has no legal power but can inform you of any complaints of past instances of poor performance and does arbitrate some disputes. No longer a free service, the call to their new number, (900) 463-6222, will cost 85¢ per minute. As a general rule, always find out what a particular store's policy is regarding return of a purchased item. Is it a final sale or is it returnable for credit or cash? In any case, always keep receipts.

DEPARTMENT STORES

Abraham & Straus
A&S Plaza, Herald Square & West 33 Street; 594-8500. And *420 Fulton Street near Hoyt St, Brooklyn; (718) 875-7200. Since 1908 this large, unpretentious store has flourished in Brooklyn. Short on hype, long on stock: The variety of styles and prices is most impressive. In 1989, A&S emerged as a contender for the dollars of the working woman in the Herald Square shopping corridor (the former site of Gimbels) with eight stories of merchandise and an attractive plaza mall of other retailers. AE, MC, V, A&S charge. *OPEN Mon, Thurs & Fri 9:45am-8:30pm; Tues & Wed till 6:45; Sat 10am-6:45pm; Sun 1-6pm. *OPEN Mon 9:45am-7pm; Tues, Wed, Fri & Sat 9:45am-6pm; Thurs till 9pm; Sun noon-5pm.*
Alexander's
731 Lexington Avenue at East 58 St. 593-0880. A patient bargain-hunter's paradise. Designer clothes without the labels and good accessory-copy shopping. Alas, not long for this world where the land is worth more than the store that's on it. AE, MC, V. *OPEN Mon-Sat 10am-9pm; Sun noon-5pm.*
Alexander's
4 World Trade Center Plaza near Church St. 466-1414. Billed as an "adult" fashion store; moderate prices. AE, MC, V. *OPEN Mon-Fri 8am-5:45pm; Sat 10am-4:45pm.*
Bergdorf Goodman
754 Fifth Avenue at 58 St. 753-7300. The lush surroundings give this store an affluent feel and the $15 million renovation has given the elegant carriage trade store and its image a lift. Now a premier player, considered by some the best department store in the world, it purveys the best

Size Comparison Chart for Clothes

Ladies' dresses, coats & skirts

American	3	5	7	9	11	12	13	14	15	16	18
Continental	36	38	38	40	40	42	42	44	44	46	48
British	8	10	11	12	13	14	15	16	17	18	20
Ladies' blouses & sweaters											
American						10	12	14	16	18	20
Continental						38	40	42	44	46	48
British						32	34	36	38	40	42
Ladies' stockings											
American						8	8½	9	9½	10	10½
Continental						1	2	3	4	5	6
British						8	8½	9	9½	10	10½
Ladies' shoes											
American						5	6	7	8	9	10
Continental						36	37	38	39	40	41
British						3½	4½	5½	6½	7½	8½
Children's clothing											
American							3	4	5	6	6X
Continental							98	104	110	116	122
British							18	20	22	24	26
Children's shoes											
American			8	9	10	11	12	13	1	2	3
Continental			24	25	27	28	29	30	32	33	34
British			7	8	9	10	11	12	13	1	2
Men's suits											
American				34	36	38	40	42	44	46	48
Continental				44	46	48	50	52	54	56	58
British				34	36	38	40	42	44	46	48
Men's shirts											
American				14	15	15½	16	16½	17	17½	18
Continental				37	38	39	41	42	43	44	45
British				14	15	15½	16	16½	17	17½	18
Men's shoes											
American				7		8	9	10	11	12	13
Continental				39½		41	42	43	44½	46	47
British				6		7	8	9	10	11	12
Men's hats											
American						6⅞	7⅛	7¼	7⅜	7½	7⅝
Continental						55	56	58	59	60	61
British						6¾	6⅞	7⅛	7¼	7⅜	7½

from the best to the best. Recent expansion: the opening of a mega men's store across Fifth Avenue (see Men's Clothes, Large Stores). AE, MC, V, Bergdorf, Neiman-Marcus charge. OPEN Mon-Wed, Fri & Sat 10am-6pm; Thurs till 8pm.

Bloomingdale's
1000 Third Avenue at East 59 St. 705-2000. A New York phenomenon (what other store would be able to sell panties with *its* name across *your* bottom?). But not the trendsetter it used to be. Frequent sales make this the first stop of a bargain hunter—believe it or not! AE, DC, MC, V, Bloomingdale's charge. OPEN Mon & Thurs 10am-9pm; Tues, Wed, Fri & Sat 10am-6:30pm; Sun noon-6pm.

Galeries Lafayette
4 East 57 Street. 355-0022. In the former Bonwit Teller flagship store, French-accented shopping. The department store, direct from Paris, features French merchandise—women's clothing and accessories only. French designer labels and private label goods, all purveyed with a French point of view. *Bonne Chance!* AE, DC, MC, V. OPEN Mon, Tues, Wed, Fri & Sat 10am-6pm; Sat till 8pm.

Henri Bendel
712 Fifth Avenue near 56 St. 247-1100. Always a unique emporium, the recent move to the landmark Coty and Rizzoli buildings has assured the mystique that its acquisition by the Limited had threatened to dispel. It's a stylish and elegant store with a luxurious array of personal services available. Whether or not the original thin and rich Bendel shopper will come back is a toss-up. AE, MC, V, Bendel charge. OPEN Mon-Wed, Fri & Sat 10am-6:30pm; Thurs till 8pm; Sun noon-6pm.

Lord & Taylor
424 Fifth Avenue at 38 St. 391-3344. A fine, sta-

ble store for classic designer sportswear leaning heavily toward contemporary American designers. Excellent sales January and July. AE, Lord & Taylor charge. *OPEN Mon & Thurs 10am-8:30pm; Tues, Wed, Fri & Sat 10am-6:30pm; Sun noon-6pm.* (If you arrive before the store opens you are treated to a seat, free coffee—served in china cups no less—and a recorded rendition of "The Star-Spangled Banner.")

Macy's
West 34 Street & Broadway. 695-4400. This huge (2.2 million feet of floor space!) full-service (post office, pharmacy, . . .) department store, excellent in so many areas, is now a fashion force to be compared to Bloomies, and the Cellar Marketplace is pure joy. Cheap to expensive. The recently restored Art Deco elegance of the main floor and the new Balcony shops are worth a visit. AE, MC, V, Macy's charge. *OPEN Mon, Thurs & Fri 10am-8:30pm; Tues, Wed & Sat till 7pm; Sun 11am-6pm.*

Saks Fifth Avenue
611 Fifth Avenue at 50 St. 753-4000. Longtime symbol of genteel retailing, this quality store is known for wide selections of elegant designer clothes or young sportswear in a conservative yet sophisticated setting. Newly expanded by 30 percent (its nine floors dip into a new office and retail tower that Saks and Swiss Bank Corporation have built), there's an inviting designer women's wear shop on three, and a newly expanded beauty salon on nine. AE, DC, MC, V, Saks charge. *OPEN Mon-Wed, Fri & Sat 10am-6:30pm; Thurs till 8pm.*

SHOPPING MALLS

This concept so prevalent across the U.S. is relatively new to Manhattan. (See also SIGHTSEEING, On Your Own: Atriums.)

A&S Plaza
Sixth Avenue & West 33 Street. 465-0500. A cheerful, neon-enhanced updating of the old site of Gimbel's. The plaza, which has the Brooklyn-originated department store as its anchor, features a clutch of moderately priced retailers including Plymouth, Au Coton, and The Limited. *OPEN Mon, Thurs & Fri 9:45am-8:45pm; Tues, Wed & Sat 9:45am-6:45pm; Sun 10am-6pm.*

Herald Center
1 Herald Square at West 34 St. 244-2555. Newcomer to the Herald Square area (Macy's country); this ten-level retail center has been plagued with problems, but a turnaround is hoped for with major new tenant Toys "R" Us. *OPEN Mon-Sat 10am-7pm.*

South Street Seaport Marketplace/Pier 17
Fulton & South Streets. In the old Seaport District: over 75 shops and restaurants and then 50 more in the glass-enclosed Pier 17 pavilion on the river containing all of the shops located in every other complex of this kind across the country—Banana Republic, Limited Express,

Sharper Image, etc. Shops: *OPEN Mon-Sat 10am-10pm; Sun noon-6pm. (See also* SIGHTSEEING, On Your Own *and* MUSEUMS & GALLERIES, Museums, Historic Museums: South Street Seaport Museum.)

Trump Tower
725 Fifth Avenue at 56 Street. The lavish pink marble atrium with its wall of water is a vertical shopping plaza devoted to high-style and even higher prices with tenants the likes of Harry Winston, Cartier, Martha, Charles Jourdan. *OPEN Mon-Sat 10am-6pm.*

CHILDREN'S CLOTHES

See KIDS' NEW YORK.

WOMEN'S CLOTHES

Shopping Services

Bendel's, Bergdorf Goodman, Bloomingdale's, Lord & Taylor, Macy's, and **Saks Fifth Avenue** offer the services of a personal shopper. Set up an appointment; make your needs, taste, and budget known, and then sit back while someone else does the legwork and brings the selections back for you to try on. There is no obligation and the service is free.

Boutiques

—Contemporary

Agnes B.
116 Prince Street near Greene St; 925-4649. And 1063 Madison Avenue near East 81 St; 570-9333. In a comfortable environment, Agnes's unpretentious, very French, and very affordable simple separates in suede, linen, leather, cotton, and silk. Sexy tees and sweaters are her forte. For women sizes 6–12; men small, medium, and large. Moderate to expensive $25–$1000. Good sales January/February, July/August. AE, MC, V. *OPEN 7 days.*

Ann Taylor
3 East 57 Street; 832-2010. And 805 Third Avenue at East 50 St; 308-5333. Also Seaport Marketplace, 25 Fulton Street, 608-5600; *2017 Broadway near West 69 St, 873-7344; and *World Financial Center, 945-1991. Well-organized and well-stocked mini "department" store for moderate to expensive contemporary clothes and their own new line of footwear for work and play. AE, MC, V, Ann Taylor charge. **OPEN 7 days.*

Barney's
Seventh Avenue & West 17 Street. 929-9000. The renowned men's store now features the newest fashions for women from Armani, Lauren, Chloe, Miyake. Shoes by Maud Frizon, Manolo Blahnik. In the Coop, lower-priced for-

ward fashions. Free alterations, delivery, parking. AE, MC. Barney's charge. *OPEN Mon-Fri 10am-9pm; Sat till 7pm; Sun noon-6pm.* NOTE: A new Barney's is coming to Madison Avenue at East 60 Street.

Benetton
805 Lexington Avenue near East 62 St; 752-5283. And 4 West 34 Street; 947-8330. Also South Street Seaport, Pier 17, 227-4252; plus additional branches. International mass merchandiser of stylish Italian sportswear separates; strong on sweater dressing. Colorful, affordable, classic. Extremely popular with the young set. AE, MC, V. *OPEN 7 days.*

Betsey, Bunky & Nini
980 Lexington Avenue near East 71 St. 744-6716. A lovely inviting shop with expensive, imaginative, sophisticated separates by Genny, Complice, Byblos, Claude Bartheleme, Malisy, Crimson, and Mariella Burani. Unique handmade sweaters from Great Britain. Sportswear to evening wear. Very personal attention. Price range: $80–$1800; sizes 4–12. AE, MC, V.

Betsey Johnson
130 Thompson Street near Prince St; 420-0169. And 248 Columbus Avenue near West 72 St; 362-3364. Also 251 East 60 Street, 319-7699. Colorful body-hugging clothes for sexy young bodies from a pro; first on SoHo's other good-shopping street, now uptown on the East and West sides. Price range: $20–$160. Also belts, gloves, "thigh-highs," crinolines, and hats to complete the picture. B.J.'s designs are also at Saks, Bloomies, Macy's, and Bergdorf's. AE, MC, V. *OPEN 7 days.*

Capezio in the Village
177 MacDougal Street near West 8 St. 477-5634. The dancer's store for everyone. Fluid, fanciful, and colorful clothes for men (upstairs) and women; great shoe selection and one of the best window displays in the Village. AE, MC, V. *OPEN Mon-Sat noon-8pm; Sun 1-6pm.*

Carol Rollo/Riding High
1147 First Avenue at East 63 St. 832-7927. One of the most extensive selections of womens' and mens' clothing from the world's leading fashion houses: Moschino, Gaultier, Claude Montana, Karl Lagerfeld, Chloe, Thierry Mugler, Byblos, and Callagan. Also, custom-made clothing. Price range: $100–$4,000; sizes 4–10. AE, MC, V. *OPEN 7 days.*

Cashmere Cashmere
840 Madison Avenue near East 69 St; 988-5252. And 595 Madison Avenue near East 57 St; 935-2522. Oh, the feel of it. Snuggle into cashmere dresses, skirts, pants, tees, robes, sweaters, scarves, socks, and shawls. For men and children, too. AE, MC, V.

Castanada
1298 Third Avenue near East 74 St. 988-8885. A full-service store in a multilevel setting for Tahari, Ellen Tracy, Tapemeasure, Vertigo, Adrienne Vittadini, and more. Dresses (for day and evening), pants, sweaters. Sizes 4–14. Also, shoes by Ann

Klein, YSL; accessories, and lingerie, too. AE, MC, V. *OPEN 7 days.*

Charivari
2315 Broadway near West 83 St; 873-1424. Sport: 201 West 79 Street; 799-8650. 72: 257 Columbus Avenue at 72 St; 787-7272. Workshop: 441 Columbus Avenue near West 81 St; 496-8700; and 16-18 West 57 Street, 333-4040. Designer fashion, much of it imported, in this clutch of West Side shops well known for innovative retailing and forward-looking fashions. Armani, Alaia, Byblos, Genny, Comme des Garçons, Claude Montana, Gianni Versace (men's), Katherine Hamnett, Jean Paul Gaultier, Shamask, Moschino, Romeo Gigli, Matsuda, Liza Bruce, Michael Kors. At 57 Street a Yohji Yamamoto boutique, as well as designer objects and accessories for the home. The Workshop, specializing in Japanese and English fashions, is the most avant-garde. All for men and women, except the first listed. Coming soon: another at Madison and East 78 Street. AE, MC, V. *OPEN 7 days.*

Chelsea Designers
128 West 23 Street. 255-8803. The exclusive designs of Peter Kent and Cathy Cunningham. Feminine, all natural fibers—cotton, linen, silk, natural rayon—one-size fashions. AE, MC, V. *OPEN 7 days.*

Compagnie Internationale EXPRESS
733 Lexington Avenue at East 58 St; 421-7246. And 691 Madison Avenue at East 62 St; 838-8787. Also 667 Madison Avenue near East 61 St, 754-4372; 321 Columbus Avenue near West 75 St, 580-5833; 7 West 34 Street, 629-6838; A&S Plaza, Broadway & West 33 Street, 971-3280; 733 Third Avenue at East 46 St, 949-9784; and South Street Seaport, Pier 17, 693-0096. The more insouciant, fast-fashion arm of The Limited. The French accent is faux (they are actually revamped Express shops), but the stylishly trendy, highly affordable fashions are real. Coordinated looks; the latest in accessories, too. AE, MC, V. *OPEN 7 days.*

F.D.R. Drive
109 Thompson Street near Spring St. 966-4827. They used to sell vintage clothing; now they do their own line of fashion (Brookoff & Mahler for F.D.R. Drive) inspired by the 20s through 40s. Beaded blouses, wool crepe suits, classic blouses and pants à la Katharine Hepburn. Wonderful looks complimented by vintage and new-for-them accessories. Also carried by Barneys and Bergdorf. AE, MC, V. *OPEN Tues-Sun 1-7pm.*

Gallery of Wearable Art
43 East 63 Street. 425-5379. A boutique/gallery of one-of-a-kind fantasy clothing and accessories by more than 800 talented artisan designers. Price range: $150–$4,000. High visual impact, especially the evening wear. Also, bridal and custom-made. AE, MC, V.

Henry Lehr
772 Madison Avenue near East 66 St. 535-1021.

Trendy casual "seasonless" sportswear separates for women, men, and kids, too. Lehr's own designs plus the likes of Katherine Hamnett. Large jeans stock. AE, MC, V. *OPEN 7 days.*

Honeybee
7 East 53 Street. 688-3660. Very popular midtown shop with an excellent easy-to-shop stock of well-priced sportswear, dresses, and accessories on two levels. Catalog available. AE, CB, DC, MC, V, Honeybee charge.

IAN'S
1151 Second Avenue near East 60 St; 838-3969. And 5 St. Mark's Place near Third Ave; 420-1857. Pioneer punker. For the adventurous woman who wants to stop traffic. Decadent designer dress-up in plastic, leather, and lycra. Jewelry and accessories to match. Price range: $25-$200. AE, MC, V. *OPEN 7 days.*

Ibiza
46 University Place near East 10 St. 533-4614. Gorgeous colorful now fashions. Great feminine style and pulled-together looks; exclusive designs from Ibiza, Spain, as well as from Bali, England, and the work of contemporary designers. Terrific accessories, shoes, too, and the prettiest shop and windows in the Village. Moderate to very expensive. AE, MC, V. *OPEN Mon-Sat 11am-8pm; Sun 1pm-7pm.*

Indios
88 Christopher Street near Bleecker St. 989-4488. Colorful and fashionable (without being trendy) all-natural-fiber clothing—wool, cotton, silk. Wonderful sweaters. Moderate prices. AE, MC, V. *OPEN 7 days.*

In Wear/Matinique
394 West Broadway near Broome St. 219-8187. Two shops in one: Danish sportswear separates in coordinated colors for men and women; and their own designs in shoes, socks, hats, scarves, and belts. AE, MC, V. *OPEN Mon-Fri 11am-7pm; Sat 11am-8pm; Sun noon-7pm.*

Jimmy's
1226 Kings Highway at 13 St, Brooklyn. (718) 645-9685. Where high fashion lives in Brooklyn; the best of Milan and Paris: Ungaro, Valentino, Claude Montana, Azzedine Alaia, Complice, Ferre, Genny, Vikki Till. For men and women and it's not cheap. AE, CB, DC, MC, V.

Jonal
25 East 73 Street. 879-9200. Now housed in a charming Victorian-era town house complete with fireplaces, it's most appealing place to shop for their ready-to-wear or custom-made dresses, suits, maternity clothes, evening wear, and bridal gowns. AE, MC, V.

Julie: Artisan's Gallery
667 Madison Avenue near East 62 St. 688-2345. In reality an art gallery featuring fanciful but wearable arts and crafts—clothes and adornments—created by talented contemporary craftspeople. Each piece is an original handmade work of art and is sure to turn heads.

Kleinfeld
82 Street at Fifth Ave, Brooklyn. (718) 833-1100.

A fabulous selection of special occasion dresses. All the latest cocktail dresses and formal wear from top-name designers including Zandra Rhodes, Bob Mackie, Fabrice, and Scaasi. But for 50 years they have been known as the best place to buy bridal gowns. This longtime family-run business sells more than 600 wedding gowns a month! Great sales. MC, V. *OPEN Tues & Thurs 11am-9pm; Wed & Fri 11am-6pm; Sat 10am-6pm by appointment only.*

Laura Ashley
21 East 57 Street; 752-7300. And *398 Columbus Avenue at West 79 St; 496-5151. Also *South Street Seaport, 4 Fulton Street, 809-3556; and Macy's. A floral oasis straight from London. Inexpensive and charming mainly all cotton and corduroy flower-print fashions for the young-at-heart woman. Children's fashions and home furnishings, including fabric and wallpaper. Bridal department upstairs at 57 Street store. AE, MC, V. *OPEN 7 days.*

The Limited
691 Madison Avenue at East 63 St; 838-8787. And South Street Seaport; 619-2922. The nationwide sportswear specialty chain's mammoth flagship store, in a 1928 McKim, Mead & White landmark, features the fashionable, moderately priced merchandise for which it is known, much of it their own Forenza and Outback Red lines. Terrific sales staff, helpful without being pushy, and terrific sales. Also at this location is an **Express**, for youngish flair (*see also* Compagnie Internationale EXPRESS), and a boudoir-closet-sized **Victoria's Secret** lingerie. P.S.: This is the new owner of Bendel's. AE, MC, V. *OPEN 7 days.*

Moga
715 Madison Avenue near East 64 St. 751-7506. Classic, well-tailored French contemporary wear. Specializes in a coordinated color range of separates. AE, MC, V.

Nancy & Co.
1242 Madison Avenue near East 89 St. 427-0770. Imported high-fashion designer sportswear. AE, MC, V.

Off Broadway
139 West 72 Street. 724-6713. Incredible selection of well-priced American and imported separates, swimsuits, shoes, bags; free alterations, too. AE, CB, DC, MC, V, Off Broadway charge.

Patches by Fonda
758A Madison Avenue near East 65 St. 628-9748. Stunning one-of-a-kind jackets and skirts—short and long—made from antique fabrics, linens, and kimonos. Victorian whites, including beautiful artwork pieces, transformed into highly wearable contemporary styles including minis. Unique. AE, MC, V. *OPEN 7 days.*

Patricia Field
10 East 8 Street. 254-1699. Innovative trendsetter on the cutting edge of fashion. Unusual, whimsical, colorful, and most of it quite affordable. Avant-garde makeup, jewelry, and wigs, too. New: the sexy lingerie for men and women. Interesting help, music, and artwork abounds.

AE, MC, V. *OPEN Mon-Sat noon-8pm; Sun 1-7pm.*

Plenda
208 Third Avenue near East 18 St. 982-8640. Small Gramercy Park area shop. Casual simplicity in separates and dresses with easy lines; lots of one-size-fits-all. Joan Vass, Blue Fish, Angel Heart; Sarah Arizona sweaters. Wonderful accessories including American Indian jewelry. Moderate prices. AE, MC, V. *OPEN Tues-Sat 11:30am-7pm.*

Pop Shop
292 Lafayette Street near Houston St. 219-2784. Giddy shop dedicated to the late graffitti artist Keith Haring. Tees, sweatshirts, jackets, and more all with the familiar images of babies and interlocking figures he's known for. AE, MC, V. *OPEN Tues-Sun noon-7pm.*

Robert Brascomb Unlimited
304 East 5 Street. 353-9649. A wide variety of unstructured, easy-to-wear fashions in fabulous prints and fabrics by talented in-house designer Robert Brascomb. AE, MC, V. *OPEN Mon-Sat 1-7pm.*

San Francisco Clothing
975 Lexington Avenue near East 71 St. 472-8740. Excellent all-natural-fabric tailoring for women in an attractive, unique setting. Their own collection of fashion directional clothing every season as well as Betsey Johnson and Urban Outfitters. Price range: $15-$600; sizes 4-14. AE, MC, V.

Stella Flame
850 Lexington Avenue near East 64 St. 879-5438. A winning collection of fashionable clothing, both ready-to-wear or custom-made, contemporary and vintage, for men and women. Boldly patterned hand-knit sweaters are a specialty, and so is the eclectic selection of antiques and collectibles that make this such an interesting place to shop. AE, MC, V.

Street Life
470 Broadway near Grand St; 219-3764. And 422 Columbus Avenue near West 80 St; 769-8858. Their own line of casual wear with a youthful flair. Good accessories, too. Great end-of-season sales. AE, MC, V. *OPEN 7 days.*

Unique Clothing Warehouse
726 Broadway at Washington Pl. 674-1767. A "specialty department store" for street-chic styles as well as New Wave fashions. Not quite as cheap as the original except for the accessories, but the street trends show up here first— and for the lowest prices. MC, V. *OPEN Mon-Thurs 10am-10pm; Fri & Sat 10am-midnight; Sun noon-8pm.*

Urban Outfitters
628 Broadway near Houston St; 475-0009. And *394 Sixth Avenue at Waverly Pl; 677-9350. A general store for the 90s. On one level, clothing and accessories for the entire young urban family. Also, whimsical novelties, housewares, books, kids' and adult toys. AE, MC, V. *OPEN Mon-Sat 10am-10pm; Sun 10am-8pm. *Mon-Thurs 10am-10pm; Fri & Sat 10am-11pm; Sun noon-8pm.*

Zara
750 Lexington Avenue at East 59 St. 754-1120. Via Spain, the latest trends, well coordinated and priced to sell to savvy budget-minded young women. The stock is constantly being updated with new shipments. AE, MC, V. *OPEN 7 days.*

—Conservative

Brooks Brothers
346 Madison Avenue near East 44 St; 682-8800. And 1 Liberty Plaza; 267-2400. Since 1818 the consummate men's tailor—now for women on four. AE, DC, Brooks charge.

Jaeger International
818 Madison Avenue at East 69 St; 628-3350. And 19 East 57 Street; 753-0370. The English-made classic sportswear in beautiful fabrics for women, sizes 6-16. No surprises but great quality. AE, DC, MC, V.

Paul Stuart
Madison Avenue at East 45 St. 682-0320. Mainly clones of the men's classics for women. Dresses, and casual wear, too. AE, DC, MC, V.

The Smiths
454 Broome Street at Mercer St. 431-0038. Beautifully cut, classic women's and men's clothes; soft fabrics, clean lines. AE, MC, V. *OPEN 7 days.*

Sport & Travel
511 Madison Avenue at East 53 St. 758-0881. Tailored sports and outerwear for the conservative woman. Custom-made and ready-to-wear; ultrasuede, leather, cashmere, and wool coats; fur-lined all-weather coats; sheepskins. AE, CB, DC, MC, V.

Tahari
802 Madison Avenue near East 67 St; 535-1515. And *2 World Financial Center; 945-2450. Known for beautifully tailored jackets and suits in gabardine, silk, and rayon. Also, dresses and blouses. AE, DC, MC, V. *OPEN 7 days.*

—Designer

Alaia New York
131 Mercer Street near Prince St. 941-1166. The designer famed for his taut sexy body-hugging fashions. In a dramatic shop designed by artist Julian Schnabel and his wife, Jacqueline, who runs the shop. See the shop even if your silhouette or pocket can't handle the clothes. AE, MC, V. *OPEN Tues-Sat noon-7pm; Sun noon-6pm.*

Chanel
5 East 57 Street. 355-5050. Everything Chanel and only Chanel under one roof at No. 5 (that's no coincidence). Women's clothing—couture and ready-to-wear—perfume, costume jewelry, shoes, scarves, men's ties and sweaters, and those much-imitated quilted chain-handled bags. Appropriately expensive. AE, MC, V.

Christian Dior
703 Fifth Avenue at 55 St. 223-4646. The 4,000-square-foot duplex is a replication of the original Dior salon on Avenue Montaigne in Paris. The line, now designed by Gianfranco Ferre, includes day and evening ready-to-wear, costume

jewelry, accessories, and cosmetics. Exorbitantly priced. AE, DC, MC, V.

Comme des Garçons
116 Wooster Street near Prince St. 219-0661. Stark, bunkerlike setting in SoHo for Rei Kawakubo's intriguing avant-garde fashions from Tokyo. For the avant-garde woman and man. Also found at Barney's, Bergdorf, Charivari, and Bloomies. Price range: $20-$1,500. AE, DC, MC, V. *OPEN 7 days.*

Emanuel Ungaro
803 Madison Avenue at East 68 St. 249-4090. Ungaro's exquisite luxurious fabrics, imaginatively mixed prints, sexy yet elegant styling, stratospheric prices. AE, DC, MC, V.

Emilio Pucci
24 East 64 Street. 752-8957. Emilio, Emilio, Emilio all over his colorful print clothing and accessories now enjoying renewed popularity with a whole new generation of shoppers. Vivara perfume, too. (Still my favorite.) AE, DC, MC, V.

Gianni Versace Boutique
816 Madison Avenue near East 68 St. 744-5572. Modern shop for Versace's entire luxurious collection for women and men; shoes, leather goods, accessories, jewelry, perfume. AE, DC, MC, V.

Giorgio Armani
815 Madison Avenue near East 68 St. 988-9191. Armani's perfectly executed tailoring on three floors: street level for women and accessories, second for men, and third for Emporio Armani, a less-expensive sportswear line. AE, MC, V.

Givenchy
954 Madison Avenue at East 75 St. 772-1040. Audrey Hepburn's longtime French favorite; his ready-to-wear clothes and accessories, for day and evening. AE, MC, V.

Gucci
685 Fifth Avenue at 54 St. 826-2600. Four levels of Gs around a central atrium. Accessories and luxurious classic apparel for men and women, now being renewed by Dawn Mello, former Bergdorf president and fashion maven. AE, DC, MC, V.

Hanae Mori
27 East 79 Street. 472-2352. Beautiful, sophisticated Japanese-inspired fashions. Ready to wear and couture. Accessories and men's, too. AE, MC, V.

Joseph Tricot
804 Madison Avenue near East 68 St. 570-0077. Via London's South Molton Street, Joseph Ettedgui's knits designed to mix and match and layer. Simple shapes, interesting textures, inventive accessories from England. Price range: $75-$800. AE, MC, V.

Kenzo Boutique
824 Madison Avenue at East 69 St. 737-8640. Direct from Paris, Kenzo's stylish and vibrantly colorful clothes and accessories, for women and men. Accessibly priced. AE, MC, V.

Koos van den Akker Couture
34 East 67 Street. 249-5432. Well known for his elaborate fabric collages to wear. Imaginative

and expensive. Also, individually designed items by commission. AE, MC, V.

Krizia
805 Madison Avenue near East 67 St. 628-8180. The complete collection from evening gowns and suits to the signature feline sweaters. For men as well. AE, DC, MC, V.

Martha
475 Park Avenue at East 58 St; 753-1511. And Trump Tower, 725 Fifth Avenue at 56 St, 3rd and 4th levels; 826-8855. The best of the best: Beene, Blass, de La Renta, Lagerfeld, Lacroix, Biagiotti, Ferre, McFadden, Montana, Bob Mackie, Carolyn Roehm, Valentino, Mugler—in elegant settings for pampered perusing and purchasing. Sizes 4-14. At the adjacent **International Boutique,** 473 Park Avenue (371-7400), younger more cutting designers at more affordable prices. AE, DC, MC, V.

Matsuda
*156 Fifth Avenue near 21 St; 979-5100. And 461 Park Avenue at East 57 St; 935-6969. In stark high-tech settings, Mitsuhiro Matsuda's unconstructed understated New Wave fashions for men and women. Shoes and accessories, too. AE, DC, MC, V. *OPEN 7 days.*

Missoni
Westbury Hotel, 836 Madison Avenue at East 69 St. 517-9339. Sleek, modern, all-black setting, the better to appreciate the fabulous distinctively hued, imaginatively patterned knits. Their entire masterful collection for women and men is here. AE, MC, V.

OMO Norma Kamali
11 West 56 Street. 957-9797. Now housed in a 100-year-old building. To the delight of Kamali fans (legions), it has six levels for her imaginative extremely feminine clothes, including bridal dresses. Also her hats, shoes, socks, bathing suits, fake furs, and one-of-a-kind evening clothes. AE, MC, V.

Polo/Ralph Lauren
867 Madison Avenue at East 72 St. 606-2100. The old Rhinelander mansion with a $14 million facelift in order to better purvey the well-bred classic looks that Lauren has universalized. Wander from room to room for a glimpse (especially on the home furnishings-filled fourth floor) of his vision of gracious living. Women's things from country clothes to executive dressing are on three. P.S.: Don't miss the ladies room. AE, DC, MC, V.

Romeo Gigli
21 East 69 Street. The Italian designer's wares from the nearly ecclesiastical coats for $30,000 to his more humanely priced resort collection and the lower priced G. Gigli collection for men and women. On several floors. AE, MC, V.

Saint Laurent Rive Gauche
855 Madison Avenue at East 71 St. 988-3821. Ready to wear from the influential master of fanciful dressing. Good end-of-season sales. AE, DC, MC, V.

Sonia Rykiel Boutique
792 Madison Avenue at East 67 St. 744-0880.

Famed French designer finally has her own showcase for her easy-to-wear knit classics; accessories, too. AE, DC, MC, V.

Valentino
823 Madison Avenue at East 67 St. 421-7550. Lavish high fashion at high prices from the designer who has over the last 30 years dressed Liz, Sophia, and Jackie. Suits for men, too. AE, DC, MC, V.

Yohji Yamamoto
103 Grand Street at Mercer St. 966-9066. Cavernous dramatic space for the well-regarded Japanese designer's pricey avant-garde fashions for women and men. AE, DC, MC, V. *OPEN 7 days.*

Zoran
214 Sullivan Street, 3rd floor. 674-6087. The Yugoslavian designer's expensive minimalist creations in the finest fabrics. The epitome of easy luxury. Famed for his tees in cashmere, silk, satin, and chamois. *By appointment only.*

—Discount & Off-price

Though discount designer-wear can now be found all over town, the traditional bargain-hunting area is the Lower East Side. Orchard Street has the highest concentration of shops selling from chic to schlock and everything in between. Sunday is a hectic but very New York experience and not to be missed. Orchard Street itself becomes a pedestrian mall closed to cars on that day. If you can, leave your car at home.

Berent & Smith
94 Rivington Street near Orchard St. 254-0900. Large, chaotic Lower East Side shop for off-price (at least 30-50 percent off) ladies dresses, suits, sportswear, and coats. Brand names, sizes 4-46. AE, MC, V. *OPEN Sun-Thurs 9:30am-5:30pm; Fri till 2pm.*

Bolton's
19 East 8 Street; 475-9547. And 53 West 23 Street; 924-6860. Also 1180 Madison Avenue at East 86 St, 772-4419; 225 East 57 Street, 755-2527; 27 West 57 Street, 935-4431; and 2251 Broadway near West 81 St, 873-8545; plus more branches. Well-known no-nonsense discount chain store with many high-quality labels, including Ralph Lauren and Anne Klein; dresses by Karin Stevens, Belle France, and others, all at 20-50 percent off. Good weekly sales. Sizes 4-16. AE, MC, V. *OPEN 7 days.*

Breakaway
125 Orchard Street near Delancey St. 598-4455. Ellen Tracy, Harve Bernard, Nicole Miller plus Italian and French imports. There's an automatic markdown system. AE, CB, DC, MC, V. *OPEN 7 days.*

Chez Aby
77-79 Delancey Street near Allen St. 431-6135. Classic French and Italian fashions. Dresses, separates, and coats, too. Good buys. Wide price range, goes way up. AE, MC, V. *OPEN Sun-Fri.*

Daffy's
111 Fifth Avenue at 18 St; 529-4477. And 335

Madison Avenue near East 44 St; 557-4422. Off-price retailer from New Jersey fills 35,000 square feet of selling space on three floors with fashionable finds at 40-80 percent off. For women, men, and children. Communal dressing rooms; long lines at the cashier. MC, V. *OPEN Mon-Sat 10am-9pm; Sun 11am-6pm.*

The Dress Shop
70 East 9 Street. 260-4963. Great prices for this season's pieces (sometimes up to 60 percent off) from Michael Lamy, Gamma, Axis, Peabody, Vanda Mazzeo, Ann Pinkerton. If you loved Williwear, you will love their own Dress Shop line. AE, MC, V. *OPEN Mon-Sat 11am-8pm.*

Filene's Basement
Fresh Meadows Shopping Center, 187-04 Horace Harding Expressway, Fresh Meadows, Queens. (718) 479-7711. A longtime Boston tradition comes to New York. Nearly perfect merchandise from some of the country's top retailers including Neiman Marcus, I. Magnin, and Sakowitz. Clothes and shoes for women and men. AE, MC, V, Filene's charge. *OPEN Mon-Sat 10am-9:30pm; Sun 11am-6pm.*

Fishkin
314 Grand Street at Allen St; 226-6538. And 318 Grand Street. Good longtime reliable Lower East Side shop for European and American dresses and sportswear including cashmere sweaters, designer boots and shoes, all at 20 percent below list price. Vittadini, Harve Bernard, Christian Dior, Regina Potter, Liz Clairborne, Carol Little. Lines are usual on Sunday. AE, DC, MC, V. *OPEN Sun-Fri.*

Friedlich
196 Orchard Street near Houston St. 254-8899. Discounted famous-name Seventh Avenue designer and French and Italian sportswear for ladies sizes 5-15, 4-16. Hectic, few amenities, but bargains make it worthwhile. AE, MC, V. *OPEN 7 days.*

Gabay's Outlet
225 First Avenue near East 13 St. 254-3180. This secret bargain source in the East Village sells overstock, end-of-season, flawed, or returned merchandise from the best-name uptown department stores. Cacharel blouses, Perry Ellis and Ralph Lauren sweaters, Maud Frizon shoes, Fendi and Judith Leiber bags. The catch: It's all thrown on tables and prices depend on whether damaged and how badly, generally 70 percent off. Smart, careful shoppers do well here, but it's not for the faint of heart or stamina. Best to go with a veteran shopper. New merchandise daily, but Saturday morning is best. MC, V. *OPEN 7 days.*

Hit or Miss
415 Fifth Avenue near 38 St; 889-0726. And *2232 Broadway at West 80 St; 595-4559. Several branches in the Financial District. Harve Bernard, Fenn Wright Mason, Calvin Klein, Evan Picone, Cathy Hardwick, Regina Porter, Wayne Rogers, French Connection—all at 20-50 percent off. New shipments two or three times a week. AE, MC, V. **OPEN 7 days.*

Labels for Less
639 Third Avenue at East 41 St; 682-3330. And
*130 East 34 Street; 689-3455. Also *1345 Sixth
Avenue near West 54 St, 956-2450; 130 West 48
Street, 997-1032; plus other branches. Good
spots for discounted junior and misses' sportswear. Merchandise varies a bit with the neighborhood. MC, V. *Mon-Fri., *OPEN 7 days.*

Loehmann's
5740 Broadway at West 236 St, Riverdale; 543-
6420. And 19 Duryea Place near Beverly Rd,
Brooklyn; (718) 469-9800. Also 60-06 99 Street
near Horace Harding Expressway, Rego Park,
Queens, (718) 271-4000. Legendary Loehmann's is more than a store, it's a tradition
handed down from one generation of New York
women to another. Everything a bargain-hunter
could want and put up with: outrageously low
prices, uneven selections, communal dressing
rooms, and hints of designer labels still attached.
Some women go daily (2,400 new garments arrive each day). Beware: no refunds, no exchanges. MC, V. *OPEN 7 days.*

Ms, Miss, or Mrs
462 Seventh Avenue at West 35 St, 3rd floor. 736-
0557. Well-known wholesaler (Ben Farber) for
moderate to expensive designer dresses for day
and evening, separates and coats. Huge stock,
excellent discounts, sizes 2-20. *OPEN Mon-Fri
9am-5:30pm; Sat till 4pm; Sun 10am-4pm.*

S&W
165 West 26 Street; 924-6656. And 287 Seventh
Avenue; 924-6656. This clutch of stores is a top
discount source for the best American designer
sportswear. The prices are 25-40 percent off,
but there are always sales to accommodate the
seasonal flows of merchandise. Up-to-the-
minute styles by names you'll recognize. At 287
Seventh Avenue, designer boots, shoes, and
handbags as well as designer coats; also a
range of more moderate merchandise. AE, MC,
V. *OPEN Sun-Fri. CLOSES Fri at 3pm.*

Spitzer's Corner Store
101 Rivington Street at Ludlow St; 477-4088. And
156 Orchard Street at Rivington St; 473-1515.
Large selection of junior suits, jackets, coats,
and casual dresses well below retail price. AE,
MC, V. *OPEN Sun-Fri. CLOSES Fri at 3pm.*

Syms
42 Trinity Place near Rector St. 797-1199. Famed
off-price retailer for name sportswear from Ralph
Lauren, Ellen Tracy, Calvin Klein, and more.
Shoes from 9 West and Maud Frizon; handbags,
too. Lingerie by Lily of France, Warners, Bali at
50 percent off. There's even more for men. *OPEN
Tues & Wed 8am-6:30pm; Thurs & Fri till 8 pm;
Sat 10am-6:30pm; Sun 11:30am-5:30pm.*

Three Wishes
365 West Broadway near Spring St. 226-7570.
An off-price store in SoHo is a rarity, but this
shop sells their own label and others you will
recognize at 30 percent off retail. Also, good
contemporary jewelry selection. Certainly worth
a look while gallery-shopping. AE, MC, V. *OPEN
7 days noon-7pm.*

—Ethnic

Back from Guatemala
306 East 6 Street. 260-7010. A most unusual but
highly wearable stock of fashions, jewelry, and
artifacts, not only from Guatemala but from
China, Bali, Afghanistan, South America, and Tibet as well. AE, MC, V. *OPEN Mon-Sat noon-
11pm; Sun 2-11pm.*

Craft Caravan
63 Greene Street near Spring St. 431-6669. Traditional African handicrafts, clothing, bags, jewelry, sculpture, baskets, furniture, toys, ceramics, and handloomed fabrics fill this huge SoHo
shop. AE, MC, V. *OPEN Tues-Sun.*

Paracelso
414 West Broadway near Prince St. 966-4232. In
this exotic SoHo bazaar you'll find contemporary
and antique European and Asian natural-fiber
clothes, jewelry, and curios much of which you
won't find elsewhere. All with a timeless, seasonless appeal. AE, MC, V. *OPEN 7 days.*

Putumayo
857 Lexington Avenue at East 65 St; 734-3111.
And 339 Columbus Avenue near West 76 St;
595-3441. Also 147 Spring Street near Wooster
St; 966-4458. Welcoming shops for moderately
priced handmade imports from Bolivia, Chile,
Iceland, Tibet, and Afghanistan. Wonderful accessories. AE, MC, V. *OPEN 7 days.*

Sermoneta
740 Madison Avenue near East 64 St. 744-6551.
A sweet shop for good-value pretty imports from
Peru, Ecuador, and India. AE, MC, V.

Surma
11 East 7 Street. 477-0729. Exquisite albeit expensive hand-embroidered Romanian peasant
blouses among beautiful traditional Ukrainian
handicrafts in the Little Ukraine section of the
East Village. Also books and music.

—Resale

Encore Resale Dress Shop
1132 Madison Avenue near East 84 St, upstairs.
879-2850. Resale consignment shop specializing in excellent-condition designer and couture,
including Galanos, Chanel, Armani, and Ungaro;
used clothing at 30 percent off original prices.
Sophisticated recycling. (Consigning time: Tuesday to Saturday, from 11am to 5pm.) *OPEN 7
days.*

Exchange Unlimited
563 Second Avenue at East 31 St. 889-3229.
Secondhand contemporary clothing, some designer, on consignment. Good stock of accessories. Note for nonsmokers: The owners do and
the clothes reek.

Michael's Resale Dress Shop
1041 Madison Avenue near East 79 St, 2nd floor.
737-7273. Pragmatic snob appeal! Nothing
older than a year, meticulous-condition designer
and better clothing on consignment. MC, V.

—Vintage

*Most "antique" clothing shops have a final-sale
policy, so purchase carefully and wisely. The*

East Village and lower Broadway are the best areas for vintage values. (See also Men's Clothes, Vintage & Surplus *and* Specialty Shops & Services, Antiques, Antique & Flea Markets.)

Alice Underground
380 Columbus Avenue at West 78 St; 724-6682. And 481 Broadway near Broome St; 431-9067. In the original large basement shop, inexpensive and highly wearable vintage clothes and accessories from the 40s and 50s, some 60s. MC, V. ($25 minimum). OPEN 7 days.

Antique Boutique
712-714 Broadway near Washington Pl; 460-8830. And 227 East 59 Street; 752-1680. A top spot on lower Broadway (a hot place to shop) for a trip through a fashion time capsule in this, the city's largest used-clothing store. Over 30,000 vintage and retro wear, including party dresses, tuxedo shirts, 40s gab shirts, 50s capris and leather motorcycle jackets, 60s minis—for men and women. Price range: $1-$800. AE, DC, MC, V. OPEN Mon-Thurs 11am-10pm; Fri & Sat till midnight; Sun noon-8pm.

Bogie's Antique Clothing
Bogie is gone and now the shop is gone, too, but his wife goes on with great vintage bargains every Sunday at the Flea Market, Sixth Avenue and West 25 Street (in the free lot).

Canal Jean Company
504 Broadway near Spring St. 226-3663. A supermarket of cheap chic from underwear to actionwear to eveningwear, plus the ubiquitous antique man's tweed overcoat, among other vintage duds. A fun place. AE, DC, MC, V. OPEN Sun-Thurs 11am-8pm; Fri & Sat 11pm-9pm.

Cheap Jack's Antique Clothes
841 Broadway near East 14 St. 777-9564. Filled to the rafters with 40s, 50s, and 60s vintage clothes for women and men. Coats, suits, jackets, dresses. Wide range of quality and price. Good updates include the cashmere zipper jackets made from old coats for men and women. Some imaginative current youth trends concocted on the premises. AE, MC, V; personal checks. OPEN Mon-Sat 11am-8pm; Sun noon-7pm.

Dorothy's Closet
335 Bleecker Street near Christopher St. 206-6414. Small welcoming spot for quality good-condition antique clothing, mainly 40s to 60s. Long on lingerie and accessories. Good prices. For him, too. AE, MC, V. OPEN 7 days 1-9pm.

Gerry Nichol
132 East 45 Street, suite 7B. 949-1008. Vintage clothing and opulent decorative textiles, mid-19th century to 1930s. Wide price range; retail and to the trade. By appointment only.

Harriet Love
412 West Broadway near Spring St. 966-2280. Women's designer clothing inspired by the past and some stellar vintage pieces from the woman who made vintage respectable. Vintage and antique jewelry and alligator purses. Accessories for men, too. Price range: $50-$1,000. AE, MC, V. OPEN 7 days noon-7pm.

Jana Starr-Jean Hoffman Antiques
See Antiques.

Joia
1151 Second Avenue near East 60 St. 754-9017. One of the few uptown sources for a good selection of mint condition 1930s to 1940s jewelry and clothes at not-bad (for the location) prices. Outstanding collection of American Indian jewelry from the 40s. AE, MC, V.

Liza's Place
132 Thompson Street near Prince St. 477-6027. Aficionados will appreciate the quality and range—if not the prices. The 1920s-1950s are represented. Exquisite evening and wedding gowns, beaded, lace, and velvet dresses. High-priced perfect accessories and jewelry, too. OPEN Tues-Sun noon-7pm.

Love Saves the Day
119 Second Avenue at East 7 St. 228-3802. Much funk from the 50s and 60s; the best older stuff hangs from the ceiling. The windows—always of a theme—are traffic stoppers. Yes! This is the shop from Desperately Seeking Susan. Weird, tasteless, and amusing novelties; some collectibles, dolls, etc. All with a loud pulsating rock beat. AE, MC, V. OPEN 7 days noon-midnight.

O Mistress Mine
143 Seventh Avenue South at Charles St. 691-4327. A very good selection of vintage clothing for men and women, including some exemplary dresses and jackets form the 30s and 40s, at surprisingly affordable prices. Also shoes, hats, jewelry, all in a low-key, welcoming shop. OPEN Mon-Wed 1-8pm; Thurs & Fri 1-10pm; Sat 1-9pm; Sun 2-6pm.

Opal White
131 Thompson Street near Prince St. 677-8215. A perfect collection of antique bridal gowns, 1890-1950. A treat for lovers of the fine fabrics and styles of the past. Moderate to expensive. AE only. OPEN Wed-Sun by appointment.

Panache
525 Hudson Street near West 10 St. 242-5115. High-quality, well-organized, well-priced selection of antique clothing and accessories for women and men. Also vintage quilts, drapery and upholstery fabrics. AE, MC, V. OPEN 7 days noon-7pm.

Reminiscence
74 Fifth Avenue near 13 St. 243-2292. Very busy big-business operation, and their new store, a mini department store, has it all. The pioneer in street chic follows fashion trends and manufactures updates of old favorites for both men and women. Best: the Hawaiian shirts, linen jackets, and pleated trousers for both sexes. Also authentic vintage oldies, as well as shoes, bags, jewelry, children's wear, vintage toys, and collectibles; cosmetics, too. Price range: $3-$150. (Reminiscence brand also carried at **Macy's** and **Bloomies**.) Visit their other two stores, 175 MacDougal Street and 109 Avenue B, for close-outs and sale items. AE, MC, V. OPEN Mon-Sat 11am-8pm; Sun 1-7pm.

Furs

New York's wholesale, and to some extent retail, fur district is centered around Seventh Avenue and West 30 Street. On weekdays the area bustles with activity as merchandise is carted or carried through the streets.

Ben Kahn
150 West 30 Street, 18th floor. 279-0633. Expensive traditional furrier renowned for quality and workmanship. AE, DC, MC, V.

Daniel A Furs (Antonovich)
333 Seventh Avenue at West 28 St, 2nd floor. 244-5875. New York's largest fur factory and showroom for savings of up to 50 percent. Blackglama mink is their forte, but there are thousands of furs to choose from for both men and women. AE, CB, DC, MC, V. *OPEN Sun-Fri.*

Fur & Sport by Albert Gompertz
352 Seventh Avenue near West 29 St, 2nd floor. 594-8873. Designer and manufacturer of contemporary furs for men and women, with all the services of a fine retail shop. Custom designs, expert alterations. Storage, cleaning, repairs. Price range: $500-$50,000 (for sable). AE, MC, V. *OPEN Mon-Sat by appointment.*

The Fur Vault
581 Fifth Avenue near 47 St. 765-3877. Yes, there is a "Fred the furrier," the man who brought furs within the reach of "Carole" and "Susan," the working woman. He offers some of the lowest prices in town for furs from 60 manufacturers in 30 countries. Incredible variety and value, watch for monthly sales. AE, MC, V. *OPEN 7 days.*

Hy Fisherman Furs
305 Seventh Avenue near West 27 St, 6th floor. 244-4948. Fashionable furs direct from this designer-manufacturer at huge savings of up to 30-60 percent below retail. Thousands of coats, sizes 3-18, in stock. Repairs, renovating, cleaning. AE, DC, MC, V.

Maximilian Fur Company
20 West 57 Street, 3rd floor. 765-6290. Famed as New York's most expensive and prestigious furrier. High society's favorite. AE, MC, V.

Michael Forrest
345 Seventh Avenue near West 28 St, 9th floor. 564-4726. Their own high-fashion line of furs sold in the better stores, direct to you at 30 to 40 percent off. AE only.

Revillon Fur Salon
Saks Fifth Avenue, 611 Fifth Avenue at 50 St, 3rd floor. 753-4000. The ultimate luxury furs, be it a sable parka or a skunk trenchcoat. Casual styling, costly pricing. Good February sales. AE, MC, V, Saks charge.

—Resale Furs

Ritz Thrift Shop
107 West 57 Street. 265-4559. Respected source for good "gently worn" furs at affordable prices. Price range: $500-$5,000 (a few dazzlers at $20,000). Everything has been cleaned and glazed, and there are free alterations and free storage with purchase. Men's furs, too. AE, MC, V.

Gloves

The department stores have the largest and best selections of gloves. ***Alexander's*** *is a good source for inexpensive imported leather gloves. Flea markets are treasure troves of fashionable 40s and 50s originals from a time when gloves were de rigueur.*

Handbags

The department stores have large selections of handbags in all price ranges. ***Bloomingdale's*** *and* ***Saks*** *have excellent handbag sales.* ***Alexander's*** *has a good range of lower-priced yet stylish leather bags, many of which are designer copies. See also Specialty Shops & Services, Leather Goods & Luggage.*

Artbag
See Handbag Repairs.

Barbara Shaum
69 East 4 Street. 254-4250. This longtime talented East Village artisan designs and handcrafts elegant, fashionable, and very well-priced leather handbags. Sandals and handmade belts, too. AE only. *OPEN Wed-Fri 1-8pm; Sat 1-6pm or by appointment.*

Bottega Veneta
635 Madison Avenue near East 59 St. 371-5511. Fine leather bags, shoes, and accessories from Italy, "when your own initials are enough." AE, MC, V.

Cachet
1159 Second Avenue at East 61 St. 753-1650. Current handbag styles for day or evening; belts and scarves, too. AE, MC, V. *OPEN 7 days.*

The Coach Store
754 Madison Avenue near East 63 St; 319-1772. And South Street Seaport, 193 Front St; 947-1727. The familiar American-classic Coach-brand leather handbags as well as briefcases, wallets, diaries, planners, and belts. Catalog available. Price range: $18-$250. AE, MC, V. *OPEN 7 days.*

Fine & Klein
119 Orchard Street near Delancey St. 674-6720. Lower East Side institution for expensive, well-known day and evening bags at great discounts (at 30 percent off). They will often special-order what you want, come with a picture. Also upstairs for shoes. Sunday is madness, try for a weekday. *OPEN Sun-Fri.*

Gucci
685 Fifth Avenue at 54 St. 826-2600. The famed signature Gs on a wide variety of handbags and accessories. Luggage, jewelry, scarves, and gifts. AE, DC, MC, V.

Jacomo
25 East 61 Street. 832-9038. Extremely expensive evening bags, most in exotic leathers. Day

bags for less, belts, and some Deco-era jewelry. Good sales. AE, MC, V.

La Bagagerie
727 Madison Avenue near East 64 St. 758-6570. Every color, style, and fabric of fashion bags. Also belts, luggage, and briefcases. AE, MC, V.

Lederer
613 Madison Avenue near East 58 St. 355-5515. Long-established shop for fashionable leather handbags, accessories, and luggage from France and Italy. Expensive. AE, MC, V.

Louis Vuitton
51 East 57 Street; 371-6111. And Saks Fifth Avenue; 753-4000. Quality leather and luggage maker since 1896. The ultimate albeit overexposed status "LV" initials on well-made bags, belts, accessories, and luggage. Now there is a new line for the secure—no "LVs"! Also new bright hues. AE, DC, MC, V.

Suarez
26 West 54 Street. 315-5614. Longtime source for very fine European bags, wide selection at very good prices (up to 20 percent lower than elsewhere). AE, MC, V.

Tony Bryant Design
339 Lafayette Street at Bleecker St. 254-5743. Smart selection of handcrafted leather and canvas bags. Vibrant colors, original designs. Wallets and belts, too. AE, MC, V. *OPEN 7 days noon-7:30pm.*

—**Handbag Repairs**

Artbag
735 Madison Avenue near East 64 St. 744-2720. The expert, albeit expensive, handbag repairers. Also finely crafted lower-priced copies of expensive (not on repairs) designer bags; custom work. Price range: $80-$3,000. AE, MC, V.

Barbara Schaum
See Handbags.

Leather

Hermès
11 East 57 Street. 751-3181. Spacious shop for the leather and silk luxuries synonymous with this 146-year-old saddlery. In addition to the saddles, there's sportclothes for men and women, perfume, and the famed equestrian-theme scarves now enjoying extraordinary popularity. And, of course, the legendary Kelly bag. AE, DC, MC, V.

Loewe
711 Madison Avenue at East 63 St. 308-7700. Exquisitely crafted and luxurious ladies' and men's leather clothing, shoes, handbags, luggage, and accessories from this leading Spanish firm. AE, DC, MC, V.

New York Leather Company
33 Christopher Street near Sixth Ave. 243-2710. High-fashion leather, beautiful colors and styles. Bags and belts, many handmade on premises. AE, MC, V. *OPEN 7 days.*

North Beach Leather
772 Madison Avenue at East 66 St. 772-0707.

For women and men: eye-catching, distinctively styled, buttery soft leather and suede clothing and accessories for all seasons. AE, MC, V.

Tannery West
South Street Seaport, 191 Front Street; 509-6095. And Trump Plaza, 1040 Third Avenue near East 61 St; 319-5112. Also 586 Columbus Avenue near West 88 St, 874-2130. A glamorous collection of year-round suedes and leathers in high styles and hot colors; for women and men. AE, CB, DC, MC, V. *OPEN 7 days.*

—**Leather Cleaning**

Leathercraft Process
212 West 35 Street. 564-8980. (Located in Marvel Cleaners.) Since 1919, specialists in cleaning shearlings, sheepskins, suede, and leather garments. MC, V. *OPEN Mon-Fri 7:30am-6:30pm.*

Leathermaster
176 Second Avenue near East 11 St. 674-6651. Expert cleaning, tailoring, repair of leather, suede, shearling. 24-hour service available.

Lingerie & Nightwear

The department stores have lovely lingerie departments now that pretty sexy underthings have made a respectable comeback. **Bloomingdale's**, **Bergdorf Goodman**, *and* **Macy's** *Private Lives are standouts.* (*See also* Vintage Clothing, *for antique undies.*)

AM/PM
109 Thompson Street near Prince St. 219-0343. Small but well-stocked SoHo shop for traditional to sexy lingerie including Hanro's all cotton comfort. Silk boxer shorts and pj's, sensational bustiers. AE, MC, V. *OPEN 7 days noon-7pm.*

A. W. Kaufman
73 Orchard Street near Grand St. 226-1629 or -1788. For over 65 years shoppers have gotten great buys on major designer's lingerie, loungewear, and sleepwear. Also an imported Swiss line for women and men. Big discounts. AE, MC, V. *OPEN Sun-Fri. CLOSES Fri at 2pm.*

Enelra Lingerie
48½ East 7 Street. 473-2454. A first for this Ukrainian neighborhood (which has seen almost everything): high-price, high-style, sexy, and sensuous European and American lingerie. Also silk tees and boxer shorts for him. AE, MC, V. *OPEN Sun-Wed noon-8pm; Thurs-Sat till 10:30pm.*

Fogal
680 Madison Avenue near East 62 St; 759-9782. And 510 Madison Avenue at East 53 St; 355-3254. Swiss-made pantyhose, stockings, socks, and bodystockings. More than 100 colors, fabrics like silk and cashmere, and the top of the line "tuxedo" with a stripe of Swarovski crystals on each leg. Extra small to extra, extra large. Price range: $8-$280. AE, DC, MC, V.

Goldman & Cohen
55 Orchard Street near Hester St. 966-0737. Good Lower East Side source for brand-name and designer lingerie and loungewear at 20-50

percent below usual retail prices. Bali, Warner, Vanity Fair, Maidenform. AE, MC, V. *OPEN Sun-Fri. CLOSES Fri at 3pm.*

L'Affaire
226 Third Avenue near East 19 St. 254-1922. Fanciful undies and nighties from France, England, Italy, and Switzerland in a tiny shop. Luxurious styles and fabrics. AE, MC, V. *OPEN 7 days.*

La Lingerie
792 Madison Avenue near East 67 St. 772-9797. Sheer indulgences fit for a princess and requiring a dowry. Luxurious silk, lace, satin, and cashmere—much of it from Italy and France. Exquisite hand-embroidery. Silk stockings. Trousseau-oriented (there's a registry). AE, MC, V.

La Petite Coquette
52 University Place near East 10 St. 473-2478. Charming little Greenwich Village shop for luxurious cotton and fine-silk designer lingerie from around the world. AE, MC, V.

Lauren Bogen
1044 Lexington Avenue near East 74 St. 570-9529.Sensual and sensible underthings. Lounge and leisurewear, swimsuits, too. Ora Feder, Fernando Sanchez, La Peria, Lore. AE, MC, V.

Lee Baumann Specialty Shop
38 East 8 Street. 473-3548. This well-stocked well-run neighborhood Village shop has all the latest in lingerie from the routine to the risqué. Active and exercisewear, too. AE, CB, MC, V.

Leggiadro
700 Madison Avenue near East 62 St. 753-5050. A wide selection of colorful pantyhose, stockings, and socks from Italy, Germany, and Austria. AE, MC, V.

Mendel Weiss
91 Orchard Street at Broome St. 925-6815. Famous-name brands including Warner, Bali, Olga, and Maidenform at 25 percent off. MC, V. *OPEN Sun-Fri. CLOSES Fri at 2pm.*

Montenapoleone
789 Madison Avenue near East 67 St. 535-2660. Very expensive and luxuriously seductive Italian lingerie, including the finest pure silk. Also custom orders. Now, Italian swimwear, too. AE, MC, V.

Roberta
1252 Madison Avenue near East 90 St. 860-8366. Exquisite lingerie in a wide price range. Silk stockings as well as swimwear. Very personal service. AE, MC, V.

Samantha Jones
1074 Third Avenue near East 63 St. 308-6680. Elegant, very personal romantic shop for seductive luxurious lingerie. AE, MC, V. *OPEN 7 days.*

Victoria's Secret
34 East 57 Street; 758-5592. And 691 Madison Avenue at East 62 St; 838-8787. Emporium of the well-known mail-order catalog. For her: a large luxurious selection of silk and lace intimate apparel and sleepwear. For him: a selection of silk boxer shorts, robes, pj's, and more. Wide price range. AE, MC, V. *OPEN 7 days.*

Maternity Wear

All the large stores have maternity departments.

Balloon
1321 Madison Avenue near East 93 St. First American outlet of a French maternity store chain. High-fashion designs for the office, for play, and for evening. Moderate to expensive. AE, MC, V.

Jonal
25 East 73 Street. 879-9200. In an inviting town house setting, custom-made, well-designed maternity clothes in sumptuous fabrics. Also elegant daywear sizes 6-12 and made to measure. Price range: $275-$300. AE, MC, V.

Lady Madonna
793 Madison Avenue at East 67 St, second floor. 988-7173. The pioneer in the well-dressed-though-pregnant idea. Everything everyone else wears for the mother-to-be. Tasteful yet imaginative. AE, MC, V.

Mothers Work Maternity
50 West 57 Street, 2nd floor. 399-9840. Dress-for-success-though-pregnant. Businesslike maternity suits and dresses; casual sportswear and lingerie. Wonderful idea for the working mother-to-be! MC, V. *OPEN Thurs till 7:30pm.*

Patent Pending
1178 Lexington Avenue near East 80 St; 988-3996. And 2007 Broadway near West 68 St; 769-2232. Trendy moderately priced sportswear, as well as career and party clothes for the mother-to-be. Activewear, including swimsuits. AE, MC, V. *OPEN 7 days.*

Reborn Maternity
1449 Third Avenue at East 82 St; 737-8817. And 564 Columbus Avenue near West 87 St; 362-6965. Everything a pregnant woman might want to wear, including designer fashions. One of the largest selections in the city. Good sales. Catalog available. AE, MC, V. *OPEN 7 days.*

Raincoats

All the major department stores have a wide selection of raincoats. (See also Men's Clothes, Rainwear.)

Rental

One Night Stand
905 Madison Avenue near East 72 St. 772-7720. Short and long eveningwear by top European and American designers not for sale here. It's rental only. Choose from over 700 dresses sizes 2-16. The fashions are the latest and the range for a three-day rental is $120-$350, with a rather steep deposit. AE, MC, V. *OPEN Mon-Sat by appointment only.*

Shoes & Boots

Eighth Street between Fifth and Sixth Avenue has a high concentration of shoe stores, wide price and quality range.

Anbar's
93 Reade Street near Church St. 227-0253. Discounted styles from the large stores can be found at this discount shoe house located in the old shoe manufacturing district (now TriBeCa). Name brands include Charles Jourdan, Martinique, some Anne Klein, Clergie, Petra, and Bandolino up to 50 percent off retail. *OPEN Mon-Fri 8am-5:25pm; Sat 11am-5pm.*

Bally of Switzerland
689 Madison Avenue at East 62 St. 751-2163. The famed classic import for women. Price range: $150 and up. Also leather accessories. AE, DC, MC, V.

Botticelli
612 Fifth Avenue near 49 St. 582-6313. Fine, handmade Italian women's shoes and boots, both trendy and conservative. Luggage and accessories. AE, MC, V. *OPEN 7 days.*

Carrano
677 Fifth Avenue at 53 St; 752-6111. And 750 Madison Avenue near East 65 St; 570-9020. Moderate to expensive high-quality high-fashion Italian shoes, boots, and handbags. AE, CB, DC, MC, V.

Charles Jourdan
Trump Tower, 725 Fifth Avenue at 56 St; 644-3830. And 769 Madison Avenue at East 66 St; 628-0133. Also at Macy's, 560-4403. The French fashion pacesetter. Fabulous shoes for men and women; accessories; women's and men's ready to wear, too. AE, CB, DC, MC, V. *OPEN 7 days.*

Ecco Shoes
111 Thompson Street near Prince St; 925-8010. And 324 Columbus Avenue near West 75 St; 799-5229. Also 94 Seventh Avenue near 15 St, 675-5180; and 1024 Third Avenue near East 61 St, 759-2868. A clutch of well-located shoe stores popular for their fun, stylish, and well-priced shoes and boots. Terrific end-of-season sales. AE, MC, V. *OPEN 7 days.*

Ferragamo
717 Fifth Avenue at 56 St. 759-3822. Top-quality classically elegant shoes crafted in Florence for women who put comfort above fashion. No heel higher than 3½ inches. Clothes and accessories, too. AE, DC, MC.

Giordano's
1118 First Avenue near East 61 St. 688-7195. Specializes in ladies shoe sizes 4-6 medium and 5½-6½ AA only. Anne Klein, Andrew Geller, YSL, Beene Bags, Julianelli, Calvin Klein, Garolina, Liz Claiborne. AE, MC, V.

Gucci
689 Fifth Avenue at 54 St. 826-2600. Their classic loafers with the signature horsebit are making a fashion comeback. For men and women, $260. AE, MC, V.

Helene Arpels
470 Park Avenue near East 57 St. 775-1623. Wives of presidents have bought their flats here. Evening shoes, too. High quality and expensive. AE, MC, V.

Joan & David
816 Madison Avenue near East 69 St. 772-3970.

All their wonderfully handsome shoes, boots, bags, belts, and luggage under one roof. For women and men. AE, DC, MC, V.

Kenneth Cole
353 Columbus Avenue near West 76 St; 873-2061. And 95 Fifth Avenue at 17 St; 675-2550. Stylish yet eminently comfortable and affordable shoes and boots for men and women. Price range: $40-$200. Also, small leather goods, belts, briefcases, ties, and socks. Great ad campaign's from this talented designer and son-in-law of Governor Cuomo. AE, MC, V. *OPEN 7 days.*

Lace-Up Shoe Shop
110 Orchard Street at Delancey St. 475-8040. Top-name fashionable designer shoes and boots well discounted, albeit size choices are limited. Joan & David, Liz Claiborne, Evan Picone, Charles Jourdan, MC, V. *OPEN Sun-Fri.*

Leslie's Bootery & Designer Shoes
319 Grand Street near Orchard St. 431-9196. Discount designer shoes, boots, and running shoes by Bally, Perry Ellis, Kenneth Cole, Cole-Haan, 9 West, Calvin Klein, Via Spiga at least 20 percent off. Men's shoes, too. MC, V. *OPEN Sun-Fri.*

Manolo Blahnik
15 West 55 Street. 582-3007. Also at Bergdorf. Innovative pricey shoe fashions handmade in Italy. AE, MC, V.

Mario Valentino
645 Fifth Avenue at 51 St. 486-0322. Via Milano. An elegant shoe store for women and men. Leather and suede shoes and clothing; small leather goods and scarves. AE, DC, MC, V.

Maud Frizon
19 East 69 Street. 249-5368. Very expensive, imaginative, beautifully detailed—in many cases exotic—creations. Special orders in special cases. Men's and a new collection of costly children's shoes, too. AE, MC, V.

Perry Ellis
680 Madison Avenue near East 61 St; 980-7012. And 1136 Madison Avenue at East 85 St; 570-9311. The Perry Ellis couture line for women only. Price range: $92-$450 (crocodile). AE, MC, V.

Peter Fox
378 Amsterdam Avenue at West 78 St; 874-6399. And 105 Thompson Street near Prince St; 431-6359. Exclusive lavish offbeat look of long-time past by this English designer. The lace-up ankle shoes, satin pumps, buckles and bows make this appear at first glance to be a vintage shop. AE, MC, V. *OPEN 7 days.*

Sacha London
294 Columbus Avenue near West 74 St; 873-5788. And 714 Lexington Avenue near East 58 St; 759-0140. Patterned and amusingly adorned flats and heels from England for the young and whimsical. AE, MC, V. *OPEN 7 days.*

Shoe Steal
116 Duane Street near Church St. 964-4017. TriBeCa store for dress and sport shoes, sandals, and boots at a discount of 30-50 percent. Sizes 5-12; AAA-E widths. Naturalizer, Caressa,

Red Cross, Bass, Nina, Nickels, 9 West. *OPEN Mon-Fri 8am-5:30pm; Sat 11am-5pm.*

Susan Bennis/Warren Edwards
440 Park Avenue at East 56 St. 755-4197. A well-known award-winning team for beautifully designed, unusual, extravagant, and appropriately expensive ($250-$1,250) shoes and boots for women and men. Luggage and clothes, too. AE, MC, V.

Tucson Leather
128 Thompson Street near Prince St. 228-2857. Handmade cowboy boots by Stewart, Larry Mehan, and others. Also shoes by Utility, French Dressings, and NaNa. For men, too. AE, MC, V. *OPEN 7 days.*

Village Cobbler
60 West 8 Street. 673-8530. Small shop with a huge stock of all the very latest fashions in youthful casual and trendy shoes and boots. Lower prices than uptown. AE, CB, DC, MC, V. *OPEN 7 days.*

Walter Steiger
739 Madison Avenue near East 65 St. 570-1212. The ultimate craftsman. Elegant, unusual, and (of course) expensive shoes for women and men. The patterned fabric shoes are very fine indeed. AE, MC, V.

Wendy's Footwear
1227 Third Avenue near East 71 St; 472-2775. And *49 West 39 Street; 391-2926. Osvaldo, Clergerie, Bandolino, Nickels, Jazz—at discount. Good seasonal sales as well. AE, MC, V. *OPEN 7 days. *Mon-Fri.*

Swimsuits

Department stores have year-round swim- and cruisewear departments as well as swimwear in the lingerie department.

Water Wear
1349 Third Avenue at East 77 St; 570-6606. And 1225 Madison Avenue at East 84 St; 439-7877. Full line of swimsuits year-round. Leading designer labels and imports. One piece with a range of cup sizes and bikini tops and bottoms sold individually, especially appealing for those with less than perfectly proportioned figures. Also, cover-ups and sportswear. Personal service. AE, MC, V.

Unusual Sizes

Saks Fifth Avenue has a petite shop and a "12 plus" shop; Bloomingdale's and Bergdorf also have large-size departments.

Ashanti-Larger Sizes
872 Lexington Avenue near East 65 St. 535-0740. High-quality stylish elegance in large (14-26) sizes. Their own label, more individual than most for the larger woman using all natural handwoven and hand-dyed fabrics. Also jewelry and accessories. Alterations on premises. AE, DC, MC, V.

Charisma
153 East 57 Street. Large-size dressing in extravagant styles and fabrics for women up to size 26-28; some 30-32. AE, MC, V. *OPEN 7 days.*

Forgotten Woman
880 Lexington Avenue at East 66 St. 535-8848. Fashionable clothes for the large woman, sizes 14-26. Oleg Cassini, Nancy Heller, Tomatsu, and more. Day or evening dresses, sportswear, sweaters, swimsuits. AE, MC, V.

Greater N.Y. Woman
215 East 23 Street. 725-0505. Large-size ladies' apparel for day and evening, sizes 14-24. AE, MC, V.

Lane Bryant
450 Fifth Avenue at 39 St. 764-3550. Now owned by The Limited, this veteran purveyor of large-size clothing for women has a new glittering multilevel store and more fashion-conscious merchandise, sizes 14-28, made expressly for them. AE, MC, V, Lane Bryant charge. *OPEN Mon & Thurs 10am-8pm; Wed, Fri & Sat till 7pm; Sun noon-5pm.*

Piaffe Professional
Business Office, 1412 Broadway, suite 702. 921-7183. This former retailer of sophisticated clothing for petites sizes 0-14 now specializes in personal wardrobe consultation and personalized shopping for that same clientele. Shop at discount; mail order from a small catalog from national manufacturers. No fee if purchases are made. AE, MC, V.

Shelley's Tall Girl Shop
13 East 41 Street. 697-8433. Contemporary dresses and sportswear for tall girls 5 feet 7 inches to 6 feet 4 inches, sizes 7-22. Belts and jewelry, too. AE, MC, V.

MEN'S CLOTHES

Large Stores

(*See also* Department Stores.)

Barney's
Seventh Avenue & West 17 Street. 929-9000. The world's largest men's store (60,000 suits, 600 employees!) and a men's fashion institution. Excellent range for men of every taste, size, and life-style—from business conservative to European now looks. Hats to shoes; toiletries, too. But there are no bargains here—*except* at the big once-a-year sale that gets the most jaded male New Yorker to stand in line for hours. Free alterations, delivery, parking. AE, MC, Barney's charge. *OPEN Mon-Fri 10am-9pm; Sat till 7pm; Sun noon-6pm.* NOTE: Not surprising, a new store is on the boards—one block away from the new Bergdorf for Men.

Bergdorf Goodman Men
745 Fifth Avenue at 58 St. 753-7300. Billed as the ultimate gentlemen's store, the tony new store boasts a refined clubby atmosphere in which to buy both the traditional and more forward fashion looks. Featured are Romeo Gigli, Alan Flusser, Barry Keiselstein-Cord, Turnbull &

Asser, Georgio Armani, Paul Smith, and Ronaldo Shamask. Pampering for the affluent executive shopper includes custom tailoring, a concierge, a cafe, the use of portable telephones, and a putting green. AE, MC, V, Bergdorf and Neiman-Marcus charge. *Mon-Wed, Fri & Sat, 10am-6pm; Thurs 10am-8pm.*

Boutiques

Alan Flusser
14 East 52 Street, 2nd floor; 888-7100. And 50 Trinity Place, 2nd floor; 422-3100. Off the peg and custom men's clothing and men's haberdashery from one at the top. Elegant but traditional, expensive but worth it. AE, DC, MC, V.

A. Peter Pushbottom
1157 Second Avenue near East 61 St. 879-2600. For grown-ups, updated classic sweaters in wonderful colors made of handloomed cotton only. Excellent value. The rest of their stock is Pushbottom for Kids. AE, MC, V.

Beau Brummel
421 West Broadway near Prince St; 219-2666. And 410 Columbus Avenue near West 80 St; 874-6262. Also 1113 Madison Avenue near East 83 St, 737-4200. These trendy boutiques carry their own line plus Hugo Boss and Bill Kaiserman. Some great looks for the young and sure. Expensive. AE, DC, MC, V. *OPEN 7 days.*

Bijan
699 Fifth Avenue near 54 St. 758-7500. Straight to you from Rodeo Drive in Beverly Hills if you have extravagant taste and a bankroll to match, not to mention an appointment. Shirts start at $240; ties at $110!

Bobby Dazzler
1450 Second Avenue near East 76 St. 628-2287. Men's forward fashions, casual, stylish clothes. Lovely collection of cotton shirts. AE, MC, V. *OPEN 7 days.*

Brioni
55 East 52 Street. 355-1940. Luxurious inviting boutique for elegant Italian men's clothing. Sumptuous fabrics, classic European styling and cut; appropriately high priced. Made-to-measure suits, as well. AE, MC, V.

Camouflage
141 Eighth Avenue at West 17 St; 741-9118. And 139 Eighth Avenue near West 17 St; 691-1750. Top Chelsea specialty shops for classic American-made menswear with an upbeat, imaginative feel. More casual at No. 139. AE, MC, V. *OPEN Mon-Fri noon-7pm; Sat 11am-6pm; Sun 1-5pm.*

Charivari
257 Columbus Avenue at West 72 St; 787-7272. And 441 Columbus Avenue near West 81 St; 496-8700. Also 201 West 79 Street, 799-8650; and 16-18 West 57 Street, 333-4040. European and American now fashions for men, including Giorgio Armani and Gianni Versace. Well stocked, well run. AE, MC, V. *OPEN 7 days.*

Comme des Garçons
116 Wooster Street near Prince St. 219-0660. In a stark, bunkerlike environment, the loosely fitting and often asymmetrical cutting-edge fashions of Japanese designer Rei Kawakubo. AE, DC, MC, V. *OPEN 7 days.*

David Cenci
801 Madison Avenue near East 67 St. 628-5910. A handsome setting for an expensive but outstanding selection of impeccably tailored classics. Wonderful fabrics in everything from suits and sportswear to coats and formal wear. AE, DC, MC, V. *Thurs till 7:30pm.*

Emporio Armani
110 Fifth Avenue at 16 St. 727-3240. In a historic Stanford White–designed building, against a stark backdrop, the Italian master's less costly interpretations of his own fashions. Classic separates, casual sweaters, jeans, and trousers; great shoes, too. For women, too. A must stop in this newly emerging shopping area on lower Fifth. AE, MC, V. *OPEN 7 days.*

F.D.R. Drive Men
80 Thompson Street near Spring St. 966-4827. Their own line of men's fashions inspired by other times—actually cut from vintage patterns and made from vintage fabrics. Wonderful pleated trousers, jackets, vests, and crisp shirts. Period accessories. AE, MC, V. *OPEN Tues-Sun 1-7pm.*

Ferragamo Uomo
730 Fifth Avenue near 57 St. 246-6211. Two floors of high-quality Florentine ready-to-wear clothing for men. Wonderful fabrics; quality shoes. AE, MC, V. *Thurs till 7pm.*

Frank Stella
440 Columbus Avenue near West 81 St. 877-5566. Super men's fashions. Silk shirts in solids and stripes; 100 percent cotton, too. Also sweaters, hundreds of ties, and accessories. AE, MC, V. *OPEN 7 days.*

Gianpietro Boutique
207 East 60 Street. 759-2322. High-profile high-fashion Italian clothes. Costly but wonderful suits, sportswear including suede and leather jackets. AE, MC, V. *OPEN Mon & Thurs till 7:30pm.*

Giorgio Armani
815 Madison Avenue near East 68 St. 988-9191. Armani's tailoring perfection for men and women. AE, MC, V.

Jean Pierre
237 East 60 Street. 838-8680. Fine, expensive European boutique. Excellent quality and service. Women's, too. AE, MC, V.

Lanvin
872 Madison Avenue at East 71 St. 288-9210. Made in France suits, jackets, slacks, and shirts. Custom shirts, too. AE, MC, V.

Madonna
210 East 60 Street. 838-3760. Still an exclusive European trendsetter. Owner was the style consultant for the film *American Gigolo* and TV's "Miami Vice." Great sales July and August. AE, DC, MC, V. *OPEN 7 days.*

Mano A Mano
580 West Broadway near Prince St. 219-9602.
Large aggressive SoHo boutique for flamboyant,
casual, and dress clothes by European designers for the man who wants to make a "fashion
statement." AE, MC, V. *OPEN 7 days.*

Napoleon
Trump Tower, 725 Fifth Avenue at 56 St; 759-
1110. And 1048 Third Avenue at East 62 St; 308-
3000. Very expensive, stylish European tailoring.
Suits, sports jackets, fine shirts, and ties. AE,
DC, MC, V.

New Republic Clothiers
93 Spring Street near Mercer St. 219-3005. Their
own original designs in menswear based on
20th-century classics, all made in the U.S. and
England, in a shop with a time-worn feel. Accessories, shoes; womenswear, too. AE, MC, V.
OPEN 7 days noon-7pm.

Paul Smith
108 Fifth Avenue at 16 St. 627-9770. A wonderful
clubby setting for the English fashion designer's
fine tailoring, handsome fabrics, and wonderfully
idiosyncratic way of updating the classics. Fascinating accessories and furnishings for sale,
too. AE, MC, V. *OPEN 7 days.*

Polo/Ralph Lauren
867 Madison Avenue at East 72 St. 606-2100. A
stylized setting in a historic mansion for Lauren's
well-bred classic look—for men on the first and
second floors. It's all here: Polo slacks, jackets,
shirts, ties, and furnishings. AE, DC, MC, V.
OPEN 7 days.

Saint Laurent Rive Gauche for Men
859 Madison Avenue near East 71 St. 517-7400.
High-priced high fashion. AE, DC, MC, V.

Verri Uomo
802 Madison Avenue near East 67 St. 737-9200.
Elegant and distinctive Euro fashions in luxurious fabrics. AE, DC, MC, V. *Thurs till 7pm.*

Custom Tailoring

(*See also* Shirts: Custom.)

Alfred Dunhill Tailors of London
450 Park Avenue at East 57 St. 753-9292. Dunhill
tailoring perfection. Men's suits and shirts both
custom (they will come to you for a fitting) and
off-the-peg imports. Very luxurious, very expensive. Also custom-made shoes, fine gifts, leather
goods, jewelry, writing instruments, and smokers' accessories. AE, MC, V.

Chipp
342 Madison Avenue at East 43 St, 2nd floor.
687-0850. Custom tailoring, including riding
clothes. High-quality, bespoke suits, plus ready-
to-wear suits, jackets, and trousers. Very expensive. AE, MC, V.

Saint Laurie, Ltd
See Discount & Off-Price.

Sulka
430 Park Avenue near East 58 St; 980-5200. And
at the Waldorf-Astoria; 872-4592. Custom-made
shirts, silk pajamas, and the like. Rich tastes and

pockets. Off-the-peg range also, English-style
suits, sport jackets and slacks. AE, DC, MC, V.

Discount & Off-Price

BFO and BFO Plus
149 Fifth Avenue near 21 St, street & 2nd floor.
254-0059 or-0060. Prices below wholesale for
jackets, suits, coats, raincoats, trousers. From
36 regular to 48 extra large. Ralph Lauren, Cardin, Perry Ellis, Geoffrey Beene, Lanvin,
Givenchy, and a large selection of well-known
Italian designers. AE, MC, V. *OPEN 7 days.*

Dollar Bills General Store
99 East 42 Street. 867-0212. Well-located, well-
stocked, well-priced menswear, including many
designer names. Low frills, high savings. AE,
DC, MC, V.

Eisenberg & Eisenberg
85 Fifth Avenue at 16 St, 6th floor. 627-1290.
Men's clothing direct from the manufacturer at
discount prices. AE, MC, V. *OPEN 7 days.*

Emporio Antony
10 Orchard Street near Delancey St. 477-0592.
Italian designer imports for men. Jackets, suits,
shirts, cashmere coats by Basile, Ferre, Versace.
Sweaters from Spain. Well priced. AE, MC, V.
OPEN 7 days.

Fashion Center
327 Grand Street near Orchard St. 966-1105.
Name brand at discount including Adolfo,
Givenchy, Saint Laurent, Stanley Blacker, and
more. AE, MC, V. *OPEN Sun-Fri.*

Gorsart
9 Murray Street near Broadway, 2nd floor. 962-
0024. Classic traditional "natural shoulder"
clothing. No frills, low prices, free alterations.
MC, V. *Thurs till 7pm.*

LS Men's Clothing
19 West 44 Street, suite 403. 575-0933. Upper-
end men's clothing at impressive discount. Try
them first for American-made natural shoulder
and designer-styled suits, sportscoats, outerwear, and slacks—all at 40-60 percent off retail.
Tailoring on premises. AE, MC, V. *OPEN Sun-Fri.*
CLOSES Fri at 3pm.

Moe Ginsburg
162 Fifth Avenue at 21 St, 2nd to 5th floors. 242-
3482. Designer clothing at less than you would
pay at fine department stores. Large selection.
AE, MC, V. *OPEN 7 days.*

NBO
1965 Broadway at West 67 St. 595-1550. European and American designer clothes up to 65
percent off list. This classy discount store has
everything for the well-dressed man—including
shoes. AE, MC, V. *OPEN Mon-Sat 10am-9pm;
Sun 6am-6pm.*

Rothman's
200 Park Avenue South at East 17 St. 777-7400.
Excellent discounter of quality men's tailored
clothing; in season and at a 30-40 percent savings. Perry Ellis, Alexander Julian, Ralph Lauren;
excessive discounter of Hickey Freeman, Nor-

man Hilton suits. In wonderful new quarters. AE, MC, V. *OPEN 7 days.*

Saint Laurie, Ltd.
897 Broadway at East 20 St. 473-0100. Specialty: well-tailored business suits (for men and women) in fine fabrics, also sportscoats, overcoats, slacks, and skirts all made on premises. Now located in the old Lord & Taylor building; there is a huge selection, all at 30 percent off. Free alterations. Also traditional custom tailoring by appointment. The lobby features a history of tailoring exhibit. Visitors may take a self-guided tour of the workrooms. This part of town was once called the Ladies' Mile, now a designated historic district. AE, DC, MC, V. *OPEN 7 days.*

Syms
42 Trinity Place. 797-1199. Three floors of off-price (30-50 percent) men's apparel from shoes and socks to hats and coats, to swimsuits and tuxedos. Blass, Cerruti, Cardin, Hechter, After Six. Specialty: shirts (original retail-price tags on). Women's and children's wear as well. NOTE: Under age 18 not admitted without an adult. Avoid lunch hour here, it's madness.

Hats

JJ Hat Center
1276 Broadway at West 33 St. 502-5012. Extremely large Stetson hat and cap collection. Everything from Westerns to collapsible top hats; homburgs to Indiana Jones, derby to Bogie. Catalog. AE, DC, MC, V. *OPENS at 8:45am.*

Van Dyke Hatters
94 Greenwich Avenue near West 12 St. 929-5696. Wide variety, including Borsalino, Stetson, and their own brand, plus cleaning and blocking. AE, MC, V. *OPEN Mon-Fri 7:30am-6pm; Sat 9am-4pm.*

Worth & Worth Ltd.
331 Madison Avenue near East 42 St. 867-6058. The complete hatter for men: fedoras by Borsalino, Cavanagh, Stetson, Christy's of London. Caps and walking hats in cashmere, shetland, viyella, and Harris tweed. Catalog. AE, DC, MC, V.

Leather

(See also Women's Clothes, Leather.*)*

Academy
See Vintage & Surplus.

Bridge Merchandise Corporation
74 Orchard Street near Grand St. 674-6320. Large selection of leatherwear substantially discounted. AE, MC, V. *OPEN Sun-Fri.*

East Village Leather
27 St. Marks Place. 533-8330. The biker look in leather. Jackets, boots, accessories for men and women. AE, MC, V. *OPEN 7 days noon-8pm.*

Leather Man
111 Christopher Street near Bleecker St. 243-5339. Custom-designed leather jackets, pants, vests, tees, and briefs, too. Moderately expensive. AE, MC, V. *OPEN 7 days noon-midnight.*

Rainwear

Aquascutum of London
680 Fifth Avenue at 54 St. 975-0250. English clothing firm famed for its trenchcoats and the luxurious tailoring of its cashmere and tweed coats for men and women. Cashmere sweaters and blouses, too. AE, DC, MC, V. *Thurs till 7pm.*

British American House
488 Madison Avenue near East 51 St. 752-5880. Specializes in English rainwear; overcoats by Burberry. AE, MC, V. *Thurs till 8pm.*

Burberry
9 East 57 Street. 371-5010. The famed trenchcoats, checked scarves, umbrellas, and accessories as well as men's wear and women's country clothes. Five floors to sell the classic English look. AE, DC, MC, V. *Thurs till 7pm.*

Rentals

Herman's
28 West 48 St. 719-2278. Latest styles, rental and sales. After Six, Adolfo, Bill Blass, Yves Saint Laurent, Lord West. Same-day service; free pickup and delivery. AE, CB, DC, MC, V. *Mon, Thurs & Fri till 7pm.*

Zeller Tuxedos
201 East 56 Street, 2nd floor. 355-0707. Traditional to trendy formalwear. Ungaro, Ferragamo, Valentino, Bally, Canali. Formal accessories, too. Alterations, delivery. AE, MC, V.

Shirts

Addison on Madison
698 Madison Avenue near East 62 St. 308-2660. A small shop sells private label pure-cotton-only French-made shirts; also all-silk ties. Shirts $59-$65, sizes 14½-17½; ties $27-$30. *OPEN 7 days.*

Ascot Chang
7 West 57 Street. 759-3333. Ready-to-wear and custom shirts from the renowned Hong Kong shirtmaker. Vast choice of glorious fabrics, twelve collar styles. Also Italian made-to-measure suits, dressing gowns, and pjs; handcrafted umbrellas. AE, MC, V.

Bancroft Haberdashers
363 Madison Avenue near East 45 St. 687-8650. Branches. Largest selection of ready-to-wear men's shirts and neckwear in New York. AE, CB, DC, MC, V.

Turnbull & Asser
Bergdorf Goodman Men, 745 Fifth Avenue at 58 St. 753-7300. London's legendary haberdasher. AE, MC, V, Bergdorf and Neiman-Marcus charge.

Victory The Shirt Experts
96 Orchard Street near Delancey St. 677-2020. These 100 percent cotton shirts sell under department stores' private labels. Here they are 25 percent less costly direct from the manufacturer. Sizes 14/32-18½/36. Also silk ties, "braces," and

accessories. AE, MC, V. *OPEN Sun-Fri 9am-5pm.*

—Shirts: Custom

(*See also* Custom Tailoring.)
Chris-Arto Custom Shirt Company
39 West 32 Street, 6th floor. 563-4455. Choose from nearly 500 natural fabrics. Six-shirt minimum order; four-week delivery. Also, custom-made pajamas and boxers. *OPEN Mon-Fri 8am-5pm.*

Custom Shop
338 Madison Avenue near East 44 St; 867-3650. And 555 Lexington Avenue at East 50 St; 759-7480. Also 618 Fifth Avenue near 49 St, 245-2499; *1400 Broadway near West 38 St, 244-2748; 1364 Sixth Avenue at West 55 St, 582-4950; and *115 Broadway near Pine St, 267-8535. Custom-made shirts at no extra charge (minimum of four). Choose from over 300 cotton and cotton-blend fabrics. Six-week delivery. Ready-to-wear as well. AE, DC, MC, V. *Mon-Fri.*

Duhamell
437 Park Avenue South near East 30 St. 684-1300. Custom shirts and pajamas made of the finest imported cotton and silks. Six-shirt minimum. Three-week delivery. Also fine custom-tailored suits and leather clothing. Expensive. AE, MC, V.

Shoes & Boots

(*See also* Sports Clothes & Shoes.)
Bally of Switzerland
711 Fifth Avenue near 55 St; 751-9082. And 645 Madison Avenue near East 59 St; 832-7267. Also 347 Madison Avenue near East 45 St, 986-0872; and *2 World Financial Center, 385-0995. Classic yet stylish, high-quality shoes imported from Switzerland. AE, DC, MC, V. *OPEN 7 days.*

Benedetti Custom Shoes
530 Seventh Avenue near West 39 St. 719-5075. Expensive men's footwear, including special made-to-orders. AE, MC, V.

Botticelli
666 Fifth Avenue near 53 St. 582-2984. Fine expensive Italian shoes in elegant surroundings. AE, DC, MC, V. *Thurs till 8pm.*

Church's English Shoes
428 Madison Avenue near East 49 St. 755-4313. Classic fine-quality English shoes, good sales. AE, CB, DC, MC, V.

Gucci
689 Fifth Avenue at 54 St. 826-2600. The statusy Italian shoes for men and women; fashions and accessories, too. AE, DC, MC, V.

J. M. Weston
42 East 57 Street. 308-5655. Exclusive bootmakers in Paris since 1865. Known for styling and fit; 80 percent of each shoe is made by hand. Sixty styles, 24 sizes, and five widths. Price range: $375-$1,600. AE, DC, MC, V.

Leslie's Bootery
319 Grand Street near Orchard St. 431-9196. Lower East Side store for minimum 20 percent discount on Bally, Rockport, Cole-Haan, Bostonian, Bass, Reebok, Timberland, Frye, Clarks. Sizes 7-13. For women, too. AE, MC, V. *OPEN Sun-Fri. CLOSES Fri at 4:30pm.*

Lord John Bootery
428 Third Avenue near East 30 St. 532-2579. This store runs a wide fashion gamut of discounted (10-50 percent) shoes and boots for men and women. Western boots by Dan Post, Acme, Justin, Frye; shoes by Dexter, Timberland, Deerstag, and others. AE, MC, V.

McCreedy & Schreiber
37 West 46 Street; 719-1552. And *213 East 59 Street; 759-9241. One of the best selections of boots (including Lucchese) and shoes for casual and dress wear in this excellent longtime emporium. Frye, Timberland, Cole-Haan, Sperry, Rockport, Sebago, Alden, Allen Edmonds, Dan Post, Justin, Tony Lama, Larry Mehan at competitive prices. AE, DC, MC, V. *OPEN 7 days.*

Nino Gabriele
169 East 60 Street. 421-3250. For high-priced, luxurious, au courant men's shoes. AE, DC, MC, V. *Mon & Thurs till 9pm.*

St. Marks Leather Company, Ltd.
17 St. Marks Place near Third Ave. 982-3444. Terrific selection of trendy footwear. Boots and shoes by Dan Post, Tony Lama, Justin, NaNa, Stewart, Acme. Discounts (10-20 percent) on all boots. Birkenstocks, too. AE, MC, V. *OPEN 7 days noon-8pm.*

To Boot
*256 Columbus Avenue at West 72 St; 724-8249. And at Bergdorf Goodman Men, 3rd floor. The famed boot selection, including handmade exotic leathers, has been joined by casual, leisure, business, and formal footwear for men. Eighty-five percent of the stock is their own design and manufacture; also an exclusive line by Italy's Cesare Paciotti. AE, DC, MC, V. *OPEN 7 days.*

Sports Clothes & Shoes

Abercrombie & Fitch
*South Street Seaport, 199 Water Street at Fulton St; 809-9000. And Trump Tower, 725 Fifth Avenue at 56 St; 832-1001. The sporting goods specialist—established in 1892—returns to New York. Amid the books, games, and globes, casual sportswear for men, mainly updated classics. AE, MC, V. *OPEN 7 days.*

ACA Joe
744 Broadway near Astor Pl; 529-8775. And Pier 17, South Street Seaport; 406-0770. Colorful, prewashed, casual 100 percent natural fiber sportswear. Seasonless, unisex, and highly affordable. AE, MC, V. *OPEN 7 days.*

Athlete's Foot
170 West 72 Street near Broadway; 874-1003. And 16 West 57 Street; 586-1936. Also 739 Third Avenue near East 46 St, 697-7870; and *34 East 8 Street, 260-0750; plus other branches. Incredible selection of moderately priced athletic footwear. Reebok, Nike, Adidas, New Balance, Avia, Converse. Some related accessories and

clothes. For women and men. Price range: $20-$110. AE, MC, V. *OPEN 7 days.*

Billy Martin's
812 Madison Avenue at East 68 St. 861-3100. Unique custom-made Western shirts, jackets, hats, boots, buckles, and belts. Indian jewelry. Fur parkas, Avirex jackets. AE, DC, MC, V.

The Gap
354 Sixth Avenue at Washington Pl; 777-2420. And 133 Second Avenue at St. Marks Pl; 353-2090. Also *145 East 42 Street near Lexington Ave, 286-9490; 734 Lexington Avenue near East 58 St, 751-1543; 1535 Third Avenue near East 86 St, 427-2155; 22 West 34 Street, 695-2521; *545 Madison Avenue near East 55 St, 421-7610; 113 East 23 Street, 533-6670; and 2109 Broadway near West 73 St, 787-6698. The jean store now emphasizes youthful, color-coordinated, moderately priced casual sportswear for men and women. AE, MC, V. *OPEN 7 days.*

Herman's
110 Nassau Street near Beekman St; 233-0733. And 845 Third Avenue at East 51 St; 688-4603. Also *39 West 34 Street, 279-8900; and 135 West 42 Street, 730-7400. Huge selection of athletic shoes, clothes, and equipment. Good sales. AE, DC, MC, V. *OPEN 7 days.*

J. Crew
South Street Seaport, 203 Front Street. 385-3500. The timeless, clean-cut, all-American outdoors look long purveyed in their successful catalog now in their first retail outlet, a huge duplex located in a historic seaport building. From swimsuits to raincoats, and everything in between; accessories, too, for men and women. AE, MC, V. *OPEN 7 days.*

Modell's
243 West 42 Street. 575-8111. Branches. Bargain store for casual clothes; jeans, workshirts, and shoes. AE, MC, V. *OPEN 7 days.*

New York Army & Navy
1598 Second Avenue at East 83 St; 737-4661. And 328 Bleecker Street at Christopher St; 242-6665. Also 110 Eighth Avenue near West 15 St, 645-7420; and 221 East 59 Street, 755-1855. Inexpensive outdoor clothes, shoes, and equipment for active people. AE, MC, V. *OPEN 7 days.*

Robbins Men's-Boys' Wear
1717 Broadway near West 55 St; 581-7033. And 48 West 14 Street; 691-2573. Other branches. Real buys on active clothes, some name brands. Patience required. *OPEN 7 days.*

Ties

Allen Street between Delancey and Houston streets on the Lower East Side has five necktie stores featuring nice, low-priced ties.

Countess Mara
445 Park Avenue near East 56 St. 751-5322. Well known for expensive ties ($35-$125). Casual shirts, too. AE, DC, MC, V.

Tie City
412 Lexington Avenue at East 43 St. 599-1121. Choose from 10,000 well-priced ties—silk and poly. Shirts, belts, socks, too. AE, MC, V. *OPEN Mon-Fri 8am-6pm.*

Trade Center Tie Company
118 Liberty Street near Greenwich St. 964-9742. Good value and selection. Belts, too. MC, V. *OPEN Mon-Fri 8am-6pm.*

—Tie cleaning

Tiecrafters
116 East 27 Street, 6th floor. 867-7676. Neck ties only; they will remove even the most difficult stains. They will also narrow, widen, and shorten ties. *OPEN Mon-Fri 8:30am-5pm.*

Traditional Clothing

(See also Large Stores.)

Brooks Brothers
346 Madison Avenue near East 44 St; 682-8800. And *1 Liberty Plaza near Wall St; 682-8595. The consummate classic men's store—America's oldest—established 1818. On six floors moderate to expensive men's clothing, furnishings. Good sales January, June, and August. AE, DC, Brooks charge. *Thurs till 7pm. *CLOSED Sat.*

F. R. Tripler & Company
366 Madison Avenue at East 46 St. 922-1090. Long-established (1886) store for fine-quality men's apparel and shoes. Largest selection of hand-tailored Hickey-Freeman in U.S. Made-to-measure custom suits and shirts, too. Women's department on three. AE, MC, V, Tripler charge.

H. Herzfeld, Inc.
507 Madison Avenue near East 53 St. 753-6756. High-quality traditional men's clothing in fine fabrics. AE, MC, V.

J. Press
16 East 44 Street. 687-7642. For 90 years, the quintessential Ivy League clothes. Ready-to-wear and bespoke. AE, MC, V.

Paul Stuart
Madison Avenue at East 45 St. 682-0320. Unstuffy conservative. Natural fabrics, sophisticated tailoring. Custom-made shirts. Expensive. Women's clothing on the mezzanine. AE, DC, MC, V, Paul Stuart charge. *OPENS Mon-Fri at 8am for before-work shopping.*

Wallach's
555 Fifth Avenue near 46 St; 687-0106. And *150 Broadway at Liberty St; 513-7660. Comfortable favorite of businessmen for famous-label suits (including the largest selection of Hart Schaffner & Marx in the world), imported sportswear, free alterations. Moderate to expensive. AE, DC, MC, V, Wallach's charge. *Thurs till 7:30pm. *CLOSED Sat.*

Underwear

Under Wares
1098 Third Avenue near East 64 St. 535-6006; (800) 237-8641. Solely devoted to men's underwear, boasting the world's largest collection. Also men's loungewear, sleepwear, and Euro-

pean swimwear. From sexy to silly—100 percent silk boxers and bikinis to Mickey Mouse–embellished briefs. Sociological note: 80 percent of their customers are women. Catalog available. AE, MC, V. *OPEN 7 days.*

Unusual Sizes

Imperial Wear
48 West 48 Street. 719-2590. Large selection of quality clothing and accessories for the big or tall man including Burberry's, Adolfo, Halston, Izod LaCoste, Perry Ellis, Bill Blass, London Fog; Bally shoes. Free alterations. AE, DC, MC, V. *Thurs till 8pm.*

Vintage & Surplus

(*See also* Women's Clothes, Vintage.)
Academy
1703 Broadway at West 54 St. 765-1440. Newly expanded but still clutterful as well as cheerful spot for never-been-worn vintage men's wear. Special orders, free alterations by on-premises tailor. Sometimes, some women's clothes (call first). Also a well-priced source for leather—motorcycle jackets to trenchcoats. AE, DC, MC, V.
Chameleon
270 Bleecker Street at Charles St. 924-8574. Specialty of this vintage emporium: military and aviator leather jackets, WWII and Vietnam era; other good oldies, including Harris tweed and cashmere overcoats, hand-painted tuxedo jackets. Well priced, but stiff staff for where and what they purvey. MC, V. *OPEN Sun-Thurs noon-9pm; Fri & Sat till midnight.*
Church Street Surplus
327 Church Street near Canal St. 226-5280. New and used government issue and civilian surplus and vintage clothing fill the store and the overflowing bins on the street. Dusty bargains. AE, MC, V.
The Cockpit
595 Broadway near Houston St. 925-5456. Authentic nylon or leather sheepskin-lined air force jackets, flight jumpsuits; aviator sunglasses, accessories, military insignias. Outlet store in Long Island City, (718) 482-1997. AE, DC, MC, V. *OPEN Mon-Sat 11:30am-7pm; Sun 12:30-6pm.*
Reminiscence
75 Fifth Avenue near 13 St. 243-2292. Their newly expanded mini-department store has it all, but best here for men, their own modern translations of vintage vests, linen and wool pleated trousers, Hawaiian and silk collarless shirts. Also antique and surplus shoes. AE, MC, V. *OPEN Mon-Sat 11am-8pm; Sun 1-6pm.*
Unique Clothing Warehouse
726 Broadway near Washington Pl. 674-1767. Don't miss this one—it's street-chic headquarters. War surplus, new and renewed: athletic wear, industrial uniforms, colorfully dyed duds.

Good prices. AE, MC, V. *OPEN Sun-Fri 10am-10pm; Sat 10am-midnight; Sun noon-8pm.*
Weiss & Mahoney
142 Fifth Avenue at 19 St. 675-1915. An authentic army/navy surplus-clothing shop from the precheap chic era (1924). Good buys on fatigues, pea coats, jumpsuits, sweaters, and leather flight jackets. AE, MC, V. *OPEN 7 days.*

BEAUTY

Beauty Specialists

Many of the following have half-and whole-day beauty packages. Call for details.
Anushka
241 East 60 Street, 2nd & 3rd floors. 355-6404. In-town spa featuring every aspect of beauty and body care, including nutritional guidance, cellulite treatments, body sluffs, seaweed wraps, acupressure facial, waxing, shiatsu massage, manicures, pedicures, electrolysis, and makeup application. Free consultation. AE, MC, V. *OPEN Mon-Sat 9am-8pm by appointment.*
Christina & Carmen
128 Central Park South at West 59 St. 757-5811. Traditional techniques from this Romanian mother and daughter team. Deep-pore cleansing facials, holistic plant-based products, body sloughing with paraffin, stress-relieving Shiatsu massage. AE, MC, V.
Christine Valmy
767 Fifth Avenue at 58 St; 752-0303. And 101 West 57 Street; 581-9488. Renowned skin-care expert who helped American women discover skin care. Uses Swiss fresh-cell therapy. Two-hour facials for men and women. Special post–plastic surgery care; makeup and foot massage, too. Special pretheater special: facial, manicure, shampoo, and blow-dry. At the Valmy school for aestheticians, lower-priced facials done by supervised students are available Monday to Friday, from 9am to 3pm, and Monday, Tuesday and Wednesday at 6 and 7pm; call 581-1520 for an appointment. AE, DC, MC, V (except at school).
Diane Young
38 East 57 Street. 753-1200. Beautiful setting for holistic skin care: facials, treatments, herbal aromotherapy, expert nutritional advice. Makeup lessons, manicures, pedicures, Swedish massage. Waxing, electrolysis (with disposable needles). Day of Beauty available as well as the "ultimate makeover." AE, MC, V.
Elizabeth Arden/The Salon
691 Fifth Avenue near 54 St. 486-7900. Behind the red door, a Manhattan mini-spa for head-to-toenail pampering. Expert facials, free makeup application. Treat yourself or a loved one to a Miracle Morning or a Main Chance Day for sauna, body massage, haircut and styling, facial, manicure and pedicure, eyebrow shaping, and makeup. AE, MC, V.

Georgette Klinger Skin Care
501 Madison Avenue near East 52 St; 838-3200. And 978 Madison Avenue near East 77 St; 744-6900. Expert skin treatment including surface peeling, deep-pore cleansing, and scalp care for men and women. New full day, full body "intensive curriculum" at 978 Madison. For men, too. The only drawback: the heavy sell on product line. AE, MC, V.

Ilona of Hungary Institute of Skin Care
629 Park Avenue near East 65 St. 288-5155. Well-trained aestheticians give facials, body skin treatments. Individualized care; cosmetic peeling. Climate-keyed all natural products. AE, MC, V.

Janet Sartin
480 Park Avenue near East 58 St. 751-5858. Consultation and product/treatment prescription from a world-famed skin expert (the fee for Sartin herself is $400) for a 90-minute pore-cleansing facial). Well-trained staff. A stellar social clientele. AE, MC, V.

Lia Schorr Skin Care
686 Lexington Avenue near East 57 St. 486-9670. Ms. Schorr analyzes every client's skin prior to treatment. Her restorative day of beauty includes facial, body massage, manicure, pedicure; makeup and a snack. Sensible care, especially for sensitive and acne-plagued skin. For men, too.

Mario Badescu Skin Care
320 East 52 Street. 758-1065. Expert analysis and skin care for women and men. He is sadly gone but his methods and natural formula products still have a loyal following. Also manicures, pedicures, body massage, waxing, and electrolysis. MC, V.

Moi Cosmetology, Ltd.
498 West End Avenue near West 84 St. 877-6128. Expert skin treatments, specializing in problem skin. Deep cleansing facials, exfoliating peel, waxing. Nail specialist as well (she is the author of *Beautiful Nails*). For men and women. *Tues-Sat by appointment.*

Trish McEvoy
800A Fifth Avenue near 61 St. 758-7790. Deep-pore cleansing facials, body buffs and waxing, makeup application and lessons. On her client list—Madonna and model Kim Alexis.

Fragrance & Toiletries

Major department stores carry a full line of fragrances for both men and women on their main floor. (See also Specialty Shops & Services, Pharmacies.*)*

Note: Counterfeit fragrances, packaged to look like the real thing, are showing up all over town. To avoid getting fooled, buy in shops you know.

Aveda Aromatherapy Esthetique
509 Madison Avenue near East 52 St. 832-2416. From Europe, hair and skin care products, makeup, and bath preparations, fragrance for the home—of all natural ingredients. Also, massage.

The Bath House
215 Thompson Street near Bleecker St. 533-0690. Culled from all over the world, natural bath products and accessories. Custom blending of scents—bath oils, bubble bath, and body lotion. Gift baskets, mail order. Perfume recipe file. AE, MC, V ($15 minimum). *OPEN Sun-Thurs 11am-10pm; Fri & Sat 11am-11pm.*

The Body Shop
South Street Seaport, 16 Fulton Street; 480-9876. And 747 Broadway near Astor Pl; 979-2944. Also A&S Plaza, 901 Sixth Avenue at West 33 St, 268-7424; 773 Lexington Avenue at East 61 St, 755-7851; 485 Madison Avenue at East 52 St, 832-0812; and 2159 Broadway at West 76 St, 721-2947. A hugely successful worldwide toiletry and cosmetics chain whose welcoming shops sell all natural products that do not pollute the environment, use biodegradable or recyclable packaging, and are never tested on animals. Along with the save the earth message the products cleanse, polish, and protect the skin and hair—no promises about beauty. AE, MC, V. *OPEN 7 days.*

Cambridge Chemists
21 East 65 Street. 734-5678. British toiletries (also French, Swiss, and German) including Floris of London, Penhaligons, Cyclax, Innoxa, Sabona of London, Simpson shavebrushes. AE, MC, V.

Caswell-Massey Co
518 Lexington Avenue at East 48 St. 755-2254. In business since 1752! This is the oldest apothecary in the U.S. The cologne, specially blended for George and Martha Washington and Lafayette, the cold cream made for Sarah Bernhardt, and the world's largest collection of imported soaps—including pure Castile by the pound—are for sale in this pretty and fragrant shop. Also, one-of-kind silver jars, wood and faux ivory brushes. Now also at the *Seaport Marketplace, 608-5401, and World Financial Center, 945-2630. AE, CB, DC, MC, V. *OPEN 7 days.*

Crabtree & Evelyn
30 East 67 Street; 734-1108. And *1310 Madison Avenue near East 92 St; 289-3923. England's famed all-natural toiletries and comestibles—beautifully presented and packed. Gift baskets made to order. AE, MC, V. *OPEN 7 days.*

Floris
703 Madison Avenue near East 62 St. 935-9100. Used by the English gentry since the 1700s—they carry the royal seal. In their first American outlet the complete luxurious line of English bath and body products. AE, MC, V.

Giorgio Beverly Hills
47 East 57 Street. 319-5660. A fragrance and a phenomenon—direct from Rodeo Drive at $150 an ounce and selling like crazy. Lavish gifts. Also the new Giorgio Suntan line for that "Beverly Hills" tan. Luxurious clothing line as well. AE, CB, DC, MC, V.

Jean Laporte Perfumers
870 Madison Avenue near East 70 St. 517-8665. *L'artisan parfumeur*, a master of perfumes. Jean

Laporte's enchanting natural scents in a small enchanting parfumerie. Also new and old perfume bottles, jewelry, picture frames. AE, DC, MC, V.

Kiehl's Pharmacy
109 Third Avenue near East 13 St. 677-3171; 475-3698. Since 1851 this fascinating pharmacy, now a New York institution, has carried a large selection of pure essences (including one called Rain), perfumes, homeopathics, and cosmetics (only foundation and lipcolor filled with vitamins and sunscreen), all natural ingredients for remedies to cure what ails you. They make all their own products on the premises, including the "age-deterrent" cream. Alas, they no longer carry leeches, but they do stock over 300 different treatments for hair, body, skin, and nails. Knowledgeable and helpful staff. Also mail order. AE, CB, DC, MC, V.

Perfumer's Workshop
Saks Fifth Avenue, 611 Fifth Avenue at 50 St. 753-4000. Have the pleasure of creating your very own personal fragrance. AE, DC, MC, V, Saks charge.

Ross Sales Company
58 Third Avenue near East 10 St. 475-8470. An almost secret source, this shop where professionals buy their hair-styling products and tools also sells to you and me. Name-brand shampoos, conditioners, tints, and dyes—including the trendiest, like the punk hues of Manic Panic—as well as Solis hair dryers at less than retail. AE, MC, V. *OPEN Mon-Fri 8am-5:30pm; Sat 10am-5:30pm.*

Soap Opera
30 Rockefeller Plaza, lower concourse; 245-5090. A wonderful variety of soap, bath oil, bubble bath, potpourri. Specializing in gift baskets and custom blending of oils, bath gels, and body lotions. AE, MC, V.

Hair

—Hairdressers for Men and Women

Astor Place Barber Stylist
2 Astor Place at Broadway. 475-9854 or-9790. Success story: 1940s family-owned barbershop finds new life as the "in" place to have your tresses trimmed—that is if you're young and/or adventuresome. Choose from the Guido, Detroit, Little Tony, Punk, Mohawk, James Dean, Fort Dix, Sparkle Cut, What-the-Hell, Spike, Spina di Pesce, or...Cheap and fun, but expect a wait of up to two hours on weekends. The street scene is interesting in and of itself. P.S.: They still give shaves and now have an annex for perms, manicures, pedicures, facials, etc. *OPEN Mon-Sat 8am-8pm; Sun 9am-6pm.*

Bruno Le Salon
16 West 57 Street, 3rd floor. 581-2760. Easy-to-maintain natural looks dominate. Individualized approach. Good color department. MC, V.

Bruno Pittini
746 Madison Avenue near East 64 St. 517-9660.

Formerly creative director of Bruno Dessange; for hairstyles to express your individuality. Clients Catherine Deneuve, Meryl Streep, Jodie Foster.

Configero
1099 Second Avenue near East 57 St. 688-3894. Haircuts to suit your facial structure.

Frederic Fekkai Beauty Center at Bergdorf Goodman
1 West 57 Street, 7th floor. 753-9500. A fashion world darling in his own wonderful salon with quiet private rooms. For feminine elegant looks. Clients include Kelly McGillis, Sigourney Weaver, and super-model Cindy Crawford. Full service including massage. AE, MC, V, Bergdorf and Neiman-Marcus charge.

Hair Power
124 Second Avenue near East 7 St. 982-6300. For East Village—creative cuts and colors for men and women. *OPEN 7 days 10am-10pm.*

John Frieda
30 East 76 Street, 2nd floor. 879-1000. The salon of lionized London hairstylist who has created looks for no less than Princess Diana, not to mention Mick Jagger and Jane Seymour. For Frieda himself $200 and a long wait.

John Louis David
303 Park Avenue South at East 23 St; 260-3628. And Madison Avenue & East 46 Street; 808-9115. Also 1385 Broadway near West 38 St, 869-6250; and 2113 Broadway near West 74 St, 721-6661. A "quick service" streamlined time- and cost-conscious approach. Designer cut, style, perm, and color—low-priced, under an hour, no appointment necessary.

John Sahag
18 East 53 Street. 371-4777. The favorite stylist of cover girls like Brooke Shields and actresses Demi Moore and Melanie Griffith. He "sculpts" hair with his dry-cut. Cuts, conditioning, color only.

Julius Caruso
22 East 62 Street. 759-7574. Wash-and-wear cuts for all types and lengths of hair styled to suit one's life-style. Manicures, pedicures, waxing. AE, MC, V.

Kenneth
Waldorf-Astoria, Park Avenue & East 50 Street. 752-1800. The lovely town house salon of the famed hair stylist burned down but now the longtime favorite of Jackie O. is based at the venerable hotel. In addition to quality hair care there are complete makeover days available.

La Beaute
142 East 49 Street. 754-0048. Small full-service salon better priced than its better-known neighbors. Expert hair styling, cuts, and color. European four-layer Repêchage facials; antiaging collagen treatments; body waxing and electrolysis. AE only.

La Coupe
694 Madison Avenue near East 62 St. 371-9230. Elaborate updos, braids, and chignons a specialty. Many models take their tresses to this dy-

namic savvy salon. Facials, manicures, pedicures, too.

Larry Mathews
536 Madison Avenue near East 54 St, upstairs. 246-6100. Sixties retro. Reasonably priced salon special for its hours—very early to late; Sunday, too. AE, MC, V. OPEN Mon-Sat 7am-10pm; Sun 9am-5pm.

Louis Guy D.
41 East 57 Street, 2nd floor. 753-6077. Expert staff to deal with both curly and straight hair. Perms, cuts, and superior coloring.

Louis Licari Color Group
797 Madison Avenue near East 67 St. 517-8084. For blended tone-on-tone coloring resulting in a beautifully healthy, natural look. He's the tops. Just ask Christie Brinkley, Ellen Barkin, and Jessica Lange. Free consultation Monday to Friday from 9am to 5pm. AE, MC, V.

Michel Kazan
16 East 55 Street. 688-1400. Haircuts and styles to fit one's life-style. Longtime full-service salon. AE, MC, V.

Oribe at Elizabeth Arden
691 Fifth Avenue at 54 St. 407-1000. Now firmly esconced behind the Red Door. Book months in advance for Oribe himself, who is usually at photo shoots tending the model's tresses. It's the trendiest salon in town for individualized feminine sexy looks like those of . . . Kelly Klein, Darryl Hannah, hot model Linda Evangelista.

Pierre Michel/Lancome Institute de Beaute
Trump Tower, 725 Fifth Avenue at 56 St. 593-1460. And at the Plaza Hotel. Longtime specialist in treatment and styling of long hair. Full-service beauty treatment salon for men and women. AE, MC, V.

Pipino-Buccheri
601 Madison Avenue near East 57 St, 4th floor. 759-2959. Easy-care natural cuts. Color, perms, makeup application.

Private World of Leslie Blanchard
19 East 62 Street. 421-4564. Hair-coloring expert. Results are natural, and the price is right. Consultations Tuesday to Saturday. Full-service salon. MC, V.

Richard Stein
1018 Lexington Avenue near East 73 St. 879-3663. Expert hair care in this full-service salon. MC, V.

Rose Reti
673 Madison Avenue near East 61 St, upstairs. 355-3152. Longtime renowned coloring specialist. Sophisticated blondes in the know go here (male and female). Full-service. AE, MC, V.

Thomas Morrissey Salon
787 Madison Avenue near East 67 St. 772-1111. Full-service salon of Kenneth defector. Shapes the tresses of Carolyn Kennedy, Nancy Kissenger, Pat Buckley, and other social circuit notables.

Vidal Sassoon
767 Fifth Avenue at 59 St; 535-9200. And 90 Fifth Avenue near 15 St; 229-2200. The man who liberated hair, 32 stylists, popular, good service

spot for men and women; cuts, color, and perms. AE, MC, V.

—Hair Removal

Alise Spiwak
20 East 68 Street. 535-6878. Expert waxing. By appointment.

Allana of New York
160 East 56 Street. 980-0216. Electrolysis salon very highly recommended. Private treatment room. Professional staff.

Diane Young
See Beauty Specialists.

Edith Imre
33 East 65 Street. 772-3351. Longtime waxing specialist. But the focus now is on wigs and hairpieces for fashion and medical reasons.

Lucy Peters
150 East 58 Street. 486-9740. Relatively painless, no scarring, permanent.

—Hair Treatment

Philip Kingsley
16 East 53 Street. 753-9600. Damaged hair revitalized by the British expert in hair and scalp care. Consultation and treatment. Candice Bergen sings his praises, so do Liza Minnelli and Cher. AE, MC, V.

Makeup

Each of the department stores devotes most of its main floor to cosmetics. All of the major names are represented, and often there are sample demonstrations, free makeovers, and promotional gifts available.

Boyd Chemists
655 Madison Avenue near East 60 St. 838-6558. Dazzling array of European makeup and treatment products, their own line as well. Experts in residence give beauty advice, makeup demonstrations, lessons, and encouragement. A mecca for the beautiful people and those who aspire to be. Now also a salon facility for hair, facials, and waxing. P.S.: They also still fill prescriptions. AE, CB, DC, MC, V.

Cosmetics Plus
518 Fifth Avenue near 43 St; 221-6560. And 275 Seventh Avenue at West 26 St; 727-0705. Also 515 Madison Avenue near East 53 St, 644-1911; and 666 Fifth Avenue near 53 St, 757-2895. Other branches, too. Largest selection of cosmetics and fragrances in the city, at discount.

Favia Cosmetics
832 Lexington Avenue near East 63 St. 751-1505. Fragrance-free cosmetics and skin-care products. AE, MC, V.

Il Makiage
107 East 60 Street. 371-3992. Upper East Side trendsetter. Over 200 eye and cheek colors, updated seasonally. Very special makeover programs from an elementary eye primer to a full makeup consultation. AE, MC, V. OPEN Sun-Fri.

Kiehl's Pharmacy
See Fragrance & Toiletries.

M.A.C
14 Christopher Street near Sixth Ave; 243-4150. And at Bendels. Make-Up Art Cosmetics, created by makeup artist Frank Toskan in 1984. Popular because they contain no mineral oil or fragrance, are vitamin-enriched, are not tested on animals, and boast a variety of textures as well as tints. They also recycle their containers. Geared to makeup professionals but fans include Cher, Madonna, Gloria Estafen, and Paula Abdul. AE, MC, V. *OPEN Tues-Sat noon-7pm; Sun 1-6pm.*

Makeup Center, Ltd.
150 West 55 Street; 977-9494. And 1013 Third Avenue near East 60 St; 751-2001. Wonderful spot to get your face "done" by a professional. Learn techniques for contouring and shading, all for a reasonable fee. Great makeup selection; also facials, manicures, pedicures, waxing, and eyelash dying. MC, V. *Thurs till 8pm.*

Merle Norman Cosmetic Studio
640 Lexington Avenue near East 54 St. 752-7985. Make an appointment for a free makeup consultation and lesson. AE, DC, MC, V.

Patricia Field
10 East 8 Street. 254-1699. Raw materials for the downtown avant-garde look—nonsmudge matte liners; matte lipsticks and lip pencils; lip paint from Japan. They'll make you over so even your mother won't recognize you. AE, MC, V. *OPEN Mon-Sat noon-8pm; Sun 1-7pm.*

Visage Beaute
Bergdorf Goodman, 754 Fifth Avenue at 58 St. 753-7300. Custom-designed lipsticks, blush, and eye shadows—you choose the hue. Gloss, matte, or pearl tones. Computerized system makes reorders easy. AE, MC, V, Bergdorf and Neiman-Marcus charge.

FOOD

Appetizing Stores

Very special New York institutions originating on the Lower East Side at the turn of the century, when the pushcarts became stores that carried the staple foods the Middle European Jewish residents craved. Yesteryears' version of a gourmet shop; some are still going strong.

Russ & Daughters
179 East Houston Street near Orchard St. 475-4880 or-4881. Grandfather Russ started it in 1909, and the third generation carries on. Appetite-teasing aromas from the many barrels filled with herrings and sour pickles. The lox, smoked cod, carp, whitefish, and lake sturgeon are all traditional; the Nova Scotia and Scotch salmon, and the fresh caviar are modern additions. A nostalgic and taste treat, the best of the genre, due in part to its Lower East Side locale. *OPEN Mon-Sat 9am-7pm; Sun 8am-6pm.*

The following represent three more fine examples of the tradition:

Barney Greengrass "The Sturgeon King"
541 Amsterdam Avenue near West 86 St. 724-4707. Over 50 years on the Upper West Side. Tops for the double-smoked Nova; herring cured and pickled on premises. Take out or eat in. *OPEN Tues-Sat 8:30am-5:45pm; Sun 8am-4:30pm.*

Murray's Sturgeon Shop
2429 Broadway near West 89 St. 724-2650. *OPEN Tues-Fri & Sun 8am-7pm; Sat till 8pm. CLOSES Sun at 2pm, July-Aug.*

Schacht
99 Second Avenue near East 6 St. 420-8219. Newly refurbished and under new management but still a good appetizing source for Nova, sable, and many flavored bagels. Now has fresh pasta and large cheese selection. Good hours for late-night East Village noshing. AE, DC, MC, V. *OPEN 7 days 7am-1am.*

Baked Goods

Black Forest
177 First Avenue at East 11 St. 254-8181. Wonderful European confections. The rum truffle and Black Forest cakes are delicious. *OPEN 7 days.*

Bonte Patisserie
1316 Third Avenue near East 75 St. 535-2360. Delicious French pastries from this popular patisserie never fail to please. Seasonal specialties. *CLOSED Aug.*

Colette
1136 Third Avenue near East 66 St. 988-2605. Croissants, brioches, plus mousse cakes, petit fours, chocolate charlottes, and fresh fruit tarts served in some of New York's finest restaurants.

Creative Cakes
400 East 74 Street. 794-9811. A "portrait-likeness" three-dimensional cake of a person, pet, building, car, or any shape or design you can think of (they have beautifully re-created the cover of this book). Buttercream outside, chocolate fudge inside only. Expensive but delicious, as well as fabulously creative. Allow two weeks. *OPEN Tues-Fri 8am-4:30pm; Sat 9am-11pm.*

Dumas Patisserie
1330 Lexington Avenue near East 88 St. 369-3900. Excellent French patisserie. All natural ingredients. Great croissants and fruit strips.

Ecce Panis
1120 Third Avenue near East 65 Street. 535-2099. Bread, glorious bread (light and dark sourdough; double walnut bread; plain or rosemary neo-Tuscan bread; sweet, savory, or olive foccaccia; and on Friday and Saturday only—to prevent addiction—chocolate bread) from the ovens that provide the Sign of the Dove, Arizona 203, Contrapunto, and Yellowfingers di Nuovo. The aroma makes it impossible to walk past the place, and why should you? Also, unusual biscotti, fresh pastas, and special items at holiday times. *OPEN Mon-Fri 10am-8pm; Sat & Sun 10am-6pm.*

Encore
141 Second Avenue near East 9 St. 505-1188.
Popular blueberry and cranberry zucchini muffins; prētzelbred; six-grain, mozzarella, and Black Forest breads. Lovely fruit mousses; opera cake coated with real 24K gold; chocolate truffle cake; and the best coffee to go. *OPEN 7 days.*

Erotic Baker
582 Amsterdam Avenue near West 88 St. 362-7557. X-rated baked goodies, handsculpted in marzipan. Good for a giggle. Custom-ordered cakes (nonerotic designs, too). They deliver. MC, V.

Gisella's Secrets
The Farmer's Market, Union Square West near East 16 St. Specialty: salt-free, sugarless, preservative-free pastries—and they're still yummy. If you're not watching your waistline go for the chocolate chip cookies. *OPEN year-round Wed, Fri & Sat 7am-5pm.*

Kramer's
1643 Second Avenue near East 85 St. 535-5955. There are those who travel uptown to Yorkville just for this old German bakery's butter and chocolate cookies, not to mention the fruit pies.

La Boulange
712 Third Avenue near East 45 St. 949-7454. A French bakery plus. Old-fashioned authentic breads (made with natural yeast), delicious croissants, brioches, pastries. Quiches, soups, salads, gratins, and other French-accented daily deli specials. They deliver and cater breakfast, cold lunches, and teas. AE only. *OPEN Mon-Fri 7am-6pm.*

Les Delices Guy Pascal
1231 Madison Avenue at East 89 St; 289-5300. And at Zabar's, Broadway & West 80 Street; 874-5400. Lemon tarts, mocha buttercream cake, and fudge roulade—yum. Also for lunch simple pâtés, salads, and sandwiches. AE, DC. *OPEN 7 days.*

Moishe's Homemade Kosher Bakery
181 East Houston Street near Orchard St; 475-9624. And 115 Second Avenue near East 7 St; 505-8555. One of the oldest and finest kosher Jewish bakeries and its newer branch. Very special corn bread, egg challah, homemade bagels (some call them the only authentic ones in the city—preservative free, great for teething babies), ruggelah, and hamentaschen year-round. *OPEN Sun-Thurs 7am-8:30pm; Fri till 5pm.*

Mrs. Fields
**233 Broadway near Park Pl; 619-2450. And *333 Sixth Avenue near West 4 St; 675-7558. Also **30 Rockefeller Plaza, 247-0514; *1776 Broadway near West 58 St, 586-3242; 943 Second Avenue at East 50 St, 935-6822; 2891 Broadway near West 112 St, 864-5350; and at Bloomies. Move over David, the lady is a champ. The chocolate chip cookie of the day made fresh and oh so tasty. *OPEN 7 days. **Mon-Fri.*

Ninth St. Bakery
350 East 9 Street. 777-0667. An eccentric little place in the East Village for lovers of Russian black, sourdough pumpernickel, raisin challah, and cheese babka. Low prices. *OPEN 7 days.*

Orwasher's
308 East 78 Street. 288-6569. Since 1916, over 35 varieties of handmade breads and rolls, baked on premises in hearth ovens, using no preservatives, no additives. Specializes in Hungarian potato bread and Vienna twists. They are the originators of raisin pumpernickel and marble bread. Cheeses, coffees, teas, and condiments, too. Certified kosher. *OPEN Mon-Sat 7am-7pm.*

Patisserie Lanciani
271 West 4 Street near Perry St; 929-0739. And 177 Prince Street near Thompson St; 477-2788. One of the city's best. Beautiful baked goods (great sacher torte). To take out or eat in the cafe. AE only. *OPEN Tues-Thurs 8am-11pm; Fri & Sat till midnight; Sun till 9pm.*

Poseidon Confectionery Company
629 Ninth Avenue near West 44 St. 757-6173. The best in Greek pastries. Spinach and cheese pies. Also stuffed vine leaves and nuts. *OPEN Tues-Sun.*

Veniero's Pasticceria
342 East 11 Street. 674-7264. Well-known and longtime (since 1894) Italian sweets as tasty as they are beautiful. Cannoli, fogliatelle, gelato, marzipan miniature fruits. Always jammed cappuccino and espresso cafe. *OPEN Sun-Thurs 8am-midnight; Fri & Sat till 1am.*

Vesuvio Bakery
160 Prince Street near West Broadway. 925-8248. White, whole wheat, and seeded Italian bread baked in the coal-fired ovens in the basement, without sugar, fat, or preservatives. In SoHo, just follow your nose.

William Greenberg, Jr., Bakery
1100 Madison Avenue near East 82 St; 744-0304. And 337 Columbus Avenue; 362-8627. Also *1377 Third Avenue near East 78 St, 535-7118; and 912 Seventh Avenue near West 57 St, 307-5930. The best brownies in the city. Spectacular custom-coated cakes at Third Avenue store. Select items may be shipped Federal Express. *OPEN 7 days.*

Zito & Sons
259 Bleecker Street near Seventh Ave. 929-6139. The best-seller is the delicious crusty whole-wheat loaf followed closely by the Sicilian loaf. Frank Sinatra has it delivered fresh to the Waldorf when he's in town. *OPEN Mon-Sat 6am-6pm; Sun till noon.*

Candy/Chocolate

Au Chocolat
Bloomingdale's, East 59 Street entrance. 705-2953. Domestic and European chocolates and candies. The best of the boxed, plus loose, filled confections including Godiva, Perugina, Laderach, Lindt, Corne, Dalloyen, Hershey, and Bloomies own private label. Custom gift basket service. AE, CD, Bloomie's charge. *OPEN 7 days.*

The Basket Shop
21 Barclay Street near Broadway. 349-3895. Candies by the handful or pound. Godiva, Perugina, Lindt chocolates. Extensive seasonal and holiday selection. Elegant custom-made gift baskets for all occasions are their specialty. Also coffees, teas, nuts, and dried fruit. AE, MC, V. *OPEN Mon-Fri.*

Chez Chocolat
Citicorp Market, 153 East 53 Street, lower level. 935-6495. Hand-dipped fresh strawberries, chocolates, nuts, novelties. AE, MC, V.

Chocolate Photos
637 West 27 Street (10001). 714-1880. Two hundred and fifty pieces of sweet or semisweet chocolate impressed with the likeness of your favorite person or your company logo, or, as a wedding favor, embossed with the names of the bride and groom. Gift boxed. After they receive the snapshot, allow two to four weeks. Call for specifics. *OPEN Mon-Fri.*

Davies Candies
101-07 Jamaica Avenue, Richmond Hill, Queens. (718) 849-7750. Homemade and hand-dipped. Over 60 varieties, all in dark and milk chocolate. Creams, marshmallows, nut and fruit, caramels, small peppermint patties, and combinations of all of the above. An old-fashioned best. Mails everywhere. *OPEN Tues-Sat 1-6pm.*

Elk Candy
240 East 86 Street. 650-1177. The specialty of this shop is delicious homemade marzipan, flavored or chocolate-coated. *OPEN 7 days.*

Evelyn Chocolates
4 John Street near Broadway. 267-5170. Handmade chocolate sculptures. AE, MC, V. *OPEN Mon-Fri 7:30am-6:30pm.*

Godiva Chocolatier
*701 Fifth Avenue near 55 St; 593-2845. And *793 Madison Avenue at East 67 St; 249-9444. Also 560 Lexington Avenue at East 50 St, 980-9810; **85 Broad Street, 514-6240; **33 Maiden Lane, 809-8990; and the *World Financial Center, 945-2174. Elaborately boxed sweets from the famed 80-year-old Belgian chocolatier. AE, MC, V. *OPEN 7 days. **Mon-Fri.*

La Maison du Chocolat
25 East 73 Street. 744-7117. Expensive, exquisitely flavorful light and dark chocolate morsels filled with cinnamon, honey, mint, lemon, marzipan, kirsch, and more, from famed Parisian chocolatier Robert Linxe. By the piece or the pound. They ship anywhere. AE, MC, V.

Li-Lac Chocolates
120 Christopher Street near Bleecker St. 242-7374; (800) 624-4874. Homemade milk and dark chocolates made with cream, butter, chocolate, and no preservatives. Great French mint patties, hazelnut truffles, almond bark, and extremely edible hand-molded milk, dark, and white Empire State Buildings and Statues of Liberty. Made on premises since 1923. AE, MC, V. *OPEN Tues-Sun noon-8pm.*

Macy's Marketplace
Herald Square, The Cellar. 695-4400. A dream (or nightmare, depending upon your waistline). Every imaginable boxed chocolate plus the likes of Michel Guerard, Godiva, Neuhaus, Perugina—loose. Over 2,000 square feet of candy! AE, MC, V, Macy's charge. *OPEN 7 days.*

Mondel Home Made Chocolates
2913 Broadway at West 114 St. 864-2111. For over 45 years, this family business has produced an amazing array of homemade chocolates, natural flavored—mint, orange, coffee, amaretto, and chocolate with a very low fat content. Beautiful boxes and baskets for presentations; also stuffed animals. AE, MC, V.

Perugina
637 Lexington Avenue at East 54 St. 688-2490. Italian chocolate baci and lovely gift-packaged candies. Loose at Zabar's and Macy's Cellar. AE, MC, V.

St. Moritz
200 Liberty Street. 945-0445. The name has changed but the unique tasty Kron chocolate specialties handmade from only natural ingredients are the same. Female torsos, yard sticks, computers, and golf balls—all in chocolate! Plus a sweet calling card or chocolate corporate logos. Also fresh fruit dipped daily. AE, MC, V. *OPEN Mon-Fri.*

Teuscher Chocolates of Switzerland
25 East 61 Street; 751-8482. And 620 Fifth Avenue at 50 St; 246-4416. The ultimate Swiss chocolate treats, including champagne truffles (yes, you can buy just one). Flown in weekly from Switzerland. The best! AE, MC, V.

Caterers

(See also Gourmet Shops *and* RESTAURANTS, *most of which will, for a price, prepare foods for a gathering.)*

Glorious Food
504 East 74 Street. 628-2320. The hottest society caterer in town right now. Known for elegant and innovative creations. Cocktails (35 or more), buffets (20 or more), dinner (16 or more). Beautiful food, beautifully presented.

Jeffrey B. Starr
214 Riverside Drive, suite 608. 864-3188. Cocktails, buffets, dinners. Very personalized custom catering built around a client's needs and/or budget.

Manganero Hero Boy
492 Ninth Avenue near West 38 St. 947-7325. The original party heros from two to six feet long! Simple but fun way to cater your own party. The six-footer serves 40 hungry folks. Delivered with breadboard and knife; side fixings. They require 24 hours' notice. AE, DC. *Available 7 days.*

New York Parties
22 East 13 Street. 777-3565. (Formerly Breadline.) Full-service catering specializes in lavish corporate and private parties.

Remember Basil
11 Old Fulton (Cadman Plaza West), Brooklyn. (718) 858-3000. Longtime all-purpose caterers.

Cocktails for 10 to 2000; buffet or sit-down dinners as well.

Paplisky Caterers
666 West End Avenue. 724-3761. Glatt kosher on an elegant scale for large affairs.

William Poll
1051 Lexington Avenue near East 61 St. 288-0501. This caterer is a fine-food take-out gourmet pioneer. Known for the smoked salmon, caviar, hors d'oeuvres, handmade truffles; their own aged cheeses; interesting sandwiches. AE, DC.

Cheese

Macy's Cellar carries a nice selection of imported cheeses, so do *Dean & DeLuca, Balducci's,* and *Zabar's.* (*See* also Gourmet Shops.)

Alleva Latticini
188 Grand Street at Mulberry St. 226-7990. Wonderful family-run cheese dairy in Little Italy, established in 1892. Specializes in mozzarella (both plain and smoked), fresh ricotta, and formaggio fresco, a white cheese formed in baskets. Made fresh daily. Imported cheeses, too. *CLOSES Sun at 3pm.*

Ben's Cheese Shop
181 East Houston Street near Houston. 254-8290. Renowned for his homemade farmer cheese baked with vegetables, or scallions, or raisins, or blueberries, or strawberries, or pineapple. Also homemade cream cheese with either chives, caviar, lox, or herbs and garlic. *OPEN Sun-Fri. CLOSES Fri at 4pm.*

Cheese of All Nations
153 Chambers Street near West Broadway. 732-0752. Famed for its international variety and stock of fine cheese and the prices at 50-60 percent less than elsewhere. Also has breads, crackers, and hors d'oeuvres. Will ship anywhere. AE, MC, V.

Cheese Unlimited
240 Ninth Avenue near West 24 St. 691-1512. Over 400 varieties from all over the world.

Di Palo's Dairy Store
206 Grand Street at Mott St. 226-1033. Fresh-ground Parmesan cheese and smoked mozzarella. Homemade ricotta-cheese-filled ravioli. Take a number and join the crowd, it's well worth it. *CLOSES Sun at 2pm.*

East Village Cheese Store
34 Third Avenue near East 9 St. 477-2601. A neighborhood shop where prices for imported and domestic cheeses can't be beat. Weekly specials abound, so do the lines; half-pound minimum purchase. Also cold cuts, pâtés, coffee beans, crackers, jams, extra virgin olive oil—all well priced. *OPEN 7 days.*

Fairway
2127 Broadway near West 75 St. 595-1888. Along with the freshest fruits and vegetables, Fairway stocks one of the best selections of cheeses in the city, including an extensive array of goat cheese. *OPEN 7 days 7am-midnight.*

Ideal Cheese
1205 Second Avenue near East 63 St. 688-7579. Top-rated cheese shop for imported and domestic cheeses. Over 300 varieties. Also pâtés.

La Marca Cheese Shop
161 East 22 Street. 673-7920. Wide variety of cheeses cut to order; fresh-baked farmer cheese with various fruit fillings, good croissants.

Coffees

See Teas & Coffee.

Ethnic Foods: Markets & Stores

New York's markets, whether a concentration of outdoor stalls or small stores, reflect the diversity of its population and are unmatched for color, vitality, variety, and friendliness.

Atlantic Avenue
Atlantic Avenue from Henry to Court Street, Brooklyn. Exotic delights of the Middle East such as Turkish coffees, Lebanese pita breads, humus, stuffed grape leaves, halvah, baklava.

Belmont
Arthur Avenue & East 187 Street, Bronx. Large Italian area for baked goods, homemade pasta, and pepperoni; pastry shops and cafes.

Bensonhurst
Eighteenth Avenue from 61 to 86 Street, Brooklyn. A thriving Italian shopping area for salamis, sausages, cheeses, prosciutto, and pizza rustica.

Chinatown
South of Canal Street, west of the Bowery. A wealth of Chinese restaurants, tea parlors, bakeries, and gift shops. Main street is Mott Street.

Indian Area
Lexington Avenue near East 28 Street. Indian spices, condiments, sweets, and saris.

La Marqueta
Park Avenue from East 110 to East 116 Street. An aromatic Latin American market with over 250 stalls displaying colorful exotic fruits and vegetables; grains, spices, hot sauces, smoked meats, and fish.

Little Athens
Ditmars Avenue from 31 to 38 Street, Astoria, Queens. The largest Greek community outside of Greece. Greek tavernas, coffeehouses (*raffenion*), restaurants, and churches; bouzouki music; baklava; and thick, rich Greek coffee.

Little Italy
West of Bowery, north of Canal Street, all along Mulberry Street. Restaurants, pastry and espresso cafes, cheese and pasta shops, outdoor food and a fun festival yearly in September (*see* ANNUAL EVENTS).

Lower East Side
East Houston Street to Delancey Street. A few remnants of the area's Jewish era prevail. Shops purveying knishes, schmaltz herring from a barrel, pastrami, corned beef, pickles, and bagels share the spotlight with the discount clothing stores.

Paddy's Market
Ninth Avenue from West 37 to West 42 Street. Stores with sidewalk stands have replaced the pushcarts. Once predominantly Italian and Greek, it is now a United Nations of food. The scene of an annual food fair in May (*see* ANNUAL EVENTS).

Ukrainian and Polish Area
Vicinity of First Avenue at East 7 Street. In the East Village, wonderful pierogi, blintzes, kielbasa, headcheese, babka, and black bread. Ukrainian Fair every May (*see* ANNUAL EVENTS).

Yorkville
Lexington Avenue to York Avenue, mainly on East 86 Street. The German area has nearly disappeared but there are still a few restaurants serving home-style hearty foods and bock beer, *Konditorei* serving exquisite pastries, and shops for specialty foods. A small Hungarian enclave exists within this district.

Fish

Balducci's
424 Sixth Avenue at West 9 St. 673-2600. More interesting than most purveyors. High quality. *OPEN 7 days.*

Central Fish Company
527 Ninth Avenue near West 39 St. 279-2317. Paddy's Market–area fishmonger known for its enormous variety of fresh fish. *OPEN Mon-Fri.*

Fulton Market Retail Store
South Street Seaport, 11 Fulton Street near Front St. 608-2920. One of the best sources for freshness and variety. You can't get much closer to the catch. *OPEN Mon-Sat 8am-8pm; Sun 10am-6pm.*

Jefferson Market
455 Sixth Avenue near West 10 St. 675-2277. The very freshest of each season's seafoods; knowledgeably and courteously purveyed. *OPEN 7 days.*

Leonard's
1241 Third Avenue near East 72 St. 744-2600. Exquisite selection. Smoked salmon, caviar, crabmeat, poached salmon, boiled lobster. Free delivery. AE, MC, V ($18 minimum).

Lobster Place
487 Amsterdam Avenue near West 84 St. 595-7605. Specialists for lobsters—great variety of sizes. Now also a large selection of fresh fish. AE, MC, V.

Pisacane
940 First Avenue near East 52 St. 355-1850. Good selection, high quality.

Gourmet Shops

Macy's has a very fine gourmet department in The Cellar.

A la Russe Catering
315 West 54 Street. 246-6341. Authentic regional Russian specialties: best borscht, herring forsimak, eggplant caviar, chicken Kiev, cabbage rolls; homebaked black Russian rye bread. Carry-out; full-catering service. Phone orders accepted.

Balducci's
424 Sixth Avenue at West 9 St. 673-2600. Greenwich Village gourmet giant; since 1948. Renowned for quantity, variety, and atmosphere. Hard-to-find items, exotic fruits, fresh breads and pastries, fresh meats, game in season, fresh caviar, exquisite in- and out-of-season produce, and an amazing assortment of cheeses; imported chocolates, prepared foods. National mail order. Full-service catering. AE, MC, V. *OPEN 7 days 7am-8:30pm.*

Call Cuisine
1032 First Avenue near East 57 St. 752-7070. Gourmet dinners prepared daily (14 to 16 to choose from) to take away. Party and corporate catering large and small. Will coordinate all amenities. AE, MC, V.

Caviarteria
29 East 60 Street. 759-7410; from out of New York (800) 4-CAVIAR. Caviar specialist, stocks eight varieties of fresh, six preserved. Importers of Scotch salmon; Nova Scotia sold as well. Also foie gras. They ship anywhere in the U.S. overnight, if desired. AE, MC, V.

Chelsea Foods
198 Eighth Avenue at West 20 St. 691-3948. Great Chelsea take-out charcuterie and cafe. AE, MC, V. *OPEN Mon-Fri 9am-9pm; Sat & Sun till 6pm.*

Danal Provisions
2 Bank Street near Greenwich Ave. 691-8083. Fax 691-8093. For beautifully presented produce, quality coffees and teas, and a fresh-daily selection of breads in this new but oh so old-fashioned service-oriented market. Also, a full range of groceries, a sandwich bar, and fresh flowers. For the truly busy, delivery of home-cooked meals; catering, too. All from the creators of Danal (*see* RESTAURANTS, Afternoon Tea *and* Cafes). *OPEN 7 days 10am-9pm.*

Dean & DeLuca
560 Broadway at Prince St. 431-1691. SoHo's gorgeous gourmet grocery. Everything is state of the art: the 175 cheeses, the olives, the oils, the vinegars, pâtés, the herbs and spices; in short, the best of everything, beautifully presented, knowledgeably purveyed. New additions: a cafe; also a branch at the Paramount Hotel, 235 West 46 St. AE, MC, V. *OPEN 7 days 8am-8pm..*

E.A.T.
1064 Madison Avenue near East 80 St. 772-0022. Handsome food shop for high-priced, lovely imported food items. Daily specials, good assortment of pâtés, cheeses, coffees, and breads. Magnificent chocolate roulade cake. AE only. *OPEN 7 days 7am-10pm.*

Grace's Marketplace
1237 Third Avenue near East 71 St. 737-0600. Similar in spirit to her father's fancy emporium downtown. Produce, prepared foods, cheeses, charcuterie, smoked fish, fancy groceries,

breads and pastries. No fresh meat or fish. Catering. AE, DC, MC, V. *OPEN Mon-Sat 7am-8:30pm; Sun 8am-7pm.*

Maison Glass
111 East 58 Street. 755-3316. Smoked Scotch and Nova Scotia salmon, Smithfield ham, foie gras, cheeses, canned and packaged gourmet items. AE, CB, DC, MC, V.

Myers of Keswick
634 Hudson Street near Jane St. 691-4194. It may be a stretch to call it gourmet, but Anglophiles will love the authentic small English village–grocer feel and the goods purveyed. Sausage rolls, kidney pie, pork pies, Scotch eggs, Stilton cheese, and Aberdeen kippers. Packages and tins of Brit foods, cookies, and candy. AE, MC, V. *OPEN 7 days.*

Old Denmark
133 East 65 Street. 744-2533. Wonderfully friendly spot for Scandinavian delicacies: meatballs, cold cuts, meat or fish salads, cheeses, and fresh breads. Catering. Eat-in lunch (set menu) daily 11am to 4pm. *OPEN Mon-Sat 9am-5:30pm.*

Petak's
1244 Madison Avenue near East 89 St. 722-7711. A carry-out gourmet shop with an appetizing section that pays homage to the first generation of Petak's in the Bronx. Vegetable pastas, salads, cheeses, deli, and coffees. AE only. *OPEN 7 days.*

Russian Delights
223 East 14 Street. 674-7979. Tasty Russian specialties to go in this Manhattan branch of a Brighton Beach, Brooklyn, shop. AE, MC, V.

Silver Palate
274 Columbus Avenue near West 73 St. 799-6340. In this tiny but famed jewel of a food emporium everything for a gourmet feast, imaginative, fresh daily entrees, hors d'oeuvres, and their own party products. Their own cookware, cookbooks, and video—and none of it has gone to their heads. AE, MC, V. *OPEN Mon-Fri 10:30am-9:30pm; Sat & Sun till 7:30pm.*

Todaro Brothers
555 Second Avenue near East 31 St. 532-0633. Complete gourmet line, 20 varieties of fresh bread, 300 cheeses, Italian cold cuts, pastas, coffees, spices, confections, catering. Mail order. AE, MC, V. *OPEN Mon-Sat 8am-9pm; Sun 8am-8pm.*

Word of Mouth
1012 Lexington Avenue near East 72 St. 734-9483. International gourmet array of main courses daily. Tasty vegetable dishes, beautifully prepared entrees, consistently high quality. AE, MC, V. *OPEN Mon-Fri 10am-7pm; Sat till 6pm; Sun 11:30am-5:30pm.*

Zabar's & Co.
2245 Broadway near West 80 St. 787-2000. Humbly begun as a deli/cheese store, it's now the undisputed champ! A mind-boggling array of cheeses, meats, smoked fish, coffees, teas, and entrees; plus a wide array of mail order, kitchenwares, and gourmet gadgetry 20-40 per-

cent off retail (on the mezzanine; open only till 6pm). Go for the sights, smells, the fun of it all. Sociological note: a Saturday-morning singles hope-to-meet place. AE, DC, MC, V. *OPEN year-round Mon-Fri 8am-7:30pm; Sat till midnight; Sun 9am-6pm.*

Health Food

Brownies Foods
91 Fifth Avenue near 16 St. 242-2199. Since 1936, renowned health food source. Stocks over 5,000 natural organic-diet foods including vitamins, nuts, grains, herbs, teas, breads, dried fruit. AE, MC, V.

Commodities
117 Hudson Street at North Moore St. 334-8330. A super supermarket in TriBeCa. Over 5,000 square feet of variety and quantity in natural foods: 125 tea choices, 24 types of granola, 30 bins of grains, 50 kinds of honey. Fresh organically raised produce. MC, V. *OPEN 7 days 10am-8pm.*

Gramercy Natural Food Center
427 Second Avenue near East 24 St. 725-1651. Organically grown unsprayed fruit and vegetables, unmedicated free-range chicken and turkey, farm fresh eggs, all natural frozen food section. Fresh daily special sandwiches; full line of natural groceries. Vitamins at 20-50 percent off.

Native Farms Organic
322 East 11 Street. 614-0727. Inviting storefront for a wonderful selection of most attractively purveyed organic produce that must meet their high standards for taste and appearance. Also hearth-baked breads. *OPEN 7 days 10am-10pm.*

Pete's Spice
174 First Avenue near East 10 St. 254-8773. A wonderful fourth-generation East Village establishment for basic foods. Burlap sacks full of spices, grains, coffees, brown rice, nuts, flour (25 different kinds!), dried fruit. Fresh breads, natural vitamins. Also for ethnic cooking: bulghar, poppy, lekvar, peeled wheat. *OPEN Mon-Sat 10am-7:30pm; Sun 12:30-5pm.*

Whole Foods in SoHo
117 Prince Street near Wooster St. 673-5388. Complete natural-food market, specializing in produce and chicken and fish. Large bulk department; gourmet takeout and herb selection. Natural cosmetics and vitamins. AE, MC, V. *OPEN 7 days 9am-9:30pm.*

Herbs & Spices

(*See also* Health Food.)

Aphrodisia Products
282 Bleecker Street near Seventh Ave South. 989-6440. Over 800 herbs and spices and a good selection of essential oils. Loose herbal teas without caffeine. Books on holistic health. Herbal skin-care preparations. AE, MC, V. *OPEN 7 days.*

Kalustyan's
123 Lexington Avenue near East 28 St. 685-3451. New York's oldest Indian store. Grains, nuts, and spices in bulk. AE, MC, V. *OPEN 7 days.*

Meadowsweet Herbal Apothecary
77 East 4 Street. 254-2870. Herbs, herbal medicines, essential oils, ointments, liniments; Bach flower remedies. Herbology classes available. *OPEN only Fri & Sat noon-7pm.*

Paprikas Weiss Importer
1546 Second Avenue near East 80 St. 288-6903. It started 94 years ago with paprika (they have hot, half sweet, and sweet) and other Hungarian food and cooking products from "home," now there are hundreds of imported herbs and spices, foie gras, cheese, and meat from around the world and so much more. Good housewares selection. Mail order. AE, MC. V.

Meat & Fowl

Kurowycky Meats
124 First Avenue near East 7 St. 477-0344. This family-run shop, in business for 33 years, prepares and purveys some of the city's finest smoked (on premises) and cured meats. Baked hams, unusual sausage (including all ham, with caraway seeds, or the spicy Ukrainian kielbasy). Also dark Lithuanian bread, homemade Polish mustard, and sauerkraut.

Morris Lobel and Sons Prime Meats
1096 Madison Avenue near East 82 St. 737-1372. Buffalo, rabbit, venison, grouse, quail, wild turkey, and guinea hen among more traditional fare. AE, MC, V.

Nevada Meat Market
2012 Broadway near West 68 St. 362-0443. Smoked pheasant, duck, goose, wild turkey, quail, and guinea hens; fresh in season, frozen all year.

Ottomanelli Brothers
1549 York Avenue near East 82 St. 772-7900. Prime cuts and fresh game in season. They deliver in the area.

Regent Foods
1174 Lexington Avenue near East 80 St. 744-3450. Meat specialists. Fresh quail, partridge, and pheasant in season, as well as hard-to-find meats.

Store 48 for Steak
48 Ninth Avenue near West 14 St. 924-3043. Gourmet shop for shell steaks, filets, brochettes, lamb and pork chops, cutlets, and roasts. Chicken Kiev and cordon bleu, lobster tails and jumbo shrimp, ready to heat and serve. Gift-boxed; telephone orders taken. AE, DC. *OPEN Mon-Fri 8am-6pm.*

—Washington Market

Washington Market, from Gansevoort Street to West 14 Street between Ninth and Tenth avenues, is the city's wholesale meat district servicing hotels and restaurants. But many of the outlets do sell retail. For the adventuresome nonvegetarian it's a hectic, colorful experience, and the selection and savings are incomparable.

Basior Schwartz Meat Products
421 West 14 Street. 929-5368. The most retail-oriented outlet in the wholesale meat district. Fresh meats as well as cheese, fish, imported canned goods, dried fruit, and nuts. Excellent prices on all. *OPEN Mon-Fri 4am-10am only.*

Nuts & Seeds

(*See also* Candy/Chocolate; Gourmet Shops; *and* Health Food.)

Broadway Nut Shoppe
2246 Broadway near West 80 St. 874-5214. Georgia pecans, black walnuts in season, pignoli nuts, macadamias, and Indian nuts. Cashews, almonds, pistachios, and filberts roasted on premises. Imported candies and dried fruits, too. Will ship anywhere. *OPEN 7 days.*

Sahadi Importing Company
187 & 189 Atlantic Avenue near Court St, Brooklyn. (718) 624-5762. Purveyors of nuts and dried fruit since 1895. The selection—over 90 varieties—is impressive and worth a trip to this Middle Eastern area of Brooklyn. Also extensive specialty food selection.

Treat Boutique
200 East 86 Street. 737-6619. Stocked with candies, nuts, dried fruit, and assorted gourmet items. Fudge made on premises. They ship anywhere. AE only. *OPEN Sun-Fri 11am-10:30pm; Sat till midnight.*

Pasta

Borgatti's Ravioli
632 East 187 Street near Arthur Ave, Bronx. 367-3799. Wonderful family business. Every thickness of fresh egg and spinach noodle available daily. Pastas lightly flavored with whole wheat, tomato, and carrot are interesting. Stuffed pastas, too. *CLOSES Sun at 1pm.*

Bruno Ravioli Co.
653 Ninth Avenue near West 45 St; 246-8456. And *2204 Broadway near West 78 St; 580-8150. Pasta makers since 1905. Fresh specialties: manicotti; tortellini; vegetable lasagna; egg fettuccine; sun dried tomato-, shiitaki mushroom-, and pesto-filled ravioli. Sauces, too. Supplier to many restaurants and caterers. *OPEN 7 days.*

Piemonte Homemade Ravioli Company
190 Grand Street near Mulberry St. 226-0475. In the heart of Little Italy, a variety of fresh pastas made daily, including gluten-free macaroni for those allergic to gluten. *OPEN Tues-Sat 8:30am-6pm; Sun 8:30am-3pm.*

Raffetto's Corporation
144 West Houston Street near Sullivan St. 777-1261. Long-established (since 1906) Village shop for fresh pasta, egg and spinach noodles, cut to your specifications as you watch. Ravioli stuffed with cheese or meat are prepared daily.

Nobody does it better or for less. *OPEN Tues-Sat 8am-6pm.*

Picnics

City picnic baskets, like city picnic sites, tend to be sophisticated and unusual. Also see Gourmet Shops for where to buy do-it-yourself fixings.

Balducci's
424 Sixth Avenue at West 9 St. 673-2600. Picnics include a potpourri of tasty treats. Order 48 hours in advance. AE, Balducci's charge. *Available year-round Mon-Sat 8am-5pm.*

Burke & Burke
2 Lincoln Center at West 66 St. 799-7000. And other branches. Boxed lunches of sandwich, salad, fruit, dessert, and a soft drink or mineral water. An upscale version adds pâté, salmon caviar, and cheese. Half-hour notice. AE only. *OPEN Mon-Fri 7am-midnight; Sat & Sun 8am-10pm.*

Brasserie
100 East 53 Street. 751-4840. For years they have offered a choice of six French Picnique boxes; order three hours in advance. They deliver for 6 or more. AE, CB, DC, MC, V. *Available year-round. NEVER CLOSES!*

Remi to Go
145 West 53 Street. 581-7115. Attractive and tasty picnics with choice of cold pasta salad, a hearty country bread sandwich, or a dinner from soup to nuts—they're flexible—from the revered Venetian restaurant's take-out shop. Order by noon for late afternoon or evening pickup. AE, MC, V. *OPEN Mon-Fri 7:30am-7pm.*

Silver Palate
274 Columbus Avenue near West 72 St. 799-6340. Delectable picnics from a choice of nine, or they will make up one of your choosing. Two days' notice. AE, MC, V. *Available year-round.*

Seltzer

Before Perrier there was seltzer—filtered water and CO_2 gas. Delivered to your door like in the old days.

Gimme Seltzer
(718) 786-7800. On the West Side, deliveries Tuesday and Thursday; on the East Side, Wednesday and Friday; and in Brooklyn, every other Wednesday. Beer and soda, too.

Teas & Coffees

Zabar's and Macy's Cellar have shops that sell a variety of fresh and packaged teas and coffees. (See also Gourmet Shops and RESTAURANTS, Afternoon Tea and Cafes.)

Danal
90 East 10 Street. 982-6930. In this charming cafe and gift shop, you'll find over 32 teas available (some in bulk, others gift boxed) including aromatics from France (try the four red berries), classics from India and China, decaf teas, and herbal infusions. Standouts: Taganda, an exclu-

sive from Zimbabwe. Also packaged teas by G. Ford and Barrow's unblended Darjeeling. The only coffee they sell is the high-quality Sumantra blend that they serve in the cafe, also available in decaf. AE only. *OPEN Tues-Fri 8:30am-6pm; Sat 11am-6pm; Sun 11:30am-6pm. (See also* RESTAURANTS, Afternoon Tea *and* Cafes.)

McNulty's Tea & Coffee Company
109 Christopher Street near Bleecker St. 242-5351. Well-known Village shop established in 1895. Offers rare teas and over 200 choice imported coffees, sold straight or custom blended for you. Imported jams and jellies. Mail order. AE, DC, MC, V. *OPEN Mon-Sat 10am-9pm; Sun 1-7pm.*

Porto Rico Importing Co.
201 Bleecker Street near Sixth Ave; 477-5421. And *40½ St. Marks Place; 533-1982. Since 1907, high-grade teas and coffees. They roast 50 different coffees each week. Custom blends; Jamaican Blue Mountain; decaffeinated espresso. In stock, 120 types of tea. Every conceivable coffee and tea accessory at 30-50 percent discount. Mail order. AE, MC, V ($15 minimum). *OPEN Mon-Sat 9:30am-9pm; Sun noon-7pm. *Mon-Sat 10am-7pm.*

Schapira Coffee Company
117 West 10 Street. 675-3733. Coffee roasting and tea blending since 1903. Good coffee source, including the coveted and expensive Jamaica Blue Mountain. Hand grinders, espresso pots. Mail order. AE, MC, V. *OPEN Mon-Fri 9am-6:30pm; Sat 9am-5:30pm; Sun 11am-4pm.*

Sensuous Bean
66 West 70 St. 724-7725. A pretty place where the friendly folks who run the shop will blend from a wide variety of coffees. AE, MC, V.

HOME

Bath, Bathrooms

(See also Linens *for discount towels and bathroom accessories.)*

Elegant John
812 Lexington Avenue near East 62 St. 935-5800. In an elegant setting, a superior selection of everything for the bath; striped and printed toilet tissue, too. AE, MC, V.

Hastings
230 Park Avenue at East 19 St. 674-9700. Bold designs in bathrooms plus all the fittings including artful designer tiles. Kitchens, too. The whole store is a knockout. MC, V.

Sherle Wagner International
60 East 57 Street. 758-3300. The world's most elegant and expensive bathroom fixtures. AE, MC, V. *OPEN Mon-Fri 9:15am-5pm.*

Brass

Brass Antique Shoppe
32 Allen Street near Canal St. 925-6660. Trea-

sure hunt for 19th-century American and European brass fixtures. Old Russian candlesticks, silver Judaica. Good bargains. MC, V. *OPEN Sun-Fri 10am-4pm.*

Brass Loft
499 Broadway near Broome St. 226-5467. One of the largest selections of brass giftware, this factory outlet specializes in brass and copper fireplace equipment, candlesticks, planters, and chandeliers at substantial discounts. MC, V. *OPEN 7 days 11am-6:30pm.*

Charles P. Rogers Brass Beds
899 First Avenue near East 50 St. 935-6900. Specializes in brass beds in both contemporary and traditional styles; they manufacture them using molded castings resulting in heavier, sturdier beds. Also reproduction iron beds. Range: $699-$5,000. AE, MC, V. *OPEN 7 days.*

Isabel Brass
200 Lexington Avenue near East 32 St. 689-3307. Custom manufacturers of solid brass beds and other furnishings. Expensive. AE, MC, V. *OPEN Mon-Fri 9am-4pm.*

Carpets & Rugs

Macy's and *Bloomingdale's* carry a selection of Oriental rugs.

ABC Carpet Company
888 Broadway at East 19 St. 677-6970. Since 1897. Oriental, designer, area, scatter, or rag rugs. Over 5,000 rolls of national brands plus a large selection of remnants in a variety of fibers, colors, and sizes. All in two of the largest showrooms anywhere. Immediate delivery and installation. Now also a wonderful source for antique furniture and accessories as well as contemporary linens. AE, MC, V. *OPEN 7 days.*

A. Beshar & Co.
611 Broadway near Bleecker St, room 405. 529-7300. Since 1898, handsome Oriental rugs plus cleaning and repair service.

Aronson's
135 West 17 Street. 243-4993. A floor-covering supermarket for all your flooring needs: carpeting remnant, close-out, or custom-cut; tile and linoleum. MC, V.

Berdj Abadjian
201 East 57 Street. 688-2229. Persian, Turkish, and Caucasian antique and semi-antique rugs. Four generations of experience. Rug restoration and cleaning.

Central Carpet
426 Columbus Avenue near West 81 St. 787-8813. Go here first! This is a great source for low-priced (they guarantee New York's lowest) antique, semi-antique, and new handmade Chinese, Persian, and Caucasian rugs. Large collection of Art Deco Chinese rugs and flat weave Indian dhurries. Also modern Belgian rugs. Huge selection—over 5,000 rugs on two floors—with prices ranging from $19 to $10,000. It's quite a place. MC, V. *OPEN Mon-Wed 9am-6pm; Thurs 10am-7:30pm; Sat 9am-5pm; Sun 11am-5pm.*

Dildarian, Inc.
595 Madison Avenue near East 57 St, 3rd floor. 288-4948. Since 1916. Antique and decorative Oriental and European rugs and tapestries. The largest retailer of fine rugs in New York. *OPEN Mon-Fri.*

Doris Leslie Blau
15 East 57 Street, 5th floor. 759-3715. Antique and exemplary Oriental and European carpets and tapestries. *OPEN Mon-Fri by appointment only.*

Einstein-Moomjy
150 East 58 Street. 758-0900. A carpet department store for new Orientals, broadlooms, area rugs. MC, V.

Rug Tower
399 Lafayette Street at East 4 St. 677-2525. Huge selection of antique, old and new Oriental rugs and kilims. AE, MC, V. *OPEN 7 days.*

Rug Warehouse
220 West 80 Street. 787-6665. For over 50 years, a best-price guarantee—for Caucasians, Persians, Art Deco Chinese, dhurries, kilims, both antique and modern. MC, V. *OPEN 7 days.*

Ceramic Tiles

(*See also* Paint *and* Hardware.)

Country Floors
315 East 16 Street. 627-8300. Specializes in fine hand-painted tiles—antique and modern—mainly imported from Italy, France, Holland, Peru, Finland, Spain, and Portugal. Also sinks designed to match tiles. Special orders. MC, V. *OPEN Mon-Fri.*

Ideal Tile
405 East 51 Street. 759-2339. Importers of Italian ceramic tiles. Expert installation or a do-it-yourself guide. MC, V.

The Quarry
192 East 32 Street. 679-2559. New York's largest stock of reasonably priced Spanish, Dutch, French, Portuguese, and Mexican tiles in bright colors and patterns. Installation or do-it-yourself guidance and supplies. Bathroom and kitchen accessories, too. Also a complete line of wallpaper. AE, MC, V. *CLOSES Sat at 3pm.*

China, Glassware, Porcelain, Pottery

Fine china can be found in the large department stores; even finer at **Tiffany's** *and* **Cartier.**

Baccarat, Inc.
625 Madison Avenue near East 58 St. 826-4100. The famed, expensive imported French crystal plus china by Limoges, Ceralene, Raynaud; pewter by Etains du Manoir; silver by Christofle and Puiforcat. Bridal registry. AE, MC, V.

Ceramica
182 Hester Street near Mulberry St; 966-3170. And 59 Thompson Street near Spring St; 941-1307. Imported directly from Italy to these cheerful charming chock full of china shops—hand-painted ceramics and reproduction majolica.

New shipments every three months. AE, MC, V. *OPEN Tues-Sun*

Fishes Eddy
889 Broadway near East 19 St; 420-9020. And 551 Hudson Street near Perry St; 627-3956. Highly whimsical shops for china and glassware from the 1930s and 1940s once belonging to corporations, restaurants, hotels, private clubs, and the government—making for some fascinating logos. Also sugar bowls, creamers, and other vintage kitchen/dining accessories. Always some interesting collectibles on hand; all at low prices. Extremely browsable. MC, V. *OPEN 7 days 10am-11pm.*

Greater New York Trading Company
81 Canal Street near Allen St. 226-2808. China, crystal, and silver including Lenox, Wedgwood, Rosenthal—at discount. MC, V. *OPEN Sun-Fri. CLOSES Fri at 3pm.*

Hoya Crystal Gallery
450 Park Avenue near East 57 St. 223-6335. The world's largest collection of this respected Japanese firm's art and functional pieces. Known for the low iron content—the result is glass with no discolorations or bubbles. Price range: $30-$30,000. AE, DC, MC, V.

Lalique
680 Madison Avenue near East 61 St. 355-6550. The famed extremely beautiful French crystal. AE, MC, V.

Lanac Sales Company
73 Canal Street at Allen St. 226-8925. Imported and domestic china and crystal at discount. Also sterling and stainless flatware. MC, V. *OPEN Sun-Fri. CLOSES Fri at 2pm.*

Mad Monk
500 Sixth Avenue near West 13 St. 242-6678. Longtime Greenwich Village source for interesting handmade pottery and mirrors. *OPEN 7 days.*

Orrefors Crystal Gallery
58 East 57 Street. 753-3442. Exclusive home of the entire collection of the world-renowned Swedish crystal. Gift registry. AE, MC, V.

Piccola Cucina
334 East 11 Street. 982-7471. A tiny oasis of Italian rustic charm purveying colorful Deruda and Vietro ceramic dinnerware; platters, pitchers, and other country kitchen wares, plus more modern designs. Also Italian kitchen linens, cookbooks, and tapes. It's a charmer. AE, MC, V. *OPEN 7 days.*

Pottery Barn
117 East 59 Street; 753-5424. And 1292 Lexington Avenue near East 87 St; 289-2477. Also 250 West 57 Street, 315-1855; 2109 Broadway near West 73 St, 595-5573; 1451 Second Avenue near East 76 St, 988-4228; 51 Greenwich Avenue near Seventh Ave South, 807-6321; 700 Broadway at East 4 St, 505-6377; and South Street Seaport, 233-2141. The source for great-value contemporary glasses, dishes, cutlery. Now expanded into stylish decorative houseware and furnishings (watch out Conrans) thanks to new owners Williams-Sonoma. Excel-

lent sales several times a year (*see also* House- & Kitchenwares: Williams-Sonoma Outlet Center). Catalog. AE, MC, V. *OPEN 7 days.*

Royal Copenhagen Porcelain
683 Madison Avenue near East 61 St. 759-6457. Danish china, Orrefors and Kosta Boda crystal, plus Georg Jensen silver flatware and jewelry. AE, MC, V.

Steuben Glass
715 Fifth Avenue at 56 St. 752-1441. Unique glass sculpture and functional pieces. Browse—it's like a museum. AE, DC, MC, V.

Wolfman-Gold & Good
116 Greene Street at Prince St. 410-7000. In a very appealing rustic country setting, a well-groomed yet stylish mainly all-white look for the table. Dinnerware, glassware, linens, stainless flatware, tabletop gifts, oddities, and collectibles; dried floral topiaries. AE, MC, V. *OPEN Mon-Sat 11am-6pm; Sun noon-5pm.*

Wooden Indian
60 West 15 Street. 243-8590. Glassware—every shape and size—in a low-frills space with prices to match. China including some old pieces. Friendly, helpful management. *OPEN Tues-Sat.*

—China: Restorers, Repairers, Searchers

Hess Restorations
200 Park Avenue South near East 17 St. 260-2255. "Repairers of the irreparable"—china, crystal, ivory, jade, wood, mother-of-pearl, paintings, lamps, boxes, etc. Recommended by the Metropolitan Museum of Art, Tiffany's, and leading galleries. *OPEN Mon-Fri 10:30am-4pm.*

Pattern Finders
P.O. Box 206, Port Jefferson Station, N.Y. (11776). (516) 928-5158. They seek matching china and stemware patterns. They stock many or they will trace for a reasonable fee. Mail order only. Also appraisal service. MC, V.

Cutlery & Gadgetry

(*See also* House- & Kitchenwares *and* Specialty Shops & Services, Hardware.)

Hammacher Schlemmer
147 East 57 Street. 421-9000. Established on the Bowery in 1848, on 57 Street since 1926. Six floors devoted to unique gadgets, conveniences, and indulgences for the home (every room), the car, the sauna, or your yacht or airplane. Phone orders: 937-8181. Catalog, toll free (800) 543-3366. AE, CB, DC, MC, V.

Hoffritz
331 Madison Avenue near East 43 St; 697-7344. And 203 West 57 St; 757-3431. Also World Trade Center, concourse level, 757-3497; Grand Central Terminal, Park Avenue at East 42 Street, 682-7808; Penn Station Main Terminal, West 33 Street & Seventh Avenue, 736-2443; and 30 Rockefeller Plaza, concourse level, 757-3497. The most impressive selection of cutlery and gadgetry to be found under one roof. AE, MC, V.

The Sharper Image
4 West 57 Street; 265-2550. And Pier 17, South

Street Seaport; 693-0477. The gadget-filled catalog comes to life. Here are all the intriguing
upscale items you can surely live without—but
don't want to. Massage chairs, a robot to serve
hors d'oeuvres, a safari hat with a built-in fan, a
talking scale, and so much more. AE, DC, MC, V.
OPEN 7 days.

—Cutlery: Knife & Scissors Sharpener

Fred de Carlo
(201) 945-7609. A knife- and scissors-sharpener
who walks his territory—East 52 to East 92 Street,
Fifth Avenue to the East River. To be sure to
catch him, call around 6pm for an appointment.

Furniture

Lord & Taylor, Bloomingdale's, and *Macy's*
have a large variety of home furnishings, contemporary and traditional as well as antique.
*Bloomingdale's model rooms are always spe-
cial. (See also* Brass; Plastic; Wicker; *and* Specialty Shops & Services, Antiques.)

—Furniture: Antique & Collectible

Better Times Antiques
500 Amsterdam Avenue at West 84 St. 496-
9001. Always an interesting selection of 19th-
century pine and other hardwood furnishings
and accessories. Knowledgeably purveyed.
MC, V. *CLOSED Wed.*

Eileen Lane Antiques
150 Thompson Street near Houston St. 475-
2988. Spacious quarters for a lovely well-priced
selection of Swedish and Viennese Biedermeier
and Art Deco furniture. Also period art glass and
alabaster lighting. AE, DC, MC, V. *OPEN 7 days
11am-7pm.*

Evergreen Antiques
1249 Third Avenue at East 72 St; 744-5664. And
*120 Spring Street near Greene St; 966-6458.
The rustic 18th-and 19th-century pine furniture
of Scandinavia, some with its original hand-
painted finishing. Also such accents as rag rugs,
pottery, and wooden boxes. AE, MC, V. *OPEN 7
days.*

Fifty/50
793 Broadway near East 10 St. 777-3208. Designer furniture and objects of the 30s, 40s, and
50s. Eames, Nelson, Noguchi, Miller, Knoll, and
the master himself, Wright. Scandinavian and
Italian, including Vennini, glass. Also American
silver jewelry from the 50s. AE, DC, MC, V.

Florian Papp
962 Madison Avenue near East 76 St. 288-6770.
Since 1900, a source for William and Mary,
Sheraton, and other periods of fine English and
European furniture. Now also Victorian.

French & Company
17 East 65 Street. 535-3330. Museum-quality
French and English 18th-century furniture. *By
appointment only.*

Howard Kaplan Antiques
827 Broadway near East 12 St. 674-1000. From
an early purveyor of the Rustic French look now

with a broader range of French (including country) and 19th-century English furnishings; and the
most luscious group of decorative accessories in
a beautiful shop. AE, MC, V. *OPEN Mon-Fri.*

Hyde Park Antiques
836 Broadway near East 12 St. 477-0033. The
finest selection of 18th-century English furniture
and accessories. Also a major collection of English marine and sporting paintings. *CLOSES
Sat at 2:30pm.*

Israel Sack
15 East 57 Street, 3rd floor. 753-6562. Established in 1905. Specialists in fine 17th- and 18th-
century American furniture.

Macklowe Gallery, Ltd.
667 Madison Avenue near East 60 St. 644-6400.
Specializes in Art Deco, Art Nouveau, and Vienna Secession decorative arts including furniture, art glass, Tiffany lamps, sculpture, and carpets. AE, MC, V.

Newel Art Galleries
425 East 53 Street. 758-1970. Six stories of the
most extensive collection of antique furnishings
from Renaissance to Art Deco, with an emphasis
on the unusual and whimsical. Accommodates
people in the trade, stylists scouting props, and
those who know *exactly* what they want. *OPEN
Mon-Fri 8am-5pm.*

Philip Colleck of London, Ltd.
830 Broadway near East 12 St. 505-2500. Fine
formal English antique furniture and accessories. *OPEN Mon-Fri.*

Pierre Deux Antiques
369 Bleecker Street at Charles St. 243-7740. Exquisite 18th- and 19th-century country French
furniture and accessories. AE, MC, V.

Pine Country Antiques
71 Mercer Street near Broome St. 274-9663. Imported Danish pine, custom cabinetry, painting,
and upholstery. *OPEN 7 days.*

Retro Modern Studio
88 East 10 Street, upstairs. 674-0530. European
and American designer Art Deco furniture, lighting, and fine art objects.

Salvage Barn
525 Hudson Street near West 10 St. 929-5787.
Often a good source for well-priced used and
some antique furniture. An eclectic selection and
fast turnover. *OPEN 7 days.*

Secondhand Rose
270 Lafayette Street near Prince St. 431-7673.
Twentieth-century American decorative arts:
Donald Desky, Gilbert Rohde, R. T. Frankl, Paul
Evans, Charles Eames. Also antique wallpaper
and fabrics. A splendid collection if it's your cup
of tea. AE only. *OPEN 7 days.*

Stair & Company, Inc.
942 Madison Avenue near East 74 St. 517-4400.
Top-quality antiques, especially 18th-century
English furniture, Chinese export porcelain, English porcelain. Restoration workshop.

Vernay & Jussel, Inc.
625 Madison Avenue near East 58 St. 308-1906.
America's oldest established art dealer. English
furniture of the Georgian period and rare clocks.

—Furniture: Contemporary

The Bombay Company
Third Avenue at East 63 Street; 759-7212. And 1018 Madison Avenue near East 79 St; 650-0556. Also 2001 Broadway at West 68 St, 721-7701. Butler's tray tables, Biedermeier consoles, tole lamps, Verona mirrors—an heirloom look in home furnishings, accessories, and wall decor at great value prices. True, it isn't heirloom quality, but that's for your heirs to worry about. AE, MC, V. OPEN 7 days.

Bon Marche
55 West 13 Street, 6th and 7th floors; 620-5550. And 1060 Third Avenue near East 63 St; 620-5592. Contemporary furniture, lighting, and accessories. Good value. MC, V.

Brancusi
938 First Avenue near East 51 St. 688-7980. Large selection of modern tables in glass, chrome, brass, stainless steel, and forged iron. MC, V. Mon & Thurs till 7pm.

Castro Convertibles
43 West 23 Street; 255-7000. And branches. One of New York's largest selection of convertible sofas, recliners; wall units. AE, MC, V. OPEN 7 days.

Conran's Habitat
The Market at Citicorp Center, 160 East 54 Street; 371-2225. And 2 Astor Place; 505-1515. Also Broadway & West 81 Street, 873-9250. Via England. A complete home furnishings store featuring affordable well-designed furniture and accessories, much of which you can carry out. Also kitchenware, glassware, china, linens, gifts. Mail order. Good sales. AE, MC, V. OPEN 7 days.

Devon Shop
111 East 27 Street. 686-1760. Formerly just for decorators, they now offer their beautiful custom-made hand-carved traditional furniture, as well as a complete design service, to the public. OPEN 7 days.

Door Store
210 East 51 Street; 753-2280. And 1 Park Avenue at East 33 St; 679-9700. Also 123 West 17 Street, 627-1515. Low-priced contemporary furniture design. Very extensive chair selection. MC, V. OPEN 7 days.

Gothic Cabinet Craft
547 Hudson Street near Perry St; 645-7828. And 1655 Second Avenue near East 85 St; 288-2999. Also branches. Unpainted stock and custom-built furniture. Fast, reliable, reasonable. MC, V. OPEN 7 days.

J & D Brauner Butcher Block
302 Bowery near Houston St; 477-2830. And branches. The solid, sturdy butcher block translated into contemporary furnishings. AE, MC. V. OPEN 7 days.

Jensen-Lewis
89 Seventh Avenue at West 15 St; 929-4880. And 1496 Third Avenue near East 84 St; 439-6440. Low-key Chelsea store started out featuring the director's chair in every shape, height, and color imaginable. Personalized if desired. Now contemporary furniture and accessories and contemporary canvas in 34 colors by-the-yard. AE, MC, V. OPEN 7 days.

Maurice Villency
200 Madison Avenue near East 35 St. 725-4840. High-quality contemporary furniture. MC, V. OPEN 7 days.

Norsk
114 East 57 Street. 752-3111. Scandinavian furniture, Rya rugs, crystal, porcelain, silver, and jewelry. AE, CB, DC, MC, V. OPEN 7 days.

Old World Warehouse
35 East 10 Street. 674-6753. Howard Kaplan, longtime purveyor of French country antiques, now manufactures his own line of reproduction furnishings, ceramics, fabrics, and decorative accessories—all authentically French accented. AE, MC, V.

OOPS
528 LaGuardia Place near Bleecker St. 982-0586. Originals On Permanent Sale. The originals are designer samples of contemporary furnishings—some overstocks, some bruised, some canceled orders. AE, MC, V. OPEN 7 days.

Palazzetti
515 Madison Avenue at East 53 St, 2nd floor. 832-1199. The classics of modern furniture. Marcel Breuer, Joseph Hoffman, Le Corbusier, Charles Rennie MacKintosh, Alvar Aalto, Rene Herbst, Pierre Chareau, and many more. AE, MC, V.

Shabby Chic
93 Greene Street near Spring St. 274-9842. Custom slip-covered furniture with a homey, lived-in look. Throw pillows, slipcovers, linens, period accessories follow through on the well-used look. Interesting. AE, MC, V. OPEN 7 days.

Workbench
470 Park Avenue South near East 32 St; 481-5454. And 161 Sixth Avenue at Spring St; 675-7775. Also branches. Attractive American and European contemporary furniture at reasonable prices. Excellent sales. MC, V. OPEN 7 days.

—Furniture: Rental

A.F.R. The Furniture Rental People
71 Third Avenue near East 44 St, 2nd floor. 867-2800. Rents groups or single pieces of furniture. Long or short term. AE, DC, V.

IFR
345 Park Avenue at East 51 St. 421-0340. Five showrooms; short- or long-term leasing. AE, MC, V.

House- & Kitchenwares

The large department stores have good selections of kitchenware. The Bowery, near Cooper Square and below Grand Street, is where the restaurant-equipment suppliers are located. Find good buys on practical, no-frills professional cooking implements. (See also Cutlery & Gadgetry.)

Bridge Kitchenware
214 East 52 Street. 688-4220. No-nonsense shop for great-priced best-quality professional equipment for the home: copperware (they do retinning), earthenware, woodware, French porcelain baking supplies, restaurant-size stockpots, and more. Know what you want before you go—they have over 40,000 items—but do go. Julia Child does. MC, V.

Broadway Panhandler
520 Broadway near Spring St. 966-3434. Extensive collection of first-quality gourmet cookware, cutlery, and gadgets at low prices. Huge stock of bakeware—cake molds and decorating implements are a specialty. Special orders taken. AE, MC, V. *OPEN 7 days.*

The Cellar at Macy's
West 34 Street & Broadway, downstairs. 695-4400. A cook's tour de force. Beautifully stocked series of "shops" dedicated to housewares and food. There are gourmet foods and baked goods, coffees and teas, as well as the utensils and equipment for creative cookery. Cooking demonstrations, free food samples, and special events throughout the year. *OPEN 7 days.*

D. F. Sanders
386 West Broadway near Broome St; 925-9040. And 952 Madison Avenue near East 75 St; 879-6161. Contemporary high-tech housewares, home furnishings, gadgets, and gifts in a spacious SoHo setting. Well stocked. A registry for the modern bride. AE, MC, V. *OPEN 7 days.*

Dot Zero
165 Fifth Avenue at 22 St. 533-8322. Design-oriented high-style high-tech gadgets and furnishings for the home. AE, MC, V. *OPEN 7 days.*

Empire Restaurant Supply
114 Bowery at Grand St. 226-4447. Discount headquarters for professional and restaurant cookware, equipment including Vulcan stoves, Buffalo and Hall china (glassware is sold in quantity only). Will special order. MC, V. *OPEN Mon-Fri 8am-5pm.*

Hold Everything
104 Seventh Avenue near West 16 St; 633-1674. And 1311 Second Avenue at East 69 St; 535-9446. What a great idea! This division of Williams-Sonoma stocks the wherewithal for you to store almost anything in a neat, attractive manner. *See also* Williams-Sonoma Outlet Center. AE, MC, V. Catalog. *OPEN 7 days.*

Kitschen
15 Christopher Street near Greenwich Ave. 727-0430. The kitchenwares we all grew up with. Chockar block with vintage (circa 1920-60) mixing bowls, cookie jars, pitchers, waffle irons, salt and pepper shakers, plates for corn on the cob, and other dedicated kitchenware, all displayed in color-coordinated tableaux. AE, MC, V. *OPEN 7 days.*

Main Course
Bloomingdale's, Third Avenue & East 59 Street, 6th floor. 355-5900. A total environment of 16 shops features all the accoutrements for gourmet cooking, serving, dining, and entertaining from heavy-duty cookware to the dining-table candles. Demonstrations, special events. AE, Bloomie's charge.

Williams-Sonoma
20 East 60 Street. 980-5155. First New York retail outlet of the famed San Francisco–based kitchen supply shop. Attractive, well stocked, and welcome. There's a culinary consultant on hand; cooking demonstrations, too. AE, MC, V. *OPEN 7 days.* (*See also* Williams-Sonoma Outlet Center *below.*)

Williams-Sonoma Outlet Center
231 Tenth Avenue near West 24 St. 206-8118. A dream come true—outlet shopping in Manhattan! The one-time Pottery Barn Warehouse Store now carries the excess and marked-down merchandise from Williams-Sonoma's mail-order catalogs and stores, including **Chambers** (bed and bath linens), **Gardner's Eden** (garden accessories), **Hold Everything** (organization and storage), **Williams-Sonoma** (cookware), and **Pottery Barn** (tabletop and decorative accessories). Huge selection in a bare bones warehouse on three floors, for savings of 30 to 70 percent. AE, MC, V. *OPEN Mon-Fri 11am-7pm; Sat 10am-6:30pm; Sun noon-5pm.*

Zabar's
2245 Broadway near West 80 St. 787-2000. The gourmet giant's housewares department is on the mezzanine. AE, DC, MC, V. *OPEN 7 days.*

—Kitchenware Repair

Retinning & Copper Repair
525 West 26 Street, 4th floor. 244-4896. City's oldest tinsmithery; since 1916. Repairs cookware; restores copper, tin, steel, cast iron, and brass. *OPEN Mon-Fri.*

Lamps/Lighting

Department stores stock modern and traditional lamps. Inexpensive, modern light fixtures can be found at many neighborhood houseware/hardware stores. The Bowery from Delancey to Grand Street is the cash-and-carry discount lamp and light fixture district. Shop after shop offers what's new and modern in most cases, tacky and tasteless in others, all at below-list prices. All are OPEN Sunday.

Barry of Chelsea
154 Ninth Avenue near West 19 St. 242-2666. Original American lighting from 1880 to 1940. *OPEN Tues-Sat noon-7pm.*

Bon Marche
1060 Third Avenue near East 63 St; 620-5592. And *55 West 13 Street, 7th floor; 620-5550. Contemporary lamps, good value. MC, V. *Thurs till 9pm.*

Bowery Lighting
132 Bowery near Grand St. 966-4034. Emphasis on very contemporary lighting; Italian designs. All at 30 percent off list price. AE, MC, V. *OPEN 7 days.*

Gallery 91
91 Grand Street near Greene St. 966-3722. Designs by an international array of contemporary artisans in table, wall, and hanging lamps. *OPEN Tues-Sat noon-6pm.*

George Kovacs Lighting
330 East 59 Street. 838-3400. Classic contemporary design including Robert Sonneman, Tamarkin Techler, David Winfield Willson, Peter Hamburger, Michael DiBlasi, Milo Baughman, Kevin Schopfer in a wide price range. The exclusive representative of the Woka series from Austria. AE, MC, V.

Just Bulbs
938 Broadway at East 22 St. 228-7820. In the Flatiron District you'll find just that—nearly 3,000 light bulbs of every description for every need. Great for the hard-to-find. AE, MC, V. *OPEN Mon-Fri 8am-5pm.*

Just Shades
21 Spring Street at Elizabeth St. 966-2757. New York's largest selection of just shades. Every size and material at 20-30 percent discount. Or recover your old one. *OPEN Thurs-Tues 9:30am-4pm.*

Thunder 'n Light
171 Bowery near Delancey St. 219-0180. Track lighting and innovative Italian and Venetian light fixtures and glass. MC, V. *OPEN 7 days.*

Uplift Lighting
506 Hudson Street near Christopher St. 929-3632. Original and reproduction Art Deco chandeliers, floor lamps, torcheres, table lamps. Large selection of restored antique lighting from teens through 30s. Repros 10-30 percent off retail. MC, V. *OPEN 7 days 1:30-8pm.*

—Lamp Repair

Grand Brass Lamp Parts
221 Grand Street at Elizabeth St. 226-2567. Family-run enterprise has been fixing and/or replacing broken or missing parts for lamps for over 90 years. They rewire, resolder, refinish. *OPEN Tues-Sat.*

Linens

Bergdorf, Bloomies, Macy's, and Saks have good linen departments, and the time to shop in them for bargains is during the January and August white sales. Year-round bargains can be found on the *Lower East Side: Grand Street from Allen to Forsyth* streets for first-quality seconds and discontinued designer lines. Though CLOSED on Saturday, all are OPEN Sunday, but be prepared for crowds that day.

For shops selling antique linens, see Women's Clothes: Vintage *and* Specialty Shops & Services, Antiques.

ABC Carpet & Home
888 Broadway at East 19 St. 677-6970. A gallery of shops with a wonderful selection of imported and domestic bed and bath linens. Custom-made as well. AE, MC, V. *OPEN 7 days.*

Ad Hoc Softwares
410 West Broadway at Spring St. 925-2652. Terrific modern SoHo shop for the finest in contemporary accessories for bed and bath. Distinctive European and American bedding in cotton and linen. AE, MC. V. *OPEN 7 days.*

Descamps
723 Madison Avenue near East 64 St. 355-2522. French linen boutique for their own 100 percent cotton; pastel, solids, delicate prints; two collections a year. Seamstress to alter duvets and dust ruffles to match. Table linens, too. Expensive. AE, DC, MC, V. *OPEN 7 days.*

Ezra Cohen
307 Grand Street at Allen St. 925-7800. Famed far and wide for its splendid selection of discount merchandise on two floors. Every brand-name sheet in current styles is represented, plus famous-maker bedspreads. Ready- and custom-made down comforters. Everything for the bed and bath, at 15-30 percent off retail. AE, MC, V. *OPEN Sun-Fri 9am-5pm.*

Frette
787 Madison Avenue near East 67 St. 988-5221. Sleek shop for Italian bed and table linens: pique, damask, voile, silk. For the well-dressed bed. AE, MC, V.

Harris Levy
278 Grand Street near Eldridge St. 226-3102. Hectic-but-worth-it Lower East Side spot for discounts (20-40 percent) on name-brand bed linens, imported tablecloths, and anything you might need for the bathroom. Second floor: custom- and ready-made curtains, bedspreads, dust ruffles, throw pillows, lamp shades, and draperies. AE, MC, V. *OPEN Sun-Fri. CLOSES Fri at 3pm.*

Porthault
18 East 69 Street. 688-1660. The Rolls-Royce of sheets. Exclusive and extravagantly expensive line of 100 percent cotton floral and print bed linens. Choose from 600 prints in a variety of colors. Also table and bath linens; a collection of exquisite children's clothes and gift items. AE, DC, MC, V.

Pratesi Shop
829 Madison Avenue at East 69 St. 288-2315. Their own fine bed, bath, and table linens manufactured in Florence, since the turn of the century. Also infant linens and clothes. Very expensive. AE, MC, V.

Schweitzer Linen
1132 Madison Avenue near East 84 St. 249-8361. Specialists in fine imported linens. Sleep pillows, both down and poly, custom-made to odd sizes. AE, DC, MC.

Paint & Wallpaper

Hardware stores carry basic paints and supplies; the extent of stock usually depends on the size of the shop. The stores below are specialists.

Janovic Plaza
161 Sixth Avenue near Spring St; 627-1100. And

*1150 Third Avenue at East 67 St; 772-1400. Also 159 West 72 Street, 595-2500; 213 Seventh Avenue near West 23 St, 243-2186; and *96-36 Queens Boulevard, Rego Park, Queens, (718) 897-1600. Wholesale and retail paint and wallpaper center; 15,000 wallpaper patterns available and they will mix paint to match any of them. Bath and fabric departments and window coverings, too. Expert professional staff. Free delivery. MC, V. *OPEN 7 days.

Pintchik
478 Bergen Street at Flatbush Ave, Brooklyn; (718) 783-3333. And 278 Third Avenue near East 22 St; 982-6600. Also 2475 Broadway near West 92 St; 769-1440. Enormous selection of major-brand paints at discount prices. New York's most extensive wallpaper stock. All at great prices. Great sales during inventory. Accessories, too. AE, MC, V. OPEN 7 days.

Sheila's Wall Styles
274 Grand Street near Eldridge St. 966-1663. Up to 70 percent discount on large selection of decorator wallpapers, overruns, discontinueds, and closeouts. This manufacturer of wallpaper also makes draperies, blinds, and fabrics to match. Half-price Levelors, woven-wood blinds. AE, MC, V. OPEN Sun-Fri. CLOSES Fri at 3pm.

Pillows

The major department stores have good selections of decorative pillows. For down pillow makers, see also Quilts: Modern.

Economy Foam Center
173 East Houston Street at First Ave. 473-4463. Foam cut to size and shape while you wait or shredded by the pound for "piller filler." Polyester fiberfill, too. Ready-made sleep and decorative pillows; foam mattresses, designer sheets, spreads, all closeout at 30-50 percent off retail. Custom covers; wall covering and upholstery fabric and vinyl. Also carries futons. OPEN Sun-Fri.

Gerry Nichol
132 East 45 Street, suite 7B. 949-1008. Exquisite decorative pillows made from period antique fabrics and trim. Retail and to the trade. By appointment only.

Harris Levy
278 Grand Street near Eldridge St. 226-3102. This longtime Lower East Side source for discount linens stocks a huge selection of throw pillows. They will also custom make or embellish with cording, scallops, monograms, etc. AE, MC, V. OPEN Sun-Fri. CLOSES Fri at 3pm.

I. Itzkowitz
174 Ludlow Street near Houston St. 477-1788. Custom-made seat cushions, decorative and sleeping pillows in every size and shape; choice of fillings. (See also Quilts: Modern.) OPEN Sun-Fri 8am-4pm.

The Pillowry
19 East 69 Street, 3rd floor. 628-3844. Unusual pillows made of antique textiles and rugs including kilims from Persia, Afghanistan, Turkey, Russia, Romania. Also needlepoint, old silk, damask, Ikat, homespun, Aubusson, and lace. Tapestries and rugs, too. Expert restoration. MC, V. OPEN Mon-Fri; Sat by appointment.

Quilts

—Quilts: Antique

Most antique stores have a few quilts in stock. The following have outstanding collections in terms of quality, originality, and quantity.

American Hurrah
766 Madison Avenue at East 66 St. 535-1930. American textile folk art: hooked rugs, samplers, and the largest, most impressive selection of quilts anywhere. Also expert restoration and mounting. In addition, specialists in 19th-century American Indian rugs, blankets, weavings, and beadwork. OPEN Tues-Sat.

Gazebo
127 East 57 Street. 832-7077. A beautiful must. American quilts mainly from the 1920s and 1930s; and new ones in traditional patterns (custom orders, too). Vintage wicker furnishings and accessories, old and new baskets, silk flowers, and other pretty accessories. AE, MC, V. OPEN 7 days.

Kelter Malce Antiques
361 Bleecker Street near Charles St. 989-6760. Very large, very fine collection of antique American quilts. Folk art, rag rugs, antique American Indian textiles and pottery. AE, MC, V. OPEN Mon-Sat 11am-7pm, but call first.

Laura Fisher
Manhattan Art & Antiques Center, 1050 Second Avenue at East 55 St. 838-2596. An exciting collection of pieced and appliquéd quilts circa 1830-1930, including Amish and crib quilts. Also paisley shawls, woven coverlets, Marseilles bedspreads, hooked and American Indian rugs, needlework and decorative Victorian accessories. AE, MC, V. OPEN Mon-Sat 11:30am-5:30pm.

Susan Parrish Antiques
390 Bleecker Street near Perry St. 645-5020. Lovely selection of pretty quilts, original 18th- and 19th-century painted country American furniture and American Indian weavings. Knowledgeable and caring owner. AE, MC, V. OPEN Mon-Sat 1-7pm.

Sweet Nellie
1262 Madison Avenue near East 90 St. 876-5775. A charming Carnegie Hill shop for American country, mainly originals, some reproductions. Quilts, pillows made from antique paisleys, new game boards, crib quilts, and hooked rugs. AE, MC, V.

Thos. K. Woodard
835 Madison Avenue near East 69 St, 2nd floor. 988-2906. Well-known well-respected source for antique American quilts from the 1850s on. Also hooked rugs, samplers, game boards, baskets, and so much more mint Americana. AE, MC, V.

—Quilts: Modern

The linen department of the major stores carry ready-made quilts in a wide range of fillings and prices.

The Down Shop
673 Madison Avenue at East 61 St. 759-3500. Large selection of ready-made down-filled all-cotton Continental quilts in all sizes and colors. AE, MC, V.

European Feather Importing Company
85 Allen Street near Broome St. 226-2282. Buy white goose down by the pound and ticking by the yard—they do the rest. *OPEN Sun-Thurs 9am-2pm; Fri till noon.*

I. Itzkowitz
174 Ludlow Street near Houston St. 477-1788. The best quilt man in America. You pick the filling and the covering, for new or refurbishing. He's the last of a breed. *OPEN Sun-Fri 8am-4pm.*

J. Schachter
85 Ludlow Street near Delancey St. 533-1150; (800) 468-6233. Longtime Lower East Side source in new digs, for custom- and ready-made comforters and quilts. Choose the filling, the design, the covering, or have your favorite patchwork quilt made into a comforter . . . or they'll recover and sterilize your old down comforters and pillows. Also a full line of current domestic and imported linens at 25-40 percent off. MC, V. *OPEN Sun-Fri. CLOSES Fri at 3pm.*

Wicker

—Wicker: Antique

Wicker Garden
1318 Madison Avenue near East 93 St. 410-7000. This lovely Carnegie Hill shop specializes in expensive 19th- and early 20th-century wicker furnishings, hand-painted country furniture, quilts, and accessories. Potpourri, too. MC, V.

—Wicker: Contemporary

Azuma and similar import shops all carry inexpensive contemporary wicker furnishings and accessories.

Bazaar
125 West 3 Street near Sixth Ave; 673-4138. And 1453 First Avenue near East 75 St; 737-2003. Also 501 Second Avenue near East 28 St, 683-2293; 1362 Third Avenue near East 77 St, 861-5999; 1145 Third Avenue near East 66 St, 988-7600; 1037 Lexington Avenue near East 74 St, 734-8119; *1186 Madison Avenue near East 86 St, 348-3786; 2025 Broadway near West 69 St, 873-9153; 540 Columbus Avenue near West 86 St, 362-7335; and 107-25 Continental Avenue, Forest Hills, Queens, (718) 263-2310. Large selection of wicker furnishings at reasonable prices. Also full line of housewares. AE, MC, V. *OPEN 7 days. *CLOSED Sun.*

Deutsch, Inc.
31 East 32 Street. 683-8746. Lovely and unusual collection of new wicker and rattan furnishings.

Pier 1 Imports
Fifth Avenue at 40 St. 447-1610. The only Mnahattan store of this source for basic home furnishings including a stylish selection of wicker imports. Well-priced and good frequent sales. AE, MC, V, Pier 1 charge. *OPEN Mon-Fri 9am-9pm; Sat & Sun 11am-6pm.*

SPECIALTY SHOPS & SERVICES

Acting Schools

American Academy of Dramatic Arts
120 Madison Avenue near East 30 St. 686-9244. Acting, speech, voice, movement, mime.

Herbert Berghof Studio
120 Bank Street near Hudson St. 675-2370. Founded by actors Uta Hagen and Herbert Berghof. For beginners and advanced students.

Lee Strasberg Theater Institute, Inc.
115 East 15 Street. 533-5500. Founded by creative genius Lee Strasberg; Pacino and De Niro are alumni.

Adult Education

The following offer an extensive selection of courses in a wide variety of fields, geared to adult interests and life-styles.

Columbia University School of General Studies
303 Lewisohn Hall, West 116 Street & Broadway. 854-3331. Day; some evening credit and some noncredit courses.

Fordham University at Lincoln Center
113 West 60 Street. 636-6000. Their "Excel" program offers the opportunity to use life experience for credit toward a degree.

New School for Social Research
66 West 12 Street. 741-5629. America's first university for adults. Over 1,700 courses in the most amazing array of subjects; Saturday and Sunday classes, too. For intellectual stimulation, career advancement, degree credit (or not).

New York University School of Continuing Education
25 West 4 Street. 998-7080. Most classes are evening and not for credit. "Life experience" program.

YMCA of Greater New York
Daytime and evening classes at over 30 coed YMCAs in the New York area, in fine arts, fitness, sports, dance, photography, crafts, or languages.

Antiques

New York has hundreds of antiques shops, only some of which sell antiques; others sell nostalgia, memorabilia, collectibles, bric-a-brac. This list is representative of the best, brightest, wittiest, most highly rated, or just plain funky.

Throughout this shopping section, antiques are also listed under specific categories (e.g., Furniture, Silver).

Several areas are particularly rich in antiques shops: Bleecker Street west of Sixth Avenue; Second Avenue in the East 50s; Madison Avenue in the East 60s to 80s; University Place to Broadway, East 11 to 13 Street (the highest concentration in the city, both retail and to the trade); East 57 Street. In Brooklyn, Atlantic Avenue from Court to Clinton Street; Coney Island Avenue from Beverly Road to Avenue M.

See also Women's Clothing, Vintage

—Antique Shops

Accents Unlimited, Ltd.
360 Amsterdam Avenue and 2211 Broadway near West 79 St. 580-8404. Steve Mohr has one of the best eyes in the business and his wonderful shops are brimming over with late-19th- to early-20th-century French and English decorative antiques with a bent toward the Victorian. Paisleys, wonderful handpainted china, beadwork, bamboo furnishings, rugs, screens, and an eclectic selection of jewelry, 1840 to 1940. AE, MC, V. *OPEN Mon-Fri noon-7:30pm; Sat 11am-6pm; Sun 11am-5pm.*

A la Vieille Russie, Inc.
781 Fifth Avenue at 59 St. 752-1727. Exquisite Russian art and antiques: clocks, art objects—especially Fabergé, icons, Russian silver and porcelain, antique jewelry and snuff boxes. AE only.

Amdur Antiques
1026-1028 Lexington Avenue near East 73 St. 472-2691. A well-stocked treasure trove of wonderful decorative antiques and accessories. Much antique bamboo, beaded footstools, Victorian picture frames, match strikers, and more. AE, MC, V.

America Hurrah
766 Madison Avenue at East 66 St. 535-1930. Americana source: magnificent patchwork quilts and textiles, weather vanes, folk sculpture, painted American country furniture, and American Indian art. *OPEN Tues-Sat.*

Antiques By Patrick
64 East 13 Street. 254-8336. In new high-celinged quarters, an eclectic range of furniture, silver, porcelain, paintings, and jewelry, from the 15th century to the 1950s. Accessibly priced, have a browse.

Back Pages
125 Greene Street near Prince St. 460-5998. SoHo source for antique amusement and slot machines, plus Wurlitzer jukeboxes, Coca-Cola vending machines, players pianos, and other large items. Restoration available. *OPEN 7 days.*

Bernard & S. Dean Levy, Inc.
24 East 84 Street. 628-7088. Lovely town house gallery for top-quality late 17th- to early 19th-century American antiques, furniture, silver, paintings, and decorative wares. *OPEN Oct-May, Tues-Sat; June-Sept, Mon-Fri.*

Bertha Black
80 Thompson Street near Spring St. 966-7116. Tiny SoHo shop for American antique painted furniture, folk art, and country dining accessories. Extensive collection of Mexican *retablos* and *santos*, 1820-1900. AE only. *OPEN Wed-Sun 2-7pm.*

Chick Darrow's Fun Antiques
309 East 61 St. 838-0730. Antique toys of every description for the Peter Pans among us. Automobilia, wind-ups, mechanical banks, carousel animals, toy soldiers, gambling devices, arcade machines. Price range: $2-$5,000. AE, MC, V. *OPEN Mon-Fri 11:30am-7pm; Sat 11:30am-4pm; and by appointment.*

Cobblestones
314 East 9 Street. 673-5372. A lot of fun old "stuff." Kitchen utensils, costume jewelry, books, glassware, sunglasses, hats, cigarette cases, evening bags. You never know what you might find. Have a browse. AE, MC, V. *OPEN Tues-Sun.*

D. Leonard & Gary Trent
950 Madison Avenue near East 75 St. 737-9511; 879-1799. Twentieth-century decorative arts. Art Nouveau and Art Deco: Tiffany lamps, glass, posters, bronzes, and mirrors; English and French cameo glass. AE only.

Dullesville
143 East 13 Street. 505-2505. Jewelry, pottery, decorative objects from 1900 through the 1960s. Much Russell Wright and one of the largest collections of Bakelite in the country. AE, MC, V. *OPEN 7 days.*

Eclectiques
55 Wooster Street at Broome St. 966-0650. Aptly named. Deco, Nouveau, 1920s Mica lamps, Mission furniture, 20th-century oils and illustrations, paisley shawls and vintage Vuiton luggage. AE, MC, V. *OPEN 7 days 12:30-6pm.*

Hubert des Forges
1193 Lexington Avenue near East 81 St. 744-1857. Lovely French/English antiques and decorative accessories. AE, MC, V. *OPEN Mon-Fri.*

Irreplaceable Artifacts
14 Second Avenue at Houston St; 777-2900. And *259 Bowery near Houston St; 982-5000. Original spectacular architectural ornamentation for interior and exterior use—stained glass, mantel pieces, fountains, wrought iron, paneling, and much, much more. MC, V. *OPEN 7 days. *OPEN by appointment only.*

Irving Barber Shop Antiques
210 East 21 Street. (No phone.) Cramped quarters overflowing with glassware, costume jewelry, beaded evening bags, prints, and sometimes antique linens, quilts, and vintage cloths. Browsable (gingerly). *OPEN Mon-Fri 12:30-6:30pm.*

Jana Starr-Jean Hoffman Antiques
236 East 80 Street. 861-8256; 535-6930. Jampacked with turn-of-the-century to 1950s wedding dresses, focus 1900-1930. Also in these tight quarters, beautiful embroidered antique table and bed linens. Plus jewelry, hats, gloves,

dressing table items, bags, antique laces and textiles, walking sticks. All obviously gathered with care. Rental of period props. AE, MC, V. *OPEN Mon-Sat noon-6pm; evenings by appointment.*

Le Fanion
299 West 4 Street at Bank St. 463-8760. French country antiques and contemporary ceramics in a shop that transports you to Provence without having to leave the city. AE only. *OPEN Mon-Sat noon-7pm.*

Leo Kaplan Ltd.
967 Madison Avenue near East 75 St. 249-6766. Extensive selection of French and American modern paperweights; 18th-century English pottery and porcelains, Russian enamels; English and French cameo glass of the Art Nouveau period and contemporary studio glass. AE, MC, V.

Lillian Nassau
220 East 57 Street. 759-6062. *The* place for Art Nouveau and Art Deco, especially Tiffany glass, rare art glass, as well as furniture and sculpture. AE.

Linda Horn
1015 Madison Avenue near East 78 St. 772-1122. Opulent treasures from the 18th and 19th centuries in a setting to match. Linda has quite an eye for the unusual. AE, MC, V.

Mood Indigo
181 Prince Street. 254-1176. The 30s and 40s are done justice in this inviting shop full of Russell Wright, Fiesta and Harlequin ware, Art Deco chrome accessories, and a wonderful selection of Bakelite jewelry. AE, MC, V. *OPEN Tues-Sun noon-7pm.*

Moriah
699 Madison Avenue near East 62 St, 2nd floor. 751-7090. Filled with antique Judaica, prints, engravings, curios. *OPEN Mon-Fri. CLOSES Fri at 3pm.*

Old Versailles, Inc.
315 East 62 Street. 421-3663. French and continental antiques and furniture. *OPEN Mon-Fri noon-5pm.*

Philip Suval, Inc.
517-8293. Antique English porcelain and pottery, paintings. China trade porcelain, English furniture and glass from the 19th century. *By appointment only.*

Price Glover, Inc.
59 East 79 Street, 3rd floor. 772-1740. English pewter and pottery and brass, circa 1690 through 1820. Also early 19th-century English brass light fixtures and Chinese furniture 1600 to 1700. *OPEN Mon-Fri 10am-5:30pm.*

Primavera Gallery
808 Madison Avenue near East 68 St. 288-1569. Twentieth-century decorative arts: paintings, furniture, glass, and jewelry, 1900s-1950s. AE, MC, V.

Sarajo
98 Prince Street near Mercer St. 966-6156. Large and impressive selection of textiles, antique furniture, and objects from Central Asia, Africa, the Far East, and Central and South America. AE, MC, V. *OPEN 7 days.*

Thos. K. Woodard
835 Madison Avenue near East 73 St, 2nd floor. 794-9404; 988-2906. Extensive and prime selection of Americana antique quilts, country furniture, and folk art. Rag rugs, both old and woodweave reproductions. AE, MC, V.

Trouvaille Française
737-6015. Treasures from France and Belgium in the form of antique bed and table linens, laces, curtains, christening gowns, and so much more, collected and purveyed with loving care by Muriel Clark. *By appointment only.*

Urban Archaeology
285 Lafayette Street near Houston St; 431-6969. And *210 Elizabeth Street near Spring St; 941-4800. Gargoyles and other grand bygone architectural embellishments, all saved from the wrecker's ball. Americana from 1880s to 1925, focus mainly on New York City. Major dealer in Art Deco interiors and exteriors. Also antique slot and arcade machines. AE, MC, V. *Indoors and outdoors.

Vitto Giallo
966 Madison Avenue near East 76 St. 535-9885. Tastefully chosen antiques from the 18th and 19th centuries fill this tiny shop: quilts, paisleys, Staffordshire, fountain pens, and small treasures from the past. Fast turnover. AE, MC, V.

Waves
32 East 13 Street. 989-9284. Vintage radios, wind-up phonographs, old telephones, neon clocks—sold, repaired, rented. Also 78 rpm records and advertising memorabilia. MC, V. *OPEN Tues-Sat noon-6pm.*

—Antique & Flea Markets

With escalating rents forcing out many small businesses, flea markets are becoming the last bastion of affordable goods.

Annex Antiques Market
West 26 Street & Sixth Avenue. 243-5343. Outdoors, year-round in nearly every kind of weather. A serious dealers' market: good antiques and collectibles. Strong on silver, jewelry, vintage clothes, glasss, Americana, Victoriana, ephemera, and more. Varies from week to week since most of the dealers are itinerant and go where the action is. Free parking; $1 admission charge. NOTE: One block south there's a more chaotic lot with a preponderance of junk, but worth a look for good vintage clothes and the occasional quilt; no admission charge. Both *OPEN year-round every Sun 9am-6pm.*

Antiques, Flea & Farmer's Market
P.S. 183, East 67 Street & First Avenue. 737-8888. A friendly spot for some good quality antiques and collectibles, including jewelry and linens. Also new goods and fresh produce. Indoors and outdoors. Free admission. *OPEN year-round Sat 9am-5pm.*

Greenflea's Market on Columbus
Columbus Avenue & West 76 Street. 316-1088. Two hundred vendors selling antiques, collectibles, old clothes, jewelry, and new merchandise, too. Rivals 26 Street as the Sunday flea to go to.

Indoors and outdoors. Free admission. *OPEN year-round Sun 10am-6pm.*

Manhattan Art & Antique Center
1050 Second Avenue near East 56 St. 355-4400. This is a class act. Over 100 shops and galleries featuring antiques and fine art objects from around the world. Price range: $10-$300,000. Great selection under one roof. Indoors. Free admission. *OPEN year-round Mon-Sat 10:30am-6:15pm; Sun noon-6pm.*

Place des Antiquaires
125 East 57 Street. 758-2709. An impressive array of 75 international antiques shops in a deluxe setting. Changing exhibits as well. Restaurant on premises. *OPEN Tues & Wed, Fri & Sat 11am-7pm; Thurs 11am-8pm; Sun noon-5pm.*

Tower Flea Market
Broadway & East 4 Street. Mainly young and earnest artisans and designers selling tees, clothes, jewelry, hats, and other adornments. *OPEN year-round Sat & Sun 9am-6pm.*

—Antiques: Shows

Check the New York Times *Weekend section on Friday for current calendar. For major shows, see* ANNUAL EVENTS.

Art Schools

Art Students' League
215 West 57 Street. 247-4510. Founded in 1875. Learn to draw, paint, or sculpt. No entrance exam or prerequisites. Saturday classes.

Manhattan Graphics Center
476 Broadway near Grand St, 4th floor. 219-8783. Classes and workshops; silk-screening, lithography, photoprinting, etching.

School of Visual Arts
209 East 23 Street. 683-0600. Drawing, painting, graphic design, illustration. Check for requirements. Evenings and weekends. MC, V.

Art Supplies

Arthur Brown & Bro, Inc.
2 West 46 Street. 575-5555. Long-established, superior art and drafting supply store, the largest in America. Fantastic pen department. AE, MC, V.

Charrette
215 Lexington Avenue at East 33 St. 683-8822. (Formerly Eastern Artists.) Incredibly extensive selection of art supplies discounted at 20 percent off. Fine custom framing, too. AE, MC, V.

Kate's Paperie
See Stationery.

New York Central
62 Third Avenue near East 11 St. 473-7705. This superior shop carries everything for the artist. The finest materials including handmade papers, parchment; 3,000 different pastels, 200 different canvases; 20-40 percent less than elsewhere. For over 80 years they have been serving the artist, including finding the "impossible." AE, DC, MC, V.

Papers Etc.
See Stationery.

Pearl
308 Canal Street near Broadway. 431-7932. World's largest art and graphics discount center. Wonderful source for artists' and crafts materials as well as house and industrial paints at 20-50 percent off list. Nine floors, MC, V. *OPEN 7 days.*

Sam Flax, Inc.
25 East 28 Street; 620-3040. And 233 Spring Street near Sixth Ave; 620-3060. Also 425 Park Avenue at East 55 St, 620-3060; and 12 West 20 Street, 620-3038. Very complete art supply store. School and office, too. AE, MC, V.

Auction Houses

Christie's & Christie's East
502 Park Avenue at East 59 St; 546-1000. And *219 East 67 Street; 606-0470. New York branches of famed London house. Auctions of fine art, furnishings, tapestries, books, and manuscripts. Free art appraisals. Inquiries on current sale, call 546-1178. *"Low-end" antiques and collectibles.

Great Gatsby's
91 University Place near East 12 St. 260-2000. Located adjacent to the antiques area. Estate auctions every other Tuesday at 11am (viewing for four days prior). American and European antiques and decorative arts.

Harmer
14 East 33 Street. 532-3700. Coin and antiquities auctions, three or four a year.

Lubin Galleries
30 West 26 Street. 924-3777. Auctions of estates of varying quality every two weeks on Saturday throughout the year. Good buys on holiday weekends especially. They sell items from as little as $5 up to $5,000. Sales every other Saturday. Viewing Thursday and Friday.

Phillips
406 East 79 Street. 570-4830. Founded in London in 1796. Fine art and estate sales. Items are on exhibit two to three days prior to actual auction. Check their ads.

Sotheby's
411 East 76 Street. 606-7000. World-famous auctioneer and appraiser since 1744. Paintings, jewelry, furniture, silver, books, porcelain, Orientalia, rugs, and more. Exciting to visit even if you're not buying. For 24-hour auction and exhibition information, call 606-7245. The **Arcade**, 1334 York Avenue at East 72 St, 606-7245, is their low-end outlet, sells 20th-century reproductions.

Tepper Galleries
110 East 25 Street. 677-5300. Large and lively, popular with collectors. Furniture, paintings, rugs, accessories, jewelry. Auction every other Saturday year-round. Viewing on Thursday and Friday.

William Doyle Galleries
175 East 87 Street. 427-2730. Specializes in es-

tates. Eighteenth- and 20th-century decorative and fine arts, including furniture, paintings, rugs, and accessories. Auction every other Wednesday year-round. Viewing Saturday to Tuesday. Tag sale next door yields "bargains."

Baskets

Adele Lewis
227 West 29 Street. 594-5075. Full of beautiful, pricey baskets as well as imported pottery and crafts items such as twig furniture. Mainly wholesale but you will be welcome. *OPEN Mon-Fri 8am-5pm.*

Azuma
415 Fifth Avenue near 37 St; 889-4310. And 666 Lexington Avenue near East 56 St; 752-0599. Also 25 East 8 Street, 673-2900; *387 Sixth Avenue near Waverly Pl, 989-8690; and 251 East 86 Street, 369-4928. Excellent source for wide selection of inexpensive imported baskets. *OPEN 7 days.*

Be Seated
66 Greenwich Avenue near Seventh Ave South. 924-8444. For over 30 years, an inviting little place for inexpensive and unusual baskets in all sizes and shapes, antique and new. MC, V.

Bicycles

Bicycles Plus
1400 Third Avenue near East 79 St; 794-2929. And 204 East 85 Street; 794-2201. A complete bike store. Sells, rents, repairs every speed bike. Will beat any price in town. AE, DC, MC, V. *OPEN 7 days.*

14th Street Bicycles
332 East 14 Street. 228-4344. Three-, 5-, and 10-speed bikes; sale, rental, repair. AE, MC, V. *OPEN 7 days.*

Gene's Bicycle Shop
242 East 79 Street. 249-9218. Low prices on major brands and a vast stock makes this a top spot for bikes. Sales, rentals, trades. Reliable repairs. Lessons, too. *OPEN 7 days.*

Pedal Pusher Bike Shop
1306 Second Avenue near East 69 St. 288-5592. Rents three-and 10-speed ATB/city bikes; repairs. Tours, racks, locks, clothing, and shoes. Private lessons available. AE, MC, V. *CLOSED Tues.*

Stuyvesant Bicycle
349 West 14 Street. 675-2160; 254-5200. Since 1939. Large selection of all types of bikes: Atala, Bottecchia, City Bikes, Raleigh—12-, 10-, 6-, and 3-speed. Touring, city, mountain, ATB, children's bikes. Repairs, parts, accessories. Shoes and clothes imported from Italy. AE, MC. V. *OPEN 7 days.*

Books

Fifth Avenue has the largest concentration of bookstores in the city.

—Books: Chain Stores

Barnes & Noble, Inc.
105 Fifth Avenue at 18 St. 807-0099. Booksellers since 1873. The most comprehensive store for new and used textbooks. *OPEN 7 days.*

Barnes & Noble Discount Bookstores
170 Broadway near Maiden Lane. And 38 Park Row at Beekman St. Also 879 Sixth Avenue at 33 St; 385 Fifth Avenue at 36 St; 109 East 42 Street at the Grand Hyatt; 1521 Broadway at West 45 St; Seventh Avenue at West 33 St; 750 Third Avenue at East 47 St; 2105 Broadway at West 73 St; 2300 Broadway at West 83 St; 120 East 86 Street; Albee Square Mall, Kings Plaza, Brooklyn; 107-24 Continental Avenue, Forest Hills, Queens; 91-20 59 Avenue, Elmhurst, Queens; 39-01 Main Street, Flushing, Queens.

Barnes & Noble Sale Annexes
*128 Fifth Avenue at 18 St; 807-0099. And 600 Fifth Avenue near East 48 St; 765-0590. Up to 35 percent discount on current fiction and nonfiction. The best for bargains. Good art books, remainders, classical records, too. AE, MC, V. *OPEN 7 days.*

B. Dalton
666 Fifth Avenue near 52 St; 247-1740. And 369 Sixth Avenue & West 8 St; 674-8780. Also 109 East 42 Street, 490-7501. Well-designed store has 300,000 books arranged by author on two floors. Personalized, helpful service. AE, MC, V. *OPEN 7 days.*

Doubleday
724 Fifth Avenue near 57 St; 397-0550. And South Street Seaport, 13 Fulton St; 571-1284. Also Citicorp, Third Avenue at East 53 St, 223-3301. Very well run and stocked. The Fifth Avenue shop has books galore, classical and show records. Excels in performing arts and travel books. Telephone and special orders. AE, CB, DC, MC, V. *OPEN 7 days.*

Waldenbooks
57 Broadway near Rector St; 269-1139. And 931 Lexington Avenue near East 69 St; 249-1327. Large general bookstore with current titles. AE, MC, V.

—Books: General

Books & Co.
939 Madison Avenue near East 74 St. 737-1450. More interested in literature than best-sellers. Stocks an author's complete works; autographed volumes, too. Many special literary events. Strong on philosophy. AE, MC, V. *OPEN 7 days.*

Brentano's Book Store
597 Fifth Avenue near 48 St. 826-2450. They're back on Fifth in the city's most beautiful bookstore (longtime former home of Scribner's), a landmark by Earnest Flagg. Personalized service; strong in history, biography, travel, local interest. AE, MC, V.

Classic Bookshop
1212 Sixth Avenue at West 48 St; 221-2252. And 133 World Trade Center Concourse; 466-0668.

Good midtown source for paperbacks, current and otherwise. Excellent sales of remaindered books. *New York Times* best-sellers at 25 percent off. They special order, gift wrap, and ship. AE, MC, V. *OPEN 7 days.*

Coliseum Books, Inc.
1771 Broadway at West 57 St. 757-8381. Huge, well-located, well-stocked, well-run store for current paperbacks, hardcover, reference books, and a good variety of remainder books including many for one dollar (except November to February). AE, DC, MC, V. *OPEN 7 days.*

The Corner Bookstore
1313 Madison Avenue at East 93 St. 831-3554. This welcoming Carnegie Hill store specializes in literature, art books, architecture, and children's books—primarily a general bookstore. They will special order with next-day delivery and do out-of-print searches; free gift wrap. They offer house and children accounts. MC, V. *OPEN 7 days.*

Endicott Booksellers
450 Columbus Avenue at West 81 St. 787-6300. Books in a charming setting. Literature, good paperback backlists, small press. A children's room; frequent author reading. Special orders and free gift wrapping. AE, MC, V. *OPEN Sun & Mon noon-8pm; Tues-Sat 10am-9pm.*

Gotham Book Mart and Gallery
41 West 47 Street. 719-4448. Once a literary mecca, it endures. Strong on theater, general literature especially fiction and standard classics; 20th-century first editions; the city's largest poetry collection; film and philosophy. Both new and out of print. Also 250 literary and small press magazines. Search service. Wise men—and women—do fish here. AE, MC, V.

St. Marks Bookshop
12 St. Marks Place near Third Ave. 260-7853. One of the finest bookstores in the city. Literature, poetry, drama, criticism, women's studies, contemporary theory; foreign and small press. Spoken word records and tapes. Mail order. AE, MC, V. *OPEN 7 days 11am-11:30pm.*

Three Lives & Co.
154 West 10 Street. 741-2069. Three women own this lovely bookshop named for the Gertrude Stein work. Dedicated to literature. Salon readings by noted authors are a special feature. AE ($15 minimum), MC, V ($10 minimum). *OPEN 7 days.*

Tower Books
383 Lafayette at East 4 St (above Tower Video). 228-5338. Extremely well stocked in every area; a good downtown browsing spot—note the hours. Policy: 30 percent off best-sellers, 20 percent off all hardcovers, 10 percent off all paperbacks. Also author readings, signings, special events. AE, DC, MC, V. *OPEN 7 days 9am-midnight.*

—Books: Antiquarian, Old & Used

(*See also* Books: Special Interest.)
Gryphon Book Shop
2246 Broadway near West 80 St. 362-0706.

Used and rare paperbacks; special interest in the performing arts. Pre-1940 children's books. Search service. Sale annex at *246 West 80 Street, 4th floor (724-1541). MC, V. *OPEN 7 days 10am-midnight. *noon-10pm.*

Pageant Book & Print Shop
109 East 9 Street. 674-5296. Good store for used books; literature, fiction, Americana; extensive selection of old prints, engravings. Film buffs will recognize the store from Woody Allen's *Hannah and Her Sisters.* AE, MC, V.

Strand
828 Broadway at East 12 St; 473-1452. Also at the *Seaport, 159 John Street; 809-0875. Eight miles of books (2 million books) in America's largest secondhand bookstore. Downstairs for review copies of new books 50 percent off. Excellent new and used history, art, and Americana. Warning, you'll spend more time and money than you had intended. AE, MC, V. *OPEN Mon-Sat 9:30am-9:20pm; Sun 11am-9:20pm. *Mon-Sat 10am-9pm; Sun 10am-8pm.*

—Books: Kiosks

Fifth Avenue and 60 Street on the park side: Bookstalls from Strand and Barnes & Noble. Also at Bryant Park.

—Books: Special Interest

Argosy Book Store
116 East 59 Street. 753-4455. Established in 1821. Strong in out-of-print history. European and American biographies. Search service. MC, V. *OPEN Mon-Fri.*

Books of Wonder
See KIDS' NEW YORK, Children's Specialty Shopping, Books.

Brunner/Mazel, Inc.
19 Union Square West near East 15 St. 924-3344. Psychiatry, psychotherapy texts, and other psychological material. AE, MC, V.

Chartwell Booksellers
In the Park Avenue Plaza arcade, 55 East 52 Street. 308-0643. A civilized place for literature and Sir Winston Churchill. Readings, tea dances, photography exhibits. AE, DC, MC, V. *OPEN Mon-Fri & 3rd Sat of every month.*

Civilized Traveler
1072 Third Avenue near East 63 St. 758-8305. Everything one might need for a civilized trip, starting with the guidebooks, maps, and videos, then on to travel-worthy, travel-sized items such as coffee makers, irons, security devices, converters, binoculars, games, and specialty luggage items. It's a civilized spot. MC, V. *OPEN 7 days.*

The Complete Traveller Bookstore
199 Madison Avenue at East 35 St. 685-9007. A shop completely devoted to travel: guides, maps, foreign-language dictionaries for near and far afield. Some posters; art books, too. Also current, classics, and used and rare. Will order. Annual catalog. AE, MC, V. *OPEN Mon-Fri 9am-7pm; Sat 10am-6pm; Sun noon-5pm.*

Drama Book Shop
723 Seventh Avenue near West 48 St, 2nd floor.

944-0595. Books on the theater, films, TV, published plays. Strong on criticism; well organized. Also vocal scores and sheet music from Broadway musicals; mail order worldwide; special orders. AE, MC, V. *OPEN 7 days.*

East West Books
78 Fifth Avenue near 14 St. 243-5994. Eastern religion and philosophy; mental and physical well-being. AE, MC, V. *OPEN 7 days.*

Eeyore's Books for Children
See KIDS' NEW YORK, Children's Specialty Shopping, Books.

General Medical Book Company
310 East 26 Street. 532-0756. Dental, medical, nursing, and veterinary books. MC, V.

Hacker Art Books
45 West 57 Street, 5th floor. 688-7600. Large bookstore with art, architecture, crafts books—both new and old and rare. Reprints of important art books.

Jaap Rietman
134 Spring Street near Wooster St, 2nd floor. 966-7044. In a SoHo loft. All areas of fine arts with particular emphasis on the 20th century and contemporary avant-garde. Art periodicals, exhibition catalogs, and small press publications. Free quarterly catalogs of new art and architecture titles, upon request. AE, MC, V ($30 minimum).

Kitchen Arts & Letters
1435 Lexington Avenue near East 93 St. 876-5550. Books from everywhere on food, cooking, and wine. Food ephemera; original art and photography related to food; kitchen-related stationery goods. Mail and phone orders. MC, V ($40 minimum). *OPEN Mon 1-6pm; Tues-Fri 10am-6:30pm; Sat 11am-6pm.*

Maritime Book Shop
24 Beaver Street near Broadway. 425-0123. Nautical technical books. AE, MC, V. *OPEN Mon-Fri.*

The Military Bookman
29 East 93 Street. 348-1280. Military, naval, and aviation history. Out-of-print and rare books. *OPEN Tues-Sat.*

M. M. Einhorn Maxwell, Books
80 East 11 Street, room 404. 228-6767; 477-5066. Used, out-of-print, and antiquarian books on food and drink; cookbooks, gastronomy, and oenology. Large selection of regional American cookbooks. Essentially mail order. *By appointment only.*

Morton Books
989 Third Avenue near East 59 St. 421-9025. All the current books and periodicals on design, decorating, gardening, and architecture in one place. AE, MC, V ($25 minimum).

Murder Ink
2486 Broadway near East 92 St. 362-8905. Mystery and suspense novels, new, used, and out-of-print. AE, MC, V ($25 minimum). *OPEN Sun-Thurs 10am-8pm; Fri & Sat till 10pm.*

Mysterious Bookshop
129 West 56 Street. 765-0900. Mystery, murder, mayhem. New, used, out-of-print hardcover and paperback. Rare-book search service. Mystery paraphernalia. Will order. AE, MC, V ($20 minimum).

New York Astrology Center
545 Eighth Avenue near West 37 St, 10th floor. 947-3609. Complete line of astrology books. Also acupuncture and healing arts. AE, MC, V.

New York Bound Bookshop
50 Rockfeller Plaza. 245-8503. This wonderful shop sells used, old, rare, and out-of-print—and now, current—books, ephemera, maps, photos, and graphics related to New York City and New York State. Knowledgeable and accommodating. Book search. AE, MC, V.

Oscar Wilde Memorial Bookshop
15 Christopher Street near Greenwich Ave. 255-8097. Specializes in gay and lesbian books. Also papers, cards, records, t-shirts, jewelry. AE, MC, V. *OPEN 7 days noon-7:30pm.*

Paraclete Book Center
146 East 74 Street. 535-4050. Theological bookstore. All faiths represented. *OPEN Tues-Sat.*

Richard Stoddard Performing Arts Books
See Memorabilia.

Rizzoli
31 West 57 Street (in the Sohmer building); 759-2424. And 454 West Broadway near Prince St; 674-1616. Also World Financial Center, 200 Vesey Street, 385-1400. Strong on art, architecture, photography, and university press. French, Italian, and German books; translations; foreign magazines and newspapers; classical recordings. AE, DC, MC, V. *OPEN 7 days till 8pm.*

Samuel Weiser, Inc.
132 East 24 Street, downstairs. 777-6363. The largest bookstore for the metaphysical, occult, Eastern philosophy. Current and out-of-print. MC, V. *OPEN 7 days.*

Science Fiction Shop
163 Bleecker near Thompson St. 473-3010. Longtime source in larger quarters, filled with books on science fiction, fact, and fantasy; new and old. MC, V. *OPEN 7 days.*

Sky Books International
48 East 50 Street, 2nd floor. 688-5086. Aviation, military, naval books, magazines, prints. AE, DC, V.

South Street Seaport Book & Chart Store
209 Water Street. 669-9455. Charming shop for nautical and New York books. Also maritime periodicals, posters, prints, and charts. AE, MC, V. *OPEN 7 days 10am-7pm.*

Traveller's Bookstore
22 West 52 Street, lobby. 664-0995. An intelligently organized bookshop for the best in travel guides as well as fiction and nonfiction about every country under the sun. Wonderful travel-sized and/or travel-related merchandise such as diaries, currency converters, electrical adapter/convertors, ponchos, carry bags, and flashlights. AE, MC, V.

Trinity Bookshop
74 Trinity Place near Rector St. 349-0376. Good

selection of technical and financial books. AE, MC, V. *OPEN Mon-Fri.*

Urban Center Books
457 Madison Avenue near East 51 St. 935-3595. Operated by the Municipal Art Society. Specializes in architecture, urban design and planning, and historic preservation. MC, V. *OPEN Mon-Thurs 11am-7pm; Fri & Sat 10am-6pm.*

Weyhe Art Books
794 Lexington Avenue near East 61 St. 838-5466. Art books, especially 20th century, out-of-print, used, and new. *CLOSED Aug.*

Wittenborn Art Books, Inc.
1018 Madison Avenue near East 78 St, 2nd floor. 288-1558. Large selection of books on fine and decorative arts; scholarly works. Antiquity, medieval, the Renaissance, and modern. Foreign publishers well represented. MC, V.

—Book Binding & Restoration

Associated Bindery
405 East 70 Street. 879-5080. Fine leather binding, European craftsmanship. *OPEN Mon-Fri. CLOSES Fri at 2pm.*

Buttons

They're becoming harder to find in New York; **Macy's** *has a small supply in their notions department. See also* Notions.

Gordon Button Co.
222 West 38 Street. 921-1684. Ten million buttons and buckles, 5,000 varieties. Classic to novelty—10 cents to $2. Service with a smile here. *OPEN Mon-Fri.*

Reliable Buttonworks
65 West 37 Street, 2nd floor. 869-0560. Factory for leather- or fabric-covered buttons—by the dozen. Also covered buckles and belts. Same-day service. Rhinestones, metal studs, belt buckles, too. *OPEN Mon-Fri 8am-5:30pm.*

Tender Buttons
143 East 62 Street. 758-7004. On display, every kind of button imaginable, including sets of the old and rare in this very special shop. Antique buckles and cuff links. Price range: 25¢-$3,500.

Candles

Azuma *shops and most large greeting-card stores have a good selection of candles.*

Candle Shop
118 Christopher Street near Bleecker St. 989-0148. The best. Every color, shape, size, and for every occasion. Holders, too. AE, MC, V. *OPEN Mon-Sat noon-8pm; Sun 1-7pm.*

Coins

Macy's
Herald Square, Broadway & West 34 Street, 7th floor. 736-1045. Rare U.S. and foreign coins bought and sold. AE, MC, V, Macy's charge. *OPEN 7 days.*

Stack's
123 West 57 Street. 582-2580. America's oldest and largest coin dealers. Rare coins, U.S., foreign, and ancient gold, silver, and copper coins sold retail. Eight auctions a year. *OPEN Mon-Fri 10am-5pm.*

Costume Rental

(See also Women's Clothes, Vintage.*)*

Abracadabra
10 Christopher Street near Greenwich Ave. 627-5745. Huge inventory of costumes, also masks, magic, and makeup. AE, MC, V.

Eaves-Brooks Costume Co.
21-07 41 Avenue near 21 St, Long Island City, Queens, 1st, 2nd & 3rd floors. (718) 729-1010. Longtime renter of theatrical costumes. Thousands in very good condition. Will also manufacture to your specifications. AE, MC, V. *OPEN Mon-Fri 10am-4:30pm. (Longer hours at Halloween, of course.)*

Gene London Studios
897 Broadway near East 20 St, 5th floor. 533-4105. Does this make sense! Everyone from the bride to the mother-in-law can rent their wedding outfits from this magnificent collection of wedding and evening wear, some of it worn in your favorite films of yesteryear. *OPEN Mon-Fri by appointment only.*

Crafts

(See also Needlework & Needlework Materials.*)*

Clayworks Pottery
332 East 9 Street. 677-8311. Retail shop; studio and classes in stoneware and earthenware in the evening. MC, V. *Hours vary; call first.*

Elder Craftsmen
850 Lexington Avenue at East 64 St. 861-5260. Skilled craftsmen over age 60 who can do anything that can be done by hand, including finishing something you've started.

Greenwich House Pottery
16 Jones Street near West 4 St. 242-4106. Courses and weekend workshops in ceramics year-round.

The Lighthouse Craft Shop
111 East 59 Street. 355-2200. Features over 300 handmade, mainly hand-knit, items created by blind craftspeople. MC, V. *OPEN Mon-Fri.*

Discount Merchandise

These stores make it easy to go broke saving money. (See also Women's Clothes: Discount & Off-price.*)*

Century 21
22 Cortlandt Street at Church St. 227-9092. Three floors of discounted merchandise including brand names: clothing, electronics, toys, and more. AE, MC, V. *OPEN Mon-Fri 7:45am-7pm; Sat 10am-6pm.*

Demitzer Bros.
5 Essex Street at Canal St. 254-1310. Small—
and large—appliances at small prices. Hectic;
know what you want. AE, MC, V. *OPEN Sun-Fri.
CLOSES Fri at 2pm.*

Job Lot Trading Company
140 Church Street near Chambers St. 962-4142.
Two floors of unbelievable buys on whatever they
can acquire: from salamis to greeting cards; discount jeans to hardware; perfume to pool cues.
Very busy at noontime. MC, V. *OPEN 7 days.*

Odd Job Trading Corp
*7 East 40 Street; 686-6825. And 66 West 48
Street; 575-0477. Also *149 West 32 Street,
564-7370. Closeouts of brand-name consumer
goods. Best buys for sports gear and small appliances. MC, V. *OPEN Mon-Fri 8am-6pm. *Sun-
Fri.*

Exercise

(*See also* Health Clubs.)

Alex & Walter Physical Fitness
30 West 56 Street, 3rd floor. 265-7270. Fitness
and fun: combination gymnastics, floor exercises, stretching for strength, coordination, and
balance. Small classes; coed. First class free.

Barbara Pearlman Slendercises
9 East 78 Street, 5th floor. 249-4590. Call for
one-on-one consultation with the well-known fitness expert. Program worked out to fit your life-
style. *Call for appointment.*

Body Designs by Gilda
187 East 79 Street; 737-8440. And 65 West 70
Street; 799-8540. Designed by fitness expert
Gilda Marx. Choose from high impact, low impact, or step aerobics; or stretch and firm for
flexibility, toning, balance, and coordination.
Done to music. Classes every hour in the am,
lunchtime, and pm depending on the location.
Coed. AE, MC, V. *Open 7 days.*

Elinor Coleman
153 Mercer Street near Houston St. 226-5767.
Dance-based low impact; expert teachers; small
classes. Ethnic (belly), modern, ballet, also self-
defense.

Integral Yoga Institute
227 West 13 Street. 929-0586. Open classes in
Hatha yoga for beginners, advanced, and very
advanced. Coed.

Lotte Berk Method Limited
23 East 67 Street, 2nd floor. 288-6613. Rigorous
combination of ballet, yoga, orthopedic exercises for the back. Abdominal and pelvic muscle
toning for shape-up or slim-down; stretch and
strengthen. Limited classes for men and women
by appointment. *OPEN 7 days.*

Molly Fox Studio
27 West 20 Street. 807-7266. For the highly mo-
tivated a potpourri of classes from high impact,
to Pace Circuit Training, to Afro/Brazilian Aerobics, and, of course, her famed "Killer Abs,
Thighs, and Buns" (there's a video version of the
latter). MC, V. *OPEN 7 days.*

—Exercises for Pregnant Women

Exercise Plus
19 East 48 Street. 935-2677. For before, during,
and after pregnancy. Free baby-sitting during
some classes. AE, MC, V.

Sports Training Institute
239 East 49 Street. 752-7111. One on one with a
professional.

Fabric

Macy's has an excellent large fabric department.

Beckenstein
130 Orchard Street near Delancey St. 475-4525;
677-3797. The widest variety of well-priced fabrics on the Lower East Side. From bridal materials to upholstery velvets and imported cashmere
and mohair. Upstairs: window treatments, upholstery, carpeting, wallpaper. Across the street at
121 Orchard: men's fabric. AE, MC, V. *OPEN 7
days*

Conran's
Citicorp Center, 160 East 54 Street; 371-2225.
And 2 Astor Place near Broadway; 505-1515.
Good selection of crisp modern fabrics. AE, MC,
V. *OPEN 7 days.*

Diamond Fabric Discount Center
165 First Avenue near East 10 St. 228-8189.
Stocks of spandex and leopard distinguish this
East Village fabric emporium, but there are all
the usuals, too. All at discount prices. AE, MC, V.
OPEN 7 days.

Fabric Alternative
78 Seventh Avenue, Brooklyn. (718) 857-5482.
High-quality fabrics at a discount. Home decorating, children's fabrics, imported laces, Schu-
macher, Waverly, and Riverdale. They will sew
for you, too. MC, V. *OPEN 7 days.*

Fabric World
283 Grand Street near Eldridge St. 925-0412.
Lovely line of fabrics at discount prices. The bonus: They will convert your fabric into wallpaper.
OPEN Sun-Fri. CLOSES Fri at 3pm.

Island Fabric Warehouse
406 Broadway near Canal St. 431-9510. Three
floors of every type of fabric imaginable. Designer, upholstery, and some imported fabrics.
Also a good selection of notions. Fantastic savings. Custom service, too. MC, V. *OPEN 7 days.*

Laura Ashley
714 Madison Avenue near East 63 St; 371-0606.
And 398 Columbus Avenue at West 79 St; 496-
5110. The finest purveyor of the English country-
house look. Delicate floral and geometric prints
on natural cotton fabrics with wallpapers and
home furnishings to match. AE, MC, V.

Le Petit Trianon
1270 Third Avenue near East 73 St. 472-1803.
European fabrics for the home; custom interiors
for wall, ceilings, windows. AE, MC, V.

Liberty of London
630 Fifth Avenue near East 51 St. 459-0080. The

famed English prints by the yard. Wide range of upholstery, drapery, and dress fabrics including glazed chintz. Also Liberty print clothing, scarves, ties, and gift items. AE, MC, V.

Pierre Deux
870 Madison Avenue at East 71 St. 570-9343. Exclusive American outlet for Souleiado hand-screened Provençal print fabric. Also furniture reproductions and beautiful accessories. Custom designing of window and bed treatments. AE, MC, V.

Silk Surplus, Inc.
223 & 235 East 58 Street. 753-6511. Designer silk, velvet, and brocades for draperies, upholstery, and slipcovers. Scalamandre closeouts and seconds; popular with the trade. MC, V.

Flowers

The wholesale flower market, a four-block area at the intersection of Avenue of the Americas and West 28 Street, with 25 outlets. Almost everyone will sell retail. Go early to find a wide variety. (See also Plants.*)*

Flower Cart
Grand Central Station, concourse level. 599-1492. To apologize for your train being late. AE, MC, V. *OPEN 7 days.*

Madderlake
478 Broadway near Broome St. 941-7770. Top creative party florist now in a gorgeous cavernous downtown space. Fresh flowers only, amid a unique eclectic selection of decorative antique pieces, all for sale. AE, MC, V.

Rialto Florist
707 Lexington Avenue near East 57 St. 688-3234. Full-service florist with delivery in Manhattan till midnight every day. AE, CB, DC, MC, V.

Renny
159 East 64 Street. 288-7000. Landscape architect and designer adorns the parties of a discriminating clientele. Lovely skylit setting.

Ronaldo Maia Ltd.
27 East 67 Street. 288-1049. Expensive and inventive floral creations in natural cachepots or baskets; elegant simple centerpieces. Wonderful potpourri and candles. AE, MC, V.

Sura Kayla
484 Broome Street near Wooster St. 941-8757. A mini botanical garden for artfully arranged fresh and dried flowers; topiaries. Also log and twig furniture and special gifts. AE, MC, V. *OPEN 7 days.*

Surroundings
224 West 79 Street. 580-8982. Well-thought-of West Side floral designers.

Framing

A. I. Friedman
14 West 45 Street. 719-2720. Ready-made wood, plexi, metal frames. Over 2,000 styles at 20 percent off list. Also custom-made. AE, MC, V. *OPEN Mon-Fri.*

A.P.F., Inc.
783 Madison Avenue near East 66 St. 988-1090. Their own factory supplies a variety of custom frames, museum-quality reproductions as well as contemporary styles. AE, MC, V.

J. Pocker & Son
824 Lexington Avenue at East 63 St. 838-5488. Expert framing since 1926. Custom work including conservation. Wide choice of styles from ornate hand-carved gilt to plexi. Pickup and delivery. Prints and posters in their gallery. AE, MC, V.

Yale Picture Frame & Moulding Corp.
770 Fifth Avenue at 28 St, Brooklyn. (718) 788-6200. Imports and manufactures picture frames; over 400 moldings for custom-made frames at 25 percent below retail. Also over 20,000 ready-made frames from which to choose. MC, V. *OPEN Sun-Fri. CLOSES Fri at 3pm.*

Gifts

Aris, Mixon & Company
381 Amsterdam Avenue near West 79 St. 724-6904. Beautiful shop for old, new, and renewed treasures. Good gift source for others and yourself. Wide price range. MC, V. *OPEN 7 days noon-7pm.*

Hudson Street Papers
581 Hudson Street near Bank St. 243-4221. It's a wonderful closet-sized general store for gifts (you'll go for someone else but I'll bet you buy something for yourself. Imported stationery items, books, jewelry, handcrafted decorative things for the home, novelties, potpourri, and much more. AE, MC, V. *OPEN 7 days.*

Il Papiro
1021 Lexington Avenue near East 73 St; 288-9330. And *World Financial Center; 385-1688. A charmer direct from Italy for delightful gift and stationery items all made with hand-marbled Florentine papers. Picture frames, desk accessories, varied-shaped boxes, albums, and more. AE, MC, V. *OPEN 7 days.*

Jenny B. Goode
1194 Lexington Avenue near East 81 St. 794-2492. Pace-setting, trendy gift boutique. Accessories and home furnishings; things for children, too. Price range: $1-$1,500. AE, DC, MC, V.

Little Rickie
49½ First Avenue at East 3 St. 505-6467. Irreverent and witty shop for the old and the new. Toys, games, books, and hundreds of original dime-store novelties from your childhood, and a working black-and-white photo booth for true nostalgics. African and Mexican handmade jewelry, nun dolls and other religious memorabilia, "outside" art by Southern artists, tees, boxers, and pjs, Elvis items, lava lamps, and...*W* loves it, but it's not for the humorless or easily offended. Price range: $10-$1,000. AE, MC, V. *OPEN 7 days.*

Matt McGhee
22 Christopher Street near Greenwich Ave. 741-

3138. Old and new, tiny and not so, treasures. Mainly from China, including porcelains, baskets, miniatures, fans. Also hand-blown German glass. Seasonal specialties; a wonderful must at Christmastime. AE, MC, V. *OPEN 7 days.*

Mythology
370 Columbus Avenue near West 77 St. 874-0774. Upper West Side treat for eye and heart. Eclectic mix of unusual, colorful toys and objects—old, new, and rare chosen for their graphic sense. Books on style and pop culture. Price range: 25¢-$5,000. AE, MC, V. *OPEN Mon-Sat 11am-11pm; Sun till 6pm.*

Only Hearts
386 Columbus Avenue at West 79 St. 724-5608. For shameless romantics. If you "gotta have heart," this is where to find it. On everything from small collector's items, cards, balloons, and party favors to sportswear, accessories, and underwear (hand-painted). AE, MC, V. *OPEN 7 days.*

Sointu
20 East 69 Street. 570-9449. A gallerylike shop for modern design objects from around the world chosen for their functional and aesthetic excellence—sleek housewares, glassware, clocks, stainless-steel pens, jewelry, unusual objects. AE, MC, V.

Star Magic
743 Broadway near East 8 St; 228-7770. And 275 Amsterdam Avenue at West 79 St; 769-2020. A celestial supermarket via California (where else?). Futuristic, scientific, and high-tech toys; kaleidoscopes, holograms, telescopes, space maps, and books; electronic music; pyramids, prisms, quartz crystals to meditate by. AE, MC, V. *OPEN 7 days.*

Think Big
390 West Broadway near Spring St. 925-7300. You'll feel like a Lilliputian in this shop filled with outsized versions of everyday objects—a 1½ foot paper clip, a 5-foot crayon, or a 6-foot pencil! Customized products, too. Price range: $10-$300. AE, MC, V. *OPEN 7 days.*

The Ultimate Basket
140 West 83 Street. 877-3291. Clever theme baskets shipped anywhere in the U.S. Interesting, expensive. Same-day delivery in Manhattan. AE, MC, V. *OPEN Mon-Fri 9am-5pm.*

United Nations Gift Center
United Nations Headquarters, First Avenue & East 46 Street, downstairs. 963-7700. Handicrafts, jewelry, gifts from most of the member nations. Also U.N. logo merchandise. Wide price range. Bonus: no sales tax on purchases here. AE, MC, V. Traveler's checks very welcome. *OPEN 7 days 9am-5pm.*

William-Wayne & Co.
324 East 9 Street. 477-3182. A tiny treasure of a shop with a space-defying array of well-chosen decorative objects and gifts, mainly imported and new, with a choice few antiques for good measure. AE, MC, V. *OPEN Mon-Sat noon-7pm; Sun 1-5pm.*

Zona
97 Greene Street near Spring St. 925-6750. Surely the most appealing shop in SoHo. Attractive earth-toned decorative accessories and handcrafted rustic furnishings of the American Southwest. Also Solari bells, potpourri, beeswax candles, soaps and fragrances, wonderful gardening tools. Very affordable style. Go! You'll love it. AE, MC, V. *OPEN Tues-Sun.*

—Gifts: Personalized

Frank Bara
787-7515. Commissioned, highly personalized wooden jigsaw puzzles. Intricate, witty way to tell someone's life story. *By appointment.*

Jill Gill
362-8440. Your brownstone's facade or interior or a New York street painted in ink and watercolor. *By appointment.*

Hardware

For true hardware buffs, Canal Street from Lafayette Street to West Broadway offers a mind-boggling array of nuts, bolts, screws, wiring, gadgets, and widgets.

Albert Constantine & Son
2050 Eastchester Road near Pelham Parkway, Bronx. 792-1600. Specializes in woodworking materials and tools; furniture-building kits, plans, and books. AE, MC, V. *Thurs till 8pm; Sat till 3pm.*

Brookstone
South Street Seaport, Schermerhorn Row, 18 Fulton Street. 344-8108. Famed New Hampshire purveyor of hard-to-find tools and gadgets. A sample of everything is on display. Pick up a clipboard upon entering—it's your order form. Goods then quickly appear. AE, MC, V. *OPEN 7 days.*

Canal Hardware
305 Canal Street near Broadway. 226-0825. If you need it, they have it. AE, MC, V. *OPEN 7 days.*

Reliable Hardware
303 Canal Street at Broadway. 966-4166. Experts in many trades, including plumbing and electrical. Also glass cut to size. Reasonable prices, free advice. Custom service is their specialty. AE, MC, V. *OPEN 7 days.*

Simon's Hardware
421 Third Avenue near East 30 St. 532-9220. Busy, well-regarded, well-stocked source for decorative hardware for the home plus tools and supplies. They're problem solvers. AE, MC, V.

Health Clubs

(See also Exercise.*)*

Manhattan Plaza Swim & Health Club
484 West 43 Street, 2nd floor. 563-7001. A 75-foot glass-enclosed swimming pool; weight room; Nautilus, aerobics, African dance, jazz, and stretch classes. Coed. MC, V. *OPEN 7 days.*

New York Health & Racquet Club
1433 York Avenue at East 76 St; 737-6666. And
*24 East 13 Street; 924-4600. Also *20 East 50
Street, 593-1500; 132 East 45 Street, 986-3100;
110 West 56 Street, 541-7200; 39 Whitehall
Street, 269-9800: Swimming pool, whirlpool,
sauna, steam room; Nautilus equipment; over
100 classes including dance, yoga, calisthenics,
karate. Coed. Facilities for racquet sports including an outdoor beach and tennis club with free
tennis, outdoor pools, outdoor dining and dancing. Also HRC Tennis: their large air-conditioned
facilities with Hartru and Supreme courts. If
you're in this for the social aspects they also
have a 75-foot "party yacht." AE, DC, MC, V.
*OPEN 7 days from 7:30am.

Profile Fitness Club for Women
52 East 42 Street. 697-7177. Nautilus and Uni-
versal equipment, one-on-one training. Classes
throughout the day. Also facials and massage.
Women only. AE, DC, MC, V. OPEN 7 days.

Russian & Turkish Baths
268 East 10 Street. 473-8806. And now for something different: This is the last of the old traditional Russian-Turkish baths that served the immigrant population on the Lower East Side at the
turn of the century. This schvitz (Yiddish slang
for steam bath) may not be glamorous, but it's
authentic. Steam, sauna, ice-cold pool, Swedish
shower. Spring for the platzka, a vigorous scrub
with an oak-leaf brush, then cool off with a shot
of Stolichnaya at the bar. There are lockers, an
exercise room, and a sun deck; restaurant for
Eastern European food. Wednesdays are reserved for ladies; Thursdays and Sundays are
men only; coed the balance of the week. The
clientele runs the gamut from rabbis to rock
stars. Admission charge includes robe, slippers,
towels, etc. OPEN 7 days 8:45am-9:45pm.

Sports Training Institute
239 East 49 Street. 752-7111. One-on-one personalized exercise with a trainer. Nautilus and
Eagle equipment. Work on spots or the whole
body for cardio fitness, strength, and flexibility.
Staff nutritionist. Coed.

Vertical Club
330 East 61 Street; 355-5100. And 139 West 32
Street; 465-1750. Also East 43 Street between
Madison & Vanderbilt, 983-5320; and 350 West
50 Street, 265-9400. State-of-the-art health club;
on seven floors with neon lighting, contemporary
music. Classes all day; a 40-foot pool; 3 racquetball and tennis courts (61 St only); free weights,
Nautilus; 1/10-mile indoor running track; rooftop
sun deck; restaurant and bar for the affluent well-
toned members to meet one another. Coed.
Membership only.

Y's
YMCA: McBurney, 215 West 23 Street, 741-
9210; Vanderbilt, 224 East 47 Street, 755-2410;
West Side, 5 West 63 Street, 787-4400.
YM/YWHA: 1395 Lexington Avenue at East 92
St. 427-6000.
  Though details vary, these all have good swim-
ming pools, tracks, gymnasiums, classes, and
sports facilities. Coed. Membership required.

Horsedrawn Carriages

Chateau Stables
608 West 48 Street. 246-0520. The largest working collection of horsedrawn vehicles in America. For a romantic evening, party event, or gas
saver. Choose from 200 varieties of horsedrawn
carriages: pony cart; hayride wagon; stage-
coach; hearse; vintage ice, bread, or milk
wagon; or a fancy open or glass-enclosed carriage. OPEN 7 days.

Hansom Cabs
Fifth Avenue & Central Park South. The limousines of a former era. A wide variety of coaches
await you; some drivers even sport top hats. The
traditional most romantic, most sensible—for you
and the horse—ride is through Central Park.
Don't take it anywhere else (there is nothing romantic about New York traffic or a dead horse).
NOTE: Rates should be clearly visible on cab; pay
only what is posted. Available 7 days unless the
temperature is 90° or more, in deference to the
animal.

Jewelry

New York's wholesale and retail jewelry (diamond) center, West 47 Street from Fifth Avenue
to Sixth Avenue, offers a dazzling selection of
gold, silver, precious stones; antique, traditional,
and modern designs. The concentration of
shops and stalls makes comparison shopping
an easy and pleasurable task, and since prices
are not necessarily firm, a practical one as well.
  The large department stores carry good selections of gold and silver jewelry. (See also Silver.)

—Jewelry: Antique & Estate

(See also Antiques.)

The Antique Buff
321½ Bleecker Street near Christopher St. 243-
7144. Tiny quarters well stocked with Victorian,
Art Nouveau, and Art Deco jewelry; wide selection of rings from 1800s to 1930s. Also silver,
crystal, walking sticks, and collectibles. AE, MC,
V. OPEN Mon-Fri 1-7pm, Sat noon-6pm.

B. Harris & Sons
See Jewelry: Repair & Restoration.

Fred Leighton, Ltd.
773 Madison Avenue at East 66 St; 288-1872.
And Trump Tower, 765 Fifth Avenue at 56 St, 3rd
floor; 751-2330. Exclusively devoted to luxurious
and rare antique and estate jewelry. Emphasis is
on the 20s, featuring extravagant Cartier pieces,
but there are pieces from the 1800s and some
from the 1950s. AE, DC, MC, V.

Ilene Chazenof
254-5564. Late 19th- to mid-20th-century jewelry
and objets at very good prices. Victorian, Art

Deco, Art Nouveau, Retro Moderne. Also Arts-and-Crafts Movement jewelry, metalwork, and furniture; 1950s Scandinavian and Italian glass. Price range: $1-$5,000. Services include research, shipping, appraisals, rentals, and a knowledgeable and lovely purveyor. *OPEN Mon-Sat 11am-6pm by appointment only.*

Macklowe Gallery
982 Madison Avenue near East 76 St. 288-1124. Impressive selection of Georgian, Victorian, Art Nouveau, and Art Deco jewelry. AE, CB, DC, MC, V.

Massab Brothers Jewelers
782 Lexington Avenue at East 61 St. 752-7139. Good longtime source for antique and estate jewelry. Beautiful, extensive collection of Georgian, Victorian, Art Deco, and Art Nouveau pieces. Jewelry repair, too. AE, MC, V.

Norman Crider Antiques
Trump Tower, 725 Fifth Avenue, level 5. 832-6958. Vintage costume jewelry from the 1920s to 1960s. AE, DC, MC, V.

Primavera Gallery
808 Madison Avenue near East 68 St. 288-1569. A steller selection of Art Deco, Art Nouveau, and Victorian jewelry. AE, DC, MC, V.

Ruzi
299 East 11 St. 473-0460. A designer and old-world craftsman who works in silver and gold. Wonderful creations mixing antique elements. An impressive selection of antique jewelry as well. *OPEN Tues-Sat 12:30-6pm.*

Sylvia Pines Uniquities
1102 Lexington Avenue near East 77 St. 744-5141. An exquisite array of antique and estate jewelry—Victorian to Deco, some Georgian pieces. Especially strong in Deco marquisite. Also a spectacular collection of beaded and jeweled bags, bronzes, picture frames, and enameled boxes. MC, V.

—Jewelry: Contemporary

Aaron Faber
666 Fifth Avenue near 53 St. 586-8411. Imaginative contemporary designs in gold. Every eight weeks the upstairs gallery shows the work of a particular artist. Custom work and a fine collection of vintage wristwatches, too. Repair and restoration. AE, CB, DC, MC, V.

Artwear
456 West Broadway near Prince St; 673-2000. And 409 West Broadway (**Robert Lee Morris-Artwear**); 431-9405. Also AT&T Arcade, 550 Madison Avenue near East 56 St, 593-3388. Dramatic space for unique handcrafted jewelry and objects of art by 30 contemporary artists including Robert Lee Morris. At no. 409, the work of Morris exclusively; uptown, an edited selection of his work. These adornments are also art works; necklaces, bracelets, earrings, belt buckles, hair ornaments—all beautiful creations and all for sale. Special orders taken. AE, MC, V. *OPEN 7 days.*

Astro Minerals
155 East 34 Street. 889-9000. A gallery of fine jewelry including a large selection of low-priced semi-precious jewelry. Also lovely collection of exotic jewelry, a well-priced collection of minerals and crystals. New addition, African art. AE, CB, DC, MC, V. *OPEN 7 days.*

Buccellati
Trump Tower, 725 Fifth Avenue at 56 St; 308-5533. And 46 East 57 Street; 308-2900. Famed Milanese silver- and goldsmith; each piece is uniquely handcrafted. Finely created artisan pieces with precious stones and a medium range (it's relative) of gold pieces. AE, DC, MC, V.

Bulgari
730 Fifth Avenue at 57 St; 315-9000. And Pierre Hotel, 2 East 61 Street; 486-0326. Prestigious international name for fine precious jewels. AE, MC, V.

Cartier
653 Fifth Avenue at 52 St; 753-0111. And Trump Tower, 725 Fifth Avenue at 56 St; 308-0840. Also the Westbury Hotel, Madison Avenue at East 69 Street, 249-3240. Internationally famed in a beautiful former mansion traded to Cartier for two strands of Oriental pearls. Housed within: jewelry, silver, fine porcelain, picture frames; "Les Must" prestige items that have become modern classics, too. AE, DC, MC, V.

David Webb
445 Park Avenue at East 57 St. 421-3030. The distinctive and extravagant 18K-gold gem-studded jewelry most copied in costume. Large, expensive pieces, often beautiful animal images. AE, V.

Fortunoff
681 Fifth Avenue near 54 St. 758-6660. "The Source." Four floors of gold, silver, diamonds, watches, flatware, and pewter. Antique and contemporary, all at very special prices. Georg Jensen, Oneida, Reed & Barton, Dansk, among others. AE, DC, MC, V. *Thurs till 8pm.*

Guy Dolen
3 West 87 Street. 595-1744. This talented designer/craftsman works in silver, producing unique yet very affordably priced rings, bracelets, and necklaces; custom designs as well. *By appointment only.*

Harry Winston
718 Fifth Avenue at 56 St. And Trump Tower, 725 Fifth Avenue at 56 St, 2nd level; 245-2000. Jewelry as an investment for the wealthy. The rarest, largest, and best gems in the world are behind these lovely locked doors. AE only.

Gallery of Exciting Jewelry/Jerry Grant, Ltd.
276 Columbus Avenue at West 73 St. 496-5050. Precious and semi-precious stones, 14K and 18K gold, some silver, in sleek ultramodern designs—their own, the work of creative young designers, as well as imports. Custom orders taken. Also, large selection of contemporary watches. Unique service: diamonds reset without having to leave the stones. AE, MC, V. *OPEN Mon-Sat noon-10pm; Sun till 7pm.*

Mishon Mishon
899 Madison Avenue near East 72 St. 288-7599.

The most current contemporary designer-jewelry in precious metals with precious and semi-precious stones. Expensive but good sales may yield a "buy." AE, DC, MC, V.

Tiffany & Co.
727 Fifth Avenue at 57 St. 755-8000. The prestigious treasure house (now in its 100th year) for fine gold and silver jewelry, including the designs of Jean Schlumberger, Elsa Peretti, Paloma Picasso; diamond engagement rings; famous-name watches; gems; crystal; china and sterling silver; clocks and stationery. Newest additions: their own scarves and perfume. Don't be intimidated, there are some very reasonably priced items here. The windows are almost as famous as the interior. Have a look at both. AE, DC, MC, V.

Underground Jeweler
147 East 86 Street in the Lexington Ave subway arcade. 348-7866. Extensive selection of ethnic and fine jewelry from around the world: Egypt, Israel, Romania, Russia, France, Italy. Also 19th-century antique gold jewelry, vintage watches. Ear piercing and repairs. Good value. AE, MC, V.

Van Cleef & Arpels
744 Fifth Avenue at 57 St. 644-9500. The name is synonymous with perfection and price. Tiny setting in Bergdorf but equal to a king's ransom of diamonds, rubies, emeralds, pearls, and platinum. AE, DC, MC, V.

—Jewelry: Costume

Large department stores and many boutiques have wide selections of au courant costume jewelry.

Ciro of Bond Street
711 Fifth Avenue near 55 St; 752-0441. And 6 West 57 Street; 581-0767. Also 791 Madison Avenue at East 67 St, 628-1290. Fabulous fakes, though by no means cheap. AE, DC, MC, V.

Jolie Gabor
699 Madison Avenue near East 62 St. 838-3896. Expensive but high-quality costume jewelry. Copies of the best designs from Van Cleef & Arpels, Bulgari, Harry Winston, and David Webb. AE, CB, DC, MC, V.

Kenneth Jay Lane
Trump Tower, 725 Fifth Avenue at 56 St. 751-6166. The costume jewelry master and society darling. Original and copies; earrings, bracelets, necklaces, rings, belts, and hair ornaments. The *courrant* top seller, the faux pearls sported by the First Lady and nearly every other lady on Mad Ave. Price range: $25-$600. AE, MC, V.

Ylang-Ylang
806 Madison Avenue near East 67 St; 879-7028. And 4 West 57 Street; 247-3580. Glitz lives! Trays and trays of faux baubles, bangles, and beads. Not for the shrinking violet. AE, DC, MC, V.

—Jewelry: Repair & Restoration

Macy's does repair work on watches and antique jewelry.

B. Harris & Sons
25 East 61 Street. 755-6455. Antique-jewelry repair specialist. Sells mainly Georgian and Victorian pieces; remodels, appraises, and buys both contemporary and antique.

Kites

Big City Kites
1201 Lexington Avenue near East 81 St; 472-2623. Your spirits will soar in this joyful store full of 200 varieties of colorful kites for every level of expertise and aspiration. Also kite-making supplies and air toys. Price range: $2-$200. AE, MC, V.

Language Schools

Most schools with adult-education programs offer foreign-language and English courses. (See also Adult Education.)

American Italy Society
38 East 57 Street, 5th floor. 838-1561. Proven, practical method to learn Italian, for beginners, intermediates, advanced students. Group, private, and conversational classes.

Berlitz
40 West 51 Street; 765-1000. And 61 Broadway near Exchange Pl; 425-3866. World-famous language experts. Total immersion courses, private and group instruction. All spoken languages! MC only.

French Institute/Alliance Française
22 East 60 Street. 355-6100. Native French teachers, small conversational classes. You will speak French the first day; all levels up to fluent taught in a thorough manner. Nonprofit.

International English Language Institute of Hunter College
695 Park Avenue at East 68 St. 722-4290. English as a second language: conversation, pronunciation, grammar, business English, reading, writing. Intensive or part-time programs available. Beginner to advanced. Day, evening, and Saturday classes. MC, V.

Parliamo Italiano
132 East 65 Street. 744-4793. Italian taught in a lovely town house setting. All levels; day, evening, and Saturday. Nonprofit.

Vanderbilt YMCA
224 East 47 Street. 755-2410. English for the foreign-born as well as French, German, Italian, and Spanish.

Leather Goods & Luggage

The department stores offer a wide range of luggage, briefcases, and leather accessories for pocket, purse, home, or office. (See also Women's Clothes, Handbags.)

Altman Luggage
135 Orchard Street near Delancey St. 254-7275. Large selection of most name-brand luggage, trunks, and small leather goods at a discount; for over 30 years. Lark, Boyt, American Tourister,

Samsonite, Tumi, Ventura, Delsey, Schlesinger, Atlas, and Renwick. Also fine stock of pens—Mount Blanc, Waterman, Pelikan. Catalog; mail and phone orders filled. Expert repairs. AE, DC, MC, V. *OPEN 7 days.*

Bettinger's Luggage Shop
80 Rivington Street near Allen St. 475-1690. A nostalgic cluttered Lower East Side shop that grew from a pushcart to become, in 1914, New York's first discount luggage store. A good selection of famous-brand luggage and leather goods, attaché cases, too—all at substantial discount. Schlesinger, Tumi, Boyt, and more. AE, DC, MC, V. *OPEN Sun-Fri.*

Crouch & Fitzgerald
400 Madison Avenue at East 48 St. 755-5888. Since 1839. Top-quality domestic and imported luggage including any shape or size of Louis Vuitton luggage or trunk. Also in stock the best name handbags. Very desirable anniversary sale in spring (excluding Vuitton). AE, CB, DC, MC, V.

Gucci
683 Fifth Avenue at 54 St. 826-2600. High quality, high price. World-renowned luggage, handbags, shoes—with or without the status initials. AE, DC, MC, V.

Innovation Luggage
10 East 34 Street; 685-4611. And 300 East 42 Street; 599-2998. Also 1755 Broadway near West 56 St, 582-2044; 866 Third Avenue at East 52 St, 832-1841; and World Trade Center, concourse level, 432-1090. Billed as America's largest luggage dealer, they carry every major popular brand including Samsonite, Ventura, Lark, Hartmann, Le Sportsac, and American Tourister luggage in every size, style, and color at reduced prices, often 20-50 percent off suggested retail prices. Catalog (800) 631-0742. *OPEN 7 days.*

Mark Cross
645 Fifth Avenue near 51 St; 421-3000. And *World Financial Center; 945-1411. Since 1845. The distinctive and expensive "MC" luggage, desk accessories, shoes, gloves, and belts. AE, CB, DC, MC, V. *OPEN 7 days.*

T. Anthony, Ltd.
480 Park Avenue at East 58 St. 750-9797. Famed leather shop for exclusive, expensive items including leather luggage and business cases. AE, DC, MC, V.

Magic

Abracadabra
10 Christopher Street near Greenwich Ave. 627-5745. Magic, illusions, trick cards, masks, gags, gifts, and gadgets. Large stock of costumes. AE, MC, V. *OPEN 7 days.*

Flosso-Hornman Magic Company
45 West 34 Street, 6th floor. 279-6079. America's oldest magic shop, established in 1865. For a time it was owned by Houdini. Every trick in the books, plus the books. MC, V. *CLOSES Sat at 4pm.*

Louis Tannen, Inc.
6 West 32 Street, 4th floor. 239-8383. In business 60 years, it's the world's largest supplier of magic illusions and magic books to the trade, retail, and wholesale. For amateurs and professionals; full-time demonstrators, custom-made illusions. Customers included the late Cary Grant. AE, MC, V. *CLOSES Sat 4pm.*

Magical Childe
35 West 19 Street. 242-7182. Over 250 fresh imported herbs and nearly 300 oils and extracts in this specialized occult witchcraft shop. Love potions concocted to order. AE, MC, V. *OPEN Mon-Sat 11am-8pm; Sun noon-6pm.*

Mostly Magic
See NIGHTLIFE, Nightclubs.

Maps

(*See also* Memorabilia: Old Print Shop.)
Argosy Bookstore, Inc.
116 East 59 Street. 753-4455. Colorful and decorative original antique maps on the 2nd floor. MC, V. *OPEN Mon-Fri.*

Hagstrom Map & Travel Center
57 West 43 Street. 398-1222. Since 1910. Road and street maps. Nauticals, aeronauticals, topographicals; maps, globes, charts; domestic and foreign travel books. AE, MC, V. *OPEN Mon-Fri.*

Rand McNally Map & Travel Store
150 East 52 Street. 758-7488. Globes, atlases, topographical maps, domestic and foreign travel guides, including video and language, and maps of all publishers. AE, MC, V. *OPEN Mon-Fri.*

Memorabilia

(*See also* Antiques *and* Posters.)
Ballet Shop
1887 Broadway near West 63 St. 581-7990. Specialty: ballet memorabilia, including rare programs, in- and out-of-print signed books, autographs, records, art, and sculpture. Opera and theater ephemera, too. AE, DC, MC, V. *OPEN Mon-Sat 11am-7:30pm; Sun noon-5pm.*

Jerry Ohlinger's Movie Material Store
242 West 14 Street. 989-0869. Still photos from every movie and TV show ever made. Movie posters, too. Great helpful research source. MC, V ($50 minimum). *OPEN 7 days 1-8pm.*

Movie Star News
134 West 18 Street. 620-8160. One of the world's largest collections of movie star photos, reissues, and originals. Posters, too. AE, MC, V.

Old Print Shop
150 Lexington Avenue near East 30 St. 683-3950. Old prints, advertising memorabilia, maps, and cards. MC, V.

Richard Stoddard Performing Arts Books
18 East 16 Street, room 305. 645-9576. Excellent selection of old, rare, and out-of-print books and ephemera relating to the performing arts. Vintage playbills, autographs, original scenic and

costume designs, photographs, and memorabilia. *CLOSED Wed & Sun.*

Miniatures

(*See also* Antiques *and* Toys: Collectible.)
Dollhouse Antics, Inc.
1343 Madison Avenue at East 94 St. 876-2288. Dollhouses and all the miniature furnishings (including very fine hand-painted pieces by Natasha), accessories, and occupants. Electrification and interior decoration. AE, MC, V.
Manhattan Doll Hospital
176 Ninth Avenue at West 21 St. 989-5220. Big selection of dollhouse furnishings from modern Lucite to Colonial maple. All handcrafted. Fine array of dolls and dollhouses. AE, MC, V. *OPEN 7 days.*
Soldier Shop
1222 Madison Avenue near East 88 St. 535-6788. For the collector, old toys, rare and unusual soldiers, and military miniatures. Military books, helmets, and swords. Price range: $100-$5,000. AE, MC, V.
Tiny Doll House
146 Lexington Avenue near East 79 St. 744-3719. Everything conceivable in miniature for a dollhouse. Specialty: one-inch to one-foot supplies; electrification and wallpapering. AE, MC, V. *Thurs till 7pm.*

Music & Musical Instruments

West 48 Street between Fifth and Sixth avenues is the musical-instrument district.
Brown's Music
61 West 62 Street. 541-6236. Long-established source (formerly Schirmer's) for sheet music, books, musical gifts, and instruments. AE only. *OPEN 7 days.*
Havivi Violins
130 West 57 Street. 265-5818. Violins, cellos, violas, bows. Repair, strings, accessories. Sales and appraisals.
Matt Umanov Guitars
273 Bleecker Street near Seventh Ave South. 675-2157. Large selection of new and used string instruments in a wide price range. Excellent repair department. AE, MC, V. *OPEN 7 days.*
Music Inn
169 West 4 Street near Sixth Ave. 243-5715. Longtime Village source for new and used guitars; also banjos, mandolins, dobros, dulcimers, sitars, balalaikas, flutes, tabla drums, zithers, and more. Expert guitar repairs. Ethnic art, too. AE, DC, MC, V. *OPEN Tues-Fri 1-7pm; Sat noon-7pm.*
Music Store at Carl Fischer
62 Cooper Square at East 7 St. 677-0821; 777-0900. Music of all publishers: classical, jazz, choral, pop, rock, folk. Accessories, musical gifts, supplies. MC, V.
Sam Ash
155, 160 & 166 West 48 Street. 719-2299, -2625, or -5109. Since 1924. Popular with professional musicians, this clutch of shops boasts a wide inventory of electronic keyboards, guitars and amplifiers, horns, and drums. Good prices. Rentals, too. Books on music; musical scores. MC, V.
Steinway & Sons
109 West 57 Street. 246-1100. Longtime home of Steinway—soundproof rooms for practice.

Music Boxes

(*See also* Antiques.)
The Last Wound Up
889 Broadway at West 19 St. 529-4197. In this outpost of whimsy: antique, restored, and new music boxes. AE, MC, V. *OPEN 7 days.*
Rita Ford Music Boxes
19 East 65 Street. 535-6717. The best collection of working antique music boxes in the world, 1830-1910. Contemporary boxes, too. Handcrafted carousels and other one-of-a-kind items made expressly for this shop. Wide price range. Restores and repairs as well. MC, V.

Music Schools

Greenwich House Music School
46 Barrow Street near Seventh Ave South. 242-4770. Community music school offers a variety of instrumental classes; music appreciation, too. Preschool program in music and art. Free concerts and recitals. For age 2-82.
Manhattan School of Music
120 Claremont Avenue near West 122 St. 749-2802. Superior conservatory offering fine advanced training in jazz and classical music performance.
92 Street YM/YWHA
1395 Lexington Avenue. 427-6000. Well-respected school. Private and group instruction, wide range of subjects relating to musical theory and practice. MC, V.
Third Street Music School Settlement
233 East 11 Street. 777-3240. Since 1894. Private and group instruction in music, art, dance, adult opera workshop. Age 21 months to adult. Concert series for adults, and outdoors in summer. MC, V for lessons paid in full only.

Needlework & Needlework Materials

(*See also* Crafts.)
Erica Wilson, Needleworks
717 Madison Avenue near East 63 St, 2nd floor. 832-7290. All needle arts and supplies. Crocheting, knitting, embroidery, needlepoint, crewel. Custom canvases. AE, MC, V. *Thurs till 7pm.*
Sunray Yarn Company, Inc.
349 Grand Street near Essex St. 475-9655. Reasonably priced supplies and yarns for needlepoint, knitting, rug-hooking. *OPEN Sun-Fri.*
Yarn Center
1011 Sixth Avenue near West 37 St, 2nd floor. 719-5648. Good discount yarn store in midtown. Needlepoint kits, finishing, and framing. Knitting

and crochet classes. Books and accessories. AE, MC, V. *Thurs till 7pm.*

Newspapers & Magazines: Foreign and Out-of-Town

Eastern Newsstand
Pan Am Building, 200 Park Avenue at East 45 St. 687-1198. Magazines—2,500-3,000 different titles including foreign language.

Hotaling's: Foreign & Domestic
142 West 42 Street. 840-1868. Over 200 out-of-town newspapers, over 35 foreign language newspapers; large selection of magazines. Language books and maps. *OPEN Mon-Fri 7:30am-9:30pm; Sat & Sun 7:30am-8pm.*

—Magazines: Backlist

Jay Bee Magazines
134 West 26 Street, downstairs. 675-1600. Over 2 million backdated magazines and periodicals; some go back as far as 1888. *TV Guides* 1953 to present. Cluttered setting, helpful search service. Good research source. Now fully computerized and there's a catalog. MC, V. *OPEN Mon-Fri 10am-4pm; Sat noon-3pm.*

Notions

The large stores have small notions departments, but this city has a notions street! On West 38 Street between Fifth Avenue and Avenue of the Americas there are 20 stores that carry trimmings. Listed below are a few of the best.

Hyman Hendler & Sons
67 West 38 Street. 840-8393. Full to the brim with ribbons of every variety: satin, grosgrain, velvet, silk in every color, size, width. *OPEN Mon-Fri.*

M&J Trimming
1008 Sixth Avenue near West 37 St. 391-9072. All the trimmings for any day's fashion accessories. Rhinestones, studs, feathers, cords, buttons, bindings, satin ribbons, lace, eyelet, embroidered trim, silk ropes, large feather boas. You supply the imagination. At no. 1014 Sixth, home-decorating accessories. AE, CB, DC, MC, V.

Tinsel Trading Company
47 West 38 Street. 730-1030. Metallic yarns, threads, lamés, gauzes, tassels, fringe, rosebud trimmings, buttons, antique ribbons, embroideries, and fabrics. Much from the 20s and 30s. MC, V.

Office Furnishings

On West 23 Street between Ninth and Tenth avenues there are many suppliers of new and used office furniture.

Office Supplies

(*See also* Stationery.)

Airline Stationery Company, Inc.
284 Madison Avenue at East 40 St. 532-6525. Long-established reputable firm. Will supply ev-

erything from a paper clip to a filing system. AE, DC, MC, V.

Kroll Stationers, Inc.
145 East 54 Street. 750-7720. Fine stationery and office-supply store; printing and engraving. Computer and word-processor supplies. Chairs and desks, too. AE, MC, V.

Typex Business Machines
23 West 23 Street. 243-8086. Need a Hebrew, Greek, or Russian typewriter? Or perhaps one with mathematical or astrological symbols? This is the place. MC, V. *OPEN Mon-Fri. CLOSES Fri at 2pm.*

Party

For children's party information, see KIDS' NEW YORK, Parties. *For party foods, see* Food, Caterers.

—Party Help

Great Performances
125 Crosby Street. 219-2800. Professional performers who produce a perfect party. Waitresses and waiters, male and female bartenders, all with theatrical aspirations. Catering, too, from cocktail parties to full dinners.

Lend-a-Hand
362-8200. Aspiring actors and actresses who have bartending, waitressing, and baby-sitting experience. Also available: clowns, Santas, belly dancers, piano players. Four-hour minimum. *Available 7 days a week.*

Manhattan Party Package
Barbara Gillen. 741-0567. This capable gracious lady will create a cocktail buffet or small wedding party from invitations and flowers to rental of her own dramatic Greenwich Village town house with garden for special occasions. Maximum 70 people.

World Yacht Cruises
929-8540. Caters private parties aboard luxury yachts; for 2 to 250 people.

—Party Music

The Black Tie Strings & Orchestra
(718) 478-2982. Traditional dinner and dancing music featuring Barbara and Joseph, Fiddlers Two. Music "from Vienna to Broadway." Last-minute inquiries welcome.

Juilliard School
144 West 66 Street. 799-5000, ext 313. Will send student musicians who can play Bach, Beethoven, or Beatles.

Manhattan School of Music
120 Claremont Avenue near West 122 St. 749-2802. School acts as mini concert bureau.

Stoy Mobile Discotheque
279 East 44 Street. 557-1588. For a disco evening: a d.j., 5,000 of the most recent and oldie discs, and lights, too.

—Party Paraphernalia

Broadway Famous Party Rental
868 Kent Avenue, Brooklyn. (718) 783-2700. All

boroughs. Can fill orders on a day's notice for china, glassware, silverware, tables and cloths, napkins, chairs, coatracks, and bars.

The Paper House
18 Greenwich Avenue at West 10 St; 741-1569. 1370 Third Avenue at East 78 St; 879-2937. Also 180 East 86 Street, 410-7950; 269 Amsterdam Avenue near West 72 St, 724-8085; and 2235 Broadway near West 79 St, 595-5656. Everything for a party in paper: invitations, hats, plates, napkins, favors. RSVP and thank-you cards. Toys, favors, masks, gift wraps, and holiday specialty items. MC, V. *OPEN 7 days.*

Party Bazaar Dennison
390 Fifth Avenue near 36 St; 695-6820. And 30 Rockefeller Center, concourse and upstairs; 581-0310. The original party store. Plates, favors, napkins, hats, cards, settings, wrapping paper, and stationery items. Imprinting; personalized gifts. Party consultants, too. AE, MC, V.

Party Time
82-33 Queens Boulevard, Elmhurst, Queens. 682-8838; (718) 457-1122. For more than 50 years. Services all five boroughs. Rents china (Ginori if you wish, or kosher), glassware, tablecloths and napkins, chairs, coatracks, bars, wishing wells, bars, hot dog or ice cream wagons. Free pickup and delivery. Brochure available.

Service Party Rental
521 East 72 Street. 288-7384. Services Manhattan only. Silverware, china, tablecloths, napkins, chairs (plain or ballroom), and bars. Needs a week's notice in the holiday season. *OPEN Mon-Fri.*

Shackman
85 Fifth Avenue at 16 St. 989-5162. Antique-styled paper goods, invites, greeting cards, and other old-fashioned items; small toys and novelties, great for favors.

Toy Balloon Corporation
204 East 38 Street. 682-3803. Will imprint balloons of all shapes and sizes. Minimum three dozen. Order must be in person or prepaid in the mail. Helium tank rental. *OPEN Mon-Fri.*

Pens

Flea markets and antique shops are the best places to go for a vintage pen. (See also Art Supplies; Office Supplies; *and* Stationery.)

Arthur Brown & Bro., Inc.
2 West 46 Street. 575-5555. One of the world's largest pen selections. The International Pen Shop carries every brand you can name from Anson to Waterman, including Mont Blanc, Staedtler, Garland, etc., in a wide variety of styles. Authorized Parker repair shop. Catalog available. AE, DC, MC, V.

Sam Flax
55 East 55 Street. 620-3050. Pens from $2.95 to $1,300. Leather desk accessories, too. AE, MC, V.

Pets

(For animals in transit, see TRAVEL & VACATION INFORMATION.)

—Pets: Adoption

Bulletin boards in veterinarians' offices and the classified sections of the New York Times *and* Village Voice *offer pets free to anyone who can provide a good home.*

A.S.P.C.A.
441 East 92 Street. 876-7700. To adopt a cat or dog you must have I.D. and be over age 18. They will spay or neuter your pet for a small fee. *OPEN 7 days.*

Bide-a-Wee Home Association
410 East 38 Street. 532-4455. To adopt, you must be over 18 and have two pieces of I.D. *OPEN 7 days.*

Humane Society of New York City
306 East 59 Street. 752-4840. There is a small fee to adopt a cat or dog, but it's well worth it. Reasonably priced medical care also available. A caring agency. *OPEN 7 days.*

—Pets: Grooming

Karen's
1220 Lexington Avenue near East 82 St. 472-9440. Specializes in hand plucking of terriers. MC, V.

New York School of Dog Grooming
248 East 34 Street. 685-3777. All breeds groomed at low prices by supervised students. *By appointment.*

—Pets: Supplies

Animal Feeds, Inc.
3255 Park Avenue at 163 St, Bronx. 293-7750. A supermarket of pet food for more than 50 years. Over 300 varieties of pet food available. Easy parking. MC, V. *Thurs till 7pm.*

Beasty Feast
605 Hudson Street near West 12 St; 620-7099. And *237 Bleecker Street near Sixth Ave; 243-3261. Also 140 Ninth Avenue near West 19 St, 929-4337. Good prices on pet food. Natural dog food; accessories, too. Delivery available. MC, V ($30 minimum). *OPEN 7 days.*

Karen's
1220 Lexington Avenue near East 82 St. 472-9440. Carries upscale doggie fashions: t-shirts, raincoats, boots, and accessories. Pet grooming. MC, V.

—Pets: Training

City Dog
158 West 23 Street, 3rd floor. 255-3618. Basic group obedience classes to solve housebreaking and chewing problems. For puppies and dogs of all ages. Observe a lesson free.

New York Academy of Dog Training
379-8844. Highly recommended for its caring training techniques. In your home. Takes four to six weeks.

—Pets: Treatment

Animal Medical Care Center
510 East 62 Street. 838-8100. A bit impersonal, but very skilled staff. Emergency service 24 hours a day, 7 days a week. AE, MC, V.

A.S.P.C.A.
441 East 92 Street. Emergency information: day, 876-7701; evening, 876-7711.

Friends of Animals
11 West 60 Street. 247-8077. Private agency dedicated to humane animal treatment. Free information regarding spaying, neutering, and declawing. Membership available.

Mobile Veterinary Unit
Brooklyn, (718) 373-0240; Queens, (718) 575-5152. House calls for basic exams or emergency. Services Brooklyn, Lower Manhattan, Staten Island, and Queens. AE, MC, V.

Pharmacies

Bigelow Pharmacy
414 Sixth Avenue near West 8 St. 533-2700. Lovely landmark Greenwich Village chemist shop in business since 1838. For prescriptions, surgical supplies, cosmetics, perfumes, boutique and gift items. Free delivery. AE, MC, V. *OPEN year-round.*

Cambridge Chemists
21 East 65 Street. 734-5678. Exclusive purveyor of Cyclax of London, Queen Elizabeth's favorite beauty products, as well as Floris of London soaps and a wide variety of toiletries, treatment preparations, and cosmetics from Europe. Such a civilized place. AE, MC, V.

Duane Reade
*19 Park Place near Broadway; 349-5175. And 50 Pine Street near Water St; 425-3720. Also *90 John Street near Gold St, 349-1285; 300 Park Avenue South near East 22 St, 533-7580; *360 Park Avenue South near East 26 St, 685-6717; *1412 Broadway near West 39 St, 354-2553; 370 Lexington Avenue near East 41 St, 683-9704; 20 East 46 Street, 682-2448; 485 Lexington Avenue near East 47 St, 682-5338; and 1150 Sixth Avenue near West 44 St, 221-3588. Excellent chain for good values on prescriptions, cosmetics, vitamins, perfumes, and beauty-care products. Windows display current good buys. New York trivia: The name is a meeting of two downtown streets. *CLOSED Sat & Sun.*

Freeda Pharmacy
36 East 41 Street. 685-4980. The highest-quality nutritional supplements including Freeda; vegetarian "born free"; no sugar or artificial color or flavor. Prescriptions. Senior discounts. AE, MC, V. *OPEN Mon-Fri.*

Kaufman Pharmacy
557 Lexington Avenue at East 50 St. 755-2266. Make a note of this one; it never closes! Good for emergency prescriptions; delivers, too. AE, MC. *OPEN 24 hours a day, 7 days a week.*

Photographic Equipment

If you are shopping for the best price, check the Sunday New York Times *Arts and Leisure section, where camera stores advertise their weekly specials.*

Camera Discount Center
45 Seventh Avenue near West 14 St. 206-0077. Discounts on name-brand cameras. Will meet or beat any price advertised. Repairs, too. MC, V. *OPEN Sun-Fri. CLOSES Fri at 3pm.*

Forty-seventh St. Photo, Inc.
67 West 47 Street, 2nd floor; 398-1410. And 115 West 45 Street; 398-1410. Also 38 East 19 Street, 260-4410; and 116 Nassau Street at Ann St, 608-8080. Perhaps the lowest prices in the city. Good value and selection, weekly specials. Also TVs, VCRs, and video games; typewriters. Know exactly what you want before you go. It's hectic, but worthwhile for the savings. MC, V. *OPEN Sun-Fri. CLOSES Fri at 2pm.*

Nikon House
620 Fifth Avenue near 50 St. 586-3907. Information center regarding Nikon cameras, lenses, and accessories. Hands-on demonstrations; technical consultation. Nothing is for sale, and the expert knowledge and information to be found here are free. Also a Nikon repair center. *OPEN Tues-Sat.*

Willoughby's
110 West 32 Street. 564-1600. Large well-established top camera and audio department store with complete range of cameras, lighting and darkroom equipment, and secondhand department. Eighty-six years and still going strong. AE, DC, MC, V. *OPEN 7 days.*

Plants

The wholesale plant district, Sixth Avenue from West 25 to West 30 Street, is a good place to shop for plants, especially on Sunday. Most new shipments arrive on Monday and many times room is needed, which means even lower prices.

—Plants: Stores

Farm & Garden Nursery
2 Sixth Avenue at White St. 431-3577. Established in 1939, this large, well-stocked indoor and outdoor garden center is open year-round. Sells trees, bushes, potted plants, and trays of flowering plants; landscaping and maintenance. Service uneven, sometimes rushed. AE, MC, V. *OPEN 7 days.*

Grass Roots Garden
131 Spring Street near Greene St. 226-2662. Very complete source for tropical and semi-tropical plants, trees, and exotic plantings. Materials and services. AE, MC, V. *OPEN Tues-Sun.*

—Plants: Planters

(See also Baskets.*)*

Clay Craft
807 Sixth Avenue at West 28 St, 2nd floor. 645-1701. In the heart of the flower district. If you've

got the plant, they've got the pot. Italian terracotta planters, also fiber-glass urns. All reasonably priced. MC, V. *OPEN 7 days.*

Lexington Gardens
1008 Lexington Avenue near East 72 St. 861-4390. An enchanting garden accessory shop with a variety of new and antique planters and window boxes, also custom designed. Garden furniture, bird feeders, gardening implements, and books. AE, MC, V.

Veen & Pol
399 Bleecker Street near Perry St. 727-3988. A unique selection of imported plant containers including interesting terra-cotta pots, alabaster urns, wood and concrete planters—all in a small space. Topiaries and custom design as well. MC, V. *OPEN Tues-Sun noon-6pm.*

Postcards

(*See also* Memorabilia.)

Untitled
159 Prince Street near West Broadway. 982-2088. This small SoHo store, here for 25 years and still going strong, stocks the city's largest collection of museum art postcards and more. A small delight. Now also in larger quarters with a good stock of art books, at 680 Broadway near Great Jones St, 982-1145. AE, MC, V. *OPEN 7 days.*

Posters

Most museum gift shops carry high-quality posters of artworks in their permanent collections as well as special exhibition posters. (See also Memorabilia and MUSEUMS & GALLERIES, Galleries, Prints & Original Posters.)

Motion Picture Arts Gallery
133 East 58 Street, 10th floor. 223-1009. Original vintage movie posters, silent era through the present, with the emphasis on older material, American and European. Price range: $20-$10,000. MC, V. *OPEN Tues-Sat.*

Poster America
138 West 18 Street. 206-0499. Original old posters, American and European, 1890 to 1960. Also advertising graphics; custom framing. Friendly, knowledgeable people. AE, DC, MC, V. *OPEN Tues-Sat.*

Reinhold-Brown Gallery
26 East 78 Street. 734-7999. Fine posters: Bayer, Beggarstaffs, Bradley, Cassandre, Hohlwein, Klimt, Lautrec, Lissitzky, Macintosh, Mucha, Tschichold, Van de Velde. *OPEN Tues-Sat.*

Triton Gallery
323 West 45 Street. 765-2472. Huge inventory of Broadway, off- and off-off-Broadway theatrical posters; West End London productions; and dance. Custom framing; trees and notecards. AE, MC, V.

Records, Tapes & CDs

Colony Records
1619 Broadway at West 49 St. 265-2050. A Broadway institution; carries the new but spe-

cializes in hard-to-get items. Rare, out-of-print LPs; cassettes and CDs. AE, CB, DC, MC, V. *OPEN 7 days 10am-1am.*

Discorama
186 West 4 Street; 206-8417. And 40 Union Square; 260-8616. Large selection of discounted compact discs. Also 12-inch dance records; tapes and videos, too. AE, MC, V. *OPEN 7 days.*

HMV
2084 Broadway near West 72 St; 721-5900. And *1280 Lexington Avenue at East 86 St; 348-0800. English chain giving Tower a run for its money. Over 300,000 recordings; the Lexington location is the largest record store in North America. Well-stocked in all areas. Helpful service. *OPEN year-round Mon-Sat 10am-midnight; Sun noon-midnight. *Mon-Thurs 10am-10pm; Fri & Sat 10am-midnight; Sun noon-10pm.*

J & R Music World
23 & 33 Park Row. 732-8600. Large comprehensive stores. At no. 33, Classical CDs (349-0062) and a good selection of jazz (349-8400), including LPs. Also a closeout clearance center for records and tapes. AE, MC, V. *OPEN Mon-Sat 9am-6:25pm; Sun 11am-6pm.*

Record Hunter
507 Fifth Avenue near 42 St; 697-8970. And *893 Broadway at East 19 St; 533-4030. An independent discount store established in 1945. Well stocked in spoken-word, international, and children's records; carries a full line of domestic and imported record labels. AE, CB, DC, MC, V. *OPEN 7 days.*

Sam Goody
1011 Third Avenue at East 60 St; 751-5809. And 666 Third Avenue near East 43 St; 986-8480. Also 1290 Sixth Avenue near West 51 St, 246-8730. Large stock selections, including some that are hard to find. Video and audio equipment, too. Great weekly sales on current recordings. Full label-line sales as well; check Sunday *New York Times* Arts and Leisure section for listings. AE, MC, V. *OPEN 7 days.*

Tower Records
*Broadway at East 4 St; 505-1500. And 1965 Broadway & West 66 Street; 799-2500. Mammoth record emporium with more than 500,000 titles! From the current hot rock to the obscure import. Well stocked in all areas including jazz and classical. *Classical annex around the corner on Lafayette for bargains. AE, MC, V. *OPEN year-round 9am-midnight.*

—Records: Specialized

Bleecker Bob's Golden Oldies
118 West 3 Street. 475-9677. Specializes in New Wave music, independent labels, British imports. Very knowledgeable re "what's happening" in music today. *OPEN Sun-Thurs noon-1am; Fri & Sat till 3am.*

Dayton's
799 Broadway at East 11 St. 254-5084. Specializes in out-of-print records. Huge selection of movie sound tracks, original-cast shows, and

spoken-word records. Used rock, jazz, classical.

Downstairs Records
35 West 43 Street, upstairs. 354-4684. They specialize in the hard-to-get with a very large, well-organized selection of oldies stocked—and there's a phonograph on which to play your choice. Helpful, music lovin' staff. Mail orders, too. AE, MC, V. *Fri till 8pm.*

Finyl Vinyl
89 Second Avenue near East 5 St. 533-8007. Well-stocked, well-organized shop featuring sounds of the 30s to the 70s. From Robert Johnson to Bootsy Collins. AE, MC, V. *OPEN "8 days a week."*

Footlight Records
113 East 12 Street. 533-1572. Wonderful East Village outpost for out-of-print and hard-to-find Broadway cast albums, movie sound tracks, big band, jazz, and vocalists, 1940s through 60s. They will search for items. AE, MC, V. *OPEN 7 days.*

G & A
139 West 72 Street. 877-5020. Over 100,000 titles of that fast disappearing item—the LP vinyl record; all gently used. Vintage and contemporary classical, jazz, Broadway cast albums, and sound tracks. Mail orders filled. They buy, too. MC, V.

Golden Disc
239 Bleecker Street near Sixth Ave. 255-7899. "World's largest oldies shop." Rock, sound tracks, blues, reggae, and jazz LPs and 45s, CDs. Color and photo discs available, too. AE, MC, V. *OPEN 7 days.*

Gryphon Record Shop & Annex
251 West 72 Street, 2nd floor; 874-1588. Annex: 246 West 80 Street; 724-1541. Over 50,000 rare and out-of-print LPs, specializing in classical and jazz. At the **Annex**, Broadway cast albums, film sound tracks, spoken word and international. Good prices. They welcome want lists. MC, V. *OPEN 7 days.*

Jazz Record Center
135 West 29 Street, 12th floor. 594-9880. Old, rare, out-of-print jazz records, books, and magazines. Major and independent labels; domestic and foreign. Free search service, listening room; will ship anywhere. Now also jazz CDs and videos. AE, MC, V. *OPEN Tues-Sat.*

Music Inn
169 West 4 Street near Sixth Ave. 243-5715. Obscure international and ethnic records, tapes, and CDs, including English, Irish, and Celtic folk music. Strong on African music. Also jazz, blues, folk, and comedy. AE, DC, MC, V. *OPEN Tues-Sat 1-7pm.*

Nostalgia and All That Jazz
217 Thompson Street near Bleecker St. 420-1940. A nostalgic collection of jazz, movie sound tracks, and early radio broadcasts. Also posters and movie stills. *OPEN 7 days.*

Venus Records
13 St. Marks Place. 598-4459. From the late 50s to current American and imported rock. AE, MC, V. *OPEN 7 days.*

Vinylmania
43 & 60 Carmine Street near Bleecker St. Used records, collector's items, LPs and 45s, but the specialty is the 12-inch dance records. No. 43 (473-7120) has CDs, cassettes, and jazz, r&b and rock albums; No. 60 (924-7223) is dance headquarters with club music, rap, and reggae. AE, MC, V. *OPEN 7 days.*

Silver

(*See also* Antiques *and* Jewelry: Antique & Estate.)

Asprey & Co., Ltd.
Trump Tower, 725 Fifth Avenue at 56 St. 688-1811. The prestigious London establishment known for its exclusive silver patterns; antique and modern silver, crystal, china. Luxurious gift items such as hand-bound books, rare first editions, 18K gold beard combs, and custom-made leather goods. AE, MC, V.

Eastern Silver Co.
54 Canal Street near Orchard St, 2nd floor. 226-5708. Large selection of silver articles. Repairs and replating, too. *OPEN Sun-Thurs.*

Fortunoff
681 Fifth Avenue near 54 St. 758-6660. Impressive antique silver department for American, Georgian, Russian, and Chinese silverware, tea services, and *objets*. Also contemporary flatware in sterling as well as plate and stainless. AE, DC, MC, V. *Thurs till 8pm.*

James Robinson
15 East 57 Street. 752-6166. For over 70 years the premier purveyor of fine 17th- to 19th-century English hallmark silver, rare porcelain dinner sets, and antique jewelry. Also known for their own hand-forged silver flatware. Upstairs: the less formal, less expensive **James II Galleries** for 19th-century bibelots.

Jean's Silversmiths
16 West 45 Street. 575-0723. The largest selection of discontinued silver patterns (over 900), plus new ones at lower prices than most other shops (flat and hollowware). MC, V. *OPEN Mon-Fri. CLOSES Fri at 3:30pm.*

Michael C. Fina
3 West 47 Street. 869-5050. Well-known store features an extensive stock of silver at substantial savings. Jewelry, sterling silver flatware, tea sets, giftware, clocks, and more. AE, DC, MC, V. *Thurs till 7pm.*

S. J. Shrubsole
104 East 57 Street. 753-8920. The best selection of silver in New York. Antique English and early American silver, jewelry. AE, MC, V.

S. Wyler, Inc.
941 Lexington Avenue at East 69 St. 879-9848. Established 1890, it's the oldest silver dealer in the U.S. Antique and modern silver, fine porcelain, and antiques. Replating service. AE only.

Tudor Rose Antiques
28 East 10 Street. 677-5239. A small shining spot for Victorian-era silver flatware and hollowware. Also frames, candlesticks, tea services, and serving trays. AE, DC, MC, V.

—Silver: Repairs

Brandt & Opis Silversmiths
46 West 46 Street, 5th floor. 245-9237. Silver and gold replating; removal of dents, bruises, and monograms. *OPEN Mon-Thurs 8am-6pm; Fri till 2pm.*

Columbia Lighting & Silversmiths
493 Third Avenue near East 33 St. 725-5250. Since 1935, silver replating and repair; 24K gold replating, too. Also, commercial, residential, indoor and outdoor lighting. AE, MC, V.

Restore-All Silversmiths
44 West 47 Street, room 3F. 719-1330. In business for 45 years. Repairs, replates, restores, and polishes precious metals. Accepts repairs via the mail. *OPEN Mon-Fri. CLOSES Fri at 2pm.*

Thome Silversmiths
49 West 37 Street, suite 605. 764-5426. Established 1931. This restorer of antiques will repair, polish, replate silver and gold; remove or add monograms. Also copper, pewter, and brasswork. Buys and sells silverware. *OPEN Mon-Fri 8:30am-5:30pm. CLOSED 1-2:30pm for lunch.*

Sports Equipment

—Sports Equipment: General

Macy's has a large department for sporting and exercise equipment.

Herman's World of Sporting Goods
*135 West 42 Street; 730-7400. And *845 Third Avenue near East 51 St; 688-4603. Also 110 Nassau Street near Fulton St, 233-0733; and *39 West 34 Street, 279-8900. Leading merchandiser of low-priced sporting goods and apparel from running shoes to boxing equipment, exercise bikes to baseball mitts. Good selections for men, women, and children; good sales, too. AE, DC, MC, V. **OPEN 7 days.*

Paragon Sporting Goods
867 Broadway at East 18 St. 255-8036. Since 1908, the city's most impressive selection of clothes and equipment for every imaginable sport. In-depth stocks of down jackets, track shoes, and shorts; baseball, lacrosse, golf, and hockey equipment; football gear, skates, skis, and swimwear; camping, fishing, and backpacking departments. Great values. Mail and phone orders. AE, DC, MC, V. *OPEN Mon-Fri 10am-8pm; Sat 10am-7pm; Sun noon-6pm.*

—Sports Equipment: Boating

Goldberg's Marine
12 West 37 Street. 594-6065. The source for marine supplies—at discount. The necessities plus foul weather apparel. AE, MC, V.

Hans Klepper Corporation
35 Union Square West near West 16 St. 243-3428. Inflatable boats, easy to carry, fast to assemble. MC, V.

—Sports Equipment: Camping & Mountaineering

EMS The Outdoor Specialists
611 Broadway near Houston St; 505-9860. And 20 West 61 Street; 397-4860. The speciality is backpacking and climbing, and it's well-stocked for both. Other outdoor sports represented are downhill and cross-country skiing, tennis, and running. AE, MC, V. *OPEN 7 days.*

Greenman's Down East Service Center
240 Lafayette Street near Spring St. 925-2632. Knapsacks, tents, hiking publications. Not so incidentally, expert cleaning and repair of down vests and jackets. AE, MC, V.

—Sports Equipment: Fishing

Capitol Fishing Tackle Co.
218 West 23 Street. 929-6132. The fisherman's friend since 1897. Equipment for freshwater, saltwater, deep-sea, and big-game fishing. Big discounts. MC, V. *OPEN Mon-Fri 8am-5:30pm; Sat 9am-4pm.*

Hunting World
16 East 53 Street. 755-3400. The Angler's World department has a fine selection of fly-fishing equipment. AE, MC, V.

Orvis New York
355 Madison Avenue at East 45 St. 697-3133. Complete line of fly rods, reels, and accessories, from the oldest rod-building company in the U.S. AE, MC, V.

Urban Angler
118 East 25 Street, 3rd floor. 979-7600. Fly-fishing rods and reels from a caring specialist. MC, V. *OPEN Mon-Fri.*

—Sports Equipment: Golf

Al Lieber's World of Golf
147 East 47 Street, 2nd floor. 755-9398. The latest in well-priced golf equipment.

Richard Metz Golf Studio
35 East 50 Street, 2nd floor. 319-0023. Golf equipment and supplies for men and women. Expert instruction, too. MC, V.

—Sports Equipment: Riding

Hermès
11 East 57 Street. 751-3181. Though for most New Yorkers they are synonymous with chic silk items with a horsey motif, this fine French firm has been making saddles and bridle equipment for over 150 years. AE, MC, V.

H. Kaufman & Son Saddlery Co.
419 Park Avenue South at East 29 St. 684-6060; (800) 872-6687. Longtime saddler housed in new quarters. Mostly Western-, some English-style, riding paraphernalia. Fine selection of authentic Western duds. Mail order from their catalog. AE, DC, MC, V.

Miller's
123 East 24 Street. 673-1400. Everything for the

horse and rider. Equipment, clothing, and accessories. Informed source; official outfitter of the U.S. equestrian team. AE, DC, MC, V.

M. J. Knoud
716 Madison Avenue near East 63 St. 838-1434. In the English riding tradition, britches, hats, boots, jackets, crops, blouses. AE, V.

—Sports Equipment: Running

Athlete's Foot
170 West 72 Street; 874-1003. And 1089 Lexington Avenue near East 76 St; 861-3700. Also in A&S Plaza. Every type of running and walking shoe available for men and women. Also a line of active sports basics. AE, MC, V. *OPEN 7 days.*

Super Runner's Shop
1170 Third Avenue at East 68 St; 249-2133. And 360 Amsterdam Avenue near West 77 St; 787-7666. Also 1337 Lexington Avenue at East 89 St, 369-6010. Well stocked with running gear primarily. Knowledgeable staff. AE, MC, V. *OPEN 7 days.*

—Sports Equipment: Skating

Paragon Sporting Goods Company
867 Broadway at East 18 St. 255-8036. Excellent stock and custom indoor and outdoor skates plus paraphernalia, including safety gear. Knowledgeable staff. AE, DC, MC, V. *OPEN 7 days.*

Peck & Goodie
919 Eighth Avenue near West 54 St. 246-6123. Longtime, well-regarded skate shop. Large variety of ice and roller skates for men and women. AE, MC, V. *OPEN 7 days.*

—Sports Equipment: Skiing

Bogner
655 Madison Avenue at East 60 St. 752-2282. The people who revolutionized the slopes—with stretch pants (in the 1950s). Ski fashions and Bogner ready-to-wear from Germany. AE, MC, V.

Scandinavian Ski & Sports Shop
40 West 57 Street. 757-8524. Top city source for ski equipment on three floors. Brand-name skiwear as well. In late October they sponsor a ski clinic. AE, DC, MC, V.

—Sports Equipment: Tennis

Grandstand
1149 Second Avenue near East 60 St; 755-5297. And 588 Columbus Avenue near West 88 St; 874-5297. All the best names in this well-organized service-oriented store used to dealing with the pro. Rackets, restringing, shoes, and accessories. AE, MC, V.

Mason's Tennis Mart
911 Seventh Avenue near West 57 St. 757-5374. Rackets, balls, bags, restringing, and high-fashion European tennis wear. Also in season skiwear. AE, DC, MC, V. *Thurs till 8pm.*

Stationery

*Each of the major department stores, plus **Tiffany's** and **Cartier's**, has a line of sta-*
tionery. (See also Art Supplies and Office Supplies.)

Browne & Co., Stationers
South Street Seaport, 211 Water Street. 669-9400. A restored 1836 stationer complete with an antique hand printing press that works! Handmade quality stationery for sale including hand-printed cards, also broadsides and books. AE, MC, V. *OPEN 7 days.*

Dempsey & Carroll
38 East 57 Street. 486-7508. Fine stationers since 1878. Needless to say, they know their business. Hand-engraved stationery from over 200 monogram styles. AE, MC, V.

Jam Envelope & Paper Company
*770 Second Avenue at East 41 St; 986-6000. And 621 Sixth Avenue at West 19 St; 255-4593. Also 111 Third Avenue near East 14 St, 473-6666. *Great* source for basic to unusual-hued stationery. Over 150 colors in stock and for long-distance mail try the map stationery. Also stop in at their warehouse outlet store at 125 Fifth Avenue near 19th St; 388-9189. *OPEN Mon-Fri.*

Kate's Paperie
8 West 13 Street. 633-0570. Handmade fine arts papers for artists, photographers, and mere mortals. Glorious spacious store for those who love paper—in all varieties; for writing, for wrapping, and for making collages. Also gorgeous desk accessories, diaries, photo albums, storage boxes, and much more to delight the spirit. AE, MC, V.

Papers Etc.
510 Broome Street near West Broadway. 431-7720. (Formerly 80 Papers.) Owner Wendy Stewart specializes in handmade paper with an impressive stock including Japanese rice, Italian marbled, and the more unusual with silver threads imbedded in the sheets. In addition, lovely handbound albums and journals, handmade stationery, boxes, and masks. AE, MC, V. *OPEN 7 days.*

Stereo & Sound Systems

*Good value sound systems can also be found at **Radio Shack**, with branches throughout the city.*

ABC Trading Company
31 Canal Street near Essex St. 228-5080. Stocks most major brands and will order what they don't have. Good discounts. *OPEN Sun-Fri. CLOSES Fri at 1pm.*

Goodman Electronics
37 Essex Street near Grand St. 673-3220. Substantial discounts available on Sony, Panasonic, KLH, Fisher, and Garrard. Call with model number. AE, MC, V. *OPEN Sun-Fri. CLOSES Fri at 2pm.*

Grand Central Radio
155 East 45 Street. 682-3869. Established in 1925, this friendly shop sells Bang & Olufsen, Proton, KEF, McIntosh, Mission, Denon, Dalquist, Thorens, Nakamichi, Sony ES, NAD, Mitsubishi, plus many other famous makers stocked at this audio showroom. AE, CB, DC, MC, V.

Harvey Electronics
2 West 45 Street. 575-5000. Audio and video electronic specialists. Knowledgeable help in creating the perfect system for the perfectionist. AE, MC, V, own charge.

Uncle Uncle Electronics
343 Canal Street near Church St. 226-4010. Low prices on stereo equipment, plus TV and video recorders. Sound room available. *OPEN 7 days.*

—**Stereo Repair**

Analogique Systems Laboratories
17 West 17 Street, 10th floor. 989-4240. Very professional servicing and repair, plus custom designing of sound systems. Authorized service agency for a host of manufacturers. *OPEN Mon-Fri 9am-6pm.*

Telegrams: Unusual

The fax has practically made the standard telegram obsolete, but here are some ways to entertainingly get your message across.

Balloons to You™
466-9274; (516) 868-2325. For a lighthearted greeting, two Mylar balloons, imprinted with your message, sent anywhere in the U.S. via UPS. Solicitations, invitations, centerpieces, customized promotions, too.

Eastern Onion
268-3900. Singing telegrams or looney balloons delivered in person by a costumed messenger. Choice of a pink gorilla, French maid, belly dancer, or a singing and dancing cake. AE, MC, V. *Call 7 days 9am-9pm.*

Western Union has resumed its national singing-telegram service albeit only for the standard Happy Birthday (can be adapted for Anniversary and Graduation) and only on the telephone (one hours' notice); followed up with a mailgram. For details, call (800) 325-6000.

Yenta-gram
475-0566. For a little gelt—a lot of guilt.

Theatrical

(*See also* Costumes *and* Memorabilia.)
One Shubert Alley
1 Shubert Alley, 944-4133. Posters, buttons, t-shirts, sweatshirts, theatrical theme jewelry, duffles, recordings of current Broadway and off-Broadway productions. Plus souvenirs of past hits. Mail order, nationwide and overseas. AE, MC, V. *OPEN 7 days.*

The Shops at Lincoln Center
The Metropolitan Opera Shop, Metropolitan Opera House, north lobby; Performing Arts Shop, Lincoln Center Concourse Level. Gifts, stationery, jewelry, and books with an opera, dance, or performing arts theme. Recordings, videos, and more. AE, MC, V. *OPEN 7 days.*

Thrift Shops

There's a heavy concentration of thrift shops from East 75 Street and Second Avenue/Third

Avenue to East 89 Street and Third Avenue. They all offer secondhand and some unused merchandise of varying quality. Some bargains can be found, and the proceeds do go to charity. Caveat: Not all shops with thrift in their names are charity stores.

Tobacconists

Alfred Dunhill of London
450 Park Avenue near East 57 St. 753-9292. And at Bloomingdale's. Famed tobacconist. Custom-blended tobaccos, pipes, humidors, cigars, and gifts, including, of course, their famed expensive lighters. AE, DC, MC, V. *Thurs till 8pm.*

Connoisseur Pipe Shop
1285 Avenue of the Americas at West 51 St, concourse level. 247-6054. Established in 1917. Unique pipes, custom- and handmade: one-of-a-kind unstained unvarnished natural-finish pipes; skillful pipe repairs. Hand-blended tobacco mixtures and a full range of tobacco pouches, humidors, racks, and accessories. Free mail order service; catalog upon request. Price range: $27.50-$4,200. AE, MC, V. *OPEN Mon-Fri 8am-6pm.*

Davidoff of Geneva
535 Madison Avenue near East 54 St. 751-9060. Fine tobaccos and smoking accessories. AE, DC, MC, V.

J. R. Tobacco Corporation
11 East 45 Street; 983-4160. And *1410 Broadway near West 39 St; 921-9360. Also *219 Broadway near Barclay, 233-6620. The world's largest cigar store with a stock of over 2,800 different sizes, shapes, and colors; from nickel cigars to the rare expensive ones. Discount; catalog available. MC, V. *OPEN Mon-Fri 7:45am-5:55pm; Sat till 4pm. *CLOSED Sat.*

Nat Sherman Cigars
711 Fifth Avenue at 55 St. 751-9100. Pipe tobacco, an imported selection of cigars in their walk-in humidor, and 30 blends of cigarette tobacco to be wrapped in your choice of paper color, with your name or company named imprinted if you wish. Large choice of pipes and cigarette lighters, too. AE, CB, DC, MC, V.

Tobacco Products
137 Eighth Avenue near West 16 St. 989-3900. Longtime family-run operation. Custom-blended cigars using tobaccos from Brazil, the Dominican Republic, Nicaragua, Mexico. Pipe and lighter seleciton. AE, MC, V.

Toys: Collectible

For new, strictly children's toys, see KIDS' NEW YORK, Children's Specialty Shopping, Toys. These shops are mainly for collectors. (See also Antiques.)
Burlington Antique Toys
1082 Madison Avenue near East 81 St (in Burlington Books). 861-9708. Downstairs—turn-of-the-century to 60s tin soldiers, miniature fighter planes, wooden boats, racing cars, die-cast

model cars, old and new. New as well as collectible. AE, MC, V.

Chick Darrow's Fun Antiques
309 East 61 Street. 838-0730. Longtime nostalgia mecca, founded in 1964 by Chick Darrow and now lovingly tended by his son. Vintage wind-up toys, rare robots, tiny trucks and cars, vending machines, arcade games, carousel figures, character watches, and campaign buttons. AE, MC, V.

Iris Brown's Victorian & Miniature Shop
253 East 57 Street. 593-2882. Antique dolls repaired, bought, sold, and loved. Specializes in Victorian dollhouses and miniature furniture with which to fill them. Also antique Christmas ornaments and sample furniture. AE, MC, V. *OPEN Mon-Fri 11am-5:30pm; Sat 12:30-5:30pm.*

Second Childhood
283 Bleecker Street near Seventh Ave South. 989-6140. For kids of all ages. Charming but expensive tin and iron toys, soldiers, carousel figures; miniatures; 1850s to 1950s. Some less collectible, less costly items. AE, MC, V.

Umbrellas

The large stores and many boutiques and handbag shops carry a line of umbrellas. Most rainy days someone on a busy street corner will be selling $2 umbrellas, guaranteed to get through that rainstorm at least!

Gloria Umbrella Mfg. Co.
39 Essex Street near Hester St. 475-7388. A manufacturer of umbrellas features a huge selection of famous-brand folding, even beach-fashion umbrellas at substantial discount. Recovers and repairs, too. Special orders filled. *OPEN Sun-Thurs; Fri till 2pm.*

Salwen
45 Orchard Street near Grand St. 226-1693. An extremely friendly well-established spot for Knirps and designer umbrellas, including Givenchy, at a minimum of 25 percent off. Also a fine diverse line of handbags and small leather goods. AE, MC, V. *OPEN Sun-Fri.*

Uncle Sam
161 West 57 Street. 582-1976. Stocks 50,000 umbrellas and 1,000 walking canes: every color, size, and description, including beach and garden. Expert, reasonably priced recovering and repairs, too. Since 1866. AE, DC, MC, V.

Video

RKO Warner Video
1608 Broadway at West 49 St; 581-6260. And 2300 Broadway near West 83 St; 721-0600. Also 168 West 96 Street, 222-0005; 288 First Avenue at East 17 St, 477-0022; 507 Third Avenue at East 34 St, 686-1004; 574 Third Avenue at East 38 St, 490-4411; 1295 Second Avenue at East 68 St, 472-2300; 1650 First Avenue at East 86 St, 772-3200; 1309 Lexington Avenue at East 88 St, 410-9800; 1675 Third Avenue near East 93 St, 289-1122; 58 East 8 Street, 475-4500; 143 Sec-

ond Avenue at East 9 St, 979-9191; and 93 Greenwich Avenue near West 12 St, 691-2200. Largest videocassette retailer and renter in New York. Over 6,000 different titles in stock. One free for every 10 rentals. AE, CB, DC, MC, V. *OPEN 7 days.*

Tower Video
215 East 86 Street; 369-2500. And Broadway & West 67 Street; 496-2500. Also Tower Records Store, downstairs, Broadway & East 4 Street, 505-1166. Video sales and rentals; great hours. No club to join; no membership fee. AE, MC, V. *OPEN every day till midnight.*

Watches

—Watches: Contemporary

The large department stores stock a variety of watches in the inexpensive to moderate price range, with the accent on fashion. (See also Jewelry.)

Tourneau
500 Madison Avenue at East 52 St. 759-1141. Handsome, elegant, and famous Swiss watches for the fashion-conscious. Rolex, Cartier, Piaget, Omega, Corum, Patek Philippe, Baume & Mercier, Vaucheron Constantin, among many others. Expensive, but there is a free lifetime battery replacement. Also a quality vintage watch selection. AE, CB, DC, MC, V.

—Watches: Antique & Vintage

Aaron Faber
666 Fifth Avenue at 53 St. 586-8411. Very large selection of antique and vintage wristwatches—turn of the century to the 1960s: Elgin, Hamilton, Patek Philippe, Rolex. For men and women. Catalog available. AE, CB, DC, MC, V.

Clock Hutt
1050 Second Avenue near East 55 St. 759-2395. Eighteenth- and 19th-century clocks from France, England, Germany. Vintage watches 1920s through 1940s. Repair and restoration work also done. AE, MC, V. *OPEN 7 days.*

Fanelli Antique Timepieces
1131 Madison Avenue at East 84 St. 517-2300. Large selection of antique timepieces, including pocket and wristwatches, wall clocks, shelf clocks, tall case clocks, and carriage clocks. The quality is high and the rare abounds. Also appraisals and expert repairs. Price range: $225-$50,000.

Time Will Tell
962 Madison Avenue near East 75 St. 861-2663. A shop full of beautiful one-of-a-kind classic timepieces (1920s-1950s) for the wrist. Audemars Piguet, Cartier, Hamilton, Bulova, Rolex, Tiffany, Patek Philippe. Also bands made of alligator, ostrich, and lizard. Some pocket pieces. Price range: $300-$40,000. Repairs as well. AE, MC, V.

—Watch Bands

George Paul Jewelers
51 East 58 Street. 308-0077. Large selection of

fine leather watch straps, including alligator, lizard, crocodile, pig, buffalo, snake, bird. Stock or made to order. AE, MC, V. *OPEN Mon-Fri 11am-5:30pm; Sat till 4pm.*

Wines & Spirits

Astor Wines & Spirits
12 Astor Place at Lafayette St. 674-7500. The largest liquor store in New York State and a must for bargain-hunting oenophiles. Good selections. Their own label is well priced and of comparable quality. Good special sales several times during the year. Get on their mailing list for special values. Order by phone, free delivery for purchases over $60. MC, V. *OPEN Mon-Sat 9am-9pm.*

Beekman Liquor Store
500 Lexington Avenue near East 47 St. 759-5857. Largest discount liquor store in midtown. AE, MC, V. *OPEN Mon-Sat 8am-11pm.*

Morrell & Company
535 Madison Avenue near East 54 St. 688-9370. Beautiful, knowledgeably run wine shop. Large collection of port and excellent selection of California wines. Wine catering; personalized service. AE, MC, V.

Sherry Lehmann, Inc.
679 Madison Avenue near East 61 St. 838-7500. One of the best. Knowledgeable salespeople, excellent stock. AE, MC, V. *OPEN Mon-Sat 9am-7pm.*

SoHo Wines and Spirits
461 West Broadway near Prince St. 777-4332. Attractive, spacious, well-organized SoHo shop for wines; strong in Bordeaux. Largest selection of malt Scotch whiskey. Reliable delivery service (Manhattan). AE, MC, V. *OPEN Mon-Sat 10am-9pm.*

Zippers

Notions departments in most large stores and tailor shops carry zippers.

A. Feibusch Zippers
33 Allen Street near Canal St. 226-3964. Every length, in any color, with thread to match. Cut to order if not stocked. Also shoulder pads. *OPEN Sun-Fri 10am-4pm.*

Harry Kantrowitz, Inc.
555 Eighth Avenue near West 38 St. 563-1610. Large selection of zippers for all purposes: heavy-duty to delicate. *OPEN Mon-Fri.*

24-HOUR
NEW YORK

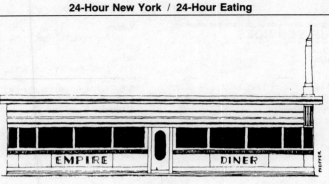

Empire Diner

24-HOUR EATING

Unless otherwise noted, everything listed is OPEN 24 hours a day, 7 days a week.

Bakeries

Bagels on the Square
7 Carmine Street near Sixth Ave. 691-3042.
Donut Pub
203 West 14 Street. 929-0126.
H & H Bagels
2239 Broadway at West 80 St; 595-8000. Lox and cream cheese, too!
Kossar's Bialystocker Kuchen
367 Grand Street near Essex St. 473-4810.
Mazzola's Bakery
192 Union Street near Henry St, Brooklyn. (718) 643-1719.

Coffee Shops & Restaurants

(See also RESTAURANTS, Bars & Burgers *and* Late Night & 24 Hours.)
Around the Clock Cafe
8 Stuyvesant Street (Third Ave & East 9 St). 598-0402. (*See* RESTAURANTS, Late Night & 24 Hours.)
Astor Riviera Restaurant
454 Lafayette Street at Fourth Ave. 677-4461.
Brasserie
100 East 53 Street. 751-4840. (*See* RESTAURANTS, Late Night & 24 Hours.)
Carnegie Delicatessen & Restaurant
854 Seventh Avenue near West 55 St. 757-2245. *OPEN 6:30am-3:30am.* (*See* RESTAURANTS, Delicatessen.)
Chelsea Square
368 West 23 Street. 691-5400.
Cheyenne
411 Ninth Avenue at West 39 St. 465-8750. (*See* RESTAURANTS, Late Night & 24 Hours.)
Coffee Shop
29 Union Square West. 243-7969. *OPEN Mon-Fri 7am-6am; Sat 9am-6am; Sun 10am-6am.* (*See* RESTAURANTS, Latin American.)
Cooper Square
87 Second Avenue at East 5 St. 420-8050.
Cosmos
248 East 23 Street at Second Ave. 679-1290.
Empire Diner
210 Tenth Avenue at West 22 St. 243-2736. (*See* RESTAURANTS, Late Night & 24 Hours.)
Florent
69 Gansevoort Street near Washington St. 989-5779. (*See* RESTAURANTS, Late Night & 24 Hours.)
Gemini
641 Second Avenue near East 5 St. 532-2143.
Green Kitchen Restaurant
1477 First Avenue at East 77 St. 988-4163.
Hong Fat
63 Mott Street. 962-9588. *OPEN 10am-5am.*
Kiev International
117 Second Avenue at East 7 St. 674-4040. (*See* RESTAURANTS, Late Night & 24 Hours.)
Lox Around the Clock
676 Sixth Avenue at West 21 St. 691-3535. (*See* RESTAURANTS, Late Night & 24 Hours.)
Pizza Joint, Too
70 West 77 Street. 799-4444. *OPEN 10am-5am.*
Roxy Coffee Shop
20 John Street near Broadway. 349-4704. *CLOSED Sat 1pm-Mon 5am.*
Silver Star
1236 Second Avenue near East 65 St. 249-4250.
Soup Burg
1347 Second Avenue at East 71 St. 879-4814. *OPEN 6am-2am.*
Tivoli
515 Third Avenue near East 36 St. 532-3300.
Tramway Coffee House
1143 Second Avenue at East 60 St. 758-7017.
Veselka Coffee Shop
144 Second Avenue at East 9 St. 228-9682. (*See* RESTAURANTS, Breakfast/Brunch.)
Washington Square
150 West 4 Street at Sixth Ave. 533-9306.

24-HOUR SERVICES

Auto Rental

Avis
217 East 43 Street. 593-8378; (800) 331-1212.
This all-night office requires 30 minutes' notice.
Also at LaGuardia, JFK International, and New-
ark International airports, *available 24 hours a
day.*
Hertz
223 East 40 Street. 486-5060; (800) 654-3131.
OPEN 7 days 7am-midnight at JFK International,
LaGuardia, and Newark International airports.

Credit Cards—Lost

American Express: (800) 528-2121.
Carte Blanche and Diners' Club: (800) 525-
9135.
MasterCard and Visa: Call the bank your cards
are registered with to get the appropriate phone
number.

Food Stores

*On nearly every street corner in every neighbor-
hood there's a Korean-owned and -operated
food store with all the usuals plus a salad bar,
fresh fruit, and flowers. They are all OPEN 7
days, 24 hours.*
—Supermarkets

Food Emporium
*OPEN 24 hours a day Mon-Fri; Sat till midnight.
Reopens Sun 7am.*
316 Greenwich Street near Duane St. 285-
9268.
501 Sixth Avenue at West 13 St. 989-9454.
215 Park Avenue South at East 18 St. 473-
9281.
221 Lexington Avenue & East 33 St. 689-1660.
1172 Third Avenue near East 68 St. 650-1964.
228 West End Avenue near West 70 St. 874-
8223.
1331 First Avenue near East 72 St. 794-8866.
1498 York Avenue near East 79 St. 650-0824.
1450 Third Avenue near East 82 St. 650-9724.
Pathmark
OPEN 24 hours a day.
  Manhattan
  227 Cherry Street at Pine St. 227-8988.
  410 West 207 Street. 569-0600.
  Bronx
  1851 Bruckner Boulevard. 892-0100.
  1880 Bartow Avenue. 320-2902.
  Brooklyn
  2965 Cropsey Avenue. (718) 266-2705.
  111-10 Flatlands Avenue. (718) 649-8224.

  Queens
  31-06 Farrington Street, Whitestone. (718)
  886-4488.
  Staten Island
  1351 Forest Avenue near Crystal Ave. (718)
  981-1900.
  2875 Richmond Avenue near Yukon Ave.
  (718) 761-8400.
  2660 Hylan Boulevard. (718) 987-6188.

Locksmiths

*All will require identification and proof of resi-
dency before they will help you get into an apartment; proof of ownership with a car.*
Eagle Master Locksmith
307 Third Avenue. 532-1075.
Night & Day Locksmith
1335 Lexington Avenue. 722-1017.

Newsstands

24-Hour, Saturday Only
Seventh Avenue South & Grove Street at Sheridan Square.

24-Hour, 7 Days a Week
Delancy & Essex Streets.
Sixth Avenue at West 8 Street.
Seventh Avenue South at Sheridan Square.
Gem Spa, Second Avenue & St. Marks Place
(They also make New York's best egg cream!)
Third Avenue & St. Marks Place.
Third Avenue & East 23 Street.
Eighth Avenue & West 23 Street.
Port Authority Bus Terminal, Eighth Avenue &
West 41 Street.
Broadway & West 42 Street.
Eighth Avenue & West 46 Street.
Sixth Avenue & West 48 Street.
Third Avenue & East 54 Street.
Second Avenue & East 61 Street.
Broadway & West 72 Street.
Broadway & West 79 Street.
First Avenue & East 65 Street.
Lexington Avenue & East 64 Street.
Broadway & West 96 Street.
Broadway & West 104 Street.

Pharmacies

Kaufman Pharmacy
557 Lexington Avenue at East 50 St. 755-2266.
Pharmacist on duty round the clock. Deliveries
within a five-block radius. *Never closes!*

Telephone Out of Order

Dial 611.

TRAVEL & VACATION INFORMATION

Grand Central Terminal

PASSPORTS

During peak travel periods, apply at least four weeks in advance of scheduled departure. Some renewals can be done through the mail, call before going to the office. If you have left an inadequate amount of time before your trip, bring your airline ticket with you to the office. An emergency need for a passport after hours or on weekends requires a call to the passport duty officer at the State Department in Washington, call (202) 647-4000.

United States Passport Office
630 Fifth Avenue at 50 St, room 270. 541-7700 (recording); 541-7710 (questions, information). One of life's more frustrating experiences. The only place where you can get a passport in 24 hours. For first-timers proof of U.S. citizenship is required as well as an I.D. with a photo or a description plus two identical photos (see below). Be prepared to wait up to five hours in peak periods. Payment by personal check or money order in exact amount. *OPEN Mon-Fri 7:30am-4pm. CLOSED Sat, Sun & holidays.*

County Clerk's Office
60 Centre Street near Pearl St, lower level. 374-3289; 374-8361. For a renewal of a passport at least three weeks in advance of departure—the secret is out: There are NO LINES here. Check the County Clerk's Office in the other boroughs; they perform the same service. Payment by personal check or money order. *OPEN Mon-Fri 9am-1pm, 2-3pm. CLOSED Sat, Sun & holidays.*

Passport Photographs

Two identical recent photos, 2-inch square, are needed. These can be done by any photographer as long as they fit the required specifications. For requirements, call 541-7700.

Acme Passport Photos
630 Fifth Avenue near 50 St, lower shopping concourse. 247-2911. In the same building as the Passport Office. Accommodating spot for color or black-and-white photos while you wait. *OPEN Mon-Fri 7:15am-4:45pm.*

INOCULATIONS & VACCINATIONS

To ascertain what vaccinations are required for the countries you intend to visit, call the U.S. Government International Vaccination Information line, (718) 917-1685.

International Health Care Service
New York Hospital–Cornell Medical Center, 440 East 69 Street. 746-1601. Devoted exclusively to the medical needs of international travelers. Provides worldwide health information, immunizations when required; provides post-travel tests and treatment if required. Staffed by infectious-disease specialists. Fees vary; worthwhile investment for those traveling to lesser-developed countries. Appointment required four to five weeks before departure. *OPEN Mon, Wed & Thurs 4-8pm, by appointment only.*

Kennedy International Medical Office
Building 198 near South Cargo Road & 150 Street. (718) 656-5344. Vaccinations and inoculations available for a fee, daily 8am to 10pm. No checks. AE, MC, V. *OPEN 7 days, 24 hours for emergencies.*

OTHER IMPORTANT NUMBERS

Information & Naturalization Service
206-6500
U.S. Customs Service, General Information
466-5550

CURRENCY EXCHANGE

New York City banks do not as a policy exchange foreign currency, so it's best to arrive with some American dollars. At the JFK International Arrivals Building, second floor, there is a **Thomas Cook Foreign Exchange,** (718) 656-8444. *OPEN 7 days 9am-10pm. If you are going abroad, it's best to buy some foreign currency. You can purchase the currency at the following exchange offices:*

Bank Leumi
Convenient locations throughout the city; foreign exchange department in all branches—no commission or fees. Call 912-6262 and their service-oriented staff will be happy to give rates for buying and selling foreign currency; they will also estimate the amount of currency you will be getting in any exchange, as well as direct you to the branch nearest you.

Thomas Cook Currency Services (formerly Deak)
630 Fifth Avenue near 51 St. 757-6915. *OPEN Mon-Fri 9am-5pm; Sat 10am-3pm.*
41 East 42 Street. 883-0400. OPEN Mon-Fri 9am-5pm; Sat 10am-3pm.
Herald Center, West 34 Street & Herald Square. 736-9790. OPEN Mon-Fri 9:30am-5:30pm; Sat 10am-3pm.
29 Broadway near Morris St. 820-2470. OPEN Mon-Fri 9am-5pm.

TRAVELER'S CHECKS

Banks and almost all shops accept them. Photo I.D. may be required.
American Express Travel Service
65 Broadway near Wall St. 493-6500.
199 Water Street, Seaport Plaza. 943-6947.
150 East 42 Street. 687-3700.
374 Park Avenue near East 53 St. 421-8240.
822 Lexington Avenue near East 63 St. 758-6510.
Macy's, Herald Square, Broadway & West 34 Street, balcony. 695-8075.
For refunds for lost or stolen American Express Traveler's Cheques, call (800) 221-7282.
Thomas Cook
For traveler's checks in dollars or in foreign currency, see Thomas Cook under Foreign Exchange. Refund information: (800) 223-7373.

LOST PROPERTY

Railroads

Pennsylvania Station: (718) 990-8384
Grand Central Station: 340-2555

New York City Subways

(718) 625-6200. *OPEN Mon-Fri 9am-4:45pm.*

New York City Buses

Queens, Brooklyn, Staten Island: (718) 625-6200. *OPEN Mon-Fri 9am-4:45pm.*
Manhattan, Bronx: 605 West 132 Street. 690-9638.

Port Authority Bus Terminal

41 Street & Eighth Avenue. 435-7000.

Airports

JFK International Airport
Lost property would be held by the airline on which you traveled. If loss occurred on airport grounds or at the International Arrivals Building, call (718) 656-4120.
LaGuardia Airport
Lost & Found: (718) 476-5115. Also call the airline on which you traveled.
Newark International Airport
Lost & Found: (201) 961-2235. Also call the airline on which you traveled.

Taxicabs

By law, anything left in a taxi must be turned in to the police station closest to where you were dropped off. To report a loss, call the **Taxi & Limousine Commission Lost & Found**, 869-4513, only if you have the medallion number or driver's name and license number. Otherwise, call 374-5084.

TRAVELER'S AID

Traveler's Aid Society of New York
The International Arrivals Building, Kennedy Airport. (718) 656-4870 (recording). Nationwide service helps crime victims, stranded travelers, wayward children. Works closely with the police. *OPEN year-round Mon-Fri 10am-10pm; Sat 1-10pm. CLOSED Sun.*
Crime Victims' Hotline, 577-7777, offers counseling and information.

Lost Anywhere

Contact the nearest police station. Addresses are located in Help!, page 290.

Lost Child

Police: 911

Lost or Found Dog

A.S.P.C.A.
441 East 92 Street. 876-7700. Also put up notices in shops in the area of loss with a description and/or photo of pet and your phone number *only*. Ads in local neighborhood publications are also helpful.

TOURIST OFFICES (INTERNATIONAL)

For literature and helpful travel information.

Antigua Department of Tourism & Trade
610 Fifth Avenue at 49 St. 541-4117.
Argentine National Tourist Office
330 West 58 Street. 765-8833.
Austrian National Tourist Office
500 Fifth Avenue near 43 St. 944-6880.
Belgian National Tourist Office
745 Fifth Avenue near 57 St. 758-8130.
Bermuda Department of Tourism
310 Madison Avenue near East 41 St. 818-9800.
Brazilian Tourism Bureau
2 West 45 Street. 575-8484.
British Tourist Authority
40 West 57 Street. 581-4700.
Caribbean Tourism Association
20 East 46 Street. 682-0435.
Cayman Islands Department of Tourism
420 Lexington Avenue near East 43 St. 682-5582.
Colombian Government Tourist Office
140 East 57 Street. 688-0151.
Curacao Tourist Board
400 Madison Avenue near East 47 St. 751-8266.
Cyprus Tourism Organization
13 East 40 Street. 683-5280.
Czechoslovakia Travel Bureau
10 East 40 Street. 689-9720.
Dominican Republic Tourist Information Center
485 Madison Avenue near East 52 St. 826-0750.
Egyptian Government Tourist Office
630 Fifth Avenue near 50 St. 246-6960.
French Government Tourist Office
628 Fifth Avenue near 49 St. 757-1125.
French West Indies Tourist Board
610 Fifth Avenue near 49 St. 757-1125.
German National Tourist Office
747 Third Avenue near East 46 St. 308-3300.
Ghana International
19 East 47 Street. 832-1300.
Greek National Tourist Organization
645 Fifth Avenue near 51 St. 421-5777.
Grenada Tourist Information Office
820 Second Avenue. 687-9554.
Haiti Government Tourist Bureau
18 East 41 Street. 779-7177.
Hong Kong Tourist Association
590 Fifth Avenue. 869-5008.
India Government Tourist Office
30 Rockefeller Plaza near West 49 St. 586-4901.
Irish Tourist Board
757 Third Avenue near East 47 St. 418-0800.
Israel Government Tourist Office
Empire State Building, 350 Fifth Avenue at 34 St. 560-0650.
Italian Government Tourist Office (E.N.I.T.)
630 Fifth Avenue near 50 St. 245-4822.
Jamaica Tourist Board
2 Dag Hammarskjold Plaza near East 46 St. 688-7650.

Japan National Tourist Organization
630 Fifth Avenue near 50 St. 757-5640.
Kenya Tourist Office
424 Madison Avenue near East 49 St. 486-1300.
Korean Tourist Office
460 Park Avenue at East 58 St. 752-1700.
Luxembourg National Tourist Office
801 Second Avenue near East 42 St. 370-9850.
Mexican Government Tourism Office
405 Park Avenue at East 45 St. 838-2949.
Monaco Government Tourist Bureau
845 Third Avenue. 759-5227.
Moroccan National Tourist Office
20 East 46 Street. 557-2520.
Netherlands Board of Tourism
437 Madison Avenue. 223-8141.
Norwegian Tourist Board
655 Third Avenue near East 42 St. 949-2333.
Philippine Tourism
556 Fifth Avenue near 45 St. 575-7915.
Portuguese National Tourist Office
548 Fifth Avenue near 45 St. 354-4403.
Puerto Rico Tourism
1290 Avenue of the Americas near West 51 St. 246-3397.
Quebec Government House
17 West 50 Street. 397-0220.
Romanian National Tourist Office
573 Third Avenue at East 38 St. 697-6971.
Scandinavian Tourist Board
655 Third Avenue near East 42 St. 949-2333.
Spanish National Tourist Office
665 Fifth Avenue near 53 St. 759-8822.
Swedish National Tourist Board
655 Third Avenue near East 42 St. 949-2333.
Swiss National Tourist Office
608 Fifth Avenue near 49 St. 757-5944.
Taiwan Visitors Association
1 World Trade Center. 466-0691.
Turkish Tourism & Information Office
821 United Nations Plaza near East 46 St. 687-2194.
Virgin Islands Government Tourist Office
1270 Avenue of the Americas near West 50 St. 582-4520.
Yugoslav National Tourist Office
630 Fifth Avenue near 50 St. 757-2801.

ANIMALS IN TRANSIT

Animalport, A.S.P.C.A.
Air Cargo Center, JFK International Airport, Jamaica, Queens. (718) 656-6042. Care and feeding of large and small animals—"from canaries to elephants"—in transit. Veterinarian on call. Also a boarding kennel for vacationers' pets. Immunization proof required. *OPEN 7 days, 24 hours.*

PASSENGER SHIP LINES

The New York Passenger Ship Terminal is on the Hudson River at West 52 Street. Check the

New York Times *for daily listings of arrivals and departures.*
ACT/Pace Line
1 World Trade Center, suite 8101. 775-1500; (800) 221-8164.
Bergen Line
505 Fifth Avenue. 986-2711; (800) 323-7436.
Celebrity & Chandris Fantasy Cruises, Inc.
900 Third Avenue near East 55 St. 223-3003; (800) 621-2100.
Classical Cruises
132 East 70 Street. 794-3200; (800) 252-7745.
Cunard Line, Ltd.
555 Fifth Avenue near 46 St. 880-7500; (800) 221-4770.
Epirotiki Lines
551 Fifth Avenue, suite 605. 599-1750; (800) 221-2470.
EuroCruises
303 West 13 Street. 691-2099; (800) 688-3876.
Floating Through Europe
271 Madison Avenue. 685-5600; (800) 221-3140.
Ivarian Lines
1 Exchange Plaza. 809-1220; (800) 535-1861.
Raymond & Whitcomb
400 Madison Avenue. 759-3960; (800) 245-9005.
Regency Cruises
260 Madison Avenue. 972-4774; (800) 388-9090.
STC Bennett Scenic Cruises
270 Madison Avenue. 447-1520; (800) 759-7226.
Sun Line Cruises
1 Rockefeller Plaza. 397-6400; (800) 872-6400.

CAR HIRE

Drive Yourself

Avis
Nationwide reservations & information: (800) 331-1212. International: (800) 331-1084
Kennedy International Airport: (718) 244-5400
LaGuardia Airport: (718) 507-3600
Newark Airport: (201) 961-4300
Budget Rent-a-Car
Local Reservations & Information: 645-9310
Kennedy International Airport: (718) 565-6010
LaGuardia Airport: (718) 639-6400
Newark Airport: (201) 961-2990
Out of Town: (800) 527-0700
Hertz
24-hour information and reservations domestic and worldwide: (800) 654-3131

Chauffeur Driven

Carey
(718) 937-3100. Lincolns, Cadillacs, stretch limos, and chauffeurs. Hourly rates. *Available 24 hours a day.* AE, CB, DC, MC, V.

Fugazy Limousine Ltd.
661-0100. Limousines and sedans with courteous, uniformed chauffeurs. *Available 24 hours a day.* AE, DC, MC, V.
Smith Limousine
636 West 47 Street. 247-0711. Located in Manhattan. Cadillac and Lincoln—limos, stretches, and sedans. *Available 24 hours a day.* AE, CB, DC, MC, V.

BUS STATIONS

George Washington Bridge Bus Station
West 178 Street & Broadway. 564-1114.
Port Authority Bus Terminal
West 41 Street & Eighth Avenue. 564-8484.

TRAIN STATIONS

Grand Central Station
Lexington Avenue & East 42 Street. MetroNorth Info: 532-4900.
Pennsylvania Station
West 33 Street & Seventh Avenue. Amtrak: 736-4545; LIRR: (718) 454-5477.

AIRPORTS

These are the three major airports serving New York City:
JFK International Airport
Jamaica, Queens. (718) 656-4520.
LaGuardia Airport
Flushing, Queens. (718) 476-5000.
Newark International Airport
Newark, New Jersey. (201) 961-2000.

AIRLINES

*The **Central Airlines Ticket Office,** 100 East 42 Street, 986-0888, handles all the major airlines, and can arrange for tickets and answer questions.*
AeroMexico
37 West 57 Street. 754-2140.
Air Canada
869-1900
Air France
666 Fifth Avenue near 52 St. 621-0300.
Air India
400 Park Avenue near East 52 St. 407-1416.
Air New Zealand
(800) 262-1234
Alaska Airlines
(800) 426-0333
Alitalia Air Lines
666 Fifth Avenue near 52 St. 903-3300.

American Airlines
(800) 433-7300
100 East 42 Street.
World Trade Center, North Tower lobby.
875 Third Avenue near East 53 St.
166 West 32 Street.
1 East 59 Street.
Waldorf-Astoria Hotel, Park Avenue at East 50 St.
1384 Broadway near West 39 St.
18 West 49 Street.
New York Hilton Hotel, Sixth Avenue & West 53 Street.
200 Montague Street, Brooklyn.
Austrian Airlines
608 Fifth Avenue near 49 St. 265-6350.
Avianca Airlines
6 West 49 Street. 246-5241.
British Airways
(800) 247-9297
British West Indian Airlines (BWIA)
5 West 49 Street. 581-3200.
China Airlines
630 Fifth Avenue. 399-7877.
Continental Airlines
100 East 42 Street. 974-9494.
Czechoslovak Airlines (CSA)
545 Fifth Avenue near 45 St. 682-5833.
Delta Airlines
400 Madison Avenue near East 47 St. 239-0700.
100 East 42 Street.
120 Broadway near Wall St.
1 East 59 St.
New York Hilton Hotel, Sixth Avenue & West 53 Street.
1384 Broadway near West 39 St.
1 World Trade Center.
875 Third Avenue near East 53 St.
Egyptair
720 Fifth Avenue near 56 St. 586-2678.
El Al Airlines
120 West 45 Street. 768-9200.
Finnair-Finnish Airlines
10 East 40 Street. 889-7070.
Hawaiian Airlines
708 Third Avenue near East 44 St. 355-4843.
Iberia Airlines
509 Madison Avenue. 644-8848.
Icelandic Air
610 Fifth Avenue. 967-8888.
Irish International Airlines (Aer Lingus)
122 East 42 Street. 557-1110.
Japan Airlines
655 Fifth Avenue near 52 St. 838-4400.
KLM Royal Dutch Airlines
437 Madison Avenue near East 49 St. 759-3600.
Lan Chile Airlines
630 Fifth Avenue. 582-3250.

Lufthansa Airlines
(718) 895-1277
Mexicana Airlines
500 Fifth Avenue near 42 St. 840-2344; (800) 531-7921.
Northwest Airlines
100 East 42 Street. Domestic: 225-2525; International: 736-1220.
299 Park Avenue near 49 St.
1 World Trade Center.
Olympic Airways
647 Fifth Avenue near 52 St. 838-3600.
Qantas Airlines
542 Fifth Avenue near 45 St. (800) 227-4500.
Royal Air Maroc
666 Fifth Avenue near 53 St. 974-3850.
Sabena Belgian World Airlines
720 Fifth Avenue near 55 St. 247-8880.
Scandinavian Airlines
1270 Avenue of the Americas near West 51 St. (718) 657-7700.
Singapore Airlines
535 Fifth Avenue near 44 St. (800) 742-3333.
Swissair
608 Fifth Avenue near 48 St. (718) 990-4500.
TAP Air Portugal
521 Fifth Avenue near 43 St. 944-2100.
Trans World Airlines (TWA)
624 Fifth Avenue near 50 St. Domestic: 290-2121; International: 290-2141.
1384 Broadway near West 39 St.
1 World Trade Center.
1 East 59 Street.
100 East 42 Street.
166 West 32 Street.
120 Broadway near Wall St.
Waldorf-Astoria Hotel, Park Avenue at East 50 St.
United Airlines
437 Madison Avenue near 50 St. (718) 803-2200.
100 East 42 Street.
120 Broadway near Wall St.
166 West 32 Street.
1 East 59 Street.
1 World Trade Center.
USAir
100 East 42 Street. 736-3200.
1 World Trade Center.
1 East 59 Street.
Varig Brazilian Airlines
634 Fifth Avenue near 51 St. 340-0205.
Viasa Venezuelan International Airways
18 East 48 Street. (800) 327-5454.
Yugoslav Airlines
630 Fifth Avenue near 50 St. 765-4056.
Zambia Airways
400 Madison Avenue. 685-1112.

HELP!

EMERGENCY

Emergency Services 24 hours, 7 days.

Ambulance, Fire, Police

Dial 911 or 0.
Deaf emergency: TTY (800) 342-4357.

Abused Child

(800) 342-3720.

AIDS Hotline

(718) 485-8111; National: (800) 342-2437.

Desperate/Suicidal

Help Line. 532-2400.
Suicide Prevention Hotline. (718) 389-9608.
The Samaritans. 673-3000.

Doctors on Call

(718) 748-7000 or (718) 238-2100. Private service for house calls by doctors in all five boroughs.

Domestic Violence Hotline

(800) 942-6906.

Poison

340-4494 or 764-7667 (POISONS).

Public Assistance/NYC Emergency Assistance Unit

513-8859.

Rape

267-7273.

Police Stations

Emergency: Dial 911.
Below is a listing of Manhattan police precincts and their direct numbers for questions and help.
1st Precinct
16 Ericsson Place near Canal St. 334-0611.
5th Precinct
19 Elizabeth Street near Canal St. 334-0711.
6th Precinct
233 West 10 Street. 741-4811.
7th Precinct
19½ Pitt Street near Broome St. 477-7311.
9th Precinct
321 East 5 Street. 477-7811.
10th Precinct
230 West 20 Street. 741-8211.

13th Precinct
230 East 21 Street. 477-7411.
Midtown South
357 West 35 Street. 239-9811.
17th Precinct
167 East 51 Street. 826-3211.
Midtown North
524 West 42 Street. 760-8300.
19th Precinct
312 East 94 Street. 860-1550.
20th Precinct
120 West 82 Street. 580-6411.
Central Park
86 Street & Transverse Road. 570-4820.
23rd Precinct
164 East 102 Street. 860-6411.
24th Precinct
151 West 100 Street. 678-1811.
25th Precinct
120 East 119 Street. 860-6511.
26th Precinct
520 West 126 Street. 678-1311.
28th Precinct
2271 Eighth Avenue near West 123 St. 678-1611.
30th Precinct
451 West 151 Street. 690-8811.
32nd Precinct
250 West 135 Street. 690-6311.
34th Precinct
4295 Broadway near West 182 St. 927-9711.

Police Services

Available 24 hours, 7 days. For location of nearest precinct, call 374-5000.
    For general information concerning police services: 374-6700.

Ambulance

In emergency, dial 911 and a city ambulance will respond free of charge to the patient. The ambulance will take the patient to one of the 13 municipal hospitals in the city according to geographic location and hospital specialty.
    If a specific, nonpublic hospital is preferred, **Keefe & Keefe** provides 24-hour service on a fee-pay basis (covers all five boroughs), call 988-8800.

Hospital Emergency Rooms

Beekman Downtown Hospital
Gold Street at Beekman Street. 312-5000. Mobile intensive care, two paramedic units operating Monday to Friday from 9am to 5pm, another Basic EMT unit 24 hours, 7 days; coronary intensive care unit.
Bellevue Hospital Center
East 27 Street at First Avenue. 561-4347. Intensive care units include coronary, surgical (trau-

ma), pediatric, psychiatric, neurosurgical, and alcohol detoxification.

Beth Israel Medical Center
East 16 Street & First Avenue. 420-2840. Coronary care, neonatal intensive care, alcohol and drug detoxification.

Cabrini Medical Center
East 20 Street between Second & Third Avenues. 995-6000. Coronary care unit, trauma intensive care unit, alcohol detoxification and drug overdose units, psychiatric facility.

Columbia Presbyterian Medical Center
622 West 168 Street at Fort Washington Ave. 305-2500. Metabolic, neurosurgical, pediatric intensive care units.

Harlem Hospital
506 Lenox Avenue at East 135 St. 491-8360. Coronary care, neonatal, and respiratory critical care units; alcohol and drug detoxification. Crisis intervention center for battered wives and children and rape victims.

Lenox Hill Hospital
100 East 77 Street between Park & Lexington Aves. 439-2345. Coronary and neonatal intensive care units.

Manhattan Eye, Ear & Throat Hospital
210 East 64 Street between Second & Third Aves. 838-9200. Ear, eye, nose, and throat emergencies.

Mount Sinai Hospital
Fifth Avenue & 100 Street. 241-7171. Coronary, trauma, and medical intensive care units, dental emergencies; emergency pharmacy till midnight.

New York Eye & Ear Infirmary
310 East 14 Street between First & Second Aves. 979-4000. 24-hour emergency service for eye, ear, nose, or throat problems.

New York Hospital-Cornell Medical Center
East 70 Street between York Avenue & East River. 472-5050. 24-hour paramedic unit. Burn, coronary, neurological, neonatal intensive care; high-risk infant transport unit and treatment.

New York University Medical Center
560 First Avenue at East 33 St. 340-5550. Coronary care.

St. Clare's Hospital & Health Center
West 52 Street between Ninth & Tenth Avenues. 586-1500. Coronary, medical, surgical intensive care units.

St. Luke's Hospital Center
West 114 Street between Amsterdam Avenue & Morningside Drive. 932-8236. Coronary, trauma, neonatal intensive care; alcohol detoxification; rape intervention team; 24-hour psychiatric emergency room.

St. Luke's-Roosevelt Hospital
West 58 Street off Ninth Avenue. 523-4000. Coronary, surgical, neonatal intensive care units; alcohol detoxification.

St. Vincent's Hospital & Medical Center of New York
Seventh Avenue at West 12 Street. 790-7000. Coronary, spinal-cord trauma, and psychiatric intensive care units, alcohol detoxification.

ASSISTANCE

These organizations help and advise anyone in need—the ill, the lonely, the victimized, the desperate, and those people who simply need solutions to problems. Remember that 24 hours a day, 7 days a week, there is police assistance.

General

New York City Human Resources Administration
250 Church Street. 553-5997. *Mon-Fri 9am-5pm.* **Emergency Assistance Unit:** 513-8859. *24 hours, 7 days.* This city agency provides public assistance in many areas. Call for referral to appropriate divisions. Below is a list of departments covered by HRA:
  Child Services:
  Foster and adoption.
  Medicaid/Medicare:
  Medical-insurance benefits.
  Family & Adult Services:
  Home care, foster care for adults.
  Office of Income Support:
  Child support from absent parents.
  General Social Services:
  Referral, interceding unit, outreach center.
  Crisis Intervention Unit:
  Emergency housing, food, clothing.

Citizens Advice Bureau
2050 Grand Concourse near Burnside Ave, Bronx. 731-0720. An information, referral, and problem-solving center regarding housing, welfare, Medicaid, and Social Services. *OPEN Mon-Fri 9am-3:30pm.*

Mayor's Action Center
61 Chambers Street. 566-5700. Handles and expedites complaints regarding the public's interaction with city agencies. *OPEN Mon-Fri 9am-5pm; till 7pm by phone.*

Salvation Army of Greater New York
242-7770. Information and referral for family problems, foster homes, adoption, alcohol and drug rehabilitation, senior citizen residence problems. Two social workers on duty *Mon-Fri 8:30am-4pm.* Thirty-three centers throughout the city; summer camps, and a general hospital in Flushing, Queens.

United Neighborhood Houses
481-5570. Information and referral for family and individual counseling, day care, nurseries, and senior citizens programs. *OPEN Mon-Fri 8:30am-5:30pm.*

Alcoholism

Alcoholics Anonymous
683-3900. Support system for alcoholics who want to stop.

Alcoholism Council of Greater New York
979-6277. New York affiliate of the National Council on Alcoholism. Information and referral hotline: 979-1010.

Crime Victims

Crime Victims Board of New York State
270 Broadway near Chambers St, 2nd floor. 587-5160. Financial aid, out-of-pocket medical expenses reimbursed for victims of crime. *OPEN Mon-Fri 9am-5pm.*
Crime Victims Hotline
577-7777. Bilingual counseling, advice, and referral for crime victims. *OPEN 24 hours, 7 days.*

Disaster Relief

American Red Cross in Greater New York
787-1000. Financial assistance, food, shelter, and clothing given to meet family needs caused by disaster. *24 hours, 7 days.*

Drug Abuse

Daytop Village
54 West 40 Street. 354-6000 (Mon-Fri 9am-5pm). Rehabilitational facilities to help addicts with drug and related problems. Hotline: (718) 474-3800. *OPEN 24 hours, 7 days.*
New York State Division of Substance Abuse Services
(800) 522-5353. Referrals to appropriate treatment programs, clinics, and hospitals. *OPEN 24 hours, 7 days.*

Odyssey House
309-11 East 6 Street. 477-9630.
Ward's Island, Building #3. 860-6460.
Respected residential rehabilitation drug abuse centers. Vocational training, reeducation, and integration into society stressed. *OPEN 24 hours, 7 days.*
Phoenix House Foundation
164 West 74 Street. 595-5810. City's largest drug-free residential rehabilitation program. Five facilities. Encourages responsibility, self-dependence, and trust. *OPEN 24 hours, 7 days.*

Rape

New York Women Against Rape
477-0819. Hotline: 777-4000. Counseling and referral service for rape victims as well as victim advocacy. Group trains hospital staff and police in the care of rape victims.

Tenants' Rights

If you have problems in a rent-controlled or rent-stabilized apartment, call 519-5797 *or* 903-9500.
Metropolitan Council on Housing
198 Broadway. 693-0550 (Mon, Wed & Fri 1:30-6:30pm) or (718) 739-6400. Advises tenants in rent-controlled and rent-stabilized apartments on their rights. Organizes tenants.

INDEX

A

Acting schools, 254
Addresses, Manhattan address locator, 4
Adult education, 254
Airline offices, 287–288
Airport
  major airports, 287
  transportation to, 5–6
Alcoholism information, 291
Ambulance, 290
Amusement parks, 119
Animal preserves, 118–119
Annual events
  art events, 83
  listing by month, 37–46
  sporting events, 133
Antiques
  antique/collectible furniture, 249
  antique shops, 255–256
  flea markets, 256–257
  jewelry, 265–266
  quilts, 253
  toys, 277–278
  watches, 278
Appetizing stores, 239
Aquariums, 110
Art
  alternative exhibition spaces, 100–101
  annual events, 83
  art and science museums, 87–88
  art tours, 27
  galleries, 92–100
  general art museums, 83–87
  See also Galleries; Museums
Art schools, 257
Art supplies, 257
Atriums, locations of, 30
Auction houses, 257

B

Baby care, 131
Baby-sitters, 131
Baked goods, 239–240
Bakeries, 24-hour, 281
Banks, 6
Baseball, 133
Basketball, 133–134
Baskets, 258
Bath/bathroom accessories, 246
Beaches, 109
  Brooklyn, 109
  Long Island, 109
Beauty
  beauty treatments, 235–236
  fragrance and toiletries, 236–237
  hairdressers, 237–238
  hair removal, 238
  makeup, 238–239
Bed & breakfast, 22–23
Bicycles, shops for, 125, 258
Bicycling
  bicycle tours, 134
  bike rentals, 134
Billiards, 134–135
Bird watching, 111–112
Blues clubs, 156
Boating, 135
Boat trips, 33–34
Boccie, 135
Books
  antiquarian, 259
  book binding/restoration, 261
  chain stores, 258
  for children, 125–126
  general books, 258–259
  special interest, 259–261
Boroughs, 48
Botanical gardens, 108–109
Boutiques
  for children, 123–124

for men, 230–231
for women, 217–224
Bowling, 135
Boxing, 135–136
Brass accessories, 246–247
Bridges, 80–81
Bronx
  facts about, 48
  parks, 106–107
  restaurants, 172
  swimming pools, 142
  tennis courts, 143
Brooklyn
  beaches, 109
  facts about, 48
  historic areas/buildings, 59–60
  parks, 106
  restaurants, 172
  swimming pools, 142
  tennis courts, 143
Buses
  bus stations, 287
  coach tours, 26–27
  public, 2
Buttons, 261

C

Cabarets, 156–157
Camp clothing, 124
Candles, 261
Candy/chocolate, 240–241
Carpets and rugs, 247
Car rental, 287
  chauffeur-driven, 287
  24-hour, 282
Caterers, 241–242
Ceramic tiles, 247
Chauffeur-driven autos, 287
Cheese shops, 242
Children
  amusement parks, 119
  baby care, 131
  baby-sitters, 131

Other I LOVE city guides
by Marilyn J. Appleberg

America's most acclaimed urban travel books—
in new, updated editions

I Love Boston
I Love Chicago
I Love Los Angeles
I Love San Francisco
I Love Washington

NOTES

NOTES

NOTES

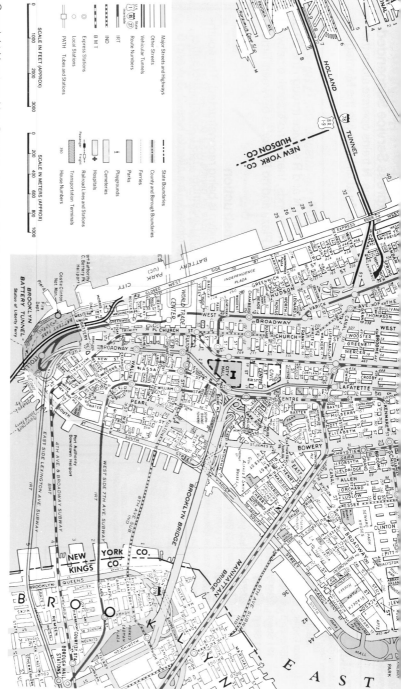

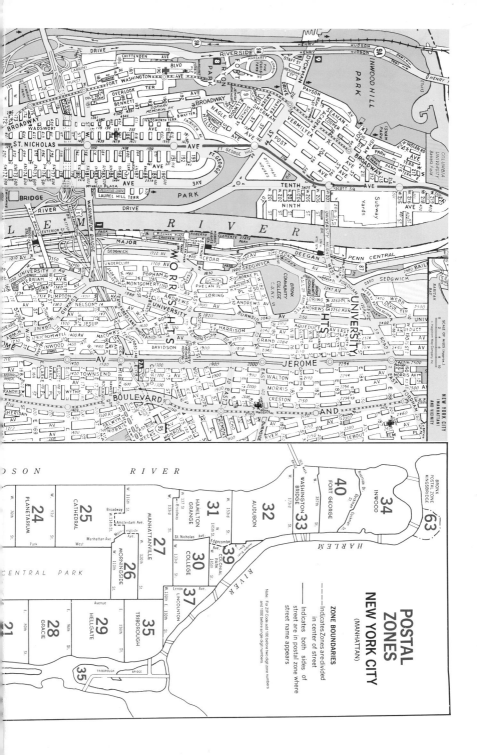

POSTAL ZONES
NEW YORK CITY
(MANHATTAN)

ZONE BOUNDARIES
Indicates Zones are divided
in center of street
Indicates both sides of
street are in postal zone where
street name appears

Note: For ZIP Code add 100 before two-digit zone numbers
and 1000 before single digit numbers